Business Calculus

Business Calculus

Backward and Forward

First Edition

Michel Mallenby and James W. Carlson

Creighton University

 cognella® | ACADEMIC PUBLISHING

Bassim Hamadeh, CEO and Publisher
Kristina Stolte, Acquisitions Editor
Alisa Munoz, Project Editor
Susana Christie, Developmental Editor
Christian Berk, Production Editor
Emely Villavicencio, Graphic Designer
Trey Soto, Licensing
Celeste Paed, Production Assistant
Natalie Piccotti, Director of Marketing
Kassie Graves, Vice President of Editorial
Jamie Giganti, Director of Academic Publishing

www.cognella.com   800-200-3908

Contents

A Note to Instructors

This text is not in the usual order for calculus textbooks—i.e., limits, derivatives, integrals. In fact, we refer to it casually as "Calculus Backward." Our order is definite integrals, limits, derivatives, indefinite integrals. We have settled on this order as the best way to reach students because the concept of area is much more intuitive for them than the concept of slope. Understanding area, more students "stay with the program" longer and enjoy it more before the weaker ones begin to struggle with the product, quotient, and chain rules. At the end we return to indefinite integrals. It makes a nice closed loop, a nice review, and integrates the beginning topics back into the course. (Pun possibly intended.)

Further, this text is written for business students, many of whom are not strong math students. Instead of attaching the review material in an appendix or an introductory chapter, we have embedded it throughout the text just before the sections in which it will first be used extensively. The review sections have an "R" in the section titles. Those with a "C" contain calculus topics. You may or may not wish to include the material from the review sections in exams. Dr. Carlson does. Dr. Mallenby doesn't.

The drawback to this nontraditional order is that we can't provide a proof, only an algorithm when it comes to definite integrals, although we promise the students that they will understand the origin of the algorithm before the end of the course. While this lack of justification may be worrisome for instructors, the business students don't mind. We do provide other proofs throughout the text in the usual places, including the Fundamental Theorem of Calculus.

Because this is a text designed for business students, we felt numerous business-related exercises should be included. So that the exercise sections could progress from easier to harder problems, from those with neat coefficients to more realistic ones, nearly all the exercises contain data from imaginary companies. Don't look for them in the Fortune 500.

Finally, have fun teaching Calculus Backward. We've tested the material for years and have found the students are more receptive and engaged with this order and appreciative of the algebra reviews. Our hope is that you will, too.

Chapter 1

Perhaps this page should be titled "A Note to Students" or even "Introduction," but we were afraid you wouldn't read it with those titles, and this is very important.

Rather than putting all the review material in an appendix or in an introductory chapter, we elected to embed review material in each unit just before the content in which you will begin to use it. Sections containing review material have an "**R**" in the section title, e.g., IR3. The "**I**" indicates the section is in Unit I. The "**R**" indicates it is a review section, and the "**3**" indicates it is the third section in Unit I. Section titles with "**C**", e.g. IVC3, contain calculus content.

You should have seen the material in the "**R**" sections in algebra classes, so if you find the R-sections boring, think of it as a good sign. While the review material introduced in Unit I is especially helpful for doing exercises in that unit, it will be needed throughout the text. The same is true for most review sections.

We have included the solutions to every odd problem and the answers to every even problem, because we don't want you to spend hours doing exercises only to find out you've done them wrong. However, doing the exercises will not be beneficial if you do them with the solutions in front of you. Do each problem without looking, then check your answer. Honestly! You'll never be able to do the exam problems if you can't do the homework problems without looking at the answers. Makes sense, right?

One last thing—this is the first edition of this text, and even though both professors have proofread it several times and a fifteen-year-old grandson, Bruce, has agreed to work all the problems in exchange for an acknowledgment (hi, Bruce!) and enlightenment, there will still be typos and (horrors!) even mistakes. If you find one, please let us know at 1-(402) 280-4720.

UNIT I

IR1

Graphing Linear and Quadratic Equations in Two Variables

LINEAR EQUATIONS

Linear equations have terms that contain only a single variable or a constant. **The graph of a linear equation is a straight line**, hence the term *linear*. An example of a linear equation is:

$$3x - 5y = 15$$

Another example is: $\qquad\qquad y = -5x + 10$

(Terms are the parts of an algebraic expression that are separated by a plus or a minus sign.) Linear equations can be plotted by finding two points. To find two points on the equation $3x - 5y = 15$, we choose a value for x and then solve for y. Suppose we choose 0 for x.

Then the equation becomes: $3(0) - 5y = 15$

$$-5y = 15 \qquad \text{Dividing both sides by } -5, \text{ we have}$$

$$y = -3$$

We can keep track of our "points" on a chart:

The second row indicates that the point $(0, -3)$ is on the line.

x	y
0	−3

If we choose $x = 2$, we can solve for y again:

$3(2) - 5y = 15$ Subtracting 6 from both sides, we have

$-5y = 9$ Dividing both sides by -5, we obtain

$y = -\dfrac{9}{5}$, or $y = -1.8$

We can add this point to the chart:

We now have two points on the line: $(0, -3)$ and $(2, -1.8)$.

If we plot these two points and connect them, we have our line.

x	y
0	−3
2	−1.8

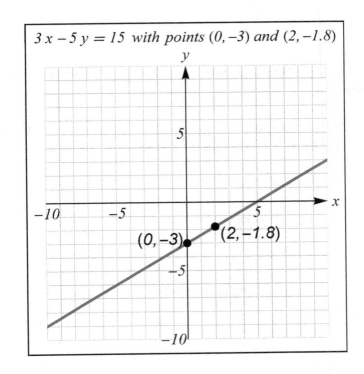

The two ordered pairs we found, $(0, -3)$ and $(2, -1.8)$, are called **solutions** of the equation. For the solution $(0, -3)$, if we substitute the 0 for x in our equation and we substitute -3 for y in our equation, we get a true statement.

$$3x - 5y = 15 \qquad \text{original equation}$$

$$3(0) - 5(-3) = 15 \qquad \text{substituting}$$

$$15 = 15$$

Similarly, for the solution $\left(2, -\dfrac{9}{5}\right)$, if we substitute 2 for x in the original equation and $-\dfrac{9}{5}$ for y, we get:

$$3(2) - 5\left(-\frac{9}{5}\right) = 15$$

$$6 + 9 = 15$$

$$15 = 15 \qquad \text{which is also a true statement.}$$

If a point is a solution of the equation, it means it is a point that lies on the graph of the equation.

When we are looking for points so we can plot a line, it is also legal to choose a value for y and then solve for x. If we choose 0 for y, we get:

$$3x - 5(0) = 15$$

$$3x = 15 \qquad \text{Dividing both sides by 3, we get}$$

$$x = 5$$

We can summarize all three points in the table.

x	y
0	−3
2	−1.8
5	0

In many cases, picking zero for one value leads to an easy solution for the other variable. These points are also easy to plot because they represent the y-intercept (when $x = 0$) and the x-intercept (when $y = 0$). The graph crosses the y-axis at the y-intercept, and it crosses the x-axis at the x-intercept.

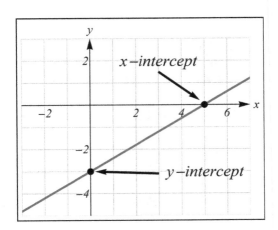

The equation $x = 2$ is also a linear equation. No matter what values we choose for y, the x value will equal 2.

This is because we could write the equation as:

$$x + 0y = 2.$$

x	y
2	0
2	4
2	−4

Notice that the points (2, 0), (2, 4), and (2, −4) are all solutions for the equations:

$$x + 0y = 2.$$

Note that the graph of the equation $x = 2$, or $x + 0y = 2$, is a vertical line.

The equation $y=2$ is another linear equation. No matter what values we choose for x, the y value will equal 2. This is because we could write the equation as:

x	y
0	2
4	2
−4	2

$$0x + y = 2.$$

Notice that all three points (0, 2), (4, 2), and (−4, 2) are all solutions for the equation

$$0x + y = 2.$$

Note that the graph of the equation is a horizontal line.

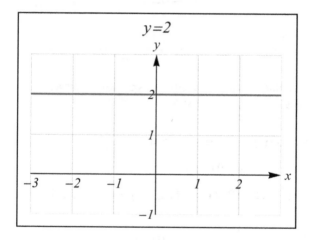

Note that the *y*-value of an equation is the *height* on a graph.

QUADRATIC EQUATIONS

Quadratic equations are equations with terms of at most degree 2. That is, the variable exponents are whole numbers, and the sum of the exponents of the variables in any term is less than or equal to 2. An example would be:

$$3x^2 + 2x - 5y^2 + 3y + 8xy = 22$$

Depending on the coefficients involved, the graphs of general quadratics are parabolas, circles, ellipses, hyperbolas, or pairs of lines.

We will consider only equations with no y^2 or xy term; that is, those of the form

$$y = ax^2 + bx + c$$

For example, $y = 3x^2 - 9x + 2$ is graphed at right.

The graphs of these types of quadratic equations are *parabolas.*
If a parabola opens upward, the vertex is the lowest point, as in the graph at the right.

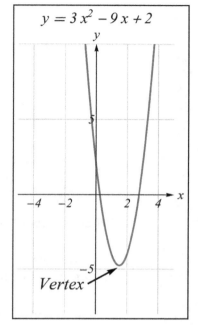

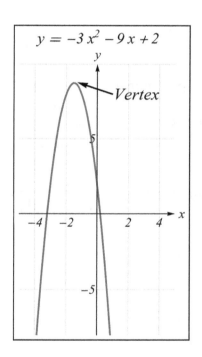

If a parabola opens downward, the vertex is the highest point, as in the graph at left.

We begin by looking at the parabola: $y = x^2$. By choosing numbers for x and solving for y, we get the table of points at right.

If we plot these points, we get the parabola $y = x^2$, graphed below.

Note the vertex is a minimum and is located at (0,0).

x	y
0	0
1	1
2	4
−1	1
−2	4

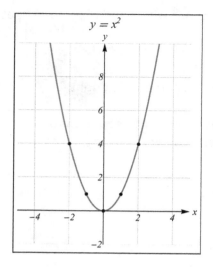

When the coefficient of x^2 is a negative number, the graph is turned upside down.

Consider: $y = -x^2$. Again, we choose numbers for x and solve for y to get the table at right.

If we plot these points, we get the parabola $y = -x^2$, graphed below. It opens downward, and the vertex is a maximum at $(0,0)$. This graph is a vertical reflection of the graph $y = x^2$

x	y
0	0
1	−1
2	−4
−1	−1
−2	−4

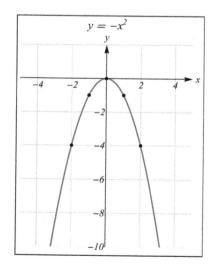

We can add a constant to the equation to move the graph up or down. The new quadratic equation has the form: $y = x^2 + k$. These graphs are *vertical translations* of the original equation $y = x^2$.

For example, for the equation: $y = x^2 + 2$, every y-value on the chart is increased by 2 units.

The graph of $y = x^2 + 2$ looks exactly like the graph of $y = x^2$, only moved up 2 units.

The graph of $y = x^2 - 3$ looks exactly like the graph of $y = x^2$, only moved down 3 units.

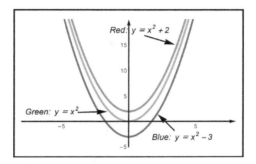

The graph of $y = -x^2 + 2$ looks exactly like the graph of $y = -x^2$, only moved up 2 units.

The graph of $y = -x^2 - 3$ looks exactly like the graph of $y = -x^2$, only moved down 3 units.

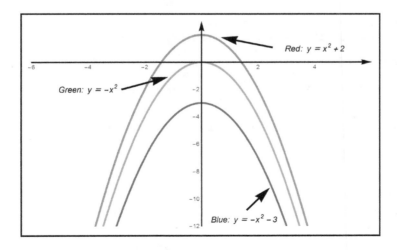

We can add a constant to the equation to move the graph right or left. The new quadratic equation has the form: $y = (x - b)^2$. These graphs are *horizontal translations* of the original equation $y = x^2$.

The graph of $y = (x + 2)^2$ looks exactly the same as the graph of $y = x^2$, only it is shifted two units to the *left*.

The graph of $y = (x - 3)^2$ looks exactly the same as the graph of $y = x^2$, only it is shifted three units to the *right*.

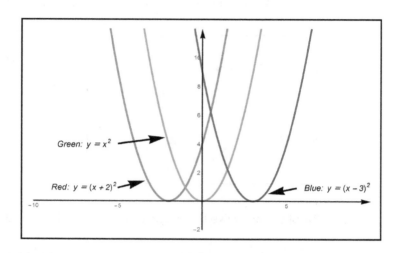

Green: $y = x^2$

Red: $y = (x + 2)^2$

Blue: $y = (x - 3)^2$

ASIDE

This is why $y = (x + 2)^2$ is shifted to the *left*. Replace x with -2.

Do you agree that $y = 0$ when $x = -2$ in the equation $y = (x + 2)^2$?

Remember that y-values are heights on a graph. So the height of the graph is 0 when $x = -2$.

Thus, the vertex of the graph is at $x = -2$ now (a shift to the left), instead of at $x = 2$.

Consider quadratic equations with the perfect square form: $y = (x - h)^2 + k$. The h designates a shift to the right or left, and the k designates a shift up or down.

Consider the graph of the equation: $y = -(x - 2)^2 + 1$.

It is the same as the graph of $y = -x^2$, only shifted 2 units to the right and up 1 unit.

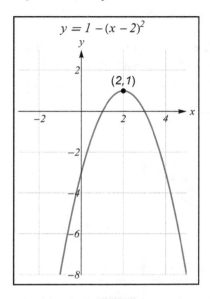

Consider the graph of the equation: $y = (x+4)^2 - 3$.

It is the same as the graph of the equation: $y = x^2$, only shifted left 4 units and down 3 units.

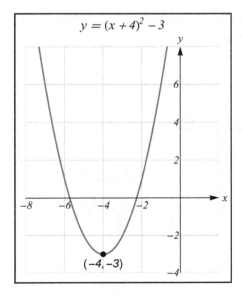

By adding a coefficient to the x^2 term, we can compress or expand the graph; i.e., we can make the parabola open wider or narrower.

For the equation $y = 2x^2$, every y value on our chart (except 0) is two times greater/higher than it was on the chart for $y = x^2$; y (= the height) rises faster, so the resulting parabola is narrower.

x	y
0	0
1	2
2	8
−1	2
−2	8

Consider the graph of $y = \dfrac{x^2}{3}$, which is equivalent to: $y = \left(\dfrac{1}{3}\right)x^2$.

At $x = 1$, $y = \dfrac{1^2}{3} = \dfrac{1}{3} \approx 0.33$. At $x = 2$, $y = \dfrac{2^2}{3} = \dfrac{4}{3} \approx 1.33$.

If the coefficient is less than 1, the graph will rise more slowly, so the parabola will be wider.

x	y
0	(1/3)(0)2 = 0
1	(1/3)(1)2 = 0.33
2	(1/3)(2)2 = 1.33
−1	(1/3)(−1)2 = 0.33
−2	(1/3)(−2)2 = 1.33

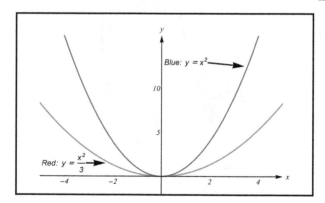

If we put the compressions, expansions, translations, and vertical reflections together, we get the perfect square form for a quadratic equation: $y = a(x-h)^2 + k$.

Consider the equation: $y = 4(x-2)^2 + 5$.

It is already in perfect square form, and a would be 4; h would be 2; and k would be 5.

The vertex of the graph is shifted 2 units right, 5 units up, and is narrower than $y = x^2$. By plotting a second point, we can set the width. In the equation above, if we let $x = 0$, then $y = 21$.

Parabolas are symmetrical about a vertical line through the vertex.

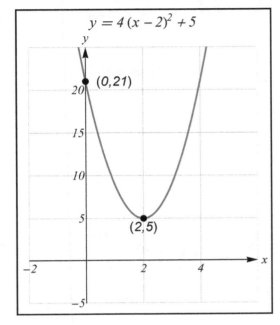

Consider the equation: $y = -3(x+1)^2 - 5$, or $y = -3(x-(-1))^2 - 5$

The a would be -3, telling us this parabola is narrower than the basic graph of $y = -x^2$, or compressed, and the graph opens downward because a is negative.

The graph is shifted 1 unit to the left. The h would be -1 in this form.

The k would be -5, telling us the graph is shifted down 5 units.

If $x = 0$, then $y = -8$.

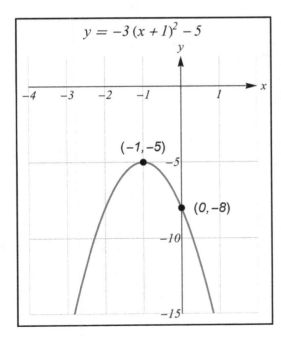

Consider the equation $y = 0.3(x-83)^2 + 194$.

The graph is shifted 83 units to the right, up 194 units, and because of the coefficient 0.3, it is wider than the basic graph of $y = x^2$.

The vertex is at the point $(83, 194)$.

If we let $x = 0$, then $y = 2260.7$.

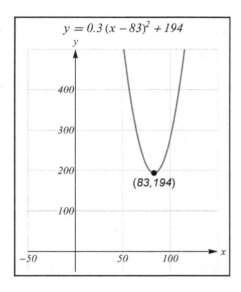

Quadratic equations in the perfect square form $y = a(x-h)^2 + k$ can be graphed fairly easily.

CONVERTING QUADRATIC EQUATIONS TO PERFECT SQUARE FORM

The equation $y = x^2 + 6x + 5$ is also a quadratic equation. Its graph would also be a parabola.

In this form, i.e., $y = ax^2 + bx + c$, it is not so easy to graph. There is a method for converting a graph in this form into the form: $y = a(x-h)^2 + k$. It's called **Completing the Square**.

EXAMPLE: Consider $y = x^2 + 6x + 5$.

There are five steps.	$y = x^2 + 6x + 5$
1) Find the coefficient of the x-term. Take one half of this coefficient, and then square it.	The x-term is $6x$ and its coefficient is 6. $\dfrac{6}{2} = 3$ $3^2 = 9$
2) Add and subtract this term after the x-term. (If we add and subtract the same number, we are adding a net of zero, which doesn't change the original equation.)	$y = x^2 + 6x + 9 - 9 + 5$
3) The first three terms can then be factored into a perfect square.	$y = (x+3)(x+3) - 9 + 5$
4) Write the equation in perfect square form.	$y = (x+3)^2 - 4$

The equation $y = (x+3)^2 - 4$ is now in perfect square form and can be graphed.

This parabola has a vertex shifted 3 units left and down 4 units. It opens upward.

If we let $x = 0$, then $y = 5$, giving another point on the graph.

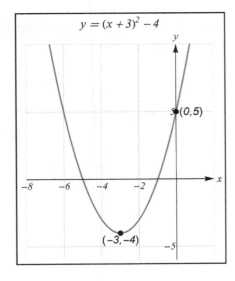

$y = (x+3)^2 - 4$

$\bullet (0,5)$

$(-3,-4)$

Admittedly, completing the square is easier when the coefficient of the x-term is an even number, but we can still perform these steps on odd coefficients.

EXAMPLE: Consider $y = x^2 + 5x + 3$

Step 1: Find the coefficient of the x-term. Take one half of this coefficient, and then square it.	The coefficient of the x-term is 5. Half of 5 is $\dfrac{5}{2}$. $\left(\dfrac{5}{2}\right)^2 = \dfrac{25}{4}$.
Step 2: Add and subtract $\dfrac{25}{4}$.	$y = x^2 + 5x + \dfrac{25}{4} - \dfrac{25}{4} + 3$
Step 3: We factor, and we also convert 3 to $\dfrac{12}{4}$ for an easier combination of like terms.	$y = \left(x + \dfrac{5}{2}\right)\left(x + \dfrac{5}{2}\right) - \dfrac{25}{4} + \dfrac{12}{4}$ It's also a good idea to FOIL $\left(x + \dfrac{5}{2}\right)\left(x + \dfrac{5}{2}\right)$ to be sure it equals $x^2 + 5x + \dfrac{25}{4}$.
Step 4: Combining $-\dfrac{25}{4}$ and $\dfrac{12}{4}$:	$y = \left(x + \dfrac{5}{2}\right)^2 - \dfrac{13}{4}$ or $y = (x + 2.5)^2 - 3.25$

The vertex on this graph is shifted 2.5 units left and 3.25 units down.

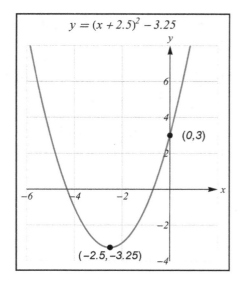

$$y = (x + 2.5)^2 - 3.25$$

Did you notice that we said there would be five steps, but we only presented four?

The zero step occurs if the leading coefficient is not 1; e.g., $y = 2x^2 + 4x + 3$.

This is still a quadratic equation, the graph is still a parabola, and we can still complete the square, *if* we add the zero step.

EXAMPLE: Consider $y = 2x^2 + 4x + 3$.

	$y = 2x^2 + 4x + 3$
Step 0: Factor the leading coefficient from both the x^2-term and the x-term.	$y = 2(x^2 + 2x) + 3$
Step 1: Find the coefficient of the x-term. Take one half of this coefficient, and then square it.	The coefficient of the x-term is 2. Half of 2 is 1, and $1^2 = 1$
Step 2: Add and subtract, but here's the tricky part: *Note that we actually added two times one 2(1), so we had to subtract 2(1).*	$y = 2(x^2 + 2x + 1) - 2(1) + 1$
Step 3: Factor.	$y = 2(x + 1)(x + 1) - 2 + 1$
Step 4: Write in perfect square form.	$y = 2(x + 1)^2 - 1$

The graph would be a parabola with the vertex shifted 1 unit left, down 1, and narrower than usual.

If $x = 0$, then $y = 1$, giving another point on the graph.

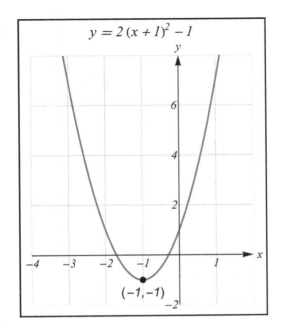

$$y = 2(x + 1)^2 - 1$$

$(-1, -1)$

Here's one last example: Consider $y = -x^2 + 4x - 3$.

Once again, the leading coefficient is not one. It is (-1), so we have to employ the zero step.

Step 0: Factor the leading coefficient from the x^2-term and the x-term.	$y = -1(x^2 - 4x) - 3$
Step 1: Find the coefficient of the x-term. Take one half of this coefficient, and then square it.	The coefficient of the x-term is -4. Half of -4 is -2, then squaring: $(-2)^2 = 4$
Step 2: Add and subtract. Tricky part: We really added $(-1)(4)$, so we had to subtract $(-1)(4)$. Rewriting, we have:	$y = -1(x^2 - 4x + 4) - (-1)(4) - 3$ $y = -1(x^2 - 4x + 4) + 4 - 3$
Step 3: Factor.	$y = -(x - 2)(x - 2) + 4 - 3$
Step 4: Write in perfect square form.	$y = -(x - 2)^2 + 1$

This quadratic equation gives us a parabola that opens downward, with the vertex shifted 2 units to the right and up 1 unit. If $x=0$, then $y=-3$.

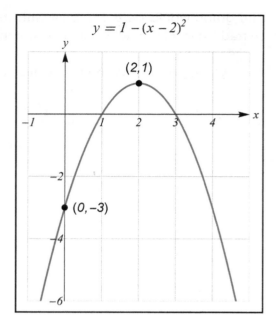

USING THE COEFFICIENTS FROM THE QUADRATIC GENERAL FORM TO PLOT PARABOLAS

Here is another method to find the perfect square form: $y=a(x-h)^2+k$ of $y=ax^2+bx+c$. This method finds the vertex, the x-intercepts, and the y-intercept for quadratic equations in the form $y=ax^2+bx+c$. You may find it easier than using the previous five steps.

The perfect square form of the equation $y=ax^2+bx+c$ is $y=a(x-h)^2+k$. The x-component of the vertex, h, is found by computing $h=-\dfrac{b}{2a}$, and the y-component of the vertex, k, is found by computing $k=ah^2+bh+c$.

Consider graphing $y = 3x^2 + 12x - 5$.

Step 1:

Compute $h = -\dfrac{b}{2a}$. For this parabola, $h = -\dfrac{12}{2 \cdot 3} = -2$.

Compute $k = ah^2 + bh + c$. For this parabola, $k = 3(-2)^2 + 12(-2) - 5 = -17$.

The vertex of the parabola $y = 3x^2 + 12x - 5$ is $(-2, -17)$.

Step 2:

Find a second point on the parabola that is not the vertex.

For example, using the value 0 for x, $y = -5$.

So, another point on the graph is $(0, -5)$.

Step 3:

Plot a parabola through the points $(0, -5)$ and $(-2, -17)$ that is symmetrical about the vertical line through the vertex.

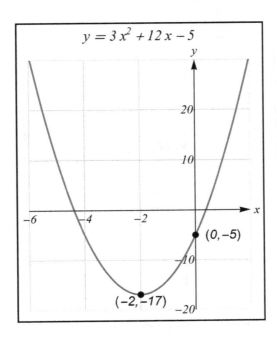

Consider graphing $y = -2x^2 + 7x + 8$.

Step 1:

Compute $h = -\dfrac{b}{2a}$. For this parabola, $h = -\dfrac{7}{2 \cdot (-2)} = \dfrac{7}{4}$.

Compute $k = ah^2 + bh + c$. For this parabola, $k = -2\left(\dfrac{7}{4}\right)^2 + 7\left(\dfrac{7}{4}\right) + 8 = \dfrac{113}{8}$.

The vertex of the parabola is the point $\left(\dfrac{7}{4}, \dfrac{113}{8}\right)$.

Step 2:

Find a second point on the parabola that is not the vertex.

For example, using the value 0 for x, $y = 8$.

So, another point on the graph is $(0,8)$.

Step 3:

Plot a parabola through the points $(0,8)$ and $\left(\dfrac{7}{4}, \dfrac{113}{8}\right)$ that is symmetrical about the vertical line through the vertex.

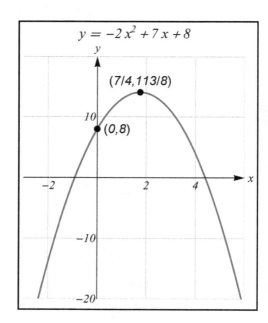

Besides the shape and vertex of a parabola, the intercepts are also important. The y-intercept occurs when $x=0$. The x-intercepts occur when $y=0$.

Revisiting the graph of $y=3x^2+12x-5$, we have already found the y-intercept, $(0,-5)$. The x-intercepts occur when $y=0$; in this case, when $0=3x^2+12x-5$.

We can solve $0=3x^2+12x-5$ using the quadratic formula.

Recall: the quadratic formula gives the solutions to $0=ax^2+bx-c$ as $x=\dfrac{-b\pm\sqrt{b^2-4ac}}{2a}$.

For $0=3x^2+12x-5$, $a=3$, $b=12$, and $c=-5$, giving $x=\dfrac{-b\pm\sqrt{b^2-4ac}}{2a}$

$$=\frac{-12\pm\sqrt{12^2-4(3)(-5)}}{2(3)}=\frac{-12\pm\sqrt{204}}{2(3)}=\frac{-12\pm2\sqrt{51}}{2(3)}$$

$$=\frac{-6\pm\sqrt{51}}{3}, x\approx0.3805,-4.3805.$$

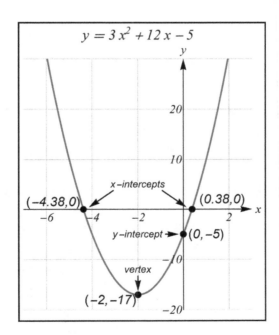

IR1 GRAPHING LINEAR AND QUADRATIC EQUATIONS EXERCISES

Note: The solutions follow at the end of the section and should be checked after each problem to avoid wasting time using the wrong methods, but it is best to do each exercise before checking the answer. Unless you can do the problem correctly without looking at the solution, you haven't learned the method.

Make quick sketches by hand without the use of an electronic graphing device.

1. Sketch the graphs of the following equations without plotting individual points.

    a. $y = 4$
    c. $y = -2$

    b. $x = -3$
    d. $x = 5$

2. Sketch graphs for the following equations. Plot only two points for each.

    a. $y = -3x + 1$
    c. $2x + y = 6$

    b. $y = \dfrac{x}{3} - 1$

3. Sketch graphs for the following equations.

    a. $y = x^2 - 2$
    c. $y = -x^2 + 5$
    e. $y = -(x-2)^2$
    g. $y = (x-1)^2 + 2$
    i. $y = (x+5)^2 + 1$

    b. $y = 4x^2 - 3$
    d. $y = (x+3)^2$
    f. $y = -(x-1)^2 + 2$
    h. $y = -(x+1)^2 - 4$

4. Complete the squares, then sketch the graphs. Plot the vertex on the graph, then, if desired, plot the x and y intercepts.

    a. $y = x^2 + 6x + 10$

    c. $y = x^2 + 2x + 2$

    b. $y = x^2 - 8x + 14$

    d. $y = x^2 - 3x + \dfrac{11}{4}$

5. Sketch the graphs of the following equations. Plot the vertex and intercepts (if the points are within the bounds of the graph) on the graph.

    a. $y = 4x^2 - 24x + 30$
    c. $y = 5x^2 - 10x - 4$

    b. $y = -3x^2 - 9x + 2$
    d. $y = -5x^2 + 11x + 2$

IR1 GRAPHING LINEAR AND QUADRATIC EQUATIONS SOLUTIONS TO THE EXERCISES

1. Sketch the graphs of the following equations without plotting individual points.

    a. $y = 4$

    b. $x = -3$

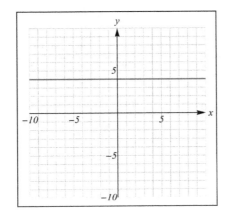

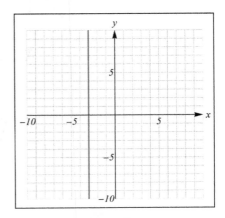

    c. $y = -2$

    d. $x = 5$

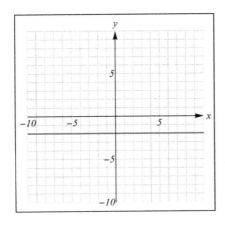

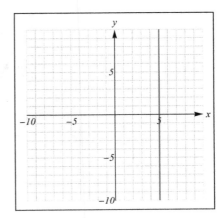

2. Sketch graphs for the following equations. Plot only two points for each.

   a. $y = -3x + 1$

   b. $y = \dfrac{x}{3} - 1$

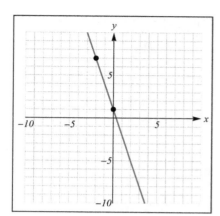
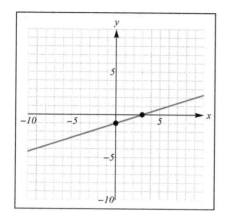

   c. $2x + y = 6$

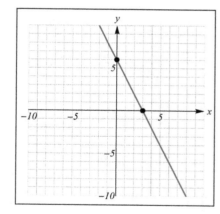

3. Sketch graphs for the following equations.

a. $y = x^2 - 2$

b. $y = 4x^2 - 3$

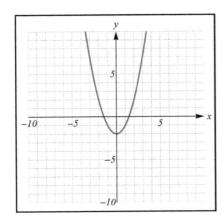

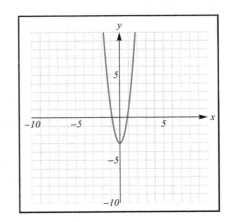

c. $y = -x^2 + 5$

d. $y = (x+3)^2$

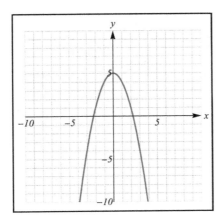

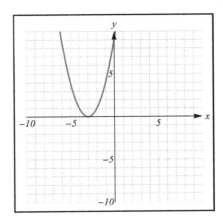

e. $y = -(x-2)^2$

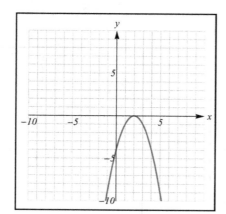

f. $y = -(x-1)^2 + 2$

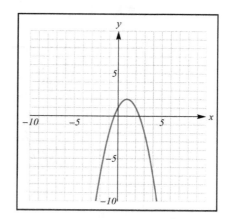

g. $y = (x-1)^2 + 2$

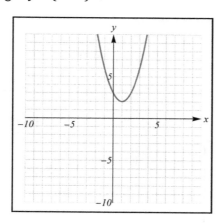

h. $y = -(x+1)^2 - 4$

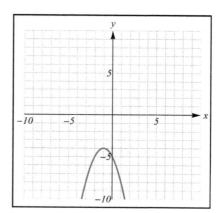

i. $y=(x+5)^2+1$

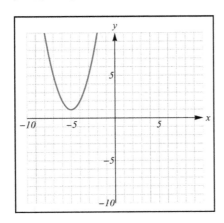

4. Complete the squares, then sketch the graphs. Plot the vertex on the graph; then, if desired, plot the x and y intercepts.

a. $y=x^2+6x+10$

$y=(x+3)^2+1$

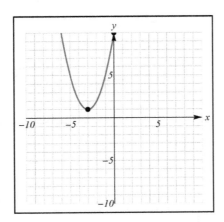

b. $y=x^2-8x+14$

$y=(x-4)^2-2$

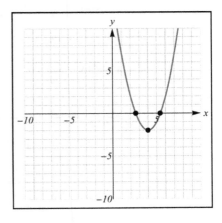

c. $y = x^2 + 2x + 2$

$y = (x+1)^2 + 1$

d. $y = x^2 - 3x + \dfrac{11}{4}$

$y = \left(x - \dfrac{3}{2}\right)^2 + \dfrac{1}{2}$

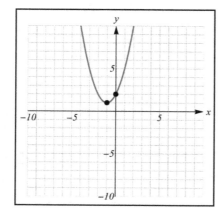

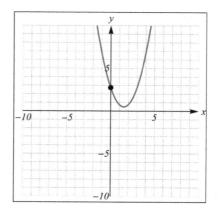

5. Sketch the graphs of the following equations. Plot the vertex and intercepts (if the points are within the bounds of the graph) on the graph.

a. $y = 4x^2 - 24x + 30$

$y = 4(x-3)^2 - 6$

b. $y = -3x^2 - 9x + 2$

$y = -3\left(x + \dfrac{3}{2}\right)^2 + \dfrac{35}{4}$

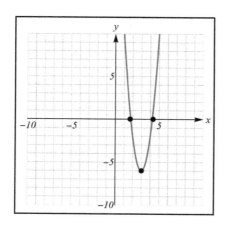

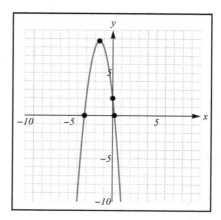

c. $y = 5x^2 - 10x - 4$

  $y = 5(x-1)^2 - 9$

d. $y = -5x^2 + 11x + 2$

  $y = -5\left(x - \dfrac{11}{10}\right)^2 + \dfrac{805}{100}$

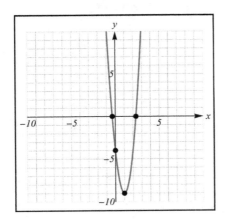

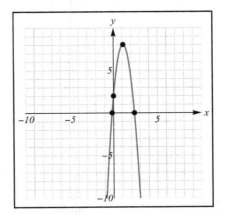

IR2

Sketching Power Functions

A **power function** is a function of the form $y = cx^n$, such as $y = 5x^3$.

The coefficient c and the exponent n must be constants, and the variables are x and y.

In $y = 5x^3$, both the coefficient, 5, and the exponent, 3, are constants.

When the coefficient c is equal to zero, then the power function is simply $y = 0$, the horizontal x-axis. We will proceed with the assumption the coefficient c is not zero.

When the exponent n equals 0, as in $y = 4x^0$, the graph is a straight line because $x^0 = 1$,

so $y = 4x^0$ is equivalent to $y = 4(1)$, which is equivalent to $y = 4$.

The graph of $y = 4$ is the horizontal line at right.

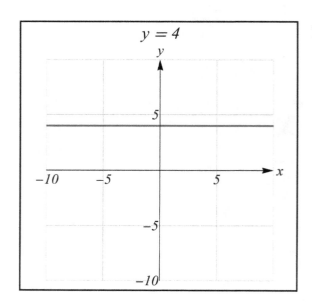

When the exponent n equals 1, as in $y = 4x^1$,

which is equivalent to $y = 4x$,

we have a linear equation, and the graph is a straight line.

It is graphed at right.

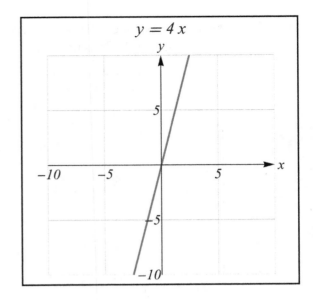

When the exponent n equals 2, as in $y = 4x^2$, we have a quadratic equation opening upward with a vertex at (0, 0).

It is graphed at right.

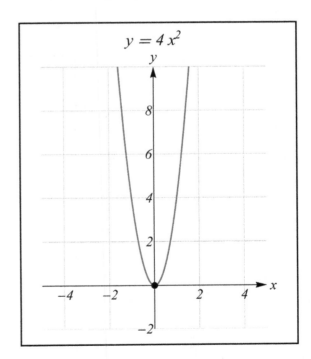

When the exponent n is an even number greater than 2, such as $y = 4x^4$ or $= 4x^6$, the graphs resemble flattened parabolas.

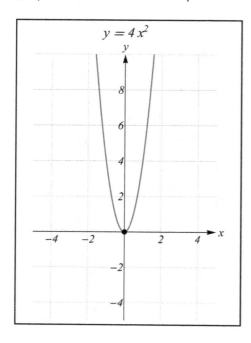

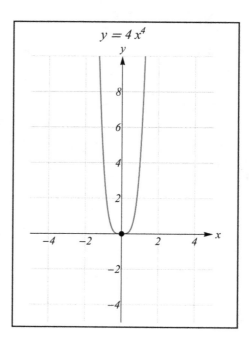

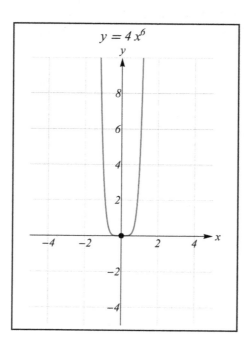

For the graphs above, as the x-values go farther and farther to the right, the y-values, i.e., the corresponding "heights" on the graph, get higher and higher. The y-values go up forever; or, we could say, the y-values approach infinity.

As the x-values go farther and farther to the left, the y-values, i.e., the corresponding "heights" on the graph, go up forever; or, we could say, the y-values approach infinity.

In mathematical notation: as $x \to \infty$, $y \to \infty$ and as $x \to -\infty$, $y \to \infty$.

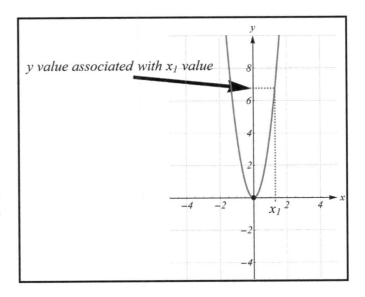

y value associated with x_1 value

This statement would be read: as x approaches infinity, y approaches infinity, and as x approaches negative infinity, y approaches infinity.

For $y = cx^n$, whenever the leading coefficient c is negative and the exponent n is even, the graph opens downward.

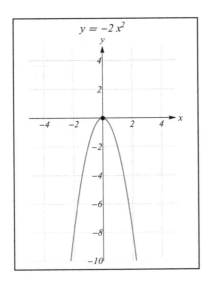

$$y = -2x^2$$

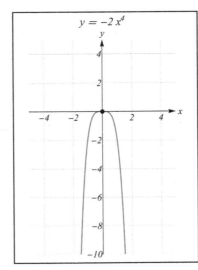

$$y = -2x^4$$

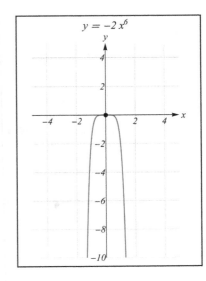

$$y = -2x^6$$

For the graphs above, as the x-values go farther and farther to the right, the y-values, i.e., the corresponding "heights" on the graph, go down forever; or, we could say, the y-values approach negative infinity.

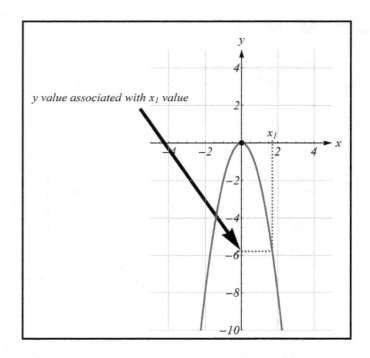

y value associated with x_1 value

As the x-values go farther and farther to the left, the y-values, i.e., the corresponding "heights" on the graph, go down forever. We could say, the y-values approach negative infinity.

In mathematical notation: as $x \to \infty$, $y \to -\infty$ and as $x \to -\infty$, $y \to -\infty$.

This statement would be read: as x approaches infinity, y approaches negative infinity, and as x approaches negative infinity, y approaches negative infinity.

We can translate these graphs vertically and horizontally as we did before. We can also compress or expand them.

Consider: $y = -0.5(x+3)^4 - 2$.

The -2 shifts the vertex down two units. The $+3$ shifts the vertex to the left three units. The coefficient 0.5 expands the width of the graph, and the leading negative sign means the graph will open downward. The vertex is now at $(-3, -2)$.

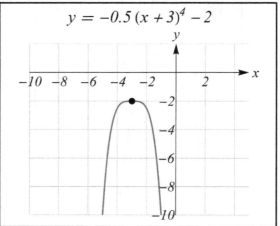

$$y = -0.5(x+3)^4 - 2$$

Consider: $y = 4.2(x - 2.3)^6 + 3.4$.

The $+3.4$ shifts the vertex up 3.4 units. The -2.3 shifts the vertex to the right 2.3 units. The leading coefficient 4.2 compresses the graph, and because the leading coefficient is positive, the graph opens upward. The vertex is now at the point (2.3, 3.4).

Would you agree that as $x \to \infty$, $y \to \infty$, and as $x \to -\infty$, $y \to \infty$? It's true.

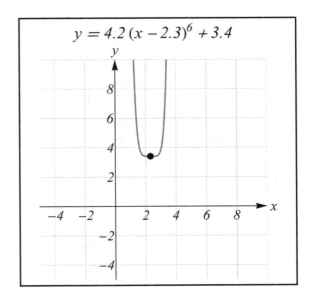

$$y = 4.2\,(x - 2.3)^6 + 3.4$$

We return to the general equation $y = cx^n$, to consider the case when the exponent n equals 3.

Consider $y = x^3$. We can make a table to plot several points.

On this graph, the point (0, 0) is called the inflection point (because that is where the concavity changes, but more about that later).

x	y
0	0
1	1
2	8
−1	−1
−2	−8

This graph goes up as we move right from (0, 0), and it goes down as we move left from (0, 0).

In other words, as x goes farther and farther to the right, the graph goes up forever, or as $x \to \infty$, $y \to \infty$.

But as x goes farther and farther to the left, the graph goes down forever, or as $x \to -\infty$, $y \to -\infty$.

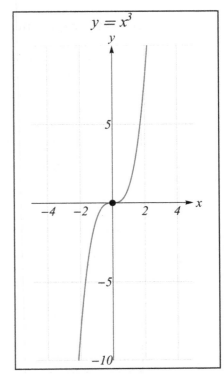

$$y = x^3$$

Now consider the graph of $y = -x^3$.

Notice that when the leading coefficient is negative (in this case, it is -1), the graph goes down as we move right from the point $(0, 0)$ and the graph goes up as we move left from $(0, 0)$, i.e., as $x \to \infty$, $y \to -\infty$, and as $x \to -\infty$, $y \to \infty$.

x	y
0	0
1	−1
2	−8
−1	1
−2	8

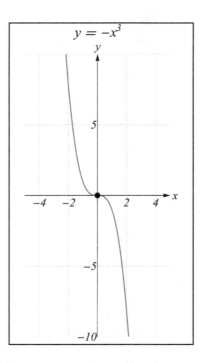

When the exponent n is an odd number greater than 2, this pattern occurs.

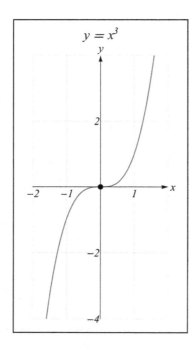

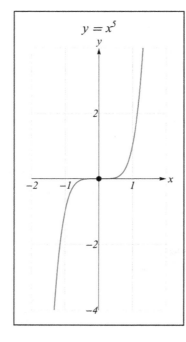

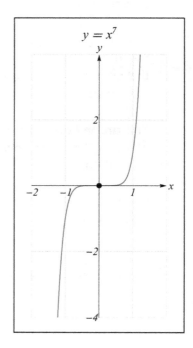

Again, we can translate the graph up or down, right or left, and we can compress or expand it as before:

Consider: $y = 3(x - 2)^3 + 4$.

We note first that the exponent is 3. Because of the +4, the inflection point is shifted up four units. Because of the −2, the inflection point is shifted two units to the right. Because of the 3, the graph is compressed, and because the leading coefficient 3 is positive, the graph goes up to the right and down to the left, or as $x \to \infty$, $y \to \infty$, and as $x \to -\infty$, $y \to -\infty$.

The inflection point is at (2, 4).

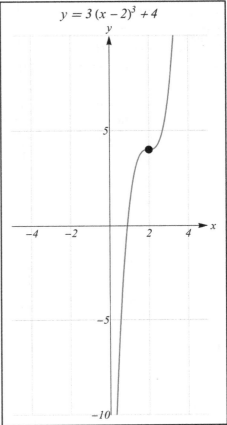

$y = 3(x - 2)^3 + 4$

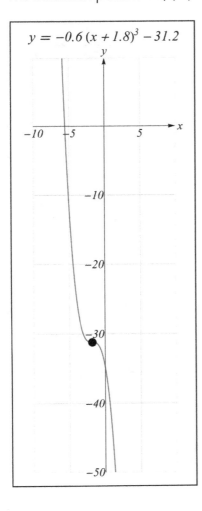

$y = -0.6(x + 1.8)^3 - 31.2$

Consider: $y = -0.6(x + 1.8)^3 - 31.2$.

We note first that the exponent is 3. The −31.2 shifts the inflection point down 31.2 units. The 1.8 shifts the inflection point 1.8 units to the left. The −0.6 expands the graph because it is less than one, and the negative means the graph goes up to the left and down to the right, or as $x \to \infty$, $y \to -\infty$, and as $x \to -\infty$, $y \to \infty$.

The inflection point is at $(-1.8, -31.2)$.

FOR FUTURE REFERENCE—POLYNOMIALS OF ODD DEGREE

Some third degree equations cannot be forced into the general form: $y = cx^3$ or even into $y = c(x-h)^3 + k$. The graphs of these equations can have a dip. The dip (relative minimum) is paired with a peak (relative maximum) like the graph at right.

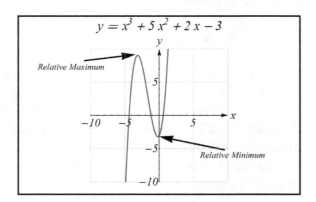

Fifth degree equations can have one or two dips. The dips need not have equal heights or widths. The graph at right has two relative maxima and two relative minima.

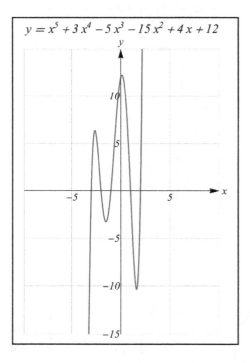

Seventh degree equations can have one, two, or three dips. The dips are paired with an equal number of peaks. Do you see a pattern here?

FOR FUTURE REFERENCE—POLYNOMIALS OF EVEN DEGREE

Many fourth degree equations do not fit the general form $y = cx^4$ or even $y = c(x-h)^4 + k$. The graphs of these equations also have relative maxima and relative minima. The graph of the fourth degree equation at right has two dips, making two relative minima and one relative maximum. The graphs of fourth degree equations with a positive leading coefficient can have one dip (one relative minimum) or two dips (two relative minima).

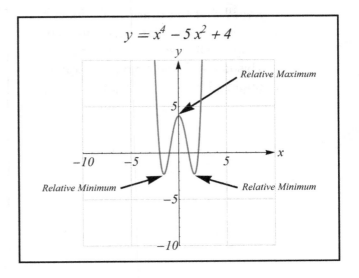

$$y = x^4 - 5x^2 + 4$$

Relative Maximum

Relative Minimum   Relative Minimum

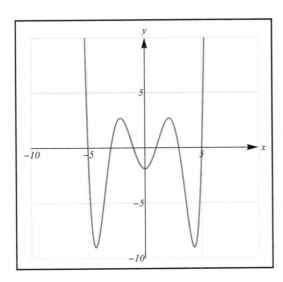

The figure at left is the graph of a sixth degree equation. Graphs of sixth degree equations with a positive leading coefficient can have one dip (one relative minimum), two dips (two relative minima), or three dips (three relative minima). There will be one less peak than dips. The dips need not be at the same height.

Do you notice another pattern?

SIDEWAYS PARABOLAS—GRAPHS OF THE FORM $y = a(x-h)^{1/2} + k$

Recall that the graphs of a function and its inverse relationship are mirror images reflected across the line $y = x$. This is a 45° line going through the origin. (See graph at right.)

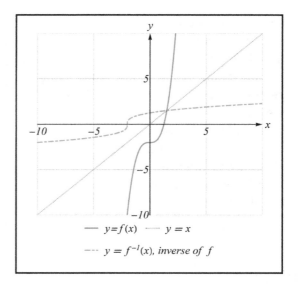

Recall that you can generate the inverse relationship of a function by changing all its 'y's into 'x's and all its 'x's into 'y's.

Consider the parabola $y = x^2$.

Its inverse relationship would be $x = y^2$.

The graph of $x = y^2$ would look like the sideways parabola at right.

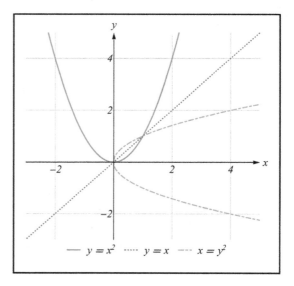

We also know that by convention, most equations are not solved for x. They don't begin with "x = ...". They begin with "y =...". Therefore, we need to solve the equation, $x = y^2$, for y.

Taking the square root of both sides, we get:

$\pm\sqrt{x} = y$, or equivalently: $y = \pm\sqrt{x}$.

Remember that the parabola $y = x^2$ opened upward, and the graph of $y = -x^2$ reflected the graph so that the parabola opened downward.

When we sketch $y = +\sqrt{x}$, we get the top half of the sideways parabola,

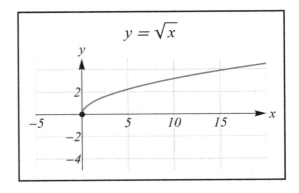

and when we sketch $y = -\sqrt{x}$, we get the bottom half of the sideways parabola.

Another way to write the equation $y = \sqrt{x}$ is $y = x^{1/2}$.

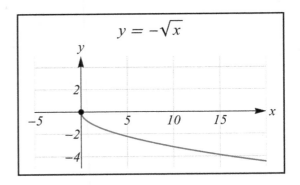

Consider the graph of $y = \sqrt{x} + 3$. The graph of $y = \sqrt{x}$ is shifted 3 units upward. The endpoint is (0, 3).

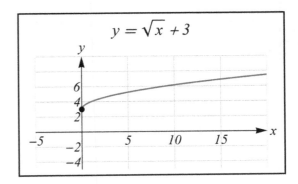

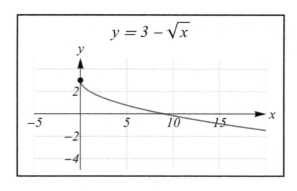

$$y = 3 - \sqrt{x}$$

Consider the graph of $y = -\sqrt{x} + 3$. The graph of $y = -\sqrt{x}$ is shifted three units upward. The endpoint is again at (0, 3), but it is the bottom half, i.e., the negative reflection.

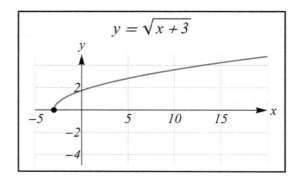

$$y = \sqrt{x + 3}$$

Consider the graph of $y = \sqrt{x + 3}$, also written $y = (x + 3)^{1/2}$. The graph of $y = \sqrt{x}$ is shifted three units to the left. The endpoint is at (−3, 0).

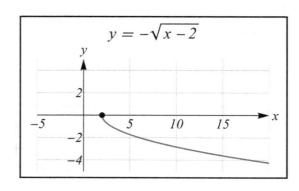

$$y = -\sqrt{x - 2}$$

Consider the graph of $y = -\sqrt{x - 2}$, also written $y = -(x - 2)^{1/2}$. The graph of $y = -\sqrt{x} - 2$ is shifted two units to the right and is the negative reflection. The endpoint is at (2, 0).

Consider the graph of $y = 3\sqrt{x}$, or $y = 3(x)^{1/2}$. This graph rises more steeply than $y = \sqrt{x}$.

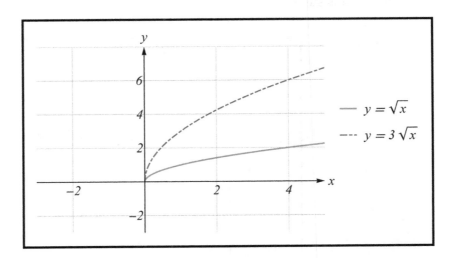

The graph of $y = 0.2\sqrt{x}$ rises less steeply than $y = \sqrt{x}$.

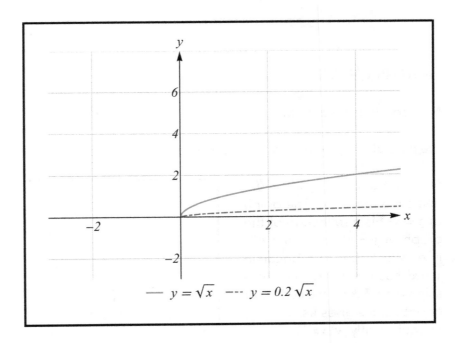

Now consider the graph of $y = -2.4\sqrt{x+2} - 3$. This graph is shifted two units left and three units down. The endpoint is at $(-2, -3)$. It is the bottom half of the sideways parabola, and it is steeper than $y = -\sqrt{x}$.

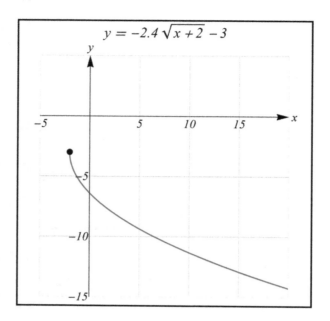

GRAPHS OF THE FORM $y = a(x-h)^{1/m} + k$

Now consider $y = x^{1/m}$, where m is a positive whole number greater than one.

We have already examined the graph when $m = 2$; that is, $y = x^{1/2}$.

Now let's use $y = x^{1/3} = \sqrt[3]{x}$ (the cube root of x). The graph of $y = x^{1/3}$ is a reflection of the graph of $y = x^3$ through a 45° line. We know this because $y = x^3$ has the inverse relationship $x = y^3$. Taking the cube root of both sides gives us: $x^{1/3} = y$, or equivalently, $y = x^{1/3}$.

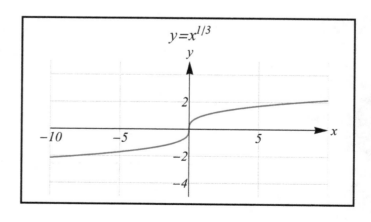

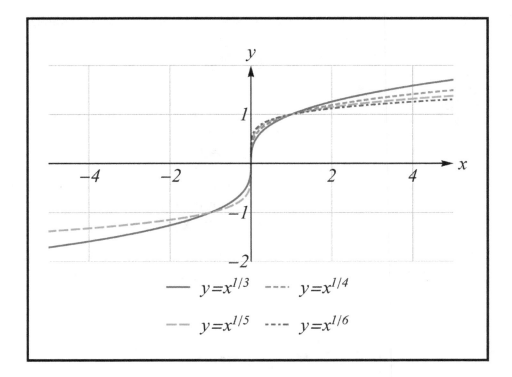

$$y=x^{1/3} \quad y=x^{1/4}$$
$$y=x^{1/5} \quad y=x^{1/6}$$

Notice that when m is an even number, the graph exists only on the side where $(x-h)$ is positive, because we can't take the 2nd, or 4th, or 6th root—i.e., an even root—of a negative number. When m is an odd number, the graphs of $y=(x-h)^{1/m}$ will exist on both halves of the x-axis because we can take odd roots of both positive and negative numbers.

KITTY-CORNER HYPERBOLAE—GRAPHS OF THE FORM $y=a(x-h)^{-1}+k$

Consider the equation $y=cx^{n}$ once again. When the exponent is −1, the graph is that of a kitty-corner hyperbola. When the exponent is the negative of a whole number greater than one, the graph is similar to a kitty-corner hyperbola, but with sharper corners.

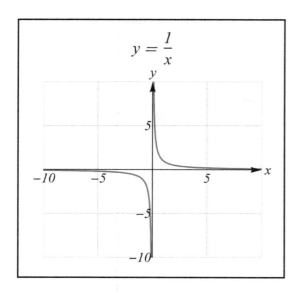

Do you agree with the following statements?

– The graph has no intercepts.

– The x-axis and y-axis are both asymptotes.

– The line $x = 0$ is a vertical asymptote, and the line $y = 0$ is a horizontal asymptote.

–The graph approaches the x-axis when x becomes larger and larger, but never reaches it, i.e., as $\to \infty$, $y \to 0$, and as $x \to -\infty$, $y \to 0$.

–The graph approaches the y-axis when x approaches 0 but never reaches it.

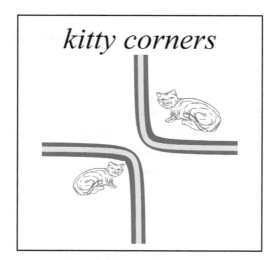

The graph of $y = \dfrac{1}{x} + 2$ shifts the kitty-corner hyperbola up two units. We start by shifting the horizontal asymptote up two units. The graph of $y = \dfrac{1}{x} - 3$ shifts the graph down three units. Again, we begin by shifting the horizontal asymptote down 3 units.

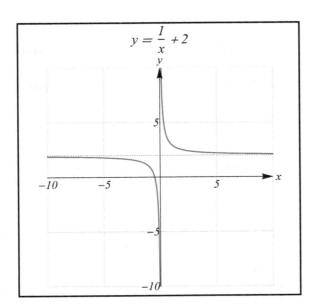

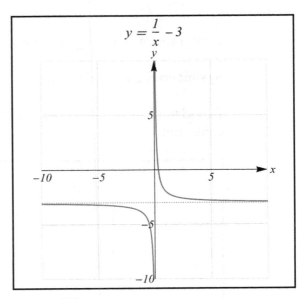

Note that the equation $y = \dfrac{1}{x} + 2$ can be written $y = \dfrac{1+2x}{x}$.

This is accomplished by putting both terms over a common denominator.

$y = \dfrac{1}{x} + 2$ We multiply the numerator and denominator of the second term by x.

$y = \dfrac{1}{x} + 2\dfrac{x}{x}$ Since both terms now have the same denominator, we can add up the numerators.

$y = \dfrac{1+2x}{x}$

That graph of $y = \dfrac{1}{(x+2)}$ is the graph of $y = \dfrac{1}{x}$ shifted two units to the left. We start by shifting the vertical asymptote two units left. The graph of $y = \dfrac{1}{(x-3)}$ is the graph shifted three units to the right. Again, we start by shifting the vertical asymptote three units right.

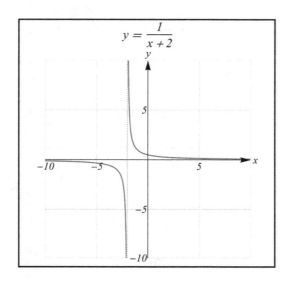

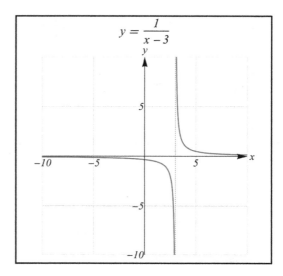

Adding coefficients to the numerator will make the hyperbolae rise more steeply or more slowly.

SUMMARY

Now that you know how to sketch graphs of linear equations, quadratic equations, and power functions, you'll soon be able to find the areas under these curves by integrating. We just have a few more review topics, and then we'll get right to that.

Steam Power Function

IR2 SKETCHING POWER FUNCTIONS EXERCISES

Sketch graphs of the following equations; make quick sketches by hand without using an electronic graphing device. Do not plot more than two points. Label or use hatch marks on the axes to indicate the position of the vertex, inflection point, or end point. Indicate any asymptotes with a dashed line.

1. $y = x^3 + 4$

2. $y = (x-2)^3$

3. $y = -x^3 + 1$

4. $y = -x^2 + 1$

5. $y = (x+1)^3 - 2$

6. $y = (x-2)^3 + 4$

7. $y = (x+3)^3 - 2$

8. $y = -2$

9. $y = (x+3)^2 - 2$

10. $y = \dfrac{1}{x}$

11. $y = \dfrac{1}{x-3}$

12. $y = \dfrac{1}{x+3}$

13. $y = \dfrac{4}{x+3}$

14. $y = \dfrac{1}{x+3} + 2$

15. $y = \dfrac{1}{x-2} - 1$

16. $y = \dfrac{-3}{x-2} - 1$

17. $y = x^2 + 2x - 1$

18. $y = \sqrt{x} + 1$

19. $y = \sqrt{x-3}$

20. $y = \sqrt{x+2} - 1$

21. $y = -\sqrt{x+2} - 1$

22. Match each equation with its graph

A.
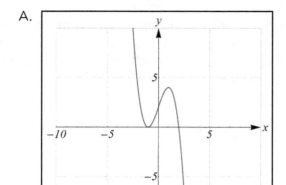

B.
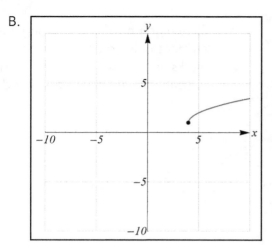

C.
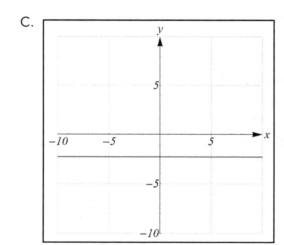

D.
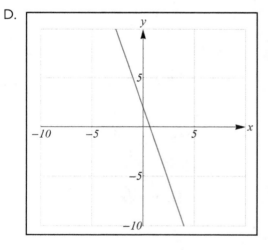

E.
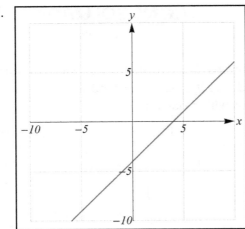

F.
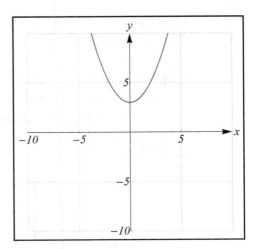

G.
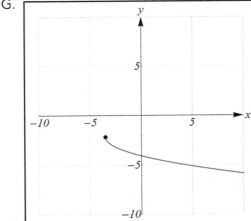

a. _____ $y = x - 4$

b. _____ $y = -3x + 2$

c. _____ $y = -x^3 + 3x + 2$

d. _____ $y = \sqrt{x - 4} + 1$

e. _____ $y = \dfrac{x^2}{3} + 3$

f. _____ $y = -\sqrt{x + 3.5} - 2.2$

g. _____ $y = -2.3$

IR2 SKETCHING POWER FUNCTIONS SOLUTIONS TO EXERCISES

Sketch graphs of the following equations. Do not plot more than two points. Label or use hatch marks on the axes to indicate the position of the vertex, inflection point, or endpoint. Indicate any asymptotes with a dashed line.

1. $y = x^3 + 4$

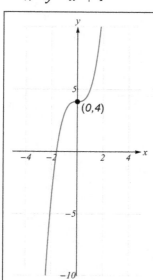

2. $y = (x-2)^3$

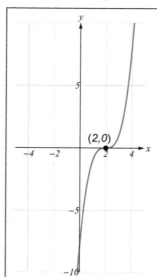

3. $y = -x^3 + 1$

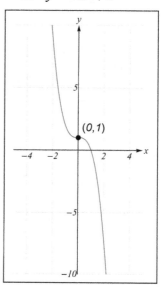

4. $y = -x^2 + 1$

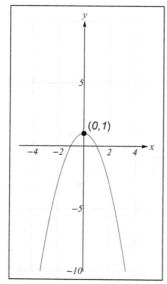

5. $y = (x+1)^3 - 2$

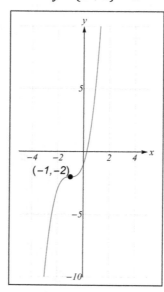

6. $y = (x-2)^3 + 4$

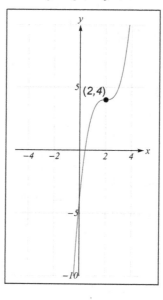

7. $y = (x+3)^3 - 2$

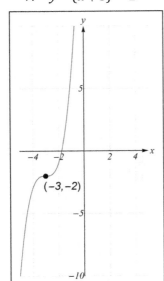

8. $y = -2$

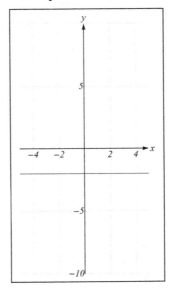

9. $y = (x+3)^2 - 2$

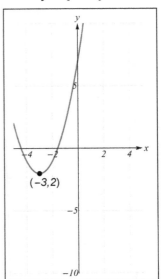

10. $y = \dfrac{1}{x}$

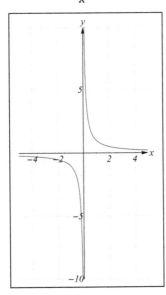

11. $y = \dfrac{1}{x-3}$

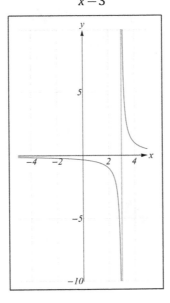

12. $y = \dfrac{1}{x+3}$

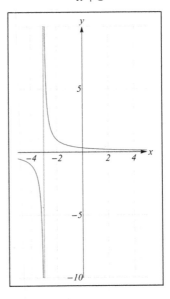

13. $y = \dfrac{4}{x+3}$

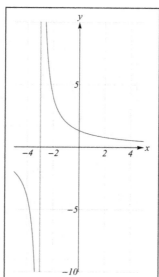

14. $y = \dfrac{1}{x+3} + 2$

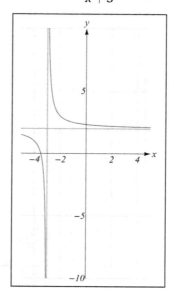

15. $y = \dfrac{1}{x-2} - 1$

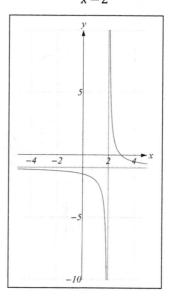

16. $y = \dfrac{-3}{x-2} - 1$

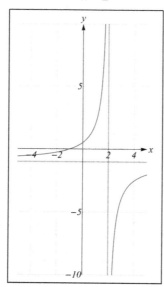

17. $y = x^2 + 2x - 1$

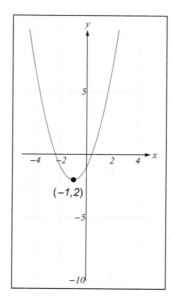

18. $y = \sqrt{x} + 1$

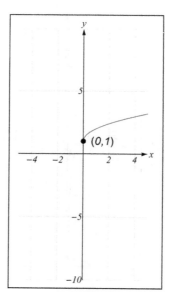

19. $y = \sqrt{x-3}$

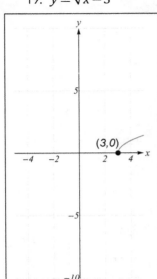

20. $y = \sqrt{x+2} - 1$

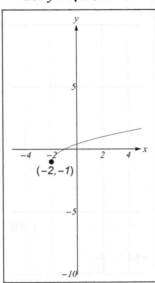

21. $y = -\sqrt{x+2} - 1$

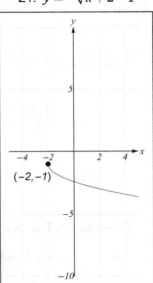

22. Match each equation with its graph

a. __E__ $y = x - 4$

b. __D__ $y = -3x + 2$

c. __A__ $y = -x^3 + 3x + 2$

d. __B__ $y = \sqrt{x-4} + 1$

e. __F__ $y = \dfrac{x^2}{3} + 3$

f. __G__ $y = -\sqrt{x+3.5} - 2.2$

g. __C__ $y = -2.3$

IR3

Exponents

Consider 3^4. This is a shorthand way to write $(3)(3)(3)(3)$, or $3\cdot3\cdot3\cdot3$.

The three is the *base* in the expression 3^4, and four is the *exponent*.

The expression 3^4 itself is called a power; in this case, the 4th power of 3.

Similarly, $(5)(5)(5)(5)(5)(5) = 5^6$, or $5\cdot5\cdot5\cdot5\cdot5\cdot5 = 5^6$,

and $10^8 = 10\cdot10\cdot10\cdot10\cdot10\cdot10\cdot10\cdot10$ and $x^4 = x\cdot x\cdot x\cdot x$.

If the table is a "base" is the vase an "exponent"?

In general, x^n is a *power* with *base x* and *exponent n*.

In our examples so far, *n* is a whole number (the number of factors), but we can extend x^n to cases where the exponent is any real number (e.g., $x^{-2.3}$) and represents something more than a direct count of factors. We will look at this extension, but first, we will look at basic exponent rules when operations are performed with powers.

MULTIPLICATION OF POWER EXPRESSIONS

The multiplication of the powers x^2 and x^3, that is, x^2x^3, can be written as $(x\cdot x)(x\cdot x\cdot x)$, which equals $x\cdot x\cdot x\cdot x\cdot x$, or x^5,

$$\text{i.e., } x^2x^3 = x\cdot x\cdot x\cdot x\cdot x = x^5.$$

We can reach x^5 without going through the middle step because we know x^2x^3 will give us a string of $2 + 3$ 'x's, which would be 5 'x's. We can write a product of 5 'x's as x^5.

In other words, when multiplying two factors with the same base, we can add the exponents.

> In general, the rule: $x^m x^n = x^{m+n}$ holds for exponents that may be any real numbers.
>
> (There are a few exceptions for x, but we will not address these here.)

Example 1:

a. $(x^5)(x^8) = x^{13}$

b. $(x^{1.2})(x^{3.6}) = x^{4.8}$

c. $\left(x^{1/2}\right)\left(x^{1/2}\right) = x^1 = x$

 (Note: x^1 equals only one 'x'
 or just: x)

d. $(x^{-6})(x^8) = x^{-6+8} = x^2$

e. $(x^8)(x^{-11}) = x^{8-11} = x^{-3}$

f. $((x+y)^{15})(x+y)^{-11}) = (x+y)^{15+-11} = (x+y)^4$

Be sure to note that x^1 is **x** one time, so x^1 equals plain old **x**, and **x** equals x^1. Therefore:

$$(x^{11})x = (x^{11})(x^1) = x^{11+1} = x^{12}.$$

INTRA-SECTION EXERCISES:

Simplify the following expressions.

1. $(x^4)(x^7) = $ _____

2. $(x^4)(x^{-7}) = $ _____

3. $(x^{-4})(x^7) = $ _____

4. $(x^{-4})(x^{-7}) = $ _____

5. $(3^{18})(3) = $ _____

6. $(3^{6.2})(3^{2.4}) = $ _____

7. $(5^{-2.6})(5^{7.2}) = $ _____

8. $(a-b)^5(a-b)^{11} = $ _____

$$(🐶)^5(🐶)^3 = (🐶)^8$$

9. In a particular US state, each county can issue a number of license plates equal to $26^3 10^3$. If there were 10 counties, how many license plates in total could be issued?

Solutions

1. $x^{4+7} = x^{11}$ 4. $x^{-4+-7} = x^{-11}$ 7. $5^{-2.6+7.2} = 5^{4.6}$

2. $x^{4-7} = x^{-3}$ 5. $3^{18+1} = 3^{19}$ 8. $(a-b)^{5+11} = (a-b)^{16}$

3. $x^{-4+7} = x^{3}$ 6. $3^{6.2+2.4} = 3^{8.6}$ 9. $(26^{3}10^{3})(10^{1}) = 26^{3}10^{4}$

MULTIPLICATION OF POWER EXPRESSIONS—MULTIPLE VARIABLES

Consider simplifying $(4x^2y)(x^3)$, which is just four algebraic expressions multiplied together.

Using the Associative Law for Multiplication: $(4x^2y)(x^3) = (4)(x^2)(y)(x^3)$.

Using the Commutative Law for Multiplication, we can change the order:

$$(4)(x^2)(x^3)(y).$$

Adding the exponents for x^2 and x^3, we can simplify the expression to:

$$(4)(x^2)(x^3)(y) = 4x^5y.$$

The middle steps aren't usually necessary. We can see at a glance that there are two factors with a base of 'x' and simplify the expression by adding the exponents for these two "x-factors."

$$\text{i.e., } (4x^2y)(x^3) = 4x^5y.$$

Consider simplifying: $(3\times10^4)(2\times10^5).$

This expression is also just four expressions, in this case, numbers, multiplied together:

$$(3)(10^4)(2)(10^5).$$

Using the Commutative Law for Multiplication of Numbers, we can change the order to:

$$(3)(2)(10^4)(10^5).$$

Since there are two factors with base 10, we can add their exponents to get:

$$(3)(2)(10^{4+5}) = (3)(2)(10^9).$$

We can also multiply the "3" times the "2" to get: $(6)(10^9)$, which we can write as: 6×10^9.

A number written as a factor times a "Base 10 number" is often said to be in *scientific notation* or *exponential notation*.

Base 10?

INTRA-SECTION EXERCISES:

Simplify the expressions below.

10. $(7x^5 y)(5xy^4)$

11. $(8x^{1.2} y^{3.4})(2x^{-0.3} y^{1.1})$

12. $(4 \times 10^{15})(1.3 \times 10^{-46})$

Solutions

10. $(7)(5)(x^5)(x)(y)(y^4) = 35x^6 y^5$

11. $(8)(2)(x^{1.2})(x^{-0.3})(y^{3.4})(y^{1.1}) = 16x^{0.9} y^{4.5}$

12. $(4)(1.3)(10^{15})(10^{-46}) = 5.2 \times 10^{15-46} = 5.2 \times 10^{-31}$

Units follow the same rules for exponents. For example, a bathroom tile that is 4 inches by 6 inches has an area of:

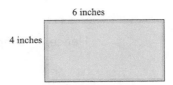

6 inches

4 inches

(4 inches)(6 inches) = 24 inches², which is read 24 inches squared, or 24 square inches. *Area is always represented by squared units of length*, like square feet, square inches, or square meters.

A box that is 2 feet wide by 2 feet long and 4 feet deep has a volume of: $(2ft)(2ft)(4ft) = 16ft^3$, read 16 feet cubed, or 16 cubic feet.

Volume is always represented by cubic units of length, such as cubic meters, cubic inches, or cubic feet.

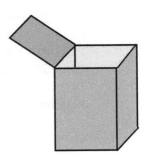

INTRA-SECTION EXERCISES:

13. How many cubic feet will the freezer compartment of a refrigerator contain if the inside is 1.5 feet wide by 2 feet deep by 3 feet high?

14. A metal box that holds tea bags is 4 cm by 17 cm by 3 cm. What is its volume?

Solutions

13. $(3ft)(2ft)(1.5ft) = 9ft^3$

14. $(4cm)(17cm)(3cm) = 204cm^3$

DIVISION OF POWER EXPRESSIONS

Consider simplifying: $\dfrac{x^5}{x^3}$. This is a shorthand way to write: $\dfrac{x \cdot x \cdot x \cdot x \cdot x}{x \cdot x \cdot x}$

Since $\dfrac{x}{x}$ reduces to "1," we can simplify to get: $\dfrac{x}{1} \cdot \dfrac{x}{1} \cdot \dfrac{x}{x} \cdot \dfrac{x}{x} \cdot \dfrac{x}{x} = x \cdot x \cdot 1 \cdot 1 \cdot 1 = x^2$.

Hence, $\dfrac{x^5}{x^3}$ simplifies to x^2. We see this procedure is subtracting the "bottom" exponent

from the "top" exponent to get: $\dfrac{x^5}{x^3} = x^{5-3} = x^2$.

In general, the rule $\dfrac{x^m}{x^n} = x^{m-n}$ holds for exponents that may be any real numbers.

(There are a few exceptions for x, but we will not address these here.)

Following the rule above, $\dfrac{x^3}{x^5} = x^{3-5} = x^{-2}$ but

$$\dfrac{x^3}{x^5} \quad \text{also equals} \quad \dfrac{x \cdot x \cdot x}{x \cdot x \cdot x \cdot x \cdot x} = \dfrac{1}{x} \cdot \dfrac{1}{x} \cdot \dfrac{x}{x} \cdot \dfrac{x}{x} \cdot \dfrac{x}{x} = \dfrac{1}{x}\dfrac{1}{x} \cdot 1 \cdot 1 \cdot 1 = \dfrac{1}{x^2}$$

Therefore, for the system to remain consistent,

x^{-2} *must equal* $\dfrac{1}{x^2}$.

Thus, $x^{-3} = \dfrac{1}{x^3}$, and $x^{-5} = \dfrac{1}{x^5}$.

Also, $\dfrac{1}{x^{-4}} = x^4$ because $\dfrac{1}{x^{-4}} = 1 \div x^{-4} = 1 \div \dfrac{1}{x^4} = 1 \cdot \dfrac{x^4}{1} = x^4$.

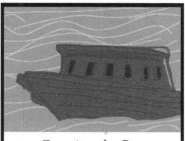

Crossing the Bar
is also a
nautical term
and a poem by
Alfred Lord Tennyson

In summary, "crossing the bar" causes the exponent to change its sign.

Example 2:

a. $\dfrac{x^6}{x^4} = x^{6-4} = x^2$

b. $\dfrac{x^6}{x^{-4}} = x^{6-(-4)} = x^{6+4} = x^{10}$

c. $\dfrac{x^{-6}}{x^4} = x^{-6-4} = x^{-10}$ *or* $\dfrac{1}{x^{10}}$

d. $\dfrac{3}{x^{11}} = 3x^{-11}$

e. $\dfrac{7}{x^{-11}} = 7x^{11}$

f. $\dfrac{(a-b)^{14}}{(a-b)^{-11}} = (a-b)^{14-(-11)} = (a-b)^{25}$

INTRA-SECTION EXERCISES:

15. $\dfrac{x^{14}}{x^{10}}$ 16. $\dfrac{x^{14}}{x^{-10}}$ 17. $\dfrac{x^{-14}}{x^{10}}$ 18. $\dfrac{x^{10}}{x}$ 19. $\dfrac{x^{-10}}{x^{-14}}$ 20. $\dfrac{x^{4.6}}{x^{2.8}}$ 21. $\dfrac{x^{-5.4}}{x^{-2.3}}$

Solutions

15. $x^{14-10} = x^4$

16. $x^{14-(-10)} = x^{14+10} = x^{24}$

17. $x^{-14-10} = x^{-24}$

18. $x^{10-1} = x^9$

19. $x^{-10-(-14)} = x^{-10+14} = x^4$

20. $x^{4.6-2.8} = x^{1.8}$

21. $x^{-5.4-(-2.3)} = x^{-5.4+2.3} = x^{-3.1}$

Whenever the numerator equals the denominator, a fraction equals 1.

For example: $\frac{3}{3}=1$ and $\frac{x}{x}=1$. Similarly, $\frac{x^5}{x^5}=1$.

But if we follow the rule above: $\frac{x^5}{x^5}=x^{5-5}=x^0$, which must also equal 1.

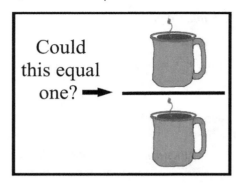

Could this equal one? ➡

Therefore, for the system to be consistent, $x^0=1$.

For the same reason, any (nonzero) number with the exponent "0" equals 1.

Consider simplifying: $\frac{4x^3y}{x^5}$. If we combine the two factors with base "x," we have

$$\frac{4x^3y}{x^5}=4x^{3-5}y=4x^{-2}y, \text{ or } \frac{4y}{x^2}.$$

INTRA-SECTION EXERCISES:

Simplify the fractions (aka rational expressions) below.

22. $\dfrac{x^8}{x^8}$ 23. $\dfrac{x^{-3}}{x^{-3}}$ 24. $\dfrac{3xy^7}{6x^4y^6}$ 25. $\dfrac{10x^{-4}y^{5.5}}{2x^4y^{1.1}}$

Solutions

22. $x^{8-8}=x^0=1$

24. $0.5(x^{1-4})(y^{7-6})=0.5x^{-3}y$ or $\dfrac{y}{2x^3}$

23. $x^{-3--3}=x^{-3+3}=x^0=1$

25. $2(x^{-4-4})(y^{5.5-1.1})=2x^{-8}y^{4.4}$ or $\dfrac{2y^{4.4}}{x^8}$

In the expression: $\frac{3x^4}{y}$, note that the constant 3 (aka the number 3) does not have an exponent.

The exponent 4 refers only to the x. It would take the expression: $\frac{(3x)^4}{y}$ to give 3 an exponent of 4.

DIVISION OF POWER EXPRESSIONS—ANOTHER VIEWPOINT

What is the meaning of a power with a negative exponent? For a power with a positive exponent such as x^3, we start with 1 and add in three factors of x by multiplication:

$$1; \ x; \ x \cdot x = x^2; \ x^2 \cdot x = x^3.$$

So, x^{-3} means to start with 1 and take away 3 factors of x by division:

$$1; \ x^{-1} = 1 \div x = \frac{1}{x}; \ x^{-2} = \frac{1}{x} \div x = \frac{1}{x^2}; \ x^{-3} = \frac{1}{x^2} \div x = \frac{1}{x^3}$$

> The general rule is: $\quad x^{-n} = \dfrac{1}{x^n}$.
>
> To change the sign of the exponent, the power is "flipped" from top to bottom in a fraction. "Crossing the bar" (fraction bar) changes the sign of the exponent.
>
> Another way to say this is that a power with an exponent $-n$ is the reciprocal of the power with exponent n.

> The general rule is $x^0 = 1$ for any real number, except that 0^0 is not defined.

Example 3:

    a. $\ x^{-7} = \dfrac{1}{x^7}$
    c. $\ x^5 = \dfrac{1}{x^{-5}}$
    e. $\ y^{-p} = \dfrac{1}{y^p}$

    b. $\ 8^0 = 1$
    d. $\ w^0 = 1$
    f. $\ (xyz)^0 = 1$

AN EXPRESSION WITH AN EXPONENT THAT IS THEN RAISED TO A POWER

Consider simplifying $(x^2)^3$. The exponent "3" tells us this expression $(x^2)^3$ is a product of 3 factors.

$$(x^2)^3 = (x^2)(x^2)(x^2).$$

We can expand further.

$$(x^2)^3 = (x^2)(x^2)(x^2) = (x \cdot x)(x \cdot x)(x \cdot x) = x \cdot x \cdot x \cdot x \cdot x \cdot x = x^6$$

The expression $(x^2)^3$ gives us three groups of two 'x's each, or 2 times 3 'x's, which is 6 'x's.

Therefore, when an expression with an exponent is raised to a power, we can multiply the exponents.

In general, the rule $(x^m)^n = x^{mn}$ holds for exponents that may be any real numbers.

(There are a few exceptions for x, but we will not address them here.)

Also note that the outside exponent applies to everything inside parentheses. For example:

$$(2x^5 y)^3 = (2^3)(x^5)^3(y^3) = 8x^{15} y^3.$$

Example 4:

a. $(x^5)^8 = x^{40}$

b. $(x^5)^{1/2} = x^{5/2}$

c. $(x^6)^{-3} = x^{-18}$ or, if you wish, you can write it $\dfrac{1}{x^{18}}$.

d. $(x^{1/2})^2 = x^{2/2} = x^1 = x$

e. $(xy^4)^{7.2} = x^{7.2} y^{(4)(7.2)} = x^{7.2} y^{28.8}$

f. $(x^3)^{-1} = \dfrac{1}{x^3}$ or, if you wish, you can write: x^{-3}.

INTRA-SECTION EXERCISES:

Simplify the expressions below.

26. $(x^8)^4$ 27. $(x^{-3})^5$ 28. $(y^{1.1})^{-2}$ 29. $(4^{-2.5})^{-2}$ 30. $(3x^6 y^2)^3$

Solutions

26. x^{32} 27. x^{-15} 28. $y^{-2.2}$ 29. 4^5 or 1024   30. $3^3 x^{18} y^6$ or $27x^{18} y^6$

Notice that the exponent "−1" results in an expression that is flipped over.

For example: $5^{-1} = \dfrac{1}{5}$, $: x^{-1} = \dfrac{1}{x}$, $: (x^3)^{-1} = \dfrac{1}{x^3}$, and $: \left(\dfrac{4y^4}{x^2}\right)^{-1} = \dfrac{x^2}{4y^4}$

Even $\left(\dfrac{8}{9}\right)^{-1} = \dfrac{9}{8}$ because $\left(\dfrac{8}{9}\right)^{-1} = \dfrac{8^{-1}}{9^{-1}} = 8^{-1} \div 9^{-1} = \dfrac{1}{8} \div \dfrac{1}{9} = \dfrac{1}{8} \cdot \dfrac{9}{1} = \dfrac{9}{8}$.

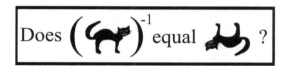

Again, note that the *exponent* applies to everything inside the parentheses.

For example: $\left(\dfrac{4y^4}{x^2}\right)^3 = \dfrac{4^3 y^{12}}{x^6} = \dfrac{64 y^{12}}{x^6}$

A WORD OF CAUTION

In an expression such as $\dfrac{1}{4x^{-6}}$, if the power is moved across the fraction bar,

do not accidentally include the four in the power. $\dfrac{1}{4x^{-6}} = \dfrac{x^6}{4}$, but $\dfrac{1}{4x^{-6}} \neq 4x^6$.

ANOTHER WORD OF CAUTION

Consider the expressions: $(-3)^2$, which equals 9, and -3^2, which equals -9.

The first expression equals 9 because $(-3)^2 = (-3)(-3)$.

The second expression equals -9 because $-3^2 = -(3)(3)$.

Caution: The exponent does not apply to the initial minus sign if it is not included in parentheses.

INTRA-SECTION EXERCISES:

Simplify so that there are no negative exponents.

31. 4^{-1} 33. $(9x^2)^{-1}$ 35. $(14x)^{-1}$ 37. $\left(\dfrac{x^2}{5}\right)^{-1}$

32. x^{-1} 34. $14x^{-1}$ 36. $\left(\dfrac{7}{5}\right)^{-1}$

Solutions

31. $\dfrac{1}{4}$ 33. $\dfrac{1}{9x^2}$ 35. $\dfrac{1}{14x}$ 37. $\dfrac{5}{x^2}$

32. $\dfrac{1}{x}$ 34. $\dfrac{14}{x}$ 36. $\dfrac{5}{7}$

EXPONENTS THAT ARE FRACTIONS

Recall that $(x^{1/2})(x^{1/2}) = x$.

Also recall that $(\sqrt{x})(\sqrt{x}) = x$.

Therefore, for the system to be consistent, $x^{1/2}$ must equal $\sqrt{x}$.

Similarly, $x^{1/3} = \sqrt[3]{x}$ because $(x^{1/3})(x^{1/3})(x^{1/3}) = x^{3/3} = x^1 = x$ and $\sqrt[3]{x} \cdot \sqrt[3]{x} \cdot \sqrt[3]{x} = x$.

In general, $x^{1/n} = \sqrt[n]{x}$.

ANOTHER VIEWPOINT REGARDING EXPONENTS THAT ARE FRACTIONS

What should $x^{1/2}$ mean? From $3 \cdot 3 = 9$, we see that 3 makes up half of the factors of 9.

Half of the factors of 9 should be indicated by $9^{1/2}$, and $3 = 9^{1/2}$.

We also say that 3 is the square root of 9 since $3^2 = 3 \cdot 3 = 9$. So $3 = 9^{1/2} = \sqrt{9}$.

For any non-negative number x, $x^{1/2}$ should be half of the factors of x; in other words, the square root of x;

$$x^{1/2} = \sqrt{x}$$

More generally, $x^{1/n}$ should indicate one-nth of the factors of x; that is, the nth root of x.

In general, $x^{1/n} = \sqrt[n]{x}$

Consider $(16)^{-3/4}$. It would also equal $\left(\left((16)^{-1}\right)^3\right)^{1/4}$.

Remember the Commutative Law for Multiplication? We can multiply the exponents in any order we want, so

$\left(\left((16)^{-1}\right)^3\right)^{1/4}$ also equals $\left(\left((16)^3\right)^{1/4}\right)^{-1}$ or $\left(\left((16)^{1/4}\right)^{-1}\right)^3$ or $\left(\left((16)^{1/4}\right)^3\right)^{-1}$.

Let's use this version: $\left(\left((16)^{1/4}\right)^3\right)^{-1}$. We have three things to do.

We have to take the 4th root of 16, then cube it, then flip it over.

The 4th root of 16 is 2, so we can replace $(16)^{1/4}$ with 2 to get: $(2^3)^{-1}$.

4throot

We can replace 2^3 with 8, to get $(8)^{-1}$, and finally,

we invert the 8 to get the final answer: $\dfrac{1}{8}$.

Try $8^{5/3}$. This would be the same as $(8^{1/3})^5$.

We take the cube root of 8 to get 2, and 2^5 equals 32.

For exponents that are fractions of the form $\dfrac{m}{n}$, we can use the rule $(x^{1/n})^m = x^{m/n}$.

Example 5:

a. $16^{\frac{1}{2}} = 4$

c. $16^{\frac{5}{4}} = \left(16^{\frac{1}{4}}\right)^5 = 2^5 = 32$

b. $16^{\frac{1}{4}} = 2$

d. $16^{-5/4} = (16^{1/4})^{-5} = 2^{-5} = \dfrac{1}{2^5} = \dfrac{1}{32}$

INTRA-SECTION EXERCISES:

38. $9^{-1/2}$

39. $\left(\dfrac{4}{25}\right)^{-1/2}$

40. $\left(\dfrac{4}{25}\right)^{3/2}$

41. $\left(\dfrac{4}{25}\right)^{-3/2}$

Solutions

38. Take the square root (square root of 9 is 3) and flip it over; hence, $9^{-1/2} = \dfrac{1}{3}$.

39. Take the square root (square root of $\dfrac{4}{25}$ is $\dfrac{2}{5}$) and flip it over; hence, $\left(\dfrac{4}{25}\right)^{-1/2} = \dfrac{5}{2}$.

40. Take the square root (square root of $\dfrac{4}{25}$ is $\dfrac{2}{5}$) and cube it; hence, $\dfrac{8}{125}$.

41. Take the square root (square root of $\dfrac{4}{25}$ is $\dfrac{2}{5}$) and cube it; (cube of $\dfrac{2}{5}$ is $\dfrac{8}{125}$),

then flip it over; hence, $\left(\dfrac{4}{25}\right)^{-3/2} = \dfrac{125}{8}$.

A WORD OF CAUTION

$\sqrt[3]{x}$ is $x^{1/3}$; it is not x^{-3}; and $\dfrac{1}{x^3}$ is x^{-3}; it is not $x^{1/3}$.

Do not confuse $x^{-n} = \dfrac{1}{x^n}$ with $x^{1/n} = \sqrt[n]{x}$.

Both rules involve a fraction, and by mistake, sometimes x^{-n} is replaced by $x^{1/n}$ instead of $\dfrac{1}{x^n}$.

For example, $x^{-3} = \dfrac{1}{x^3}$, but $x^{-3} \neq x^{1/3}$.

MOVING FACTORS IN RADICALS OUTSIDE THE RADICAL

To simplify $\sqrt{98}$, we begin by breaking 98 into prime factors:

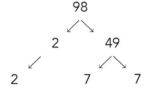

So, we can replace $\sqrt{98}$ with $\sqrt{2 \cdot 7 \cdot 7}$, or $\sqrt{2 \cdot 7^2}$.

Whenever a number or variable appears under the square root sign twice, we can move it outside the radical sign.

Because there is a pair of "7's", $\sqrt{2 \cdot 7 \cdot 7}$ becomes $7\sqrt{2}$.

To understand why we can do this, consider $\sqrt{x^2} = \sqrt{xx}$. But in exponent form, $\sqrt{x^2} = (x^2)^{1/2} = x^1 = x$. Since $(x^2)^{1/2} = x$, then it is equivalent, $\sqrt{x^2}$ must also equal x.

We can see that because a radical expression has an equivalent power expression, the rules for exponents have counterparts that are rules for radicals. One of them is:

$$\sqrt[n]{x^n} = (x^n)^{1/n} = x$$

Hence: $\quad \sqrt{x^2} = (x^2)^{1/2} = x$

or: $\qquad \sqrt{x^2} = x$

$\qquad\qquad \sqrt[3]{x^3} = x$

$\qquad\qquad \sqrt[4]{x^4} = x$

$\qquad\qquad \sqrt[5]{x^5} = x$

Another general rule: $\quad x^{1/n} = \sqrt[n]{x}$

This rule allows us to write a radical expression as a set of factors times a radical expression that has the least number of factors in the radical.

Recall: $\sqrt{98} = \sqrt{2 \cdot 7 \cdot 7}$, or $\sqrt{2 \cdot 7^2}$. Further, $\sqrt{2 \cdot 7^2} = \sqrt{2} \sqrt{7^2} = \sqrt{2} \cdot 7 = 7\sqrt{2}$

The radical $\sqrt{98}$ is now written as: $7\sqrt{2}$, an expression that has the least whole number in the radical. This was accomplished by noticing that pairs of factors are squares and can be written as a number without a radical.

Let's follow the same process for $\sqrt{24}$.

Factor 24 as $2 \cdot 2 \cdot 2 \cdot 3$.   So $\sqrt{24} = \sqrt{2 \cdot 2 \cdot 2 \cdot 3}$.

Pair up factors where possible. $\sqrt{2 \cdot 2 \cdot 2 \cdot 3} = \sqrt{2^2 \cdot 2 \cdot 3}$

Break the radical into paired factors and nonpaired factors: $\sqrt{2^2} \sqrt{2 \cdot 3}$.

Square roots of paired factors become whole numbers: $2\sqrt{2 \cdot 3} = 2\sqrt{6}$.

This process for moving factors outside a square root, even if the factors are symbols, is:

- Factor the expression under the square root to prime factors.
- Separate the factors into those that can be grouped in sets of two identical factors (pairs) and factors that cannot be grouped into pairs.
- Take the square root of the factors that are paired, moving them outside the square root.
- *If necessary, multiply* together the factors outside the square root, and multiply together the factors inside the square root.

Example 6:

     a. $\sqrt{18} = \sqrt{2 \cdot 3 \cdot 3} = \sqrt{2} \sqrt{3^2} = \sqrt{2} \cdot 3 = 3\sqrt{2}$

     b. $\sqrt{x^5} = \sqrt{x^2 x^2 x} = \sqrt{x^2 x^2} \sqrt{x} = xx\sqrt{x} = x^2\sqrt{x}$

     c. $\sqrt{12x^5 y^6} = \sqrt{2 \cdot 2 \cdot 3 \cdot x \cdot x \cdot x \cdot x \cdot x \cdot y \cdot y \cdot y \cdot y \cdot y \cdot y}$

$$= \sqrt{2^2} \sqrt{3} \sqrt{x^2} \sqrt{x^2} \sqrt{x} \sqrt{y^2} \sqrt{y^2} \sqrt{y^2} = 2xxyyyy\sqrt{3x} = 2x^2 y^3 \sqrt{3x}$$

     d. $\sqrt{5x^{22} y^{13}} = \sqrt{5x^{11} x^{11} y^6 y^6 y} = \sqrt{x^{11} x^{11} y^6 y^6} \sqrt{5y} = x^{11} y^6 \sqrt{5y}$

For cube roots, the process is the same, except look for groups of three identical factors instead of two. Move factors outside the cube root by taking cube roots of groups of three identical factors.

For example,

- $\sqrt[3]{243} = \sqrt[3]{3 \cdot 3 \cdot 3 \cdot 3 \cdot 3} = \sqrt[3]{3 \cdot 3 \cdot 3} \sqrt[3]{3 \cdot 3} = 3\sqrt[3]{3 \cdot 3} = 3\sqrt[3]{9}$

- $\sqrt[3]{12x^6 y^5} = \sqrt[3]{2 \cdot 2 \cdot 3 \cdot x^3 x^3 y^3 y^2} = \sqrt[3]{x^3 x^3 y^3} \sqrt[3]{2 \cdot 2 \cdot 3 y^2}$

  $= x \cdot x \cdot y\sqrt[3]{12 y^2} = x^2 y\sqrt[3]{12 y^2}$

The process works for any nth root, replacing groups of two for square roots with groups of n.

Example 7:

a. $\sqrt[4]{243} = \sqrt[4]{3 \cdot 3 \cdot 3 \cdot 3 \cdot 3} = \sqrt[4]{3 \cdot 3 \cdot 3 \cdot 3} \sqrt[4]{3} = \sqrt[4]{3^4} \cdot \sqrt[4]{3} = 3\sqrt[4]{3}$

b. $\sqrt[4]{12x^6 y^5} = \sqrt[4]{2 \cdot 2 \cdot 3 \cdot x^4 x^2 y^4 y^1} = xy\sqrt[4]{12x^2 y}$

c. $\sqrt[5]{243} = \sqrt[5]{3 \cdot 3 \cdot 3 \cdot 3 \cdot 3} = \sqrt[5]{3^5} = 3$

d. $\sqrt[5]{12x^6 y^5} = \sqrt[5]{2 \cdot 2 \cdot 3 \cdot x^5 x^1 y^5} = xy\sqrt[5]{12x}$

e. $\sqrt[5]{* * * * * * *} = \sqrt[5]{*^5 *^2} = *\sqrt[5]{*^2}$

REPEATED WORD OF CAUTION

Do not confuse $\sqrt[n]{x} = x^{1/n}$ with $\dfrac{1}{x^n} = x^{-n}$.

Expressions under radical signs have exponents that are fractions.

A negative exponent causes the expression to "cross the bar," not hide under a $\sqrt{\ }$.

e.g., $x^{-17} = \dfrac{1}{x^{17}}$ and $x^{1/17} = \sqrt[17]{x}$.

INTRA-SECTION EXERCISES:

Move the greatest number of factors outside the radical sign.

42. $\sqrt{54x^5 y^6}$ 43. $\sqrt[3]{54x^5 y^6}$ 44. $\sqrt[4]{54x^5 y^6}$ 45. $\sqrt{72xy^{22}z^{19}}$ 46. $\sqrt{44x^3 y}$

Solutions

42. $3x^2 y^3 \sqrt{6x}$ 43. $3xy^2 \sqrt[3]{2x^2}$ 44. $xy\sqrt[4]{54xy^2}$ 45. $6y^{11}z^9 \sqrt{2xz}$ 46. $2x\sqrt{11xy}$

IR3 EXPONENTS EXERCISES

Simplify.

1. $3x^5x^4$

2. $5x^4x^{13}$

3. $6y^5y^{-4}$

4. $7y^{-8}y^{10}$

5. $x^7(4x^{-9})$

6. $x^{-9}(3x^7)$

7. $x^{7.2}x^{4.3}$

8. $x^{5.2}x^{6.6}$

9. $z^{\frac{1}{2}}z^{\frac{3}{4}}$

10. $z^{\frac{2}{3}}z^{\frac{5}{3}}$

11. $5x^0-(5x)^0$

12. $(6x)^0-5x^0$

13. $\dfrac{x^8}{x^6}$

14. $\dfrac{x^{10}}{x^7}$

15. $\dfrac{x^8}{x^{-6}}$

16. $\dfrac{x^{10}}{x^{-7}}$

17. $\dfrac{4x^{\frac{3}{4}}}{x^{\frac{1}{2}}}$

18. $\dfrac{5x^{\frac{3}{8}}}{x^{\frac{1}{4}}}$

19. $\dfrac{5x^{\frac{1}{4}}}{x^{\frac{3}{4}}}$

20. $\dfrac{6x^{\frac{1}{2}}}{x^{\frac{3}{4}}}$

21. $(5\times10^8)(6.1\times10^{-4})$

22. $(6\times10^7)(4.1\times10^{-5})$

23. $(x^5)^{1.2}$

24. $(x^{1.5})^2$

25. $(3y^2)^2$

26. $(5y^3)^2$

27. $3(z^3)^5$

28. $5(z^3)^4$

29. $\dfrac{\sqrt{4x^2}}{2x^3}$

30. $\dfrac{\sqrt{6x^3}}{2x^2}$

31. $\left(\dfrac{4}{3}xy^2\right)^3$

32. $\left(\dfrac{5}{2}xy^3\right)^2$

33. $\dfrac{4(x+y)^3}{(x+y)^2}$

34. $\dfrac{5(x-y)^5}{(x-y)^4}$

35. $5\dfrac{x^5}{x^3}$

36. $4\dfrac{y^8}{y^3}$

37. $5\dfrac{z^3}{z^5}$

38. $4\dfrac{x^3}{x^8}$

39. $5(x+y)^5(x+y)^3$

40. $2(x-y)^6(x-y)^2$

Write with negative exponents.

41. $\dfrac{2}{3x^5}$

42. $\dfrac{3}{4x^6}$

43. $\dfrac{3}{x^4}$

44. $\dfrac{4}{x^3}$

Convert to exponent form.

45. $5\sqrt{x}$

46. $7\sqrt[3]{x}$

47. $2\sqrt[5]{x^3}$

48. $2\sqrt{x^5}$

Convert to a single integer.

49. $9^{-\frac{3}{2}}$

50. $4^{-\frac{3}{2}}$

51. $8^{\frac{2}{3}}$

52. $27^{\frac{2}{3}}$

Evaluate.

53. Find $-4x^2$ for $x=-1$

54. Find $5y^2$ for $y=-1$

55. Find $(-4x)^2$ for $x=-1$

56. Find $(-5y)^2$ for $y=-1$

IR3 EXPONENTS SOLUTIONS TO EXERCISES

1. $3x^9$

2. $5x^{17}$

3. $6y$

4. $7y^2$

5. $4x^{-2}$

6. $3x^{-2}$

7. $x^{11.5}$

8. $x^{11.8}$

9. $z^{\frac{5}{4}}$

10. $z^{\frac{7}{3}}$

11. $5(1) - 1 = 4$

12. -4

13. x^2

14. x^3

15. x^{14}

16. x^{17}

17. $4x^{\frac{1}{4}}$

18. $5x^{\frac{1}{8}}$

19. $5x^{-\frac{1}{2}}$

20. $6x^{-\frac{1}{4}}$

21. $30.5 \times 10^4 = 3.05 \times 10^5$

22. 2.46×10^3

23. $x^{6.0}$

24. $x^{3.0}$

25. $9y^4$

26. $25y^6$

27. $3z^{15}$

28. $5z^{12}$

29. $\dfrac{1}{x^2} = x^{-2}$

30. $\dfrac{\sqrt{6x}}{2x}$

31. $\dfrac{64}{27}x^3y^6$

32. $\dfrac{25}{4}x^2y^6$

33. $4(x + y)$

34. $5(x - y)$

35. $5x^2$

36. $4y^5$

37. $\dfrac{5}{z^2}$ or $5z^{-2}$

38. $\dfrac{4}{x^5}$ or $4x^{-5}$

39. $5(x + y)^8$

40. $2(x - y)^8$

41. $\dfrac{2x^{-5}}{3}$

42. $\dfrac{3x^{-6}}{4}$

43. $3x^{-4}$

44. $4x^{-3}$

45. $5x^{\frac{1}{2}}$

46. $7x^{\frac{1}{3}}$

47. $2(x^3)^{\frac{1}{5}} = 2x^{\frac{3}{5}}$

48. $2x^{\frac{5}{2}}$

49. $(((9)^{\frac{1}{2}})^3)^{-1} = ((3)^3)^{-1} = 27^{-1} = \dfrac{1}{27}$

50. $\dfrac{1}{8}$

51. $((8)^{\frac{1}{3}})^2 = 2^3 = 4$

52. 9

53. $-4(-1)^2 = -4(1) = -4$

54. 5

55. $[(-4)(-1)]^2 = 4^2 = 16$

56. 25

IR4

Functions

Human beings naturally look for relationships as a way to order their worlds. Even toddlers at play will pair big plastic ponies with little plastic ponies to make family units. They will group red blocks together and yellow blocks together.

Even when we're older, relationships are common phenomena of our lives. Suppose we have a group of math students studying together. Suppose their names are Ann, Bob, Curt, Dan, and Ed. Suppose both Ann and Curt have Dr. Zen for their math professor, while Bob and Ed have Dr. Young, and Dan has Dr. Xan.

We pair each student with his or her teacher by using a set of ordered pairs.

(Ann, Zen), (Curt, Zen), (Bob, Young), (Ed, Young), (Dan, Xan).

These ordered pairs describe the relationship: (student, student's math professor).

We might also think about these matchings as who is in a math professor's class:

(Zen, Ann), (Zen, Curt), (Young, Bob), (Young, Ed), (Xan, Dan).

These pairs are reversed from the pairs above and is not the same relationship but is the inverse relationship. The *inverse* of a relationship is obtained by reversing the order of the pairs.

FROM RELATIONSHIPS TO FUNCTIONS

Let's begin with the definition of a function

A *function* can be defined as a rule (or you could say a set of ordered pairs, a relationship, or a mapping) that associates each member of one set, which we call the *Domain*, to a member of another set, which we call the *Range*, such that every element *x* in the Domain is associated with (or you could say relates to or is mapped to) exactly one element *y* in the Range.

The set of ordered pairs above (student, student's math professor) would be a function because each student is mapped to exactly one math professor. But notice that the inverse relationship (math professor, professor's student) is not a function because Dr. Zen, for example, can be mapped to more than one student; i.e., to Ann and Curt. Therefore, the relationship (math professor, professor's student) would not be a function.

Relationships need not involve people. On a certain electric stovetop Range, when the dial reads "warm", the temperature of the coil burner is 200°F. At "low", the temperature of the coil burner is 300°F. At "medium", the temperature is 350°F. At "medium high", the temperature is 400°F. At "high", the temperature reaches 500°F. We can show this relationship by:

(warm, 200°F), (low, 300°F), (medium, 350°F), (medium high, 400°F), (high, 500°).

If only one temperature is associated with each setting (warm, low, medium, medium high, and high), then the stovetop burner relationship is a function.

Here's one more example. Carla is a waitress. She constantly notes the relationship between a customer and his or her order; e.g. (tall man, coffee with cream) (blond, black coffee) (man with baseball cap, Diet Coke).

Functions are desirable when we want a single controlled output. When a customer orders "coffee black," he wants to be certain that Carla will bring coffee without cream or sugar. She won't ever bring coffee with sugar, coffee with cream, coffee with both, black tea, or any other beverage when the customer orders "coffee black." The beverage he receives is a function of his order. The input is his order. The output is his beverage. A function indicates that the output is controlled by the input. When the customer orders "coffee black," he wants Carla to bring the same beverage every time—coffee without cream or sugar.

The Domain is the set of possible inputs. For the study group, the Domain was the set {Ann, Bob, Curt, Dan, and Ed}. The Range is the set of corresponding outputs. For the study group, the Range is the set {Xan, Young, Zen}.

For the stovetop burner, the Domain was the set {warm, low, medium, medium high, high}. The Range (no pun intended) is the set {200°F, 300°F, 350°F, 400°F, and 500°F}. For the waitress, the Domain is the set of possible orders, and the Range is the set of items offered on the menu.

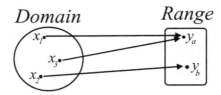

The set of arrows represents the function; that is, the rules that take each 'x' to only one 'y'. The Domain is $\{x_1, x_2, x_3\}$, and the Range is $\{y_a, y_b\}$.

ANOTHER EXAMPLE

We might observe that there appears to be a relationship between the year in which someone is born and his or her age. (We're very clever.)

We let the Domain be the set of all birth years. The Range will be the set of ages we generate from the birth years.

Assume that this is the year 2017.

We can map the birth year 1950 to the age 67.

We can map the birth year 2000 to the age 17.

Clearly, we can map every element in the Domain {every birth year} to an element in the Range {every age}. Because each birth year gets mapped to only one age, the relationship between birth year and age is a function.

In this case, we can even find an equation to relate birth year to age:

2017 − (birth year) = age.

If we let x represent the birth year and we let y represent the age, we can write the equation in a form that looks more familiar, i.e.,

$$2017 - x = y$$

or using the Law of Symmetry, we can turn this around to get:

$$y = 2017 - x.$$

For a function, we can use the notation $f(x)$ instead of y. It's read "f of x."

That is, $f(x)$ is another way to write y when we have an equation that's a function. Also, just as y represents a "height" on the graph of an equation, $f(x)$ also represents the y-value or height on the graph of the function.

Consider: $y = 3x + 2$

where we let the Domain be the set of all real numbers. The Range will also be the set of all real numbers.

Every x we plug into the equation generates only one value of y. Therefore, this equation is a function, and we can write:

$$f(x) = 3x + 2 \quad \text{instead of } y = 3x + 2.$$

The funky-looking equation $x = \sqrt{y^2}$ does not represent a function because the x generates two values of y.

$$2 = \sqrt{2^2}, \text{ so } y \text{ could equal 2.}$$

$$\text{and} \quad 2 = \sqrt{(-2)^2}, \text{ so } y \text{ could also equal } -2.$$

Why would we want to replace a perfectly good y with an $f(x)$?

We can use this notation to see easily what value we're going to substitute for x.

Suppose $(x) = 3x + 2$.

Then $f(1)$ means we will replace every x with a 1, i.e.,

$$f(1) = 3(1) + 2$$

$$f(1) = 5.$$

Similarly,
$$f(-6)=3(-6)+2$$

$$f(-6)=-18+2=-16$$

and
$$f(5j)=3(5j)+2$$

$$f(5j)=15j+2$$

and
$$f(x+16)=3(x+16)+2 \quad \text{Distributing the 3, we get:}$$

$$f(x+16)=3x+48+2$$

$$f(x+16)=3x+50$$

If we expand the Domain and Range a little, we can even get:

$$f(🌢)=3(🌢)+2$$

Also note:
$$f(x+\Delta x)=3(x+\Delta x)+2 \quad \text{Distributing the 3, we get:}$$

$$f(x+\Delta x)=3x+3(\Delta x)+2$$

Be especially sure you understand the last example since this substitution occurs again and again in calculus, and you will be doing the substitution.

Note: Δx, read "delta x" is one variable. It is not a "delta" times an "x", or a Δ times an x.

Watch the next example closely, too. Recall we're using $f(x)=3x+2$.

$$f(x+\Delta x)-f(x)=[3(x+\Delta x)+2]-[3x+2] \quad \text{Distributing the 3 and the negative gives us:}$$

$$f(x+\Delta x)-f(x)=3x+3\Delta x+2-3x-2. \quad \text{By combining } 3x \text{ and } -3x, \text{ and 2 with } -2,$$

$$f(x+\Delta x)-f(x)=3(\Delta x) \text{ or just } 3\Delta x.$$

Here's one more using $(x)=3x+2$:

$$f(z(x))=3(z(x))+2 \quad \text{i.e., we replaced the } x \text{ with } z(x).$$

Example 1:

For $f(x)=4x-1$, find $f(2)$, $f(a)$, $f(x+h)$, and $f(x+\Delta x)$.
$f(2)=4(2)-1=8-1=7$
$f(a)=4a-1$
$f(x+h)=4(x+h)-1=4x+4h-1$
$f(x+\Delta x)=4(x+\Delta x)-1=4x+4\Delta x-1$

Example 2:

For $f(x)=x^2+6$, find $f(-1)$, $f(z)$ and $f(x-h)$.
$f(-1)=(-1)^2+6=1+6=7$
$f(z)=z^2+6$
$f(x-h)=(x-h)^2+6=(x-h)(x-h)+6=x^2-2xh+h^2+6$

Example 3:

For $f(x)=x^2+4x+6$, find $f(3)$, and $f(x+\Delta x)$.
$f(3)=3^2+4(3)+6=9+12+6=27$
$f(x+\Delta x)=(x+\Delta x)^2+4(x+\Delta x)+6=(x+\Delta x)(x+\Delta x)+4x+4\Delta x+6$
$\qquad = x^2+2x\Delta x+\Delta x^2+4x+4\Delta x+6$

Example 4:

For $g(t)=4t-1$, find $g(0)$ and $g(5+t)$.
$g(0)=4(0)-1=-1$
$g(5+t)=4(5+t)-1=20+4t-1=19+4t$

GRAPHS OF FUNCTIONS

To repeat, the *Domain* of a function is the set of all values we are allowed to put in (i.e., to substitute) for *x*. That is, the *Domain* of a function is all values of *x* for which $f(x)$ is defined.

For $y=3x+2$, we used the Domain *all real numbers*. In Interval Notation, *all real numbers* is written $(-\infty, \infty)$.

Every real number we substitute for *x* produces a single real number *y*. The *Range* of a function is the set of values *y* that can be computed from $f(x)$.

We know that the graph of $y = 3x^2 - 6x + 5$; that is: $f(x) = 3x^2 - 6x + 5$ is a parabola that opens upward. Its vertex is at $= 1$.

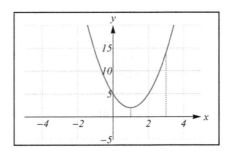

Each value of x has a corresponding y-value, i.e., a height, generated by the equation:

$height = y = f(x) = 3x^2 - 6x + 5.$

When $x = 1$, the corresponding y-value, or height, is 2. When $x = 3$, the corresponding y-value, or height, is 14.

The collection of these y-values is the *Range* of the function.

For every value of x, there is exactly one corresponding height on the graph. Hence, if the graph of an equation meets the Vertical Line Test—i.e., *any vertical line crosses the curve in no more than one point*—then the equation is a function. It is a function because every x-value is associated with only one y-value, or height.

Consider the graphs below. Which ones are the graphs of functions?

A. $y = 2x + 3$

B. $y = \dfrac{1}{x}$

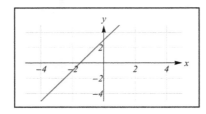

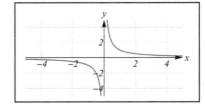

C. $y = x^2 - 3$

D. $y = 3\sqrt{x}$

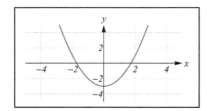

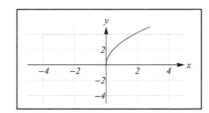

E. $x = y^2$

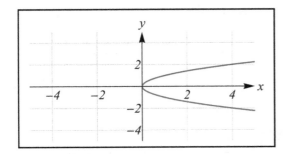

A is a function because any vertical line you draw will cross the curve in no more than one point.

B is a function because any vertical line will cross in no more than one point. A vertical line through the y-axis will not cross at all, but since zero points is not more than one, B still meets the Vertical Line Test.

C is a function. Again, any vertical line drawn will cross the curve in no more than one point.

D is a function. Vertical lines drawn anywhere left of the y-axis will not cross the curve, but since zero points are not more than one point, the Vertical Line Test is met, and the equation is a function.

It is possible to draw a vertical line that crosses E in two points; hence the Vertical Line Test is not met, and E is not a function.

If a graph meets the vertical line test *and* the Horizontal Line Test, it is the graph of a special kind of function called a One-to-one Function. To meet the Horizontal Line Test, any horizontal line drawn may cross the curve in no more than one point. Hence, any x-value will correspond to only one y-value, or height (shown by the Vertical Line Test), and any y-value will correspond to only one x-value (shown by the Horizontal Line Test).

Which of the following graphs below depict one-to-one functions?

A. $y = 2x + 3$

B. $y = \dfrac{1}{x}$

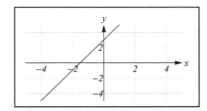

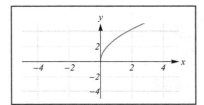

C. $y = x^2 - 3$

D. $y = 3\sqrt{x}$

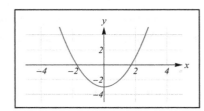

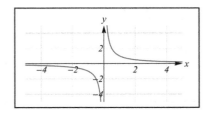

E. $x = y^2$

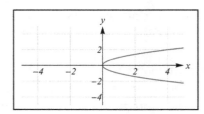

For the equations above, A, B, and D are one-to-one functions because they meet the Vertical Line Test *and* the Horizontal Line Test. It is possible to draw a horizontal line on C that crosses the curve twice, so it does not meet the Horizontal Line Test, and $y = x^2 - 3$ is not a one-to-one function, even though it is a function. Curve E is not a function, so it cannot be a one-to-one function.

INTRA-SECTION EXERCISES:

Sketch the graphs below. Which ones are functions? Which ones are one-to-one functions?

1. $y = -x^2 + 3$ 2. $y = x^3 - 4$ 3. $x = 5$ 4. $y = -1$ 5. $y = -\sqrt{x+3}$

Solutions

1. $y = -x^2 + 3$
   A function, but not a one-to-one function.

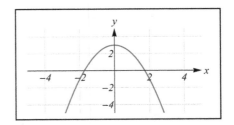

2. $y = x^3 - 4$
   One-to-one function.

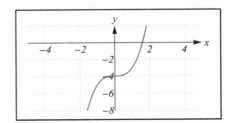

3. $x = 5$
   Not a function. A vertical line drawn through the graph where $x = 5$ would cross an infinite number of times, which is definitely more than 1, so the Vertical Line Test is not satisfied.

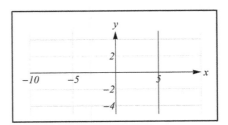

4. $y = -1$

This is a function, but not a one-to-one function. A horizontal line drawn through the graph where $y = -1$ would cross at an infinite number of points, so the Horizontal Line Test is not satisfied.

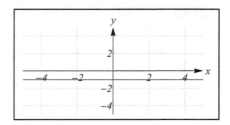

5. $y = -\sqrt{x+3}$

One-to-one function.

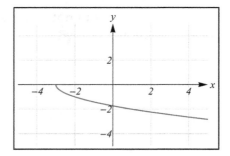

FINDING THE DOMAIN AND RANGE ON A GRAPH

Consider the graph $y = -x^2 - 3$ at right. It meets the Vertical Line Test, indicating that the equation is a function, so we could write: $f(x) = -x^2 - 3$.

Now determine which values of x have corresponding points on the curve.

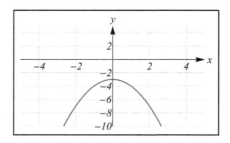

We see that at $x=1$, there is a corresponding point on the curve, so 1 is a member of the Domain of the function $f(x)=-x^2-3$.

We see that at $x=2.5$, there is a corresponding point on the curve, so 2.5 is also a member of the Domain.

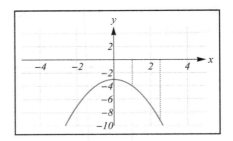

In fact, you can see that every value of x will have a corresponding point on the curve. The collection of all these x-values is the Domain of $f(x)=-x^2-3$. In this case, the Domain is the set of all real numbers. In interval notation, we would say the Domain is $(-\infty, \infty)$.

We found the Domain by looking along the x-axis and dropping (or raising) vertical lines from every value of x to determine which values of x had corresponding points on the curve. (Some of the vertical lines were just in our minds.)

Consider the graph of the function $(x)=\dfrac{-1}{x-3}$, at right.

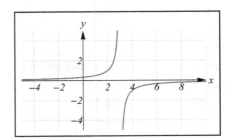

Now consider which values of x have corresponding points on the curve. Some example values of x are used below. We can see that every x-value will have a corresponding point on the curve except for $x=3$. We could say the Domain is the set of all real numbers but $x \neq 3$. In interval notation, we would write this set: $(-\infty, 3) \cup (3, \infty)$

The parentheses around the 3 indicate that 3 is not included in this interval. We would use square brackets, as in $[3, \infty)$, if the 3 were included as an endpoint of the interval. The symbol $\cup$ means the union of the sets. It's similar to a plus sign for sets. For the Domain, the interval $(-\infty, \infty)$ represents x-values along the x-axis from left to right.

Round brackets, i.e., parentheses, are always used around ∞, because infinity can't be enclosed.

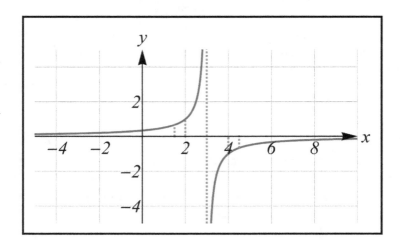

Now let's talk about finding the Range from graphs. Consider $f(x) = -x^2 - 3$ once again and its graph at right. We want to locate all the values of y that have corresponding points on this curve. We can see that at the y-value, or height, 2, there is no corresponding point on the graph. At $y = -5$, there are two corresponding points on the curve. We could say that all the values of y less than or equal to -3 have corresponding

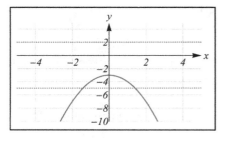

points on the curve. Since the Range is the collection of y-values with corresponding points on the curve, the Range is the set of y-values less than or equal to -3. In interval notation, this would be: $(-\infty, -3]$. For the Range, interval notation indicates y-values from the bottom of the y-axis to the top. All y-values would be indicated by the interval $(-\infty, \infty)$. (Note: We used a square bracket around -3 because it was included in the set.)

We found the Range by looking along the y-axis and considering horizontal lines from every value of y to determine which values of y had corresponding points on the curve. (Again, some of the horizontal lines were just in our minds since there are an infinite number of them.)

INTRA-SECTION EXERCISES:

Sketch the curve and find the Domain and Range for each graph below.

6. $f(x) = x^2 - 4$ 7. $f(x) = -x^3 + 2$ 8. $f(x) = 2x - 4$

9. $f(x) = \sqrt{x+2}$ 10. $f(x) = \dfrac{1}{x+2}$

Solutions

6.

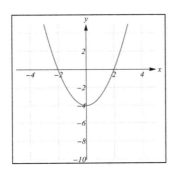

Domain: $(-\infty, \infty)$
Range: $[-4, \infty)$

7.

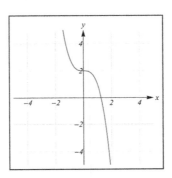

Domain: $(-\infty, \infty)$
Range: $(-\infty, \infty)$

8.

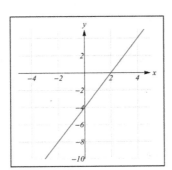

Domain: $(-\infty, \infty)$
Range: $(-\infty, \infty)$

9.

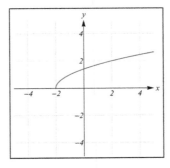

Domain: $[-2, \infty)$
Range: $[0, \infty)$

10.

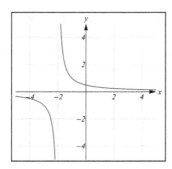

Domain: $(-\infty, -2)\cup(-2, \infty)$
Range: $(-\infty,0)\cup(0,\infty)$

THREE MORE EXAMPLES

Example 5:

If $f(x)=2x-3$, for what value of x is the height of the function 11?

Solution:

Since heights are y-values, this is another way of saying: If $f(x)=2x-3$, for what value of x does y equal 11? We also know that we can replace $f(x)$ with y, writing the equation as:

$$y=2x-3$$

So we want to know: What is x when y is 11? We simply replace y with 11 and solve for x

$11=2x-3$ We add 3 to both sides,

$14=2x$ and divide by 2 to get:

$7=x$.

We conclude that when $x=7$, y (the height) $=11$.

Example 6:

If $f(x) = x^2 + 3x + 2$, where are the x-intercepts?

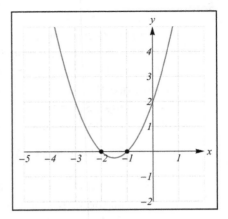

Solution:

We know that at the x-intercepts, the curve crosses the x-axis.

At the x-intercepts, the y-values, or heights, equal zero. To find the x-intercepts then, we simply replace the y with 0.

$$f(x) = x^2 + 3x + 2$$

$$y = x^2 + 3x + 2$$

$0 = x^2 + 3x + 2$ Since this is a quadratic equation, we factor, if possible, or else use the Quadratic Formula.

$0 = (x+1)(x+2)$ Therefore,

$(x+1) = 0$ or $(x+2) = 0$

$x = -1$ or $x = -2$

Therefore, the x-intercepts are at $x = -1$, and $x = -2$,

or we could say that the x-intercepts are the points $(-1, 0)$ and $(-2, 0)$.

Example 7:

Where do the curves $f(x) = 2x - 3$ and $g(x) = x^2 + 5x - 1$ intersect?

Solution:

At the points of intersection, both curves have the same x-values and the same y-values, so this is another way of saying: Where are the x's equal? Or where are the y's equal? Since the functions are each solved for y, let's set the y-values equal.

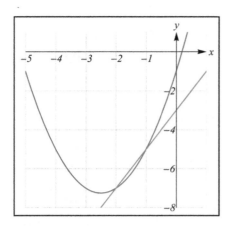

$$2x - 3 = x^2 + 5x - 1$$

Since this is a quadratic equation, we need to move all the terms to one side, so we'll subtract 2x from each side and add 3.

$0 = x^2 + 3x + 2$ Factoring, we get:

$0 = (x + 2)(x + 1)$ Setting each factor equal to zero gives us:
                      and then solving for x we have:

$0 = x + 2$ or $0 = x + 1$

$x = -2$ or $x = -1$,

which tells us the x-coordinates of the points of intersection are at -1 and -2. But since we are asked to find "points," we need both the x-coordinate and the y-coordinate for each point.

To find the y-coordinate when $x = -1$, we simply substitute -1 for x into either equation since the y-values are the same for each curve at the points of intersection. Let's use $y = 2x - 3$.

$$y = 2(-1) - 3 = -2 - 3 = -5.$$

So now we know that when $x = -1$, $y = -5$ and one of the points of intersection is $(-1, -5)$.

For the other point, we find y when $x = -2$.

$$y = 2(-2) - 3 = -7$$

This gives us the other point of intersection as $(-2, -7)$.

IR4 FUNCTIONS EXERCISES

For numbers 1 through 5, sketch $y = f(x)$ and list the Domain and Range.

1. $f(x) = 3x + 6$

2. $f(x) = x^2 + 6$

3. $f(x) = x^2 + 4x + 6$

4. $f(x) = \dfrac{3}{x-2}$

5. $g(z) = -\sqrt{z+3}$

For numbers 6 through 9 below, find a. $f(-1)$ b. $f(a)$ c. $f(x+h)$ d. $f(x+\Delta x)$.

6. $f(x) = 3x + 6$

7. $f(x) = x^2 + 6$

8. $f(x) = x^2 + 4x + 6$

9. $f(x) = \dfrac{3}{x-2}$

10. For $f(x) = 3x^2 - 4$ find $\dfrac{f(x+\Delta x) - f(x)}{\Delta x}$ and simplify your results.

11. $f(x) = 3x + 1;\ g(x) = -2x$

    a. Find $f(g(x))$ b. Find $g(f(x))$ c. Find $f(g(4))$

12. $f(x) = x^2;\ g(x) = x - 1$

    a. Find $f(g(x))$ b. Find $g(f(x))$ c. Find $f(g(4))$

13. If $f(x) = 4x - 2$,

    a. what is the height of the function at $x = 1$?
    b. what is the value of x when the height of the function is 10?

14. Where are the x-intercepts for the curve $f(x) = x^2 + 4x - 5$? Sketch.

15. Where do the curves $f(x) = x^2 - 4x - 5$ and $g(x) = -4x - 1$ intersect?

16. Where do the curves $y = 2$ and $f(x) = x^2 - 2x - 1$ intersect?

IR4 FUNCTIONS SOLUTIONS TO EXERCISES

1. $f(x) = 3x + 6$
   Domain: $(-\infty, \infty)$ or All Real Numbers
   Range: $(-\infty, \infty)$ or All Real Numbers

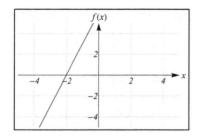

2. $f(x) = x^2 + 6$
   Domain: $(-\infty, \infty)$ or All Real Numbers
   Range: $[6, \infty)$ or $y \geq 6$.

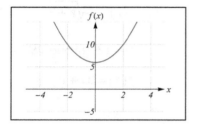

3. $f(x) = x^2 + 4x + 6$
   Complete the square: $y = (x^2 + 4x + 4) - 4 + 6$
   $$y = (x+2)^2 + 2$$
   Domain: $(-\infty, \infty)$ or All Real Numbers
   Range: $[2, \infty)$ or $y \geq 2$

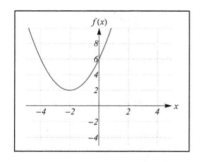

4. $f(x) = \dfrac{3}{x-2}$
   Domain: $(-\infty, 2) \cup (2, \infty)$ or All Real Numbers
   except $x \neq 2$
   Range: $(-\infty, 0) \cup (0, \infty)$ or All Real Numbers
   except $y \neq 0$

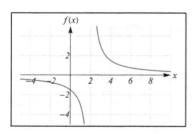

5. $g(z)=-\sqrt{z+3}$

   Domain: $[-3,\infty)$ or $z \geq -3$

   Range: $(-\infty,0]$ or $y \leq 0$

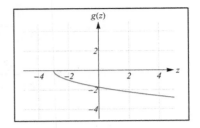

6. $f(x)=3x+6$

   a. $f(-1)=3(-1)+6=-3+6=3$

   b. $f(a)=3a+6$

   c. $f(x+h)=3(x+h)+6=3x+3h+6$

   d. $f(x+\Delta x)=3(x+\Delta x)+6=3x+3\Delta x+6$

7. $f(x)=x^2+6$

   a. $f(-1)=(-1)^2+6=1+6=7$

   b. $f(a)=a^2+6$

   c. $f(x+h)=(x+h)^2+6=(x+h)(x+h)+6=x^2+2xh+h^2+6$

   d. $f(x+\Delta x)=(x+\Delta x)^2+6=(x+\Delta x)(x+\Delta x)+6=x^2+2x\Delta x+(\Delta x)^2+6$

8. $f(x)=x^2+4x+6$

   a. $f(-1)=(-1)^2+4(-1)+6=1-4+6=3$

   b. $f(a)=a^2+4a+6$

   c. $f(x+h)=(x+h)^2+4(x+h)+6=(x+h)(x+h)+4x+4h+6$

   $\qquad =x^2+2xh+h^2+4x+4h+6$

   d. $f(x+\Delta)=(x+\Delta x)^2+4(x+\Delta x)+6=(x+\Delta x)(x+\Delta x)+4x+4\Delta x+6$

   $\qquad =x^2+2x\Delta x+(\Delta x)^2+4x+4\Delta x+6$

9. $f(x)=\dfrac{3}{x-2}$

   a. $f(-1)=\dfrac{3}{-1-2}=\dfrac{3}{-3}=-1$

   b. $f(a)=\dfrac{3}{a-2}$

c. $f(x+h)=\dfrac{3}{x+h-2}$

d. $f(x+\Delta x)=\dfrac{3}{x+\Delta x-2}$

10. For $f(x)=3x^2-4$ find $\dfrac{f(x+\Delta x)-f(x)}{\Delta x}$ and simplify your results.

$$\dfrac{3(x+\Delta x)^2-4-(3x^2-4)}{\Delta x}=\dfrac{3(x+\Delta x)(x+\Delta x)-4-3x^2+4}{\Delta x}$$

$$=\dfrac{3(x^2+2x\Delta x+\Delta x^2)-4-3x^2+4}{\Delta x}$$

$$=\dfrac{3x^2+6x\Delta x+3\Delta x^2-4-3x^2+4}{\Delta x}=\dfrac{6x\Delta x+3\Delta x^2}{\Delta x}$$

$$=\dfrac{\Delta x(6x+3\Delta x)}{\Delta x}=6x+3\Delta x$$

11. $f(x)=3x+1;\ g(x)=-2x$

a. $f(g(x))=3g(x)+1=3(-2x)+1=-6x+1$

b. $g(f(x))=-2f(x)=-2(3x+1)=-6x-2$

c. Since $g(4)=-2(4)=-8$, then $f(g(4))=f(-8)=3(-8)+1=-24+1=-23$

12. $f(x)=x^2;\ g(x)=x-1$

a. $f(g(x))=(g(x))^2=(x-1)^2=(x-1)(x-1)=x^2-2x+1$

b. $g(f(x))=f(x)-1=x^2-1$

c. Since $g(4)=4-1=3$, then $f(g(4))=f(3)=3^2=9$

13. If $f(x)=4x-2$,

a. what is the height of the function at $x=1$?
   i.e., *What is the y-value when $x=1$?*
   $$y=4(1)-2=2$$
   Therefore, when $x=1$, the height $y=2$.

b. what is the value of x when the *height* of the function is 10?
    i.e., For what x-values does $y = 10$?

$$10 = 4x - 2$$
$$12 = 4x$$
$$3 = x$$

Therefore, when the height $y = 10$, $x = 3$.

14. Where are the x-intercepts for the curve
    $f(x) = x^2 + 4x - 5$? Sketch.
    *i.e., What are the x-values when y
    (the height) $= 0$?*

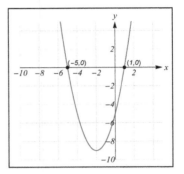

$$0 = x^2 + 4x - 5$$
$$0 = (x + 5)(x - 1)$$
$$0 = x + 5 \text{ or } 0 = x - 1$$
$$-5 = x \text{ or } 1 = x$$

*Therefore, the x-intercepts are at $x = -5$
and $x = 1$; i.e., at the points $(-5, 0)$ and $(1, 0)$.*

15. Where do the curves $f(x) = x^2 - 4x - 5$ and $g(x) = -4x - 1$ intersect?
    i.e., Where do the curves have the same heights, or y-values?

$x^2 - 4x - 5 = -4x - 1$ *Adding 4x and 1 to both sides we have:*

$x^2 - 4 = 0$ *Factoring gives us*

$(x - 2)(x + 2) = 0$
$x - 2 = 0 \text{ or } x + 2 = 0$

*Hence, $x = 2$ and $x = -2$ at the points of intersection, but we still need the
y-coordinates.*

$$y = -4(2) - 1 = -8 - 1 = -9 \text{ and } y = -4(-2) - 1 = 8 - 1 = 7$$

Therefore, the points of intersections are at $(2, -9)$ and $(-2, 7)$.

16. Where do the curves $y = 2$ and $f(x) = x^2 - 2x - 1$ intersect?
    i.e., Where do the curves have the same heights, or y-values?

$x^2 - 2x - 1 = 2$ *Subtracting 2 from both sides and then factoring:*
$x^2 - 2x - 3 = 0$
$(x - 3)(x + 1) = 0$
$x = 3, -1$

*Both corresponding y-values would be at $y = 2$, so the points of intersection
are $(3, 2)$ and $(-1, 2)$.*

IC5

Area Bound by a Curve: Definite Integral Power Rule

Many situations involve accumulating values, i.e., a summation. For example, profits per month for Joanie Cakes are recorded in the following table:

Month t	1	2	3	4	5	6
Profit p (in thousands of dollars) per month	25	36	15	22	18	14

A graph of the monthly profit is shown in the figure below.

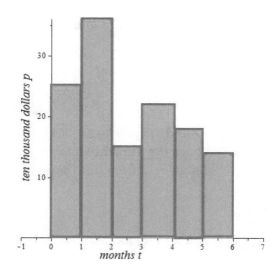

The area of each rectangle in the graph gives the profit for a month. We can calculate the area of a rectangle by length times width, so the sum of the areas of the rectangles would give us the total profit for Joanie Cakes over the given six-month period.

(Of course, we could get the total profit by adding up the profits for each month: $25+36+15+22+18+14 = 130$ thousand dollars, but we're going for a larger concept here, so please bear with us.)

We recall that the area of a rectangle is given by a product: $A = lw$

In words, the area of a rectangle equals its length (or height) times its width.

The area of the first rectangle on the graph above; i.e., its length times width, equals:

$$(\$25{,}000)(1\ month) = \$25{,}000\,/\,month.$$

The area of the second rectangle, or its length times width, equals:

$$(\$36{,}000)(1\ month) = \$36{,}000\,/\,month.$$

Joanie Cakes' total profit could be written as a function $P(t)$ where t represents the month.

In the Joanie Cake example, the values of P are fixed for large units of time (months), making $P(t)$ a discrete function. What happens if the function values could change at every instant? $P(t)$ would then be a continuous function. The area under the curve would still represent the accumulation or sum, but the computation cannot be done with a simple sum of rectangle areas.

An underground tank is to be filled with gasoline from the hose on a tanker truck. At the beginning, the valve controlling the gasoline flow is turned off, and the tank contains 20 liters of gasoline. The valve is slowly opened and then slowly closed, so that the rate of flow of gasoline changes at every instant. The variable rate of flow in liters per minute is given by: $r = -t^2 + 6t$, where time is in minutes.

How much gasoline is in the tank after six minutes? We would need to find the accumulation of gasoline at r liters per minute for six minutes.

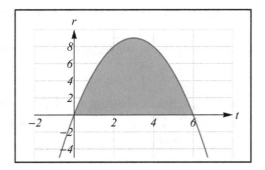

Consider the graph at right. The accumulation of gasoline is the area under the curve bounded by the function $r=-t^2+6t$ as a function of t, and by the horizontal axis between $t=0$ and $t=6$.

How can we add up (find the sum of areas) of:

$$r(t)=-t^2+6t \text{ for } 0\leq t\leq6$$

to get the total area under the curve?

In the Joanie Cake example, we could find the sum because we knew the formula for areas of rectangles. Now we have an unusual shape without a standard formula from geometry. We first present some notation and formulas; second, we compute the unusual shape's area.

The area under a curve over a given interval $a\leq t\leq b$ is given by a **definite integral**; one meaning of definite being: an exact physical quantity; and one meaning of integral being: putting parts together to make a total.

The mathematical notation devised for this integral uses the old German s, or $\int$, to signify that it is a sum. The notation also indicates how we will find the height and width of areas, the starting point for the accumulation of the area, and the stopping point for the accumulation of the area.

For the gasoline example, the height is given by $r(t)$. The width is a change in time, or t. A change in t is usually designated as Δt. In our new notation, however, the Δ is replaced by the letter d, and the width is indicated by dt. We wanted the accumulation of area to start at $t=0$ and to stop at $t=6$.

The notation for this area is: $\int_0^6 r(t)\,dt$.

It is the sum symbol with the starting point as a subscript and the stopping point as a superscript, followed by height times width.

The general notation for a definite integral is: $\int_a^b f(x)\,dx$, where a is the starting point for the sum, b is the stopping point for the sum, $f(x)$ is the height, and dx indicates the width. The dx also indicates that a and b represent endpoints of an interval on the x-axis: $a \leq x \leq b$. The starting and stopping points for the definite integral can be referred to as endpoints and, more precisely, left endpoint and right endpoint. Because of their placement in the notation, the left endpoint is called the *lower limit of integration*, and the right endpoint is the *upper limit of integration*.

(In mathematics, the word *limit* has a precise definition, and we will introduce such a definition later. The word limit used as the endpoint for a definite integral has little to do with the mathematical definition of the word limit; hence, we will avoid using the terminology *limit of integration*.)

The adjective *definite* is commonly omitted, and the definite integral is simply referred to as "the integral." The process of finding the integral is referred to as *integration*.

THE POWER RULE FOR INTEGRATION

A definite integral represents the area of a geometric shape outlined by a curve and some line segments. Most students are aware of formulas for the areas of several geometric shapes: rectangle, triangle, trapezoid, circle, ...; alas, many of the curves involved in definite integrals are not simple geometric shapes, so we will need to introduce more formulas for other areas.

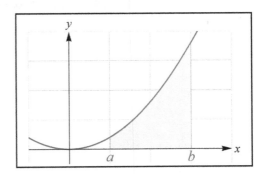

The formula for the area of the shape between a power curve $y = x^n$ (like that at right) and the x-axis, starting at point $x = a$ and ending at point $x = b$, is:

$$\int_a^b x^n \, dx = \left[\frac{1}{n+1} x^{n+1} \right]_a^b = \frac{1}{n+1} b^{n+1} - \frac{1}{n+1} a^{n+1} \text{ when } n \neq -1.$$

We will work with the case $n = -1$ in a later section.

In words, we could say that the *Power Rule for Integration* involves three steps, always remembering that this method is to be used only when we can write the function in the form:

$f(x) = x^n$, and we know some endpoints a and b.

Then, the integral is written: $\int_a^b x^n \, dx$ and we can begin.

Step 1:

> We add 1 to the exponent, and then divide by the new exponent. This gives us:
>
> $$\left[\frac{x^{n+1}}{n+1} \right]_a^b.$$
>
> Note that we have replaced the integral sign $\int$ and its bookend, dx, with square brackets. The endpoints are now indicated as a subscript and superscript on the right square bracket.

Step 2:

> We substitute the right endpoint (aka upper limit of integration) for every x, and, then we substitute the left endpoint (aka lower limit of integration) for every x.
>
> $$\frac{b^{n+1}}{n+1}, \qquad \frac{a^{n+1}}{n+1}.$$

Step 3:

> We subtract the values we have, giving us:
>
> $$\frac{b^{n+1}}{n+1} - \frac{a^{n+1}}{n+1}.$$

Example 1:

> We wish to integrate $f(x) = x^3$ from $x = 1$ to $x = 5$.
>
> **Step 1:** We set up the integral: $\int_1^5 x^3 \, dx$.

Step 2: We add 1 to the exponent and divide by the new exponent, converting the $\int$ and dx into square brackets and noting the endpoints as a subscript and superscript.

$$\int_1^5 x^3 dx = \left[\frac{1}{4} x^4 \right]_1^5$$

Step 3: We substitute the right endpoint 5 (upper "limit") in for x, and we substitute the left endpoint 1 (lower "limit") in for x.

$$\frac{1}{4} 5^4, \qquad \frac{1}{4} 1^4$$

Step 4: Subtract the expressions.

$$\frac{1}{4} 5^4 - \frac{1}{4} 1^4 = \frac{625}{4} - \frac{1}{4} = 156.$$

Here's the whole process in one stream:

$$\int_1^5 x^3 dx = \left[\frac{1}{3+1} x^{3+1} \right]_1^5 = \left[\frac{1}{4} x^4 \right]_1^5 = \frac{1}{4} 5^4 - \frac{1}{4} 1^4 = 156.$$

Example 2:

$$\int_0^1 x^4 \, dx$$

$$\int_0^1 x^4 dx = \left[\frac{1}{4+1} x^{4+1} \right]_0^1$$

We added 1 to the exponent and divided by the new exponent.

$$= \left[\frac{1}{5} x^5 \right]_0^1$$

$$= \frac{1}{5} 1^5 - \frac{1}{5} 0^5$$

Next, we substitute the right endpoint 1 (the upper limit of integration) in for x, substitute the left endpoint 0 (the lower limit of integration) in for x, and subtract the two values.

$$= \frac{1}{5} - 0 = \frac{1}{5}$$

Example 3:

$$\int_1^2 \frac{1}{x^3}\, dx$$

The function $f(x) = \dfrac{1}{x^3}$ is not in the form x^n,

the kind we can integrate with the Power Rule.

But we know that $\dfrac{1}{x^3} = x^{-3}$. If we set up our integral with this

form, we can integrate.

$$\int_1^2 x^{-3}\, dx = \left[\frac{1}{-3+1} x^{-3+1}\right]_1^2$$

We add 1 to the exponent and divide by the new exponent.

$$= \left[\frac{1}{-2} x^{-2}\right]_1^2$$

Next, we do the substitutions,

$$= \frac{1}{-2} 2^{-2} - \frac{1}{-2} 1^{-2}$$

$$= \frac{1}{-8} + \frac{1}{2} = \frac{3}{8}$$

Example 4:

$$\int_1^4 \sqrt{x}\, dx$$

Again, the function $f(x) = \sqrt{x}$ is not in the form x^n, the kind we can integrate with the Power Rule,

but we know that $\sqrt{x} = x^{1/2}$, so we use this form in our integral.

$$\int_{1}^{4} x^{1/2}\, dx = \left[\frac{1}{(1/2)+1} x^{(1/2)+1} \right]_{1}^{4}$$

We add 1 to the exponent and divide by the new exponent.

$$= \left[\frac{1}{1.5} x^{1.5} \right]_{1}^{4}$$

Then we do the substitutions. In calculus, these substitutions are called the *evaluation*.

$$= \left(\frac{1}{1.5} 4^{1.5} \right) - \left(\frac{1}{1.5} 1^{1.5} \right)$$

Using a calculator, we get:

$$= 5.3 - 0.7 = 4.6$$

How would we integrate $\int_{4}^{5} x\, dx$?

Because the function x is equal to x^1, we can still use the power rule.

$$\int_{4}^{5} x\, dx = \int_{4}^{5} x^1\, dx$$

We add 1 to the exponent and divide by the new exponent,

$$= \left[\frac{x^2}{2} \right]_{4}^{5}$$

then we do the evaluation,

$$= \frac{5^2}{2} - \frac{4^2}{2}$$

and simplify.

$$= \frac{25}{2} - \frac{16}{2} = \frac{9}{2} \text{ or } 4.5$$

ADDITIONAL INTEGRAL PROPERTIES—COEFFICIENTS

We can also use the power rule when the function we wish to integrate contains a real number coefficient. We merely pull the constant to the outside of the integral. Here's our new rule:

$$\int_a^b cf(x)\,dx = c\int_a^b f(x)\,dx$$

Example 5:

$$\int_1^5 7x^3\,dx$$

First, we pull the 7 to the outer side of the integral sign.

$$= 7\int_1^5 x^3\,dx$$

We carry on by adding 1 to the exponent, dividing,

$$= 7\left[\frac{x^4}{4}\right]_1^5$$

and then evaluating.

$$= 7\left(\frac{5^4}{4} - \frac{1^4}{4}\right) = 7(156) = 1092$$

So why does this work?

Consider the area of a rectangle with height h and width w. The area of this rectangle would be hw. If the height of this rectangle is multiplied by 7, then the height becomes $7h$ and the area becomes $7hw$. Multiplying the height by 7 results in multiplying the area by 7.

Multiplying the height by any constant c results in multiplying the area by c.

In a definite integral, $\int_a^b cf(x)\,dx$, the *heights* have been multiplied by c, so $\int_a^b cf(x)\,dx$ is the same as multiplying the *area* by c; in other words:

$$\int_a^b cf(x)\,dx = c\int_a^b f(x)\,dx.$$

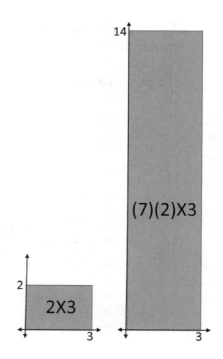

Example 6:

$$\int_{2}^{3} 5x^{-2}\,dx$$

We begin by moving the 5 to the outside of the integral sign.

$$= 5\int_{2}^{3} x^{-2}\,dx$$

Next, we do the integration,

$$= 5\left[\frac{x^{-1}}{-1}\right]_{2}^{3} = 5\left[-x^{-1}\right]_{2}^{3}$$

the evaluation,

$$= 5((-3^{-1})-(-2^{-1}))$$

and simplify.

$$= 5\left(-\frac{1}{3}+\frac{1}{2}\right) = \frac{5}{6}$$

Leading a Coefficient?

Suppose we want $\int_{5}^{6} 4\,dx$.

We can integrate because $4 = 4x^{0}$. (Of course, we recall that $x^{0}=1$).

So our integral becomes: $\int_{5}^{6} 4\,dx = \int_{5}^{6} 4x^{0}\,dx$, or $4\int_{5}^{6} x^{0}\,dx$.

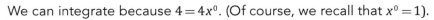

Using the Power Rule, we have: $4\left[\frac{x^{1}}{1}\right]_{5}^{6} = 4[x]_{5}^{6}$ and then evaluating:

$$4(6-5) = 4(1) = 4.$$

Usually, we don't need to add the middle steps, and just remember that:

$$\int_{a}^{b} 3\,dx = 3[x]_{a}^{b}$$

and

$$\int_{a}^{b} 11\,dx = 11[x]_{a}^{b}$$

and

$$\int_{a}^{b} -116\,dx = -116[x]_{a}^{b}$$

and, in general,

$$\int_{a}^{b} n\,dx = n[x]_{a}^{b}$$

Example 7:

$$\int_4^5 3dx = 3[x]_4^5 \qquad \text{Substitute 5 for } x \text{ and subtract the substitution of 4 for } x$$

$$= 3(5-4) = 3$$

Example 8:

$$\int_{-5}^5 12dx = 12[x]_{-5}^5 \quad \text{Substitute 5 for } x \text{ and subtract the substitution of } -5 \text{ for } x.$$

$$= 12[5-(-5)] = 12(5+5) = 120$$

INTRA-SECTION EXERCISES:

1. $\displaystyle\int_2^3 x^2\,dx$ 　　　2. $\displaystyle\int_2^3 \frac{1}{x^2}\,dx$ 　　　3. $\displaystyle\int_0^3 \sqrt[3]{x}\,dx$ 　　　4. $\displaystyle\int_{-2}^3 x\,dx$

5. $\displaystyle\int_0^3 6x^2\,dx$ 　　　6. $\displaystyle\int_3^5 2x\,dx$ 　　　7. $\displaystyle\int_1^2 \frac{2}{x^5}\,dx$ 　　　8. $\displaystyle\int_0^4 4\sqrt{x}\,dx$

Solutions

1. $\displaystyle\int_2^3 x^2\,dx = \left[\frac{x^3}{3}\right]_2^3 = \left(\frac{3^3}{3}\right) - \left(\frac{2^3}{3}\right) = \frac{27}{3} - \frac{8}{3} = \frac{19}{3}$ or ≈ 6.33

2. $\displaystyle\int_2^3 \frac{1}{x^2}\,dx = \int_2^3 x^{-2}\,dx = \left[\frac{x^{-1}}{-1}\right]_2^3 = \left[-\frac{1}{x}\right]_2^3 = -\frac{1}{3} - \left(-\frac{1}{2}\right) = -\frac{1}{3} + \frac{1}{2} = \frac{1}{6}$

3. $\displaystyle\int_0^3 \sqrt[3]{x}\,dx = \int_0^3 x^{1/3}\,dx = \left[\frac{x^{\frac{4}{3}}}{\frac{4}{3}}\right]_0^3 = \left[\frac{3}{4}\left(x^{\frac{4}{3}}\right)\right]_0^3 = \frac{3}{4}\left(3^{\frac{4}{3}}\right) - \frac{3}{4}\left(0^{\frac{4}{3}}\right) \approx 3.25$

4. $\displaystyle\int_{-2}^3 x\,dx = \left[\frac{x^2}{2}\right]_{-2}^3 = \frac{3^2}{2} - \frac{(-2)^2}{2} = \frac{9}{2} - \frac{4}{2} = \frac{5}{2}$ or 2.5

5. $\displaystyle\int_0^3 6x^2\,dx = 6\left[\frac{x^3}{3}\right]_0^3 = 6\left[\frac{3^3}{3} - \frac{0^3}{3}\right] = 6(9-0) = 54$

6. $\displaystyle\int_{3}^{5} 2x\,dx = 2\left[\dfrac{x^2}{2}\right]_{3}^{5} = [x^2]_{3}^{5} = 5^2 - 3^2 = 25 - 9 = 16$

7. $\displaystyle\int_{1}^{2} \dfrac{2}{x^5}\,dx = \int_{1}^{2} 2x^{-5}\,dx = 2\left[\dfrac{x^{-4}}{-4}\right]_{1}^{2} = \left[\dfrac{x^{-4}}{-2}\right]_{1}^{2} = \left[\dfrac{1}{-2x^4}\right]_{1}^{2}$

$\qquad\qquad = \left[\dfrac{1}{-2(2^4)} - \dfrac{1}{-2(1^4)}\right] = \dfrac{1}{-32} + \dfrac{1}{2} = \dfrac{15}{32}$ or ≈ 0.47

8. $\displaystyle\int_{0}^{4} 4\sqrt{x}\,dx = \int_{0}^{4} 4x^{\frac{1}{2}}\,dx = 4\left[\dfrac{x^{\frac{3}{2}}}{\dfrac{3}{2}}\right]_{0}^{4} = 4\left[\left(\dfrac{2}{3}\right)x^{\frac{3}{2}}\right]_{0}^{4} = 4\left[\left(\dfrac{2}{3}\right)4^{3/2} - \left(\dfrac{2}{3}\right)0^{3/2}\right]$

$\qquad\qquad = 4\left[\left(\dfrac{16}{3}\right) - 0\right] = \dfrac{64}{3}$ or ≈ 21.33

ADDITIONAL INTEGRAL PROPERTIES—SUM OF TERMS

This rule pertains to stacked functions

If a rectangle of width 3 and height 5 is stacked on top of a rectangle of width 3 and height 7, the result is a rectangle of width 3 and height 12. (See figure at right.)

- not stacked
pancakes ---
necessarily

The original rectangles have areas 5×3 and 7×3, and the resulting rectangle stack has an area that is the sum of the areas $(5\times3)+(7\times3)$. We could factor out the 3 in each term to get the resulting area: $3(5+7)$.

The definite integral $\displaystyle\int_{a}^{b} f(x)+g(x)\,dx$ represents an area where the heights $f(x)$ and $g(x)$ have been stacked on top of each other, so this is the same as the sum of two areas, i.e.,

$$\int_{a}^{b} f(x)+g(x)\,dx = \int_{a}^{b} f(x)\,dx + \int_{a}^{b} g(x)\,dx$$

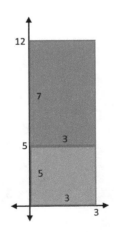

We can now integrate entire polynomials or any function that is a set of power terms. We do it term by term.

Example 9:

$$\int_1^5 x^3 + x^{-3} dx$$ We integrate each term.

$$= \left[\frac{x^4}{4} + \frac{x^{-2}}{-2} \right]_1^5$$ Then we evaluate.

$$= \left(\frac{5^4}{4} + \frac{5^{-2}}{-2} \right) - \left(\frac{1^4}{4} + \frac{1^{-2}}{-2} \right)$$ Finally, we simplify.

$$= (156.25 + -.02) - (.25 + -.5) = 156.23 - (-.25) = 156.48$$

Example 10:

$$\int_1^3 7x^3 - 2x^{-3} dx$$ We integrate,

$$= \left[7 \left(\frac{x^4}{4} \right) - 2 \left(\frac{x^{-2}}{-2} \right) \right]_1^3$$ evaluate,

$$= \left[7 \left(\frac{3^4}{4} \right) - 2 \left(\frac{3^{-2}}{-2} \right) \right] - \left[7 \left(\frac{1^4}{4} \right) - 2 \left(\frac{1^{-2}}{-2} \right) \right]$$ and simplify.

$$\approx \left[141.75 + 0.11 \right] - \left[1.75 + 1 \right] = 139.01$$

INTRA-SECTION EXERCISES:

9. $5 \int_{-3}^{-1} x^5 - x^{-4} dx$ 10. $\int_0^2 3x^5 + 6 dx$ 11. $\int_1^2 5x^3 + \frac{2}{x^3} + 4\sqrt[3]{x} \, dx$

Solutions

9. $5 \int_{-3}^{-1} x^5 - x^{-4} dx = 5 \left[\frac{x^6}{6} - \frac{x^{-3}}{-3} \right]_{-3}^{-1} = 5 \left[\frac{(-1)^6}{6} - \frac{(-1)^{-3}}{-3} \right] - 5 \left[\frac{(-3)^6}{6} - \frac{(-3)^{-3}}{-3} \right]$

$= 5 \left[\frac{1}{6} - \frac{1}{3} \right] - 5 \left[\frac{243}{2} - \frac{1}{81} \right] \approx 5(-0.167) - 5(1214.877) = -608.273$

10. $\int_0^2 3x^5 + 6 \, dx = \left[3\frac{x^6}{6} + 6x \right]_0^2 = \left[\frac{x^6}{2} + 6x \right]_0^2 = \left[\frac{2^6}{2} + 6(2) \right] - \left[\frac{0^6}{2} + 6(0) \right] = 44 - 0 = 44$

11. $\int_{1}^{2} 5x^3 + \dfrac{2}{x^3} + 4\sqrt[3]{x}\ dx = \int_{1}^{2} 5x^3 + 2x^{-3} + 4x^{1/3}\ dx = \left[5\dfrac{x^4}{4} + 2\dfrac{x^{-2}}{-2} + 4\dfrac{x^{4/3}}{4/3} \right]_{1}^{2}$

$= \left[5\dfrac{x^4}{4} - \dfrac{1}{x^2} + \left(\dfrac{3}{4}\right)4x^{4/3} \right]_{1}^{2} = \left[5\dfrac{x^4}{4} - \dfrac{1}{x^2} + 3x^{4/3} \right]_{1}^{2}$

$= \left[5\dfrac{2^4}{4} - \dfrac{1}{2^2} + 3(2)^{4/3} \right] - \left[5\dfrac{(1)^4}{4} - \dfrac{1}{1^2} + 3(1)^{\frac{4}{3}} \right] = \left[20 - \dfrac{1}{4} + 3(2)^{\frac{4}{3}} \right] - \left[\dfrac{5}{4} - 1 + 3 \right] \approx 24.06$

AREA VERSUS INTEGRAL

Exercise 9 above has an unusual negative answer. To understand it, let's revisit the example of profits per month for Joanie Cakes.

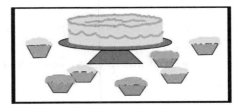

Suppose there are some months with losses, i.e., negative profit. How much total profit did Joanie Cakes have for the six months given in the table below?

Month t	1	2	3	4	5	6
Profit p (in thousands of dollars) per month	25	36	15	−22	−18	41

The total profit is the sum (accumulation) of the profit per month $p(t)$:

$$25 + 36 + 15 - 22 - 18 + 41 = 77$$

or $77,000 profit.

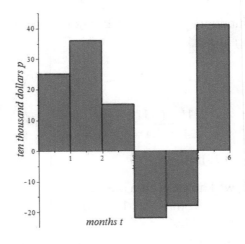

The total **area** of the rectangles in the graph above is not the total profit since the areas of the two rectangles below the axis are subtracted.

The definite integral $\int_a^b f(x)dx$ is the area of the shape between the curve $y = f(x)$ and the x-axis when the graph of $y = f(x)$ remains above the x-axis, but **not** when the graph of $y = f(x)$ dips below the x-axis. The integral $\int_a^b f(x)dx$ gives a negative value for the area of the shape that is enclosed between the x-axis and the curve $\int_a^b f(x)dx$ when the curve dips below the x-axis.

For the case of Joanie Cakes, because the integral provides positive values for the months with positive profit and negative values for the months with negative profit, it actually yields the net profit.

Consider the function $f(x) = -3x^3$ at right.

The graph of this function lies below the x-axis for $x > 0$.

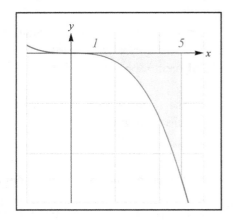

The definite integral gives a negative value.

$$\int_1^5 -3x^3\,dx = -3\left[\frac{x^4}{4}\right]_1^5$$

$$= -3\left[\frac{5^4}{4} - \frac{1^4}{4}\right]$$

$$= -3(156.25 - 0.25) = -468$$

Customarily, the term *area* is considered to be a positive quantity, so the *area* between the curve $f(x) = -3x^3$ and the x-axis is the absolute value of -468, i.e., $|-468| = 468$.

Consider the same function: $f(x) = -3x^3$, but now integrate over the interval, starting at $x = -1$ and ending at $x = 1$.

Its graph is at right.

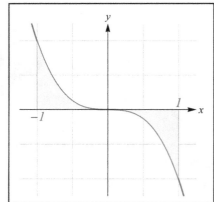

$$\int_{-1}^1 -3x^3\,dx = -3\left[\frac{x^4}{4}\right]_{-1}^1 = -3\left[\frac{1^4}{4} - \frac{(-1)^4}{4}\right]$$

$$= -3(0.25 - 0.25) = 0$$

Since the integral is 0, we know the area between the curve and the x-axis from −1 to 1 has an area above the x-axis (positive integral value) equal to the area below the x-axis (negative integral value).

For curves $y = f(x)$ that have negative values, the area bounded between $y = f(x)$ and the x-axis is given by the definite integral:

$$\textbf{Area} = \int_a^b |f(x)| dx$$

Let's return to the first example with gasoline accumulating at a rate given by $r = -t^2 + 6t$. The total amount of gasoline accumulated would be the initial 20 liters plus the definite integral.

$$r = 20 + \int_0^6 (-t^2 + 6t) dt$$

$$= 20 + \left[-\frac{t^3}{3} + 6\frac{t^2}{2} \right]_0^6 = 20 + \left[-\frac{t^3}{3} + 3t^2 \right]_0^6$$

$$= 20 + \left[-\frac{6^3}{3} + 3(6)^2 \right] - \left[-\frac{0^3}{3} + 3(0)^2 \right]$$

$$= 20 + (-72 + 108) - 0 = 56 \text{ liters}$$

MEANING OF THE "AREA UNDER THE CURVE"

So what is it we are finding when we compute the *area under the curve*?

Suppose we have a delivery truck and we track its speed as it travels through town.

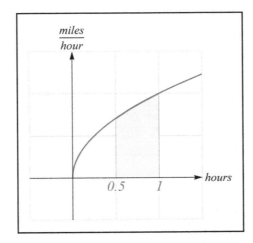

Imagine that the area under the curve—i.e., between the curve and the x-axis—is made up of the sum of the squares on the grid behind it, and we blow up one of these squares.

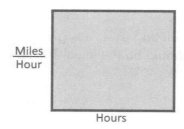

$\dfrac{\text{Miles}}{\text{Hour}}$

Hours

The vertical side, or length of each square, represents *miles/hour* and the horizontal side, or width of each square, represents hours. The area of each square (length × width) would represent:

$$\frac{miles}{hour} \cdot hours = miles$$

The sum of all the squares and partial squares under the curve between

$t = \dfrac{1}{2} hours \ and \ t = 1 \ hour$ would represent the total miles traveled by our delivery

van during that time period.

In general, the area under the curve represents:

whatever measurement unit is represented on the y-axis times whatever measurement unit is represented on the x-axis.

Example 11:

Suppose a college dining hall keeps track of how many eggs are used each day over the course of a year. The information is recorded on the graph below.

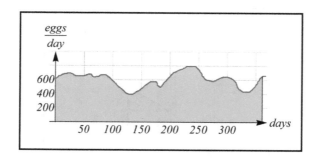

(We realize that "eggs/day" is a discrete quantity, so the graph would technically be a bar graph, but we'll assume that the large quantity of eggs and days makes the graph appear to be a smooth curve.)

The shaded area under the curve would represent $\frac{eggs}{day} \times days$; or in other words, it would represent the total number of eggs consumed over the given time period.

Example 12:

Suppose a construction firm keeps track of how many hours the men on its crew are working versus the number of men on a crew. The information is recorded on the graph below.

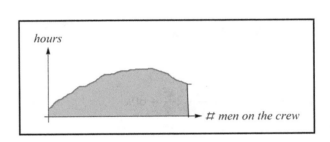

The area under the curve would represent $hours \times men = man\text{-}hours$.

Example 13:

Let's consider one final example. A professor teaches in a very large lecture hall and believes the number of students entering the room per minute follows a bell curve like that below.

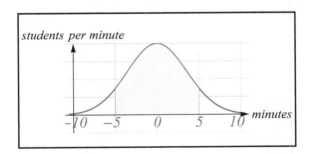

The professor is particularly interested in determining the total number of students in the lecture hall between –5 *minutes*, or 5 minutes before class starts, and 5 *minutes*, or 5 minutes after class starts. That would be the shaded area under the graph above.

The equation of a bell curve is quite complex, but the professor believes the portion of this curve between –5 and 5 can be approximated with the quadratic equation:

$$f(x) = -5x^2 + 2x + 60.$$

To find this area, the integral below is set up.

$$\int_{-5}^{5} -5x^2 + 2x + 60\,dx.$$

The integration is performed:

$$= \left[-5\frac{x^3}{3} + 2\frac{x^2}{2} + 60x \right]_{-5}^{5}$$

and then the evaluation.

$$= \left[-5\frac{5^3}{3} + 2\frac{5^2}{2} + 60(5) \right] - \left[-5\frac{(-5)^3}{3} + 2\frac{(-5)^2}{2} + 60(-5) \right]$$

$$= \left[-\frac{625}{3} + 25 + 300 \right] - \left[\frac{625}{3} + 25 - 300 \right] \approx 183.33$$

The professor finds that approximately 183 students enter the lecture hall between the interval five minutes before class starts and five minutes after it starts.

IC5 AREA BOUND BY A CURVE: DEFINITE INTEGRAL POWER RULE EXERCISES

Find each definite integral.

1. $\displaystyle\int_{-2}^{6} x^2 + 3x - 4\, dx$

2. $\displaystyle\int_{0}^{3} 4x^2 - 2x + 7\, dx$

3. $\displaystyle\int_{1}^{2} \frac{4}{x^4} + 6x\, dx$

4. $\displaystyle\int_{1}^{2} \frac{4}{x^3} + 8x\, dx$

5. $\displaystyle\int_{1}^{2} 4\sqrt{x} + 5x\, dx$

6. $\displaystyle\int_{-1}^{2} 4\sqrt[3]{x} + 5x\, dx$

7. $\displaystyle\int_{1}^{3} 6x^3 - \frac{1}{3x^3} + 4\sqrt{x} - 7\, dx$

8. $\displaystyle\int_{1}^{3} 6x^2 - \frac{1}{4x^3} + 3\sqrt{x} + 9\, dx$

Sketch the graph, shade the area indicated, set up the definite integral, integrate, and evaluate.

9. Find the area under the curve for $f(x) = 3x^2 + 1$ from $x = 0$ to $x = 2$.
10. Find the area under the curve for $f(x) = 2x + 4$ from $x = -2$ to $x = 3$.
11. Find the area under the curve for $f(x) = -3x^2 + 6$ from $x = -1$ to $x = 1$.
12. Find the area under the curve for $f(x) = -3x^2 + 1$ from $x = 0$ to $x = 0.5$.

Sketch the region represented by the definite integral, then evaluate the integral.

13. $\displaystyle\int_{0}^{4} 2x + 1\, dx$

14. $\displaystyle\int_{1}^{6} 2x - 1\, dx$

15. $\displaystyle\int_0^1 -x^3 + 2\,dx$

16. $\displaystyle\int_{-2}^0 -x^3 - 1\,dx$

17. A treehouse manufacturing firm finds that when a new crew is added, the number of treehouses per hour produced by the new crew can be represented by the function:

$$f(x) = 3.4\sqrt{x}$$

where $f(x)$ represents treehouses per hour produced, and x represents hours on the job.

  a. If $f(x)$ were sketched on a graph, what would the area under the curve represent?

  b. Sketch the function, then find the number of treehouses produced between the time the new crew begins ($x = 0$) and when the crew has completed its first four-hour shift.

18. A construction firm finds that gallons per mile used by its tractors varies with the speed of the tractors according to the function:

$$f(x) = -0.9\sqrt{x} + 14$$

where $f(x)$ represents gallons used per mile, and x represents speed in miles per hour.

  a. If $f(x)$ were sketched on a graph, what would the area under the curve represent?

  b. Sketch the function, then find the number of gallons consumed per hour as the speed increased from 10 to 20 miles per hour.

IC5 AREA BOUND BY A CURVE: DEFINITE INTEGRAL POWER RULE SOLUTIONS TO EXERCISES

1. $\displaystyle\int_{-2}^{6} x^2 + 3x - 4\,dx = \left[\frac{x^3}{3} + 3\frac{x^2}{2} - 4x\right]_{-2}^{6}$

$$= \left[\frac{6^3}{3} + 3\frac{6^2}{2} - 4(6)\right] - \left[\frac{(-2)^3}{3} + 3\frac{(-2)^2}{2} - 4(-2)\right]$$

$$= \left[102\right] - \left[11.33\right] = 90.67$$

2. $\displaystyle\int_{0}^{3} 4x^2 - 2x + 7\,dx = \left[4\frac{x^3}{3} - 2\frac{x^2}{2} + 7x\right]_{0}^{3} = \left[4\frac{x^3}{3} - x^2 + 7x\right]_{0}^{3}$

$$= \left[4\frac{3^3}{3} - 3^2 + 7(3)\right] - \left[4\frac{0^3}{3} - 0^2 + 7(0)\right]$$

$$= \left(48\right) - (0) = 48$$

3. $\displaystyle\int_{1}^{2} \frac{4}{x^4} + 6x \ dx = \int_{1}^{2} 4x^{-4} + 6x \ dx = \left[4\frac{x^{-3}}{-3} + 6\frac{x^2}{2}\right]_{1}^{2} = \left[4\frac{x^{-3}}{-3} + 3x^2\right]_{1}^{2}$

$$= \left[4\frac{2^{-3}}{-3} + 3(2)^2\right] - \left[4\frac{1^{-3}}{-3} + 3(1)^2\right] \approx (11.83) - (1.67) = 10.16$$

4. $\displaystyle\int_{1}^{2} \frac{4}{x^3} + 8x\,dx = \int_{1}^{2} 4x^{-3} + 8x\,dx = \left[4\frac{x^{-2}}{-2} + 8\frac{x^2}{2}\right]_{1}^{2} = \left[-2x^{-2} + 4x^2\right]_{1}^{2}$

$$= \left[-2(2)^{-2} + 4(2)^2\right] - \left[-2(1)^{-2} + 4(1)^2\right]$$

$$= \left(15.5\right) - (2) = 13.5$$

5. $\displaystyle\int_{1}^{2} 4\sqrt{x} + 5x\,dx = \int_{1}^{2} 4x^{1/2} + 5x\,dx = \left[4\frac{x^{3/2}}{3/2} + 5\frac{x^2}{2}\right]_{1}^{2}$

$$= \left[4\frac{(2)^{1.5}}{1.5} + 5\frac{(2)^2}{2}\right] - \left[4\frac{(1)^{1.5}}{1.5} + 5\frac{(1)^2}{2}\right]$$

$$\approx (17.54) - (5.17) = 12.37$$

6. $\displaystyle\int_{-1}^{2} 4\sqrt[3]{x} + 5x\,dx = \int_{-1}^{2} 4x^{1/3} + 5x\,dx = \left[4\frac{x^{4/3}}{4/3} + 5\frac{x^2}{2}\right]_{-1}^{2}$

$$= \left[3x^{4/3} + 5\frac{x^2}{2}\right]_{-1}^{2} = \left[3(2)^{4/3} + 5\frac{(2)^2}{2}\right] - \left[3(-1)^{4/3} + 5\frac{(-1)^2}{2}\right]$$

$$\approx (17.56) - (5.5) = 12.06$$

7. $\displaystyle\int_1^3 6x^3 - \frac{1}{3x^3} + 4\sqrt{x} - 7\,dx = \int_1^3 6x^3 - \frac{x^{-3}}{3} + 4x^{\frac{1}{2}} - 7\,dx$

$$= \left[6\frac{x^4}{4} - \frac{x^{-2}}{3(-2)} + 4\frac{x^{\frac{3}{2}}}{\frac{3}{2}} - 7x\right]_1^3 = \left[3\frac{x^4}{2} + \frac{x^{-2}}{6} + 4\frac{x^{1.5}}{1.5} - 7x\right]_1^3$$

$$= \left[3\frac{(3)^4}{2} + \frac{(3)^{-2}}{6} + 4\frac{(3)^{1.5}}{1.5} - 7(3)\right] - \left[3\frac{(1)^4}{2} + \frac{(1)^{-2}}{6} + 4\frac{(1)}{1.5} - 7(1)\right]$$

$$= (114.38) - (-2.66) = 117.04$$

8. $\displaystyle\int_1^3 6x^2 - \frac{1}{4x^3} + 3\sqrt{x} + 9\,dx = \int_1^3 6x^2 - \frac{x^{-3}}{4} + 3x^{\frac{1}{2}} + 9\,dx$

$$= \left[6\frac{x^3}{3} - \frac{x^{-2}}{4(-2)} + 3\frac{x^{\frac{3}{2}}}{\frac{3}{2}} + 9x\right]_1^3 = \left[2x^3 + \frac{x^{-2}}{8} + 2x^{1.5} + 9x\right]_1^3$$

$$= \left[2(3)^3 + \frac{(3)^{-2}}{8} + 2(3)^{1.5} + 9(3)\right] - \left[2(1) + \frac{(1)^{-2}}{8} + 2(1) + 9(1)\right]$$

$$\approx (91.4) - (13.1) = 78.3$$

Sketch the graph, shade the area indicated, set up the definite integral, and then integrate and evaluate.

9. Find the area under the curve for $f(x) = 3x^2 + 1$ from $x = 0$ to $x = 2$.

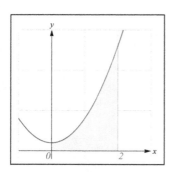

$$\int_0^2 3x^2 + 1\,dx = \left[3\frac{x^3}{3} + x\right]_0^2$$
$$= [x^3 + x]_0^2$$
$$= [2^3 + 2] - [0^3 + 0]$$
$$= 10$$

10. Find the area under the curve for $f(x) = 2x + 4$
    from $x = -2$ to $x = 3$.

$$\int_{-2}^{3} 2x + 4\,dx = \left[2\frac{x^2}{2} + 4x\right]_{-2}^{3} = [x^2 + 4x]_{-2}^{3}$$
$$= \left[3^2 + 4(3)\right] - \left[(-2)^2 + 4(-2)\right] = (21) - (-4) = 25$$

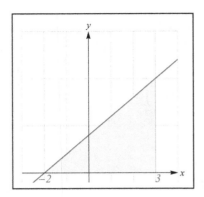

11. Find the area under the curve for
    $f(x) = -3x^2 + 6$ from $x = -1$ to $x = 1$.

$$\int_{-1}^{1} -3x^2 + 6\,dx = \left[-3\frac{x^3}{3} + 6x\right]_{-1}^{1} = \left[-x^3 + 6x\right]_{-1}^{1}$$
$$= \left[-1^3 + 6(1)\right] - \left[-(-1)^3 + 6(-1)\right]$$
$$= 5 - (-5) = 10$$

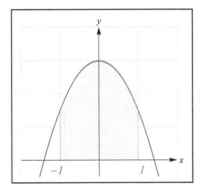

12. Find the area under the curve for
    $f(x) = -3x^2 + 1$ from $x = 0$ to $x = 0.5$.

$$\int_{0}^{.5} -3x^2 + 1\,dx = \left[-3\frac{x^3}{3} + x\right]_{0}^{.5} = [-x^3 + x]_{0}^{.5}$$
$$= -(.5)^3 + .5] - [-0^3 + 0]$$
$$= .375 - 0 = .375$$

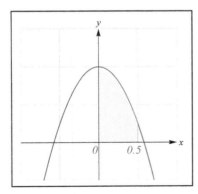

Sketch the region represented by the definite integral, then evaluate the integral.

13. $\displaystyle\int_0^4 2x+1 \; dx = \left[2\dfrac{x^2}{2}+x\right]_0^4 = \left[x^2+x\right]_0^4$

$= \left[4^2+4\right]-\left[0^2+0\right]=20$

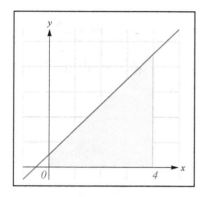

14. $\displaystyle\int_1^6 2x-1 \; dx = \left[2\dfrac{x^2}{2}-x\right]_1^6 = [x^2-x]_1^6$

$= [6^2-6]-[1^2-1]=30$

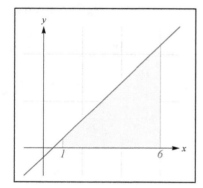

15. $\displaystyle\int_0^1 -x^3+2dx = \left[-\dfrac{x^4}{4}+2x\right]_0^1$

$= \left[-\dfrac{1^4}{4}+2(1)\right]-\left[-\dfrac{0^4}{4}+2(0)\right]$

$= 1.75$

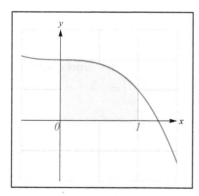

16. $\displaystyle\int_{-2}^{0} -x^3 - 1\,dx = \left[-\frac{x^4}{4} - 1x\right]_{-2}^{0}$

$$= \left[-\frac{0^4}{4} - 1(0)\right] - \left[-\frac{(-2)^4}{4} - 1(-2)\right]$$

$$= (0) - (-4 + 2) = 2$$

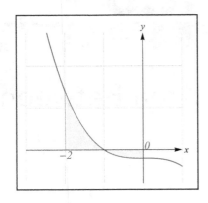

17. a. $\dfrac{treehouses}{hour} \times hours = $ total treehouses produced

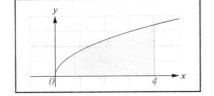

   b. $\displaystyle\int_{0}^{4} 3.4\sqrt{x}\,dx = \int_{0}^{4} 3.4x^{\frac{1}{2}}\,dx$

$$= \left[3.4\frac{x^{1.5}}{1.5}\right]_{0}^{4}$$

$$= \left[3.4\frac{4^{1.5}}{1.5}\right] - \left[3.4\frac{0^{1.5}}{1.5}\right]$$

$$\approx 18.13 - 0 \approx 18 \ treehouses$$

18. a. $\dfrac{gallons}{mile} \times \dfrac{miles}{hour} = \dfrac{gallons}{hour} = $ total gallons used per hour

   b. $\displaystyle\int_{10}^{20} -0.9\sqrt{x} + 14 = \int_{10}^{20} -0.9x^{1/2} + 14\,dx = \left[-0.9\frac{x^{1.5}}{1.5} + 14x\right]_{10}^{20}$

$$= \left[-0.9\frac{(20)^{1.5}}{1.5} + 14(20)\right] - \left[-0.9\frac{(10)^{1.5}}{1.5} + 14(10)\right]$$

$$\approx (226.3) - (121) = 105.3$$

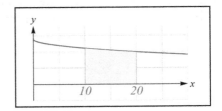

IC6

Area Between Curves

We have looked at the area bounded between a curve and the x-axis. Now we will look at the area bounded between two curves.

Consider the curves $y = x^2$ and $y = 2x + 3$.

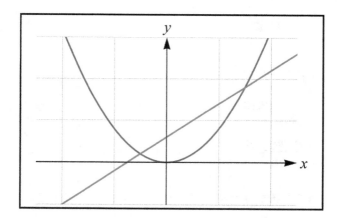

Suppose we want to find the area between the curves from $x = 1$ to $x = 2$.

At $x = 1$, we draw a vertical line up and down until we connect both curves. We do the same at $x = 2$ to obtain the graph below. The area bounded between the curves $y = x^2$ and $y = 2x + 3$ from $x = 1$ to $x = 2$ is shaded in the following graph.

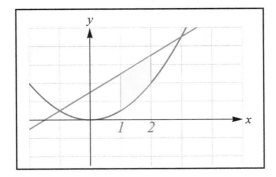

Now we set up an integral to determine the shaded area:

$$\int_{1}^{2} (2x+3)-(x^2)\,dx.$$

The subscript of the integral is the left endpoint $x=1$, and the superscript of the integral is the right endpoint $x=2$. The dx indicates there is width for the area, that the endpoints are along the x-axis, and the curves are given by functions that depend on the variable x.

The function to integrate is the difference between the top curve and the bottom curve within the area of interest. This gives us the height of the area.

Consider any vertical line that lies within our shaded region. The "top curve" is the highest curve on that vertical line. The "bottom curve" is the lowest curve on that vertical line.

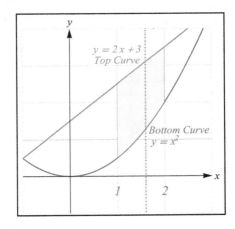

The height of the area is given by the difference between the top curve and the bottom curve: $(2x+3)-(x^2)=3+2x-x^2$. We get the area by adding up the heights over the interval width from $x=1$ to $x=2$:

$$\int_1^2 (2x+3)-(x^2)dx = \int_1^2 3+2x-x^2 dx$$

We integrate as before:

$$\left[3x+2\frac{x^2}{2}-\frac{x^3}{3}\right]_1^2 = \left[3x+x^2-\frac{x^3}{3}\right]_1^2$$

then evaluate:

$$\left[3(2)+2^2-\frac{2^3}{3}\right]-\left[3(1)+1^2-\frac{1^3}{3}\right]$$

and simplify to get:

$$\approx(7.33)-(3.67)=3.66$$

To find the area between curves, we employ the following steps.

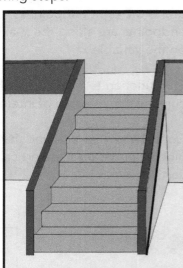

Not those ⟶

Step 1:

Sketch the curves. This will allow us to determine which curve is on top (the highest) and which is at the bottom (the lowest) within the area of interest.

Step 2:

Set up the integral. Remember it's the "top" function minus the "bottom" function.

Distribute the negative and collect like terms.

Step 3:

Integrate.

Step 4:

Evaluate and simplify.

<u>Another Example:</u> Find the area between the curves $f(x)=(x-2)^2+1$ and $y=3$ from $x=1$ to $x=2$.

Step 1:

We recall that the function $f(x)=(x-2)^2+1$ is a parabola opening up, with vertex shifted two units to the right and shifted up one unit. The equation $y=3$ is a horizontal line.

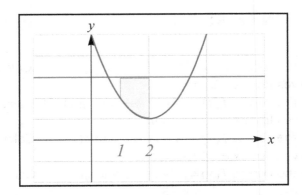

We note that within the shaded region, the horizontal line, $y=3$, is the top function (the highest), and the parabola, $f(x)=(x-2)^2+1$, is the bottom (lowest) function.

Step 2:

We set up the integral; also, distribute the negative and then collect like terms:

$$\int_1^2 3-((x-2)^2+1)dx = \int_1^2 3-(x^2-4x+5)dx =$$

$$\int_1^2 3-x^2+4x-5\ dx = \int_1^2 -x^2+4x-2\ dx =$$

Step 3:

We integrate: $\left[-\dfrac{x^3}{3}+4\dfrac{x^2}{2}-2x\right]_1^2 = \left[-\dfrac{x^3}{3}+2x^2-2x\right]_1^2 =$

Step 4:

We evaluate the integral: $\left[-\dfrac{2^3}{3}+2(2)^2-2(2)\right]-\left[-\dfrac{1^3}{3}+2(1)^2-2(1)\right]=$

$$\approx(1.33)-(-.33)=1.66$$

INTRA-SECTION EXERCISES:

1. Sketch the curves $f(x)=(x-5)^2+11$ and $g(x)=5$. Calculate the area between the curves from $x=2$ to $x=4$.
2. Sketch the curves $f(x)=(x+5)^2+6$ and $g(x)=4$. Calculate the area between the curves from $x=-4$ to $x=0$.
3. Sketch the curves $f(x)=(x+1)^3+2$ and $g(x)=1$. Calculate the area between the curves from $x=-1$ to $x=1$.
4. Sketch the curves $f(x)=(x-2)^3+1$ and $g(x)=8$. Calculate the area between the curves from $x=2$ to $x=3$.

Don't forget to use the steps!

Solutions

1. $\displaystyle\int_2^4 ((x-5)^2+11)-5 \ dx = \int_2^4 (x^2-10x+36)-5 \ dx$

$$= \int_2^4 x^2-10x+31 \ dx = \left[\dfrac{x^3}{3}-10\dfrac{x^2}{2}+31x\right]_2^4$$

$$= \left[\frac{x^3}{3} - 5x^2 + 31x\right]_2^4 = \left[\frac{4^3}{3} - 5(4)^2 + 31(4)\right] - \left[\frac{2^3}{3} - 5(2)^2 + 31(2)\right]$$

$$\approx (21.3 - 80 + 124) - (2.7 - 20 + 62) = (65.3) - (44.7) = 20.6$$

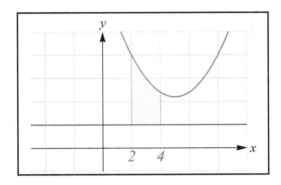

2. $\displaystyle\int_{-4}^{0} ((x+5)^2 + 6) - 4 \ dx = \int_{-4}^{0} (x^2 + 10x + 31) - 4 \ dx$

$$= \int_{-4}^{0} x^2 + 10x + 27 \ dx = \left[\frac{x^3}{3} + 10\frac{x^2}{2} + 27x\right]_{-4}^{0} = \left[\frac{x^3}{3} + 5x^2 + 27x\right]_{-4}^{0}$$

$$= \left[\frac{0^3}{3} + 5(0)^2 + 27(0)\right] - \left[\frac{(-4)^3}{3} + 5(-4)^2 + 27(-4)\right]$$

$$\approx (0) - (-21.33 + 80 - 108) = (0) - (-49.33) = -49.33$$

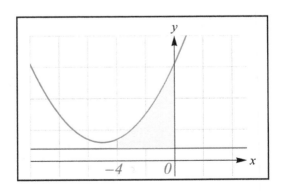

3. $\displaystyle\int_{-1}^{1}((x+1)^3+2)-1\,dx = \int_{-1}^{1}(x^3+3x^2+3x+3)-1\,dx$

$\displaystyle = \int_{-1}^{1}x^3+3x^2+3x+2\,dx \quad = \left[\frac{x^4}{4}+3\frac{x^3}{3}+3\frac{x^2}{2}+2x\right]_{-1}^{1}$

$\displaystyle = \left[\frac{x^4}{4}+x^3+3\frac{x^2}{2}+2x\right]_{-1}^{1} = \left[\frac{1^4}{4}+1^3+3\frac{1^2}{2}+2(1)\right]-\left[\frac{(-1)^4}{4}+(-1)^3+3\frac{(-1)^2}{2}+2(-1)\right]$

$= (4.75)-(-1.25)=6$

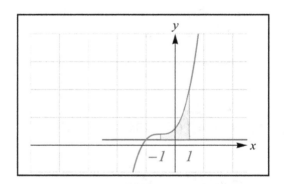

4. $\displaystyle\int_{2}^{3}8-((x-2)^3+1)\,dx = \int_{2}^{3}8-(x^3-6x^2+12x-7)\,dx$

$\displaystyle = \int_{2}^{3}-x^3+6x^2-12x+15\,dx = \left[-\frac{x^4}{4}+6\frac{x^3}{3}-12\frac{x^2}{2}+15x\right]_{2}^{3}$

$\displaystyle = \left[-\frac{x^4}{4}+2x^3-6x^2+15x\right]_{2}^{3}$

$\displaystyle = \left[-\frac{3^4}{4}+2(3)^3-6(3)^2+15(3)\right]-\left[-\frac{(2)^4}{4}+2(2)^3-6(2)^2+15(2)\right]$

$= (24.75)-(18)=6.75$

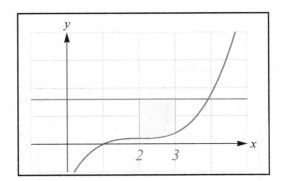

AREA BETWEEN POINTS OF INTERSECTION

Consider the two curves $y=x^2$ and $y=2x+3$ once again. They enclose a bounded area between their points of intersection.

At the points of intersection, both curves share one common point (x,y). At a common point of intersection, both curves share the same x-value and the same y-value.

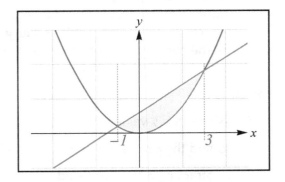

The points of intersection can be found by setting the y for $y=x^2$ equal to the y for $y=2x+3$.

$x^2=2x+3$ We subtract $2x$ and 3 from both sides.

$x^2-2x-3=0$ Factoring, we have:

$(x-3)(x+1)=0$ [*Note: If the resulting quadratic equation didn't factor, we would need to use the Quadratic Formula.*]

$x=3,\ x=-1$ The points of intersection occur at $x=-1$ and at $x=3$.

The left endpoint for the interval is at $x=-1$, and the right endpoint is at $x=3$.

The area of the region bounded by $y=x^2$ and $y=2x+3$ can be found with the integral:

$$\int_{-1}^{3}(2x+3)-(x)^2\,dx$$

Using the steps, we can find the area.

$$\int_{-1}^{3}(2x+3)-(x)^2\,dx=\left[2\frac{x^2}{2}+3x-\frac{x^3}{3}\right]_{-1}^{3}=\left[x^2+3x-\frac{x^3}{3}\right]_{-1}^{3}$$

$$=\left[(3)^2+3(3)-\frac{(3)^3}{3}\right]-\left[(-1)^2+3(-1)-\frac{(-1)^3}{3}\right]\approx(9)-(-1.67)=10.67.$$

INTRA-SECTION EXERCISES:

5. Sketch the curves $y=x^2+2$ and $y=6$; then calculate the area bounded by the curves between their points of intersection.
6. Sketch the curves $f(x)=x^2+3$ and $y=2x+6$; then calculate the area bounded by the curves between their points of intersection.

Solutions

5. We set the y-values equal

    to find the points of intersection; $x^2+2=6$

    Subtracting 6 from both sides; $x^2-4=0$

    and factoring; $(x+2)(x-2)=0,$

    we find that $x=-2,\ x=2.$

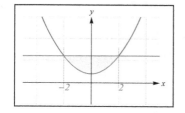

We set up the integral, noting that the horizontal line is the top (highest) function within the bounded region of interest:

$$\int_{-2}^{2}6-(x^2+2)dx=\int_{-2}^{2}6-x^2-2\ dx=\int_{-2}^{2}-x^2+4\ dx=$$

We integrate: $\left[-\frac{x^3}{3}+4x\right]_{-2}^{2}=$

and evaluate $\left[-\frac{2^3}{3}+4(2)\right]-\left[-\frac{(-2)^3}{3}+4(-2)\right]\approx5.33-(-5.33)=10.66$

6. We set the y-values equal to find the points of intersection. $x^2+3=2x+6$

    Subtracting 2x and 6 from both sides $x^2-2x-3=0$

    and factoring, $(x+1)(x-3)=0$

    we find that $x=-1, \; x=3$

we set up the integral, noting that the straight line is the top (highest) function within the bounded region of interest:

$$\int_{-1}^{3} 2x+6-(x^2+3)dx = \int_{-1}^{3} 2x+6-x^2-3 \; dx$$

$$= \int_{-1}^{3} -x^2+2x+3 \; dx =$$

We integrate: $\left[-\dfrac{x^3}{3}+\dfrac{2x^2}{2}+3x \right]_{-1}^{3} =$

and evaluate $\left[-\dfrac{3^3}{3}+3^2+3(3) \right] - \left[-\dfrac{(-1)^3}{3}+(-1)^2+3(-1) \right] \approx 9-(-1.67)=10.67$

TWO NOTES ABOUT FACTORING

Consider the equation: $ab=0.$

We know that a could equal zero because: $(0)b=0$

or b could equal zero because: $a(0)=0$

or a and b could both equal zero because: $(0)(0)=0$

An annihilator - not a terminator

There is actually a mathematical term for values that act in this way. Zero is an *annihilator*. It is truly a mathematical term. Now consider the equation:

$$ab=6.$$

Does this mean that a must equal six, or b must equal 6?

Of course not. The factor a might equal 12 while b equals $1/2$ because $(12)\left(\dfrac{1}{2}\right)=6$, or a could equal -2 while b equals -3 because $(-2)(-3)=6$.

It is only when one side of an equation equals zero that we can set each factor equal to the other side of the equation (zero).

Now consider the equation:

$$x^2+x=6.$$

It is possible to factor out an x from each term on the left: $x(x+1)=6$, but it would be "illegal" to set each factor equal to 6. We must have a zero on the right side.

Therefore, we need to subtract 6 from both sides: $\qquad x^2+x=6$

$$x^2+x-6=0$$

Then we can factor: $\qquad\qquad\qquad\qquad\qquad (x+3)(x-2)=0$

and set each factor equal to zero: $\qquad\qquad (x+3)=0,\ \ (x-2)=2$

giving us the answers: $\qquad\qquad\qquad\qquad x=-3$ or $x=2$.

Now consider the curves: $y=x^2+2$ and $y=2x+3$ (graphed at right). We want to find the area bounded by the two curves between their points of intersection.

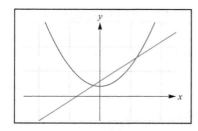

As before, we begin by setting the functions of the curves equal to each other so that we can find the x-values of the points they share.

$$x^2+2=2x+3$$

Since this is a quadratic equation (the variable with the highest degree is 2), we can set one side of the equation equal to zero.

We subtract $2x$ and 3 from both sides. Since this equation doesn't factor, we can use the Quadratic Formula to solve for x.

$$x^2-2x-1=0$$

You probably recall from a basic algebra course that for an equation in the form:

$$ax^2 + bx + c = 0,$$

we can find x with the formula: $x = \dfrac{-b \pm \sqrt{b^2 - 4ac}}{2a}.$

In our equation: $x^2 - 2x - 1 = 0$, $a = 1$, $b = -2$, and $c = -1$.

Inserting these values in the Quadratic Formula gives us: $x = \dfrac{--2 \pm \sqrt{(-2)^2 - 4(1)(-1)}}{2(1)}.$

This formula gives us both values of x: $\dfrac{2 + \sqrt{8}}{2} \approx 2.41$ and $\dfrac{2 - \sqrt{8}}{2} \approx -0.41.$

After noting that the "top" equation in the area of interest is $y = 2x + 3$, and the "bottom" equation is $y = x^2 + 2$, we can now set up the integral to find the area between the curves from $x = 2.41$ to $x = -0.41$.

$$\int_{-0.41}^{2.41} 2x + 3 - (x^2 + 2)\,dx$$

As before, we would compute the area by distributing the negative, collecting like terms, integrating, and evaluating the integral.

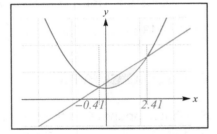

ONE FINAL EXAMPLE

Suppose the projected fuel cost (in thousands of dollars) for a fleet of delivery trucks in 2020 is:

$$C_1 = 488.60 + 9.25t \quad \text{where } t = 0 \text{ corresponds to the year 2020.}$$

If the cost of crude oil is expected to decrease due to the completion of a new pipeline from Canadian oil sands, the projected cost will be:

$$C_2 = 380.40 + 7.08t.$$

How much will the company save on fuel over the years 2020 to 2025 if the pipeline is completed?

Imagine graphing the two functions, where the horizontal axis represents time in years and the vertical axis represents fuel cost. The area between the curves would represent the difference in fuel costs over the given years, i.e., the savings in fuel costs.

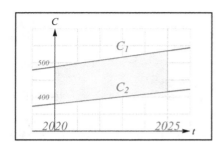

To find this area, we set up the integral:

$$\int_0^5 (488.60 + 9.25t) - (380.40 + 7.08t)\,dx$$

Distributing and collecting like terms give us: $\int_0^5 (108.20 + 2.17t)\,dx$

which we can integrate to get: $\left[108.20t + 2.17\frac{t^2}{2} \right]_0^5$

and evaluate to get: $\left[108.20(5) + 2.17\frac{5^2}{2} \right] - \left[108.20(0) + 2.17\frac{0^2}{2} \right] = 568.13 - 0,$

or \$568.13 saved on fuel costs.

CROSSING CURVES

So what happens when the curves cross? Consider the curves $f(x) = x^3 - 10x^2 + 24x + 5$ and $g(x) = x + 2$, graphed below. Suppose we want to find the area between the curves from $x = 0$ to $x = 7$.

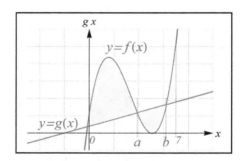

We notice that from $x = 0$ to $x = a$, $f(x)$ lies above the straight line, $g(x)$. Then from $x = a$ to $x = b$, $g(x)$ lies above $f(x)$. From $x = b$ to $x = 7$, $f(x)$ is once again above $g(x)$. We will need to set up three integrals—another reason we sketch the curves.

$$\int_0^a f(x) - g(x)\,dx + \int_a^b g(x) - f(x)\,dx + \int_b^7 f(x) + g(x)\,dx$$

However, we will consider crossed curves beyond the scope of this text.

IC6 AREA BETWEEN CURVES EXERCISES

1. Sketch the curves; then determine the area between the curves: $f(x) = (x-2)^2 + 6$ and $g(x) = 3$ from $x = 1$ to $x = 4$.

2. Sketch the curves; then determine the area between the curves: $f(x) = (x+2)^2 + 6$ and $g(x) = 2$ from $x = -4$ to $x = -1$.

3. Sketch the curves; then determine the area bounded by the curves between their points of intersection: $f(x) = x^2 + 3$ and $g(x) = 2x + 3$.

4. Sketch the curves; then determine the area bounded by the curves between their points of intersection: $f(x) = x^2 + 6$ and $g(x) = 3x + 4$.

5. Sketch the curves; then determine the area between the curves: $f(x) = -(x-3)^2 + 5$ and $g(x) = 2$ from $x = 2$ to $x = 4$.

6. Sketch the curves; then determine the area between the curves: $f(x) = -(x+4)^2 + 5$ and $g(x) = -2x - 4$ from $x = -4$ to $x = -2$.

7. Sketch the curves; then determine the area between the curves from $x = 3$ to $x = 4$. $f(x) = -(x-3)^3 + 1$ and $g(x) = 2x - 5$.

8. Sketch the curves; then determine the area between the curves from $x = 3$ to $x = 4$. $f(x) = (x-3)^3 + 1$ and $g(x) = 2x - 5$.

9. Sketch the curves; then determine the area bounded by the curves between their points of intersection. $f(x) = (x+2)^2 + 4$ and $g(x) = -2x + 5$.

10. Sketch the curves; then determine the area bounded by the curves between their points of intersection. $f(x) = (x+2)^2 + 7$ and $g(x) = -2x + 12$.

11. A causeway has blocked the natural outflow of water and sediment so that the bay is silting up at a rate of $0.013t^3 + 8.2t + 36.4$ cubic meters of silt per year. If concrete conduits are installed through the causeway every 100 meters, it is estimated that the silting up can be reduced to a rate of $0.0004t^3 + 6.3t + 15.4$ cubic meters per year. If the conduits can be completed in 2020 ($t = 0$), what will be the total reduction in cubic meters of silt over the next 10 years, starting in 2020?

IC6 AREA BETWEEN CURVES SOLUTIONS TO EXERCISES

1. $\displaystyle\int_{1}^{4}((x-2)^2+6)-3\,dx = \int_{1}^{4}(x^2-4x+10)-3\,dx$

$$= \int_{1}^{4} x^2-4x+7\,dx = \left[\frac{x^3}{3}-4\frac{x^2}{2}+7x\right]_{1}^{4} = \left[\frac{x^3}{3}-2x^2+7x\right]_{1}^{4}$$

$$= \left[\frac{4^3}{3}-2(4)^2+7(4)\right]-\left[\frac{1^3}{3}-2(1)^2+7(1)\right]$$

$$\approx (17.3)-(5.3)=12$$

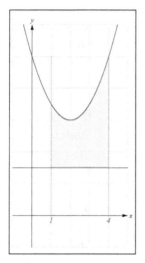

2. $\displaystyle\int_{-4}^{-1}((x+2)^2+6)-2\,dx = 15$

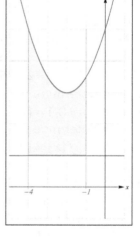

3. Points of intersection: $\quad 2x+3=x^2+3$
$$0=x^2-2x$$
$$0=x(x-2)$$
$$x=0,\,2$$

$$\int_{0}^{2}(2x+3)-(x^2+3)dx = \int_{0}^{2}-x^2+2x\,dx = \left[-\frac{x^3}{3}+2\frac{x^2}{2}\right]_{0}^{2}$$

$$= \left[-\frac{x^3}{3}+x^2\right]_{0}^{2} = \left[-\frac{2^3}{3}+(2)^2\right]-\left[-\frac{0^3}{3}+(0)^2\right]$$

$$\approx (1.33)-(0)=1.33$$

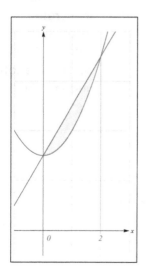

4. Points of intersection: $x = 1, 2$.

$$\int_1^2 (3x+4)-(x^2+6)\,dx \approx 0.16$$

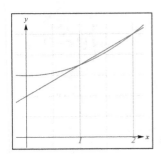

5. $$\int_2^4 (-(x-3)^2+5)-(2)\,dx = \int_2^4 (-x^2+6x-4)-(2)\,dx$$

$$= \left[-\frac{x^3}{3}+6\frac{x^2}{2}-6x\right]_2^4 = \left[-\frac{x^3}{3}+3x^2-6x\right]_2^4$$

$$= \left[-\frac{4^3}{3}+3(4)^2-6(4)\right]-\left[-\frac{2^3}{3}+3(2)^2-6(2)\right]$$

$$\approx (2.67)-(-2.67)=5.34$$

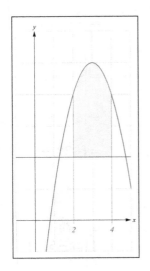

6. $$\int_{-4}^{-2} (-x^2-8x-11)-(-2x-4)\,dx \approx 3.34$$

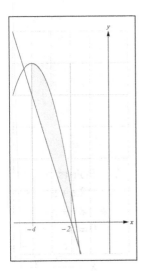

7. $\displaystyle\int_3^4 (2x-5)-(-(x-3)^3+1)dx$

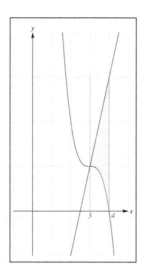

$\displaystyle = \int_3^4 (2x-5)-(-x^3+9x^2-27x+28)dx$

$\displaystyle = \int_3^4 x^3-9x^2+29x-33\,dx = \left[\frac{x^4}{4}-9\frac{x^3}{3}+29\frac{x^2}{2}-33x\right]_3^4$

$\displaystyle = \left[\frac{x^4}{4}-3x^3+29\frac{x^2}{2}-33x\right]_3^4$

$\displaystyle = \left[\frac{4^4}{4}-3(4)^3+29\frac{4^2}{2}-33(4)\right]-\left[\frac{3^4}{4}-3(3)^3+29\frac{3^2}{2}-33(3)\right]$

$= [64-192+232-132]-[20.25-81+130.5-99]$

$= (-28)-(-29.25) = 1.25$

8. $\displaystyle\int_3^4 (2x-5)-((x-3)^3+1)\,dx = 0.75$

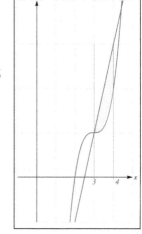

9. Points of intersection:
$-2x+5 = (x+2)^2+4$
$-2x+5 = x^2+4x+8$
$0 = x^2+6x+3$ We must use the quadratic formula

$$x = \frac{-6\pm\sqrt{(-6)^2-4(1)(3)}}{2(1)} \approx -5.45, -0.55$$

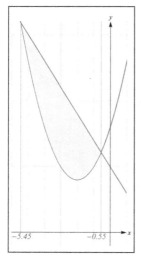

$$\int_{-5.45}^{-0.55} (-2x+5)-(x^2+4x+8)dx = \int_{-5.45}^{-0.55} -x^2-6x-3dx$$

$$= \left[-\frac{x^3}{3}-6\frac{x^2}{2}-3x\right]_{-5.45}^{-.55} = \left[-\frac{x^3}{3}-3x^2-3x\right]_{-5.45}^{-0.55}$$

$$= \left[-\frac{(-0.55)^3}{3}-3(-0.55)^2-3(-0.55)\right]-\left[-\frac{(-5.45)^3}{3}-3(-5.45)^2-3(-5.45)\right]$$

$$\approx = (0.80)-(-18.80)=19.6$$

10. Points of intersection: $x=.16, -6.16$

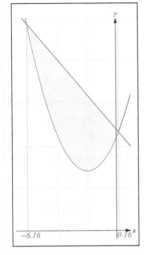

$$\int_{-6.16}^{.16} (-2x+12)-(x^2+4x+11)dx$$
$$\approx (.08)-(-197.91)=197.99$$

11. $\int_{0}^{10}(0.013t^3+8.2t+36.4)-(0.0004t^3+6.3t+15.4)dx$

$$= \int_{0}^{10}(0.0126t^3+1.9t+21)\,dx = \left[0.0126\frac{t^4}{4}+1.9\frac{t^2}{2}+21t\right]_{0}^{10}$$

$$= \left[0.0126\frac{10^4}{4}+1.9\frac{10^2}{2}+21(10)\right]-\left[0.0126\frac{0^4}{4}+1.9\frac{0^2}{2}+21(0)\right]$$

$$= 336.5 \text{ cubic meters}$$

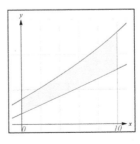

IR7

Exponential Functions

We have looked at exponents, powers, and power functions. Power functions are of the form: $y = x^n$

where the base x is the variable, and the exponent n is a fixed value e.g., $y = x^6$.

Again, we are going to define a class of functions using exponents and bases, but the base b is a fixed value, and the exponent x is the variable.

Another kind of function with more power

The general form of this *exponential function* is: $y = b^x$.

Consider the exponential function $y = 3^x$.

We can make a chart of points belonging to this graph: $y = 3^x$.

x	$y = 3^x$	(x, y)
0	$3^0 = 1$	$(0, 1)$
1	$3^1 = 3$	$(1, 3)$
2	$3^2 = 9$	$(2, 9)$
100	$3^{100} = 5.15 \times 10^{47}$, = Reallllly big number!	$(100, 5.15 \times 10^{47})$
-1	$3^{-1} = 1/3$	$(-1, 1/3)$
-2	$3^{-2} = 1/9$	$(-2, 1/9)$
-100	$3^{-100} = 1.94 \times 10^{-48}$, = Realllly small number!	$(-100, 1.94 \times 10^{-48})$

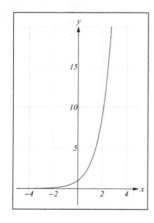

Note:

1. The values of y are positive. Making the exponent negative does not change the sign of y, e.g., $y = 3^{-2}$ equals $1/9$. One ninth is small, but it's a positive number.
2. The values of y become extremely large as the values of x become very large positive numbers. Look at the row in the chart when $x = 100$.
3. The values of y become extremely close to zero as the values of x become very large *negative* numbers. The line $y = 0$, i.e., the x-axis, is an asymptote. Look at the row in the chart when $x = -100$.

Now consider the exponential function: $y = -3^x$. All the values of y would be negative.

Remember that even with a negative exponent, 3^x remains a positive number, so $-(3^x)$, or -3^x, would be a negative number for every value of x.

x	$y = -3^x$	(x, y)
0	$-3^0 = -1$	$(0, -1)$
1	$-3^1 = -3$	$(1, -3)$
2	$-3^2 = -9$	$(2, -9)$
100	$-3^{100} = -5.15 \times 10^{47}$, = Realllllly low!	$(100, -5.15 \times 1047)$
-1	$-3^{-1} = -1/3$	$(-1, -1/3)$
-2	$-3^{-2} = -1/9$	$(-2, -1/9)$
-100	$-3^{-100} = -1.94 \times 10^{-48}$, = Reallllly small and close to zero!	$(-100, -1.94 \times 10^{-48})$

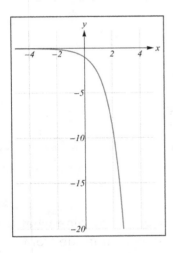

The graph of $y = -3^x$ is the graph of $y = 3^x$ turned upside down.

What about the exponential function $y = 3^{-x}$? How does it vary?

Plotting points, we can see that where $y = 3^x$ produces big numbers, $y = 3^{-x}$ produces small numbers, and vice versa.

x	$y = 3^x$	−x	$y = 3^{-x}$
0	$3^0 = 1$	0	$3^0 = 1$
1	$3^1 = 3$	−1	$3^{-1} = 1/3$
2	$3^2 = 9$	−2	$3^{-2} = 1/9$
100	$3^{100} = 5.15 \times 10^{47}$, = Really Big!	−100	$3^{-100} = 1.94 \times 10^{-48}$ = Really Small
−1	$3^{-1} = 1/3$	1	$3^{--1} = 3^1 = 3$
−2	$3^{-2} = 1/9$	2	$3^{--2} = 3^2 = 9$
−100	$3^{-100} = 1.94 \times 10^{-48}$, = Really Small!	100	$3^{--100} = 3^{100} = 5.15 \times 10^{47}$ = Really Big

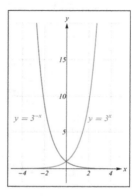

We can imagine what the fourth variation, $y = -3^{-x}$, would look like. The negative sign in the front would make the graph of $y = 3^{-x}$ flip over because every positive value would become negative. These two exponential functions are graphed below.

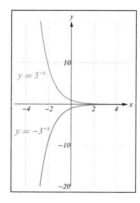

What if we choose a different base, say, 7?

How would the graph of $y = 7^x$ compare with our graph of $y = 3^x$?

For one thing, both graphs would contain the point (0,1) since $y = 7^0 = 1$, as does $y = 3^0$.
In fact, every graph of the form $y = b^x$ contains the point (0,1), if $b > 1$. Right?

The exponential functions $y = 15^x$, $y = 7^x$, and $y = 3^x$ are all graphed on the same axes at right.

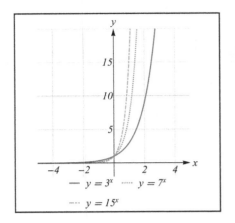

We can see that the greater the base, the steeper the graph.

What if our base b is less than one? What if $b = \frac{1}{3}$, for example?

Then we would have the equation $y = \left(\frac{1}{3}\right)^x$, but since $\frac{1}{3} = 3^{-1}$, our equation would become $y = (3^{-1})^x$, which equals $y = 3^{-x}$, a form we have already explored.

To summarize, the four variations of $y = b^x$ we have investigated are shown below.

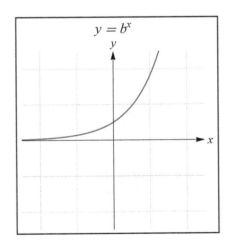

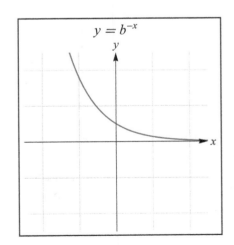

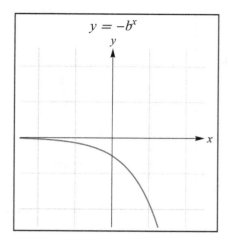

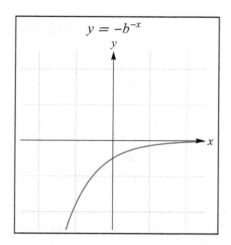

Altogether, they are quite stunning.

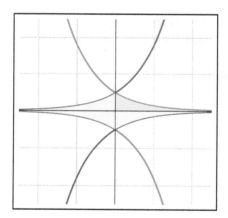

THE SPECIAL NUMBER *e*

You are probably familiar with the constant number π. It represents the ratio of the circumference to the diameter of a circle, making the number π occur naturally in many formulas. The constant number *e* is also a special number that occurs naturally in many formulas because of its relationship to a ratio. The properties of *e* are so natural mathematically and scientifically that it is called the *natural number*. Later, when derivatives have been introduced, the special properties of *e* will be more fully explained.

The number e is approximately 2.7183. The value 3 may be used for a quick, rough approximation to e.

The graph of $y=e^x$ looks like the graph of $y=3^x$, since e is roughly approximated by 3. Similarly, the graph of $y=e^{-x}$ looks like the graph of $y=3^{-x}$, etc.

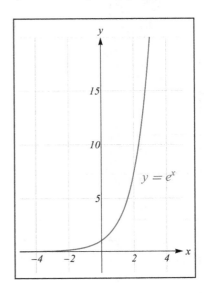

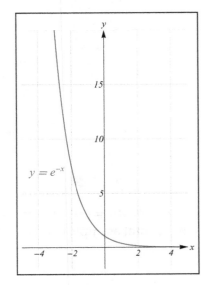

While the graph of $y=e^x$ contains the point $(0,1)$, the graph of $y=2e^x$ contains the point $(0,2)$ because when $x=0$, $y=2e^x=2e^0=2(1)=2$.

[Both $y=e^x$ and $y=2e^x$ are graphed at right.]

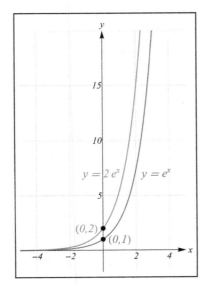

The graph of $y = e^x + 1$ has the shape of $y = e^x$ with a horizontal asymptote of $y = 1$. [graph at right]

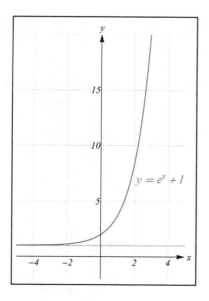

The graph of $y = e^x - 3$ has the shape of $y = e^x$ with a horizontal asymptote of $y = -3$. [graph at right]

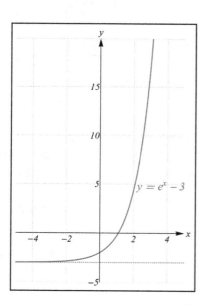

The graph of $y = e^{x+2}$ is shifted two units to the left [graph at right]. Notice that instead of the point $(0,1)$, the graph now goes through the point $(-2,1)$.

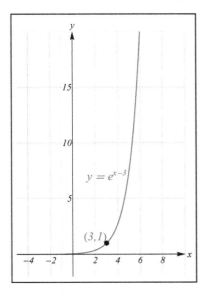

The graph of $y = e^{x-3}$ is shifted three units to the right [graph at right]. Instead of going through the point $(0,1)$, it goes through $(3,1)$.

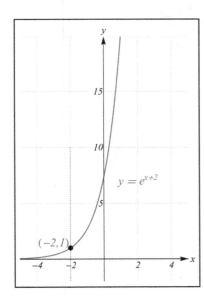

The graph of $y=e^{-x-3}$ or $y=e^{-(x+3)}$ falls as x goes from left to right, just like $y=e^{-x}$, but it is shifted three units left [graph at right]. It contains the point $(-3,1)$.

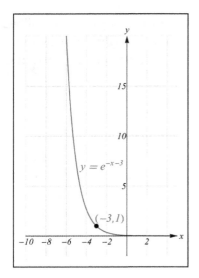

The graph of $y=e^{-x+2}$ or $y=e^{-(x-2)}$ is similar to the graph $y=e^{-x}$, but it is shifted two units to the right [graph at right]. It contains the point $(2,1)$.

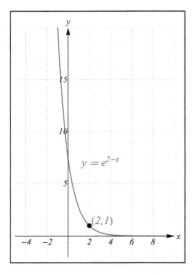

INTRA-SECTION EXERCISES:

1. Sketch the graph of: $y=e^{-x}+2$
2. Sketch the graph of: $y=-e^{x}-1$
3. Sketch the graph of: $y=e^{-x+2}$

4. Sketch the graph of: $y = -e^{-x+2}$
5. Sketch the graph of: $y = -e^{x-1}$
6. Sketch the graph of: $y = e^{-x+3} - 4$
7. Sketch the graph of $y = -3e^{x}$

Solutions

1.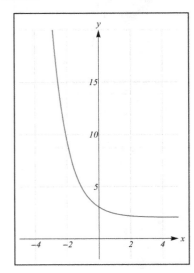

2.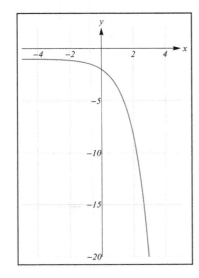

3.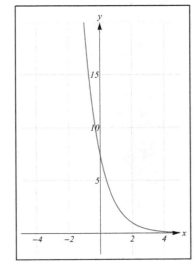

4.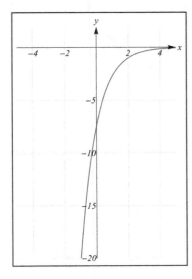

5.

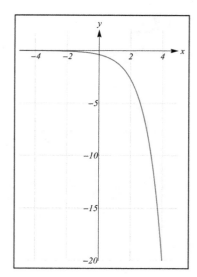

6.

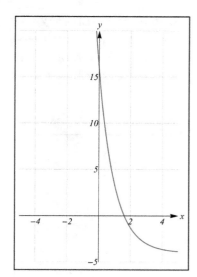

7.

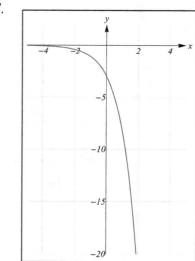

WHY ARE EXPONENTIAL FUNCTIONS IMPORTANT (AND SOMETHING SPECIAL ABOUT e)?

POPULATION GROWTH

Let's look at a population growth setting to get a basis for understanding exponential functions. Suppose we have four rabbits and they reproduce every month at a rate that triples the population every month. At the beginning, there are 4 rabbits; after one month, there are 12 rabbits; after two months, there are 36 rabbits; after three months, there are 108 rabbits … We can follow this process mathematically: let $P_0 = 4$ be the initial population size of four rabbits.

Month	Population Size	Size Using P_0
0, start	4	P_0
1	$4 \cdot 3 = 12$	$P_0 \cdot 3 = P_0 \cdot 3^1$
2	$4 \cdot 3 \cdot 3 = 12 \cdot 3 = 36$	$P_0 \cdot 3 \cdot 3 = P_0 \cdot 3^2$
3	$4 \cdot 3 \cdot 3 \cdot 3 = 36 \cdot 3 = 108$	$P_0 \cdot 3 \cdot 3 \cdot 3 = P_0 \cdot 3^3$
4	$4 \cdot 3 \cdot 3 \cdot 3 \cdot 3 = 108 \cdot 3 = 324$	$P_0 \cdot 3 \cdot 3 \cdot 3 \cdot 3 = P_0 \cdot 3^4$
5	$4 \cdot 3 \cdot 3 \cdot 3 \cdot 3 \cdot 3 = 324 \cdot 3 = 972$	$P_0 \cdot 3 \cdot 3 \cdot 3 \cdot 3 \cdot 3 = P_0 \cdot 3^5$

Following the pattern, after t months, the constant multiplier 3 is applied t times, and the population of rabbits would be

$$4 \cdot 3 \cdot 3 \cdot 3 \cdot 3 \cdots \cdots 3 = 4 \cdot 3^t,$$

or, for a general initial population size P_0, the population after t months is $P_0 \cdot 3^t$. Now let's use $P(t)$ to represent the function that gives the population after t weeks, $P(t) = P_0 \cdot 3^t$.

From this example, we can see that basic population growth is modeled by an exponential function of the form $P(t) = P_0 K^t$, where K would be the constant growth multiplier. In particular, for every unit of time, if $K=2$, the population doubles, or if $K=3$, the population triples.

Populations can also decay (that is, get smaller) due to deaths in the population. For instance, a population $P(t)$ could be losing half of its population each month. Then population size from one month to the next would follow a pattern of repeatedly applying the multiplier $1/2$. The basic population decay function becomes $P(t)=P_0\left(\frac{1}{2}\right)^t=P_0(2^{-1})^t=P_0 2^{-t}$ where the constant decay multiplier K is $1/2$ or 2^{-1}.

COMPOUND INTEREST

A basic business model for exponential growth is compound interest. For example, suppose $1000 is invested at a yearly interest rate of 2% compounded monthly (interest is added to the total once a month). The interest rate for each month would  be $0.02/12$, the yearly interest rate 0.02 divided by the number of months (compound periods) in a year. Initially, there is the amount $A_0=\$1000$. After one month, interest is computed as $\$1000(0.02/12)$ and then added to the present amount: $A_1=\$1000+\$1000(0.02/12)=\$1000(1+0.02/12)$; the last step factors out the common factor $1000. At the end of two months, interest is computed on the new present amount $\$1000(1+0.02/12)$ as $\$1000(1+0.02/12)(0.02/12)$ and then added to the present amount $\$1000(1+0.02/12)$ resulting in the new total amount of $A_2=\$1000(1+0.02/12)+\$1000(1+0.02/12)(0.02/12)=\$1000(1+0.02/12)(1+0.02/12)=\$1000(1+0.02/12)^2$. There is a pattern here we can follow:

Month	Current amount	Amount with interest added at end of month
0, start	$1000	$1000(1+0.02/12)
1	$1000(1+0.02/12)	$1000(1+0.02/12)^2
2	$1000(1+0.02/12)^2	$1000(1+0.02/12)^3
3	$1000(1+0.02/12)^3	$1000(1+0.02/12)^4
4	$1000(1+0.02/12)^4	$1000(1+0.02/12)^5
5	$1000(1+0.02/12)^5	$1000(1+0.02/12)^6

Usually, in financial formulas, time is measured in years, so for every t years there are $12t$ months. Following the pattern in the table, after t years, the constant multiplier $1+0.02/12$ is applied $12t$ times, and the amount would be

$$\$1000(1+0.02/12)^{12t}.$$

The general formula for compound interest is $A = A_0\left(1 + \frac{r}{m}\right)^{mt}$, where A_0 is the initial amount invested, r is the yearly interest rate, m is the number of times a year interest is added to the amount, and t is the number of years. Every time interest is added to the invested amount, the amount grows by a factor of $\left(1 + \frac{r}{m}\right)$. The amount A is given by an exponential function $A(t) = A_0 K^t$ where $K = \left(1 + \frac{r}{m}\right)^m$ is the yearly constant growth multiplier.

For an example, suppose $1000 is invested at a yearly interest rate of 2% for 4 years compounded monthly. Then $A_0 = \$1000$, $m = 12$, $r = 0.02$, and $t = 4$, so
$$A = 1000\left(1 + \frac{0.02}{12}\right)^{(12)(4)} \approx 1000(1.001667)^{48} \approx \$1083.21.$$

In the rabbit population example, time was treated discretely. Population size was computed once at the end of each month without any use of population size in between the beginning and the end of a month. The values of time were $t = 0,1,2,3,4,5, \dots$. Values of time between the whole numbers were not considered. Compound interest was also treated with discrete time; the amount did not change between the beginning and the end of a month.

Other settings for exponential growth or decay require the consideration of time at every possible instant. That is, continuously over all real number values instead of discretely at separated values. If interest is compounded continuously, the formula for compound interest becomes $A(t) = A_0 e^{rt}$.

VOLUME AND FLOW

At the beach, you blow up your beach ball and have a relaxing afternoon. In the evening, you are getting ready to go home, but you need to let the air out of your beach ball. When you open the valve to let the air out, the air flows out quickly. As time goes by, the air flows out of the ball more and more slowly. At the beginning, there is a large volume, V, of air in the ball that is causing the air to flow out quickly. Later, there is less air volume in the ball, and the air flows out more slowly. How fast the air escapes from the ball is proportional to how much air is in the ball; the volume of air in the beach ball decays at a constant rate. Suppose after one minute the ball has lost one third of the air volume. Note that two thirds of the air volume is left in the ball. The proportion of air lost and the proportion of air left will remain constant, so the exponential decay function for air volume is $V(t) = V_0(2/3)^t$ where V_0 is the initial volume of air in the beach ball.

The constant multiplier 2/3 is proportional to the actual constant rate at which the air flows out of the beach ball. An expression with base 2/3 can be written as an expression with another base; we could use the natural number e as the base. The volume function $V(t)=V_0(2/3)^t$ could be written in the form $V(t)=V_0 e^{kt}$. What is special using the natural number e as the base is that k is the rate at which air flows out of the beach ball.

RADIOACTIVE DECAY

For radioactive elements or compounds, the decay rate depends on the amount of radioactive material we begin with. The function that describes the amount of radioactive material is:

$$A = A_o e^{kt}$$

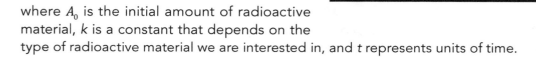

where A_0 is the initial amount of radioactive material, k is a constant that depends on the type of radioactive material we are interested in, and t represents units of time.

Let's find the constant k for carbon-14, if we know that the half-life of carbon-14 is 5,730 years. (A half-life is the length of time for half of the substance to decay.)

After 5,730 years, we will have half of the amount of carbon-14 that we started with; in other words, $A=\frac{1}{2}A_o$. If we substitute this expression into the equation above, along with a t of 5,730, we have:

$$\frac{1}{2}A_o = A_o e^{k(5730)} \quad \text{If we divide both sides by } A_0 \text{, we have:}$$

$$\frac{1}{2} = e^{k(5730)} \quad \text{or} \quad 0.5 = e^{k(5730)}.$$

Since the variable we want, t, is in the exponent, we will need to take the log or the natural log, ln, of both sides. Since the equation contains the *natural number e*, we will use the natural log. We do this because logs have a property that allows us to bring exponents around to the front of the term as coefficients. (We'll explain why later.)

$$\ln(0.5)=\ln(e^{k(5730)}) \qquad \text{We use a calculator to determine that } \ln(0.5)\approx-0.693$$
$$\text{and recall that } \ln e^v = v. \text{ (Note: } \ln e^1 = 1\text{)}$$

$-0.693 = k(5730)$ Dividing both sides by 5730 gives us:

$-0.000121 = k$ We can now use this value of k for all problems involving carbon-14 dating.

Carbon-14 dating can be used to date anything that was once alive. This includes wooden picture frames, linen cloth, and mummies. All living things retain a fairly constant level of carbon dioxide in their bodies. Most carbon dioxide contains two oxygen atoms bonded with a normal carbon-12 atom, but a small percentage contains the radioactive isotope carbon-14 instead. After death, the radioactive carbon dioxide begins to decay. In Carbon-14 dating, the percentage of carbon-14 molecules remaining in the artifact is compared to the amount expected in a living creature.

Suppose a fresco is found painted on a wooden wall in the crypt of an ancient church. The fresco is believed to date from the eighth century. A sliver from this wall is extracted and sent to be carbon dated. (In carbon dating, small samples are used because they are actually destroyed in the dating process.)

Suppose the sliver is found to contain 89% of the carbon-14 it would have had initially. Could the fresco date from the eighth century?

If the sliver has 89% of the initial C-14, we can substitute $A = 0.89A_o$ into our equation, as well as $k = -0.000121$.

$A = A_o e^{kt}$

$0.89A_o = A_o e^{-.000121t}$ We cancel A_o and take the ln of both sides.

$\ln(0.89) = \ln(e^{-.000121t})$ We find $\ln(0.89)$ and use $\ln e^v = v$.

$-0.1165 = (-0.000121t)$ We divide both sides by (-0.000121)

963 years $= t$

This would give us a date around 1050. While the fresco might be more recent than the wooden wall, it could not be older. It could not be an eighth-century fresco, but it might be an eleventh-century fresco, which is still pretty remarkable.

INTRA-SECTION EXERCISES:

8. The half-life of radium-226 (Ra^{226}) is 1,620 years.

    a. Determine the constant k for Ra^{226}.
    b. Determine the amount of Ra^{226} remaining after 1200 years.

Solution

a. At $t = 1620$, we know: $\qquad\qquad\qquad\qquad\qquad A = A_o e^{kt}$

    $$0.5A_o = A_o e^{k(1620)}$$

    Dividing both sides by A_0, we have: $\qquad 0.5 = e^{k(1620)}$

    We take the natural log of both sides: $\qquad \ln 0.5 = \ln(e^{k(1620)})$

    and use $\ln e^v = v$ to get: $\qquad\qquad\quad \ln 0.5 = k(1620)$

    and dividing both sides by 1620, we find: $\quad -0.000428 = k$

b. Using $k = -0.000428$ and $t = 1200$ we have $A = A_o e^{(-0.000428)(1200)}$ Dividing by A_0 and calculating $e^{(-0.000428)(1200)}$ gives us: $\frac{A}{A_o} = 0.598$. Therefore, after 1200 years, we will have 59.8% of the original amount of radium-226.

IR7 EXPONENTIAL FUNCTIONS EXERCISES

1. Use a calculator to compute the following:

    a. e^4
    b. e^{-7}
    c. $e^{1.3}$

2. Use a calculator to compute the following:

    a. e^{-4}
    b. e^7
    c. $e^{3.1}$

3. If $e^x = 1$, then $x = $ _____.

4. If $e^x = \dfrac{1}{e}$, then $x = $ _____.

5. If $e^x = \dfrac{1}{e^2}$, then $x = $ _____.

6. If $e^x = \dfrac{1}{e^3}$, then $x = $ _____.

7. The demand function for a product is modeled by $p = 550 - 5e^{0.003x}$ where p is the price when x units are demanded. Find the price if $x = 1000$ units.

8. The demand function for a product is modeled by $p = 6500 - 5e^{0.004x}$ where p is the price when x units are demanded. Find the price if $x = 1000$ units.

9. The population of a bacteria culture needed for a pharmaceutical is modeled by $M = \dfrac{910}{1 - e^{-0.06t}}$ where M is the weight of the culture in milligrams and t is the time in days. What is the weight of the culture after 30 days?

10. The growth of an amoeba needed by a seafood production company is modeled by $W = \dfrac{810}{1 - e^{-0.1t}}$ where w is the weight in milligrams and t is the time in days. What is the weight after 10 days?

11. Sketch the functions below.

    a. $y = 4^x$
    b. $f(x) = e^x$
    c. $f(x) = e^x + 2$

12. Sketch the functions below.

    a. $y = 5^x$
    b. $f(x) = e^x + 1$
    c. $f(x) = e^x - 4$

13. Sketch the functions below.

    a. $y = 4^{-x}$
    b. $f(x) = -e^x$
    c. $f(x) = e^{-x} - 2$

14. Sketch the functions below.

    a. $y = -4^x$
    b. $f(x) = 2e^{-x}$
    c. $f(x) = e^{-x} + 3$

15. Sketch the functions below.

    a. $y = 3^{x+2}$ b. $f(x) = e^{x-3}$ c. $f(x) = e^{-x+1}$

16. Sketch the functions below.

    a. $y = e^{x-2}$ b. $f(x) = 3^{x+3} - 2$ c. $f(x) = e^{-x+3}$

17. The Fi-D realty company owned properties worth \$226 million in the year 2010. This property was worth \$385 million in 2015. Assume the value increased exponentially.

    a. Determine the constant k for the realty company. Let $t = 0$ for the year 2010.
    b. Estimate the worth of their property in 2020.

18. The Gro-D Farm Corporation owned 4,212 acres in the year 2010. In the year 2015, they owned 10,300 acres. If $t = 0$ for the year 2010 and assuming exponential growth,

    a. determine the constant k for Gro-D.
    b. At the current rate of growth, estimate the number of acres they will own by 2020.

19. A company excavating a new subway tunnel came upon what appeared to be an ancient stone building. If the building is deemed to be of historic significance, the operation will need to shut down until archaeologists can excavate. The fire pit inside the building contained remnants of burned wood. If the wood contained 94% of the carbon-14 expected in living wood, approximately how old is the remnant? (Hint: $k \approx -0.000121$.) *Note: True carbon dating has at best a 160-year range.*

20. A construction company excavating basements in a new development finds a tunnel that is believed by some to be a remnant of the Underground Railroad. Wooden support beams contain 99.6% of the carbon-14 expected in living wood. How old is the beam? (Hint: $k \approx -.000121$.) *Note: True carbon dating has at best a 160-year range.*

IR7 EXPONENTIAL FUNCTIONS SOLUTIONS TO EXERCISES

1. a. 54.6   b. 0.000912   c. 3.67   2. a. 0.0183   b. 1096.6   c. 22.2

3. If $e^x = 1$, then $x = 0$ because $e^0 = 1$.   4. -1

5. If $e^x = \frac{1}{e^2}$, then $x = -2$ because $e^{-2} = \frac{1}{e^2}$.   6. -3

7. $p = 550 - 5e^{(0.003)(1000)} = 550 - 5(20.1) = \$449.50$ 8. \$6227

9. $M = \frac{910}{1 - e^{-.06(30)}} = \frac{910}{.835} = 1090 \text{ mg}$ 10. 1281 mg

11. Sketch the functions below.

   a. $y = 4^x$ b. $f(x) = e^x$ c. $f(x) = e^x + 2$

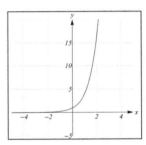   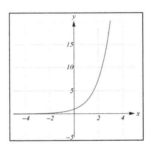   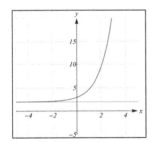

12. Sketch the functions below.

   a. $y = 5^x$ b. $f(x) = e^x + 1$ c. $f(x) = e^x - 4$

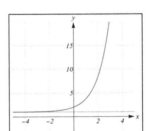      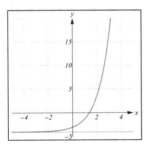

13. Sketch the functions below.

a. $y = 4^{-x}$

b. $f(x) = -e^x$

c. $f(x) = e^{-x} - 2$

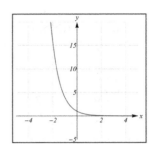
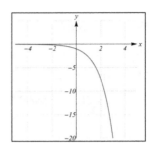
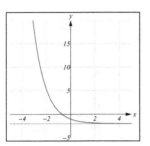

14. Sketch the functions below.

a. $y = -4^x$

b. $f(x) = 2e^{-x}$

c. $f(x) = e^{-x} + 3$

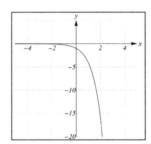
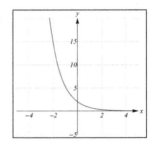
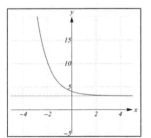

15. Sketch the functions below.

a. $y = 3^{x+2}$

b. $f(x) = e^{x-3}$

c. $f(x) = e^{-x+1}$

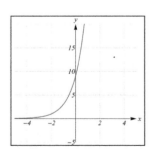
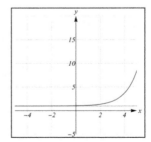
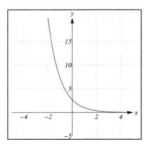

16. Sketch the functions below.

   a. $y = e^{x-2}$

   b. $f(x) = 3^{x+3} - 2$

   c. $f(x) = e^{-x+3}$

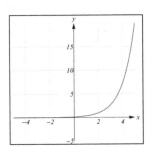
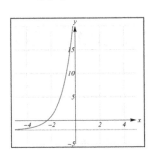
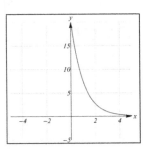

17. a. $A = A_o e^{kt}$

   We substitute $A_o = 226$; $A = 385$; $t = 5$.

   $385 = 226e^{k(5)}$

   We divide both sides by 226, and then take the natural log of both sides.

   $\ln(1.70) = \ln(e^{5k})$

   Calculating $\ln(1.70)$ and using $\ln e^v = v$ gives us:

   $0.53 = 5k$

   Dividing both sides by 5,

   $0.106 = k$

   b. In the year 2020, $t = 10$, $A_o = 226$, and $k = 0.106$.

   $A = 226e^{(.106)(10)} = \$652.32$ million

18. a. $k = 0.1788$

   b. 25,177 acres

19. $A = A_o e^{kt}$

   We substitute: $A = 0.94A_o$; $k = -0.000121$.

   $0.94A_o = A_o e^{-0.000121t}$

   We cancel the A_o's and take the natural log of both sides.

   $\ln(0.94) = \ln e^{-0.000121t}$

   We calculate $\ln(.94)$ and use $\ln e^v = v$.

   $-0.0618 = (-0.000121t)$

   We divide both sides by -0.000121.

   We find $t = 511$ years

20. $t = 33$ years

IR8

Inverses and Logarithmic Functions

Our objective is to study *logarithmic functions*, but in order to do that, we have to review some properties of *inverse functions*.

INVERSES

Suppose the local country club is sponsoring a father-daughter golf tournament. Betty has signed up to play with her father, Frank. Carol will play with her father, Abel, Enid with Hank, and Gerry with Dave.

The relationship (daughter, father of daughter) can be represented by the pairs below:

(daughter, father of daughter): (Betty, Frank) (Carol, Abel) (Enid, Hank) (Gerry, Dave).

The inverse relationship would be described by: (father, daughter of father). The set of ordered pairs would be:

(Frank, Betty) (Abel, Carol) (Hank, Enid) (Dave, Gerry).

Note the difference between (daughter, father of daughter) and (father, daughter of father).

The order is reversed, and also the relationship between the pairs is reversed—i.e., (father of daughter) becomes (daughter of father).

Consider the equation $3x - 5y = 15$. Some of the points on the line represented by this equation, i.e., by this relationship, are:

$$(0, -3), (5, 0), \left(2, -\frac{9}{5}\right), \left(-2, -\frac{21}{5}\right), (50, 27)$$

The inverse of the relationship represented by the equation would contain the points:

$$(-3, 0), (0, 5), \left(-\frac{9}{5}, 2\right), \left(-\frac{21}{5}, -2\right), (27, 50)$$

In summary, we have interchanged the 'x' coordinates and the 'y' coordinates. To generate all the pairs in the inverse of our equation, we interchange the 'x' variable and the 'y' variable.

Therefore, the inverse of our equation $3x - 5y = 15$ would be $3y - 5x = 15$.

Another way to think about inverses is that the inverses reverse the order of operations, and the inverse operations are used. In the equation above, we added, then divided. The inverse was obtained by multiplying (the inverse operation for dividing) and then subtracting (the inverse operation for adding).

 Consider the procedure: We slip our shoes on and then tie them. The inverse procedure would be to untie our shoes and then slip them off. The order of operations was reversed, and we used the inverse operation for each step, i.e., (slipping on, tying) to (untying, slipping off).

The inverse of an equation is obtained by interchanging the roles of the variables in an equation.

Consider the equation $= \dfrac{x+1}{3}$. If we are given a value for x, we would generate y by adding a 1 and then dividing the sum by 3. To get the inverse of this relationship, if we are given a number, we would multiply by 3 and then subtract 1. Therefore, the inverse of the equation above would be $y = 3x - 1$.

INVERSES OF FUNCTIONS

For a function $f(x)$, its inverse is usually denoted as $f^{-1}(x)$, but be careful of this notation.

The variable x^{-1} is equal to $\dfrac{1}{x}$, and we could write 3^{-1} as $\dfrac{1}{3}$, but $f^{-1}(x)$ **does not equal** $\dfrac{1}{f(x)}$.

In general, we will find the inverse of a function by following the four steps below.

Steps	Example: $f(x) = 2x - 3$
1. Replace $f(x)$ with y	$y = 2x - 3$
2. Interchange 'x's and 'y's. We have now found the inverse.	$x = 2y - 3$
3. Solve for y.	$x + 3 = 2y$ $\dfrac{x+3}{2} = y$
4. Replace the new y with $f^{-1}(x)$.	$f^{-1}(x) = \dfrac{x+3}{2}$

CHARACTERISTICS OF A FUNCTION AND ITS INVERSE

We've already mentioned the first characteristic: If (a,b) is a solution of $y = f(x)$, then (b,a) will be a solution of $y = f^{-1}(x)$. Alternatively, we could say that if (a,b) is a point on the graph of $y = f(x)$, then (b,a) will be a point on the graph of $y = f^{-1}(x)$.

[Not that kind of range]

Since all the 'x's of $y = f(x)$ become the 'y's of $y = f^{-1}(x)$ and vice versa, it follows that the domain of $f(x)$ is the range of $f^{-1}(x)$ and the range of $f(x)$ becomes the domain of $f^{-1}(x)$.

Consequently, the graph of the inverse of an equation is its reflection across the line $y = x$, i.e., if the line and its inverse are graphed on the same axes, and the paper is folded along the line $y = x$, then the graph of the original equation should lie exactly on top of the graph of its inverse (the scale on both axes has to be the same).

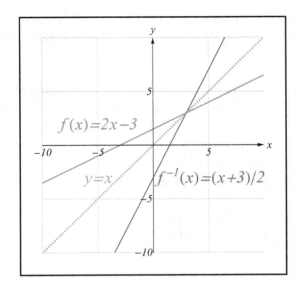

The inverse of the line $y = 2$ would be $= 2$.

Notice that when the graph of $y = 2$ is reflected across the line $y = x$, it lines up on the inverse $x = 2$. But the resulting inverse graph (or relationship) $x = 2$ is not a function.

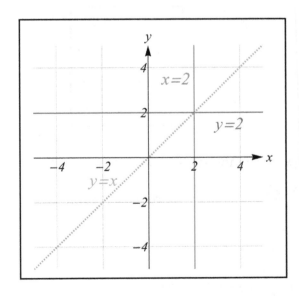

Given an equation, we can always interchange 'x's and 'y's, producing an inverse relationship. The inverse relationship is not always a function. When is the inverse relationship a function?

Remember the criteria for a one-to-one function? For each value of x there is only one corresponding value of y, and for each value of y there is only one corresponding x. If we interchange the 'x's and 'y's, then it is still true—for each value of y there is only one corresponding value of x, and for each value of x there is only one corresponding y. That gives us another characteristic of functions and their inverses. One-to-one functions have inverses, and the inverses are also one-to-one functions.

Another characteristic is that the composition of a function and its inverse always returns to the starting point, i.e., $f(f^{-1}(x)) = x$ and $f^{-1}(f(x)) = x$.

Example 1:

Try it with the function $f(x) = 2x - 3$ and its inverse function $f^{-1}(x) = \dfrac{x+3}{2}$ that we found above.

$f(f^{-1}(x)) = 2(f^{-1}(x)) - 3 =$ 　　　　We replace $f^{-1}(x)$ with $\frac{x+3}{2}$.

$2\left(\dfrac{x+3}{2}\right) - 3 =$ 　　　　　　We cancel the 2s, giving us:

$x + 3 - 3 = x$

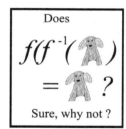

Does

$f(f^{-1}(\text{🐕}\,))$

$= 🐕$?

Sure, why not ?

Now try $f^{-1}(f(x))$ using the same two functions.

$f^{-1}(f(x)) = \dfrac{f(x)+3}{2} =$ 　　　　We replace $f(x)$ with $2x - 3$.

$\dfrac{2x - 3 + 3}{2} = \dfrac{2x}{2} = x$

Similarly, $f(f^{-1}(5)) = 5$, and $f^{-1}(f(93)) = 93$, etc.

Example 2:

Let's check to see if $y = f(x) = x^2 + 1$ is the inverse of $y = g(x) = \sqrt{x-1}$.

$f(g(x)) = (g(x))^2 + 1$ We substitute $g(x) = \sqrt{x-1}$.

$f(g(x)) = \left(\sqrt{x-1}\right)^2 + 1$ We know $\left(\sqrt{x-1}\right)^2 = \sqrt{x-1} \cdot \sqrt{x-1} = x-1$.

$f(g(x)) = x - 1 + 1 = x$

Since $f(g(x))$ returns us to the starting point, x, we know that $f(x)$ is the inverse function of $g(x)$. Now let's try $g(f(x))$.

$g(f(x)) = \sqrt{f(x) - 1}$ We substitute $f(x) = x^2 + 1$.

$g(f(x)) = \sqrt{x^2 + 1 - 1}$

$\qquad = \sqrt{x^2} = x$

There is a slight difficulty here: $f(g(0)) = f\left(\sqrt{0^2 - 1}\right) = f\left(\sqrt{-1}\right)$.

But $\sqrt{-1}$ is not defined as a real number, even though:

$g(f(0)) = g(0^2 + 1) = g(1) = \sqrt{1-1} = \sqrt{0} = 0$ *is* a real number.

We need to be more specific and say that $f(x) = x^2 + 1$ defined for $x \geq 0$ is the inverse of $g(x) = \sqrt{x-1}$ defined for $x \geq 1$.

THE MAIN EVENT—THE INVERSE OF AN EXPONENTIAL FUNCTION

Consider the equation $y=3^x$ one more time.

Its graph is at right.

We can see that the graph meets the Vertical Line Test, so we know that the equation is a function, and we can write it as:

$$f(x)=3^x.$$

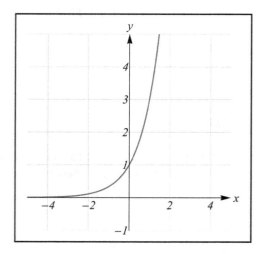

The graph also meets the Horizontal Line Test, so we know the function is a one-to-one function and therefore has an inverse.

Further, we know the graph of the inverse will be symmetrical about the line $y=x$, and since the point (0,1) is a point on $f(x)$, the point (1,0) will be a point on the inverse, $f^{-1}(x)$. It will look like the graph at right.

Now recall the steps we used to find an inverse. We'll use them to find the inverse of our function, $f(x)=3^x$.

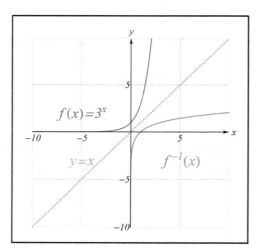

Steps	$f(x)=3^x$
1. Replace $f(x)$ with y	$y=3^x$
2. Interchange 'x's and 'y's. We have now found the inverse.	$x=3^y$
3. Solve for y.	*There's the rub. How do we do that?*

To solve for *y* we need to use **logarithms**.

$y = \log_3 x$ is another way to write $3^y = x$.
$y = \log_3 x$ is read: *y* equals log base 3 of *x*.

Take note of the relative position of the base and exponent in the two forms of the equation:

$$y = \log_3 x, \qquad x = 3^y$$
These are the bases:

$$y = \log_3 x, \qquad x = 3^y$$
These are the exponents:

Example 3:

a. $\log_2 8 = 3$ because $8 = 2^3$.
b. $\log_5 25 = 2$ because $25 = 5^2$.
c. $\log_{10} 10{,}000 = 4$ because $10{,}000 = 10^4$.
d. $\log_{10} 0.001 = -3$ because $0.001 = 10^{-3}$.
    [Remember: $0.001 = \dfrac{1}{1000} = \dfrac{1}{10^3} = 10^{-3}$.]
e. $\log_7 7^3 = 3$ because $7^3 = 7^3$.
f. $\log_e e^2 = 2$ because $e^2 = e^2$.
g. $\log_{10} 10^9 = 9$ because $10^9 = 10^9$.

Traditionally, a base of *10* is understood and remains unwritten. So $\log_{10} 10{,}000 = 4$ is written $\log 10{,}000 = 4$ and $\log_{10} 0.001 = -3$ is written $\log 0.001 = -3$. Base *10* logs are usually called **common logs**, but sometimes Briggsian logs, decadic logs, or decimal logs.

INTRA-SECTION EXERCISES:

Write the following expressions for y in a simplified form without a logarithm.

1. $\log_2 16 = y$

2. $\log_7 \dfrac{1}{7} = y$

3. $\log_6 1 = y$

4. $\log_e e = y$

5. $\log 100 = y$

6. $\log 0.01 = y$

7. $\log 10^5 = y$

8. $\log 10 = y$

Solutions

1. $y = 4$ because $2^4 = 16$

2. $y = -1$ because $7^{-1} = \dfrac{1}{7}$

3. $y = 0$ because $6^0 = 1$

4. $y = 1$ because $e^1 = e$

5. $y = 2$ because $10^2 = 100$

6. $y = -2$ because $10^{-2} = \dfrac{1}{100} = 0.01$

7. $y = 5$ because $10^5 = 10^5$

8. $y = 1$ because $10^1 = 10$

Take another look at example 3)g above: $\log 10^9 = 9$, or $\log_{10} 10^9 = 9$.

Since $f^{-1}(x) = \log_{10} x$ is the inverse function of $f(x) = 10^x$, this is actually a case of the composition of a function with its inverse, and the result is the starting value of x, in this case, a 9. Also note that $\log 10 = 1$.

Similarly, $10^{\log_{10} x} = x$, and $10^{\log_{10} 9} = 9$. These are also cases of the composition of a function with its inverse.

Consider $\log_e e = 1$. When the base is the natural number e, the $\log_e x$ is traditionally written $\ln x$. So $\log_e e = 1$ would be written $\ln e = 1$, with an understood base of e. Base e logs are usually called **natural logs**, but sometimes Naperian logs.

INTRA-SECTION EXERCISES:

Write the following expressions for y in a simplified form without a logarithm.

9. $\ln 1 = y$ 10. $\ln \dfrac{1}{e} = y$ 11. $\ln e = y$ 12. $\ln e^5 = y$

13. Give a quick approximation to $\ln 2.72 = y$.

Solutions

9. $y=0$ because $e^0=1$
10. $y=-1$ because $e^{-1}=\dfrac{1}{e}$
11. $y=1$ because $e^1=e$
12. $y=5$ because $e^5=e^5$
13. $y\approx1$ because $e^1\approx2.72$ i.e., y is about 1 because $e^1=e$ is about 2.72.

Take a look at $\ln e^5=5$.

Since $f^{-1}(x)=e^x$ is the inverse function of $f(x)=\ln x$, this is another case of the composition of a function with its inverse. Therefore, $\ln e^x=x$ and also $e^{\ln x}=x$.

Similarly, $\ln e^{11.6}=11.6$ and $e^{\ln 14}=14$.

Most calculators only provide common logs and natural logs directly. Use a calculator to solve the following problems for y.

INTRA-SECTION EXERCISES:

Give calculator approximations to the following values for y.

14. $\log 3.2=y$ 15. $\ln 3.2=y$ 16. $\log 2413=y$ 17. $\ln 0.245=y$

Solutions

14. 0.505   15. 1.16   16. 3.38   17. -1.41

PROPERTIES OF LOGARITHMS

Because logs are exponents, we can derive several properties. We've already discussed the first two properties for base 10 logs and for natural logs.

Base 5 Log ?

Property 1: $b^{\log_b x}=x$

Property 2: $\log_b b^x=x$

These two properties are a reprise of *"a function composed with its inverse."*

Property 3: $\log_v v + \log_b w = \log_b(vw)$

This one comes about because logs are exponents. Remember that $x^2 \cdot x^3 = x^{2+3}$? We could add the exponents when the bases were the same.

So $\log_3 9 + \log_3 27 = \log_3(9 \cdot 27) = \log_3 243$.

Check it out: $243 = 3^5$, resulting in $2 + 3 = 5$ for the equation above.

> **Note:** $(\log_3 9)(\log_3 27)$ *does not equal* $\log_3(9)(27)$. We can turn the sum of logs into the log of a product (if the bases are the same), but we can't turn the product of logs into the log of a product (*even if* the bases are the same).

Property 4: $\log_b v - \log_b w = \log_b \dfrac{v}{w}$

Remember that $\dfrac{x^5}{x^3} = x^{5-3}$? When the bases are the same, we can subtract the exponents, and a log is an exponent. So $\log_3 27 - \log_3 9 = \log_3 \left(\dfrac{27}{9}\right) = \log_3 3$, or $3 - 2 = 1$.

> **Note:** $\dfrac{\log_3 27}{\log_3 9}$ *does not equal* $\log_3 \dfrac{27}{9}$. We can turn the difference of logs into the log of a quotient (if the bases are the same), but we can't turn a quotient into the log of a quotient (*even if* the baes are the same).

Property 5: $\log_b x^n = n\log_b x$

Remember that $(x^2)^3 = x^{2 \cdot 3} = x^6$? We could multiply exponents. In the property above, n is an exponent, and $\log_b x$ is the other exponent. So $\log x^{4.9} = 4.9\log x$, and $\ln z^{-5.77} = (-5.77)\ln z$.

Property 6: $\log_c x = \dfrac{\log_b x}{\log_b c}$

This one lets us change to a different base. For example, $\log_{12} 46 = \dfrac{\log 46}{\log 12}$. Since the numerator and denominator are now both in base 10, we can use a calculator to compute the answer. Here's a little proof.

PROOF OF $\log_{12} 46 = \dfrac{\log 46}{\log 12}$

Let $\log_{12} 46 = y$.

Then $12^y = 46$.   We take the common log of both sides.

$\log 12^y = \log 46$ We use property 5 above.

$y \log 12 = \log 46$ We divide both sides by $\log 12$.

$y = \dfrac{\log 46}{\log 12}$ Ta-da!!

INTRA-SECTION EXERCISES:

Use the properties of logs to write the expressions below without a logarithm.

18. $e^{\ln(x-1)}$ 19. $\log 10^t$ 20. $\log_3 9t - \log_3 3t$

21. Write $\log 2t + \log 3t$ as a single logarithm of an expression.
22. Write $3\ln 2y$ as logarithm of an expression.
23. Change to natural logs: $\log_3 5.2$.
24. Change to common logs: $\log_8 17.1$.

Solutions

18. $x - 1$ (property 1)

19. t (property 2)

20. $\log_3 \dfrac{9t}{3t} = \log_3 3 = 1$ (property 4)

21. $\log(2t)(3t) = \log 6t^2$ (property 3)

22. $\ln(2y)^3 = \ln(2^3 y^3) = \ln 8y^3$ (property 5)

23. $\dfrac{\ln 5.2}{\ln 3}$ (property 6)

24. $\dfrac{\log 17.1}{\log 8}$ (property 6)

We are also allowed to take the log (any base) of each side of an equation.

For example, we can convert $3+e^6 = 82$ into $\ln(3+e^6) = \ln 82$.

We must use a log of the same base on each side. Also, we cannot distribute logs over addition.

> **Caution:** $\log(a+b) \neq \log a + \log b$ and $\ln(a+b) \neq \ln a + \ln b$

With this in mind, it would be better to subtract 3 from both sides in the example above before taking the natural log of both sides.

If we have $5^2 = 5^{x+1}$ then the bases are equal; we can set the exponents equal to each other:

$$2 = x + 1.$$

This is the result of being able to take the log base 5 of both sides.

$\log_5 5^2 = \log_5 5^{x+1}$ Using property 2, we would have:

$$2 = x + 1.$$

We can use a combination of the log properties to solve equations like those in the examples below.

Example 4:

Solve for x: $3^{2x-1} = 9$ We substitute $9 = 3^2$.

$3^{2x-1} = 3^2$ We can set the exponents equal.

$2x - 1 = 2$ We add 1 to both sides.

$2x = 3$ We divide both sides by 2.

$x = \dfrac{3}{2} = 1.5$

Example 5:

Solve for x: $4^{x-1} = 3^{3-2x}$

We take the natural log of both sides, but we could have used the common log or any log, as long as the base is the same on both sides.

$$\ln 4^{x-1} = \ln 3^{3-2x}$$

$$(x-1)\ln 4 = (3-2x)\ln 3$$

The approximate log of a number is a number we can find on a calculator.

$$(x-1)(1.39) = (3-2x)(1.10)$$ We divide both sides by (1.10)

$$(x-1)(1.26) = 3-2x$$ and distribute.

$$(1.26)x - 1.26 = 3 - 2x$$ We add $2x$ and 1.26 to both sides.

$$3.26x = 4.26$$ We divide both sides by 3.26.

$$x \approx 1.31$$

Example 6:

Solve for x: $5 = 3\log(1-2x)$

Remember that logs don't distribute. We use property 5.

$$5 = \log(1-2x)^3$$ We make both sides exponents of 10.

$$10^5 = 10^{\log(1-2x)^3}$$ We use property 1.

$$10^5 = (1-2x)^3$$ We take the cube root of both sides.

$$\sqrt[3]{10^5} = 1 - 2x$$ We calculate $\sqrt[3]{10^5} \approx 46.6$ and subtract 1, then divide by -2.

$$45.4 \approx -2x$$

$$-22.7 \approx x$$

Example 7:

Solve for t: $3^{t-2} = 16$

$$\ln 3^{t-2} = \ln 16$$

$$(t-2)\ln 3 = \ln 16$$

$$t-2 = \frac{\ln 16}{\ln 3}$$

$$t = \frac{\ln 16}{\ln 3} + 2 \approx \frac{2.77}{1.10} + 2 \approx 2.52 + 2 = 4.52$$

SKETCHING GRAPHS OF LOGARITHMS

We have already noted that the function $f(x) = 10^x$ is the inverse function of $f^{-1}(x) = \log x$. Since $y = f(x)$ contains the point (0, 1), the inverse function contains the point (1, 0). Since $f(x)$ gets closer and closer to the x-axis as x approaches $-\infty$, the inverse function gets closer and closer to the y-axis as y approaches $-\infty$. The graphs of the functions are symmetrical about the line $y = x$.

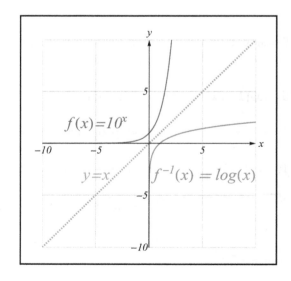

Adding a negative will "flip the graph over." The functions $y = \ln x$ and $y = -\ln x$ are below.

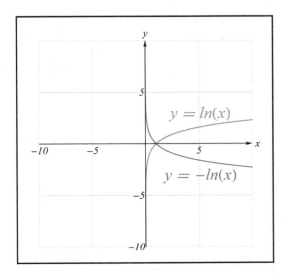

We also have the usual vertical and horizontal shifts.

The graph of $y = \ln x + 2$ will shift the graph of $y = \ln x$ up by two units and the graph of $y = \ln x - 3$ will shift the graph of $y = \ln x$ down by three units. Both are graphed at right. Note that the graph of $y = \ln x + 2$ now contains the point $(1, 2)$ and the graph of $y = \ln x - 3$ contains the point $(1, -3)$.

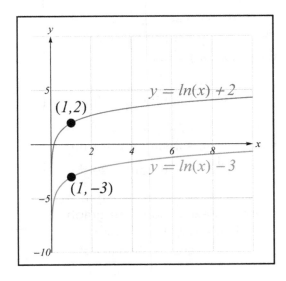

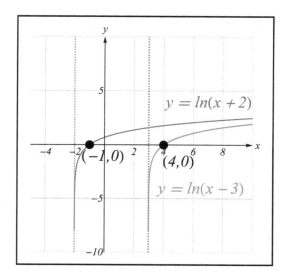

The graph of $y=\ln(x+2)$ will shift the graph of $y=\ln x$ two units to the left, and the graph of $y=\ln(x-3)$ will shift the graph of $y=\ln x$ three units to the right. Both are graphed at left. Note that the graph of $y=\ln(x+2)$ contains the point $(-1,0)$, and the line $y=-2$ is a vertical asymptote. The graph of $y=\ln(x-3)$ contains the point $(4,0)$, and the line $y=3$ is a vertical asymptote.

The graph of $y=\ln 2x$ goes through the point $(1/2, 0)$. Test it by substituting $x=\dfrac{1}{2}$ into the equation $y=\ln\left(2\cdot\dfrac{1}{2}\right)=\ln 1=0$. The coefficient of x causes a compression. The graph rises more quickly than the graph of $y=\ln x$.

The graph of $y=\ln\dfrac{x}{3}=\ln\left(\dfrac{1}{3}x\right)$ goes through the point $(3, 0)$. To test this, we substitute 3 for the x: $y=\ln\dfrac{3}{3}=\ln 1=0$. Because the coefficient of x is less than 1, it causes an expansion. The graph rises more slowly than the graph of $y=\ln x$. Both are graphed at right.

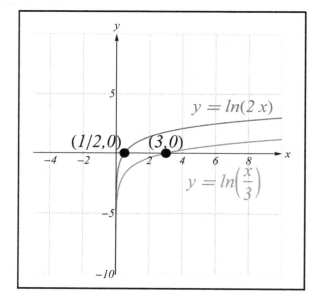

IR8 INVERSES AND LOGARITHMIC FUNCTIONS EXERCISES

For numbers 1) through 22), solve for x giving exact values.

1. $\log_9 81 = x$

2. $\log_4 16 = x$

3. $\log_2 16 = x$

4. $\log_5 125 = x$

5. $\log_9 \dfrac{1}{9} = x$

6. $\log_{12} \dfrac{1}{12} = x$

7. $\log_8 1 = x$

8. $\log_{16} 1 = x$

9. $\log \dfrac{1}{10} = x$

10. $\log \dfrac{1}{100} = x$

11. $\log 10{,}000 = x$

12. $\log 100 = x$

13. $\log 10^8 = x$

14. $\log 10^{19} = x$

15. $\log 10^{7.6} = x$

16. $\log 10^{9.6} = x$

17. $\ln e^{5.7} = x$

18. $\ln e^{-4.2} = x$

19. $\ln 2.72 = x$

20. $\ln e = x$

21. $\ln 1 = x$

22. $\log 1 = x$

For numbers 23) through 26), simplify.

23. $e^{\ln(8x+3)}$

24. $e^{\ln(x^2-1)}$

25. $10^{\log 48.3}$

26. $10^{\log 0.056}$

For numbers 27)–36), write in log notation.

27. $9 = 3^2$

28. $64 = 4^3$

29. $18 = x^5$

30. $t = 5^{1.2}$

31. $y = 14^{9.6}$

32. $y = 0.53^2$

33. $y = e^4$

34. $54.6 \approx e^4$

35. $63{,}096 \approx 10^{4.8}$

36. $z = 10^{0.22}$

For numbers 37) through 44), solve for the variable.

37. $e^{x-3} = 14.3$

38. $e^{2x} = 8.1$

39. $3^y = 15.7$

40. $12^y = 18.4$

41. $3^{3t-2} = 15.7$

42. $8^{-6t} = 19.8$

43. $10^z = 64.6$

44. $10^x = 0.74$

For numbers 45) through 48), find the inverse function.

45. $f(x) = 2.3x - 6$

46. $g(x) = 5x + 14$

47. $h(x) = 3^x + 7$

48. $f(x) = 1.6^x - 4$

For numbers 49)–58), sketch the graphs.

49. $y=\ln x$ 50. $y=2+\ln x$ 51. $y=-\ln x$ 52. $y=2-\ln x$

53. $y=(\ln x)-1$ 54. $y=\ln(x+2)$ 55. $y=\ln(x-3)$ 56. $y=\ln 3x$

57. $y=\ln\dfrac{x}{2}$ 58. $y=\ln(0.4x)$

59. The revenue per acre from growing white pine Christmas trees in Virginia can be modeled by the equation $R=1.4e^{1.000747t}$ where R represents revenue in dollars and t represents years. How much revenue would be expected after two years? After five years?

60. The original Ebbinghaus equation for memory retention r after a time period of t weeks is: $r=e^{-s/t}$ where s represents relative memory strength. If $s=0.9$, what is one's memory retention after one week? After three weeks?

IR8 INVERSES AND LOGARITHMIC FUNCTIONS
SOLUTIONS TO EXERCISES

1. $9^x = 81; x = 2$ 2. 2   3. $2^x = 16; x = 4$ 4. 3

5. $9^x = \dfrac{1}{9}; x = -1$ 6. -1 7. $8^x = 1; x = 0$ 8. 0

9. $10^x = \dfrac{1}{10}; x = -1$ 10. -2 11. $10^x = 10,000; x = 4$ 12. 2

13. $10^8 = 10^8; x = 8$ 14. 19   15. $10^{7.6} = 10^{7.6}; x = 7.6$ 16. 9.6

17. $e^x = 5.7; x = 5.7$ 18. -4.2 19. $e^x = 2.72 \approx e; x \approx 1$ 20. $x \approx 1$

21. $e^x = 1; x = 0$ 22. 0   23. $8x + 3$ 24. $x^2 - 1$

25. 48.3   26. 0.056   27. $\log_3 9 = 2$ 28. $\log_4 64 = 3$

29. $\log_x 18 = 5$ 30. $\log_5 t = 1.2$ 31. $\log_{14} y = 9.6$ 32. $\log_{0.53} y = 2$

33. $\ln y = 4$ 34. $\ln 54.6 \approx 4$ 35. $\log 63,096 \approx 4.8$ 36. $\log z = 0.22$

37. $\ln e^{x-3} = \ln 14.3$ 38. 1.05   39. $\ln 3^y = \ln 15.7$ 40. 1.17
$\quad x - 3 = \ln 14.3$ $\qquad\qquad\qquad\qquad y \ln 3 = \ln 15.7$
$\quad x - 3 \approx 2.66$ $\qquad\qquad\qquad\qquad y = \dfrac{\ln 15.7}{\ln 3} \approx \dfrac{2.75}{1.10} = 2.51$
$\quad x \approx 2.66 + 3 = 5.66$

41. $\ln 3^{3t-2} = \ln 15.7$ 42. -0.239 43. $\log 10^z = \log 64.6$ 44. -0.131
$\quad (3t - 2)\ln 3 = \ln 15.7$ $\qquad\qquad\qquad z = \log 64.6$
$\quad 3t - 2 = \dfrac{\ln 15.7}{\ln 3} \approx 3.61$ $\qquad\qquad z \approx 1.81$
$\quad 3t \approx 5.61$
$\quad t \approx 1.87$

45. $y = 2.3x - 6$ 46. $f^{-1}(x) = \dfrac{x - 14}{5}$
$\quad x = 2.3y - 6$
$\quad x + 6 = 2.3y$
$\quad \dfrac{x + 6}{2.3} = y = f^{-1}(x)$

47. $y = 3^x + 7$ 48. $f^{-1}(x) = \log_{1.6}(x + 4)$
$\quad x = 3^y + 7$
$\quad x - 7 = 3^y$
$\quad \log_3(x - 7) = y = f^{-1}(x)$

49.

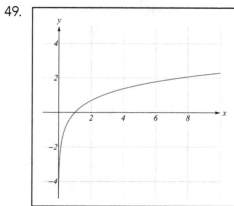

50.

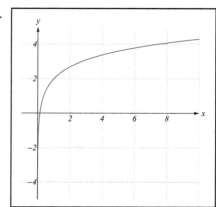

51.

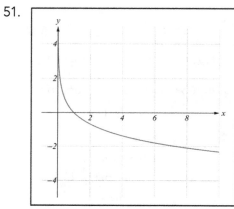

52.

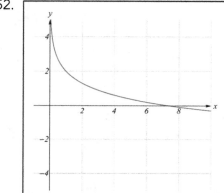

53.

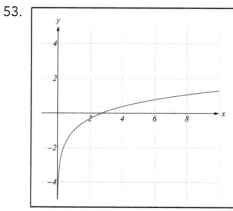

54.

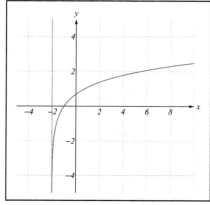

55.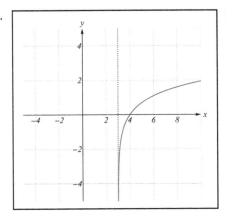

56.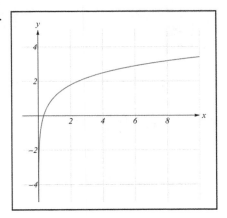

57.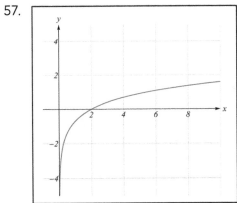

58.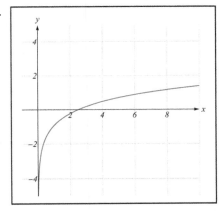

59. $R = 1.4e^{(1.000747)(2)}$
$R = 1.4e^{2.00149}$
$R = 1.4(7.4001)$
$R = 10.36$

$R = 1.4e^{(1.000747)(5)}$
$R = 1.4e^{5.003735}$
$R = 1.4(148.97)$
$R = 208.56$

60. $r \approx 0.4066$
$r \approx 0.7408$

IC9

Integrals with Exponentials and Logarithms

In this section, we add integral formulas for two more functions: $y = e^{kx}$ and $=\frac{1}{x}$. The power rule of Section IC5 does not apply since $y = e^{kx}$ is not a power function, and $y = \frac{1}{x} = x^{-1}$ is the one power function exception for the Power Rule.

INTEGRATION OF $y = e^x$ AND $y = ae^x$

The function $y = e^x$ or $f(x) = e^x$ has the distinction of being the only function that is its own integral (a property that makes e the special natural number). Hence,

$$\int_a^b e^x \, dx = [e^x]_a^b = e^b - e^a.$$

Example 1:

$$\int_0^3 e^x \, dx = [e^x]_0^3 = e^3 - e^0 \approx 20.09 - 1 = 19.09.$$

As in section IC1, we may move a leading coefficient to the outside.

Example 2:

$$\int_0^3 4e^x \, dx = 4[e^x]_0^3 = 4[e^3 - e^0] \approx 4[20.09 - 1]$$

$$= 4(19.09) = 76.36.$$

Move leading coefficients to the outside

EXIT

INTRA-SECTION EXERCISES

1. $\displaystyle\int_1^3 e^x\,dx$
            2. $\displaystyle\int_2^5 4e^x\,dx$
            3. $\displaystyle\int_{-3}^{-1} 6e^x\,dx$

Solutions

1. $\displaystyle\int_1^3 e^x\,dx = [e^x]_1^3 = e^3 - e^1 \approx 20.09 - 2.72 = 17.37$

2. $\displaystyle\int_2^5 4e^x\,dx = 4[e^x]_2^5 = 4[e^5 - e^2] \approx 4[148.41 - 7.39] = 4(141.02) = 564.08$

3. $\displaystyle\int_{-3}^{-1} 6e^x\,dx = 6[e^x]_{-3}^{-1} = 6[e^{-1} - e^{-3}] \approx 6[0.368 - 0.050] = 6(0.318) = 1.908$

INTEGRATION OF $y = e^{kx}$

To integrate $y = e^{kx}$, we will integrate in the same way as $y = e^x$, but we will divide the integral by k, the coefficient of x in the exponent.

Example 3:

$$\int_0^3 e^{4x}\,dx = \left[\frac{e^{4x}}{4}\right]_0^3 = \left[\frac{e^{4(3)}}{4}\right] - \left[\frac{e^{4(0)}}{4}\right] \approx 40688.70 - 0.25 = 40688.45$$

As before, a leading coefficient may be moved to the outside.

Example 4:

$$\int_0^3 2(e^{4x})\,dx = 2\left[\frac{e^{4x}}{4}\right]_0^3 = 2\left[\frac{e^{4(3)}}{4}\right] - 2\left[\frac{e^{4(0)}}{4}\right] \approx 81377.40 - 0.50 = 81376.90$$

INTRA-SECTION EXERCISES:

4. $\displaystyle\int_2^4 e^{0.2x}\,dx$
            5. $\displaystyle\int_{-1}^1 4e^{3x}\,dx$
            6. $\displaystyle\int_3^4 0.8e^{-x}\,dx$

Solutions

4. $\int\limits_{2}^{4} e^{0.2x}\,dx = \left[\dfrac{e^{0.2x}}{0.2}\right]_{2}^{4} = \left[\dfrac{e^{0.2(4)}}{0.2}\right] - \left[\dfrac{e^{0.2(2)}}{0.2}\right] \approx 11.13 - 7.46 = 3.67$

5. $\int\limits_{-1}^{1} 4e^{3x}\,dx = 4\left[\dfrac{e^{3x}}{3}\right]_{-1}^{1} = 4\left[\dfrac{e^{3(1)}}{3}\right] - 4\left[\dfrac{e^{3(-1)}}{3}\right] \approx 26.78 - 0.07 = 26.71$

6. $\int\limits_{3}^{4} 0.8e^{-x}\,dx = 0.8\left[\dfrac{e^{-x}}{-1}\right]_{3}^{4} = 0.8\left[\dfrac{e^{-4}}{-1}\right] - 0.8\left[\dfrac{e^{-3}}{-1}\right] \approx -0.015 - (-0.040) = 0.025$

INTEGRATION OF $y = c^x$

Suppose the base of our integrand isn't e? We integrate in the same way, but we'll need to divide by $\ln c$. In mathematical terms:

$$\int\limits_{a}^{b} c^x\,dx = \left[\dfrac{c^x}{(\ln c)}\right]_{a}^{b} = \dfrac{c^b}{(\ln c)} - \dfrac{c^a}{(\ln c)}$$

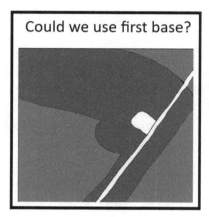

Could we use first base?

Example 5:

$$\int\limits_{1}^{3} 8^x\,dx = \left[\dfrac{8^x}{(\ln 8)}\right]_{1}^{3} = \left[\dfrac{8^3}{(\ln 8)} - \dfrac{8^{(1)}}{(\ln 8)}\right] \approx [246.22 - 3.85] = 242.37$$

Again, we may move a leading coefficient to the outside.

Example 6:

$$\int\limits_{1}^{3} (7)8^x\,dx = 7\left[\dfrac{8^x}{(\ln 8)}\right]_{1}^{3} = 7\left[\dfrac{8^3}{(\ln 8)} - \dfrac{8^1}{(\ln 8)}\right] \approx 7[246.22 - 3.85] = 1696.59$$

CAUTION:

$(7)8^x \neq [(7)(8)]^x$; $(7)8^x \neq 56^x$. The exponent x applies only to the 8.

INTRA-SECTION EXERCISES:

7. $\displaystyle\int_{1}^{2} 12^x\, dx$

8. $\displaystyle\int_{-1}^{1} (3.1)8^x\, dx$

Solutions

7. $\displaystyle\int_{1}^{2} 12^x\, dx = \left[\frac{12^x}{(\ln 12)} \right]_{1}^{2} = \left[\frac{12^2}{(\ln 12)} - \frac{12^1}{(\ln 12)} \right] \approx [57.95 - 4.83] = 53.12$

8. $\displaystyle\int_{-1}^{1} (3.1)8^x\, dx = 3.1 \left[\frac{8^x}{(\ln 8)} \right]_{-1}^{1} = 3.1 \left[\frac{8^1}{(\ln 8)} - \frac{8^{(-1)}}{(\ln 8)} \right] \approx 3.1[3.85 - 0.06] = 11.75$

INTEGRATION OF x^{-1} OR $1/x$

Again, since $f(x) = 1/x$ is the one power function where we cannot use the Power Rule to integrate.

In fact, if we attempt it, we get: $\displaystyle\int_{a}^{b} x^{-1}\, dx = \left[\frac{x^0}{0} \right]_{a}^{b}$. Clearly, this is undefined.

And yet, we know what the graph $y = 1/x$ looks like.

It's the kitty-corner hyperbola at right.

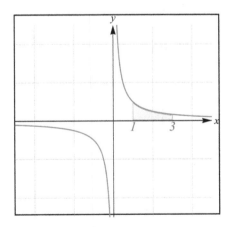

If $a = 1$ and $b = 3$, then we should be able to find an area under the curve from $x = 1$ to 3. There should be a way to integrate:

$\displaystyle\int_{1}^{3} \frac{1}{x}\, dx$ or $\displaystyle\int_{1}^{3} x^{-1}\, dx$

and fortunately, there is:

$$\int_{a}^{b} \frac{1}{x}\, dx = [\ln|x|]_{a}^{b} = \ln|b| - \ln|a|$$

Example 7:

Find the area under the curve $f(x) = \frac{1}{x}$ from $x = 2.3$ to 8.7.

$$\int_{2.3}^{8.7} \frac{1}{x} dx = \left[\ln|x|\right]_{2.3}^{8.7} = \ln|8.7| - \ln|2.3| \approx 2.16 - 0.83 = 1.33$$

As before, we can move leading coefficients to the outside.

Example 8:

Suppose we want to integrate the area under the curve.

$f(x) = \frac{5}{x}$ from $x = -6$ to -2.

We set up the integral: $\int_{-6}^{-2} \frac{5}{x} dx$.

Because we know that $\frac{5}{x} = 5\frac{1}{x}$, we can convert the integral to:

$$\int_{-6}^{-2} 5 \cdot \frac{1}{x} dx = 5 \int_{-6}^{-2} \frac{1}{x} dx.$$

We can then integrate as above:

$$5 \int_{-6}^{-2} \frac{1}{x} dx = 5\left[\ln|x|\right]_{-6}^{-2} = 5[\ln|-2| - \ln|-6|]$$

$$= 5[\ln 2 - \ln 6] = 5[0.69 - 1.79] = -5.50$$

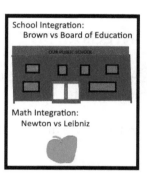

School Integration:
Brown vs Board of Education

OUR PUBLIC SCHOOL

Math Integration:
Newton vs Leibniz

INTRA-SECTION EXERCISES:

9. $\int_{4}^{5} \frac{1}{x} dx$

10. $\int_{-4}^{-1} \frac{1}{x} dx$

11. $\int_{3.6}^{4.1} \frac{7}{x} dx$

Solutions

9. $\int_{4}^{5} \frac{1}{x} dx = [\ln|x|]_{4}^{5} = \ln|5| - \ln|4| = 1.61 - 1.39 = 0.22$

10. $\int_{-4}^{-1} \frac{1}{x} dx = [\ln|x|]_{-4}^{-1} = \ln|-1| - \ln|-4| = \ln 1 - \ln 4 \approx 0 - 1.39 = -1.39$

11. $\int_{3.6}^{4.1} 7 \cdot \frac{1}{x} dx = 7 \int_{3.6}^{4.1} \frac{1}{x} dx = 7[\ln|x|]_{3.6}^{4.1} = 7[\ln|4.1| - \ln|3.6|] \approx 7[1.41 - 1.28] = 0.91$

WHAT ABOUT NEGATIVE INTEGRALS?

The graph of the function $f(x)=x^2-3e^x+\dfrac{1}{2x}-\dfrac{1}{x^2}$ resembles the graph at right. Find the area between the x-axis and the function from $x=1$ to 3.

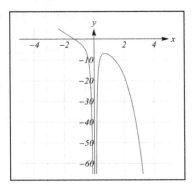

First, notice that this area lies below the x-axis. The distance from the curve to the x-axis is negative, so we expect our integral to return a negative number. Since areas are customarily defined to be positive, we will need to take the absolute value of the final answer.

Next, we set up the integral: $\displaystyle\int_1^3 x^2-3e^x+\frac{1}{2x}-\frac{1}{x^2}dx$

We can adjust the integral so that we can use the Power Rule when possible. Notice that we can't use the Power Rule for the third term because it's a case when the exponent for x would be -1. Instead, we'll have to use our new rule for integrating $\dfrac{1}{x}$ or x^{-1}.

$$\int_1^3 x^2-3e^x+\frac{1}{2}\cdot\frac{1}{x}-x^{-2}\ dx$$

$$\int_1^3 x^2-3e^x+\frac{1}{2}\cdot\frac{1}{x}-x^{-2}\,dx=\left[\frac{x^3}{3}-3e^x+\frac{1}{2}\ln|x|-\frac{x^{-1}}{-1}\right]_1^3$$

$$\left[\frac{3^3}{3}-3e^3+0.5\ln|3|+3^{-1}\right]-\left[\frac{1^3}{3}-3e^1+0.5\ln|1|+1^{-1}\right]$$

$$\approx[9-60.26+0.55+0.33]-[0.33-8.15+0+1]=[-50.38]-[-6.82]=-43.56$$

The integral is -43.56, but the *area* would be $|-43.56|=43.56$.

Example 9:

Sketch the graphs; then find the area bounded between the curves $y=2e^x$ and $y=\dfrac{3}{x}$ from $x=1$ to e.

From the graph at right, we see that the function $y = 2e^x$ lies above the function $y = \dfrac{3}{x}$, so we can set up the following integral.

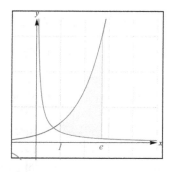

$$\int_1^e 2e^x - \frac{3}{x}\,dx = \int_1^e 2e^x - 3\frac{1}{x}\,dx$$

$$= [2e^x - 3\ln|x|]_1^e = [2e^e - 3\ln|e|] - [2e^1 - 3\ln|1|]$$

$$\approx [30.36 - 3.00] - [5.44 - 0] = 21.92$$

TO SUMMARIZE:

$$\int_a^b ce^x\,dx = c[e^x]_a^b = c[e^b - e^a]$$

and

$$\int_a^b ce^{kx}\,dx = c\left[\frac{e^{kx}}{k}\right]_a^b = c\left[\frac{e^{kb}}{k} - \frac{e^{ka}}{k}\right]$$

TO SUMMARIZE:

$$\int_a^b \frac{c}{x}\,dx = \int_a^b c\frac{1}{x}\,dx = \int_a^b cx^{-1} = [c\ln|x|]_a^b = c[\ln|b| - c\ln|a|]$$

Example 10:

In the state of Wisconsin, suppose the cranberry yield in thousands of barrels per year can be approximated by the equation $y = 21.2e^x$ where x is the year, beginning with 2005 as $x = 1$. Predict the total cranberry yield for the years 2010 to 2014.

Since the y-axis represents thousands of barrels per year and the x-axis represents years, the area under the curve will give us:

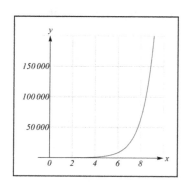

$$\frac{barrels\ (in\ thousands)}{year} \cdot years = total\ barrels\ (in\ thousands)$$

To find the area for $x = 5$ (representing the year 2010) to $x = 9$ (representing the year 2014), we set up the integral:

$$\int_{5}^{9} 21.2e^{x}dx = 21.2[e^{x}]_{5}^{9} = 21.2[e^{9} - e^{5}] = 21.2[8103.08 - 148.41] =$$

168,639 thousand total barrels produced in the years 2010 through 2014.

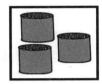

IC9 INTEGRALS WITH EXPONENTIALS AND LOGARITHMS EXERCISES

1. $\int_{1}^{2} e^x dx =$ 2. $\int_{4}^{6} e^x dx =$ 3. $\int_{-3}^{1} e^x dx =$ 4. $\int_{-4}^{2} e^x dx =$

5. $\int_{1}^{2} 6e^x dx =$ 6. $\int_{1}^{5} 3.6e^x dx =$ 7. $\int_{1}^{3} \left(\frac{1}{x}\right) dx =$ 8. $\int_{-3}^{-1} \left(\frac{1}{x}\right) dx =$

9. $\int_{-2}^{-1} \left(\frac{5}{x}\right) dx =$ 10. $\int_{1}^{3} \left(\frac{12}{x}\right) dx =$ 11. $\int_{1}^{3} \left(\frac{1}{5x}\right) dx =$ 12. $\int_{-2}^{-1} \left(\frac{1}{3x}\right) dx =$

13. $\int_{1}^{2} e^{3x} dx =$ 14. $\int_{-1}^{0} e^{2x} dx =$ 15. $\int_{-1}^{2} 4e^{0.5x} dx =$ 16. $\int_{0}^{2} 5e^{0.7x} dx =$

(Hint: The integral will subtract from the area if the integrand is negative.)

17. Sketch the curves; then find the area between them over the interval indicated. $f(x) = -x^2 + 5$ and $g(x) = e^x$ from $x = 0$ to 1.

18. Sketch the curves; then find the area between them over the interval indicated. $f(x) = x^2 + 4$ and $g(x) = e^{-x}$ from $x = 0$ to 1.

19. Sketch the curves; then find the net area between them over the interval indicated. $f(x) = e^x + 1$ and $g(x) = x^2 + 1$ from $x = 0$ to 1.

20. Sketch the curves; then find the net area between them over the interval indicated. $f(x) = e^x - 1$ and $g(x) = x^2 + 2$ from $x = 0$ to 1.

    [Hint: The integral yields the net area.]

21. Sketch the curves; then find the net area between them over the interval indicated. $f(x) = \frac{1}{x}$ and $g(x) = -1$ from $x = 1$ to 3.

22. Sketch the curves; then find the area between them over the interval indicated. $f(x) = \frac{1}{x}$ and $g(x) = 1$ from $x = 2$ to 3.

23. Sketch the curves; then find the area between them over the interval indicated. $f(x) = \frac{1}{x} + 3$ and $g(x) = 1$ from $x = 2$ to 4.

24. Sketch the curves; then find the area between them over the interval indicated. $f(x) = \frac{1}{x} + 5$ and $g(x) = 4$ from $x = 1$ to 2.

25. Sketch the curves; then find the area between them over the interval indicated. $f(x) = \frac{3}{x} + 2$ and $g(x) = 1$ from $x = 2$ to 3.

26. Sketch the curves; then find the area between them over the interval indicated.
    $f(x) = \frac{3}{x} - 2$ and $g(x) = -1$ from $x = -3$ to -2.

27. Sketch the curves; then find the area between them from the point of intersection to $x = 10$. $f(x) = \frac{1}{x}$ and $g(x) = 3$.

28. Sketch the curves; then find the area between them from the point of intersection to $x = 10$. $f(x) = \frac{6}{x}$ and $g(x) = 3$

29. Sketch the curves; then find the area between them over the interval indicated.
    $f(x) = e^x + 1$ and $g(x) = \frac{1}{x} + 1$ from $x = 1$ to 3.

30. Sketch the curves; then find the area between them over the interval indicated.
    $f(x) = e^{-x} + 1$ and $g(x) = \frac{1}{x} + 3$ from $x = 1$ to 3.

31. Sketch the curves; then find the area between them over the interval indicated.
    $f(x) = e^{-2x} + 1$ and $g(x) = \frac{2}{x} + 3$ from $x = 1$ to 2.

32. Sketch the curves; then find the area between them over the interval indicated.
    $f(x) = e^{-3x}$ and $g(x) = \frac{2}{x} + 3$ from $x = 1$ to 2.

33. Over the last three years, subscribers to the Nation's Normal News Service grew at a rate of $N(t) = 1.43e^t$, while subscribers to the Metro Model News Service grew at a rate of $M(t) = 0.86e^t$, where t equals number of years, and $N(t)$ and $M(t)$ are in thousands of subscribers. How many more customers did Nation's Normal obtain than Metro Model in the last three years?

34. The Walcote Corporation owns a retail online clothing outlet and a discount online clothing outlet. The retail outlet grew at a rate of $R(t) = 0.78e^t$ and the discount outlet grew at a rate of $D(t) = 2.13e^t$ where $R(t)$ and $D(t)$ are in thousands of dollars and t is in years. How much more did the discount outlet make over the retail outlet in the last four years?

35. The RK Realty Firm rents both warehouses and multifamily residential units. If the revenue from the warehouses can be modeled by the formula $W = 14 + 0.6e^{0.3t}$ and the revenue from the residential units can be modeled by the formula $R = 21 + 0.5e^{0.87t}$, where t represents time in years, how much more will the residential units gross than the warehouses over the next five years? W and R represent revenue in thousands of dollars.

36. If sales, in thousands of dollars, from the brick-and-mortar stores owned by a large chain can be modeled by the equation $B(t) = 4 + 0.5e^{-0.6t}$ and sales, in thousands of dollars, from its online store can be modeled by $S(t) = 5.6 + 1.2e^{0.7t}$, where t represents time in years, what will be the accumulated difference in sales at the end of the next three years?

IC9 INTEGRALS WITH EXPONENTIALS AND LOGARITHMS SOLUTIONS TO EXERCISES

1. $\int_{1}^{2} e^x dx = [e^x]_1^2 = e^2 - e^1 \approx 7.39 - 2.72 = 4.67$ 2. ≈ 348.83

3. $\int_{-3}^{1} e^x dx = [e^x]_{-3}^1 = e^1 - e^{-3} \approx 2.72 - 0.05 = 2.67$ 4. ≈ 7.37

5. $\int_{1}^{2} 6e^x dx = 6[e^x]_1^2 = 6[e^2 - e^1] \approx 6[4.67] = 28.02$ 6. ≈ 524.5

7. $\int_{1}^{3} \left(\frac{1}{x}\right) dx = [\ln|x|]_1^3 = \ln|3| - \ln|1| \approx 1.10 - 0 = 1.10$ 8. ≈ -1.10

9. $\int_{-2}^{-1} \left(\frac{5}{x}\right) dx = 5[\ln|x|]_{-2}^{-1} = 5[\ln|-1| - \ln|-2|] \approx 5[0 - 0.69] = -3.45$ 10. ≈ 13.18

11. $\int_{1}^{3} \left(\frac{1}{5x}\right) dx = \frac{1}{5}[\ln|x|]_1^3 = \frac{1}{5}[\ln|3| - \ln|1|] \approx \frac{1}{5}[1.10 - 0] = 0.22$ 12. ≈ -0.23

13. $\int_{1}^{2} e^{3x} dx = \left[\frac{e^{3x}}{3}\right]_1^2 = \left[\frac{e^{3(2)}}{3}\right] - \left[\frac{e^{3(1)}}{3}\right] \approx 134.48 - 6.70 = 127.78$ 14. ≈ 0.43

15. $\int_{-1}^{2} 4e^{5x} dx = 4\left[\frac{e^{5x}}{.5}\right]_{-1}^2 = 4\left[\frac{e^{.5(2)}}{.5}\right] - 4\left[\frac{e^{.5(-1)}}{.5}\right] \approx 21.75 - 4.85 = 16.90$ 16. ≈ 21.83

17. $f(x) = -x^2 + 5$ and $g(x) = e^x$ from $x = 0$ to 1
We first note that from $x = 0$ to 1, the $f(x)$ lies above $g(x)$.

$$\int_{0}^{1} -x^2 + 5 - e^x dx = \left[-\frac{x^3}{3} + 5x - e^x\right]_0^1$$

$$= \left[-\frac{1^3}{3} + 5(1) - e^1\right] - \left[-\frac{0}{3} + 5(0) - e^0\right] \approx 2.95$$

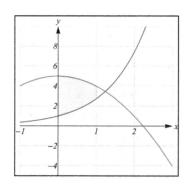

18. ≈ 3.70

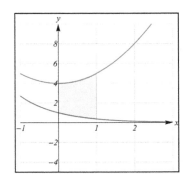

19. $f(x) = e^x + 1$ and $g(x) = x^2 + 1$ from x 0 to 1

We note that $f(x)$ lies above $g(x)$ between $x = 0$ to 1.

$$\int_0^1 (e^x + 1) - (x^2 + 1)dx = \int_0^1 e^x - x^2 dx = \left[e^x - \frac{x^3}{3} \right]_0^1$$

$$= \left[e^1 - \frac{1^3}{3} \right] - \left[e^0 - \frac{(0)^3}{3} \right] \approx 2.39 - 1 = 1.39$$

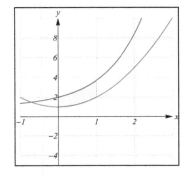

20. ≈ 1.61

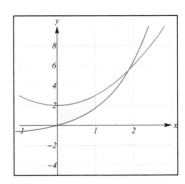

21. $f(x) = \frac{1}{x}$ and $g(x) = -1$ from $x = 1$ to 3

We note that from $x = 1$ to 3, $f(x)$ lies above $g(x)$.

$$\int_1^3 \frac{1}{x} - (-1)dx = [\ln|x| + x]_1^3 = [\ln|3| + 3] - [\ln|1| + 1]$$

$$\approx [1.10 + 3] - [0 + 1] = 3.10$$

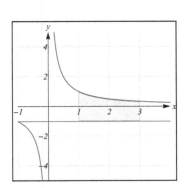

22. ≈ 0.59

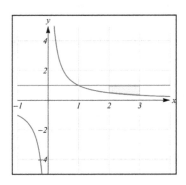

23. $f(x)=\frac{1}{x}+3$ and $g(x)=1$ from $x=2$ to 4

We note that $f(x)$ lies above $g(x)$ from $x=2$ to 4.

$$\int_2^4 \frac{1}{x}+3-1dx = \int_2^4 \frac{1}{x}+2dx = [\ln|x|+2x]_2^4$$
$$= [\ln|4|+2(4)]-[\ln|2|+2(2)]$$
$$\approx [1.39+8]-[.69+4] = 4.7$$

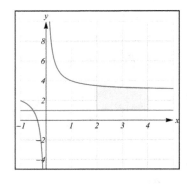

24. ≈ 1.69

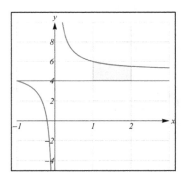

25. $f(x)=\frac{3}{x}+2$ and $g(x)=1$ from $x=2$ to 3

We note that $f(x)$ lies above $g(x)$ from $x=2$ to 3.

$$\int_2^3 \frac{3}{x}+2-1dx = \int_2^3 3\frac{1}{x}+1dx = [3\ln|x|+x]_2^3$$
$$= \left[3\ln|3|+3\right]-[3\ln|2|+2]\approx[3.30+3]-[2.08+2]$$
$$= 2.22$$

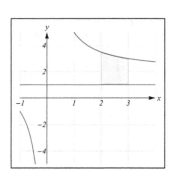

26. ≈ 2.22

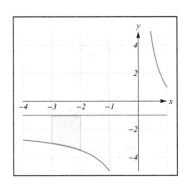

27. Point of intersection: $\dfrac{1}{x} = 3$. Multiply both sides

by x, then divide both sides by 3: $x = \dfrac{1}{3}$

$f(x) = \dfrac{1}{x}$ and $g(x) = 3$ from $x = \dfrac{1}{3}$ to 10

We note that $g(x)$ is above $f(x)$

from $x = \dfrac{1}{3}$ to 10.

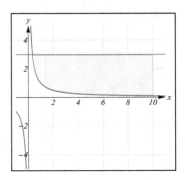

$$\int_{\frac{1}{3}}^{10} 3 - \frac{1}{x}\,dx = \Big[3x - \ln|x|\Big]_{\frac{1}{3}}^{10} =$$

$$[3(10) - \ln|10|] - \left[3\left(\frac{1}{3}\right) - \ln\left|\frac{1}{3}\right|\right]$$

$$\approx [30 - 2.30] - [1 - (-1.10)] = 27.70 - 2.10 = 25.6$$

28. ≈ 14.34

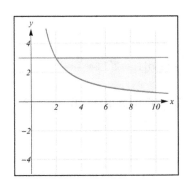

29. $f(x)=e^x+1$ and $g(x)=\dfrac{1}{x}+1$ from $x=1$ to 3

We note the curve $f(x)$ lies above $g(x)$

from $x=1$ to 3.

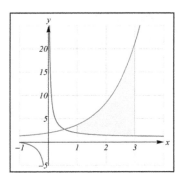

$$\int_1^3 e^x+1-\left(\frac{1}{x}+1\right)dx=\int_1^3 e^x-\frac{1}{x}dx=[e^x-\ln|x|]_1^3$$

$$=[e^3-\ln|3|]-[e^1-\ln|1|]\approx[20.09-1.10]-[2.72-0]$$

$$=16.27$$

30. ≈ 4.78

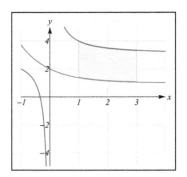

31. $f(x)=e^{-2x}+1$ and $g(x)=\dfrac{2}{x}+3$ from $x=1$ to 2

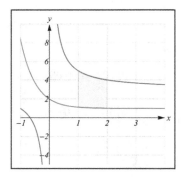

We note that $g(x)$ lies above $f(x)$ from
$x=1$ to 2.

$$\int_1^2\left(\frac{2}{x}+3\right)-(e^{-2x}+1)dx=\int_1^2\left(\frac{2}{x}+2-e^{-2x}\right)dx$$

$$=\left[2\ln|x|+2x-\frac{e^{-2x}}{-2}\right]_1^2$$

$$=\left[2\ln|2|+2(2)+\frac{e^{-2(2)}}{2}\right]-\left[2\ln|1|+2(1)+\frac{e^{-2(1)}}{2}\right]$$

$$\approx[1.39+4+.01]-[0+2+.07]=5.40-2.07=3.33$$

32. ≈ 4.37

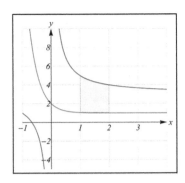

33. $\int\limits_{0}^{3} 1.43e^t - 0.86e^t\,dt = \int\limits_{0}^{3} 0.57e^t\,dt = 0.57[e^t]_0^3 = 0.57[e^3 - e^1] \approx 9.90$ thousand

34. ≈ 72.36 thousands of dollars

35. $\int\limits_{0}^{5} 21 + 0.5e^{0.87t} - (14 + 0.6e^{0.3t})\,dt = \int\limits_{0}^{5} 7 + 0.5e^{0.87t} - 0.6e^{0.3t}\,dt$

$$= \left[7t + 0.5\frac{e^{0.87t}}{0.87} - 0.6\frac{e^{0.3t}}{0.3}\right]_0^5 = \left[7(5) + 0.5\frac{e^{0.87(5)}}{0.87} - 0.6\frac{e^{0.3(5)}}{0.3}\right]$$

$$- \left[7(0) + 0.5\frac{e^{0.87(0)}}{0.87} - 0.6\frac{e^{0.3(0)}}{0.3}\right] \approx [35 + 44.53 - 8.96] - [0 + 0.57 - 2]$$

$$= 72 \text{ thousand dollars.}$$

36. ≈ 16.39 thousand dollars

UNIT II

IIR1

Factorization

It is apparent from the previous sections that there are mathematical meanings to many common words. These include *root*, *base*, and *limit*. In this section, we will consider the mathematical meaning of the words *terms* and *factors*. It would be nice if we're all on the same page, so to speak, when we discuss the math of operations yet to come.

MIND YOUR TERMS AND FACTORS

Parts of a sum are called *terms* of the expression. The terms of an expression are completely separated by an addition or subtraction sign.

The expression $x^2 + 5x + 6$ has three terms.

The first term is x^2, the second term is $5x$, and the third term is 6.

Consider the expression $(x-1)(x+2) + 3x - 5$. It also has three terms.

The first term is $(x-1)(x+2)$, the second term is $3x$, and the third term is -5. Notice that a negative, as in -5, is part of the term.

An expression can have exactly one term, as in the expression $6x^4$.

Parts of a product are called *factors* of the expression. The factors of an expression are completely separated by a multiplication or division sign.

The expression $(x+2)(x+3)$ has two factors.

The first factor is $(x+2)$, and the second factor is $(x+3)$.

The expression $(x-1)^3(x+2)$ has one factor of multiplicity 3, the $(x-1)$, because $(x-1)^3 = (x-1)(x-1)(x-1)$ represents 3 factors. The same expression has another factor of multiplicity 1, the $(x+2)$, because $(x+2)=(x+2)^1$ represents one factor.

An expression can have exactly one factor, as in the expression $6+x$.

Now, back to the expression $(x-1)(x+2)+3x-5$

The first term, $(x-1)(x+2)$, is composed of the factor $(x-1)$ and the factor $(x+2)$, but neither is a factor of the entire expression.

Many mistakes are made by using a factor of one term in an expression as a factor of an entire expression. For example, 3 is not a factor of $3x+7y$. Three is a factor only of the first term.

Similarly, $(x-1)$ is not a factor of the expression $(x-1)(x+2)+3x-5$. It, $(x-1)$, is a factor only of the first term.

We must keep our terms and factors straight. These mistakes occur often when dealing with algebraic fractions, and we will bring up these points again when we look at algebraic fractions.

INTRA-SECTION EXERCISES:

1. List the terms of each expression below.

   a. x^2-5x+7 b. $5x^3+x^2-6$ c. $5(x-1)^2+8$
   d. $4xy-14x^2y$ e. $4-(x+1)(x+2)-x+2y$

2. List the factors of each expression below.

   a. $(x+4)(8-y)$ b. $5xy$ c. $(x-6)^2$ d. $7(x-27)$ e. $3xy(5+y)$

Solutions

1. a. 1st term: x^2; 2nd term: $-5x$; 3rd term: 7
    b. 1st term: $5x^3$; 2nd term: x^2; 3rd term: -6
    c. 1st term: $5(x-1)^2$; 2nd term: 8
    d. 1st term: $4xy$; 2nd term: $-14x^2y$
    e. 1st term: 4; 2nd term: $-(x+1)(x+2)$; 3rd term: $-x$; 4th term: $2y$

2. a. 1st factor: $(x+4)$; 2nd factor: $(8-y)$
    b. 1st factor: 5; 2nd factor: x; 3rd factor: y
    c. 1st factor: $(x-6)$; it has multiplicity 2
    d. 1st factor: 7; 2nd factor: $(x-27)$
    e. 1st factor: 3; 2nd factor: x; 3rd factor: y; 4th factor: $(5+y)$

EQUIVALENT FORMS

Algebraic expressions can have several equivalent forms.

For instance, x^2+5x+6 is equivalent to $(x+2)(x+3)$.

We know these are equivalent because every number we substitute for x in the first expression yields the same number when we substitute it for x in the second expression. For example, if $x=3$, then

$$3^2+5(3)+6=9+15+6=30$$

$$(3+2)(3+3)=(5)(6)=30$$

$$30=30$$

Ta-da!

Usually, it is not practical to check every substitution for the variable, so we rely on known algebraic equivalences, i.e., some algebra rules.

The expression x^2+5x+6 is the expanded form of the expression $(x+2)(x+3)$.

The expression $(x+2)(x+3)$ is the factored form of the expression x^2+5x+6.

INTRA-SECTION EXERCISES:

Determine whether the expressions in each problem below are equivalent.

3. $(x-4)(x+11)$; $x^2+7x-44$
4. x^2-9; $(x+3)(x-3)$
5. $(x+2)^2$; x^2+4
6. $(x+6)(x-6)$; $(x-6)(x+6)$
7. $3xy^2$; $x3y^2$
8. $-3(x-5)$; $-3x+5$

9. $x^3+3x^2y+3xy^2+1$; $(x+1)^3$
10. $\sqrt{x^2+9}$; $x+3$
11. $\sqrt{(x+3)^2}$; $(x+3)$
12. $-4(4x-5)$; $-16x-20$

Solutions

(If you do not agree with the answers below, try testing numerical values for x and y.)

3. equivalent
4. equivalent
5. not equivalent
6. equivalent

7. equivalent
8. not equivalent
9. equivalent
10. not equivalent

11. equivalent
12. not equivalent

POLYNOMIALS

A *polynomial* is an expression in expanded form where the factors of each term are constants and whole number powers of variables. Here's an example:

$$x^3+5x^2-7x+8.$$

The factor of the first term is x^3.
The factors of the second term are 5 and x^2.
The factors of the third term are −7 and x.
The factor of the last term is 8.

Polynomials do not have any variables with negative exponents. They do not have any variables in a denominator (another way of saying no variables with negative exponents). They do not have variables as exponents.

The example below is *not* a polynomial.

$$x^{-3}+\frac{5}{x^2}-7^{-x}+8$$

The *degree* of a *term* is the sum of the exponents of the variables in the term.

Consider the polynomial: $x^3 + 5x^2 y^4 - 7x + 8$

The degree of the first term is 3.

The degree of the second term is 2 + 4 or 6.

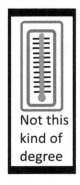

Not this kind of degree

The degree of the third term is 1 because $7x$ is the same as $7x^1$.

The degree of the fourth term, the constant, is 0 because 8 is the same as $8x^0$.

The *degree of the polynomial* is the maximum of the degrees of the terms.

For the polynomial $x^3 + 5x^2 y^4 - 7x + 8$ the degrees of the terms are 3, 6, 1, and 0, so the *degree* of the entire *polynomial* is 6.

The polynomial $3x^4 + 7x^3 + x + 9$ has a degree of 4.

INTRA-SECTION EXERCISES:

Write the degree of each term of the polynomials below and the degree of the polynomial.

13. $8x^3 - 5x + 81$
14. $3x^5 y^2 - 4x^2 y$
15. 94
16. $-8x$
17. $x(x - 3)$

Solutions

13. 1st term: degree 3; 2nd term: degree 1; 3rd term: degree 0; degree of polynomial: 3
14. 1st term: degree 7; 2nd term: degree 3; degree of polynomial: 7
15. 1st term: degree 0; degree of polynomial: 0
16. 1st term: degree 1; degree of polynomial: 1
17. First, we need to multiply the factors of this expression for the expanded form $x^2 - 3x$. Now we can see: 1st term: degree 2; 2nd term: degree 1; degree of polynomial: 2

The term of a polynomial with the greatest power is called the *leading term*, even if it is not written first.

A *monomial* is a polynomial with only one term, such as $3x^4$.

A *binomial* is a polynomial that has two terms, such as $3x + 2$.

A *trinomial* is a polynomial that has three terms, such as $x^2 + 5x + 6$.

A Treenomial?

INTRA-SECTION EXERCISES:

| a. $x^4 - 3x^2$ | b. $6x - 5 + 7x^3$ | c. $7x^5$ |

18. Choose the monomial from polynomials (a), (b), and (c) above.
19. Choose the binomial from the polynomials above.
20. Choose the trinomial from the polynomials above.
21. What are the leading terms of polynomials (a), (b), and (c)?

Solutions

18. (c)   19. (a)   20. (b)
21. (a) x^4; (b) $7x^3$; (c) $7x^5$

EQUATIONS

Placing an equal sign between two algebraic expressions creates an equation. An equation represents a complete sentence or statement: "Thing one is equal to thing two." An example of an equation would be:

$$x^2 + 3x = 8x - 6$$

Some important questions in the world are of the form, "What is true?" "When is it true?" or "When is it false?" We attempt to capture the essence of these questions as an equation. Hence, it is important to ask, "When is an equation true?," i.e., what substitutions for the variables make the equation statement true? It may be just as important to ask, "When is an equation not true?," i.e., what substitutions for the variables make the equation statement false? If we determine when an equation is false, we should have also determined when the equation is true.

A *solution* to an equation in one variable is a substitution for the variable that makes the equation true. The value of 2 substituted for the variable x in the equation:

$$x^2 + 3x = 8x - 6$$

yields the true statement:

$$2^2 + 3(2) = 8(2) - 6$$

$$4 + 6 = 16 - 6$$

$$10 = 10$$

Not this type of solution

The value of 1 substituted for the variable x in the equation $x^2 + 3x = 8x - 6$

yields the **false** statement:

$$1^2 + 3(1) = 8(1) - 6$$

$$1 + 3 = 8 - 6$$

$$4 = 2$$

The value 1 is not a solution to the equation $x^2 + 3x = 8x - 6$.

The value 3 is a solution to the equation $x^2 + 3x = 8x - 6$.

$$3^2 + 3(3) = 8(3) - 6$$

$$9 + 9 = 24 - 6$$

$$18 = 18$$

To "solve an equation" is to find all solutions to the equation. Some equations have no solutions; some equations have one solution; some equations have more than one solution; and some equations have infinitely many solutions. The set of all solutions of an equation is called the *solution set* for the equation.

INTRA-SECTION EXERCISES:

Consider the equation $x^3 + 4x = 18 - x$

22. Is 1 a solution?   23. Is 2 a solution?   24. Is -2 a solution?

Solutions

22. No; $1^3 + 4(1) \neq 18 - 1$

              $5 \neq 17$

24. No; $(-2)^3 + 4(-2) \neq 18 - (-2)$

               $-8 + (-8) \neq 18 + 2$

                    $-16 \neq 20$

23. Yes; $2^3 + 4(2) = 18 - 2$

             $8 + 8 = 18 - 2$

               $16 = 16$

COMMON FACTORS AND NEGATIVE EXPONENTS

When finding factors of an expression, the first step should be to factor out any object that is common to each term of an expression (using the Distributive Law).

For example, $3x^3 - 18x + 27 = 3(x^3 - 6x + 9)$

Another example: $5x^4 - 7x^3 + 2x^2 = x^2(5x^2 - 7x + 2)$

Notice that when we factor out the power of x, the least of the exponents 4, 3, and 2 was used—i.e., 2. The resulting powers of the remaining expression are obtained by subtracting exponents: $4 - 2 = 2$, $3 - 2 = 1$, $2 - 2 = 0$.

It can be useful to factor out common powers when negative exponents are involved. The principle is the same: **use the power with the least exponent**.

Example 1:

$5x^{-4} - 7x^{-3} + 2x^{-2}$

The least of the exponents -4, -3, and -2 is -4.

The resulting new exponents are $-4 - (-4) = 0$, $-3 - (-4) = 1$, and $-2 - (-4) = 2$.

The factorization is $5x^{-4} - 7x^{-3} + 2x^{-2} = x^{-4}(5 - 7x + 2x^2)$.

Example 2:

$$x^{-2} - 7x^{-1} + 5$$

The least of the exponents $-2, -1$, and 0 is -2.

The resulting new exponents are $-2-(-2)=0$, $-1-(-2)=1$, and $0-(-2)=2$.

The factorization is $x^{-2} - 7x^{-1} + 2 = x^{-2}(1 - 7x + 5x^2)$.

Example 3:

$$3x^2(2x-1)^{-2} + 4(2x-1)^{-1}$$

The common factor is $(2x-1)$.

The least of the exponents -2 and -1 is -2.

The resulting new exponents are $-2-(-2)=0$ and $-1-(-2)=1$.

The factorization is $3x^2(2x-1)^{-2} + 4(2x-1)^{-1}$
$$= (2x-1)^{-2} [3x^2(2x-1)^0 + 4(2x-1)^1]$$
$$= (2x-1)^{-2} [3x^2 + 4(2x-1)]$$
$$= (2x-1)^{-2} (3x^2 + 8x - 4).$$

INTRA-SECTION EXERCISES:

Factor

25. $x^{-5} - 13x^{-3} + 12x^{-1}$

26. $x^{-2} - 5x^{-1} - 12$

27. $3x(5x-2)^{-2} - (x+2)(5x-2)^{-1}$

Solutions

25. $x^{-5}(1 - 13x^2 + 12x^4)$

26. $x^{-2}(1 - 5x - 12x^2)$

27. $3x^2(5x-2)^{-2} - (x+2)(5x-2)^{-1} = (5x-2)^{-2}[3x - (x+2)(5x-2)]$
$$= (5x-2)^{-2}[3x - (5x^2 + 8x - 4)] = (5x-2)^{-2}(4 - 5x - 5x^2)$$

FOILING AND FACTORING TRINOMIAL QUADRATICS

You have probably learned the art of distributing multiplication factors over addition or subtraction in a basic algebra class. When you see $3(x+2)$, you now automatically know:

$$3(x+2)=3x+3(2)=3x+6.$$

Mathematicians FOILing?

You have probably seen the term *FOILing*, which is a method of multiplying two binomials together, as in:

$$(x+3)(2x-1)=2x^2-1x+6x-3=2x^2+5x-3.$$

FOIL is an acronym telling you to multiply the **F**irst terms in each binomial together: $x(2x)$; then the **O**utside terms together: $x(-1)$; then the **I**nside terms together: $3(2x)$; and finally, the **L**ast terms of each binomial together: $3(-1)$. After all that, you can combine the two middle terms together: $-1x+6x$, to get the finished product.

FOILing is actually just the Law of Distribution used twice. For $(x+3)(2x-1)$ we distribute the x over $(2x-1)$ and then we distribute 3 over $(2x-1)$.

$$(x+3)(2x-1)=x(2x-1)+3(2x-1)=2x^2-1x+6x-3$$

Notice that these four terms are the same as when we FOILed.

Factoring is just going backward, "un-distributing," or perhaps, "un-FOILing."

Notice that in the product $(x+3)(2x-1)=2x^2+5x-3$, the coefficient of the leading term, $2x^2$, comes from the product of the coefficients of x in the factors, and the constant term, -3, comes from the product of the constants. To reverse the process of FOILing, look for factors of the form $ux+v$ where u is a factor of the leading coefficient and v is a factor of the constant.

Consider the trinomial x^2+5x+6.

The leading coefficient is an understood 1, so the factorization has the form $(x+?)(x+?)$, or $(x+a)(x+b)$ where a and b are factors of 6. In addition, $a+b=5$, the coefficient of the middle term.

The factors of 6 are 1 and 6, which add to 7, or 2 and 3, which add to 5. *Bingo*; 2 and 3 it is.

So $x^2 + 5x + 6 = (x + 2)(x + 3)$.

Example 4:

Consider $x^2 - 5x + 6$.

Neither set of factors we considered above, 1 and 6 or 2 and 3, add to −5. However, there are two other sets of factors for 6. These are −1 and −6, which add to −7, and −2 and −3, which add to −5. We'll use −2 and −3.

$$x^2 - 5x + 6 = (x - 2)(x - 3)$$

Could you determine the factors for each example below?

$x^2 + x - 6$

$x^2 - x - 6$

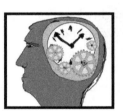

Time's up!

$x^2 - 7x + 6$

$x^2 - 5x - 6$

$x^2 + x - 6 = (x + 3)(x - 2)$

$x^2 - x - 6 = (x - 3)(x + 2)$

$x^2 - 7x + 6 = (x - 6)(x - 1)$

$x^2 - 5x - 6 = (x - 6)(x + 1)$

These examples are monic polynomials; i.e., the coefficient of x^2 is one. In this case, factoring is accomplished by finding factors of the constant term that add to the coefficient of x, the middle term.

Consider the trinomial $15x^2 + 28x + 12$.

When the leading coefficient is not one, factorization has the form $(ax + b)(cx + d)$ where a and c are factors of the coefficient of x^2. In this case, they are factors of 15. The last terms, b and d, are factors of the constant term, which is 12 in this case. One possible choice would be $a = 5$, $c = 3$ and $b = 4$, $d = 3$. The resulting factors $(5x + 4)(3x + 3) = 15x^2 + 27x + 12$ do not give a factorization of $15x^2 + 28x + 12$. Another possible choice would be $a = 3$, $c = 5$ and $b = 2$, $d = 6$. The resulting factors $(3x + 2)(5x + 6) = 15x^2 + 28x + 12$ does give a factorization of $15x^2 + 28x + 12$. The correct factorization is:

$$15x^2 + 28x + 12 = (3x + 2)(5x + 6).$$

There are algorithms we can use to find *a*, *b*, *c*, and *d*, but the most effective is probably trial and error, plus practice. Just be sure to FOIL your final answer to make sure the result of FOILing will take you back to your starting trinomial. We invite you to FOIL the factorizations below to check for their accuracy.

Example 5:

$$2x^2 + 5x - 3 = (2x - 1)(x + 3)$$

Example 6:

$$15x^2 + 8x - 12 = (3x - 2)(5x + 6)$$

Example 7:

$$10x^2 + 13x - 3 = (5x - 1)(2x + 3)$$

INTRA-SECTION EXERCISES:

Factor

28. $x^2 - 8x + 12$ 30. $x^2 + x - 12$ 32. $2x^2 - 5x - 12$

29. $x^2 - 4x - 12$ 31. $x^2 + 13x + 12$ 33. $4x^2 + 13x - 12$

Solutions

28. $(x - 2)(x - 6)$ 30. $(x + 4)(x - 3)$ 32. $(2x + 3)(x - 4)$

29. $(x - 6)(x + 2)$ 31. $(x + 12)(x + 1)$ 33. $(4x - 3)(x + 4)$

FACTORING THE DIFFERENCE OF SQUARES

Another type of polynomial, one that is easily factored, is the *difference of two squares*.

Consider the polynomial $a^2 - b^2$. This polynomial factors into $(a + b)(a - b)$. We can FOIL to check it out.

$$(a + b)(a - b) = a^2 - ab + ba - b^2$$

Because $ba = ab$ (Commutative Law for Multiplication) the two middle terms will cancel, so

$$(a+b)(a-b) = a^2 - ab + ab - b^2 = a^2 - b^2.$$

We could also factor a polynomial such as $4x^2 - 25$. Since $4x^2$ is equal to the square $(2x)^2$ and 25 equals 5^2, we have the difference of two squares again, and we can factor it as:

$$4x^2 - 25 = (2x+5)(2x-5)$$

Example 8:

a. $x^2 - 4 = (x+2)(x-2)$
b. $9x^2 - 16 = (3x+4)(3x-4)$
c. $x^2 - 7 = (x+\sqrt{7})(x-\sqrt{7})$
d. $x^2 - 1 = (x+1)(x-1)$. Recall that 1 is equal to 1^2, so it is also a square.

INTRA-SECTION EXERCISES:

Factor

34. $x^2 - 9$

35. $9x^2 - 1$

36. $36x^2 - 100y^2$

37. $x^2 - 5$

Solutions

34. $(x+3)(x-3)$

35. $(3x+1)(3x-1)$

36. $(6x+10y)(6x-10y)$

37. $(x+\sqrt{5})(x-\sqrt{5})$

ROOTS AND ZEROS

Before we consider roots and zeros, we need a brief review regarding zero, a mathematical annihilator.

A BRIEF ASIDE

Recall that when $ab = 0$, a can equal zero, because $0 \cdot b = 0$

or b can equal zero because $a \cdot 0 = 0$,

or both a and b could equal zero, because $0 \cdot 0 = 0$.

In fact, the word "or" in mathematical usage is a nonexclusive "or." It functions as an "and/or." The term "A or B" means we are dealing with A or B or both of them.

Now consider $ab = 6$. Does this mean that a must equal 6 or b must equal 6? **Of course not**.

The variable a could equal 2 and the variable b could equal 3 because $(2)(3) = 6$;

or a could equal 12 and b could equal $\dfrac{1}{2}$ because $(12)\left(\dfrac{1}{2}\right) = 6$;

or a could equal $7x$ and b could equal $\dfrac{6}{7x}$ because $(7x)\left(\dfrac{6}{7x}\right) = 6$.

There are an infinite number of possibilities when one side of the equation equals a nonzero number.

> **NOTE**
> It is only when a set of factors equals **zero** that we can set each factor equal to that constant, **zero**.

AND NOW BACK TO OUR REGULARLY SCHEDULED ROOTS AND ZEROS

A *root* of an expression such as $x^2 - 5x + 6$ is a value of x (or whatever variable is used) that makes the expression equal to zero. In other words, a root of $x^2 - 5x + 6$ is a solution or root of the equation $x^2 - 5x + 6 = 0$.

The value 3 is a root of $x^2 - 5x + 6$ because $3^2 - 5(3) + 6 = 0$.

We may solve for roots by setting the expression equal to zero. Factoring can then help us find the roots.

$$x^2 - 5x + 6 = 0$$

$$(x-2)(x-3) = 0$$

$$(x-2) = 0 \text{ or } (x-3) = 0$$

$$x = 2 \text{ or } x = 3$$

The roots are 2 and 3.

For a function, such as $y = x^2 - 5x + 6$, the roots of the expression are referred to as *zeros* of the function; i.e. the values of x that make $y = 0$. This would also make them the x-intercepts of the function. Find them on the graph below.

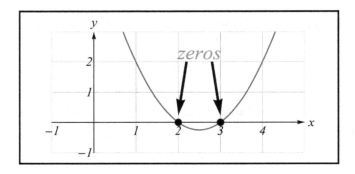

What is true: if r is a root of a polynomial, then $x - r$ is a factor of the polynomial. If a rational number, $\dfrac{m}{n}$, is a root of a polynomial, the factor $x - \dfrac{m}{n}$ could be written $\left(\dfrac{1}{n}\right)(nx - m)$, so $nx - m$ is a factor. For example, if $\dfrac{3}{5}$ is a root, then $5x - 3$ is a factor.

Further, if r_1 and r_2 are roots of a quadratic, then $(x - r_1)$ and $(x - r_2)$ is the complete set of factors (non-constant).

Even if we can't factor a quadratic, we can always find the roots by using the Quadratic Formula.

In general, if a quadratic equation is in the form: $ax^2 + bx + c = 0$, then its roots can be found using: $x = \dfrac{-b \pm \sqrt{b^2 - 4ac}}{2a}$.

The factors would be: $\left(x - \dfrac{-b + \sqrt{b^2 - 4ac}}{2a}\right)$ and $\left(x - \dfrac{-b - \sqrt{b^2 - 4ac}}{2a}\right)$.

Example 9:

Factor $x^2 - 3x - 7$ We note this quadratic is the same as $\mathbf{1}x^2 - 3x - 7$.

so $a = 1$, $b = -3$, and $c = -7$. We substitute them into the quadratic formula.

$$x = \frac{-(-3) \pm \sqrt{(-3)^2 - 4(1)(-7)}}{2(1)} = \frac{3 \pm \sqrt{9 + 28}}{2} = \frac{3 \pm \sqrt{37}}{2}.$$

The roots are: $\dfrac{3 + \sqrt{37}}{2} \approx 4.54$ and $\dfrac{3 - \sqrt{37}}{2} \approx -1.54$ and the factors are

$(x - 4.54)(x - (-1.54))$ or $(x - 4.54)(x + 1.54)$.

The factorization is $x^2 - 3x - 7 \approx (x - 4.54)(x + 1.54)$.

Example 10:

Find the roots of $2x^2 - x = 5$ using the Quadratic Formula.

Don't do this: $x(2x - 1) = 5$; $x = 5$ or $(2x - 2) = 5$

It's invalid since the right side equals five rather than zero. Instead, begin by subtracting 5 from both sides.

$2x^2 - x - 5 = 0$. For the Quadratic Formula $a = 2$, $b = -1$, $c = -5$.

$$x = \frac{-(-1) \pm \sqrt{(-1)^2 - 4(2)(-5)}}{2(2)} = \frac{1 \pm \sqrt{1 + 40}}{4} = \frac{1 \pm \sqrt{41}}{4}$$

$$x \approx 1.85, -1.35$$

Example 11:

Find the zeros and factors of $2x^2 - x - 5$.

The roots, $x = \dfrac{1 \pm \sqrt{41}}{4}$, found in the previous example, are the zeros of

the expression $2x^2 - x - 5$.

This gives the factors $x - \dfrac{1 + \sqrt{41}}{4}$ and $x - \dfrac{1 - \sqrt{41}}{4}$ for $2x^2 - x - 5$.

Note: Since the leading coefficient is 2, **the factorization requires a**

constant factor of 2:

$$2x^2 - x - 5 = 2\left(x - \frac{1 + \sqrt{41}}{4}\right)\left(x - \frac{1 - \sqrt{41}}{4}\right)$$

Example 12:

Find the roots of $2x^2 + 5x = 3$ using the quadratic formula.

$$2x^2 + 5x - 3 = 0, \quad a = 2, b = 5, c = -3$$

$$x = \frac{-(5) \pm \sqrt{(5)^2 - 4(2)(-3)}}{2(2)} = \frac{-5 \pm \sqrt{25 + 24}}{4} = \frac{-5 \pm \sqrt{49}}{4} = \frac{-5 \pm 7}{4}$$

$$x = \frac{-5 + 7}{4}, \frac{-5 - 7}{4}$$

$$x = \frac{1}{2}, -3$$

Because the roots, $\frac{1}{2}$ and -3, are rational numbers, we could have solved the equation by factoring the quadratic without using the quadratic formula.

However, the quadratic formula will work in every case, so we can always use it, whether or not we can figure out a factorization otherwise.

Example 13:

Find the zeros and factors of $2x^2 + 5x - 3$.

The roots, $x = \dfrac{1}{2}, -3$, found in the previous example, are the zeros of the expression $2x^2 + 5x - 3$.

This gives the factors, $x - \dfrac{1}{2}$ and $x + 3$. Instead of the factor $x - \dfrac{1}{2}$, use the factor $2x - 1$. The factorization is $2x^2 + 5x - 3 = (2x - 1)(x + 3)$.

Example 14:

Find the zeros and factors of $2x^2 - x + 5$ using the Quadratic Formula.

$$a = 2, b = -1, c = 5$$

$$x = \frac{-(-1) \pm \sqrt{(-1)^2 - 4(2)(5)}}{2(2)} = \frac{1 \pm \sqrt{1 - 40}}{4} = \frac{1 \pm \sqrt{-39}}{4}$$

Since we cannot take the square root of a negative number in the Real Number System, this quadratic has no roots, and the quadratic equation has no zeros. The expression has no first degree factors. If we examine the graph of the function (at right), we can see the reason why. The parabola has no x-intercepts.

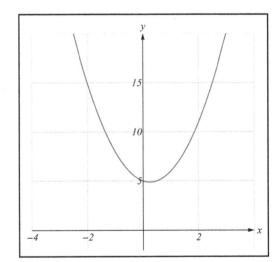

INTRA-SECTION EXERCISES:

Find the roots of the quadratic equations.

38. $x^2 - 8x + 12 = 0$
39. $x^2 - 7x = -12$
40. $x^2 - 49 = 0$
41. Find the zeros and factors of the quadratic expression $x^2 - 7x - 4$.

Solutions

38. $x^2 - 8x + 12 = 0$
$(x-6)(x-2) = 0$
$(x-6) = 0, (x-2) = 0$
$x = 6, 2$

39. $x^2 - 7x = -12$
$x^2 - 7x + 12 = 0$
$(x-4)(x-3) = 0$
$(x-4) = 0, (x-3) = 0$
$x = 4, 3$

40. $x^2 - 49 = 0$
$(x+7)(x-7) = 0$
$(x+7) = 0, (x-7) = 0$
$x = -7, 7$

41. $x^2 - 7x - 4 = 0 \quad a = 1, b = -7, c = -4$

$$x = \frac{-(-7) \pm \sqrt{(-7)^2 - 4(1)(-4)}}{2(1)} = \frac{7 \pm \sqrt{49 + 16}}{2} = \frac{7 \pm \sqrt{65}}{2}; \ x \approx 7.53, -0.53$$

These are the zeros.
The factors would be: $(x - 7.53)(x - (-0.53))$, which we would write as
$(x - 7.53)(x + 0.53)$.

IIR1 FACTORIZATION EXERCISES

Factor the algebraic expressions below.

1. $x^2 - 8x + 12$
2. $x^2 - 8x + 15$
3. $x^2 + 7x + 12$
4. $x^2 + 8x + 15$

5. $x^2 - 4x - 12$
6. $x^2 - 2x - 15$
7. $x^2 - 16x + 15$
8. $x^2 - 13x + 12$

9. $x^2 - 3x - 4$
10. $x^2 - 8x - 9$
11. $x^2 - x - 30$
12. $x^2 - x - 42$

13. $y^2 + 2y + 1$
14. $y^2 - 2y + 1$
15. $b^2 - 64$
16. $b^2 - 81$

17. $49a^2 - 16$
18. $16a^2 - 49$
19. $t^2 - 6$
20. $t^2 - 3$

21. $2x^2 + 7x + 6$
22. $2x^2 + 10x + 8$
23. $3x^2 + 11x + 6$
24. $3x^2 + 9x + 6$

Find the zeros of the functions below.

25. $y = 4x^2 - 4$
26. $y = 5x^2 - 5$
27. $y = 6x + 6$

28. $y = 8x - 8$
29. $y = x^2 - 12x - 13$
30. $y = x^2 - 14x + 13$

31. $y = x^2 - 3x$
32. $y = x^2 - 4x$
33. $y = 3x^2 - 9x$

34. $y = 7x^2 - 14x$
35. $y = 3x^2 + 2x - 8$
36. $y = 6x^2 - 4x - 2$

37. $y = 3x^2 + 7x + 2$
38. $y = 2x^2 - 9x - 18$
39. $y = x^2 + 6x - 2$

40. $y = x^2 - 6x - 2$
41. $y = 2.4x^2 + x + 3.2$
42. $y = 3.5x^2 - x + 7.2$

43. $5x^3 + 7xy - 4y^2 - 18$

   a. What is the third term?
   b. What is the constant?
   c. What is the leading term?
   d. What is the degree of the second term?
   e. What is the degree of the polynomial?
   f. What are the factors of the third term?

44. $8y^3 + 5xy - 6.5x^2 - 5.2$

   a. What is the third term?
   b. What is the constant?
   c. What is the leading term?
   d. What is the degree of the second term?
   e. What is the degree of the polynomial?
   f. What are the factors of the third term?

45. What are the factors of the expression $4x(5-y)$? How many terms does it have?
46. What are the factors of the expression $7y(x-2)$? How many terms does it have?
47. What are the factors of the second term of the expression $4(x-1)-3x^4(x+2)$?
48. What are the factors of the third term of the expression $4(x-1)-3x^4(x+2)$?

IIR1 FACTORIZATION SOLUTIONS TO EXERCISES

1. $(x-6)(x-2)$ 2. $(x-3)(x-5)$ 3. $(x+3)(x+4)$ 4. $(x+3)(x+5)$

5. $(x-6)(x+2)$ 6. $(x-5)(x+3)$ 7. $(x-1)(x-15)$ 8. $(x-12)(x-1)$

9. $(x-4)(x+1)$ 10. $(x-9)(x+1)$ 11. $(x-6)(x+5)$ 12. $(x-7)(x+6)$

13. $(y+1)(y+1)$ 14. $(y-1)(y-1)$ 15. $(b-8)(b+8)$ 16. $(b-9)(b+9)$

17. $(7a-4)(7a+4)$ 18. $(4a-7)(4a+7)$ 19. $(t-\sqrt{6})(t+\sqrt{6})$ 20. $(t-\sqrt{3})(t+\sqrt{3})$

21. $(2x+3)(x+2)$ 22. $2(x+1)(x+4)$ 23. $(3x+2)(x+3)$ 24. $(3x+3)(x+2)$

25. $y=4(x^2-1)=0$
$4(x+1)(x-1)=0$
$(x+1)=0; (x-1)=0$
$x=-1,1$
Note: $4 \neq 0$ and is not a zero

26. $x=-1,1$

27. $y=6x+6=0$
$6(x+1)=0$
$x=-1$
Note: $6 \neq 0$ and is not a zero

28. $x=1$

29. $y=(x-13)(x+1)=0$
$(x-13)=0; (x+1)=0$
$x=13,-1$

30. $x=13,1$

31. $y=x(x-3)=0$
$x=0; (x-3)=0$
$x=0,3$

32. $x=0,4$

33. $y=3x(x-3)=0$
$3x=0; (x-3)=0$
$x=0,3$

34. $x=0,2$

35. $y=(3x-4)(x+2)=0$
$(3x-4)=0; (x+2)=0$
$3x=4; x=-2$

$x=\dfrac{4}{3},-2$

36. $x=1,-\dfrac{1}{3}$

37. $y=(3x+1)(x+2)=0$
$(3x+1)=0; (x+2)=0$
$3x=-1; x=-2$

$x=-\dfrac{1}{3},-2$

38. $x=-\dfrac{3}{2},6$

39. $x=\dfrac{-6\pm\sqrt{6^2-4(1)(-2)}}{2(1)}$

$=\dfrac{-6\pm\sqrt{36+8}}{2}=\dfrac{-6\pm\sqrt{44}}{2}$

$x\approx 0.317,-6.32$

40. $x=6.3,-0.32$

41. $x=\dfrac{-1\pm\sqrt{(-1)^2-4(2.4)(3.2)}}{2(2.4)}$

$=\dfrac{-1\pm\sqrt{1-30.72}}{4.8}=\dfrac{-1\pm\sqrt{-29.72}}{4.8}$

no zeros

42. no zeros

43. a. $-4y^2$ b. -18 c. $5x^3$ d. 2   e. 3   f. -4; y^2

44. a. $-6.5x^2$ b. -5.2 c. $8y^3$ d. 2   e. 3   f. -6.5; x^2

45. 4; x; $(5-y)$; 1 *term*

46. 7; y; $(x-2)$; 1 *term*

47. -3; x^4; $(x+2)$

48. *trick question*—there are only 2 terms.

IIR2

Fraction Review Operations and Simplification

In this section you'll find a quick review of fractions, not only how to do operations with them, but why these algorithms work. Next, we'll discuss how to simplify fractions because this is one area in which we find that students frequently perform all kinds of "illegal" operations. We'll tell you what you *can* and *can't do* with fractions. But first—a note about prerequisites.

A NOTE ABOUT PREREQUISITES

Remember the multiplication tables you were supposed to memorize in third grade or thereabouts? If you attended an elementary school in which students were not allowed to use calculators, you probably remember them. But if you've forgotten them over the years due to "creeping calculator dependence" or if you never really learned your multiplication facts well to begin with, it would be a good idea to memorize them or rememorize them now before we get started. Relearn all the facts from $0 \times 0 = 0$ up through $12 \times 12 = 144$.

Yes, you will be allowed to use calculators, but it's very difficult to reduce fractions or to factor unless you have a solid knowledge of the multiplication facts, once called "times tables."

If you need a refresher, the multiplication facts are printed at the back of this section, and then the following page has a "facts run" you can use to quiz yourself. You should be able to answer the entire sheet easily within three minutes. (Be sure to check the solutions.) If not, practice some more. If you're weak on multiplication facts, think of it as a second chance to learn them.

OPERATIONS WITH FRACTIONS—MULTIPLICATION

Imagine a garden plot divided into five equal strips for planting carrots, radishes, onions, lettuce, and tomatoes. Now suppose the children want to try their hands at raising tomatoes. We decide to allot them one third of the tomato strip.

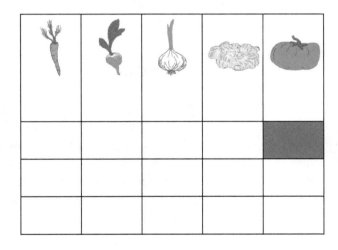

Think of dividing the garden into thirds. One third of the tomato strip is shaded. This would be 1/3 of 1/5th of the garden.

Note that the word "of" translates into "times".

Notice that each small rectangle is 1/15th of the plot.

$\dfrac{1}{3} \cdot \dfrac{1}{5} = \dfrac{1}{15}$ The children are responsible for $\dfrac{1}{15}$ th of the garden.

Suppose the kids want $\frac{2}{3}$ *rds* of the

tomatoes, or $\frac{2}{3}$ of $\frac{1}{5} = \frac{2}{3} \cdot \frac{1}{5} = \frac{2}{15}$

The kids now have 2/15th of the garden.

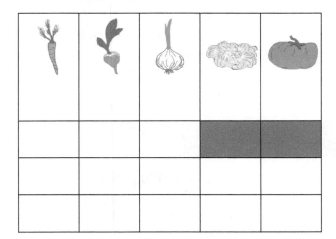

Suppose we give them tomatoes and lettuce, one third of each row, or one-third of two-fifths of the garden.

i.e. $\frac{1}{3} \cdot \frac{2}{5} = \frac{2}{15}$

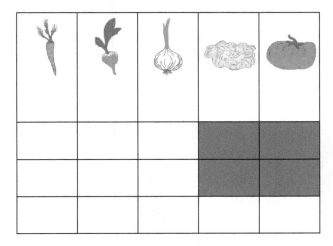

If we give them 2/3rd of the tomatoes and lettuce, i.e., 2/3 of 2/5 of the garden, they will get:

$\frac{2}{3} \cdot \frac{2}{5} = \frac{4}{15}$

The general rule for the multiplication of fractions is:

numerator x numerator over denominator x denominator;

or, in mathematical terms: $\dfrac{a}{b} \cdot \dfrac{c}{d} = \dfrac{ac}{bd}$

Recall that "ac" means "a" times "c", and "bd" means "b" times "d".

When you multiply $\dfrac{1}{3} \cdot \dfrac{1}{5} = \dfrac{1 \cdot 1}{3 \cdot 5} = \dfrac{1}{15}$, the denominator tells us the size of each small rectangle, and the numerator tells us how many of these small rectangles we have.

Suppose we have two cookies to be divided equally among 23 children. We could divide each of the two cookies into 23 parts, and then give each child 1/23rd from each cookie; in other words,

$$\dfrac{1}{23} \cdot 2 = \dfrac{2}{23} \text{ cookies to each child.}$$

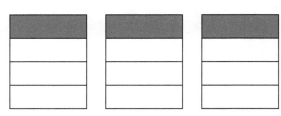

Each child would get 2/23rd of the cookie.

Again, the denominator tells us the size of each portion, and the numerator tells us how many of these portions we have.

Suppose we have 3 garden plots, and we decide to let the kids have 1/4th of each one.

We need $\dfrac{1}{4} \cdot 3$.

Remember that 3 is the same as $\dfrac{3}{1}$, so

$$\dfrac{1}{4} \cdot 3 = \dfrac{1}{4} \cdot \dfrac{3}{1} = \dfrac{3}{4}$$

Altogether, the kids have 3/4th of a plot.

Notice that 3/4th could be allotted as in the figure above (1/4th of each of the plots), or the 3/4th could be allotted from a single plot, as in the figure below. In each case, the children have the same area; i.e., 3/4th of a plot.

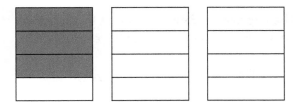

If we were to give each child ½ of each of the 3 plots, they would have:

$$\frac{1}{2} \cdot \frac{3}{1} = \frac{3}{2}$$

or three halves of a plot.

You probably remember that $\frac{3}{2} = 1\frac{1}{2}$.

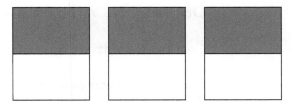

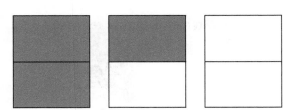

INTRA-SECTION EXERCISES:

1. $\dfrac{2}{3} \cdot \dfrac{4}{7}$ 2. $\dfrac{3}{5} \cdot 9$ 3. $\dfrac{11}{4} \cdot \dfrac{3}{5}$ 4. $\dfrac{\sqrt{3}}{x} \cdot \dfrac{\sqrt{3}}{y}$ 5. $\dfrac{(x+2)}{3} \cdot \dfrac{x}{\sqrt{x+1}}$ 6. $\dfrac{\sqrt{2}}{4} \cdot \dfrac{\sqrt{3}}{1}$

Solutions

1. $\dfrac{2}{3} \cdot \dfrac{4}{7} = \dfrac{2 \cdot 4}{3 \cdot 7} = \dfrac{8}{21}$ 2. $\dfrac{3 \cdot 9}{5 \cdot 1} = \dfrac{27}{5}$ 3. $\dfrac{11 \cdot 3}{4 \cdot 5} = \dfrac{33}{20}$ 4. $\dfrac{3}{xy}$ 5. $\dfrac{x(x+2)}{3\sqrt{x+1}}$ 6. $\dfrac{\sqrt{6}}{4}$

Take a moment to consider exercise 6) above. We can combine the radicands under

the radical sign to make a product. For example: $\sqrt{2} \cdot \sqrt{3} = \sqrt{2 \cdot 3} = \sqrt{6}$. However, we

cannot do the same with sums; for example, $\sqrt{2} + \sqrt{3} \neq \sqrt{2+3}$.

> Caution: $\sqrt{a} \cdot \sqrt{b} = \sqrt{ab}$ but $\sqrt{a} + \sqrt{b} \neq \sqrt{a+b}$

Also, remember the Commutative Law of Multiplication. This means that the order in which we multiply factors doesn't matter. $(2)(3) = (3)(2)$, and $3\pi = \pi 3$, although we usually write the rational number first. The expression $3x$ is equivalent to $x3$, but we prefer to see it in the form $3x$. The constant is called the *coefficient* of the expression $3x$.

Another thing: $\dfrac{4x}{5}$ is equivalent to $\dfrac{4}{5} \cdot x$. Think of it as "un-multiplying."

OPERATIONS WITH FRACTIONS—DIVISION

Consider 6 divided by 3.

If we have 6 chests of gold and 3 children, and we want to divide the chests among them equally, we divide 6 chests into 3 groups.

In mathematical terms, $6 \div 3 = 2$.

Again, we made 6 into 3 groups, or $6 \div 3 = 2$.

Suppose we want to make 6 into one-third of a group, i.e., $6 \div \dfrac{1}{3}$.

This means we would need 18 chests, so that $\dfrac{1}{3}$ of the 18 would be 6 chests.

Notice that we can get 18 by $6 \cdot \dfrac{3}{1} = 18$.

The general rule for dividing by fractions is to multiply by the reciprocal of the divisor, so:

$$6 \div \frac{1}{3} \text{ equals } 6 \cdot \frac{3}{1} = \frac{6}{1} \cdot \frac{3}{1} = \frac{6 \cdot 3}{1 \cdot 1} = \frac{18}{1} = 18$$

which is really more steps than we usually need. Just $6 \cdot \frac{3}{1} = 18$ should do it.

> The general rule for the division of fractions is:
> Multiply the dividend by the reciprocal of the divisor,
>
> or in math notation: $\dfrac{a}{b} \div \dfrac{c}{d} = \dfrac{a}{b} \cdot \dfrac{d}{c} = \dfrac{ad}{bc}$

Using the same rule: $6 \div \frac{5}{7} = 6 \cdot \frac{7}{5} = \frac{6}{1} \cdot \frac{7}{5} = \frac{42}{5}$,

and $6 \div \frac{1}{x} = 6 \cdot \frac{x}{1} = \frac{6}{1} \cdot \frac{x}{1} = \frac{6x}{1} = 6x$

INTRA-SECTION EXERCISES:

7. $\dfrac{2}{3} \div \dfrac{5}{7}$

8. $\dfrac{2}{3} \div 5$

9. $\dfrac{2}{x+1} \div \dfrac{x-3}{3}$

10. $x^4 \div \dfrac{2}{3}$

11. $\dfrac{x^4}{\frac{2}{3}}$

12. $\dfrac{x^4+1}{\frac{2}{3}}$

13. $\dfrac{x^4+1}{\frac{2x-1}{3}}$

Solutions

7. $\dfrac{2}{3} \div \dfrac{5}{7} = \dfrac{2}{3} \cdot \dfrac{7}{5} = \dfrac{14}{15}$

8. $\dfrac{2}{3} \div \dfrac{5}{1} = \dfrac{2}{3} \cdot \dfrac{1}{5} = \dfrac{2}{15}$

9. $\dfrac{2}{x+1} \div \dfrac{x-3}{3} = \dfrac{2}{x+1} \cdot \dfrac{3}{x-3} = \dfrac{6}{(x+1)(x-3)}$

10. $x^4 \div \dfrac{2}{3} = \dfrac{x^4}{1} \cdot \dfrac{3}{2} = \dfrac{3x^4}{2}$

11. $\dfrac{x^4}{\frac{2}{3}}$ is another way to write: $x^4 \div \dfrac{2}{3}$. Hence, $x^4 \div \dfrac{2}{3} = \dfrac{x^4}{1} \cdot \dfrac{3}{2} = \dfrac{3x^4}{2}$

12. $\dfrac{x^4+1}{\dfrac{2}{3}}$ is another way to write: $(x^4+1)\div\dfrac{2}{3}$. Hence, we have $(x^4+1)\cdot\dfrac{3}{2}=\dfrac{3(x^4+1)}{2}$.

Be sure to notice that the 3 is multiplied by the entire numerator: x^4+1. Parentheses are *very* helpful here.

13. $\dfrac{x^4+1}{\dfrac{2x-1}{3}}=(x^4+1)\div\dfrac{2x-1}{3}=\dfrac{(x^4+1)}{1}\cdot\dfrac{3}{2x-1}=\dfrac{3(x^4+1)}{2x-1}$

OPERATIONS WITH FRACTIONS—ADDITION AND SUBTRACTION— SAME DENOMINATORS

Suppose a pie is cut into sixths. Each piece is 1/6 *th* of the pie.

We note that 6/6 *th* of the pie equals one whole pie, or $\dfrac{6}{6}=1$.

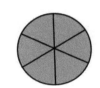

Similarly, $\dfrac{12}{12}$*ths* of a pie would equal 1 whole pie, or $\dfrac{5}{5}$*ths* or $\dfrac{8}{8}$*ths*, etc.

Whenever the numerator equals the denominator, the fraction equals one.

Let's say your dog, Igor, eats one piece, or $^1\!/_6$ *th* of the pie.

Then he gobbles down 4 more pieces, or $^4\!/_6$ *ths* before you can

catch him. Igor has eaten a total of $\dfrac{1}{6}+\dfrac{4}{6}$ or $\dfrac{5}{6}$*th* of the pie.

Notice we can only add fractions when the denominators are equal, and the process of adding doesn't change the denominator, so

$$\frac{2}{7}+\frac{3}{7}=\frac{5}{7}\text{ and }\frac{20}{51}-\frac{3}{51}=\frac{17}{51}\text{ and }\frac{3}{5}+\frac{y}{5}=\frac{3+y}{5}.$$

> The general rule is: If the denominators are equal,
> add, or subtract, the numerators,
>
> or $\dfrac{a}{c} + \dfrac{b}{c} = \dfrac{a+b}{c}$ and $\dfrac{a}{c} - \dfrac{b}{c} = \dfrac{a-b}{c}$

INTRA-SECTION EXERCISES:

14. $\dfrac{3}{5} + \dfrac{1}{5}$

15. $\dfrac{5}{x} + \dfrac{6}{x}$

16. $\dfrac{17}{x-y} - \dfrac{4}{x-y}$

17. $\dfrac{2}{x+1} - \dfrac{6+x}{x+1}$

18. $\dfrac{3+\sqrt{2}}{4} + \dfrac{\sqrt{5}}{4}$

19. $\dfrac{3}{7} + \dfrac{4}{7}$

Solutions

14. $\dfrac{3+1}{5} = \dfrac{4}{5}$

15. $\dfrac{5+6}{x} = \dfrac{11}{x}$

16. $\dfrac{17-3}{x-y} = \dfrac{13}{x-y}$

17. $\dfrac{2-(6+x)}{x+1} = \dfrac{2-6-x}{x+1} = \dfrac{-4-x}{x+1}$. Note that the use of parentheses is vital. The entire numerator "$6+x$" must be subtracted. It was necessary to distribute the subtraction minus sign to both the 6 and the x.

18. $\dfrac{3+\sqrt{2}+\sqrt{5}}{4}$. Remember that we **cannot** combine $\sqrt{2}+\sqrt{5}$. They **do not** equal $\sqrt{7}$.

19. $\dfrac{3+4}{7} = \dfrac{7}{7} = 1$. Whenever the numerator equals the denominator, the fraction equals 1.

OPERATIONS WITH FRACTIONS—ADDITION AND SUBTRACTION— DIFFERENT DENOMINATORS

Suppose we have one-sixth of a rhubarb-raspberry pie left over and two-thirds of a chokecherry cream pie. We want to add:

$$\frac{1}{6}+\frac{2}{3}$$

Unless the denominators are equal, this can't be done! But don't despair—there is a solution.

We must make the denominators equal first. We'll cut each piece of chokecherry cream pie in half, and voila! We now have $\frac{4}{6}$ ths of the chokecherry cream pie to add to $\frac{1}{6}$ th of the rhubarb-raspberry pie for a total:

$$\frac{1}{6}+\frac{4}{6}=\frac{5}{6}\text{th of a pie.}$$

Before we can understand this algebraically, we'll need to recall that $\frac{2}{2}=1$ and that 1 times any number equals that number; i.e., $(1)(2)=2$, $(1)(3)=3$, $(1)(38.1)=38.1$, $(1)(z)=z$, etc.

Multiplying a fraction by 1 does not change the original fraction.

Two-thirds of a cherry cream pie remains the same amount of pie as: $\frac{2}{3}\cdot\frac{2}{2}=\frac{4}{6}$ ths of a cherry cream pie. The fraction $\frac{2}{3}$ rds has been transformed into a fraction with the same denominator as $\frac{1}{6}$ th, allowing us to add $\frac{1}{6}$ th and $\frac{2}{3}$ rds as $\frac{1}{6}$ th and $\frac{4}{6}$ ths.

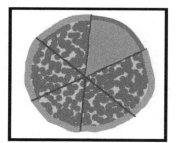

Once again, algebraically: $\dfrac{1}{6}+\dfrac{2}{3}\cdot\dfrac{2}{2}=\dfrac{1}{6}+\dfrac{4}{6}=\dfrac{5}{6}$.

Suppose we want to add $\dfrac{1}{8}+\dfrac{1}{4}$.

We want both denominators to equal 8, so we multiply $\dfrac{1}{4}$ by $\dfrac{2}{2}$. This gives us:

$$\frac{1}{8}+\frac{1}{4}=\frac{1}{8}+\frac{1}{4}\cdot\frac{2}{2}=\frac{1}{8}+\frac{2}{8}=\frac{3}{8}$$

Suppose we want to add $\dfrac{1}{7}+\dfrac{3}{5}$. Both denominators will need factors of 7 and 5.

We will need to multiply $\dfrac{1}{7}$ by $\dfrac{5}{5}$ to have a denominator with the factors (7)(5), and

we will need to multiply $\dfrac{3}{5}$ by $\dfrac{7}{7}$ to have a denominator with the factors (7)(5).

$$\frac{1}{7}\cdot\frac{5}{5}+\frac{3}{5}\cdot\frac{7}{7}=\frac{5}{35}+\frac{21}{35}=\frac{26}{35}$$

Let's add $\dfrac{3}{x}+\dfrac{y}{2}$. Both denominators will need factors of x and 2.

$$\frac{3}{x}\cdot\frac{2}{2}+\frac{y}{2}\cdot\frac{x}{x}=\frac{6}{2x}+\frac{yx}{2x}=\frac{6+yx}{2x}\text{ or }\frac{6+xy}{2x}$$

We seem to prefer variables in alphabetical order, so we also convert yx to xy.

Example 1:

Simplify: $\dfrac{1}{x^2-9}+\dfrac{x+2}{x^2-5x+6}$

$$\frac{1}{x^2-9}+\frac{x+2}{x^2-5x+6}=\frac{1}{(x+3)(x-3)}+\frac{x+2}{(x-3)(x-2)}$$

$$=\frac{1}{(x+3)(x-3)}\cdot\frac{(x-2)}{(x-2)}+\frac{x+2}{(x-3)(x-2)}\cdot\frac{(x+3)}{(x+3)}=\frac{(x-2)}{(x+3)(x-3)(x-2)}$$

$$+\frac{(x+2)(x+3)}{(x+3)(x-3)(x-2)}=\frac{x-2+x^2+3x+2x+6}{(x+3)(x-3)(x-2)}=\frac{x^2+6x+4}{(x+3)(x-3)(x-2)}$$

INTRA-SECTION EXERCISES:

20. $\dfrac{3}{5}+\dfrac{4}{15}$

21. $\dfrac{2}{3}-\dfrac{1}{9}$

22. $\dfrac{1}{2}+\dfrac{2}{11}$

23. $\dfrac{1}{4}-\dfrac{1}{z}$

24. $3+\dfrac{2}{x}$

25. $\dfrac{8}{(x-1)}+\dfrac{y}{5}$

Solutions

20. $\dfrac{3}{5}+\dfrac{4}{15}=\dfrac{3}{5}\cdot\dfrac{3}{3}+\dfrac{4}{15}=\dfrac{9}{15}+\dfrac{4}{15}=\dfrac{13}{15}$

22. $\dfrac{1}{2}+\dfrac{2}{11}=\dfrac{1}{2}\cdot\dfrac{11}{11}+\dfrac{2}{11}\cdot\dfrac{2}{2}=\dfrac{11}{22}+\dfrac{4}{22}=\dfrac{15}{22}$

21. $\dfrac{2}{3}-\dfrac{1}{9}=\dfrac{2}{3}\cdot\dfrac{3}{3}-\dfrac{1}{9}=\dfrac{6}{9}-\dfrac{1}{9}=\dfrac{5}{9}$

23. $\dfrac{1}{4}-\dfrac{1}{z}=\dfrac{1}{4}\cdot\dfrac{z}{z}-\dfrac{1}{z}\cdot\dfrac{4}{4}=\dfrac{z}{4z}-\dfrac{4}{4z}=\dfrac{z-4}{4z}$

24. $3+\dfrac{2}{x}=\dfrac{3}{1}\cdot\dfrac{x}{x}+\dfrac{2}{x}=\dfrac{3x}{x}+\dfrac{2}{x}=\dfrac{3x+2}{x}$

25. $\dfrac{8}{(x-1)}\cdot\dfrac{5}{5}+\dfrac{y}{5}\cdot\dfrac{(x-1)}{(x-1)}=\dfrac{40}{5(x-1)}+\dfrac{xy-y}{5(x-1)}=\dfrac{40+xy-y}{5(x-1)}$

ADDITION AND SUBTRACTION—AN ALTERNATIVE USING NEGATIVE EXPONENTS

$$\frac{5}{7}+\frac{2}{9}=5\cdot7^{-1}+2\cdot9^{-1}=(7^{-1})(9^{-1})(5\cdot9+2\cdot7)=(7^{-1})(9^{-1})(59)=\frac{59}{7\cdot9}=\frac{59}{63}$$

$$\frac{5}{21}+\frac{11}{18}=5\cdot21^{-1}+11\cdot18^{-1}=5\cdot(3\cdot7)^{-1}+11\cdot(2\cdot3^2)^{-1}$$

$$=5\cdot3^{-1}\cdot7^{-1}+11\cdot2^{-1}\cdot3^{-2}=(2^{-1})(3^{-2})(7^{-1})(5\cdot2\cdot3+2\cdot7)$$

$$=(2^{-1})(3^{-2})(7^{-1})(51)=\frac{51}{2\cdot3^2\cdot7}=\frac{59}{126}$$

REALLY IMPORTANT STUFF—SIMPLIFYING ALGEBRAIC FRACTIONS (I.E., REDUCING)

Pay close attention to this topic because it's where a large proportion of errors are made.

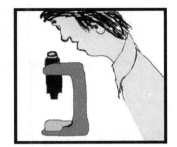

Reducing fractions is a process of removing ones.

For example, consider the fraction $\dfrac{35}{42}$.

We recognize that both numerator and denominator have factors of 7. (If you don't, be sure to review the multiplication facts at the end of this section.) We might call this "un-multiplying."

$$\frac{35}{42} = \frac{5 \cdot 7}{6 \cdot 7} \text{ Since } \frac{7}{7} = 1, \text{ the fraction reduces to } \frac{5}{6}.$$

Factoring is the inverse of distributing. Consider $4x + 4y$. Since both terms $4x$ and $4y$ have a common factor of 4, we can "un-distribute" the 4. This is more conventionally said, we can factor out the 4, or less correctly said, we can "take out" the 4.

Therefore, $4x + 4y = 4(x + y)$. Note that distributing the 4 gets us back to the original algebraic phrase, $4x + 4y$.

Now consider the rational expression, i.e., fraction: $\dfrac{2x + 6y}{18}$.

Every term has a factor of 2. We can write the fractions as: $\dfrac{2(x + 3y)}{2 \cdot 9}$. Since $\dfrac{2}{2}$ equals 1,

the fraction reduces to: $\dfrac{(x + 3y)}{9}$.

Note: We could only do this simplification because there was a 2 in every term. (Remember terms?)

Think about the fraction $\dfrac{1 + 4}{4}$. It equals $\dfrac{5}{4}$. Do you agree?

If we erroneously "cancel" the 4s in the numerator and the denominator, we would

erroneously conclude that $\dfrac{1 + 4}{4} = 1 + 1 = 2$ instead of $\dfrac{5}{4}$.

Similarly, $\dfrac{1+x}{x}$ cannot be reduced because the three terms of the numerator and

denominator do not have a factor in common.

Remember: Fractions can only be reduced if you can "take out" the same factor
             from **every** term.

Example 2:

Reduce $\dfrac{3x-9}{3}$

$$\frac{3x-9}{3}=\frac{3(x-3)}{3}=\frac{x-3}{1}=x-3$$

Shortcut: Remove 3 from every term: $\dfrac{3x-9}{3}=\dfrac{x-3}{1}=x-3$

Example 3:

Reduce $\dfrac{2x-6}{3}$

Since there is no factor common to all three terms, this fraction does
not reduce.

Example 4:

Reduce $\dfrac{x^2-5x+6}{x-3}$

$$\frac{x^2-5x+6}{x-3}=\frac{(x-3)(x-2)}{x-3}=x-2$$

Example 5:

Reduce $\dfrac{x^2-5x+6}{x+3}$

$\dfrac{x^2-5x+6}{x+3}=\dfrac{(x-3)(x-2)}{x+3}$ does **not** reduce.

Not that kind of
reducing!

Example 6:

Reduce $\dfrac{\sqrt{2}}{2}$

$\dfrac{\sqrt{2}}{2}$ does **not** reduce. We cannot "cancel" a number under a radical sign with a number outside the radical sign.

Example 7:

Reduce $\dfrac{3(x-4)+7}{(x-4)^2}$

$\dfrac{3(x-4)+7}{(x-4)^2}$ does **not** reduce.

There are three terms here. In the numerator, the two terms are: $3(x-4)$ and 7. In the denominator, there is one term: $(x-4)^2$. Unless all three terms have the same factor, we cannot reduce the fraction. In this case, two of the terms have the factor $(x-4)$, but the term 7 does not, so we cannot reduce.

Example 8:

Reduce $\dfrac{0(x-5)-5(x+5)^2}{(x+5)^4}$

$\dfrac{0(x-5)-5(x+5)^2}{(x+5)^4} = \dfrac{-5}{(x+5)^2}$

Since the first term in the numerator equals zero, we need not consider it as a term.

Example 9:

Reduce $\dfrac{4(x-2)^2 - 7x(x-2)^3}{(x-2)^6}$

$\dfrac{4(x-2)^2 - 7x(x-2)^3}{(x-2)^6} = \dfrac{4 - 7x(x-2)}{(x-2)^4} = \dfrac{4 - 7x^2 + 14x}{(x-2)^4}$

Note that we factored an $(x-2)^2$ out of every term, leaving $(x-2)^4$ in the denominator.

Also note that when the numerator has no common factors, we expand the numerator and collect any like terms. But since the denominator is

244 | Business Calculus

in factored form, we generally do not FOIL or multiply out factors in the denominator.

INTRA-SECTION EXERCISES:

Reduce to lowest terms, if possible.

26. $\dfrac{24}{16}$

27. $\dfrac{5x^2y^2}{10xy}$

28. $\dfrac{6x+8}{10}$

29. $\dfrac{6x+5}{10}$

30. $\dfrac{x}{x+3}$

31. $\dfrac{x^2-x-12}{x+3}$

32. $\dfrac{3(x-5)-2(x-5)^2}{(x-5)^4}$

Solutions

26. $\dfrac{24}{16} = \dfrac{3\cdot8}{2\cdot8} = \dfrac{3}{2}$

27. $\dfrac{5x^2y^2}{10xy} = \dfrac{xy}{2}$ A "$5xy$" was factored out of each term.

28. $\dfrac{6x+8}{10} = \dfrac{3x+4}{5}$ A 2 was factored out of each of the three terms.

29. $\dfrac{6x+5}{10}$ There is no factor common to all three terms, so this fraction cannot be reduced.

30. $\dfrac{x}{x+3}$ There is no factor common to all three terms, so this fraction cannot be reduced.

31. $\dfrac{x^2-x-12}{x+3} = \dfrac{(x-4)(x+3)}{x+3} = x-4$

32. Since all three terms contain one factor of $(x-5)$, we can remove only one $(x-5)$ from each of the three terms: $\dfrac{3(x-5)-2(x-5)^2}{(x-5)^4} = \dfrac{3-2(x-5)}{(x-5)^3} = \dfrac{3-2x+10}{(x-5)^3} = \dfrac{-2x+13}{(x-5)^3}$

We can't remove an $(x-5)$ from one term and an $(x-5)^2$ from another term. We have to **remove the same factor from every term**.

REDUCING A SPECIAL KIND OF FRACTION/RATIONAL EXPRESSION

Consider the expression $\dfrac{x-3}{3-x}$. If we factor out a '-1' from the numerator, we would have:

$$\dfrac{-1(-x+3)}{3-x} \text{ [Check by distributing.]}$$

We have commutativity for addition, so we can change the order of $(-x+3)$ to get $(+3-x)$:

$$\dfrac{-1(-x+3)}{3-x} = \dfrac{-1(3-x)}{3-x} = -1$$

This type of reducing can be done whenever the numerator and denominator have the same factors but with opposite signs.

Example 10:

Reduce $\dfrac{3(5-x)}{(x-5)(x-6)}$

$$\dfrac{3(5-x)}{(x-5)(x-6)} = \dfrac{-3(x-5)}{(x-5)(x-6)} = \dfrac{-3}{x-6}$$

It's worth noting that minus signs can migrate.

$$\dfrac{-2}{3} = -\dfrac{2}{3} = \dfrac{2}{-3}$$

As long as we don't change the number of minus signs, (one, in this case), we can shift them from the numerator to the denominator or out to the side.

Not that kind of migration!

Another fact: Fractions are equivalent if every sign is replaced with the opposite sign.

Consider the fraction $\dfrac{4x^2-2x+5}{32x^2-6y^2}$. If we multiply the fraction by $\dfrac{-1}{-1}$, we are essentially

multiplying by 1, which shouldn't change the value of the fraction, but it will now look like:

$$\dfrac{4x^2-2x+5}{32x^2-6y^2} = \dfrac{(-1)}{(-1)} \cdot \dfrac{(4x^2-2x+5)}{(32x^2-6y^2)} = \dfrac{-4x^2+2x-5}{-32x^2+6y^2}$$

INTRA-SECTION EXERCISES:

Reduce, if possible.

33. $\dfrac{14(x^2-4)}{7(4-x^2)}$

35. $-\dfrac{(2x-13)}{13-2x}$

34. $\dfrac{-6(x-1)}{1-x}$

36. Are $\dfrac{2x-3y}{-5x+8y}$ and $\dfrac{-2x+3y}{5x-8y}$ equivalent?

Solutions

33. $\dfrac{14(x^2-4)}{7(4-x^2)}=\dfrac{-14(4-x^2)}{7(4-x^2)}=-2$

35. $-\dfrac{(2x-13)}{(13-2x)}=-\dfrac{-1(13-2x)}{13-2x}=-(-1)=1$

34. $\dfrac{-6(x-1)}{(1-x)}=\dfrac{--6(1-x)}{1-x}=6$

36. Yes, all signs are reversed

SIMPLIFYING COMPLEX FRACTIONS

Consider the fraction: $\dfrac{\dfrac{1}{x}+\dfrac{1}{3}}{\dfrac{5}{y}-2}$.

This is a complex fraction because it has subordinate denominators. To simplify it, we multiply the numerator and denominator by the product of all the subordinate denominators.

$$\dfrac{\left(\dfrac{1}{x}+\dfrac{1}{3}\right)}{\left(\dfrac{5}{y}-2\right)}\cdot\dfrac{(3xy)}{(3xy)}=\dfrac{\left(\dfrac{1}{x}\right)(3xy)+\left(\dfrac{1}{3}\right)(3xy)}{\left(\dfrac{5}{y}\right)(3xy)-2(3xy)}=\dfrac{3y+xy}{15x-6xy}$$

The multiplication step eliminates all subordinate denominators. They should all cancel out if we multiply correctly.

Example 11:

Simplify $\dfrac{3+\dfrac{1}{\sqrt{2}}}{4}$

The subordinate denominator is $\sqrt{2}$, so we multiply by $\dfrac{\sqrt{2}}{\sqrt{2}}$.

$$\frac{\left(3+\dfrac{1}{\sqrt{2}}\right)}{4}\cdot\frac{\sqrt{2}}{\sqrt{2}}=\frac{3\sqrt{2}+\dfrac{1}{\sqrt{2}}\sqrt{2}}{4\sqrt{2}}=\frac{3\sqrt{2}+1}{4\sqrt{2}}$$

This fraction cannot be reduced further because no factor is common to all three terms.

Example 12:

Simplify $\dfrac{1}{\dfrac{1}{10}}$

One way to do this problem is to think of it as $1\div\dfrac{1}{10}$,

but let's approach it as a complex fraction and multiply by $\dfrac{10}{10}$.

$$\frac{1}{\dfrac{1}{10}}\cdot\frac{10}{10}=\frac{10}{1}=10$$

Similarly, $\dfrac{1}{\dfrac{1}{100}}=100$ and $\dfrac{1}{\dfrac{1}{3}}=3$, and $\dfrac{1}{\dfrac{1}{x+y}}=x+y$, but $\dfrac{1}{\dfrac{1}{x}+\dfrac{1}{y}}\neq x+y$.

Notice the difference? The last fraction has two subordinate denominators, not one.

> To simplify complex fractions,
> multiply the numerator and denominator by
> the product of all the subordinate denominators.
>
> $$\text{e.g.,} \quad \frac{\left(a+\dfrac{b}{c}\right)}{\left(d-\dfrac{e}{f}\right)} = \frac{\left(a+\dfrac{b}{c}\right)}{\left(d-\dfrac{e}{f}\right)} \cdot \frac{(cf)}{(cf)} = \frac{acf+\left(\dfrac{b}{c}\right)(cf)}{dcf-\left(\dfrac{e}{f}\right)(cf)} = \frac{acf+bf}{dcf-ce}$$

INTRA-SECTION EXERCISES:

Simplify

37. $\dfrac{\dfrac{3}{1}}{\dfrac{1}{4}}$

38. $\dfrac{3+\dfrac{1}{x}}{5}$

39. $\dfrac{\dfrac{2}{x}-\dfrac{y}{3}}{\dfrac{1}{x}+\dfrac{4}{5}}$

40. $\dfrac{\sqrt{x-1}+\dfrac{3x}{\sqrt{x-1}}}{4}$

Solutions

37. $\dfrac{\dfrac{3}{1}}{\dfrac{1}{4}} = \dfrac{3}{1}\cdot\dfrac{4}{4} = \dfrac{12}{1} = 12$

38. $\dfrac{\left(3+\dfrac{1}{x}\right)}{5}\cdot\dfrac{x}{x} = \dfrac{3x+\left(\dfrac{1}{x}\right)x}{5x} = \dfrac{3x+1}{5x}$

39. $\dfrac{\left(\dfrac{2}{x}-\dfrac{y}{3}\right)}{\left(\dfrac{1}{x}+\dfrac{4}{5}\right)}\cdot\dfrac{(3)(5)(x)}{(3)(5)(x)} \quad \dfrac{\dfrac{2}{x}(3)(5)x-\dfrac{y}{3}(3)(5)x}{\dfrac{1}{x}(3)(5)x+\dfrac{4}{5}(3)(5)x} = \dfrac{30-5xy}{15+12x}$

40. $\dfrac{\left(\sqrt{x-1}+\dfrac{3x}{\sqrt{x-1}}\right)}{4}\cdot\dfrac{\sqrt{x-1}}{\sqrt{x-1}} = \dfrac{\sqrt{x-1}\sqrt{x-1}+\left(\dfrac{3x}{\sqrt{x-1}}\right)\sqrt{x-1}}{4\sqrt{x-1}} = \dfrac{x-1+3x}{4\sqrt{x-1}} = \dfrac{4x-1}{4\sqrt{x-1}}$

NOW ON TO INFINITY

Consider the sequence: $\dfrac{1}{1}, \dfrac{1}{2}, \dfrac{1}{10}, \dfrac{1}{1,000}, \ldots, \dfrac{1}{1,000,000}$.

As the denominators get larger and larger, the fractions as a whole get smaller and smaller. If we were to put the biggest number possible in the denominator, we would expect the fraction as a whole to equal zero. Hence, we can define the expression $\dfrac{1}{\infty} = 0$.

And since $\dfrac{4}{\infty} = 4 \cdot \dfrac{1}{\infty}$, then $\dfrac{4}{\infty}$ equals zero, too.

Now consider the sequence: $-\dfrac{1}{1}, -\dfrac{1}{2}, -\dfrac{1}{10}, -\dfrac{1}{1,000}, \ldots, -\dfrac{1}{1,000,000}$.

If we were to think of them on a number line, we would realize that these numbers are also getting closer and closer to zero. Hence, we can define $-\dfrac{1}{\infty} = 0$.

In fact, $\dfrac{n}{\infty} = 0$ for any real number n.

What about the sequence $\dfrac{1}{3}, \dfrac{1}{2}, \dfrac{1}{1}, \dfrac{1}{1/10}, \dfrac{1}{1/100}, \dfrac{1}{1/1000}, \ldots, \dfrac{1}{1/1,000,000}$?

We know that $\dfrac{1}{1/10} = 10$, $\dfrac{1}{1/100} = 100$, and $\dfrac{1}{1/1,000,000} = 1,000,000$.

As the denominators are getting smaller and smaller, the fractions as a whole are getting larger and larger. If we were to make the denominator equal to zero, we should expect a very large number. In fact, we might expect: $\dfrac{1}{0}$ to equal ∞.

But these numbers

$$-\dfrac{1}{3}, -\dfrac{1}{2}, -\dfrac{1}{1}, -\dfrac{1}{1/10} = -10, \quad -\dfrac{1}{1/100} = -100, \ldots, -\dfrac{1}{1/1,000,000} = -1,000,000$$

are getting closer and closer to negative infinity $-\infty$. So does $\dfrac{1}{0}$ equal ∞? or $-\infty$?

It could be either one. If we have knowledge that a series is getting larger and larger, approaching infinity through positive numbers, then we could say $\frac{1}{0} = \infty$. On the other hand, if we know that a series is getting larger and larger, approaching infinity through negative numbers, then we could infer $\frac{1}{0} = -\infty$. If we don't know which it is, then $\frac{1}{0}$ remains undefined.

Infinity is a concept rather than a number. It has these properties.

Infinity plus any real number equals infinity; e.g., $\infty + 3 = 3 + \infty = \infty$.

Infinity minus any real number equals infinity; e.g., $\infty - 89,000 = \infty$.

Infinity multiplied or divided by any positive nonzero number equals infinity; e.g., $45(\infty) = \infty$, and $\frac{\infty}{45} = \infty$.

Infinity multiplied or divided by any negative nonzero number equals negative infinity; e.g., $-45(\infty) = -\infty$, and $\frac{\infty}{(-45)} = -\infty$.

Infinity raised to any positive nonzero exponent equals infinity; e.g., $(\infty)^{84} = \infty$.

Negative infinity raised to any positive nonzero exponents behaves like $(-1)(\infty)$, e.g. $(-\infty)^2 = \infty$, while $(-\infty)^3 = -\infty$.

If numbers close to zero, such as 1/2 and 1/4, are multiplied, the result is even closer to zero, 1/8. An infinite product of numbers close to zero is closer to zero, and $0^{\infty} = 0$.

... AND BEYOND

For some expressions, an appropriate definition cannot be determined: they are *indeterminate*.

You are probably familiar with $\frac{0}{0}$. This expression

might very well equal any real number, but we can't discern which one without further analysis.

Other indeterminate expressions are $\dfrac{\infty}{\infty}$, $0 \cdot \infty$, $\infty - \infty$, 0^0, and ∞^0.

If your calculations produce any of these expressions, you haven't finished the problem.

IIR2 FRACTION REVIEW EXERCISES

Multiply

1. $\dfrac{x}{3}\cdot\dfrac{4}{5}$ 2. $\dfrac{6}{y}\cdot\dfrac{2}{5}$ 3. $\dfrac{\sqrt{3}}{4}\cdot\sqrt{7}$ 4. $\dfrac{\sqrt{3}}{6}\cdot\sqrt{x}$ 5. $-\dfrac{x}{3}\cdot x^4$ 6. $-x\cdot\dfrac{2x}{5}$

Reduce wherever possible.

7. $\dfrac{x+2}{2}$

8. $\dfrac{1+x}{x}$

9. $\dfrac{15x+10}{5}$

10. $\dfrac{6-3x}{9}$

11. $\dfrac{2-\sqrt{6}}{2}$

12. $\dfrac{\sqrt{5}+10}{5}$

13. $\dfrac{2+\sqrt{8x}}{6}$

14. $\dfrac{3-\sqrt{18x}}{6}$

15. $\dfrac{x^2-7x-18}{x+2}$

16. $\dfrac{y^2-16}{y+4}$

17. $\dfrac{2+\dfrac{1}{x}}{3}$

18. $\dfrac{x+\dfrac{1}{3}}{4}$

19. $\dfrac{6}{\dfrac{2}{3}}$

20. $\dfrac{4}{\dfrac{1}{5}}$

21. $\dfrac{\dfrac{1}{5}}{4}$

22. $\dfrac{\dfrac{x}{6}}{2}$

23. $\dfrac{\dfrac{1}{x}-\dfrac{2}{y}}{\dfrac{3}{xy}+7}$

24. $\dfrac{\dfrac{1}{x}-8}{\dfrac{x}{2}+\dfrac{y}{3}}$

25. $\dfrac{\sqrt{x+2}+\dfrac{3}{\sqrt{x+2}}}{\sqrt{x+2}}$

26. $\dfrac{\sqrt{4-x}-\dfrac{1}{\sqrt{4-x}}}{(x-2)}$

27. $\dfrac{3x(x-1)^3-(x-1)^2}{(x-1)^6}$

28. $\dfrac{5(x+1)^2-(x+1)^3}{(x+1)^4}$

29. $\dfrac{3(x-5)+(x-5)^2}{(x-5)}$

30. $\dfrac{4(x+5)+(x+5)^2}{(x+5)}$

31. $\dfrac{-6(x^2-7)}{7-x^2}$

32. $\dfrac{x^2-11}{-4(11-x^2)}$

33. $\dfrac{44y^3-3}{3-44y^3}$

34. $\dfrac{51y^2-17}{17-51y^2}$

35. $5+\infty$

36. $1{,}000+\infty$

37. $\infty-80{,}500$

38. $\infty-42{,}000$

39. $\dfrac{14{,}327}{\infty}$

40. $\dfrac{5}{\infty}$

41. $\dfrac{-80}{\infty}$

42. $\dfrac{-14{,}000}{\infty}$

43. $(-16)(\infty)$

44. $(\infty)(-43)$

45. $-9(-\infty)^6$

46. $7(-\infty)^3$

47. $24(-\infty)^5$

48. $-4(-\infty)^{10}$

49. $\dfrac{0}{0}$

50. $\dfrac{\infty}{\infty}$

51. $6\dfrac{\infty}{\infty}$

52. $\infty-\infty$

53. Upon dissolution of the partnership, one-third of the QYY Company's value goes to each of its three founding partners. Since Partner Abel is deceased, his portion is split evenly among his four heirs. What portion of the company's value does each of these heirs receive?

54. Five state agencies, A, B, C, D, and E, are to receive one-fifth of designated tax revenues. Agency C must divide its share equally among four departments. What proportion does each department receive?

IIR2 FRACTION REVIEW SOLUTIONS TO EXERCISES

1. $\dfrac{4x}{15}$ 2. $\dfrac{12}{5y}$ 3. $\dfrac{\sqrt{21}}{4}$ 4. $\dfrac{\sqrt{3x}}{6}$ 5. $\dfrac{-x^5}{3}$ 6. $\dfrac{-2x^2}{5}$

7. cannot reduce   8. cannot reduce   9. $\dfrac{3x+2}{1}=3x+2$ 10. $\dfrac{2-x}{3}$

11. cannot reduce   12. cannot reduce   13. $\dfrac{2+2\sqrt{2x}}{6}$ 14. $\dfrac{1-\sqrt{2x}}{2}$

$=\dfrac{1+\sqrt{2x}}{3}$

15. $\dfrac{(x-9)(x+2)}{x+2}$ 16. $y-4$ 17. $\dfrac{\left(2+\dfrac{1}{x}\right)}{3}\cdot\dfrac{x}{x}$ 18. $\dfrac{3x+1}{12}$

$=x-9$

$=\dfrac{2x+\left(\dfrac{1}{x}\right)x}{3x}=\dfrac{2x+1}{3x}$

19. $\dfrac{6}{2}\cdot\dfrac{3}{3}=\dfrac{18}{2}=9$ 20. 20 21. $\dfrac{\dfrac{1}{5}}{4}\cdot\dfrac{5}{5}=\dfrac{1}{20}$ 22. $\dfrac{x}{12}$

$\dfrac{3}{}$

23. $\dfrac{\left(\dfrac{1}{x}-\dfrac{2}{y}\right)}{\left(\dfrac{3}{xy}+7\right)}\cdot\dfrac{xy}{xy}=\dfrac{\left(\dfrac{1}{x}\right)xy-\left(\dfrac{2}{y}\right)xy}{\left(\dfrac{3}{xy}\right)xy+7xy}=\dfrac{y-2x}{3+7xy}$ 24. $\dfrac{6-48xy}{3x^2y+2xy^2}$

25. $\dfrac{\left(\sqrt{x+2}+\dfrac{3}{\sqrt{x+2}}\right)}{\sqrt{x+2}}\cdot\dfrac{\sqrt{x+2}}{\sqrt{x+2}}=\dfrac{\sqrt{x+2}\sqrt{x+2}+\left(\dfrac{3}{\sqrt{x+2}}\right)\sqrt{x+2}}{\sqrt{x+2}\sqrt{x+2}}$ 26. $\dfrac{3-x}{(x-2)\sqrt{4-x}}$

$=\dfrac{x+2+3}{x+2}=\dfrac{x+5}{x+2}$

27. $\dfrac{3x(x-1)^3-(x-1)^2}{(x-1)^6}=\dfrac{3x(x-1)-1}{(x-1)^4}=\dfrac{3x^2-3x-1}{(x-1)^4}$ 28. $\dfrac{4-x}{(x+1)^2}$

29. $\dfrac{3(x-5)+(x-5)^2}{(x-5)}=\dfrac{3+(x-5)}{1}=x-2$ 30. $9+x$ 31. $\dfrac{-6(x^2-7)}{7-x^2}=\dfrac{--6(7-x^2)}{7-x^2}=6$

32. $\dfrac{1}{4}$ 33. $\dfrac{44y^3-3}{3-44y^3}=\dfrac{-(3-44y^3)}{3-44y^3}=-1$ 34. -1 35. ∞ 36. ∞ 37. ∞

38. ∞ 39. 0 40. 0 41. 0 42. 0 43. $-\infty$ 44. $-\infty$

45. $-9(\infty)=-\infty$ 46. $-\infty$ 47. $24(-\infty)=-\infty$ 48. $-\infty$ 49. indeterminate

50. indeterminate 51. indeterminate 52. indeterminate

53. $\dfrac{1}{4}$ of $\dfrac{1}{3}=\dfrac{1}{4}\cdot\dfrac{1}{3}=\dfrac{1}{12}$ 54. $\dfrac{1}{20}^{th}$

IIR2 MULTIPLICATION FACTS

Remember, we have the Commutative Law for Multiplication. That means we can rearrange the order of multiplication; e.g., (8)(12) has the same answer as (12)(8).

$(0)(0) = 0$

$(0)(1) = 0$	$(0)(2) = 0$	$(0)(3) = 0$	$(0)(4) = 0$	$(0)(5) = 0$	$(0)(6) = 0$
$(0)(7) = 0$	$(0)(8) = 0$	$(0)(9) = 0$	$(0)(10) = 0$	$(0)(11) = 0$	$(0)(12) = 0$
$(1)(1) = 1$	$(1)(2) = 2$	$(1)(3) = 3$	$(1)(4) = 4$	$(1)(5) = 5$	$(1)(6) = 6$
$(1)(7) = 7$	$(1)(8) = 8$	$(1)(9) = 9$	$(1)(10) = 10$	$(1)(11) = 11$	$(1)(12) = 12$
$(2)(1) = 2$	$(2)(2) = 4$	$(2)(3) = 6$	$(2)(4) = 8$	$(2)(5) = 10$	$(2)(6) = 12$
$(2)(7) = 14$	$(2)(8) = 16$	$(2)(9) = 18$	$(2)(10) = 20$	$(2)(11) = 22$	$(2)(12) = 24$
$(3)(1) = 3$	$(3)(2) = 6$	$(3)(3) = 9$	$(3)(4) = 12$	$(3)(5) = 15$	$(3)(6) = 18$
$(3)(7) = 21$	$(3)(8) = 24$	$(3)(9) = 27$	$(3)(10) = 30$	$(3)(11) = 33$	$(3)(12) = 36$
$(4)(1) = 4$	$(4)(2) = 8$	$(4)(3) = 12$	$(4)(4) = 16$	$(4)(5) = 20$	$(4)(6) = 24$
$(4)(7) = 28$	$(4)(8) = 32$	$(4)(9) = 36$	$(4)(10) = 40$	$(4)(11) = 44$	$(4)(12) = 48$
$(5)(1) = 5$	$(5)(2) = 10$	$(5)(3) = 15$	$(5)(4) = 20$	$(5)(5) = 25$	$(5)(6) = 30$
$(5)(7) = 35$	$(5)(8) = 40$	$(5)(9) = 45$	$(5)(10) = 50$	$(5)(11) = 55$	$(5)(12) = 60$
$(6)(1) = 6$	$(6)(2) = 12$	$(6)(3) = 18$	$(6)(4) = 24$	$(6)(5) = 30$	$(6)(6) = 36$
$(6)(7) = 42$	$(6)(8) = 48$	$(6)(9) = 54$	$(6)(10) = 60$	$(6)(11) = 66$	$(6)(12) = 72$
$(7)(1) = 7$	$(7)(2) = 14$	$(7)(3) = 21$	$(7)(4) = 28$	$(7)(5) = 35$	$(7)(6) = 42$
$(7)(7) = 49$	$(7)(8) = 56$	$(7)(9) = 63$	$(7)(10) = 70$	$(7)(11) = 77$	$(7)(12) = 84$
$(8)(1) = 8$	$(8)(2) = 16$	$(8)(3) = 24$	$(8)(4) = 32$	$(8)(5) = 40$	$(8)(6) = 48$

$(8)(7)=56$	$(8)(8)=64$	$(8)(9)=72$	$(8)(10)=80$	$(8)(11)=88$	$(8)(12)=96$
$(9)(1)=9$	$(9)(2)=18$	$(9)(3)=27$	$(9)(4)=36$	$(9)(5)=45$	$(9)(6)=54$
$(9)(7)=63$	$(9)(8)=72$	$(9)(9)=81$	$(9)(10)=90$	$(9)(11)=99$	$(9)(12)=108$
$10(1)=10$	$10(2)=20$	$10(3)=30$	$10(4)=40$	$10(5)=50$	$10(6)=60$
$10(7)=70$	$10(8)=80$	$10(9)=90$	$10(10)=100$	$10(11)=110$	$10(12)=120$
$11(1)=11$	$11(2)=22$	$11(3)=33$	$11(4)=44$	$11(5)=55$	$11(6)=66$
$11(7)=77$	$11(8)=88$	$11(9)=99$	$11(10)=110$	$11(11)=121$	$11(12)=132$
$12(1)=12$	$12(2)=24$	$12(3)=36$	$12(4)=48$	$12(5)=60$	$12(6)=72$
$12(7)=84$	$12(8)=96$	$11(12)=132$	$12(10)=120$	$12(11)=132$	$12(12)=144$

IIR2 MULTIPLICATION FACTS RUN

Do the problems below with out using a calculator. Try to do them with in three minutes.

1. $(2)(4) =$ _____ $(5)(9) =$ _____ $(0)(8) =$ _____ $(3)(9) =$ _____

2. $(1)(12) =$ _____ $(7)(4) =$ _____ $(5)(11) =$ _____ $(8)(4) =$ _____

3. $(3)(0) =$ _____ $(6)(5) =$ _____ $(4)(9) =$ _____ $(9)(2) =$ _____

4. $(8)(7) =$ _____ $(5)(5) =$ _____ $(10)(11) =$ _____ $(6)(4) =$ _____

5. $(9)(5) =$ _____ $(12)(3) =$ _____ $(6)(3) =$ _____ $(10)(5) =$ _____

6. $(2)(3) =$ _____ $(9)(9) =$ _____ $(12)(8) =$ _____ $(4)(3) =$ _____

7. $(12)(9) =$ _____ $(10)(3) =$ _____ $(8)(2) =$ _____ $(6)(0) =$ _____

8. $(5)(1) =$ _____ $(3)(3) =$ _____ $(2)(2) =$ _____ $(5)(7) =$ _____

9. $(6)(2) =$ _____ $(9)(6) =$ _____ $(7)(10) =$ _____ $(8)(5) =$ _____

10. $(11)(6) =$ _____ $(2)(12) =$ _____ $(3)(5) =$ _____ $(4)(4) =$ _____

11. $(7)(3) =$ _____ $(8)(8) =$ _____ $(9)(1) =$ _____ $(12)(11) =$ _____

12. $(6)(7) =$ _____ $(7)(2) =$ _____ $(8)(3) =$ _____ $(9)(10) =$ _____

13. $(11)(4) =$ _____ $(11)(11) =$ _____ $(4)(12) =$ _____ $(12)(7) =$ _____

14. $(7)(7) =$ _____ $(6)(8) =$ _____ $(5)(4) =$ _____ $(9)(8) =$ _____

15. $(12)(5) =$ _____ $(2)(5) =$ _____ $(6)(12) =$ _____ $(9)(7) =$ _____

IIR2 SOLUTIONS TO MULTIPLICATION FACTS RUN

Row 1	8	45	0	27
Row 2	12	28	55	32
Row 3	0	30	36	18
Row 4	56	25	110	24
Row 5	45	36	18	50
Row 6	6	81	96	12
Row 7	108	30	16	0
Row 8	5	9	4	35
Row 9	12	54	70	40
Row 10	66	24	15	16
Row 11	21	64	9	132
Row 12	42	14	24	90
Row 13	44	121	48	84
Row 14	49	48	20	72
Row 15	60	10	72	63

IIC3

Limits from Graphs

Sandra is climbing a mountain. She can see a flag at point *P* above her, but she cannot see past this point. She is attempting to reach the flag at point *P*. She expects to do so. Point *P*, the point she is aiming for, is the "limit" of her climb.

Sandra climbs closer and closer to the point on the mountain. As she moves forward, the terrain of the mountain forces her to move upward.

There are two dimensions in her ascent: forward and upward. Let *x* be the forward direction and *y* be the upward direction. Label the point *P* that Sandra is approaching (x_0, y_0). The outline of the mountain can be represented as the function $y = f(x)$. Sandra controls her forward direction, but the mountain controls her vertical direction.

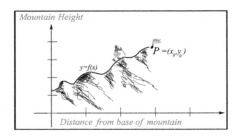

Said another way, as Sandra approaches the point (x_0, y_0), the approach of *x* to x_0 forces the approach of *y* to y_0. As Sandra's horizontal distance gets closer to x_0, her vertical distance necessarily gets closer to y_0. If we call Sandra's horizontal position *x* and her vertical distance *y*, we could say:

As *x* approaches x_0, then *y* approaches y_0.

Recall that another label for the height on $f(x)$ corresponding to x_0 is $f(x_0)$.

What will happen when Sandra reaches point *P*? She probably expects the trail to continue uninterrupted (continuously) …

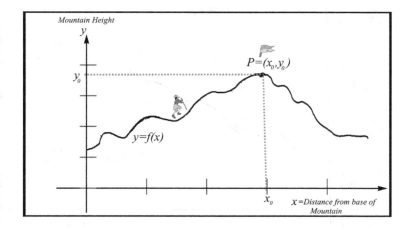

but there are other possibilities. Maybe an earthquake caused part of the mountain to give way at (x_0, y_0), dropping 50 feet and causing a discontinuity in the trail.

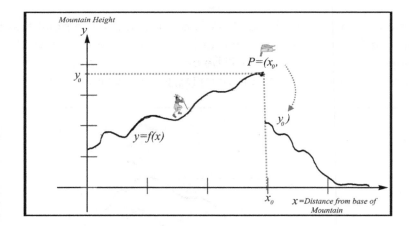

The vertical height y_0 is still where Sandra is aiming for if she climbs the mountain from the left, but it is much lower than that if she climbs the mountain from the right.

Perhaps the flag is marking the opening of an old mine shaft. As Sandra approaches her aim of x_0, the corresponding height $f(x_0)$ is no longer where she expects it to be. It is now much lower. If Sandra succeeds in reaching her aim of y_0, she will fall in. The height $f(x_0)$ is at the level of the bottom of the mine shaft. It is not the height y_0 that Sandra is aiming for and expects to reach. The height Sandra aims for, and expects to reach, would be called "the limit as x approaches x_0," which is y_0, but the actual height at x_0 is $f(x_0)$. *The limit can exist even when the actual point is in a different place.*

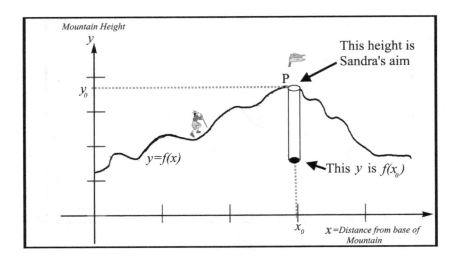

When the actual height on the mountain, $f(x_0)$, matches the height Sandra is expecting, y_0, then we say that $f(x)$ is continuous at x_0.

Suppose there is an invisible flying saucer hovering above the point that Sandra is aiming for. The flying saucer has extended a cylindrical beam above this point so that any object reaching that point will be beamed up to the spaceship. Little does Sandra know she will never reach the point (x_0, y_0) she is aiming for.

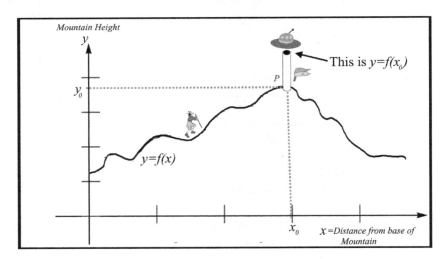

There is another discontinuity at $f(x_0)$ because it doesn't match Sandra's expected height, y_0.

Let's return to the fallen mountainside. Suppose Anders is climbing the mountain from the right.

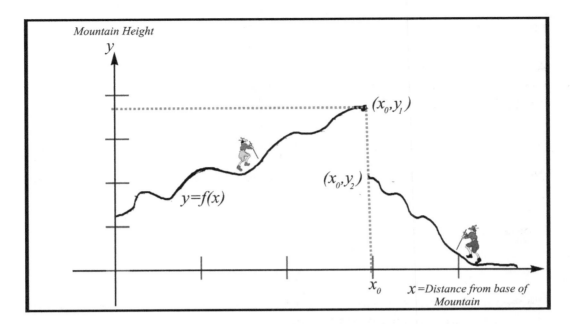

Sandra is approaching x_0 from the left, and Anders is approaching x_0 from the right. Though Sandra's expectation/limit is that she will reach the point (x_0, y_1), Anders' expectation/limit is that he will reach the point (x_0, y_2). The limit as x approaches x_0 from the left is different from the limit as x approaches x_0 from the right. When this occurs, we say the limit as x approaches x_0 does not exist.

As x approaches x_0 from the left, $f(x_0)$ is expected to be y_1, or Sandra's limit, but as x approaches x_0 from the right, $f(x_0)$ is expected to be y_2, or Anders' limit. If $y_1 \neq y_2$, then the limit does not exist. This is also a discontinuity, because there is a jump at $f(x_0)$. Discontinuities exist when there are holes, breaks, or jumps in $f(x)$.

When the limit of $f(x)$ from the left at x_0 is equal to the limit of $f(x)$ from the right at x_0, then the limit of $f(x)$ at x_0 exists and is equal to both the limit from the left and the limit from the right.

We will revisit the mountain climbers, but first we need to introduce some official mathematical notation and a procedure to determine the limit; i.e., the expected height (the y-value).

LIMIT NOTATION

As x approaches x_0 we watch the values (heights) of $f(x)$ to see if they approach some one value (some height). This is the concept of the limit in mathematics. In the mountain example, x approaches x_0 from the left. We write this limit as:

$$\lim_{x \to x_0^-} f(x)$$

We read it: The limit of $f(x)$ as x approaches x_0 from the left. Note that the superscript on x_0^- represents the direction "from the left." It is not a negative sign.

In other settings, x may approach x_0 from the right. We write this limit as:

$$\lim_{x \to x_0^+} f(x)$$

We read it: The limit of $f(x)$ as x approaches x_0 from the right. Note that the superscript on x_0^+ represents the direction "from the right."

It does not mean that x_0 is positive.

If x approaches x_0 without regard to direction, we simply write: $\lim_{x \to x_0} f(x)$.

Again, the limit of $f(x)$ at $x = x_0$ exists when the limit of $f(x)$ from the left at x_0 is equal to the limit of $f(x)$ from the right at x_0. We write this:
$$\lim_{x \to x_0^-} f(x) = \lim_{x \to x_0^+} f(x) = \lim_{x \to x_0} f(x).$$

We read $\lim_{x \to x_0} f(x) = L$: the limit of $f(x)$ as x approaches x_0 is L.

Note that L is a limit, i.e., a height. On a graph, L represents a y-value. Also remember that x_0 is a value of x.

LIMITS AS HEIGHTS ON GRAPHS

Consider the function $f(x)$ on the graph at right with a point on the x-axis designated as c.

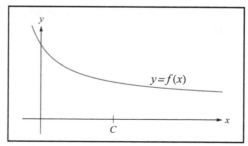

The point on the graph corresponding to the x-value c is $f(c)$. Thus, $f(c)$ represents a height, or a y-value, on the graph. We are going to give this y-value another name, L.

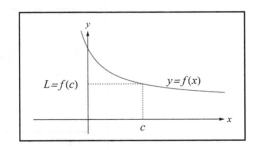

If you have the graph of a function, you can find a limit using the three-step process below.

Step 1:

Find x-values near x_0.

Step 2:

Find the corresponding y-values on the graph.

Step 3:

Find the height to which the y-values are getting closer and closer.

Example 1:

Consider the graph below. What is $\lim\limits_{x \to 2} f(x)$?

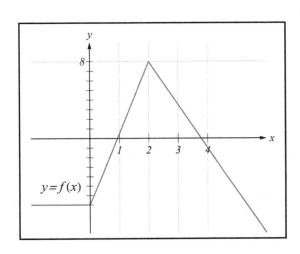

Step 1:

To find $\lim\limits_{x \to 2^-} f(x)$ we first note that the 'x's are approaching 2 from the left.

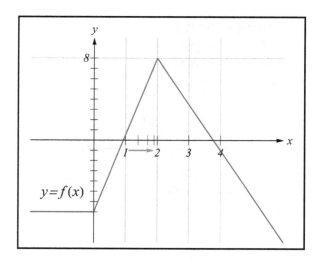

On the graph above, notice that the 'x's are zooming in toward the 2 from the left side.

Step 2:

We now trace each x upward or downward until we find its corresponding y-value on the graph.

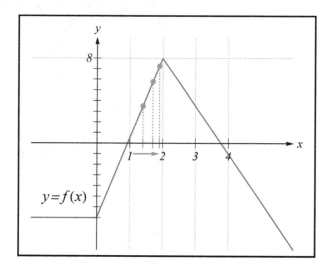

Step 3:

As the 'x's get closer and closer to 2 from the left side, the y-values are climbing up closer and closer to a height, or y-value, of 8. Imagine a tiny hiker climbing up the graph on the corresponding y-values. As the hiker's horizontal position gets closer and closer to 2, he expects to get closer and closer to a height of 8. In other words, as the value of x approaches 2 from the left, the hiker's expected height, or y-value, approaches 8.

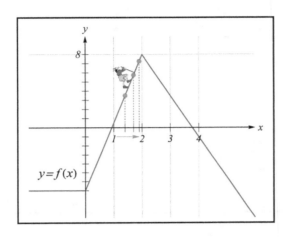

Now consider the limit as x approaches 2 from the right: $\lim\limits_{x \to 2^+} f(x)$.

Step 1:

The 'x's get closer and closer to 2 from the right; i.e., the 'x's are zooming in on 2 from the right.

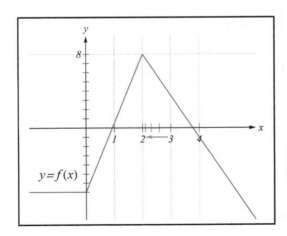

Step 2:

Find the corresponding y-values.

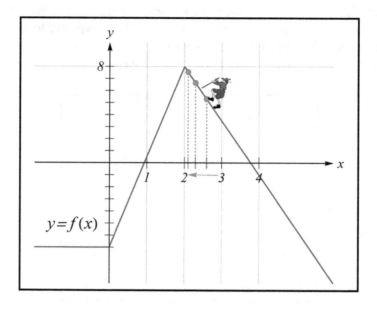

Step 3:

Once again, as the hiker's horizontal position approaches 2 from the right, he expects to reach a height of 8, or we could say: as the value of x approaches 2 from the right, the value of y approaches 8.

Since the $\lim\limits_{x \to 2^-} f(x)$ (which is 8) equals the $\lim\limits_{x \to 2^+} f(x)$ (which is 8 again), then we have

$$\lim_{x \to 2} f(x) = 8$$

Again in words, because the limit of $f(x)$, as x approaches 2 from the left equals 8, and the limit of $f(x)$ as x approaches 2 from the right, equals 8, then the limit of $f(x)$ as x approaches 2 (from both sides) equals 8.

In general, $\lim\limits_{x \to c} f(x)$ can exist only when

$$\lim_{x \to c^+} f(x) = \lim_{x \to c^-} f(x).$$

If $\lim\limits_{x \to c^+} f(x) = L$ and $\lim\limits_{x \to c^-} f(x) = L$, then $\lim\limits_{x \to c} f(x) = L$.

The limits will exist when the graph is *continuous*. A graph is continuous at x_0 if the expected height equals the actual height—that is, if:

$$\lim_{x \to x_0} f(x) = f(x_0)$$

Example 2:

Now consider the function below. Again find $\lim\limits_{x \to 2} f(x)$.

This graph is similar to the previous function, but it has a missing point at $x = 2$. The graph is not *continuous* at $x = 2$.

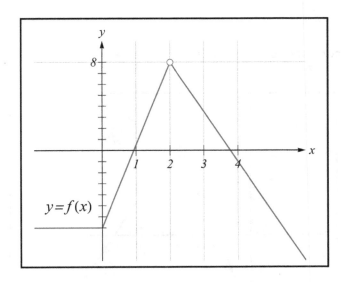

Once again, we start by finding the limit as x approaches 2 from the left; i.e., $\lim\limits_{x \to 2^-} f(x)$. Remember to use all three steps.

Step 1:

Find the x's.

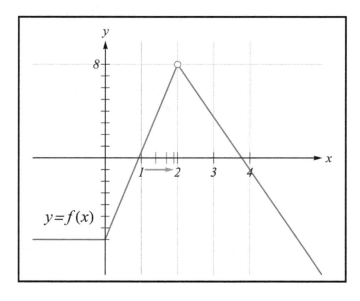

Step 2:

Find the corresponding y-values.

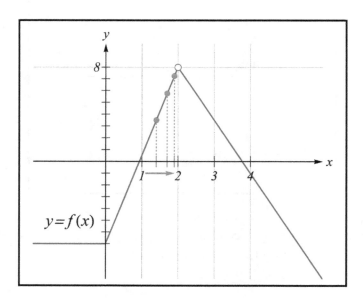

Step 3:

Find the height to which the hiker, *y*-values, are getting closer and closer.

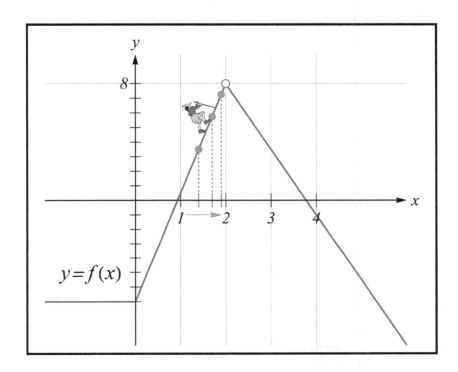

Note that even though there is a missing *y*-value corresponding to $x=2$, the hiker is still getting *closer and closer* to a height of 8, so we have a limit as *x* approaches 2 from the left; i.e., $\lim_{x \to 2^-} f(x)=8$.

If one were to ask, maybe the hiker, "What exactly is the height at $x=2$?" or in mathematical terms, "What is $f(2)$?," we would have to say $f(2)$ does not exist (DNE) because there is no corresponding *y*-value for an *x*-value of 2. *So even when $f(x_0)$ doesn't exist, there can still be a limit.*

Similarly, using the three steps, we could say $\lim_{x \to 2^+} f(x)=8$.

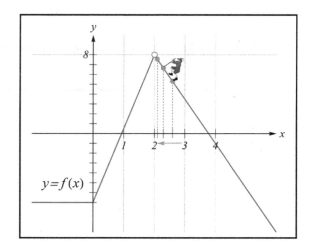

Finally, we can say that since $\lim\limits_{x\to 2^-} f(x)=8=\lim\limits_{x\to 2^+} f(x)$, then $\lim\limits_{x\to 2} f(x)=8$.

Example 3:

Now consider another similar graph. This one also has a discontinuity at $x=2$, but note that on the graph below $f(2)=10$, but what about $\lim\limits_{x\to 2} f(x)$? Again, we'll have to use the three steps and we must check both the limit as x approaches 2 from the left and the limit as x approaches 2 from the right; i.e., $\lim\limits_{x\to 2^-} f(x)$ and $\lim\limits_{x\to 2^+} f(x)$. If these are equal, then we will have a limit as x approaches 2; i.e., $\lim\limits_{x\to 2} f(x)$.

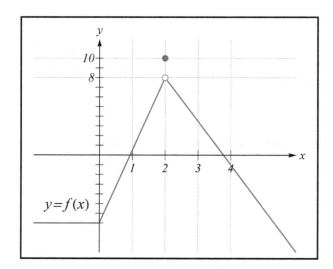

Step 1:

For $\lim\limits_{x \to 2^-} f(x)$, we find the x-values.

Step 2:

We find the corresponding y-values, or heights, on the graph.

Step 3:

We find the height that the hiker, or y-values, are getting closer and closer to.

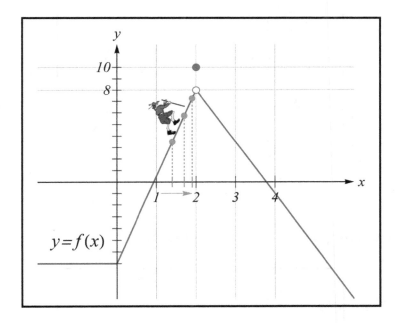

Note that our hiker is getting closer and closer to a height of 8. He can't fly. He must stay on the path arranged by the corresponding y-values as x approaches 2.

Similarly, as he approaches 2 from the right, the hiker gets closer and closer to a height of 8. That is, the corresponding y-values approach a height of 8. So even though $f(x) = 10$, we have:

$$\lim\limits_{x \to 2^-} f(x) = \lim\limits_{x \to 2^+} f(x) = 8. \text{ Therefore, } \lim\limits_{x \to 2} f(x) = 8$$

Example 4:

Using the graph above, let's find: $\lim\limits_{x \to 0} f(x)$. We'll start with $\lim\limits_{x \to 0^-} f(x)$.

Step 1:

Find the x's.

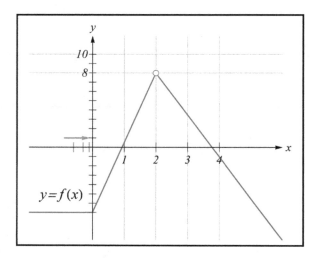

Step 2:

Find the corresponding y-values, or heights.

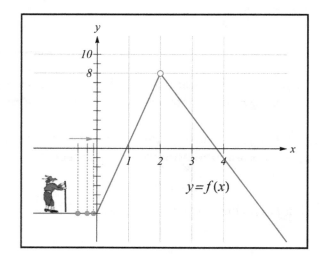

Step 3:

Since we are approaching 0 from the left, the corresponding y-values are getting closer and closer to, or actually staying at, a height of -6. The hiker expects to be at a height of -6 when he reaches the horizontal distance $x = 0$.

Next, we consider $\lim\limits_{x \to 0^+} f(x)$.

Step 1:

Find the x's.

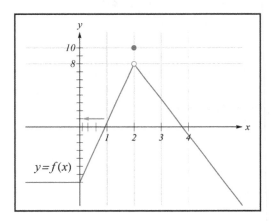

Step 2:

Find the corresponding y-values, or heights.

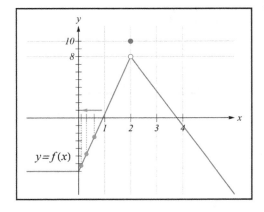

Step 3:

This time, a tiny hiker would approach a height of -6. Thus, $\lim\limits_{x \to 0^+} f(x) = -6$.

Since $\lim\limits_{x \to 0^-} f(x) = \lim\limits_{x \to 0^+} f(x) = -6$, we can conclude:

a. $\lim\limits_{x \to 0} f(x) = -6$,

b. we can also see that $f(0) = -6$.

Example 5:

For the same graph, what about $\lim\limits_{x \to \infty} f(x)$?

Step 1:

Infinity is the farthest distance to the right on the x-axis. We can't draw a line going to the right forever in order to find the x-values as x approaches infinity, but fortunately, we come equipped with minds that can imagine such a process. We'll just pinpoint some x's on their way toward ∞.

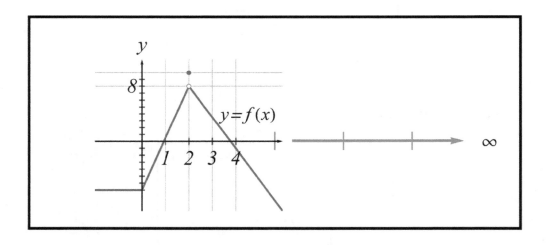

Step 2:

Next, we imagine where the corresponding *y*-values would be.

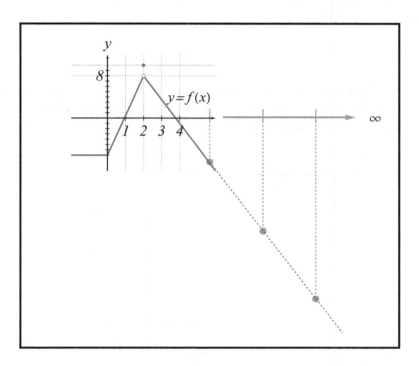

Step 3:

We can see that as *x* approaches infinity, the corresponding *y*-values are going down and down forever. They never level off or get closer and closer to one particular height, or *y*-value. We say: $\lim\limits_{x \to \infty} f(x) = -\infty$.

While " "$-\infty$" " is not an actual value, it does tell us some important information about the function $f(x)$. That is, that $f(x)$ drops forever as *x* approaches positive infinity.

Example 6:

What about $\lim\limits_{x \to -\infty} f(x)$?

Step 1:

Find the *x*-values. Again, we can only imagine them since we can't draw a line going forever to the left. We'll just pinpoint a few of the 'x's on their way to forever left.

Step 2:

We can also imagine the corresponding *y*-values. If $f(x)$ continues to be a horizontal line as *x* approaches $-\infty$, then the corresponding *y*-values will all lie on the line at a height of -6.

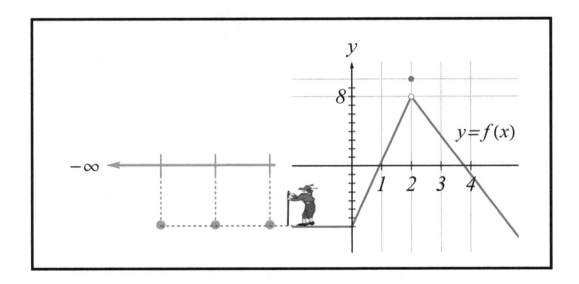

Step 3:

The corresponding *y*-values are getting closer and closer to, ... or actually staying at, a height of -6. The hiker expects to stay at a height of -6. Hence, $\lim\limits_{x \to -\infty} f(x) = -6$.

Remember: **Limits are always y-values—i.e., heights on a graph.**

INTRA-SECTION EXERCISES:

1. On the graph in Example 5, find $\lim\limits_{x \to 4} f(x)$.

2. For the function $f(x) = \dfrac{-3|x-2|}{x-2}$ (below), find $\lim\limits_{x \to 2} f(x)$.

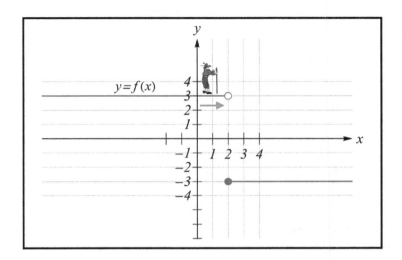

3. For the graph $f(x) = \dfrac{1}{x}$, find $\lim\limits_{x \to \infty} f(x)$.

4. For the graph $f(x) = \dfrac{1}{x}$, find $\lim\limits_{x \to -\infty} f(x)$.

5. For the graph $f(x) = \dfrac{1}{x}$, find $\lim\limits_{x \to 0^-} f(x)$.

6. For the graph $f(x) = \dfrac{1}{x}$, find $\lim\limits_{x \to 0^+} f(x)$.

7. For the graph $f(x) = \dfrac{1}{x}$, find $\lim\limits_{x \to 0} f(x)$.

Solutions

1. Using the three-step method, we find $\lim\limits_{x \to 4^-} f(x) = -1 = \lim\limits_{x \to 4^+} f(x)$. We conclude $\lim\limits_{x \to 4} f(x) = -1$

2. Using the three-step method, we find $\lim_{x \to 2^-} f(x) = 3$, but $\lim_{x \to 2^+} f(x) = -3$, so $\lim_{x \to 2} f(x)$ doesn't exist. (Graph below.)

Whenever there is a step in the graph at $x = c$, such as that at $x = 2$ below, the limit as x approaches c will not exist because the limit as x approaches c from the left will not equal the limit as x approaches c from the right.

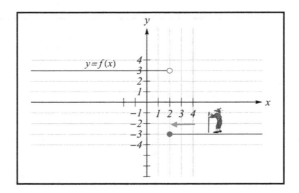

Note that though the limit could exist when the discontinuity was a hole, the limit does not exist when the discontinuity is a step. At steps, the limit as x approaches c from the right doesn't match the limit as x approaches c from the left.

3. The function $f(x) = \dfrac{1}{x}$ is graphed below. The x-axis and the y-axis are both asymptotes.

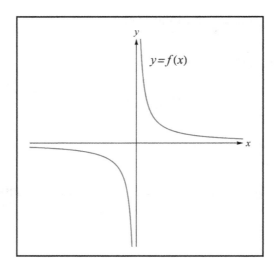

If we use the three steps, we can determine that $\lim\limits_{x\to\infty} \frac{1}{x} = 0$ because as the x's approach infinity going forever to the right, the corresponding y-values get closer and closer to a height, or y-value, of 0. The hiker expects to reach a height of 0. (See diagram below.)

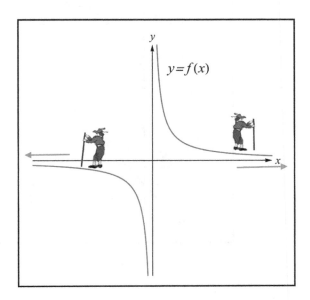

4. Similarly, if we use the three steps, we can determine that $\lim\limits_{x\to-\infty} \frac{1}{x} = 0$ because as the x's approach infinity going forever to the left, the corresponding y-values get closer and closer to a height, or y-value, of 0. The hiker expects to reach a height of 0. (See diagram above.)

5. Using the three-step method, we determine that $\lim\limits_{x\to 0^-} \frac{1}{x} = -\infty$ because the y-values continue to fall forever as x approaches 0 from the left.

6. Using the three-step method, we determine that $\lim\limits_{x\to 0^+} \frac{1}{x} = \infty$ because the y-values continue to rise forever as x approaches 0 from the right.

7. A hiker approaching 0 from the left would never meet a hiker approaching 0 from the right.

    Because $\lim\limits_{x\to 0^-} \frac{1}{x} \neq \lim\limits_{x\to 0^+} \frac{1}{x}$; that is: $-\infty \neq \infty$, we can say $\lim\limits_{x\to 0} \frac{1}{x}$ *doesn't exist.* We often abbreviate *does not exist* as DNE.

IIC3 LIMITS FROM GRAPHS EXERCISES

For numbers 1)–9), use the graph at right.

1. $\lim\limits_{x \to 3^-} f(x)$

2. $\lim\limits_{x \to 3^+} f(x)$

3. $\lim\limits_{x \to 3} f(x)$

4. $f(3)$

5. $\lim\limits_{x \to \infty} f(x)$

6. $\lim\limits_{x \to -\infty} f(x)$

7. $\lim\limits_{x \to 0^-} f(x)$

8. $\lim\limits_{x \to 0^+} f(x)$ 19–23

9. $\lim\limits_{x \to 0} f(x)$

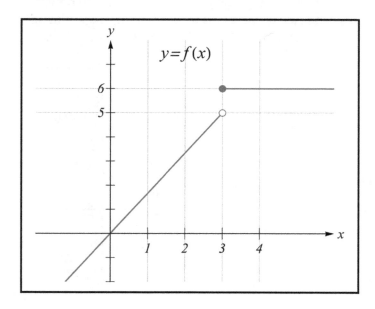

For numbers 10)–14), use the graph at right.

10. $\lim\limits_{x \to \infty} f(x)$

11. $\lim\limits_{x \to -\infty} f(x)$

12. $\lim\limits_{x \to 0^+} f(x)$

13. $\lim\limits_{x \to 0^-} f(x)$

14. $\lim\limits_{x \to 0} f(x)$

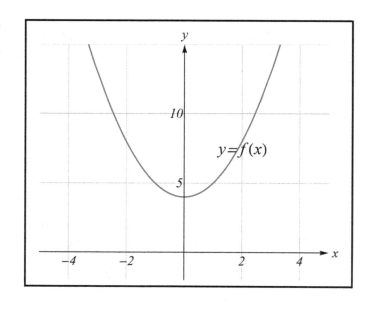

For numbers 15)–21), use the graph at right.

15. $\lim\limits_{x \to 4^-} f(x)$

16. $\lim\limits_{x \to 4^+} f(x)$

17. $\lim\limits_{x \to 4} f(x)$

18. $\lim\limits_{x \to 0^-} f(x)$

19. $\lim\limits_{x \to 0^+} f(x)$

20. $\lim\limits_{x \to 0} f(x)$

21. $\lim\limits_{x \to \infty} f(x)$

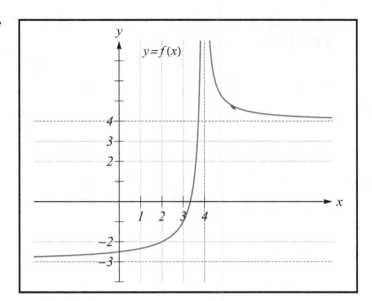

For numbers 22)–29), use the graph at right.

22. $\lim\limits_{x \to -2^+} f(x)$

23. $\lim\limits_{x \to -2^-} f(x)$

24. $\lim\limits_{x \to -2} f(x)$

25. $f(-2)$

26. $\lim\limits_{x \to 0} f(x)$

27. $\lim\limits_{x \to \infty} f(x)$

28. $\lim\limits_{x \to -\infty} f(x)$

29. $\lim\limits_{x \to 2} f(x)$

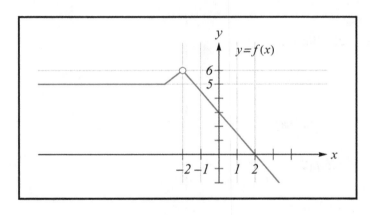

For numbers 30)–35), use the graph at right.

30. $\lim\limits_{x \to 2^+} f(x)$

31. $\lim\limits_{x \to 2^-} f(x)$

32. $\lim\limits_{x \to 2} f(x)$

33. $f(2)$

34. $\lim\limits_{x \to -\infty} f(x)$

35. $\lim\limits_{x \to \infty} f(x)$

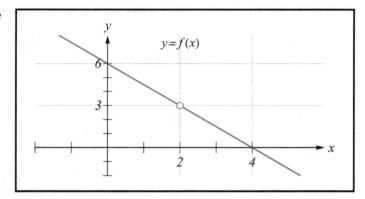

For numbers 36)–43), use the graph at right.

36. $\lim\limits_{x \to 2^-} f(x)$

37. $\lim\limits_{x \to 2^+} f(x)$

38. $\lim\limits_{x \to 2} f(x)$

39. $f(2)$

40. $\lim\limits_{x \to 3} f(x)$

41. $\lim\limits_{x \to -\infty} f(x)$

42. $\lim\limits_{x \to \infty} f(x)$

43. $f(3)$

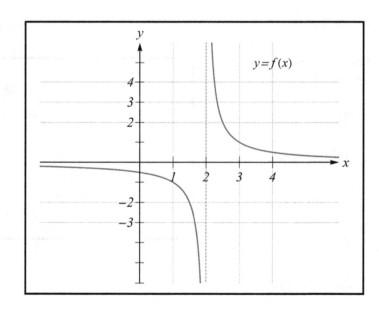

For numbers 44)–46), use the graph at right.

44. Find $\lim\limits_{x \to c^+} f(x)$ for $c = 3$.

45. Find $\lim\limits_{x \to c^-} f(x)$ for $c = 3$.

46. Find $\lim\limits_{x \to c} f(x)$ for $c = 3$.

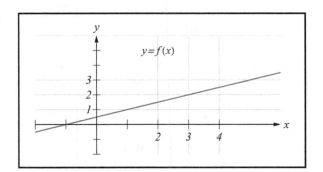

For numbers 47)–49), use the graph at right.

47. Find $\lim\limits_{x \to c^+} f(x)$ for $c = 4$.

48. Find $\lim\limits_{x \to c^-} f(x)$ for $c = 4$.

49. Find $\lim\limits_{x \to c} f(x)$ for $c = 4$.

50. Find the value of $f(c)$ at $c = 4$.

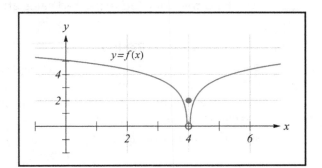

For numbers 51)–54), use the graph at right.

51. Find $\lim\limits_{x \to c^+} f(x)$ for $c = 2$.

52. Find $\lim\limits_{x \to c^-} f(x)$ for $c = 2$.

53. Find $\lim\limits_{x \to c} f(x)$ for $c = 2$.

54. Find the value of $f(c)$ at $c = 2$.

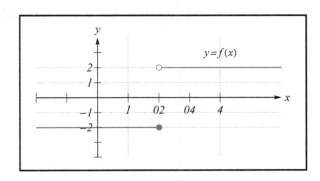

55. The Suther Company has several subsidiaries. Its projected total sales is represented by the graph at right. In 2006 a tsunami wiped out several of its stores in Indonesia.

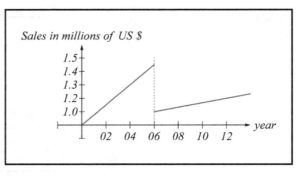

Sales in millions of US $

a. Find the expected sales for 2006, i.e., $\lim\limits_{x \to 2006^-} f(x)$.

b. Find the adjusted expected sales after the tsunami, i.e., $\lim\limits_{x \to 2006^+} f(x)$.

56. The Cuther Family Bank was experiencing rapid growth until its security was compromised in 2003. Its projected customer growth is represented by the graph at right.

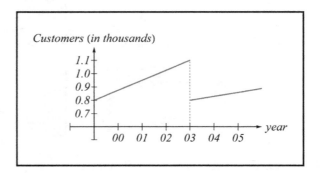

Customers (in thousands)

a. Find the expected number of customers for 2003; i.e., $\lim\limits_{x \to 2003^-} f(x)$.

b. Find the adjusted expected number of customers after the security breach, i.e., $\lim\limits_{x \to 2003^+} f(x)$.

IIC3 LIMITS FROM GRAPHS SOLUTIONS TO EXERCISES

1. 5   2. 6   3. DNE   4. 6   5. 6   6. $-\infty$

7. 0   8. 0   9. 0   10. ∞ 11. ∞ 12. 4

13. 4   14. 4   15. ∞ 16. ∞ 17. ∞ 18. -2.5

19. -2.5 20. -2.5 21. 4   22. 6   23. 6   24. 6

25. DNE   26. 3   27. $-\infty$ 28. 5   29. 0   30. 3

31. 3   32. 3   33. DNE   34. ∞ 35. $-\infty$ 36. $-\infty$

37. ∞ 38. DNE   39. DNE   40. 1   41. 0   42. 0

43. 1   44. 2   45. 2   46. 2   47. 0   48. 0

49. 0   50. 2   51. 2   52. -2 53. DNE   54. -2

55. a. $1.4 million
    b. $1.0 million

56. a. 1.1 thousand
    b. 0.8 thousand

IIC4

Limits from Algebraic Expressions

If we have the graph of a function $f(x)$, then we know how to find the limit as x approaches a given number. Suppose we have only the equation of the function, such as:

$$y = f(x) = 3x^2 - 5x + 7.$$

How would we find the limit of this $f(x)$ as x approaches 2? Or put another way, as x gets closer and closer to 2, what is our expected value of y? (Recall that on a graph, the y-value is the height.) We need to begin by examining two basic theorems and some properties of limits.

TWO BASIC THEOREMS

BASIC THEOREM A:
The limit of a constant is the constant, or in mathematical notation:

$$\lim_{x \to c} b = b$$

In this case, $f(x)$ is equal to the constant b.

Suppose we let $b = f(x) = 3$, or in other words, $y = 3$. The function is the graph of a horizontal line.

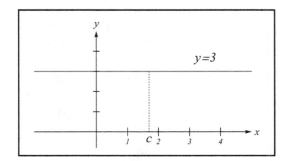

Recalling the three steps for finding limits, we consider the points approaching *c* from the left.

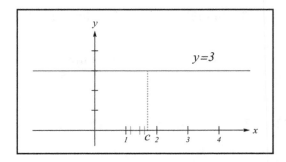

Next, we find the corresponding points on $f(x) = y$.

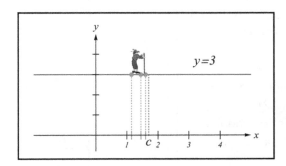

As the values of *x* approach *c* from the left, we expect the *y*-values to remain at a height of 3.

The same is true as we approach *c* from the right. The *y*-values remain at a height of 3. So

$$\lim_{x \to c} 3 = 3.$$

It doesn't matter what c we use if the graph of $f(x)$ is a horizontal line. When $f(x)$ equals a constant, such as $f(x)=3$, the height on the line will equal the constant everywhere.

For any c, $\lim_{x \to c} b = b$ or in words: the limit of a number is the number.

Therefore: $\lim_{x \to 11} 5 = 5$, and $\lim_{x \to 1.2} 83 = 83$, and $\lim_{x \to 2} 83 = 83$, and $\lim_{x \to -17} \sqrt{3} = \sqrt{3}$.

INTRA-SECTION EXERCISES:

Find the limits.

1. $\lim_{x \to 12} 93$

2. $\lim_{x \to -3} 93$

3. $\lim_{x \to \pi} 93$

4. $\lim_{x \to 12} \pi$

5. $\lim_{x \to -7.7} 21$

6. $\lim_{x \to 4} 2.8$

7. $\lim_{x \to 4} 0.33$

8. $\lim_{x \to 4} 114$

Solutions

1. 93   2. 93   3. 93   4. π 5. 21   6. 2.8   7. 0.33   8. 114

Our second basic theorem is: As x approaches c, the limit of x is c, or $\lim_{x \to c} x = c$. This time, our function $f(x)$ equals x, or $y=x$. The graph is at right.

Notice that this is the line that contains the points (1,1), (2,2), (11,11), (−4, −4), etc. Every point on the line has a y-value equal to its x-value.

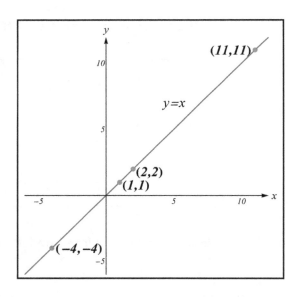

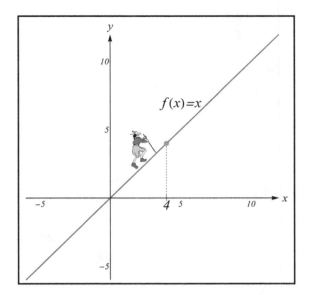

Consider an x-value of 4. As we approach 4 from the left, we expect to reach a height of 4. If we approach 4 from the right, we also expect to reach a height of 4.

If we were to choose an x-value of 8, we would expect a corresponding height of 8, or if we choose an x-value of −3, we would expect a corresponding height of −3, all because $f(x) = y = x$.

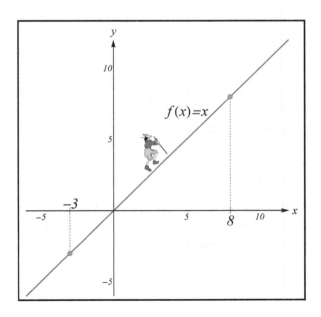

Once again, as x approaches c, the limit of $f(x)=c$.

BASIC THEOREM B:

The limit of x is c, or in mathematical notation:

$$\lim_{x \to c} x = c.$$

INTRA-SECTION EXERCISES:

"Trick Question"

Find the limits.

9. $\displaystyle\lim_{x \to 5} x$ 10. $\displaystyle\lim_{x \to 1.4} x$ 11. $\displaystyle\lim_{x \to e} x$ 12. $\displaystyle\lim_{x \to 7} 12$

Solutions

9. 5   10. 1.4   11. e 12. 12

MORE PROPERTIES OF LIMITS

Here are some other properties of limits.

a. $\displaystyle\lim_{x \to b} f(x) + \lim_{x \to b} g(x) = \lim_{x \to b}[f(x)+g(x)]$

We could say: as x approaches b, the sum of the limits is the limit of the sums.

b. $\displaystyle\lim_{x \to b} f(x) \cdot \lim_{x \to b} g(x) = \lim_{x \to b}[f(x)g(x)]$

We could say: as x approaches b, the product of the limits is the limit of the product.

c. $\displaystyle\lim_{x \to b} cf(x) = c\lim_{x \to b} f(x)$

As x approaches b, the limit of a constant times a function equals the constant times the limit of the function, or we could just remember that it's legal to pull the constant to the outside of the limit.

d. $\dfrac{\lim\limits_{x\to b} f(x)}{\lim\limits_{x\to b} g(x)}=\lim\limits_{x\to b}\dfrac{f(x)}{g(x)}$; *if* $\lim\limits_{x\to b} g(x)\neq 0$

As *x* approaches *b*, the quotient of limits is the limit of the quotient.

e. $\lim\limits_{x\to b}[f(x)^n]=[\lim\limits_{x\to b} f(x)]^n$

We could say: as *x* approaches *b*, the limit of the power of the function is the power of the limit, ... or we could remember that it's okay to pass the limit to the inside function.

EVALUATING THE LIMIT OF A POLYNOMIAL

So how do we evaluate the limit of a function; for example, how do we find:

$$\lim_{x\to 4}(x^2+3x-5)?$$

First, we use Property C to divide the limit of the sum into the sum of limits.

$$\lim_{x\to 4}(x^2+3x-5)=\lim_{x\to 4}x^2+\lim_{x\to 4}3x-\lim_{x\to 4}5$$

Next, we use Property G on the first term to shift the exponent to the outside.

$$=[\lim_{x\to 4}x]^2+\lim_{x\to 4}3x-\lim_{x\to 4}5$$

For the second term, we can use Property E to pull the constant to the outside.

$$=[\lim_{x\to 4}x]^2+3\lim_{x\to 4}x-\lim_{x\to 4}5$$

Now we can use Basic Theorem B to find the limits when $f(x)=x$.

$$4^2+3(4)-\lim_{x\to 4}5$$

Finally, we use Basic Theorem A to find the limit of the constant 5. (Drum roll, please.)

$$4^2+3(4)-5$$

$$=16+12-5$$

$$=23$$

But wait! "$4^2+3(4)-5$" looks like we simply substituted $x=4$ into $\lim\limits_{x\to 4}(x^2+3x-5)$. Surprise!!

We have actually used Basic Theorems A and B, plus Properties C, E, and G, but the process turns out to look like substitution.

For functions that yield graphs without holes or jumps—that is, continuous graphs—the limit is equal to the function value, a point where the function is continuous.

For example, the limit as x approaches 2 for the function $f(x)=3+2x-x^2$, or $\lim\limits_{x\to 2}3+2x-x^2$ is simply $f(2)=3+2(2)-2^2=3$.

For continuous functions,

$$\lim_{x\to b}f(x)=f(b).$$

Example 1:

$$\lim_{x\to 5}2x=2(5)=10$$

Example 2:

$$\lim_{x\to 2}\frac{3+2x}{x-3}=\frac{3+2(2)}{2-3}=\frac{7}{-1}=-7$$

Example 3:

$$\lim_{x\to 2}\sqrt{4+2x-x^2}=\sqrt{4+2(2)-2^2}=\sqrt{4+4-4}=\sqrt{4}=2$$

INTRA-SECTION EXERCISES:

Find the limits.

13. $\lim\limits_{x\to 1}\dfrac{x^2-4x+2}{3-x}$

14. $\lim\limits_{x\to -3}x^2-2x+7$

15. $\lim\limits_{x\to 0}\dfrac{4x^2-4x+2}{4-x}$

Solutions

13. $\dfrac{1^2-4(1)+2}{3-1}=\dfrac{-1}{2}$

14. $(-3)^2-2(-3)+7=22$

15. $\dfrac{4(0^2)-4(0)+2}{4-0}=\dfrac{2}{4}=\dfrac{1}{2}$

EVALUATING THE LIMITS AT POINTS OF DISCONTINUITY CAUSED BY DIVISION BY ZERO

Sometimes the simple evaluation of the expression in the limit does not yield a number.

For example, consider $\lim\limits_{x \to 3} \dfrac{x^2 - 9}{x - 3}$.

A simple substitution gives us: $\dfrac{3^2 - 9}{3 - 3} = \dfrac{0}{0}$. This is not a number; $\dfrac{0}{0}$ is an indeterminate form.

However, in this case, we can algebraically manipulate the expression into an expression that can be evaluated.

$$\lim_{x \to 3} \frac{x^2 - 9}{x - 3} = \lim_{x \to 3} \frac{(x+3)(x-3)}{x-3} = \lim_{x \to 3} x + 3 = 3 + 3 = 6$$

If a polynomial expression $P(x)$ evaluates to zero at c then $x - c$ is a factor of $P(x)$.

Hence, the indeterminate form $\dfrac{0}{0}$ tells us that the numerator has a factor of $x - 3$ and the denominator has a factor of $x - 3$. The indeterminate form $\dfrac{0}{0}$ tells us what to factor out and then reduce.

If you have an inquiring mind, at this point you might be wondering about the difference between the graphs $f(x) = \dfrac{x^2 - 9}{x - 3}$ and $f(x) = x + 3$. Examine both graphs below.

You'll notice that the first graph has a hole at $x = 3$. Even though $f(3)$ doesn't exist, we still have a limit at $x = 3$.

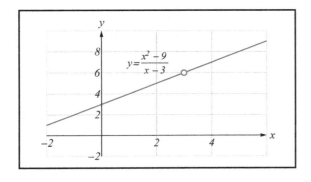

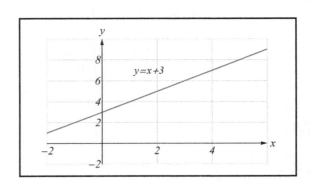

Important Point: If a limit of the form $\lim\limits_{x \to c} \dfrac{f(x)}{g(x)}$ evaluates to the indeterminant form $\dfrac{0}{0}$, then $x - c$ is a common factor of $f(x)$ and $g(x)$. Reduce the fraction and try evaluation again.

Example 4:

$\lim\limits_{x \to 0} \dfrac{x^2}{x^2}$ A simple substitution gives us $\dfrac{0}{0}$, but this isn't an answer. If we reduce $\dfrac{x^2}{x^2}$, we will have: $\lim\limits_{x \to 0} \dfrac{x^2}{x^2} = \lim\limits_{x \to 0} 1 = 1$

INTRA-SECTION EXERCISES:

Find the limits.

16. $\lim\limits_{x \to -1} \dfrac{x^2 + 5x + 4}{3x + 3}$ 17. $\lim\limits_{x \to 6} \dfrac{4x^2}{x^2}$ 18. $\lim\limits_{x \to -2} \dfrac{2 + x}{3x^2 + 5x - 2}$

Solutions

16. $\lim\limits_{x \to -1} \dfrac{(x+4)(x+1)}{3(x+1)} = \lim\limits_{x \to -1} \dfrac{x+4}{3} = \dfrac{-1+4}{3} = 1$ 17. $\lim\limits_{x \to 6} 4 = 4$

18. $\lim\limits_{x \to -2} \dfrac{x+2}{(3x-1)(x+2)} = \lim\limits_{x \to -2} \dfrac{1}{3x-1} = \dfrac{1}{3(-2)-1} = \dfrac{1}{-7}$

LIMITS RESULTING IN INFINITIES; DIVISION BY ZERO WHEN THE NUMERATOR IS NOT ZERO

Consider the function $g(x) = \dfrac{3}{14(x-1)^2}$.

The function g is not defined at $x = 1$. The graph of $g(x)$ is at right.

If we attempt to evaluate $g(x)$ at $x = 1$, we get $\dfrac{3}{14(1-1)^2} = \dfrac{3}{0}$. Unfortunately, $\dfrac{3}{0}$ is not a number.

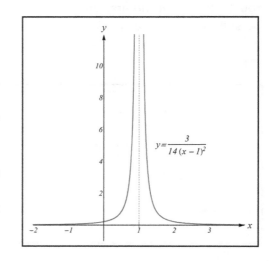

For x values near 1, such as $x = 1.0001$, we find

that $g(x) = g(1.0001) = \dfrac{3}{14(1.0001-1)^2} \approx 2.14 \times 10^7$

is a very large number.

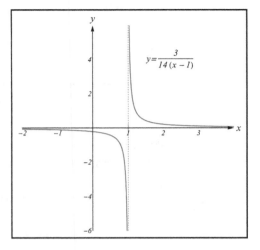

Conceptually, the limit of $\dfrac{3}{0}$ is ∞, or $\lim\limits_{x \to 1} g(x) = \infty$.

The function $G(x) = \dfrac{3}{14(x-1)}$ is also not defined at $x = 1$

and has the graph at right. Now $G(x)$ becomes both large negatively and large positively near $x = 1$, so $\lim\limits_{x \to 1} G(x)$ does not exist.

But $\lim\limits_{x \to 1^-} G(x)$ and $\lim\limits_{x \to 1^+} G(x)$ do exist:

$\lim\limits_{x \to 1^-} G(x) = -\infty$ and $\lim\limits_{x \to 1^+} G(x) = \infty$.

Now let's think about it algebraically. Consider $\lim\limits_{x \to 1^+} \dfrac{3}{14(x-1)}$ once again. We know

that x is approaching 1 from the right. The numbers are getting closer and closer to

1, but they are all a little bigger than 1.

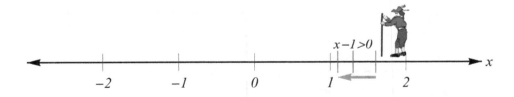

This makes $(x-1)$ a positive number, so the progression is approaching 0 through positive numbers. We will indicate this type of evaluation to zero by 0^+. Therefore,

$\lim\limits_{x \to 1^+} \dfrac{3}{14(x-1)} = \dfrac{3}{0^+}$ equals positive infinity, or ∞.

Now consider $\lim\limits_{x \to 1^-} \dfrac{3}{14(x-1)}$. This time, we know x is approaching 1 from the left. The

numbers are getting closer and closer to 1, but they are all a little smaller than 1.

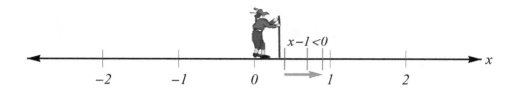

This makes $(x-1)$ a negative number, so the progression is approaching 0 through negative numbers. We will indicate this type of evaluation to zero by 0^-. Therefore,

$$\lim_{x\to 1^-}\frac{3}{14(x-1)}=\frac{3}{0^-}$$ equals negative infinity, or $-\infty$.

Example 5:

$$\lim_{x\to 5^+}\frac{4+x}{x-5}=\frac{4+5}{5-5}=\frac{9}{0^+}=\infty$$ because x approaches 5 from the right.

Example 6:

$$\lim_{x\to 5^-}\frac{4+x}{x-5}=\frac{4+5}{5-5}=\frac{9}{0^-}=-\infty$$ because x approaches 5 from the left.

Example 7:

$$\lim_{x\to 5}\frac{4+x}{x-5}=\frac{4+5}{5-5}=\frac{9}{0}$$ is undefined.

Sticky point coming up.

Example 8:

$$\lim_{x\to 5}\frac{4+x}{(x-5)^2}=\frac{4+5}{5-5}=\frac{9}{0^+}=\infty$$. Since the denominator is squared, it will always progress through positive numbers. Therefore, the limit is positive infinity. Check out the function's graph at right.

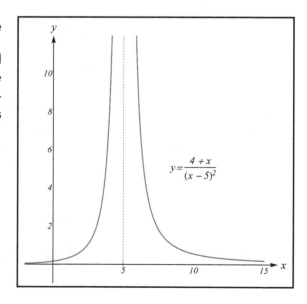

$$y=\frac{4+x}{(x-5)^2}$$

Important Point: If a limit of the form $\lim\limits_{x\to c}\dfrac{f(x)}{g(x)}$ evaluates to the form

$\dfrac{non-zero}{0}$, then $x-c$ is a factor of $g(x)$. Factor $g(x)=(x-c)^n G(x)$.

If n is even, $\lim\limits_{x\to c}\dfrac{f(x)}{g(x)}=\dfrac{f(c)}{G(c)}=\infty$. If n is odd, $\lim\limits_{x\to c^-}\dfrac{f(x)}{g(x)}=\dfrac{f(c)}{G(c)}=(-\infty)$,

$\lim\limits_{x\to c^+}\dfrac{f(x)}{g(x)}=\dfrac{f(c)}{G(c)}=\infty$, and $\lim\limits_{x\to c}\dfrac{f(x)}{g(x)}$ is undefined.

INTRA-SECTION EXERCISES:

Find the limits, if they exist.

19. $\lim\limits_{x\to 0^-}\dfrac{2}{x^3}$ 20. $\lim\limits_{x\to 0^+}\dfrac{2}{x^3}$ 21. $\lim\limits_{x\to 0}\dfrac{2}{x^3}$ 22. $\lim\limits_{x\to 0}\dfrac{x^2}{x^4}$

Solutions

19. $-\infty$ 20. ∞ 21. The limit does not exist.

22. ∞ The denominator is squared, hence always positive.

LIMIT APPLICATION

Suppose the cost to prevent 100% of the illegal transportation of drugs across the border in

a large country can be represented by the equation $C(p)=\dfrac{\$830,000p}{100-p}$ for $0\le p<100$.

To prevent 80% of the illegal drugs, it will cost $C(80)=\dfrac{\$830,000(80)}{100-80}=\$3,320,000$.

To determine the cost to prevent 100% of the drugs, we find the limit as p approaches 100.

$$\lim\limits_{p\to 100^-}\dfrac{\$830,000p}{100-p}=\lim\limits_{p\to 100^-}\dfrac{\$830,000p}{-(p-100)}=\dfrac{\$830,000(100)}{-(100-100)}=\dfrac{\$83,000,000}{-0^-}=\infty$$

IIC4 LIMITS FROM ALGEBRAIC EXPRESSIONS EXERCISES

Find the limits if they exist.

1. $\lim\limits_{x\to 0} 6$

2. $\lim\limits_{x\to 5} 7$

3. $\lim\limits_{x\to 0}\dfrac{3x}{x}$

4. $\lim\limits_{x\to 0}\dfrac{x}{4x}$

5. $\lim\limits_{x\to 3}\dfrac{x}{4x^2}$

6. $\lim\limits_{x\to 3}\dfrac{x^2}{6x}$

7. $\lim\limits_{x\to 0}\dfrac{x^2}{4x^2}$

8. $\lim\limits_{x\to 0}\dfrac{2.3x^2}{x^2}$

9. $\lim\limits_{x\to 3}\dfrac{2x^2}{6x}$

10. $\lim\limits_{x\to 1}\dfrac{5x}{x^2}$

11. $\lim\limits_{x\to 0^+}\dfrac{x}{4x^2}$

12. $\lim\limits_{x\to 0^+}\dfrac{7x}{x^2}$

13. $\lim\limits_{x\to 0^-}\dfrac{9x}{2x^2}$

14. $\lim\limits_{x\to 0^-}\dfrac{5.3x}{x^2}$

15. $\lim\limits_{x\to 1}\dfrac{5-x}{x+1}$

16. $\lim\limits_{x\to -1}\dfrac{x+7}{x-1}$

17. $\lim\limits_{x\to 2}\dfrac{5-x^2}{x+1}$

18. $\lim\limits_{x\to 2}\dfrac{5-x}{x^2+1}$

19. $\lim\limits_{x\to 2}\dfrac{x^2-4}{x-2}$

20. $\lim\limits_{x\to 3}\dfrac{x^2-9}{x-3}$

21. $\lim\limits_{x\to -3}\dfrac{x+3}{x^2-x-12}$

22. $\lim\limits_{x\to -4}\dfrac{x+4}{x^2-x-20}$

23. $\lim\limits_{x\to 3}\dfrac{x^2-9}{x^2+7x+12}$

24. $\lim\limits_{x\to 4}\dfrac{x^2-16}{x^2+7x+12}$

25. $\lim\limits_{x\to 4}\dfrac{x^2-7x+12}{x-4}$

26. $\lim\limits_{x\to 5}\dfrac{x^2-8x+15}{x-5}$

27. $\lim\limits_{x\to 2}\sqrt{4+2x-x^2}$

28. $\lim\limits_{x\to 3}\sqrt{4+3x-x^2}$

29. $\lim\limits_{x\to 7}\dfrac{4x^2-21x-49}{x-7}$

30. $\lim\limits_{x\to 7}\dfrac{3x^2-14x-49}{x-7}$

31. $\lim\limits_{x\to -3}\dfrac{x^2-7x-30}{x+3}$

32. $\lim\limits_{x\to -4}\dfrac{3x^2+7x-20}{x+4}$

33. A refinery determines its cost to add equipment that will remove p percent of the pollutants it emits is represented by the function $C(p)=\$20{,}000+\dfrac{\$2150p}{100-p}$.

   a. How much will it cost to remove 50% of the pollutants?
   b. How much will it cost to remove 100% of the pollutants?

34. A police department hires a consultant to determine how many officers are needed to eliminate all speeding in the district. The consultant determines the number of officers, $N(p)$, can be modeled by the function $N(p)=\dfrac{24p}{100-p}$, where p equals the percent reduction in speeding, and N equals the number of officers.

   a. How many officers will be needed to eliminate 80% of the speeding?
   b. How many officers will be needed to eliminate 100% of the speeding?

IIC4 LIMITS FROM ALGEBRAIC EXPRESSIONS SOLUTIONS TO EXERCISES

1. 6

2. 7

3. $\lim\limits_{x \to 0} \dfrac{3x}{x} = \lim\limits_{x \to 0} 3 = 3$

4. $\dfrac{1}{4}$

5. $\lim\limits_{x \to 3} \dfrac{x}{4x^2} = \lim\limits_{x \to 3} \dfrac{1}{4x} = \dfrac{1}{4(3)} = \dfrac{1}{12}$

6. $\dfrac{1}{2}$

7. $\lim\limits_{x \to 0} \dfrac{1}{4} = \dfrac{1}{4}$

8. 2.3

9. $\lim\limits_{x \to 3} \dfrac{2x}{6} = \lim\limits_{x \to 3} \dfrac{x}{3} = \dfrac{3}{3} = 1$

10. 5

11. $\lim\limits_{x \to 0^+} \dfrac{1}{4x} = \dfrac{1}{4(0)} = \dfrac{1}{0^+} = \infty$

12. ∞

13. $\lim\limits_{x \to 0^-} \dfrac{9}{2x} = \dfrac{9}{2(0)} = \dfrac{9}{0^-} = -\infty$

14. $-\infty$

15. $\dfrac{5-1}{1+1} = \dfrac{4}{2} = 2$

16. -3

17. $\dfrac{5-2^2}{2+1} = \dfrac{1}{3}$

18. $\dfrac{3}{5}$

19. $\lim\limits_{x \to 2} \dfrac{(x+2)(x-2)}{x-2} = 2+2 = 4$

20. 6

21. $\lim\limits_{x \to -3} \dfrac{x+3}{(x-4)(x+3)} = \dfrac{1}{-3-4} = \dfrac{-1}{7}$

22. $\dfrac{-1}{9}$

23. $\lim\limits_{x \to 3} \dfrac{(x+3)(x-3)}{(x+3)(x+4)} = \dfrac{3-3}{3+4} = \dfrac{0}{4} = 0$

24. 0

25. $\lim\limits_{x \to 4} \dfrac{(x-3)(x-4)}{x-4} = 4-3 = 1$

26. 2

27. $\sqrt{4+2(2)-2^2} = \sqrt{4} = 2$

28. 2

29. $\lim\limits_{x \to 7} \dfrac{(x-7)(4x+7)}{x-7} = \dfrac{4(7)+7}{1} = 35$

30. 28

31. $\lim\limits_{x \to -3} \dfrac{(x-10)(x+3)}{x+3} = -13$

32. -17

33. a. $C(50) = \$20{,}000 + \dfrac{2150(50)}{100-50} = \$20{,}000 + \$2150 = \$22{,}150$

    b. $C(100) = \lim\limits_{p \to 100^-} \$20{,}000 + \dfrac{\$2150p}{100-p} = \$20{,}000 + \$\dfrac{2150(100)}{100-100} = \$20{,}000 + \$\dfrac{2150(100)}{0^+}$

    $= \$20{,}000 + \infty = \infty$ i.e., it will approach an infinite amount of dollars to remove 100% of the pollutants.

34. a. 96 officers

    b. It will take an infinite number of officers to eliminate all speeding.

IIC5

Limits at Infinity, Continuity

We have seen functions $f(x)$ that tend to become large without bound near a value of x, like the one at right. As x approaches 3, the function climbs without bound. We assigned the concept of infinity to this situation, $\lim_{x \to 3} f(x) = \infty$.

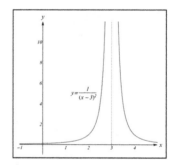

Now let x become large without bound, as $x \to \infty$, and look at the tendency of $f(x)$. In other words, let's examine $\lim_{x \to \infty} f(x)$.

Consider the polynomial $f(x) = 2x^3$.

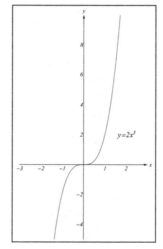

As x grows without bound, $f(x)$ grows without bound, or $\lim_{x \to \infty} f(x) = \lim_{x \to \infty} 2x^3 = \infty$.

The polynomial $f(x) = x^3 - 2x + 5$ behaves similarly as x approaches infinity. It grows without bound.

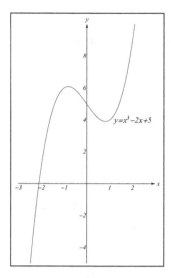

But let's think about it numerically for a moment. When we substitute a very large value of x, such as 10^6, the value becomes: $f(10^6) = (10^6)^3 - 2(10^6) + 5 = 999{,}999{,}999{,}998{,}000{,}005$. This figure is very similar to the value we would get if we used only the leading term x^3. The value of $(10^6)^3 = 1{,}000{,}000{,}000{,}000{,}000{,}000$, differs only after eleven places. The point is, for very large values of x, a polynomial is very nearly the same as its leading term. So for limits, such as,

$\lim\limits_{x\to\infty}\dfrac{3x^2 - 2x + 5}{6x^2 + 3x - 7}$, we may replace the numerator and denominator by their leading terms.

$$\lim_{x\to\infty}\frac{3x^2 - 2x + 5}{6x^2 + 3x - 7} = \lim_{x\to\infty}\frac{3x^2}{6x^2} = \lim_{x\to\infty}\frac{3}{6} = \frac{1}{2}.$$

It is very, very important to use this process only for limits as x is approaching infinity or negative infinity; i.e, only for $x \to \infty$ or $x \to -\infty$.

> For cases in which $x \to \infty$ or $x \to -\infty$
>
> polynomials can be replaced by their leading terms
>
> in the numerator and the denominator.

To use this shortcut, when $x \to \infty$ or $x \to -\infty$, don't forget that there are still three steps.

Step 1:

Consider only the $\displaystyle\lim_{x\to\infty}\frac{\text{term with the highest degree}}{\text{term with the highest degree}}$.

Step 2:

Reduce.

Step 3:

Substitute.

The leading term of a polynomial is the one with the highest degree, but the leading term might not occur first.

Now consider the function $y=f(x)=\dfrac{3}{x}$ (at right).

The function gets smaller and smaller (close to zero) as x gets larger and larger. We have:

$$\lim_{x\to\infty}f(x)=\lim_{x\to\infty}\frac{3}{x}=\frac{3}{\infty}=0.$$

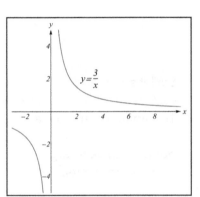

Example 1:

$y=2-\dfrac{3}{x}$ Find the limit as x approaches ∞.

$$\lim_{x\to\infty}2-\frac{3}{x}=\lim_{x\to\infty}2-\lim_{x\to\infty}\frac{3}{x}=2-\frac{3}{\infty}=2-0=2.$$

Example 2:

$y=\dfrac{2x+5}{3-7x}$ Find the limit as x approaches ∞.

$$\lim_{x\to\infty}\frac{2x}{-7x}=\lim_{x\to\infty}\frac{2}{-7}=-\frac{2}{7}$$

Example 3:

$y=\dfrac{2x^2+2x-1}{5x+3}$ Find the limit as x approaches ∞.

$$\lim_{x\to\infty}\frac{2x^2}{5x}=\lim_{x\to\infty}\frac{2x}{5}=\frac{2\infty}{7}=\infty$$

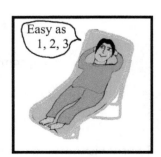

Easy as 1, 2, 3

Example 4:

$$y = \frac{2x^2 - 6x + 5}{6x^4 - 7x - 3}$$ Find the limit as x approaches ∞.

$$\lim_{x \to \infty} \frac{2x^2}{6x^4} = \lim_{x \to \infty} \frac{2}{6x^2} = \frac{2}{6(\infty)^2} = 0$$

Now consider the function $f(x) = x^3 - 2x + 5$ as x approaches $-\infty$. For very large negative values of x, there is very little difference between $g(x) = x^3$ and $f(x) = x^3 - 2x + 5$. For example,

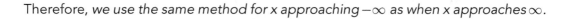

$$g(-10)^5 = ((-10)^5)^3 = 1{,}000{,}000{,}000{,}000{,}000$$

and

$$f(-10^5) = ((-10)^5)^3 - 2(-10)^5 + 5$$
$$= -1{,}000{,}000{,}000{,}200{,}005.$$

Both grow without bound in the negative y direction.

Therefore, *we use the same method for x approaching $-\infty$ as when x approaches ∞.*

Example 5:

$$y = \frac{2x^2 + 2x - 1}{5x + 3}$$ Find the limit as x approaches $-\infty$.

$$\lim_{x \to -\infty} \frac{2x^2}{5x} = \lim_{x \to \infty} \frac{2x}{5} = \frac{2(-\infty)}{7} = -\infty$$

INTRA-SECTION EXERCISES:

Find the limit as x approaches ∞.

1. $y = \dfrac{3x^4 + 2x^2 - 6}{5x^4 + 16}$

2. $y = \dfrac{3x^4 + 2x^2 - 6}{5x^5 + 16}$

3. $y = \dfrac{3x^5 + 2x^2 - 6}{5x^4 + 16}$

4. $y = 5x^3 + 2x - 6$

Find the limit as x approaches $-\infty$.

5. $y = 5x^3 + 2x - 6$

6. $y = \dfrac{3x^5 + 2x^2 - 6}{5x^4 + 16}$

Solutions

1. $\lim\limits_{x \to \infty} \dfrac{3x^4 + 2x^2 - 6}{5x^4 + 16} = \lim\limits_{x \to \infty} \dfrac{3x^4}{5x^4} = \lim\limits_{x \to \infty} \dfrac{3}{5} = \dfrac{3}{5}$

2. $\lim\limits_{x \to \infty} \dfrac{3x^4 + 2x^2 - 6}{5x^5 + 16} = \lim\limits_{x \to \infty} \dfrac{3x^4}{5x^5} = \lim\limits_{x \to \infty} \dfrac{3}{5x} = \dfrac{3}{5\infty} = 0$

3. $\lim\limits_{x \to \infty} \dfrac{3x^5 + 2x^2 - 6}{5x^4 + 16} = \lim\limits_{x \to \infty} \dfrac{3x^5}{5x^4} = \lim\limits_{x \to \infty} \dfrac{3x}{5} = \dfrac{3\infty}{5} = \infty$

4. $\lim\limits_{x \to \infty} 5x^3 = 5(\infty)^3 = \infty$

5. $\lim\limits_{x \to -\infty} 5x^3 = 5(-\infty)^3 = -\infty$

6. $\lim\limits_{x \to -\infty} \dfrac{3x^5 + 2x^2 - 6}{5x^4 + 16} = \lim\limits_{x \to -\infty} \dfrac{3x^5}{5x^4} = \lim\limits_{x \to -\infty} \dfrac{3x}{5} = \dfrac{3(-\infty)}{5} = -\infty$

ANOTHER REASON TO USE THE SHORTCUT AS x APPROACHES INFINITY

We'll use the example $\lim\limits_{x \to \infty} \dfrac{3x^4 + 2x^2 - 6}{5x^4 + 16}$.

We know that when we multiply an algebraic expression by 1, the value of the expression remains unchanged. We also know that when the numerator and denominator are equal, a rational expression equals 1. For example, $\dfrac{4}{4} = 1$, and $\dfrac{x+5}{x+5} = 1$, and $\dfrac{a}{a} = 1$.

Therefore, we choose to multiply the expression above by $\dfrac{\frac{1}{x^4}}{\frac{1}{x^4}}$. It also equals 1.

$$\lim\limits_{x \to \infty} \dfrac{3x^4 + 2x^2 - 6}{5x^4 + 16} \cdot \dfrac{\frac{1}{x^4}}{\frac{1}{x^4}}$$

Next, we distribute,

$$\lim_{x\to\infty} \frac{3x^4\dfrac{1}{x^4}+2x^2\dfrac{1}{x^4}-6\dfrac{1}{x^4}}{5x^4\dfrac{1}{x^4}+16\dfrac{1}{x^4}}$$

and then reduce,

$$\lim_{x\to\infty} \frac{3+\dfrac{2}{x^2}-\dfrac{6}{x^4}}{5+\dfrac{16}{x^4}}$$

Finally, we substitute.

$$\frac{3+\dfrac{2}{\infty^2}-\dfrac{6}{\infty^4}}{5+\dfrac{16}{\infty^4}}$$

Of course, we recall that $\infty^{(any\ positive\ exponent)}=\infty$ and $\dfrac{any\ constant}{\infty}=0$, so the rational expression becomes:

$$\frac{3+0-0}{5+0} \quad \text{which equals } \frac{3}{5}, \text{ just as it did in Example 1.}$$

In summary, the reason we can ignore the terms, other than those with the highest degree, is that they will all become zeros under this method when we do the substitution step.

AND NOW A WORD ABOUT CONTINUITY

When we look at the graph of a function like $y=2x^2-4$, there are no holes or jumps. We can move continuously across any point on the graph. We say a function $y=f(x)$ is *continuous* at $x=b$ if $f(b)=\lim_{x\to b} f(x)$. The function is defined at b and the approach to b matches the value of the function at b.

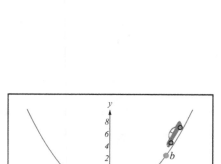

Polynomials, rational functions, roots, exponentials, and logarithms are continuous at each point where they are defined. We calculate the limit merely by evaluating the function.

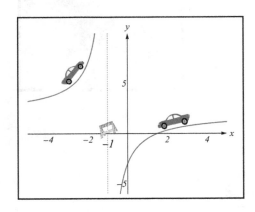

The function $f(x)=\dfrac{2x-3}{x+1}$ is continuous at each point where it is defined; i.e., wherever $x\neq-1$. Since $f(-1)$ is not defined, f cannot be continuous. Furthermore, we see that $\lim\limits_{x\to-1} f(x)$ does not exist. The function f is continuous on the interval $(-\infty,-1)$ and on the interval $(-1,\infty)$.

The function $f(x)=\dfrac{2x+2}{x+1}$ is continuous at each point where it is defined; i.e., wherever $x\neq-1$. $f(-1)$ is not defined, so f cannot be continuous, but $\lim\limits_{x\to-1}\dfrac{2x+2}{x+1}=2$ does exist. The function f is continuous on the interval $(-\infty,-1)$ and on the interval $(-1,\infty)$. The graph of f has a hole at $x=-1$.

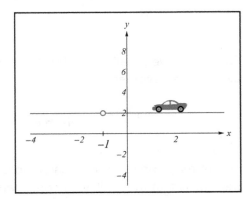

Next, we are going to consider the function $f(x)=\dfrac{|2x+2|}{x+1}$, but first a word about absolute values.

WE INTERRUPT OUR REGULAR PROGRAM TO DISCUSS ABSOLUTE VALUES

The sad news is that an absolute value problem is always two distinct problems. Think about the simple equation $y=|x|$. We have two cases.

Case I:

When x is a positive value or 0, or $x \geq 0$, then $|x| = x$, and our expression $y = |x|$ becomes simply $y = x$. We can even graph $y = x$ for $x \geq 0$.

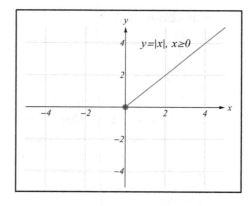

Case II:

When x is a negative value, or $x < 0$, then $|x| = -x$. If that's confusing, think of $x = -3$. Then $|-3| = -(-3)$, or since $x = -3$ then $|x| = -x$. (One minus sign is part of the x.) So we have established that when $x < 0$, our equation $y = |x|$ becomes $y = -x$.

We can also graph $y = x$ for $x < 0$.

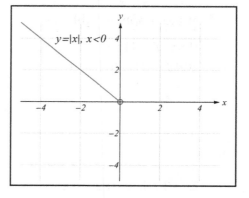

We can splice together the results of Case I and Case II to obtain a graph of $y = |x|$.

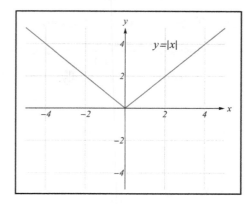

So, what about $f(x) = \dfrac{|2x+2|}{x+1}$? It's an absolute value function, so we must consider two cases.

Case I:

2x+2≥0, i.e., the value inside the absolute value signs is positive or 0. This happens when $2x \geq -2$ or $x \geq -1$.

Therefore, at $x \geq -1$, $|2x+2| = 2x+2$ and $f(x) = \dfrac{2x+2}{x+1} = \dfrac{2(x+1)}{x+1} = 2$. Look at the graph at right carefully.

Here, $f(-1)$ causes division by zero and $f(-1)$ is not defined.

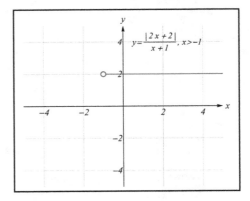

Case II:

$2x+2 < 0$, i.e., the value inside the absolute value signs is negative.

This happens when $2x < -2$ or $x < -1$.

Therefore, at $x < -1$, $|2x+2| = -(2x+2)$ and $f(x) = \dfrac{-2(x+1)}{x+1} = -2$. Look at the graph at right carefully.

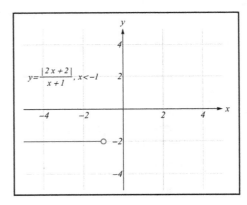

The complete graph of $f(x)=\dfrac{|2x+2|}{x+1}$ is graphed at right.

It has two parts, a y-value for $x>-1$, and a different y-value for $x<-1$. Also, the function does not have a value at $x=-1$.

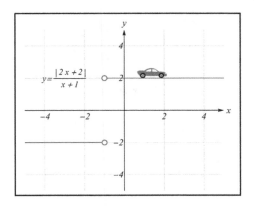

INTRA-SECTION EXERCISES:

7. Sketch the graph of: $f(x)=\dfrac{2|x+3|}{x+3}$.

8. Sketch the graph of: $f(x)=\dfrac{3x-6}{|x-2|}$.

9. Sketch the graph of: $f(x)=|3x|$.

10. Sketch the graph of: $y=|x|+2$.

11. Sketch the graph of: $y=|x+2|$.

12. Sketch the graph of: $y=-|x|$

Solutions

7. Case I:

$$f(x)=\dfrac{2(x+3)}{x+3}=2 \text{ or}$$

$$y=2 \text{ when } x\geq-3$$

Case II:

$$f(x)=\dfrac{2(-1)(x+3)}{x+3}=-2 \text{ or}$$

$$y=-2 \text{ when } x<-3$$

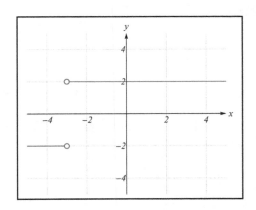

8. Case I:

$$f(x)=\frac{3x-6}{x-2}=\frac{3(x-2)}{x-2}=3 \text{ or}$$

$$y=3 \text{ for } x\geq2$$

Case II:

$$f(x)=\frac{3x-6}{-(x-2)}=\frac{3(x-2)}{-(x-2)}=-3 \text{ or}$$

$$y=-3 \text{ for } x<2$$

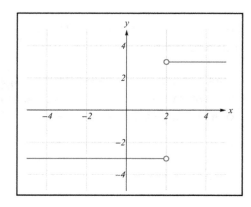

9. Case I:

$$f(x)=3x \text{ or } y=3x \text{ for } x\geq0$$

Case II:

$$f(x)=-3x \text{ or } y=-3x \text{ for } x<0$$

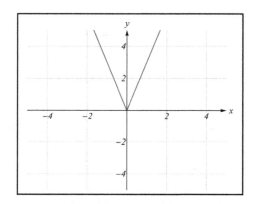

10. Case I:

$$f(x)=x+2 \text{ or } y=x+2 \text{ for } x\geq0$$

Case II:

$$f(x)=-x+2 \text{ or } y=-x+2 \text{ for } x<0$$

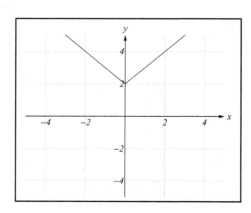

11. Case I:

$$f(x)=x+2 \text{ or } y=x+2 \text{ for } x\geq-2$$

Case II:

$$f(x)=-(x+2) \text{ or } y=-(x+2) \text{ for } x<-2$$

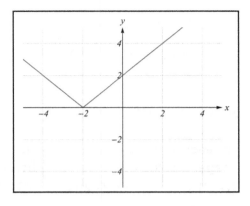

12. Case I:

$$f(x)=-x \text{ or } y=-x \text{ for } x\geq 0$$

Case II:

$$f(x)=--x \text{ or } y=x \text{ for } x<0$$

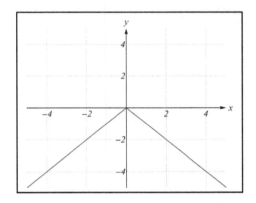

WE NOW RETURN TO OUR DISCUSSION OF CONTINUITY

The function $f(x)=\dfrac{|2x+2|}{x+1}$ is continuous at each point where it is defined; i.e., wherever $x\neq-1$. But $f(-1)$ does not exist, making the function f discontinuous (*not* continuous) at $x=-1$. Furthermore, the graph jumps at $x=-1$, more precisely, $\displaystyle\lim_{x\to-1^-}\dfrac{|2x+2|}{x+1}=-2$ and $\displaystyle\lim_{x\to-1^+}\dfrac{|2x+2|}{x+1}=2$. The limits as $x\to-1$ from the left and from the right are not equal,

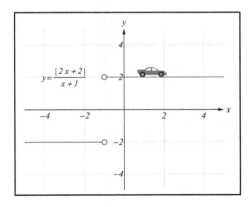

so $\lim\limits_{x \to -1} \dfrac{|2x+2|}{x+1}$ does not exist. The function f is continuous on the interval $(-\infty, -1)$ and on the interval $(-1, \infty)$.

ANOTHER EXAMPLE

For each x, the greatest integer function $g(x) = [[x]]$ is defined to be the greatest integer less than or equal to x. Therefore: $[[2.3]] = 2$, $[[0.3]] = 0$, $[[\pi]] = 3$, $[[-2.3]] = -3$, $[[-\pi]] = -4$, $[[2]] = 2$, $[[-2]] = -2$, and $[[0]] = 0$. The greatest integer function is graphed below. We see that $\lim\limits_{x \to -1^-} [[x]] = -2$ but $\lim\limits_{x \to -1^+} [[x]] = -1$, and $\lim\limits_{x \to 3^-} [[x]] = 2$ but $\lim\limits_{x \to 3^+} [[x]] = 3$. The function $g(x) = [[x]]$ is not continuous at each integer, but it is continuous between each integer; it is continuous on the intervals $(n, n+1)$ for each integer n.

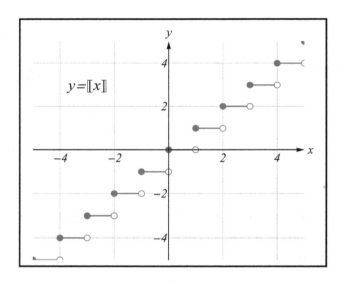

IIC5 LIMITS AT INFINITY, CONTINUITY EXERCISES

Find the following limits.

1. $\lim\limits_{x \to \infty} \dfrac{x^2 + 3x - 1}{2x^2 + 3x}$

2. $\lim\limits_{x \to \infty} \dfrac{5x^2 + 3x - 1}{x^2 + 3x}$

3. $\lim\limits_{x \to \infty} \dfrac{x^4 + 3x - 1}{2x^2 + 3x}$

4. $\lim\limits_{x \to \infty} \dfrac{x^4 + 3x - 1}{5x^2 + 3x}$

5. $\lim\limits_{x \to \infty} \dfrac{5x^2 + 3x - 1}{2x^4 - 4x + 1}$

6. $\lim\limits_{x \to \infty} \dfrac{4x^4 + 3x - 1}{2x^5 - 2x}$

7. $\lim\limits_{x \to \infty} 4x^3 - 5x + 1$

8. $\lim\limits_{x \to \infty} 3x^4 - 5x + 7$

9. $\lim\limits_{x \to -\infty} 4x^6 - 6x + 1$

10. $\lim\limits_{x \to -\infty} 7x^3 - 2x + 1$

11. $\lim\limits_{x \to \infty} \dfrac{x^4 + 1}{x^2 + 5x + 4}$

12. $\lim\limits_{x \to \infty} \dfrac{3x^3 + 1}{8x^2 + x + 4}$

13. $\lim\limits_{x \to -\infty} \dfrac{3x^3 + 1}{8x^2 + x + 4}$

14. $\lim\limits_{x \to -\infty} \dfrac{x^4 + 1}{x^2 + 5x + 4}$

15. $\lim\limits_{x \to \infty} \dfrac{x - 3}{x + 2}$

16. $\lim\limits_{x \to \infty} \dfrac{x - 5}{x + 5}$

17. $\lim\limits_{x \to 1} \dfrac{x + 4}{x - 2}$

18. $\lim\limits_{x \to 2} \dfrac{x + 3}{x + 1}$

19. The J&M Freight Firm sets its intra-island rates by the quantity of units trans-ported, so that the more a customer ships with J&M, the lower his/her per unit cost, calculated with the formula:

$$\bar{C}(x) = \frac{\$14.95 - 0.002x}{0.8x}$$

where $\bar{C}(x)$ equals the cost per unit and x represents the number of units shipped.

   a. What is the cost to ship 1 unit?
   b. What is the cost to ship 1,000 units?
   c. What is the cost per unit as $x \to \infty$?

20. The M&J Shipping Firm sets its inter-island rates by the quantity of units transported, so that the more a customer ships with M&J, the lower his/her per unit cost, calculated with the formula:

$$\bar{C}(x) = \frac{\$160.15 - 0.01x}{1.2x}$$

where $\bar{C}(x)$ equals the cost per unit and x represents the number of units shipped.

   a. What is the cost to ship 1 unit?
   b. What is the cost to ship 1,000 units?
   c. What is the cost per unit as $x \to \infty$?

IIC5 LIMITS AT INFINITY, CONTINUITY SOLUTIONS TO EXERCISES

1. $\lim\limits_{x\to\infty}\dfrac{x^2+3x-1}{2x^2+3x}=\lim\limits_{x\to\infty}\dfrac{x^2}{2x^2}=\lim\limits_{x\to\infty}\dfrac{1}{2}=\dfrac{1}{2}$

2. 5

3. $\lim\limits_{x\to\infty}\dfrac{x^4+3x-1}{2x^2+3x}=\lim\limits_{x\to\infty}\dfrac{x^4}{2x^2}=\lim\limits_{x\to\infty}\dfrac{x^2}{2}=\dfrac{\infty^2}{2}=\infty$

4. ∞

5. $\lim\limits_{x\to\infty}\dfrac{5x^2+3x-1}{2x^4-4x+1}=\lim\limits_{x\to\infty}\dfrac{5x^2}{2x^4}=\lim\limits_{x\to\infty}\dfrac{5}{2x^2}=\dfrac{5}{2(\infty)^2}=0$

6. 0

7. $\lim\limits_{x\to\infty}4x^3-5x+1=\lim\limits_{x\to\infty}4x^3=4(\infty)^3=\infty$

8. ∞

9. $\lim\limits_{x\to-\infty}4x^6-6x+1=\lim\limits_{x\to-\infty}4x^6=4(-\infty)^6=\infty$

10. $-\infty$

11. $\lim\limits_{x\to\infty}\dfrac{x^4+1}{x^2+5x+4}=\lim\limits_{x\to\infty}\dfrac{x^4}{x^2}=\lim\limits_{x\to\infty}\dfrac{x^2}{1}=\infty^2=\infty$

12. ∞

13. $\lim\limits_{x\to-\infty}\dfrac{3x^3+1}{8x^2+x+4}=\lim\limits_{x\to-\infty}\dfrac{3x^3}{8x^2}=\lim\limits_{x\to-\infty}\dfrac{3x}{8}=\dfrac{3(-\infty)}{8}=-\infty$

14. ∞

15. $\lim\limits_{x\to\infty}\dfrac{x-3}{x+2}=\lim\limits_{x\to\infty}\dfrac{x}{x}=\lim\limits_{x\to\infty}1=1$

16. 1

17. $\lim\limits_{x\to 1}\dfrac{x+4}{x-2}=\dfrac{1+4}{1-2}=\dfrac{5}{-1}=-5$ *The shortcut method can only be used when $x\to\infty$.*

18. $\dfrac{5}{3}$

19. a. $\bar{C}(1)=\bar{C}(x)=\dfrac{\$14.95-0.002(1)}{0.8(1)}=\$18.685/unit$

d. $\bar{C}(1000)=\bar{C}(x)=\dfrac{\$14.95-0.002(1,000)}{0.8(1000)}=\$0.016/unit$

e. $\displaystyle\lim_{x\to\infty}\dfrac{-0.002x}{0.8x}=\lim_{x\to\infty}\dfrac{-0.002}{0.8}=-\$0.0025,$ *J&M should cap their discount quantity.*

20. a. $133.45/unit   b. $0.125/unit

c. $-\$0.0083$/unit, *M&J should cap their discount quantity.*

IIC6

Estimating Integrals—Riemann Sums

The stream flowing through Farmer Corby's land widens out into a small lake. It is of irregular shape, but has approximately uniform depth most of the year. Corby is considering using the lake to raise trout. While the suitability of this enterprise depends on the temperature, hardness of the water, and amount of dissolved oxygen, Corby has learned that he can raise about 15 pounds of trout per gallons per minute (GPM) of water flow.

Therefore, Corby needs to compute the capacity of his lake in gallons, among other things, in order to determine if this could be a profitable venture. The volume of the lake will be its surface area times the depth, but because the lake has an irregular shape, there is no simple geometrical formula that can be used to compute surface area, and there is no equation for the perimeter of the pond that can be integrated to provide the area.

In some settings, a formula for the area under a curve is not practical. Many techniques for estimating definite integrals with finite sums have been developed. We are going to explore the technique of estimating a definite integral using the sum of the areas of rectangles called a Riemann Sum.

Consider the function $y = x^2 + 2$ over the interval from $x = -1$ to $x = 9$. In this case, we have a formula to compute the area bounded by the curve:

$$\int_{-1}^{9}(x^2 + 2)dx = \left[\frac{x^3}{3} + 2x\right]_{-1}^{9} = \left[\frac{9^3}{3} + 2(9)\right] - \left[\frac{(-1)^3}{3} + 2(-1)\right] \approx 263.33$$

Let us study Riemann Sums for this basic example before applying the technique when estimation may be necessary, as for Corby's lake. The graph for $y = x^2 + 2$ can be found below.

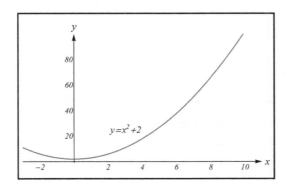

Our task is to use a Riemann Sum to estimate the area under the curve $y = x^2 + 2$ over the interval from $x = -1$ to $x = 9$, using $n = 5$ rectangles and left endpoints.

To compute a Riemann Sum, we follow six steps.

Step 1:

Sketch.

We sketch the graph of $y = x^2 + 2$ and we locate $a = -1$ and $b = 9$ on the x-axis.

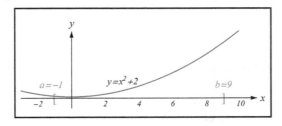

Step 2:

Find $\triangle x$.

We determine the width of each rectangle. We call this width $\triangle x$, and we find it by:

$$\triangle x = \frac{b - a}{n}$$

i.e., in our example, we take the right endpoint: 9, less the left endpoint: -1, and divide by the number of rectangles we will need: 5,

giving the width of each rectangle $\triangle x = \dfrac{9-(-1)}{5} = \dfrac{10}{5} = 2.$

We begin to build a chart. We first list rectangles # 1, 2, 3, 4, and 5, then we find the x_is.

i	x_i				
1					
2					
3					
4					
5					

Step 3:

Find the x_is.

We find the x_i for each rectangle using the left endpoint. In our example, each rectangle is 2 units long. We examine the x-axis. The first rectangle will run from $x=-1$, our starting point, and go to $x=1$, a distance of 2 units. We could say the first subinterval is [–1, 1]. We were instructed to use the left endpoint of each rectangle. The left end of the subinterval [-1 *to* 1] is -1, so $x_1 = -1$.

The second rectangle runs from $x=1$ *to* $x=3$; the second subinterval is [1, 3]. The left end of this subinterval is 1, so $x_2 = 1$.

The third rectangle runs from $x=3$ *to* $x=5$; the third subinterval is [3, 5]. The left end of this interval is 3, so $x_3 = 3$. Using this method, $x_4 = 5$ and $x_5 = 7$.

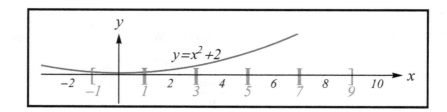

We add the x_is to our chart.

i	x_i					
1	−1					
2	1					
3	3					
4	5					
5	7					

We used the left endpoints of each x-interval, but the example could have asked us to use the right endpoints, or the midpoints, or even a different point for each subinterval.

Step 4:

Find the height of each rectangle.

The x_is tell us where we will construct our rectangles. The first rectangle is constructed from x_1 to its corresponding point on the graph $f(x_1)$. The value $f(x_1)$ gives us the y-value; that is, the height of the graph at x_1. For our first rectangle, x_1 is −1, so we construct our first rectangle at $x = -1$ and we find the corresponding height of the graph where $x = -1$; that is, we find $f(-1)$. This is the height of our first rectangle.

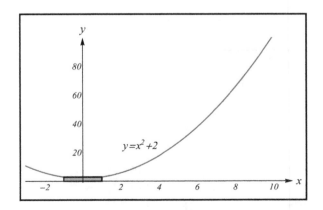

The next x_i, is x_2, which equals 1, so our second rectangle is constructed at $x_2 = 1$. The height of this second rectangle will be computed from $f(1)$.

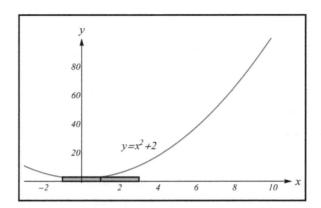

Similarly, we find the heights of rectangles 3, 4, and 5 from f(x_3), f(x_4), and f(x_5) and construct rectangles that have the subintervals as bases and heights that match the heights of the curve at the left endpoints of the subintervals.

i	x_i	Height(ht) $= f(x_i) = (x_i)^2 + 2$		
1	-1	$ht = f(-1) = (-1)^2 + 2 = 3$		
2	1	$ht = f(1) = (1)^2 + 2 = 3$		
3	3	$ht = f(3) = (3)^2 + 2 = 11$		
4	5	$ht = f(5) = (5)^2 + 2 = 27$		
5	7	$ht = f(7) = (7)^2 + 2 = 51$		

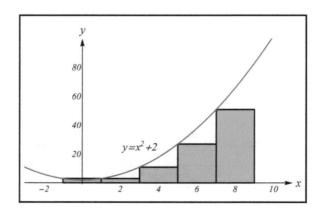

Step 5:

We add a column for $\triangle x$, the width of each of our rectangles.

i	x_i	Height(ht) $= f(x_i) = (x_i)^2 + 2$	$\triangle x$	
1	-1	$ht = f(-1) = (-1)^2 + 2 = 3$	2	
2	1	$ht = f(1) = (1)^2 + 2 = 3$	2	
3	3	$ht = f(3) = (3)^2 + 2 = 11$	2	
4	5	$ht = f(5) = (5)^2 + 2 = 27$	2	
5	7	$ht = f(7) = (7)^2 + 2 = 51$	2	

Step 6:

Find the area of each rectangle.

The area of a rectangle is its length times its width: $A = lw$. The length of each of our rectangles is its height. The width is $\triangle x$. Hence, the area of each of our rectangles is $height \times width = f(x_i)(\triangle x)$.

i	x_i	Height(ht) $= f(x_i) = (x_i)^2 + 2$	$\triangle x$	$A_i = (ht)\triangle x$
1	-1	$ht = f(-1) = (-1)^2 + 2 = 3$	2	$(3)(2) = 6$
2	1	$ht = f(1) = (1)^2 + 2 = 3$	2	$(3)(2) = 6$
3	3	$ht = f(3) = (3)^2 + 2 = 11$	2	$(11)(2) = 22$
4	5	$ht = f(5) = (5)^2 + 2 = 27$	2	$(27)(2) = 54$
5	7	$ht = f(7) = (7)^2 + 2 = 51$	2	$(51)(2) = 102$

Step 7:

Sum the areas.

We now have the area for each of our five rectangles. For the total approximate area, we just sum each of these individual areas.

i	x_i	Height(ht) $= f(x_i) = (x_i)^2 + 2$	Δx	$A_i = (ht)\Delta x$
1	-1	$ht = f(-1) = (-1)^2 + 2 = 3$	2	$(3)(2) = 6$
2	1	$ht = f(1) = (1)^2 + 2 = 3$	2	$(3)(2) = 6$
3	3	$ht = f(3) = (3)^2 + 2 = 11$	2	$(11)(2) = 22$
4	5	$ht = f(5) = (5)^2 + 2 = 27$	2	$(27)(2) = 54$
5	7	$ht = f(7) = (7)^2 + 2 = 51$	2	$(51)(2) = 102$
		Total Approximate Area:		190

We have an expression that summarizes all the steps on our chart to give us the total approximate area. It is the summation of each height times the width for rectangles 1 through n.

$$\sum_{i=1}^{n} f(x_i)(\Delta x)$$

Note that $\Delta x = (b-a)/n$.

The symbol Σ is the summation sign. It tells us to add up the areas of all the rectangles from $i = 1$ to $i = n$; i.e., from the first rectangle to the nth rectangle.

Remember we used a Riemann Sum to estimate the area under the curve $y = x^2 + 2$ over the interval from $x = -1$ to $x = 9$, using $n = 5$ rectangles and using left endpoints. Recall that a Riemann Sum gives us an *approximate area*, while the integral gives us the exact area. The exact area of the example above was:

$$\int_{-1}^{9} x^2 + 2\ dx = \left[\frac{x^3}{3} + 2x\right]_{-1}^{9} = \left[\frac{9^3}{3} + 2(9)\right] - \left[\frac{(-1)^3}{3} + 2(-1)\right] \approx 261 - (-2.33) = 263.33.$$

The difference between the approximate area and our actual area is $190 - 263.3 = -73.33$.

We have an error of –73.33, which would be a percentage error of $\dfrac{-73.33}{263.33}(100\%) \approx$ -27.85%.

Now suppose we use a Riemann Sum to estimate the area under the curve $y = x^2 + 2$ over the interval from $x = -1$ to $x = 9$, using $n = 5$ rectangles and *right* endpoints.

Again, our $\triangle x$, the width of each subinterval, is $\dfrac{9-(-1)}{5} = 2$, and the subintervals are: $[-1, 1]$, $[1, 3]$, $[3, 5]$, $[5, 7]$, and $[7, 9]$. The *right* endpoints of each subinterval are: $1, 3, 5, 7$, and 9.

We enter these values on our table and construct rectangles on the subintervals with heights that match the heights of the curve at the right endpoints.

i	x_i	Height$(ht) = f(x_i) = (x_i)^2 + 2$	$\triangle x$	$A_i = (ht)\triangle x$
1	1		2	
2	3		2	
3	5		2	
4	7		2	
5	9		2	

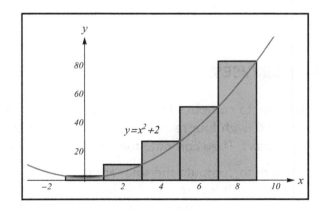

Next, we compute the height for each x_i.

i	x_i	Height(ht) $= f(x_i) = (x_i)^2 + 2$	Δx	$A_i = (ht)\Delta x$
1	1	$ht = f(1) = (1)^2 + 2 = 3$	2	
2	3	$ht = f(3) = (3)^2 + 2 = 11$	2	
3	5	$ht = f(5) = (5)^2 + 2 = 27$	2	
4	7	$ht = f(7) = (7)^2 + 2 = 51$	2	
5	9	$ht = f(9) = (9)^2 + 2 = 83$	2	

Then we compute the area for each rectangle and sum them.

i	x_i	Height(ht) $= f(x_i) = (x_i)^2 + 2$	Δx	$A_i = (ht)\Delta x$
1	1	$ht = f(1) = (1)^2 + 2 = 3$	2	6
2	3	$ht = f(3) = (3)^2 + 2 = 11$	2	22
3	5	$ht = f(5) = (5)^2 + 2 = 27$	2	54
4	7	$ht = f(7) = (7)^2 + 2 = 51$	2	102
5	9	$ht = f(9) = (9)^2 + 2 = 83$	2	166
		Total Approximate Area:		**350**

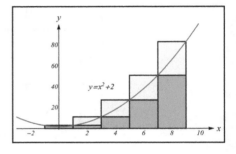

This time, we have an error of $350 - 263.33 = 86.67$. The estimate is off by $\dfrac{86.67}{263.3} \times 100\% = 32.91\%$.

INTRA-SECTION EXERCISES:

1. Use a Riemann Sum to compute the total approximate area for $f(x) = x^2 + 4$ from $x = -6$ to $x = 6$, with four rectangles, left endpoint evaluation. Make a sketch and use a chart. Then compute the actual area and the percent error.

2. Use a Riemann Sum to compute the total approximate area for $f(x) = x^2 + 4$ from $x = -6$ to $x = 6$, with four rectangles, right endpoint evaluation. Make a sketch and use a chart. Then compute the actual area and the percent error.

Solutions

1. $\Delta x = \dfrac{6--6}{4} = \dfrac{12}{4} = 3$

Subintervals are: $[-6, -3], [-3, 0], [0, 3], [3, 6]$. Left ends are: $-6, -3, 0, 3$.

i	x_i	height $= f(x_i) = (x_i)^2 + 4$	Δx	$A = f(x_i)\Delta x$
1	-6	$(-6)^2 + 4 = 40$	3	120
2	-3	$(-3)^2 + 4 = 13$	3	39
3	0	$(0)^2 + 4 = 4$	3	12
4	3	$(3)^2 + 4 = 13$	3	39
		Total approximate area:		210

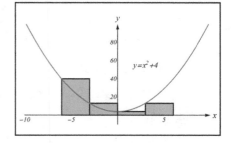

Actual area $= \displaystyle\int_{-6}^{6} x^2 + 4\ dx = \left[\dfrac{x^3}{3} + 4x\right]_{-6}^{6} = \left[\dfrac{6^3}{3} + 4(6)\right] - \left[\dfrac{(-6)^3}{3} + 4(-6)\right]$

$= 96 - (-96) = 192.$

Percent error equals $\dfrac{210 - 192}{192} \times 100\% \approx 9.4\%.$

2. $\Delta x = \dfrac{6--6}{4} = \dfrac{12}{4} = 3$

Subintervals are: $[-6, -3], [-3, 0], [0, 3], [3, 6]$. Right ends are: $-3, 0, 3, 6$.

i	x_i	height $= f(x_i) = (x_i)^2 + 4$	Δx	$A = f(x_i)\Delta x$
1	-3	$(-3)^2 + 4 = 13$	3	39
2	0	$(0)^2 + 4 = 4$	3	12
3	3	$(3)^2 + 4 = 13$	3	39
4	6	$(6)^2 + 4 = 40$	3	120
		Total approximate area:		210

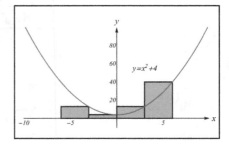

Actual area $= \int\limits_{-6}^{6} x^2 + 4 \; dx = \left[\dfrac{x^3}{3} + 4x \right]\Bigg|_{-6}^{6} = \left[\dfrac{6^3}{3} + 4(6) \right] - \left[\dfrac{(-6)^3}{3} + 4(-6) \right]$

$= 96 - (-96) = 192.$

Percent error equals $\dfrac{210 - 192}{192} \times 100\% \approx 9.4\%.$

We can improve our estimate by using more intervals. Let us use $n = 20$ rectangles with the subintervals evaluated at the left endpoints to find the total approximate area of our function $f(x) = x^2 + 2$ for $x = -1$ to $x = 9$. The width of each subinterval would be: $\Delta x = \dfrac{9 - (-1)}{20} = .5$. The subintervals would be: [–1, –0.5], [–0.5, 0], [0, 0.5], [0.5, 1], [1, 1.5], [1.5, 2], [2, 2.5], [2.5, 3], [3, 3.5], [3.5, 4], [4, 4.5], [4.5, 5], [5, 5.5], [5.5, 6], [6, 6.5], [6.5, 7], [7, 7.5], [7.5, 8], [8, 8.5], and [8.5, 9]. The left ends would be: –1, –0.5, 0, 0.5, 1, 1.5, 2, 2.5, 3, 3.5, 4, 4.5, 5, 5.5, 6, 6.5, 7, 7.5, 8, and 8.5.

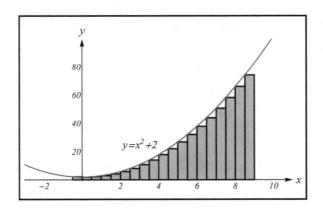

i	x_i	Height $= f(x_i) = (x_i)^2 + 2$	Δx	$A_i = (ht)\Delta x$
1	-1	$f(-1) = (-1)^2 + 2 = 3$	0.5	1.5
2	-0.5	$f(-.5) = (-.5)^2 + 2 = 2.25$	0.5	1.125
3	0	$f(0) = (0)^2 + 2 = 2$	0.5	1
4	0.5	$f(.5) = (.5)^2 + 2 = 2.25$	0.5	1.125
5	1	$f(1) = (1)^2 + 2 = 3$	0.5	1.5
6	1.5	$f(1.5) = (1.5)^2 + 2 = 4.25$	0.5	2.125
7	2	$f(2) = (2)^2 + 2 = 6$	0.5	3.0

8	2.5	$f(2.5)=(2.5)^2+2=8.25$	0.5	4.125
9	3	$f(3)=(3)^2+2=11$	0.5	5.5
10	3.5	$f(3.5)=(3.5)^2+2=14.25$	0.5	7.125
11	4	$f(4)=(4)^2+2=18$	0.5	9
12	4.5	$f(4.5)=(4.5)^2+2=22.25$	0.5	11.125
13	5	$f(5)=(5)^2+2=27$	0.5	13.5
14	5.5	$f(5.5)=(5.5)^2+2=32.25$	0.5	16.125
15	6	$f(6)=(6)^2+2=38$	0.5	19
16	6.5	$f(6.5)=(6.5)^2+2=44.25$	0.5	22.125
17	7	$f(7)=(7)^2+2=51$	0.5	25.5
18	7.5	$f(7.5)=(7.5)^2+2=58.25$	0.5	29.125
19	8	$f(8)=(8)^2+2=66$	0.5	33
20	8.5	$f(8.5)=(8.5)^2+2=74.25$	0.5	37.125
		Total approximate area:		**243.75**

This area estimate of 243.75 has an error of $243.75-263.33=-19.58$, which is off by

only $\dfrac{-19.05}{263.33}\times100\%\approx-7.44\%$. The more rectangles we use, the closer they fit the

actual curve. As the number of rectangles n approaches infinity, the width of each rectangle Δx becomes smaller, and the approximate area approaches the actual area.

We have studied special cases of Riemann Sums: the Δx's were all the same size, the x_i were endpoints, and the function f was continuous.

For these special cases, the algebraic construction, $\sum_{n=1}^{\infty} f(x_i)\Delta x$ for the approximate

area, becomes the calculus expression $\lim_{\Delta x \to 0} \sum_{n=1}^{\infty} f(x_i)\Delta x$ for the actual area. The

symbols $\lim_{\Delta x \to 0} \sum_{n=1}^{\infty}$ are replaced with the symbol $\int$, and the Δx is replaced with dx.

We now have the calculus expression for the actual area $\int_a^b f(x)dx$. Look familiar?

Now, back to Farmer Corby and the lake formed by his trout stream. He measures the distance across the lake every 10 feet. These distances are the lengths of his rectangles. He might need to hire a surveying crew, but these measurements will give him a set of rectangles with widths of 10 *feet*. If the pond is 100 feet long, he would need a set of 10 rectangles. Suppose he uses the length of the east side of each rectangle. We'll enter his measurements into a chart.

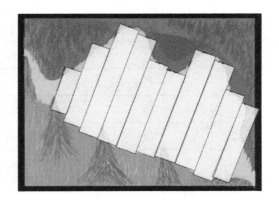

i	lengths	Δx	$A = (l)\Delta x$
1	31 ft	10 ft.	310 sq. ft.
2	56 ft	10 ft.	560 sq. ft.
3	82 ft	10 ft.	820 sq. ft.
4	80 ft	10 ft.	800 sq. ft.
5	63 ft	10 ft.	630 sq. ft.
6	54 ft	10 ft.	540 sq. ft.
7	80 ft	10 ft.	800 sq. ft.
8	72 ft	10 ft.	720 sq. ft.
9	61 ft	10 ft.	610 sq. ft.
10	55 ft	10 ft.	550 sq. ft.
			6,340 sq. ft.

Corby has effectively used a Riemann Sum to approximate the surface area of his pond. If the depth is approximately 8 *feet* uniformly, and there are 7.48 gallons per cubic foot, the volume of his pond in gallons is computed by

$$(6{,}340 \ ft^2)(8 \ ft)\left(7.48 \ \frac{gallons}{ft^3}\right) = 379{,}385.6 \ gallons.$$

At fifteen pounds of trout per gallon, he ought to be able to harvest 5,690,784 pounds of trout.

IIC6 ESTIMATING INTEGRALS—RIEMANN SUMS EXERCISES

1. For the function $f(x)=(x-2)^2+1$:

    a. Determine the Riemann Sum using $n=4$ rectangles, right interval end-points from $a=-8$ to $b=4$.
    b. Find the actual area.
    c. Find the percent error.

2. For the function $f(x)=(x+2)^2+1$:

    a. Determine the Riemann Sum using $n=4$ rectangles, right interval end-points from $a=-4$ to $b=8$.
    b. Find the actual area.
    c. Find the percent error.

3. For the function $f(x)=3x+3$:

    a. Determine the Riemann Sum using $n=6$ rectangles, left interval endpoints from $a=-1$ to $b=11$.
    b. Find the actual area.
    c. Find the percent error.

4. For the function $f(x)=4x+5$:

    a. Determine the Riemann Sum using $n=6$ rectangles, left interval endpoints from $a=-1$ to $b=11$.
    b. Find the actual area.
    c. Find the percent error.

5. Determine the Riemann Sum for the figure at right, using indicated heights and x_is.

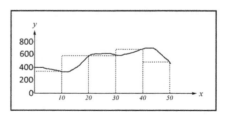

6. Determine the Riemann Sum for the figure at right, using indicated heights and x_is.

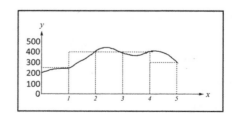

IIC6 ESTIMATING INTEGRALS—RIEMANN SUMS
SOLUTIONS TO EXERCISES

1. $\Delta x = \dfrac{4-(-8)}{4} = 3$

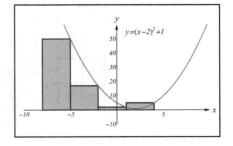

i	x_i	$ht = f(x_i) = (x_i - 2)^2 + 1$	Δx	$A = f(f_i)\Delta x$
1	−5	$ht = (-5-2)^2 + 1 = 50$	3	150
2	−2	$ht = (-2-2)^2 + 1 = 17$	3	51
3	1	$ht = (1-2)^2 + 1 = 2$	3	6
4	4	$ht = (4-2)^2 + 1 = 5$	3	15
				222

a. *Total approximate area is 222.*

b. *Actual area:* $\displaystyle\int_{-8}^{4} ((x-2)^2 + 1)\,dx = \int_{-8}^{4} (x^2 - 4x + 5)\,dx = \left[\dfrac{x^3}{3} - 4\dfrac{x^2}{2} + 5x\right]_{-8}^{4}$

$= \left[\dfrac{4^3}{3} - 4\dfrac{(4)^2}{2} + 5(4)\right] - \left[\dfrac{(-8)^3}{3} - 4\dfrac{(-8)^2}{2} + 5(-8)\right] \approx 9.33 - (-338.67) = 348.$

c. *Percent error* $= \dfrac{222 - 348}{348} \cdot 100\% \approx -36.2\%$

2.

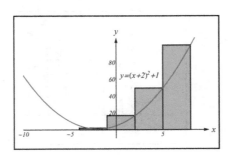

a. *Total approximate area is 510.*
b. *Actual area is 348.*
c. *Percent error is 46.6%.*

3. $\Delta x = \dfrac{11-(-1)}{6} = 2$

i	x_i	$ht = f(x_i) = 3x+3$	Δx	$A = f(x_i)\Delta x$
1	-1	$ht = 3(-1)+3 = 0$	2	0
2	1	$ht = 3(1)+3 = 6$	2	12
3	3	$ht = 3(3)+3 = 12$	2	24
4	5	$ht = 3(5)+3 = 18$	2	36
5	7	$ht = 3(7)+3 = 24$	2	48
6	9	$ht = 3(9)+3 = 30$	2	60
				180

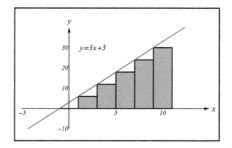

a.   Total approximate area is 180.

b.   Actual area $= \displaystyle\int_{-1}^{11}(3x+3)dx = \left[3\dfrac{x^2}{2}+3x\right]_{-1}^{11} = \left[3\dfrac{(11)^2}{2}+3(11)\right]$

$-\left[3\dfrac{(-1)^2}{2}+3(-1)\right] = 214.5 - -1.5 = 216.$

c.   Percent error $= \dfrac{180-216}{216}\cdot 100\% \approx -16.7\%.$

4.

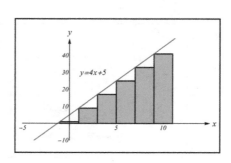

a.   Total approximate area is 252.
b.   Actual area is 300.
c.   Percent error is -16%.

5.

i	x_i	height	$\triangle x$	$A_i = (ht)\triangle x$
1	10	350	10	3500
2	20	600	10	6000
3	20	600	10	6000
4	35	700	10	7000
5	50	500	10	5000
				Total approximate area is 27,500

6. *Total approximate area is about 1750.*

UNIT III

IIIR1

Slopes and Equations of Lines

Businesses need to collect data. They keep track of sales, revenue, profits, clients, expenses of all kinds, etc.

Suppose the owner of the Rainbow Bakery is keeping track of sales. We'll call her Keani. Keani is pleased to see that sales have increased in the last quarter. Her partner, Kent, believes this might be due to an increase in advertising dollars spent. They would like to know exactly how an increase in spending on advertising is affecting sales. If an increase of $1,000 on advertising generated increased sales of $5,000, then Keani and Kent might want to increase their advertising even more (if they have additional baking capacity). On the other hand, if an increase in sales of $1,000 was the result of increasing advertising by $2,000, then increasing the advertising budget may not be a good idea.

It is helpful to know the absolute change in sales, but it is even more helpful to know the change in sales relative to advertising dollars spent. Graphs are very useful at portraying relative changes.

Kent examines the records and finds that over the first quarter of the year, the advertising budget increased by $500, and sales increased by $5,000. In the second quarter, the advertising budget was increased further by $1,000. In this quarter, sales increased by $5,000 again. In the third quarter, the advertising budget was increased by $1,000, and sales increased by $2,000.

In the fourth quarter, the advertising budget was increased by $1,000 once again, but sales increased by only $1,000.

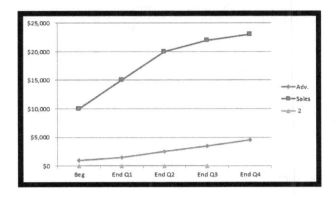

While the graph above provides a good picture of the changes in sales and advertising dollars, a more helpful graph would illustrate the change in sales per change in advertising dollars. In other words, it's important to look at the relative change. It's the slope of the graph that gives us this information on relative changes.

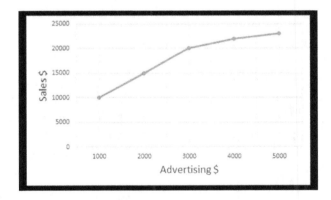

By examining the new graph, it becomes clear that increasing advertising is having less and less of an effect on sales. We can tell this because the curve is getting flatter. The "flatness" or "steepness" of the curve is its slope.

The steeper the line, the greater the slope, and the flatter the line, the smaller the slope.

Slope is a measure that tells us how the quantity portrayed on the y-axis changes per unit change in the quantity portrayed on the x-axis.

The symbol usually used to represent slope is, strangely enough, an "m."
The symbol usually used to represent "change in" is Δ.

$$\text{slope} = m = \frac{\text{change in quantity on } y-axis}{\text{change in quantity on } x-axis} = \frac{\Delta y}{\Delta x}$$

On Kent and Keani's graph of sales dollars versus advertising dollars, the slope is getting flatter and flatter. It tells them that sales per advertising dollar is flattening out, or they're no longer getting the "bang for their bucks" that they once had.

Because it's important to understand what the lines on graphs can tell us, we need to review the mathematics of lines and slopes.

Consider a straight line.
Choose any two points on the straight line.
Call them (x, y_1) and (x_2, y_2).

The slope of a straight line is the "rise," or vertical height, between the two points compared to the "run," or horizontal distance, between the two points.

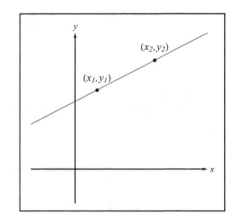

$$slope = m = \frac{rise}{run} = \frac{\Delta y}{\Delta x} = \frac{change\ in\ y\ distance}{change\ in\ x\ distance}.$$

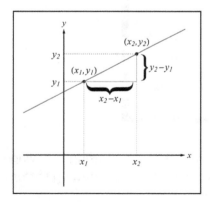

The change in y distance is the difference between the height at y_2 and the height at y_1, or $(y_2 - y_1)$. The change in x distance is the horizontal distance $(x_2 - x_1)$.
Slope can therefore be computed as:

$$slope = m = \frac{\Delta y}{\Delta x} = \frac{y_2 - y_1}{x_2 - x_1}$$

The *slope of a line* is the ratio of the length of the side parallel to the *y*-axis to the length of the side parallel to the *x*-axis.

The steeper the line, the greater the "rise" per horizontal distance, hence the greater the slope.

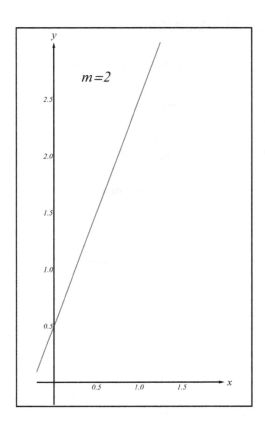

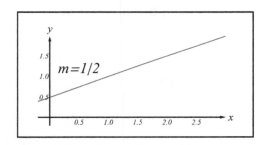

On this graph, $(y_2 - y_1)$ is a negative number, so the slope is negative. The curve falls as the x-distance goes from left to right; i.e., y_2 is less (lower) than y_1.

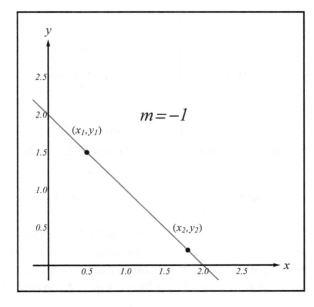

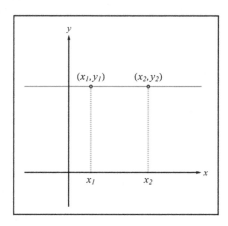

HORIZONTAL LINES

The slope of the horizontal line at left is:

$$m = \frac{y_2 - y_1}{x_2 - x_1}$$

while $(x_2 - x)$ is a nonzero distance, $(y_2 - y_1) = 0$, making the slope of the line $m = \dfrac{0}{x_2 - x_1} = 0$.

Since the change in vertical distance will equal zero between any two points on a horizontal line, **the slope of every horizontal line $m = 0$.**

VERTICAL LINES

Consider the vertical line at right.

The slope of the line is $m = \dfrac{y_2 - y_1}{x_2 - x_1}$. This time, the change in vertical distance $(y_2 - y_1)$ is a nonzero number, but the change in horizontal distance $(x_2 - x_1) = 0$. This gives us a slope of $= \dfrac{y_2 - y_1}{0}$.

A vertical line is as steep as you can get. It is infinitely steep. **Vertical lines have infinite slope.**

Keani and Kent wish to expand their bakery, so they take their sales figures to the bank to apply for a loan. Although Keani and Kent might see the data points as rising sales, the bank officials are more interested in the trend. That is, the bank officials are more interested in the slope of the sales curve. The bank officials may be concerned that the slope of the line segments between the points is decreasing. The sales curve is not a straight line with a fixed slope. We need to explore the concept of slope that varies at different points on the sales curve.

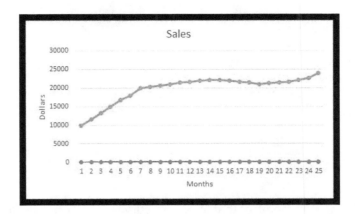

CURVES WITH POSITIVE AND NEGATIVE SLOPE

It is important to remember that lines with positive slope rise as they go from left to right. They angle upward compared to the x-axis. So far, we have considered only straight lines.

These lines have positive slope.
They can be flatter or steeper.

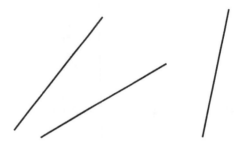

Curves that rise as they go from left to right also have positive slope.

They can curve   or this way:
this way:

They can even be wiggly.

And it is important to remember that lines and curves with negative slope fall as they go from left to right. They angle downward compared to the x-axis.
They can be straight.
They can be flatter or steeper.
They can be curved.
They can even be wiggly.

SLOPES ON STRAIGHT LINES

Suppose we want to find the slope of the line that goes through the points $(3, 5)$ and $(4, 8)$.

We let the point $(3, 5)$ be our (x_1, y_1) and we let the point $(4, 8)$ be our (x_2, y_2).

Since slope is $m = \dfrac{y_2 - y_1}{x_2 - x_1}$, we simply substitute to get: $\dfrac{8-5}{4-1} = \dfrac{3}{1} = 3$.

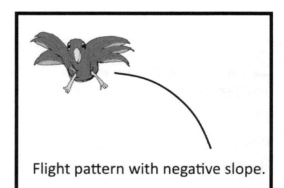

Flight pattern with negative slope.

Had we chosen to reverse the labels (x_1, y_1) and (x_2, y_2), we would have found the same slope

$$m = \frac{5-8}{1-4} = \frac{-3}{-1} = 3.$$

INTRA-SECTION EXERCISES:

1. Find the slope of the line going through the points $(4, 2)$ and $(6, 7)$.
2. Find the slope of the line going through the points $(1, 4)$ and $(-3, 2)$.
3. Find the slope of the line going through the points $(6, 3)$ and $(-8, 3)$.
4. Find the slope of the line going through the points $(-3, 11)$ and $(-3, 4)$.

Solutions

1. Let $(4, 2) = (x_1, y_1)$ and let $(6, 7) = (x_2, y_2)$. Then $m = \frac{7-2}{6-4} = \frac{5}{2}$.

2. Let $(1, 4) = (x_1, y_1)$ and let $(-3, 2) = (x_2, y_2)$. Then $m = \frac{2-4}{-3-1} = \frac{-2}{-4} = \frac{1}{2}$.

3. Let $(6, 3) = (x_1, y_1)$ and let $(-8, 3) = (x_2, y_2)$. Then $m = \frac{3-3}{-8-6} = \frac{0}{-14} = 0$.

   We know this is a horizontal line because the slope equals 0 and because both points have the same vertical distance above the x-axis, a height of 3.

4. Let $(-3, 11) = (x_1, y_1)$ and let $(-3, 4) = (x_2, y_2)$. Then $m = \frac{4-11}{-3--3} = \frac{-7}{0}$. *The slope is infinitely steep, making this a vertical line. We verify this by noting that both points have an x-distance of -3.*

DIFFERENT FORMS FOR THE EQUATION OF A STRAIGHT LINE

Using the formula for slope, we can generate the very useful equation for a straight line: $y - y_1 = m(x - x_1)$. Starting with $m = \frac{y_2 - y_1}{x_2 - x_1}$, we replace y_2 with y, and x_2 with x, giving us $m = \frac{y - y_1}{x - x_1}$. We then simply multiply both sides by $(x - x_1)$, and we have derived the point-slope form for equations of straight lines: $y - y_1 = m(x - x_1)$. We will be using this form to generate equations of tangent lines throughout the course.

The *standard form* for the equation of a line is: $Ax + By = C$. The variables are on the left side and the constant is on the right side. The equation $3x + 2y = 17$ is in the standard form.

For a line in this form, the slope can be computed by: $m = \dfrac{-A}{B}$. For example, the slope of the line $3x + 2y = 17$ would have $A = 3$ and $B = 2$, so its slope would be $m = \dfrac{-3}{2}$.

This equation for the slope can be derived by solving for y in the equation $Ax + By = C$. First, we subtract Ax from both sides to get: $By = -Ax + C$. Second, we divide both sides by B: $y = \dfrac{-A}{B}x + \dfrac{C}{B}$. The equation is now in the *slope-intercept* form: $y = mx + b$, and the slope, m, is $\dfrac{-A}{B}$. The constant $b = \dfrac{C}{B}$ is the y-intercept.

A horizontal line is parallel to the x-axis, and the y-coordinate (height) of every point on the line is exactly the same. Equations of horizontal lines have the form $y = (constant)$; e.g., $y = 32$.

A vertical line is parallel to the y-axis and the x-coordinate of every point on the line is exactly the same. Equations of vertical lines have the form $x = (constant)$. The equation $x = 3$ gives an example of a vertical line.

In general, we think you will find the point-slope form to be the most useful in finding the equations of straight lines throughout this course.

Use the formula $y - y_1 = m(x - x_1)$ to generate the equations of straight lines.

INTRA-SECTION EXERCISES:

5. Find the equation of the line passing through the points $(4, -2)$ with slope 6.
6. Find the equation of the line passing through the points $(-1, 3)$ and $(5, 1)$.

Solutions

5. We let the point $(4, -2) = (x_1, y_1)$ and we are given $m = 6$. Using $y - y_1 = m(x - x_1)$ we have $y - -2 = 6(x - 4)$. Distributing we have $y + 2 = 6x - 24$. Solving for y gives us the equation $y = 6x - 26$.
6. We are given two points but no slope, so the first task is to find the slope of the line connecting the two points. We let $(-1, 3) = (x_1, y_1)$ and $(5, 1) = (x_2, y_2)$. We can then find the slope: $m = \dfrac{1 - 3}{5 - -1} = \dfrac{-2}{6} = \dfrac{-1}{3}$. Then using $y - y_1 = m(x - x_1)$, we substitute to get: $y - 3 = \dfrac{-1}{3}(x - -1)$. Distributing, we have $y - 3 = \dfrac{-x}{3} - \dfrac{1}{3}$. Solving for y gives us the equation $y = \dfrac{-x}{3} + \dfrac{8}{3}$.

x-INTERCEPTS

The *x*-intercept is the point at which a line crosses the *x*-axis. For all points on the *x*-axis, the height, or *y*-value, equals zero. To find the *x*-intercept(s) of an equation, we let $y = 0$ and solve for *x*.

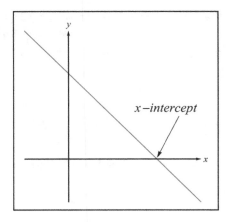

E.g.:   If $2x - 4y = 12$, we let *y* (*the height*) $= 0$.

Then we have: $2x - 4(0) = 12$, or $2x = 12$.

Dividing both sides by 2, we have $x = 6$.

Therefore, the *x*-intercept is at $x = 6$, or we can say the *x*-intercept is the point (6,0).

For quadratic equations, there can be 2, 1, or 0 *x*-intercepts.

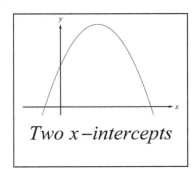

Two x−intercepts

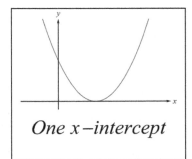

One x−intercept

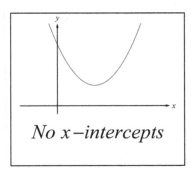

No x−intercepts

The *x*-intercepts are also the "zeros" of an equation because they tell us the value(s) of *x* that make the equation equal zero.

Suppose our quadratic equation is $y = x^2 - 3x + 2$.

To find the x-intercepts, we assign $y = 0$, giving us: $x^2 - 3x + 2 = 0$.

If we can factor, we do so. $(x-2)(x-1) = 0$. (Recall that we can only set each factor equal to the right side of the equation if the **right side equals 0**.) We have a product of factors that equal 0, so we set

$$(x-2) = 0; (x-1) = 0,$$

giving us the intercepts $x = 2$; $x = 1$, or the points $(2, 0)$ and $(1, 0)$.

We could also find the intercepts using the quadratic formula:

$$x = \frac{-b \pm \sqrt{b^2 - 4ac}}{2a}$$

which will always give us the x-intercepts; in other words, it will always give us the value(s) of x that will make $y = 0$, whether or not we can factor the equation.

y-INTERCEPTS

The y-intercepts occur where the curve crosses the y-axis.

At this point, the value of 'x' is 0. To find the y-intercept, we set x equal to 0 and solve for y.

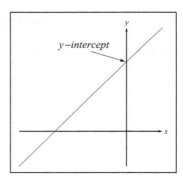

For example, if $y = 2x - 9$, we substitute 0 for x, giving us:

$$y = 2(0) - 9, \text{ or } y = -9.$$

The y-intercept for the line $y = 2x - 9$ is -9, or we could say the y-intercept is the point $(0, -9)$.

Whenever we have a line in the form $y = mx + b$, then b will give us the y-intercept. We can verify this by setting x equal to 0, giving us $y = m(0) + b$, or $y = b$.

Therefore, the line $y = 5x + 4.6$ has y-intercept 4.6. Or we could say its y-intercept is the point $(0, 4.6)$.

The line $y = \dfrac{x}{3} - 2.1$ has a y-intercept of -2.1; or we could say its y-intercept is the point $(0, -2.1)$.

A line in the form $Ax + By = C$ will have a y-intercept at $\dfrac{C}{B}$.

The line $2x - 7y = 6$ has a y-intercept of $\dfrac{6}{-7}$.

INTRA-SECTION EXERCISES:

y-interception

7. Find the x-intercept(s) for the line $y = 7x - 4$.
8. Find the x-intercept(s) for the line $y = x^2 - 4x - 12$.
9. Find the x-intercept(s) for the line $x^2 + 2x = 15$.
10. Find the y-intercept(s) for the line $y = 3x + 8$.
11. Find the y-intercept(s) for the line $y = 4.7x - 1$.
12. Find the x-intercept(s) for the line $y = 4$.
13. Find the y-intercept(s) for line $y = 4$.
14. Find the x-intercept(s) for the line $x = 9$.
15. Find the y-intercept(s) for the line $x = 9$.

Solutions

7. $0 = 7x - 4$
    $4 = 7x$
    $\dfrac{4}{7} = x$ or $\left(\dfrac{4}{7}, 0\right)$

8. $0 = x^2 - 4x - 12$
    $0 = (x - 6)(x + 2)$
    $x = 6, x = -2$
    or $(6, 0)$ & $(-2, 0)$

9. $x^2 + 2x - 15 = 0$
    $(x + 5)(x - 3) = 0$
    $x = -5, x = 3$
    or $(-5, 0)$ & $(3, 0)$

10. $y = 3(0) + 8$
    $y = 8$ or $(0, 8)$

11. $y = 4.7(0) - 1$
    $y = -1$ or $(0, -1)$

12. *Since $y = 4$ is a horizontal line at a height of 4, there is no x-intercept.*

13. *The horizontal line has a height of 4 at every value of x, including $x = 0$. The y-intercept is $(0, 4)$.*

14. *This is the equation of a vertical line. It crosses the x-axis at (9, 0).*

15. *This is a vertical line. Because it is parallel to the y-axis, it never crosses it. The line has no y-intercept.*

PARALLEL AND PERPENDICULAR LINES

Parallel lines have the same rise over run—that is, they have the same slope. Only the y-intercepts vary.

Recall that when the equation of a line is in the form:

$$y = mx + b$$

we can read the slope, "m," directly from the equation.

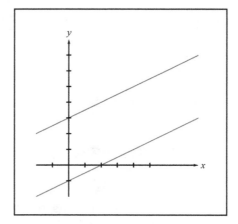

The equations of the lines above are $y = \frac{1}{2}x + 3$ and $y = \frac{1}{2}x - 1$. Both have a slope of $\frac{1}{2}$.

Perpendicular lines have slopes that are negative reciprocals. Consider the line: $y = 2x - 6$. Its slope is 2. The slope of a line parallel to this line is 2. The slope of a line perpendicular to it is $-\frac{1}{2}$.

Can you find the mistake in the chart below?

Equation of the line	Its slope	Slope of parallel line	Slope of perpendicular line
$y = -3x - \frac{2}{3}$	-3	-3	$\frac{1}{3}$
$y = -x + 7$	-1	-1	1
$y = \frac{x}{3} + 11$	$\frac{x}{3}$	$\frac{x}{3}$	$-\frac{3}{x}$

The **mistake** is in the slope of the last equation. We could write $y=\frac{x}{3}+11$ as $y=\frac{1}{3}x+11$. Now we can see that the slope is not $\frac{x}{3}$; it is $\frac{1}{3}$.

The slope of the parallel line is also $\frac{1}{3}$ and a perpendicular line would have a slope of -3.

Example 1:

Find the equation of the line going through the point $(-1,1)$ that is perpendicular to the line $y=\frac{x}{2}+6$.

The slope of this line is ½, so the slope of a line that is perpendicular would be -2.

Substituting $m=-2$ and $(x_1,y_1)=(-1,1)$ into the point-slope equation gives us:

$$y-1=-2(x--1) \text{ or } y-1=-2(x+1)$$

$$y-1=-2x-2$$

$$y=-2x-1$$

INTRA-SECTION EXERCISES:

16. Find the equation of a line going through the point $(0,4.2)$ that is perpendicular to the line $y=0.5x-8$.
17. Find the equation of a line going through the point $(9,0.5)$ that is parallel to the line $y=\frac{2}{3}x+17$.

Solutions

16. We let $(x_1,y_1)=(0,4.2)$. The slope of the given equation is 0.5, so the slope of a line perpendicular would be $-\frac{1}{0.5}=-2$. Using the formula: $y-y_1=m(x-x_1)$, we substitute to get:

$$y-4.2=-2(x-0)$$
$$y-4.2=-2x$$
$$y=-2x+4.2$$

17. We let $(x_1, y_1) = (9, 0.5)$. The slope of the given equation is $\frac{2}{3}$, so the slope of a line parallel would be $\frac{2}{3}$. Using the formula $y - y_1 = m(x - x_1)$, we substitute to get:

$$y - 0.5 = \frac{2}{3}(x - 9)$$

$$y - 0.5 = \frac{2}{3}x - 6$$

$$y = \frac{2}{3}x - 5.5$$

WE RETURN TO THE SAGA OF KEANI AND KENT

Keani and Kent wish to expand their bakery, so they take their sales figures to the bank to apply for a loan. Although Keani and Kent might see the data points as rising sales, the bank officials are more interested in the trend—that is, the bank officials are more interested in the slope of the sales curve.

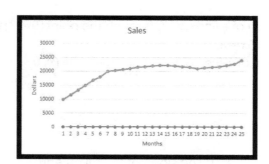

THE SLOPE OF A CURVE

The graph of Ken and Keani's sales figures is not a straight line. Direction along the curve constantly changes. What do we mean by the slope of a curve?

To examine the slope of a curve, we need to remember tangents.

Imagine an Argentinian gaucho swinging his bola in a circle around his head. The bola stays on a circular path because he applies forces to the bola. His arm resists the pull of the bola. If no forces were applied to the bola, it would follow a straight line path. The bola follows a path tangential to the circle when it is released. That is, its path will be along a tangent line to the circle.

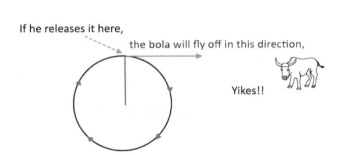

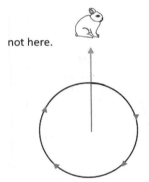

From geometry class, you might remember that tangents are always perpendicular to the radius of a circle.

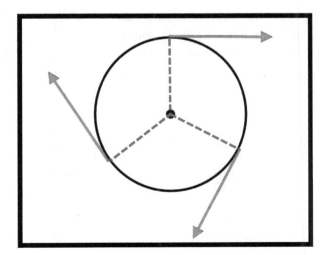

The tangents tell us the direction in which the bola is heading. We can see that on every point of its circle, it has a direction.

The slope of a curve gives the tangential direction along the curve; the direction of travel if no forces are applied.

Examples of tangents to curves (directions):

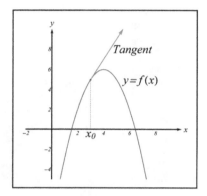
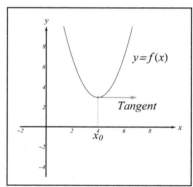
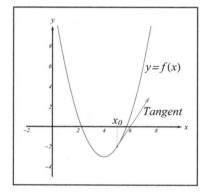

Notice that the slope of the curve at right is not constant. Around the origin it is very steep, but it gets flatter as we go from left to right. The slope continues to change. *Only the slopes of straight lines stay constant.*

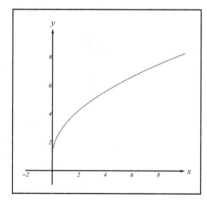

Suppose we mark the curve off at $x = 1$, $x = 2$, $x = 3$, etc. Each change in x or Δx will equal one unit. Then the slope will be the change in y-values, or rise, over the change in x-values (the run). But the x-values will be changing by just 1 each time, so the slope will be equal to the change in y-values.

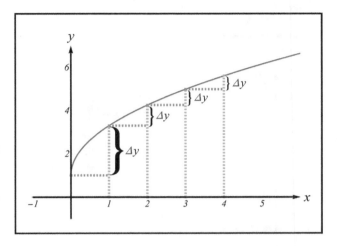

Notice that the rise, or change in heights (y-values), decreases as the curve flattens out. The *slope is decreasing* as the curve flattens out.

You can see that the slope gets flatter and flatter by examining the slopes of succeeding tangents as we go from left to right, too.

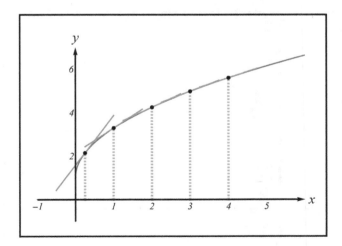

The tangents are getting flatter and flatter. The slope of the curve is decreasing.

We will use the same procedure for the curve below, marking off Δx's of 1 unit each. Once again, we can examine the slope $\left(\dfrac{\Delta y}{\Delta x} = \dfrac{change \ in \ y}{change \ in \ x} \right)$ by observing the change in y-values only. We see that each Δy is greater than the one before it. *The slope of the curve is increasing.*

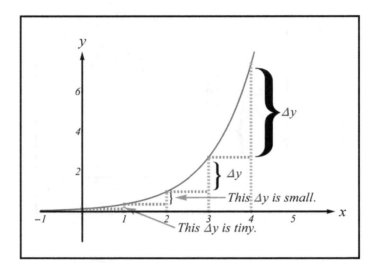

We can also see that the slope of the curve is increasing because its tangents are getting steeper and steeper.

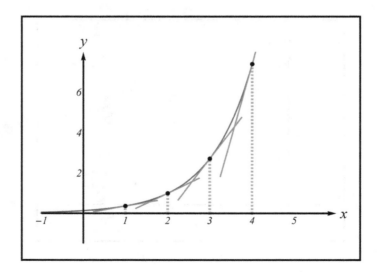

The curve below is also getting flatter and flatter, but the slope is negative. The absolute value of the slope is getting smaller and smaller.

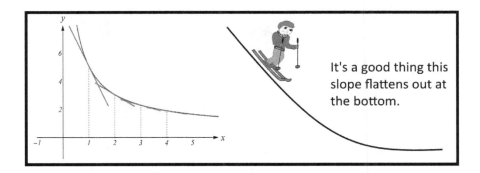

Unfortunately for the canoer below, the slope of the curve he's on is negative and getting steeper.

SLOPES AS RATES OF CHANGE

In general, a slope indicates a rate of change. It tells us how whatever is on the y-axis is changing with respect to whatever is on the x-axis. Or we could say it tells us how whatever is on the y-axis is changing per unit on the x-axis.

The graph below charts the number of vehicle accidents in a community with respect to the number of licensed teenaged drivers. While the number of accidents is increasing, the slope is getting flatter. That means the number of accidents per teen driver is decreasing.

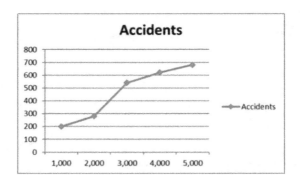

The chart below represents the median price of homes in a Midwestern community between 1982 ($t = 0$) and 2012 ($t = 20$). The slope represents change in median housing price per year. The graph indicates a steady increase in median housing prices until a drastic decline around $t = 27$ (2009). Before 2009, the slope, representing increase in median housing price per year, is nearly a straight line. The increase each year is nearly constant.

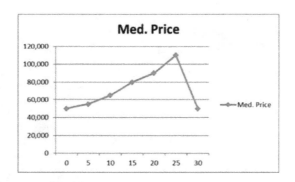

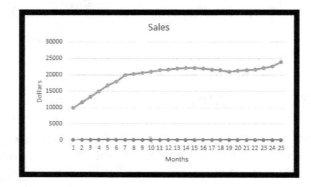

The slope on Keani and Kent's sales chart indicates $\dfrac{change\ in\ sales}{month}$. The slope shows a steady increase in sales but is beginning to flatten out. While actual sales are increasing, the *increase* in sales (change in sales per month) is getting smaller. This may be part of the normal business cycle for a new business. It may be due to seasonal variations or to conditions in the general economy. On the other hand, the decrease may be due to a falling customer base. The bank analyst will make these determinations.

Example 2:

The Bixby Company owns an apartment building. The units have an 80% occupancy rate when a monthly rent of $400/unit is charged. They have a 60% occupancy rate when a monthly rent of $550/unit is charged.

a. Write a linear equation giving the occupancy rate y, for any given rent x.
b. Predict the occupancy rate for a rent of $475.

Imagine making a graph of occupancy rate versus rent. We would expect a negative slope because of the inverse relationship between rent and occupancy rate; i.e., the higher the rate, the lower the occupancy rate. We would expect an x-intercept where the rent charged is so high that no one rents, and we would expect that at a rent of $0 we would have 100% occupancy, or even more.

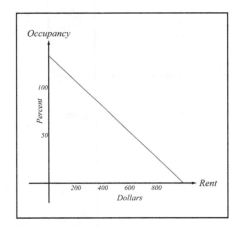

a. We are given two points for this graph of rent versus occupancy rate. These are ($400, 80%) and ($550, 60%). We can now find the slope, and then using the point-slope form, we can find a linear equation that will yield the occupancy rate for any given rent.

$$m = \frac{60\% - 80\%}{\$550 - \$400} = \frac{-20}{150} \approx -.133.$$

We'll use the point ($400, 80%) for (x_1, y_1).

$$y - 80 = -.133(x - 400)$$
$$y - 80 = -.133x + 53.2$$
$$y = -.133x + 133.2$$

b. We can now use the equation in (a) to solve for the occupancy rate y when the rent $x = \$475$.

$$y = -.133(475) + 133.2$$

$$y \approx 70\%$$

Example 3:

Kent and Keani decide to add a commercial pizza oven to their bakery, at a cost of $11,500. It should have a lifespan of 20 years and a salvage value of $400.

a. Write a linear equation given the value of the oven y for each year t.
b. What is the value of the oven after 10 years?

Because we know that the oven has a value of $11,500 when it is new, at $t = 0$, and we know that after $t = 20$ years, its value will have dropped to $400, we have two points: (0, \$11, 500) and (20, \$400) from which to find the slope of an equation. We can then use the point-slope formula to compute a linear equation for the value of the oven.

$$m = \frac{\$400 - \$11,500}{20 - 0 \ years} = \frac{-\$11,100}{20 \ years} = -\$555/year$$ We'll use the point

$$(0, 11,500) \text{ for } (x_1, t_1).$$

$$y - \$11,500 = {}^{-\$555}\!\!\big/\!_{yr} (t - 0) yrs$$

$$y - \$11,500 = {}^{-\$555}\!\!\big/\!_{yr} (t \ yrs)$$

$$y = {}^{-\$555}\!\!\big/\!_{yr} (t \ yrs) + \$11,500$$

For $t = 5$ years, $y = {}^{-\$555}\!\!\big/\!_{yr} (5 \ yrs) + \$11,500 = \$8725$

In our next section, we will discuss the calculus behind the slope of a curve.

IIIR1 SLOPES AND EQUATIONS OF LINES EXERCISES

1. Find the slope of the line passing through the points $(2, 3)$ and $(3, 6)$.

2. Find the slope of the line passing through the points $(5, 3)$ and $(6, 2)$.

3. Find the slope of the line passing through the points $(5, 6)$ and $(1, -2)$.

4. Find the slope of the line passing through the points $(4, -6)$ and $(-3, 2)$.

5. Find the equation of the line passing through the point $(2, -1)$ with slope -4.

6. Find the equation of the line passing through the point $(4, 1)$ with slope -3.

7. Find the equation of the line passing through the point $(-6, 2)$ with slope $\frac{1}{3}$.

8. Find the equation of the line passing through the point $(6, 9)$ with slope $-\frac{2}{3}$.

9. Sketch and find the equation of the line passing through the point $(2, 6)$ with slope 0.

10. Sketch and find the equation of the line passing through the point $(3, -4)$ with slope 0.

11. Find the equation of the line passing through the points $(6, 1)$ and parallel to the line $y = -\frac{x}{6} + 11$.

12. Find the equation of the line passing through the point $(1, 6)$ and parallel to the line $y = \frac{-x}{3} - 1$.

13. Find the equation of the line passing through the point $(6, 1)$ and perpendicular to the line $y = \frac{-x}{6} + 1$.

14. Find the equation of the line passing through the point $(1, 6)$ and perpendicular to the line $y = \frac{-x}{3} - 1$.

15. Find the equation of the line running through the points $(2, 3)$ and $(-2, 3)$. (Hint: A sketch might help.)

16. Find the equation of the line running through the points $(4, -5)$ and $(4, 1)$. (Hint: A sketch might help.)

17. Find the equation of the line running through the points $(1, 8)$ and $(1, -3)$.

18. Find the equation of the line running through the points $(3, -5)$ and $(1, -5)$.

19. Find the slope and y-intercept (if possible) for the equation of the line $x - 5y = 20$.

20. Find the slope and y-intercept (if possible) for the equation of the line $2x + 5y = 20$.

21. Find the slope and y-intercept (if possible) for the equation of the line $3x - y = 20$.

22. Find the slope and y-intercept (if possible) for the equation of the line $2x - y = 10$.

23. Find the x-intercept(s) (if possible) for the equation of the line $y = \frac{2}{5}x - 4$.

24. Find the x-intercept(s) (if possible) for the equation of the line $y = \frac{-1}{4}x - 4$.

25. Find the y-intercept(s) (if possible) for the equation $y = \frac{2x}{5 - x}$.

26. Find the y-intercept(s) (if possible) for the equation $y = \frac{-2x}{x - 4}$.

27. Find the x-intercept(s) (if possible) for the equation $y = 2x^2 - 8$.

28. Find the x-intercept(s) (if possible) for the equation $y = 3x^2 - 27$.

29. A heavy equipment company builds a garage to house its vehicles for $125,000. The garage has an expected lifetime of 25 years and a salvage value of $20,000 (value of the lot).
    a. Write a linear equation giving the value y of the building for any given year t.
    b. What is the value of the building after 10 years?

30. A landscaping company builds an additional greenhouse for $260,000. It has an expected lifetime of 30 years and a salvage value of $6,000.
    a. Write a linear equation giving the value y of the building for any given year t.
    b. What is the value of the building after 10 years?

31. A school builds a shop to service its school buses for a cost of $535,000. If the expected life of the building is 30 years and the salvage value is $12,000:

a. Write a linear equation giving the value y of the building for any given year t.
b. What is the value of the building after 10 years?

32. A church builds an addition for its Sunday school classes at a cost of $403,000. If the expected life of the building is 30 years and the salvage value is $7,000:
   a. Write a linear equation giving the value y of the building for any given year t.
   b. What is the value of the building after 10 years?

33. The population of Exeter County was 52,300 in the year 2010 and 48,230 in the year 2015. Assume the relationship between the population y and the year t is linear. Let $t = 0$ represent the year 2010.
   a. Write a linear model for the data. What is the slope, and what does it tell you about the population?
   b. Estimate the population in the year 2012.
   c. Predict the population in the year 2020.

34. The population of Current City was 22,800 in the year 2010 and 25,200 in the year 2015. Assume the relationship between the population y and the year t is linear. Let $t = 0$ represent the year 2010.
   a. Write a linear model for the data. What is the slope, and what does it tell you about the population?
   b. Estimate the population in the year 2012.
   c. Predict the population in the year 2020.

IIIR1 SLOPES AND EQUATIONS OF LINES
SOLUTIONS TO EXERCISES

1. $\dfrac{y_2 - y_1}{x_2 - x_1} = \dfrac{6-3}{3-2} = 3$

2. $m = -1$

3. $\dfrac{y_2 - y_1}{x_2 - x_1} = \dfrac{6 - -2}{5-1}$

   $= \dfrac{8}{4} = 2$

4. $m = -\dfrac{8}{7}$

5. $y - (-1) =$
   $-4(x-2)$
   $y + 1 =$
   $-4x + 8$
   $y = -4x + 7$

6. $y = -3x + 13$

7. $y - 2 =$
   $\dfrac{1}{3}(x - (-6))$
   $y = \dfrac{1}{3}x + 4$

8. $y = \dfrac{-2}{3}x + 13$

9. $y - 6$
   $= 0(x-2)$
   $y - 6 = 0$
   $y = 6$

10. $y = -4$

11. $m = -\dfrac{1}{6}$
    $y - 1 = -\dfrac{1}{6}(x - 6)$
    $y - 1 = -\dfrac{x}{6} + 1$
    $y = -\dfrac{x}{6} + 2$

12. $y = -\dfrac{x}{3} + \dfrac{19}{3}$

13. $m = 6$
    $y - 1 = 6(x - 6)$
    $y - 1 = 6x - 36$
    $y = 6x - 35$

14. $y = 3x + 3$

15. $m = \dfrac{3-3}{-2-2} = \dfrac{0}{-4} = 0$
    $y - 3 = 0(x - 2)$
    $y = 3$, a horizontal line

16. $x = 4$, a vertical line

17. $m = \dfrac{-3-8}{1-1} = \dfrac{-11}{0}$, a vertical line

$x = 1$

18. $y = -5$, a horizontal line

19. $A = 1, B = -5; m = -\dfrac{A}{B} = -\dfrac{1}{-5} = \dfrac{1}{5}$

$0 - 5y = 20$

$y = -4$; y-intercept: $(0, -4)$

20. $m = -\dfrac{2}{5}$; y-intercept: $(0, 4)$

21. $A = 3, B = -1; m = -\dfrac{A}{B} = -\dfrac{3}{-1} = 3$

$3(0) - y = 20$

$y = -20$; y-intercept: $(0, -20)$

22. $m = 2$; y-intercept: $(0, -10)$

23. $0 = \dfrac{2}{5}x - 4$

$4 = \dfrac{2}{5}x$

$\dfrac{5}{2}(4) = x$

$x = 10$; x-intercept: $(10, 0)$

24. x-intercept: $(-16, 0)$

25. $y = \dfrac{2(0)}{5-0} = \dfrac{0}{5} = 0$

y-intercept: $(0, 0)$

26. y-intercept: $(0, 0)$

27. $0 = 2(x^2 - 4)$

$0 = 2(x + 2)(x - 2)$

$x = -2, 2$

x-intercepts: $(-2, 0), (2, 0)$

28. x-intercepts: $(3, 0), (-3, 0)$

29. a. $(0, \$125{,}000) = (t_1, y_1)$

$(25, \$20{,}000) = (t_2, y_2)$

$m = \dfrac{\$20{,}000 - \$125{,}000}{25 - 0}$

$= \dfrac{-\$105{,}000}{25} = -\$4200$

$y - \$125{,}000 = -\$4200(t - 0)$

$y = -\$4200t + \$125{,}000$

b. $y = -\$4200(10) + \$125{,}000$

$= \$83{,}000$

30. a. $y = -\$8466.67 + \$260{,}000$

b. $\$175{,}333.33$

31. a. $(0, \$535,000)=(t_1, y_1)$

   $(30, \$12,000)=(t_2, y_2)$

   $m = \dfrac{12,000-535,000}{30-0}$

   $= \dfrac{-523,000}{30} = -\$17,433$

   $y-\$535,000 = -\$17,433(t-0)$

   $y = -\$17,433t + \$535,000$

   b. $y = -\$17,433(10) + \$535,000$
   $= \$360,670$

32. a. $y = -\$13,200t + \$403,000$

   b. $\$271,000$

33. a. $(0, 52,300) = (t_1, y_1)$

   $(5, 48,230) = (t_2, y_2)$

   $m = \dfrac{48,230-52,300}{5-0}$

   $= \dfrac{-40700}{5} = -814$

   The population is decreasing each year.

   $y - 52,300 = -814(t-0)$

   $y = -814t + 52,300$

   b. $y = -814(2) + 52,300$
   $y = 50,672$

   c. $y = -814(10) + 52,300$
   $y = 44,160$

34. a. $y = 22,800 + 480t$

   $m = 480$ *The population is increasing.*

   b. $23,760$

   c. $27,600$

Definition of the Derivative

Recall the slope of a straight line is found by the formula $m = \dfrac{y_2 - y_1}{x_2 - x_1}$.

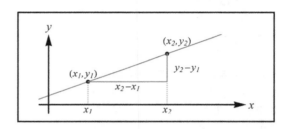

Consider the graph of the straight line below.

Suppose we let Δx be the distance between x_1 and x_2.

The y-value on the graph that corresponds to x_1 could be called $f(x_1)$, and the y-value that corresponds to x_2 could be called $f(x_2)$.

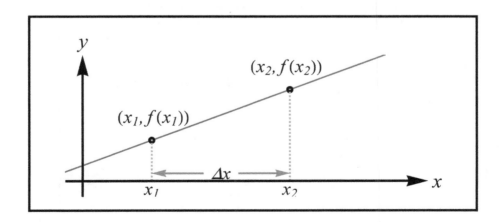

Next, we notice that x_2 could also be called $x_1 + \Delta x$. Then $f(x_2)$ could become $f(x_1 + \Delta x)$. Finally, let's replace x_1 with plain old x. Then our picture becomes:

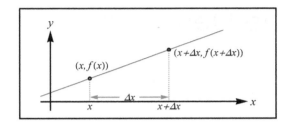

Our equation for slope is now: $\quad m = \dfrac{y_2 - y_1}{x_2 - x_1} = \dfrac{f(x + \Delta x) - f(x)}{x + \Delta x - x} = \dfrac{f(x + \Delta x) - f(x)}{\Delta x}$.

Suppose $f(x)$ is a curve and we want the slope of the curve at the point $(x, f(x))$.

If we use our old two-point equation, we will succeed only in finding the slope of the straight line that connects the two points; that is, the secant between the points.

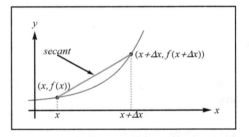

Recall that the slope of the curve at $(x, f(x))$ is the slope of the tangent to the curve at $(x, f(x))$.

Notice that as we let Δx become smaller and smaller, the secant connecting the two points gets closer and closer to the direction of the tangent line.

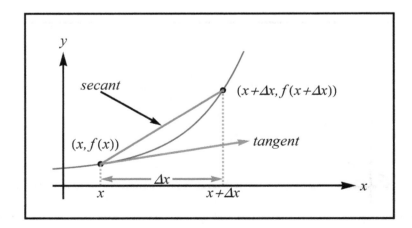

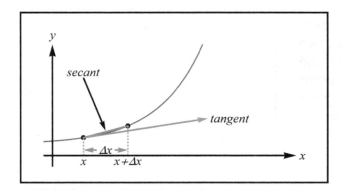

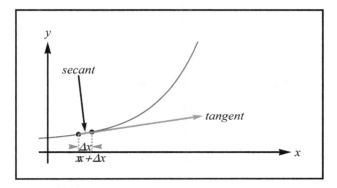

If we let Δx approach a distance of 0, then the secant will actually lie on top of the tangent. The slope of the curve at $(x, f(x))$ is therefore:

$$m = \lim_{\Delta x \to 0} \frac{f(x + \Delta x) - f(x)}{\Delta x} = f'(x) = \frac{dy}{dx}$$

This limit is called the derivative of $f(x)$. It gives us the formula for the slope of $f(x)$ at any point.

Let's consider an example. The function $y = f(x) = -x^2 + 6x - 6$ is graphed at right. Its tangent at the point $(2, f(2))$ is graphed in red. Let's try to find the equation of this tangent.

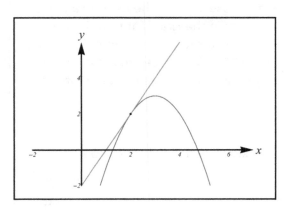

We can approximate the tangent line using a secant line through two points on the curve. We'll use the point $(2, f(2)) = (2,2)$ and the point $(3, f(3)) = (3,3)$. The secant is graphed at right in purple, and the tangent of interest is in red.

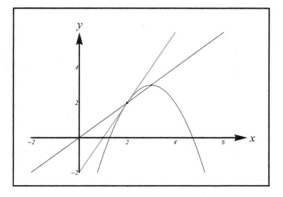

The slope of this secant will be:

$$\frac{y_2 - y_1}{x_2 - x_1} = \frac{3-2}{3-2} = 1$$

Using our formula $y - y_1 = m(x - x_1)$, we find the equation of this secant.

$$y - 2 = 1(x - 2)$$

$$y = x$$

So far, our estimation of the equation of the tangent line is $y = x$, but if we choose an x-value that is closer to $x = 2$, we can find a better approximation to the true tangent line. Suppose we choose $x = 2.5$. The new secant line appears in the graph at right in green. It passes through the points $(2, 2)$ and $(2.5, 2.75)$. We can see that it is a closer approximation to the red tangent line.

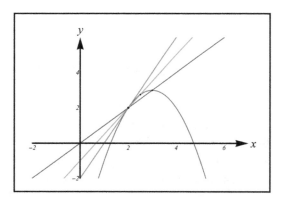

The slope of this secant will be:

$$\frac{y_2 - y_1}{x_2 - x_1} = \frac{2.75 - 2}{2.5 - 2} = 1.5$$

Using our formula $y - y_1 = m(x - x_1)$, we find the equation of this secant.

$$y - 2 = 1.5(x - 2)$$

$$y = 1.5x - 1$$

Let's do one more iteration. This time, we will choose the secant through the points (2, 2) and (2.1, 2.19). This secant has a slope $m = 1.9$ and equation of $y = 1.9x - 1.8$. It is graphed at right in orange. We can see that it is an even better approximation to the tangent.

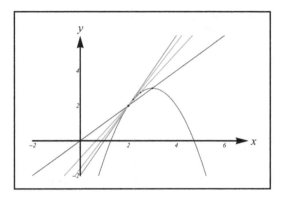

Once again, we see that as our $x + \Delta x$ values get closer and closer to x, the line connecting the corresponding points on the graph gets closer and closer to the tangent line. When we take the limit as Δx approaches 0, the line will actually lie on top of the tangent. Since we have defined the slope of a curve at the point $(x, f(x))$ to be the slope of its tangent at $(x, f(x))$, then our equation for finding this slope will be:

$$\lim_{\Delta x \to 0} \frac{f(x + \Delta x) - f(x)}{\Delta x}.$$

We are going to make one further change in the notation. We will replace the distance Δx with the letter h. (It requires fewer strokes to write. If you've ever written a page full of Δ's, you'll appreciate the difference.)

Both $f'(x)$ and $\dfrac{dy}{dx}$ are used for the derivative. We have two systems because calculus was invented independently and contemporaneously by Leibniz in Germany and Newton in England. Both systems have advantages, and both remain in common use. A hybrid symbol is also used occasionally for the derivative of y: y'.

Our formal definition of derivative is now: $\dfrac{dy}{dx} = f'(x) = \lim_{h \to 0} \dfrac{f(x + h) - f(x)}{h}$

We now know some characteristics of the derivative.

1. It gives us an equation that will compute the slope of a curve at any point.
2. It is a limit, so we can use the properties of limits when working with derivatives.
3. It gives us a rate of change. It tells us how whatever is on the *y*-axis varies per unit of whatever is on the *x*-axis.

Some examples will be helpful.

Example 1:

For $f(x) = 3x^2 - 4$, find

a. the derivative $f'(x)$.
b. the slope of the curve $f(x)$ at the point $(-2,8)$.
c. the equation of the tangent to $f(x)$ at $(-2, 8)$.

a. In order to find $\lim\limits_{h \to 0} \dfrac{f(x+h) - f(x)}{h}$, we will need to find $f(x+h)$.

In $f(x)$ we replace x with whatever is inside the parentheses; in this case, with $x + h$.

Therefore, $f(x+h) = 3(x+h)^2 - 4$.

Substituting $f(x+h)$) and $f(x) = 3x^2 - 4$ into our formal equation for the derivative, we have:

$$\lim\limits_{h \to 0} \frac{3(x+h)^2 - 4 - (3x^2 - 4)}{h}$$

Next we prepare to FOIL the $(x+h)^2$ term.

$$\lim\limits_{h \to 0} \frac{3(x+h)(x+h) - 4 - (3x^2 - 4)}{h}$$

We multiply out, or FOIL, the $(x+h)(x+h)$ terms, and we distribute the minus in: $-(3x^2 - 4)$.

$$\lim\limits_{h \to 0} \frac{3(x^2 + 2xh + h^2) - 4 - 3x^2 + 4}{h}$$

Next we distribute the leading coefficient of 3.

$$\lim\limits_{h \to 0} \frac{3x^2 + 6xh + 3h^2 - 4 - 3x^2 + 4}{h}$$

Collecting like terms gives us: $\lim\limits_{h\to 0}\dfrac{6xh+3h^2}{h}$

We still need to substitute a 0 for h, but if we do it, we get $\lim\limits_{h\to 0}\dfrac{0+0}{0}$, which we know is indeterminate. So we try factoring first.

$\lim\limits_{h\to 0}\dfrac{6xh+3h^2}{h}=\lim\limits_{h\to 0}\dfrac{h(6x+3h)}{h}$. Canceling the h gives us: $\lim\limits_{h\to 0}6x+3h$.

Now if we substitute $h=0$, we get: $6x+3(0)=6x$.

So our derivative is $f'(x)=6x$.

b. If we want to know the slope of our curve $f(x)$ where $x=-1$, we substitute -1 for x. Similarly, if we want to know the slope of our curve $f(x)$ where $x=-1.4$, we substitute -1.4 for x, or at $x=3\pi$, we use 3π for x.

In part b), we want to know the slope of the given curve $f(x)$ at the point $(-2,8)$, so we let $x=-2$ and substitute it for x in our equation for slope— that is, in the derivative, $f'(x)=6x$.

TaDa!

(Drum roll, please.) $slope=m=f'(-2)=6(-2)=-12$

c. We want to find the tangent to the curve. Since the tangent is a line, we use our line-finding equation: $y-y_1=m(x-x_1)$. We have $m=-12$ and $(x_1,y_1)=(-2,\ 8)$.

Now we just substitute.

$$y-8=-12(x--2)$$

$$y-8=-12x-24$$

$$y=-12x-16$$

In the graph below, you can see a picture of the tangent at the point $(-2,8)$. It has a steep negative slope ($m=-12$, no less) and a y-intercept at $y=-16$, which is exactly what we found.

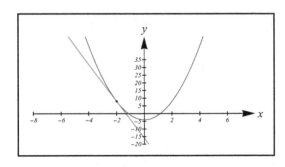

INTRA-SECTION EXERCISES:

1. The curve $f(x)=-2x^3+9x$ has derivative $f'(x)=-6x^2+9$.

   a. Find the slope of the curve at the point $(3,-27)$.
   b. Find the equation of the tangent to the curve at the point $(3,-27)$.

2. The curve $y=4x^2-5x$ has derivative $\dfrac{dy}{dx}=8x-5$.

   a. Find the slope of the curve at the point $(2,6)$.
   b. Find the equation of the tangent to the curve at the point $(2,6)$.

3. Find the derivative of the function $f(x)=4x+2$.

Solutions

1. a. $m=f'(3)=-6(3^2)+9=-45$
   b. $y--27=-45\,(x-3)$
      $y+27=-45x+135$
      $y=-45x+108$

2. a. $m=\dfrac{dy}{dx}\bigg|_{x=2}=8(2)-5=11$

   b. $y-6=11\,(x-2)$
      $y-6=11x-22$
      $y=11x-16$

3. $f(x+h)=4(x+h)+2$

   $$f'(x)=\lim_{h\to0}\frac{f(x+h)-f(x)}{h}=\lim_{h\to0}\frac{4(x+h)+2-(4x+2)}{h}=\lim_{h\to0}\frac{4x+4h+2-4x-2}{h}=$$

   $$\lim_{h\to0}\frac{4h}{h}=\lim_{h\to0}4=4$$

   The slope is 4 everywhere because $f(x)=4x+2$ is a straight line.

Example 2:

For $f(x)=\dfrac{3}{x^2}$ find

a. the derivative: $f'(x)$.
b. the slope of the curve $f(x)$ at $x=-1$.
c. the equation of the tangent to $f(x)$ at $x=-1$.

For part a), we begin by finding $f(x+h)$. It would be: $\dfrac{3}{(x+h)^2}$. Our definition for derivatives then becomes:

$$\lim_{h \to 0} \frac{\dfrac{3}{(x+h)^2} - \dfrac{3}{x^2}}{h}$$

Some people call them baby denominators.

Example 2:

We now have a complex fraction—i.e., it has subordinate denominators—so we multiply the numerator and denominator by the product of all the subordinate denominators: $(x+h)^2 x^2$.

$$\lim_{h \to 0} \frac{\dfrac{3}{(x+h)^2} - \dfrac{3}{x^2}}{h} \cdot \frac{\dfrac{((x+h)^2)(x^2)}{1}}{\dfrac{((x+h)^2)(x^2)}{1}} = \lim_{h \to 0} \frac{\dfrac{3}{(x+h)^2} \dfrac{(x+h)^2 x^2}{1} - \dfrac{3}{x^2} \dfrac{(x+h)^2 x^2}{1}}{h(x+h)^2(x^2)}$$

If we cancel out the baby denominators, I mean subordinate denominators, we have:

$$\lim_{h \to 0} \frac{3x^2 - 3(x+h)^2}{h(x+h)^2(x^2)}$$

When we have separate terms of products in the numerator, we multiply (FOIL) them out and collect like terms. However, we generally leave the factored denominators un-FOILed.

Therefore, our next step is to multiply the $(x+h)^2 = (x+h)(x+h)$ in the numerator.

$$\lim_{h \to 0} \frac{3x^2 - 3(x^2 + 2xh + h^2)}{h(x+h)^2 x^2}$$

Now we distribute the -3 to get:

$$\lim_{h \to 0} \frac{3x^2 - 3x^2 - 6xh - 3h^2)}{h(x+h)^2 x^2}$$

Collecting like terms, we have:

$$\lim_{h \to 0} \frac{-6xh - 3h^2}{h(x+h)^2 x^2}$$

Once again, if we substitute $h=0$, we get the indeterminate $\dfrac{0}{0}$, so we factor the h out of the numerator. This gives us:

$$\lim_{h \to 0} \frac{h(-6x-3h)}{h(x+h)^2 x^2}$$

If we cancel the h's we can now substitute $h=0$ to get:

$$\frac{-6x-3(0)}{(x+0)^2 x^2} = \frac{-6x}{x^2 x^2} = -\frac{6x}{x^4} = \frac{-6}{x^3}$$

Therefore, $f'(x) = -\dfrac{6}{x^3}$.

Now for part b): We want the slope of the curve at $x=-1$, so we simply substitute $x=-1$ into the derivative:

$$m = f'(-1) = \frac{-6}{(-1)^3} = \frac{-6}{-1} = 6$$

Ta Dah! We did it again!

For part c), we need to find the equation of a tangent line. To use our equation for finding a line, we need a slope, $m=6$, and a point. We have $x=-1$. We notice that this is only half of a point.

But do not despair. We know how to find the corresponding y-value when we know x. We go back to our original equation: $f(x) = y = \dfrac{3}{x^2}$.

Since we want to find y when $x=-1$, we substitute:

$$y = f(-1) = \frac{3}{(-1)^2} = 3$$

Remember that $f(x)$ gives us a y-value, or height.
The derivative $f'(x)$ gives us a slope.

Now we have both the slope ($m=6$) and a point $(-1,3)$ for (x_1,y_1). We substitute these into our equation-finding line:

$$y-y_1=m(x-x_1)$$

$$y-3=6(x--1)$$

$$y-3=6x+6$$

$$y=6x+9$$

Once again, we can inspect the graph and check out the slope and tangent at the point $(-1,3)$.

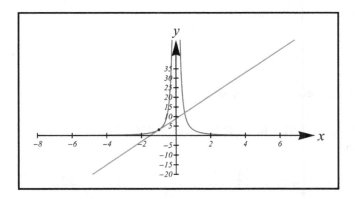

You'll notice the slope is steep and positive, $m=6$ actually, and the y-intercept appears to be at a height of 9.

Example 3:

Find the derivative of $y=f(x)=45$.

Because there is no x, $f(x+h)=45$. We substitute these values into our derivative equation.

$$f'(x)=\lim_{h\to0}\frac{f(x+h)-f(x)}{h}=\lim_{h\to0}\frac{45-45}{h}=\lim_{h\to0}0=0$$

The derivative of a constant function is zero. The constant function $y=45$ is the equation of a horizontal line. It has a slope of 0 everywhere, which the derivative confirms.

Example 4:

Find the derivative of $y=f(x)=5x-6$.

$f(x+h)=5(x+h)-6$. We substitute $f(x)$ and $f(x+h)$ into our derivative equation.

$$f'(x)=\lim_{h\to0}\frac{f(x+h)-f(x)}{h}=\lim_{h\to0}\frac{5(x+h)-6-(5x-6)}{h}=$$

$$=\lim_{h\to0}\frac{5x+5h-6-5x+6}{h}=\lim_{h\to0}\frac{5h}{h}=\lim_{h\to0}5=5$$

The function $f(x)=5x-6$ is a straight line, so its slope is constant, as confirmed by the derivative.

Example 5:

Find the derivative of $y=\sqrt{3x}-4$.

$f(x+h)=\sqrt{3(x+h)}-4$. We substitute $f(x)$ and $f(x+h)$ into our derivative equation.

$$f'(x)=\lim_{h\to0}\frac{f(x+h)-f(x)}{h}=\lim_{h\to0}\frac{\sqrt{3(x+h)}-4-(\sqrt{3x}-4)}{h}=$$

$$\lim_{h\to0}\frac{\sqrt{3x+3h}-4-\sqrt{3x}+4}{h}=\lim_{h\to0}\frac{\sqrt{3x+3h}-\sqrt{3x}}{h}$$

To clear the radical, we need to multiply the numerator and denominator by the conjugate of $\sqrt{3x+3h}-\sqrt{3x}$. That would be $\sqrt{3x+3h}+\sqrt{3x}$.

QUICK ASIDE TO REVIEW CONJUGATES

The conjugate of $\sqrt{x}-7$ would be $\sqrt{x}+7$.

The conjugate of $18-5\sqrt{2x}$ would be $18+5\sqrt{2x}$.

Conjugate
Relationship

Conjugates look exactly alike, except that the sign in the middle is the opposite. When conjugates are multiplied, the radical signs are eliminated. For example, if we FOIL $\sqrt{x} - 7$ with its conjugate, we have:

$$(\sqrt{x} - 7)(\sqrt{x} + 7) = \sqrt{x}\sqrt{x} + 7\sqrt{x} - 7\sqrt{x} - 49 = x - 49$$

The middle terms containing the radicals will cancel out. Let's try FOILing $18 - 5\sqrt{2x}$ and its conjugate.

$$(18 - 5\sqrt{2x})(18 + 5\sqrt{2x}) = 324 + 90\sqrt{2x} - 90\sqrt{2x} - 25\sqrt{2x}\sqrt{2x} =$$

$$325 - 25(2x) = 325 - 50x$$

INTRA-SECTION EXERCISES:

Find the conjugates:

    4. $3.5 - \sqrt{4x}$ 5. $\sqrt{8x} + 11$ 6. $1 - \sqrt{-3+x}$

Solutions

    4. $3.5 + \sqrt{4x}$ 5. $\sqrt{8x} - 11$ 6. $1 + \sqrt{-3+x}$

Back to Example 5:

We were about to multiply the numerator and denominator of $\lim\limits_{h \to 0} \dfrac{\sqrt{3x + 3h} - \sqrt{3x}}{h}$ by the conjugate of the numerator.

$$\lim_{h \to 0} \frac{(\sqrt{3x + 3h} - \sqrt{3x})}{h} \cdot \frac{(\sqrt{3x + 3h} + \sqrt{3x})}{(\sqrt{3x + 3h} + \sqrt{3x})} =$$

$$\lim_{h \to 0} \frac{\sqrt{3x + 3h}\sqrt{3x + 3h} + \sqrt{3x + 3h}\sqrt{3x} - \sqrt{3x + 3h}\sqrt{3x} - \sqrt{3x}\sqrt{3x}}{h} =$$

$$\lim_{h \to 0} \frac{3x + 3h - 3x}{h} = \lim_{h \to 0} \frac{3h}{h} = \lim_{h \to 0} 3 = 3$$

*A word of caution: $f(x+h)$ does not mean that we automatically add h to the end of the function. We *do* replace every x in the function with $x+h$. For example, consider the function $f(x)=5x^2-7x$. Then $f(x+h)$ **does not equal** $5x^2-7x+h$. It *does* equal $5(x+h)^2-7(x+h)$.

*Also remember to write $\lim_{h\to 0}$ for every step until you actually take the limit by substituting 0 for h.

IIIC2 DEFINITION OF THE DERIVATIVE EXERCISES

Using the limit definition of a derivative, find

     a.   the derivative of each function below.
     b.   the slope of the function at the given point.
     c.   the equation of the tangent line to the curve at the given point.

1. $f(x) = 3x^2 + 1$; at $(2, 13)$

2. $f(x) = -2x^2 + 3$; at $(2, -5)$

3. $f(x) = \dfrac{3}{x+2}$ at $x = 1$

4. $f(x) = \dfrac{1}{x-3}$ at $x = 1$

5. $f(x) = \sqrt{x} + 1$ at $(4, 3)$

6. $f(x) = \sqrt{x} - 1$ at $(4, 1)$

7. $f(x) = 4x - 6$ at $x = 0$

8. $f(x) = 2x + 6$ at $x = 0$

9. $f(x) = 2\sqrt{x}$ at $(4, 4)$

10. $f(x) = 5\sqrt{x}$ at $(1, 5)$

11. $f(x) = \dfrac{1}{x+3}$ at $(-2, 1)$

12. $f(x) = \dfrac{1}{x-4}$ at $(3, -1)$

IIIC2 DEFINITION OF THE DERIVATIVE SOLUTIONS TO EXERCISES

1. a. $f(x+h)=3(x+h)^2+1$ and $f'(x)=\lim_{h\to 0}\dfrac{f(x+h)-f(x)}{h}$

   $f'(x)=\lim_{h\to 0}\dfrac{3(x+h)^2+1-(3x^2+1)}{h}=\lim_{h\to 0}\dfrac{3(x^2+2xh+h^2)+1-3x^2-1}{h}$

   $=\lim_{h\to 0}\dfrac{3x^2+6xh+3h^2-3x^2}{h}$

   $\lim_{h\to 0}\dfrac{6xh+3h^2}{h}=\lim_{h\to 0}\dfrac{h(6x+3h)}{h}=\lim_{h\to 0}6x+3h=6x+3(0)=6x$

   b. $m=f'(2)=6(2)=12$

   c. $y-13=12(x-2)$
   $y-13=12x-24$
   $y=12x-11$

2. a. $f'(x)=-4x$ b. $m=f'(2)=-8$ c. $y=-8x+11$

3. a $f(x+h)=\dfrac{3}{x+h+2}$ and $f'(x)=\lim_{h\to 0}\dfrac{f(x+h)-f(x)}{h}$

   $\lim_{h\to 0}\dfrac{\dfrac{3}{x+h+2}-\dfrac{3}{x+2}}{h}$. We multiply by the product of the subordinate denominators.

   $\lim_{h\to 0}\dfrac{\dfrac{3}{x+h+2}-\dfrac{3}{x+2}}{h}\cdot\dfrac{(x+h+2)(x+2)}{(x+h+2)(x+2)}$

   $=\lim_{h\to 0}\dfrac{\dfrac{3}{x+h+2}(x+h+2)(x+2)-\dfrac{3}{x+2}(x+h+2)(x+2)}{h(x+h+2)(x+2)}$

   $=\lim_{h\to 0}\dfrac{3(x+2)-3(x+h+2)}{h(x+h+2)(x+2)}=\lim_{h\to 0}\dfrac{3x+6-3x-3h-6}{h(x+h+2)(x+2)}=\lim_{h\to 0}\dfrac{-3h}{h(x+h+2)(x+2)}$

   $=\lim_{h\to 0}\dfrac{-3}{(x+h+2)(x+2)}=\dfrac{-3}{(x+0+2)(x+2)}=\dfrac{-3}{(x+2)^2}$

   b. $m=f'(1)=\dfrac{-3}{(1+2)^2}=\dfrac{-3}{9}=-\dfrac{1}{3}$

c. We need to find the y-value when $x=1$: $y=f(1)=\dfrac{3}{1+2}=\dfrac{3}{3}=1$ giving us the point $(1,1)$

$$y-1=-\frac{1}{3}(x-1)$$

$$y-1=-\frac{x}{3}+\frac{1}{3}$$

$$y=-\frac{x}{3}+\frac{4}{3}$$

4. a. $f'(x)=-\dfrac{1}{(x-3)^2}$ c. at the point $\left(1,-\dfrac{1}{2}\right)$ $y=-\dfrac{x}{4}-\dfrac{1}{4}$

d. $m=f'(1)=-\dfrac{1}{4}$

5. a. $f(x+h)=\sqrt{x+h}+1$ and $f'(x)=\lim\limits_{h\to 0}\dfrac{f(x+h)-f(x)}{h}$

$$f'(x)=\lim_{h\to 0}\frac{\sqrt{x+h}+1-\left(\sqrt{x}+1\right)}{h}=\lim_{h\to 0}\frac{\sqrt{x+h}+1-\sqrt{x}-1}{h}=$$

$$\lim_{h\to 0}\frac{\left(\sqrt{x+h}-\sqrt{x}\right)}{h}\cdot\frac{\left(\sqrt{x+h}+\sqrt{x}\right)}{\left(\sqrt{x+h}+\sqrt{x}\right)}=$$

$$\lim_{h\to 0}\frac{\sqrt{x+h}\sqrt{x+h}+\sqrt{x+h}\sqrt{x}-\sqrt{x+h}\sqrt{x}-\sqrt{x}\sqrt{x}}{h\left(\sqrt{x+h}+\sqrt{x}\right)}=$$

$$\lim_{h\to 0}\frac{x+h-x}{h\left(\sqrt{x+h}+\sqrt{x}\right)}=\lim_{h\to 0}\frac{h}{h\left(\sqrt{x+h}+\sqrt{x}\right)}=\lim_{h\to 0}\frac{1}{\left(\sqrt{x+h}+\sqrt{x}\right)}=$$

$$\lim_{h\to 0}\frac{1}{\left(\sqrt{x+0}+\sqrt{x}\right)}=\frac{1}{2\sqrt{x}}$$

b. $m=f'(4)=\dfrac{1}{2\sqrt{4}}=\dfrac{1}{4}$

c. $y-3=\dfrac{1}{4}(x-4)$

$$y-3=\frac{x}{4}-1$$

$$y=\frac{x}{4}+2$$

6. a. $f'(x)=\dfrac{1}{2\sqrt{x}}$ 　　　　　 b. $m=f'(4)=\dfrac{1}{4}$ 　　　　　 c. $y=\dfrac{x}{4}$

7. a. $f(x+h)=4(x+h)-6$ and $f'(x)=\lim\limits_{h\to 0}\dfrac{f(x+h)-f(x)}{h}$

$$\lim\limits_{h\to 0}\dfrac{4(x+h)-6-(4x-6)}{h}=\lim\limits_{h\to 0}\dfrac{4x+4h-6-4x+6}{h}=\lim\limits_{h\to 0}\dfrac{4h}{h}=\lim\limits_{h\to 0}4=4$$

  b. $m=f'(0)=4$ *The slope is equal to 4 everywhere.*

  c. We first need to find the *y*-value when $x=0$;
  $y=f(0)=4(0)-6=-6$ gives us the point $(0,-6)$
  $y--6=4(x-0)$
  $y+6=4x$
  $y=4x-6$

8. a. $f'(x)=2$ 　　　　　　　　　　 c. at the point $(0,6)$, $y=2x+6$
  d. $m=2$

9. a. $f(x+h)=2\sqrt{x+h}$ and $f'(x)=\lim\limits_{h\to 0}\dfrac{f(x+h)-f(x)}{h}$

$f'(x)=\lim\limits_{h\to 0}\dfrac{2\sqrt{x+h}-2\sqrt{x}}{h}$. We multiply numerator and denominator by the conjugate.

$$\lim\limits_{h\to 0}\dfrac{(2\sqrt{x+h}-2\sqrt{x})}{h}\cdot\dfrac{(2\sqrt{x+h}+2\sqrt{x})}{(2\sqrt{x+h}+2\sqrt{x})}$$

$$=\lim\limits_{h\to 0}\dfrac{4\sqrt{x+h}\sqrt{x+h}+4\sqrt{x+h}\sqrt{x}-4\sqrt{x+h}\sqrt{x}-4\sqrt{x}\sqrt{x}}{h(2\sqrt{x+h}+2\sqrt{x})}$$

$$=\lim\limits_{h\to 0}\dfrac{4(x+h)-4x}{h(2\sqrt{x+h}+2\sqrt{x})}=\lim\limits_{h\to 0}\dfrac{4x+4h-4x}{h(2\sqrt{x+h}+2\sqrt{x})}$$

$$=\lim\limits_{h\to 0}\dfrac{4h}{h(2\sqrt{x+h}+2\sqrt{x})}=\lim\limits_{h\to 0}\dfrac{4}{(2\sqrt{x+h}+2\sqrt{x})}$$

$$=\dfrac{4}{(2\sqrt{x+0}+2\sqrt{x})}=\dfrac{4}{4\sqrt{x}}=\dfrac{1}{\sqrt{x}}$$

b. $m = f'(4) = \dfrac{1}{\sqrt{4}} = \dfrac{1}{2}$

c. $y - 4 = \dfrac{1}{2}(x - 4)$

$y - 4 = \dfrac{x}{2} - 2$

$y = \dfrac{x}{2} + 2$

10. a. $f'(x) = \dfrac{5}{2\sqrt{x}}$ b. $m = \dfrac{5}{2}$ c. $y = \dfrac{5}{2}x + \dfrac{5}{2}$

11. a. $f(x + h) = \dfrac{1}{x + h + 3}$ and $f'(x) = \lim\limits_{h \to 0} \dfrac{f(x+h) - f(x)}{h}$

$f'(x) = \lim\limits_{h \to 0} \dfrac{\dfrac{1}{x+h+3} - \dfrac{1}{x+3}}{h}$. We multiply by the product of the subordinate denominators.

$$\lim\limits_{h \to 0} \dfrac{\left(\dfrac{1}{x+h+3} - \dfrac{1}{x+3}\right)}{h} \cdot \dfrac{(x+h+3)(x+3)}{(x+h+3)(x+3)}$$

$$= \lim\limits_{h \to 0} \dfrac{\dfrac{1}{x+h+3}(x+h+3)(x+3) - \dfrac{1}{x+3}(x+h+3)(x+3)}{h(x+h+3)(x+3)}$$

$$= \lim\limits_{h \to 0} \dfrac{(x+3) - (x+h+3)}{h(x+h+3)(x+3)} = \lim\limits_{h \to 0} \dfrac{x+3-x-h-3}{h(x+h+3)(x+3)} = \lim\limits_{h \to 0} \dfrac{-h}{h(x+h+3)(x+3)}$$

$$= \lim\limits_{h \to 0} \dfrac{-1}{(x+h+3)(x+3)} = \dfrac{-1}{(x+3)^2}$$

b. $m = f'(-2) = \dfrac{-1}{(-2+3)^2} = -1$

c. $y - 1 = -1(x - -2)$

$y - 1 = -x - 2$

$y = -x - 1$

12. a. $f'(x) = \dfrac{-1}{(x-4)^2}$ b. $m = -1$ c. $y = -x + 2$

IIIC3

Derivatives of Sums of Powers—Shortcut

At the local fast food restaurant, a high percentage of the orders call for a burger, fries, and a soft drink. To speed processing, the overhead lighted menu has listed this combination as #2. When a #2 is ordered, the clerk could enter "burger," "fries," and "soft drink," but the restaurant has established a special rule for this particular order. The clerk merely pushes the button labeled "#2" to ring up this order.

In taking derivatives, there are also special rules to speed the calculations for particular classes of mathematical expressions. In particular, we want to find a rule to help us take the derivative of a function in the form $f(x) = x^n$. Let's use the definition of *derivative* from the previous section to look for a pattern that might explain the source of this rule.

We'll start with $f(x) = x^2$. Then $f(x+h) = (x+h)^2$.

$$f'(x) = \lim_{h \to 0} \frac{f(x+h) - f(x)}{h} = \lim_{h \to 0} \frac{(x+h)^2 - x^2}{h} = \lim_{h \to 0} \frac{x^2 + 2xh + h^2 - x^2}{h}$$

$$= \lim_{h \to 0} \frac{2xh + h^2}{h} = \lim_{h \to 0} \frac{h(2x+h)}{h} = \lim_{h \to 0} 2x + h = 2x + 0 = 2x$$

Now let's try $f(x)=x^3$. Then $f(x+h)=(x+h)^3$.

$$f'(x)=\lim_{h\to 0}\frac{f(x+h)-f(x)}{h}=\lim_{h\to 0}\frac{(x+h)^3-x^3}{h}=\lim_{h\to 0}\frac{x^3+3x^2h+3xh^2+h^3-x^3}{h}$$

$$=\lim_{h\to 0}\frac{3x^2h+3xh^2+h^3}{h}=\lim_{h\to 0}\frac{h(3x^2+3xh+h^2)}{h}=\lim_{h\to 0}3x^2+3xh+h^2$$

$$=3x^2+3x(0)+0^2=3x^2$$

Let's do one more. Let's try $f(x)=x^4$. Then $f(x+h)=(x+h)^4$.

$$f'(x)=\lim_{h\to 0}\frac{f(x+h)-f(x)}{h}=\lim_{h\to 0}\frac{(x+h)^4-x^4}{h}$$

$$=\lim_{h\to 0}\frac{x^4+4x^3h+6x^2h^2+4xh^3+h^4-x^4}{h}=\lim_{h\to 0}\frac{4x^3h+6x^2h^2+4xh^3+h^4}{h}$$

$$=\lim_{h\to 0}\frac{h(4x^3+6x^2h+4xh^2+h^3)}{h}=\lim_{h\to 0}4x^3+6x^2h+4xh^2+h^3$$

$$=4x^3+6x^2(0)+4x(0)^2+0^3=4x^3$$

To summarize:

When $f(x)=x^2$, then $f'(x)=2x$.

When $f(x)=x^3$, then $f'(x)=3x^2$.

When $f(x)=x^4$, then $f'(x)=4x^3$.

Notice the pattern. As the power increases, the derivative exponent is one less than the exponent of the power function, and the derivative coefficient is the exponent of the power function.

This rule can be generalized as follows.

> If $f(x)=x^n$, then the derivative becomes $f'(x)=nx^{n-1}$.
>
> In alternate notation: If $y=x^n$, then the derivative becomes $\dfrac{dy}{dx}=nx^{n-1}$.
>
> In words: to find the derivative of x^n, we multiply by the exponent and subtract one from the exponent.

We could call this method the *Burger Rule*, but it isn't. It's called the *Power Rule*.

Example 1:

If $f(x)=x^8$, then $f'(x)=8x^7$

Example 2:

If $y=x^5$, then $\dfrac{dy}{dx}=5x^4$

Example 3:

If $f(x)=x^{5.4}$, then $f'(x)=5.4x^{4.4}$

Example 4:

If $y=x^{-9.3}$, then $\dfrac{dy}{dx}=-9.3x^{-10.3}$

Note: We always subtract 1 from the exponent, even if it's negative.

Example 5:

If $f(x)=\dfrac{1}{x^5}$ we can use the Power Rule if we rewrite the function as

$f(x)=x^{-5}$. Then $f'(x)=-5x^{-6}$.

Example 6:

If $y=\dfrac{1}{x^3}$ we can use the Power Rule if we rewrite the function as

$y=x^{-3}$. Then $\dfrac{dy}{dx}=-3x^{-4}$.

Example 7:

If $f(x)=\sqrt{x}$, we can use the Power Rule ⚡ if we rewrite the function as

$f(x)=x^{\frac{1}{2}}$. Then $f'(x)=\frac{1}{2}x^{-\frac{1}{2}}$.

Note: We always subtract 1 or $\frac{2}{2}$ from the exponent, even if it's a fraction.

Example 8:

If $y=\sqrt[3]{x}$, we can use the Power Rule ⚡ if we rewrite the function as $y=x^{\frac{1}{3}}$.

Then $\frac{dy}{dx}=\frac{1}{3}x^{-\frac{2}{3}}$.

Example 9:

If $f(x)=x^{\frac{5}{3}}$, then $f'(x)=\frac{5}{3}x^{\frac{2}{3}}$.

Note: We subtracted $1=\frac{3}{3}$ from the exponent.

We could also find each of these derivatives using the formal definition from the

previous section: $f'(x)=\lim_{h\to 0}\dfrac{f(x+h)-f(x)}{h}$, but it would take longer.

INTRA-SECTION EXERCISES:

Find the derivative of each function below.

1. $f(x)=x^6$

2. $y=x^4$

3. $f(x)=x^{-3}$

4. $y=x^{-9}$

5. $f(x)=x^{1.3}$

6. $y=x^{2.2}$

7. $f(x)=\dfrac{1}{x^4}$

8. $f(x)=\dfrac{1}{x^7}$

9. $f(x)=\sqrt{x^3}$

10. $y=\sqrt[3]{x^2}$

Solutions

1. $f'(x)=6x^5$

2. $\dfrac{dy}{dx}=4x^3$

3. $f'(x)=-3x^{-4}$

4. $\dfrac{dy}{dx}=-9x^{-10}$

5. $f'(x) = 1.3x^{0.3}$

6. $\dfrac{dy}{dx} = 2.2x^{1.2}$

7. $f(x) = x^{-4}; f'(x) = -4x^{-5}$

8. $y = x^{-7}; f'(x) = -7x^{-8}$

9. $f(x) = x^{\frac{3}{2}}; f'(x) = \dfrac{3}{2}x^{\frac{1}{2}}$

10. $y = x^{\frac{2}{3}}; \dfrac{dy}{dx} = \dfrac{2}{3}x^{-\frac{1}{3}}$

"PROOF" OF THE POWER RULE WHEN THE EXPONENT IS A WHOLE NUMBER

Here's why the Power Rule works for $f(x) = x^n$.

We will prove the following: If $f(x) = x^n$, then $f'(x) = nx^{n-1}$ when n is a positive whole number.

But first, we'll need to recall *Pascal's Triangle*. Part of it can be found at right. Notice that each row begins and ends with a 1, and the other numbers are determined by adding the two numbers diagonally above it. For example, the first 3 in the fourth row is obtained by adding the numbers 1 and 2 above it.

Also, each row is symmetrical about the middle. The coefficient row for $n = 5$ begins with 1, 5, 10 and ends with 10, 5, 1.

Next, we label the rows, starting with $n = 0$.

It looks like a Christmas tree to me.

```
            1
          1   1
        1   2   1
      1   3   3   1
    1   4   6   4   1
  1   5  10  10   5   1
        ad infinitum
```

```
n = 0 .............  1
n = 1 ............  1   1
n = 2 .......... 1   2   1
n = 3 ......... 1   3   3   1
n = 4 ....... 1   4   6   4   1
n = 5 ..... 1   5  10  10   5   1
n = 6 .....1   6  15  20  15   6   1
          ad infinitum
```

Now we can observe one additional property. For each row, the second and the next-to-last number match the row number. For example, consider $n = 5$. The second number in the row is 5 and the next-to-last number is also 5.

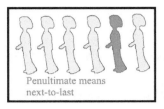

Penultimate means
next-to-last

Pascal's Triangle has many uses, but we're only going to use the fact that it gives us the coefficients of a *binomial expansion*. Check out the coefficients of each expansion below.

For $(x+h)^3$ notice that the coefficients of its expansion $1x^3+3x^2h+3xh^2+1h^3$, or **1, 3, 3, 1**, match the numbers in the row $n=3$ on Pascal's Triangle.

For $(x+h)^5$, we could multiply $(x+h)(x+h)(x+h)(x+h)(x+h)$, or we could find row $n=5$ on Pascal's Triangle, which will tell us that the coefficients are 1, 5, 10, 10, 5, *and* 1. The exponents on the x-factors begin with 5 because we're on row $n=\mathbf{5}$ and decrease in each term until they reach 0. The exponents on the h-factors begin with 0 and increase by one in each term until they reach 5.

$$(x+h)^5 = 1x^5+5x^4h+10x^3h^2+10x^2h^3+5xh^4+1h^5$$

We added the coefficients of 1, but they are understood and can be omitted.

INTRA-SECTION EXERCISES:

11. Write the row $n=7$ for Pascal's Triangle.
12. Expand $(x+h)^4$.
13. Expand $(x+h)^6$

Solutions

11. 1, 7, 21, 35, 35, 21, 7, 1
12. $(x+h)^4 = 1x^4+4x^3h+6x^2h^2+4xh^3+1h^4$
13. $(x+h)^6 = 1x^6+6x^5h+15x^4h^2+20x^3h^3+15x^2h^4+6xh^5+1h^6$

Now we'll consider the expansion of $(x+h)^n$.

It would begin with $1x^n+nx^{n-1}h + \ldots$ and it would end with $\ldots+nxh^{n-1}+1h^n$.

We don't know the third, fourth, fifth, or any of the other coefficients. We'll call them c_3, c_4, etc.

$$(x+h)^n = 1x^n+nx^{n-1}h+c_3x^{n-2}h^2+\cdots+c_{n-2}x^2h^{n-2}+nxh^{n-1}+h^n$$

This expansion will be important for our proof.

Now that we've got the expansion of $(x+h)^n$ settled, we'll get back to the proof of:

The Power Rule: 🔧 We'll also need to use our definition of the derivative from the previous section:

$$f'(x)=\lim_{h\to 0}\frac{f(x+h)-f(x)}{h}.$$

Remember that $f(x)=x^n$, so $f(x+h)=(x+h)^n$

Substituting $f(x)$ and $f(x+h)$ into our formal definition for the derivative, we get:

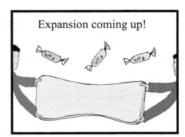

Expansion coming up!

$$f'(x)=\lim_{h\to 0}\frac{(x+h)^n-x^n}{h}.$$

Next, we expand $(x+h)^n$ to get:

$$f'(x)=\lim_{h\to 0}\frac{x^n+nx^{n-1}h+c_3x^{n-2}h^2+\cdots.nxh^{n-1}+h^n-x^n}{h}$$

We notice that we can cancel x^n and $-x^n$. We are left with:

$$f'(x)=\lim_{h\to 0}\frac{nx^{n-1}h+c_3x^{n-2}h^2+\cdots.nxh^{n-1}+h^n}{h}$$

We will need to substitute $h=0$, but if we do so now, we'll get the indeterminate:

$$\frac{0+0+\cdots+0}{0}$$

Indeterminant
and
Infamous

So we factor an h out of every term in the numerator.

$$f'(x)=\lim_{h\to 0}\frac{h(nx^{n-1}+c_3x^{n-2}h+\cdots.+nxh^{n-2}+h^{n-1})}{h}$$

Now the h's will cancel, leaving:

$$f'(x)=\lim_{h\to 0}nx^{n-1}+c_3x^{n-2}h+\cdots+nxh^{n-2}+h^{n-1}$$

and we can now substitute $h=0$ without becoming infamous.

$$f'(x)=nx^{n-1}+c_3x^{n-2}(0)+\cdots+nx(0)+0$$

Every term except the first one contained an h, hence became a 0, leaving:

TaDah!

$$f'(x) = nx^{n-1}$$

We have very cleverly shown the *Power Rule* for *Derivatives*.

BASIC PROPERTIES OF DERIVATIVES (ILLUSTRATED WITH THE POWER RULE)

Rule 1: $\dfrac{d(cf)(x)}{dx} = c\dfrac{df(x)}{dx}$ for any constant c.

Since derivatives are limits (remember the formal definition?), we can use the limit properties already noted in Unit II.

If $f(x) = cx^n$, then $f'(x) = cnx^{n-1}$, just as $\lim\limits_{x \to a} cx^n = c(\lim\limits_{x \to a} x^n)$.

Or, if $y = cx^n$ then $\dfrac{dy}{dx} = cnx^{n-1}$.

In words, the derivative of a constant times a function is the constant times the derivative of the function.

Example 10:

If $f(x) = 3x^8$ find $f'(x)$.

$f'(x) = 3(8)x^7 = 24x^7$

Example 11:

If $y = 3x^5$ find $\dfrac{dy}{dx}$.

$\dfrac{dy}{dx} = 3(5)x^4 = 15x^4$

Example 12:

If $f(x) = \dfrac{x^3}{6}$, find $f'(x)$.

$f(x) = \dfrac{1}{6}x^3$, so $f'(x) = \dfrac{1}{6}(3)x^2 = \dfrac{1}{2}x^2$ or $\dfrac{x^2}{2}$

INTRA-SECTION EXERCISES:

Find the derivatives.

14. $f(x) = 8x^{11}$

15. $y = 4x^{\frac{1}{2}}$

16. $f(x) = \dfrac{x^4}{4}$

17. $y = \dfrac{4}{x^3}$

Solutions

14. $f'(x) = 8(11)x^{10} = 88x^{10}$

15. $\dfrac{dy}{dx} = 4\left(\dfrac{1}{2}\right)x^{\frac{1}{2}-1} = 2x^{-\frac{1}{2}}$ or $2x^{-0.5}$ or $\dfrac{2}{\sqrt{x}}$

16. $f(x) = \dfrac{1}{4}x^4;\ f'(x) = \dfrac{1}{4}(4)x^3 = x^3$

17. $y = 4\dfrac{1}{x^3} = 4x^{-3};\ \dfrac{dy}{dx} = 4(-3)x^{-4} = -12x^{-4}$ or $\dfrac{-12}{x^4}$

Consider $y = 5x$. Since $5x$ can be written $5x^1$, then $\dfrac{dy}{dx} = 5(1)x^0 = 5(1) = 5$.

Similarly, the derivative of $f(x) = 7x$ is $f'(x) = 7$, and the derivative of $y = -88x$ is

$\dfrac{dy}{dx} = -88$, and the derivative of $f(x) = \pi x$ is $f'(x) = \pi$.

Rule 2: $\dfrac{d(f+g)(x)}{dx}(x) = \dfrac{df(x)}{dx} + \dfrac{dg(x)}{dx}$

Limit properties also allow us to take the derivative of a function that is the sum or difference of terms by taking derivatives term by term.

Recall: $\lim\limits_{x \to a}[f(x) + g(x)] = \lim\limits_{x \to a} f(x) + \lim\limits_{x \to a} g(x)$.

Since derivatives are limits, we can use the Power Rule ⊘ and take derivatives term by term.

In mathematical language: The derivative of a sum is the sum of the derivatives:

Example 13:

If $f(x)=3x^6+5x^2-7x$, find the derivative.

$f'(x)=3(6)x^5+5(2)x^1-7=18x^5+10x-7$.

Example 14:

If $y=\sqrt{x}+\dfrac{5}{x^2}-8x$, find the derivative.

We first rewrite the equation, putting the first and second terms in exponential form.

$$y=x^{\frac{1}{2}}+5x^{-2}-8x$$

Then, using the Power Rule: ⚡

$$\frac{dy}{dx}=\frac{1}{2}x^{-\frac{1}{2}}+5(-2)x^{-3}-8=\frac{1}{2}x^{-\frac{1}{2}}-10x^{-3}-8 \text{ or } \frac{dy}{dx}=\frac{1}{2\sqrt{x}}-\frac{10}{x^3}-8.$$

Example 15:

If $y=4\sqrt[3]{x}+2x$, find the derivative.

We first rewrite the equation, putting the first term in exponential form.

$$y=4x^{\frac{1}{3}}+2x$$

Then, using the Power Rule: ⚡

$$\frac{dy}{dx}=4\left(\frac{1}{3}\right)x^{-\frac{2}{3}}+2=\frac{4}{3}x^{-\frac{2}{3}}+2 \text{ or } \frac{dy}{dx}=\frac{4}{3\sqrt[3]{x^2}}+2$$

DERIVATIVES OF CONSTANTS

Suppose $f(x)=8$. We could write the function as $f(x)=8x^0$ because we know $x^0=1$.

Using the Power Rule ⚡, $f'(x)=(0)(8)x^{-1}=0$.

Similarly, the derivative of 12 is 0, the derivative of -97 is 0, and the derivative of π is 0.

The derivative of any real number is 0. Here's a better reason why.

If we graph $f(x)=3$ or $y=3$, we see that it is a horizontal line. We know that the derivative of the line will give us its slope at any point. We also know that the slope of a horizontal line at every point equals 0, so we would expect the derivative to equal 0. It does!

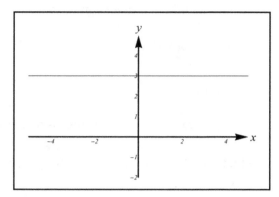

Example 16:

If $y=\sqrt{x}+\dfrac{5}{x^3}-7$, find the derivative. We rewrite the equation in exponent form, as before.

$$y=x^{\frac{1}{2}}+5x^{-3}-7$$

Then, using the Power Rule as before,

$$\frac{dy}{dx}=\frac{1}{2}x^{-\frac{1}{2}}+5(-3)x^{-4}-0=\frac{1}{2}x^{-\frac{1}{2}}-15x^{-4} \text{ or } \frac{dy}{dx}=\frac{1}{2\sqrt{x}}-\frac{15}{x^4}$$

INTRA-SECTION EXERCISES:

Find the derivatives.

18. $f(x)=3x^2-2x+4$

19. $g(t)=\dfrac{4}{t^2}+5t^3$

20. $y=\dfrac{x^4}{5}-6x+2.7$

21. $h(z)=6\sqrt{z}-14z+4$

Solutions

18. $f'(x)=3(2)x^1-2+0=6x-2$

19. $y=\dfrac{1}{5}x^4-6x+2.7; \dfrac{dy}{dx}=\dfrac{1}{5}(4)x^3-6+0=\dfrac{4}{5}x^3-6$

20. $g(t)=4t^{-2}+5t^3; g'(t)=4(-2)t^{-3}+5(3)t^2=-8t^{-3}+15t^2$ or $g'(t)=\dfrac{-8}{t^3}+15t^2$

21. $h(z)=6z^{\frac{1}{2}}-14z+4; h'(z)=6\left(\dfrac{1}{2}\right)z^{-\frac{1}{2}}-14+0=3z^{-\frac{1}{2}}-14$ or $h'(z)=\dfrac{3}{\sqrt{z}}-14$

FINDING THE TANGENT LINE TO A CURVE

If we're given the equation of a curve and a point on the curve, we can find the equation of the tangent line to the curve at the given point by using the Power Rule 🔘 to help us find the slope of the tangent.

Example 17:

For $y = x^3 + x - 1$, find the equation of the tangent at the point $(-1, -3)$.

Our equation-finding formula is: $y - y_1 = m(x - x_1)$.

We're given a point $(x_1, y_1) = (-1, -3)$.

Next, we can use the Power Rule 🔘 to find the derivative of the curve $y = x^3 + x - 1$.

$\dfrac{dy}{dx} = 3x^2 + 1 - 0 = 3x^2 + 1$

Since we want the slope of the curve where $x = -1$, we substitute -1 into the derivative to get the slope:

$m = 3(-1)^2 + 1 = 3(1) + 1 = 4$

Now we have both a point and a slope for our formula.

$y - -3 = 4(x - -1)$ We distribute the 4.

$y + 3 = 4x + 4$ Subtracting 3 from both sides.

$y = 4x + 1$

This is the equation of the tangent to the curve $y = x^3 + x - 1$ at the point $(-1, -3)$.

Example 18:

For $f(x) = 3x^2 - 4x + 5$, find the equation of the tangent at $x = 0$.

We use the Power Rule 🔘 to find the derivative: $f'(x) = 6x - 4$.

Then we use the derivative to find the slope of the curve where $x=0$:

$$m=f'(0)=6(0)-4=-4$$

Now if we only had a whole point (x_1,y_1), we could use our equation-finding formula to calculate the tangent. Instead, we only have half a point; i.e., $(x_1,y_1)=(0,?)$. We'll need to go back to the original function to find y_1. Recall that $f(x)$ is a way to write y when the equation is a function. We want to know what y is when $x=0$, so we find:

$$y=f(0)=3(0)^2-4(0)+5=5.$$

Aha!! $y=5$ when $x=0$.

Now we have the complete point: $(x_1,y_1)=(0,5)$ and a slope $m=-4$.

We substitute them into our old reliable equation-finding formula:

$$y-y_1=m(x-x_1).$$

$y-5=-4(x-0)$ We distribute,

$y-5=-4x$ and add 5 to both sides.

$y=-4x+5$ This is the equation of the tangent at $x=0$.

If we examine the graph of our original curve, $f(x)=3x^2-4x+5$, and its tangent at $x=0$, we can see that the tangent line has a negative slope and a y-intercept at $x=5$, as predicted by the equation of the tangent: $y=-4x+5$.

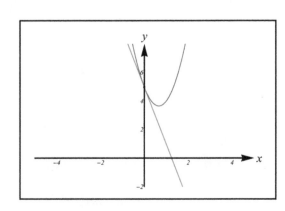

*To get y-values, or heights, we always use the original function of the curve, y or $f(x)$.
To get slopes, we use the derivative $f'(x)$.

Example 19:

Find the point where the tangent of the curve $y = 6x^2 + 12x$ is a horizontal line.

Since horizontal lines have slopes of zero, this is another way of asking:

Find the point where the tangent of the curve has a slope equal to 0.

Since we find slopes from the derivative, we could say it's also a way of asking: Where is the derivative of the curve equal to 0?

To find out, we find the derivative, $\dfrac{dy}{dx}$, and set it equal to 0.

If $y = 6x^2 + 12x$, then using the Power Rule

$\dfrac{dy}{dx} = 12x + 12$. This is the equation that gives us slope, so we set

$m = 12x + 12 = 0$.

Then $2x = -12$ and $x = -1$.

We now know that the curve $y = 6x^2 + 12x$ has a horizontal tangent where $x = -1$, but this is only half the point $(-1, ?)$. We still need the y-value. We find y when $x = -1$ by returning to the original equation. We substitute $x = -1$ in the original equation $y = 6x^2 + 12x$ to get:

$$y = 6(-1)^2 + 12(-1) = 6 - 12 = -6$$

So now we know the curve has a horizontal tangent at the point $(-1, -6)$. Check it out on the graph below.

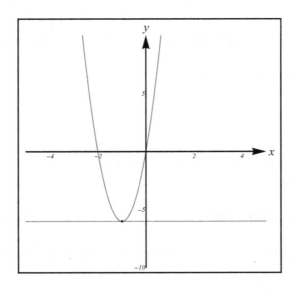

Example 20:

The number of new businesses in a growing Midwestern town has been modeled by the function $N(t) = 0.31t^2 - 0.26t + 806$, where t is the year beginning with $t = 0$ for the year 2010.

a. How many businesses are expected in the year 2020?
b. What is the rate (businesses/year) of business growth in the year 2015?

Solution for a.) To find the number of businesses (N) in the year 2020, we let $t = 10$. Then $N(10) = 0.31(10)^2 - 0.26(10) + 806 \approx 834$ businesses.

Solution for b.) Derivatives give us rates. Rates are indicated by slopes on a graph. $N'(t) = 0.31(2)t - 0.26 = 0.62t - 0.26$. For $t = 5$, $N'(5) = 0.62(5) - 0.26 = 2.84$ *businesses/year.*

IIIC3 DERIVATIVES OF SUMS OF POWERS—SHORTCUT EXERCISES

For numbers 1 through 24, find the derivatives of the functions.

1. $y = x^8$

2. $f(x) = x^{6.1}$

3. $f(x) = 3x^7$

4. $y = 4x^{-5}$

5. $y = 7$

6. $f(x) = 14$

7. $f(x) = 3x^{-5.6}$

8. $y = 2x^{6.6}$

9. $g(t) = 4.1t$

10. $h(t) = -3t$

11. $y = -4\pi x$

12. $f(x) = -7.8\pi x$

13. $g(x) = 3x^2 + 7x - 1$

14. $y = 5x^4 - 14x + 5$

15. $y = x^{-3} + x^{\frac{1}{5}} - 3x$

16. $f(x) = 4x^{-2} + x^{\frac{1}{3}} - 2x$

17. $f(x) = \dfrac{4}{x^3} + 6x - 10$

18. $y = \dfrac{3}{x^3} - 8x + 4$

19. $y = 5\sqrt{x} - \dfrac{2}{3}x^3$

20. $f(x) = 6\sqrt{x} + \dfrac{4}{3}x^{-3}$

21. $f(t) = 5t^{\frac{4}{5}}$

22. $y = 4z^{-\frac{1}{2}}$

23. $y = \dfrac{3}{(2x)^3}$

24. $f(t) = -\dfrac{4}{(2t)^2}$

For numbers 25–32, find the equation of the tangent line to the curve at the given point.

25. $y = \dfrac{5}{2}x^2 + \dfrac{1}{2}$ at $(1,3)$

26. $f(x) = \dfrac{2}{3}x^3 + \dfrac{1}{3}$ at $(1,1)$

27. $f(x) = \dfrac{x^4}{2} + 3x$ at $x = 0$

28. $y = \dfrac{x^3}{9} + \dfrac{2}{3}x$ at $x = 1$

29. $y = 3x^2 - 10$ at $x = 2$

30. $f(x) = -2x^2 + 8$ at $x = 1$

31. $f(x) = 3\sqrt{x} - x$ at $x = 4$

32. $g(t) = -4\sqrt{t} + t$ at $t = 9$

33. Where is the tangent of $f(x) = -3x^2 + 4$ a horizontal line?

34. Where is the tangent of $y = -5x^2 - 6$ a horizontal line?

35. Where is the tangent of $y = \frac{2}{3}x^3 - \frac{7}{2}x^2 + 6x$ a horizontal line?

36. Where is the tangent of $f(x) = \frac{1}{3}x^3 - 2x^2 + 3$ a horizontal line?

37. The revenue R for Zeus Running Shoes (in millions of dollars) from 2000 through 2015 can be modeled by $R = 43.2t^3 - 661.2t^2 + 4223t + 8422.1$, where $t = 0$ in 2000.

    a. At what rate was revenue growing in the year 2000? In the year 2010?
    b. In which of those two years was revenue growing the fastest?

38. The revenue for Apex Ball Caps (in thousands of dollars) from 2000 through 2015 can be modeled by $R = 86.4t^3 - 441.1t^2 + 6114t + 4155.6$, where $t = 0$ in 2000.

    a. At what rate was revenue growing in the year 2000? In the year 2010?
    b. In which of those two years was revenue growing the fastest?

39. A hospital auxiliary raises funds by selling tickets to a dinner with a nationally known speaker. Tickets are sold for $80 each. The auxiliary pays $50 for each dinner and has fixed costs of $4,000 for the speaker's fees and transportation.

    a. Write the profit P as a function of t, the number of tickets sold.
    b. Show that the derivative of the profit function is a constant equal to the increase in profit from each ticket sold.

40. A travel agency sells packages that include transportation, lodging, and tickets to the Orange Bowl New Year's Eve game. Each package sells for $1,500. The agency's costs are $800 per package, plus fixed costs of $4,000 for a chartered plane, paperwork, etc.

    a. Write the profit P as a function of x, the number of packages sold.
    b. Show that the derivative of the profit function is a constant equal to the increase in profit from each package sold.

IIIC3 DERIVATIVES OF SUMS OF POWERS—SHORTCUT
SOLUTIONS TO EXERCISES

1. $\dfrac{dy}{dx} = 8x^7$

2. $f'(x) = 6.1x^{5.1}$

3. $f'(x) = 3(7)x^6 = 21x^6$

4. $\dfrac{dy}{dx} = -20x^{-6}$ or $\dfrac{dy}{dx} = \dfrac{-20}{x^6}$

5. $\dfrac{dy}{dx} = 0$

6. $f'(x) = 0$

7. $f'(x) = 3(-5.6)x^{-6.6} = -16.8x^{-6.6}$ or $f'(x) = \dfrac{-16.8}{x^{6.6}}$

8. $\dfrac{dy}{dx} = 13.2x^{5.6}$

9. $g'(t) = 4.1t^0 = 4.1$

10. $h'(t) = -3$

11. $\dfrac{dy}{dx} = -4\pi x^0 = -4\pi$

12. $f'(x) = -7.8\pi$

13. $g'(x) = 6x + 7$

14. $\dfrac{dy}{dx} = 20x^3 - 14$

15. $\dfrac{dy}{dx} = -3x^{-4} + \dfrac{1}{5}x^{-\frac{4}{5}} - 3$ or $\dfrac{dy}{dx} = \dfrac{-3}{x^4} + \dfrac{1}{5\sqrt[5]{x^4}} - 3$

16. $f'(x) = -8x^{-3} + \dfrac{1}{3}x^{-\frac{2}{3}} - 2$ or $f'(x) = \dfrac{-8}{x^3} + \dfrac{1}{3\sqrt[3]{x^2}} - 2$

17. $f(x) = 4x^{-3} + 6x - 10;\ f'(x) = -12x^{-4} + 6$ or $f'(x) = \dfrac{-12}{x^4} + 6$

18. $\dfrac{dy}{dx} = -9x^{-4} - 8$ or $\dfrac{dy}{dx} = \dfrac{-9}{x^4} - 8$

19. $y = 5x^{\frac{1}{2}} - \dfrac{2}{3}x^3;\ \dfrac{dy}{dx} = \dfrac{5}{2}x^{-\frac{1}{2}} - 2x^2$ or $\dfrac{dy}{dx} = \dfrac{5}{2\sqrt{x}} - 2x^2$

20. $f'(x) = 3x^{-\frac{1}{2}} - 4x^{-4}$ or $f'(x) = \dfrac{3}{\sqrt{x}} - \dfrac{4}{x^4}$

21. $f'(t) = 5\left(\dfrac{4}{5}\right)t^{-\frac{1}{5}} = 4t^{-\frac{1}{5}}$ or $f'(t) = \dfrac{4}{\sqrt[5]{t}}$

22. $\dfrac{dy}{dx} = -2z^{-\frac{3}{2}}$ or $\dfrac{dy}{dx} = \dfrac{-2}{\sqrt{z^3}}$

23. $y = \dfrac{3}{8x^3} = \dfrac{3}{8}x^{-3};\ \dfrac{dy}{dx} = -\dfrac{9}{8}x^{-4}$ or $\dfrac{dy}{dx} = \dfrac{-9}{8x^4}$

24. $f'(t) = -t^{-3}$ or $f'(t) = \dfrac{-1}{t^3}$

25. $\dfrac{dy}{dx}=\dfrac{5}{2}(2)x+0=5x,\ \ m=5(1)=5;$

$\quad y-3=5(x-1),\ y-3=5x-5,\ y=5x-2$

26. $y=2x-1$

27. $f(x)=\dfrac{1}{2}x^4+3x;\ \ f'(x)=2x^3+3;\ \ m=f'(0)=2(0)^3+3=3;$

$\quad y_1=f(0)=\dfrac{1}{2}(0)^4+3(0)=0;\ \ (x_1,y_1)=(0,0);$

$\quad y-0=3(x-0),\ y=3x$

28. $y=x-\dfrac{2}{9}$

29. $\dfrac{dy}{dx}=6x;\ \ m=6(2)=12;\ \ y_1=3(2)^2-10=2,\ (x_1,y_1)=(2,2);$

$\quad y-2=12(x-2),\ y-2=12x-24,\ y=12x-22$

30. $y=-4x+10$

31. $f(x)=3x^{\frac{1}{2}}-x;\ \ f'(x)=\dfrac{3}{2}x^{-\frac{1}{2}}-1=\dfrac{3}{2\sqrt{x}}-1;$

$\quad m=f'(4)=\dfrac{3}{2\sqrt{4}}-1=\dfrac{3}{4}-1=-\dfrac{1}{4};$

$\quad y_1=f(4)=3\sqrt{4}-4=6-4=2;\ \ (x_1,y_1)=(4,2);$

$\quad y-2=-\dfrac{1}{4}(x-4),\ y-2=-\dfrac{1}{4}x+1,\ y=-\dfrac{1}{4}x+3$

32. $y=\dfrac{1}{3}t-6$

33. i.e., where is the slope equal to 0? Or where is $f'(x)=0$?
$f'(x)=-6x=0$. The tangent is horizontal at $x=0$.
For the corresponding y: $y=f(0)=-3(0)^2+4=4$
Thus, the tangent is a horizontal line at the point $(0,4)$.

34. $(0,-6)$

35. i.e., where is the slope equal to 0? Or where is $\dfrac{dy}{dx}=0$?

$\dfrac{dy}{dx}=2x^2-7x+6=0$

$(2x-3)(x-2)=0$ The tangent is horizontal at $x=\dfrac{3}{2},\ x=2$.

The corresponding y at $x=\dfrac{3}{2}$: $y=\dfrac{2}{3}\left(\dfrac{3}{2}\right)^3-\dfrac{7}{2}\left(\dfrac{3}{2}\right)^2+6\left(\dfrac{3}{2}\right)=\dfrac{27}{8}$

The corresponding y at $x=2$: $y=\dfrac{2}{3}(2)^3-\dfrac{7}{2}(2)^2+6(2)=\dfrac{10}{3}$

The tangent is a horizontal line at the points $\left(\dfrac{3}{2},\dfrac{27}{8}\right)$ and $\left(2,\dfrac{10}{3}\right)$.

36. $(0,3)$ and $\left(4,\dfrac{-23}{3}\right)$

37. $R'(t) = 129.6t^2 - 1322.4t + 4223$ = rate of growth

for $t = 0$; $R'(0) = 129.6(0)^2 - 1322.4(0) + 4223 = 4223$ *million dollars*

for $t = 10$; $R'(10) = 129.6(10)^2 - 1322.4(10) + 4223 = 3959$ *million dollars*.

Growth is faster in the year 2000.

38. for $t = 0$: $R'(0) = 6114$ *thousand dollars*

for $t = 10$; $R'(10) = 23,212$ *thousand dollars*. Revenue grew faster in 2010.

39. a. Profit = revenue ($80t$) − costs ($50t + \$4000$); $P(t) = \$30t - \$4000$

   b. $P'(t) = \$30$, which is the profit from each ticket sold ($80 - \$50$).

40. a. $P(x) = \$700x - \$4000$

   b. $P'(t) = \$700$, which is the profit on each package sold ($1500 - \$800$).

UNIT IV

IVR1

Analyzing Slopes on Graphs and Solving Inequalities

There are many statistics generated by businesses that can be presented in a graphical form, such as annual sales, monthly advertising expenses, daily cost of resources, weekly online hits, etc. These graphs help us determine at a glance if our figures are improving or declining.

INCREASING AND DECREASING FUNCTIONS AND SLOPES ON GRAPHS

The graph below represents the US national debt from 1975 through 2018. It generally continues to rise from 1975 through 2018. The slope is upward, or positive,

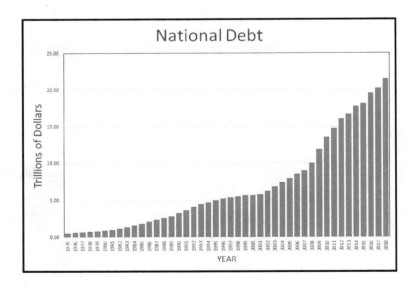

Source: TreasuryDirect.gov

408

as time increases. We could say that the curve representing the national debt is increasing.

The Bureau of Labor Statistics tracks the price of computer equipment over time as one component of consumer price data generated to determine the Computer Price Index. The graph below represents "personal computer and peripheral equipment" from 1998 through 2014.

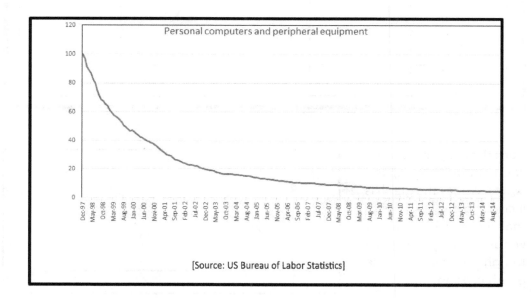

[Source: US Bureau of Labor Statistics]

As we study the graph from left to right, we notice that the curve falls. The slope is negative. We say that the curve representing the Computer Price Index is decreasing.

Informally, a function is increasing if the graph rises upward to the right and is decreasing if the graph falls downward to the right.

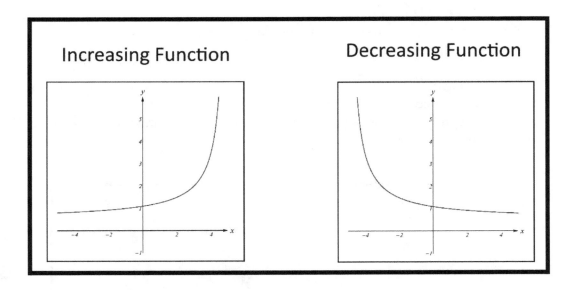

Consider the graph at right and the points (x_1, y_1) and (x_2, y_2). We say the graph is increasing if $x_2 > x_1$ implies that $f(x_2) > f(x_1)$. In other words, as we go from left to right, the height of the graph is rising.

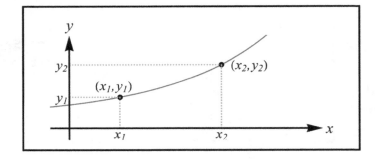

We can therefore say that a function is increasing if its slope is positive, or since we obtain the slope from the derivative, we can say:

A function is increasing if its derivative is positive; or

a function is increasing if $f'(x) > 0$.

Note that we are using the term *increasing* to mean strictly increasing.

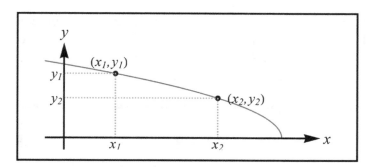

Consider the function at left. It is decreasing. In general, a function is decreasing if $x_2 > x_1$ implies $f(x_2) < f(x_1)$. In other words, as we go from left to right, the height of the graph is falling.

We can therefore say that function is decreasing if its slope is negative, or since we obtain the slope from the derivative, we can say:

> **A function is decreasing if its derivative is negative; or**
> **a function is decreasing if $f'(x) < 0$.**
> Note that we are using the term *decreasing* to mean strictly decreasing.

The graph below shows average consumer fuel prices cited by the US Energy Information Administration. The curve is increasing over the intervals [2002, 2008], [2009, 2012], and [2016, 2018]. It is decreasing over the intervals [2000, 2002], [2008, 2009], and [2012, 2016].

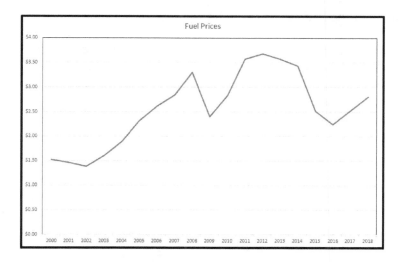

Source: US Energy Information Administration

The graph below represents a housing price index. For the main part, the curve is increasing over the interval [1986, 2007] and again after 2013. The curve is decreasing over the interval [2007, 2009]. Between 2009 and 2013, the curve has brief, rapid fluctuations in which it is increasing, decreasing, increasing, and decreasing.

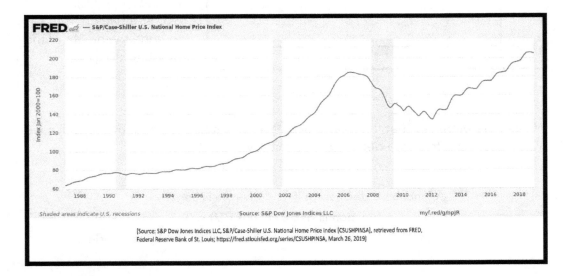

[Source: S&P Dow Jones Indices LLC, S&P/Case-Shiller U.S. National Home Price Index [CSUSHPINSA], retrieved from FRED, Federal Reserve Bank of St. Louis; https://fred.stlouisfed.org/series/CSUSHPINSA, March 26, 2019]

Let f be given by the graph at right. Assume the graph continues indefinitely to the left and right in the manner that it approaches the edge of the visible graph. The function f is increasing on the intervals (−∞, −3] and [1, ∞).

The function f is decreasing on the interval [−3, 1].

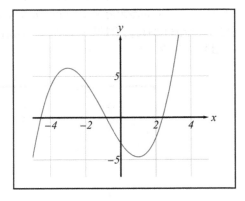

Note that the intervals are in terms of x-values.

Also note that the graph is defined at $x = -3$ and at $x = 1$, so the interval with the endpoint at -3 has a square bracket. The interval with endpoint $x = 1$ also has a square bracket. We use rounded brackets (i.e. parentheses) for the non-endpoints noted as ∞.

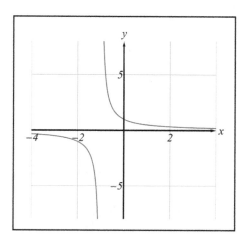

Now let f be the graph at left. The function f is decreasing on the interval $(-\infty, -1)$ and on the interval $(-1, \infty)$. This time, the graph was nonexistent at $x = -1$, so rounded brackets (parentheses) were used for the endpoints of -1.

Consider the function $f(x) = -(x-3)^2 + 1$. We want to find where the function is increasing and where it is decreasing; that is, where the function's slope, or derivative, is positive and where it is negative.

We know the function is increasing where $f'(x) > 0$, and decreasing where $f'(x) < 0$. This function is a quadratic function that we know how to graph.

We can see that the graph is increasing over the interval $(-\infty, -3]$ and it is decreasing over the interval $[3, -\infty)$. (Remember the intervals are in terms of x-values.)

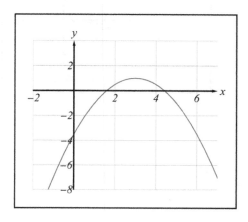

INTRA-SECTION EXERCISES

Where are the graphs in 1 through 4 increasing, and where are they decreasing?

1.

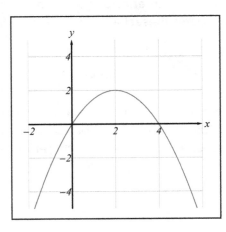

2.

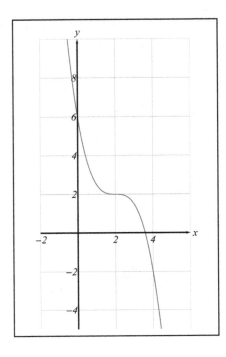

3.

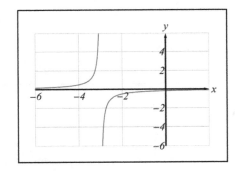

4.

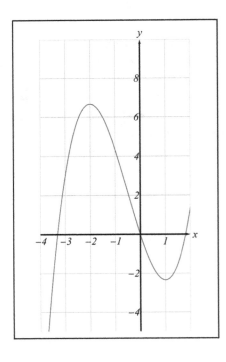

For numbers 5–7, sketch the graph, and give the intervals where the function increases and where the function decreases.

5. $f(x)=(x-4)^2-2$ 6. $f(x)=(x+1)^3+4$ 7. $f(x)=\dfrac{1}{x-2}$

Solutions

1. increasing: $(-\infty, 2]$
   decreasing: $[2, \infty)$
2. increasing: nowhere
   decreasing: $(-\infty, \infty)$
3. increasing: $(-\infty,-3),(-3,\infty)$
   decreasing: nowhere
4. increasing: $(-\infty, -2], [1,\infty)$
   decreasing: $[-2, 1]$

5.

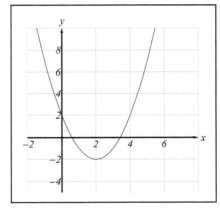

increasing: $[4,\infty)$
decreasing: $(-\infty, 4]$

6.

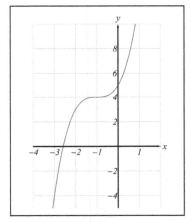

increasing $(-\infty,\infty)$
decreasing: nowhere

7.

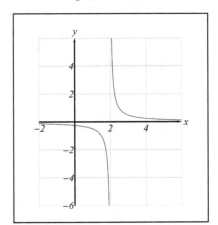

increasing: nowhere
decreasing: $(-\infty,2), (2, \infty)$

We can recognize that the graph at right is increasing over the interval $[3,\infty)$ and decreasing over the interval $(-\infty,3]$, but what if the function is not easily graphed? We'll need to analyze the slope of the function, which we find from its derivative.

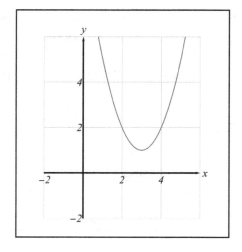

Consider the function: $f(x)=x^3-\frac{3}{2}x^2$. Suppose $f(x)$ represents the cost of certain resources we need in our jewelry-making business, and x represents the quantity ordered in hundreds of lots. As we order more materials, x, we expect the cost, $f(x)$ to rise, but we want to find out if there is an interval over which the quantity discount we receive brings the costs down a bit. We want to find for what size lots x this function $f(x)$ is increasing and decreasing. We need to know the 'x's for which $f'(x)>0$, and the 'x's for which $f'(x)<0$.

For the given function $f(x)$, its slope at any point can be computed from the derivative $f'(x)=3x^2-3x$. This derivative function is a quadratic equation.

To find $f(x) = 3x^2 - 3x > 0$ and $f(x) = 3x^2 - 3x < 0$, we need to know how to solve inequalities.

SOLVING INEQUALITIES

We'll investigate solving inequalities using the function $g(x)=x^2+x-6$. We'll solve the inequality $g(x)>0$.

Step 1:

The first step to solving an inequality is to solve the related equality: $g(x) = 0$.

$$x^2 + x - 6 = 0$$

$$(x+3)(x-2) = 0$$

$$x = -3, \ x = 2$$

The possible places where $g(x)$ can change sign from positive to negative ($g(x) > 0$ to $g(x) < 0$), or from negative to positive ($g(x) < 0$ to $g(x) > 0$), is at these values of x. In this case, the possible places are at $x = -3$ and 2.

Step 2:

The second step is to note any values where the graph of the function is discontinuous. In piecewise graphs, there are often values where the function is not defined, but for $g(x) = x^2 + x - 6$, there are no discontinuities.

Step 3:

We divide the set of real numbers into intervals using $x = -3$ and 2.

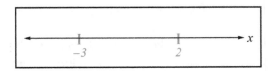

The intervals would be $(-\infty, -3)$, $(-3, 2)$, and $(2, \infty)$.

Step 4:

We choose one value from each of the intervals found in Step 3 and test each of our chosen values in $g(x) = x^2 + x - 6$.

Let's choose $x = -4$, $x = 0$, and $x = 3$.

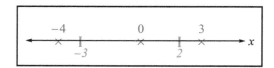

Test $x = -4$: $g(-4) = (-4)^2 + (-4) - 6 = 6$, which is a positive number. This implies that all values of x within the interval $(-\infty, -3)$ will produce positive values of $g(x)$.

Test $x = 0$: $g(0) = (0)^2 + (0) - 6 = -6$, which is a negative number.

This implies that all values of x within the interval $(-3, 2)$ will produce negative values of $g(x)$.

Test $x = 3$: $g(3) = (3)^2 + (3) - 6 = 6$, which is a positive number. This implies that all values of x within the interval $(2, \infty)$ will produce positive values of $g(x)$.

Thus, $g(x) = x^2 + x - 6 > 0$ on the intervals $(-\infty, -3)$ and $(2, \infty)$.

Note that we have round brackets around -3 and 2 because these are points where $y = 0$, and we only want to include points in our solution where $y > 0$. If we had wanted all values of x where $y \geq 0$, we would have included -3 and 2 in our solution so that the solution intervals would be $(-\infty, -3]$ and $[2, \infty)$.

Example 1:

Solve $\dfrac{2x - 5}{x + 2} \leq 0$

Step 1:

We solve $\dfrac{2x-5}{x+2}=0$.

Recall that a fraction equals 0 where its numerator equals 0.

$$2x-5=0$$

$$2x=5$$

$$x=\frac{5}{2}$$

Step 2:

We note that $\dfrac{2x-5}{x+2}$ is undefined at $x=-2$.

Recall that a fraction is undefined where its denominator equals 0.

$$x+2=0$$

$$x=-2$$

Step 3:

The values $x=\dfrac{5}{2}$ and $x=-2$ divide the real numbers into the intervals

$$(-\infty,-2),\left(-2,\frac{5}{2}\right],\left[\frac{5}{2},\infty\right).$$

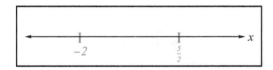

We used a parenthesis around −2 since the equation is undefined at $x = -2$, but square brackets around the endpoint $\dfrac{5}{2}$ because this is the x-value that makes the expression equal to 0, and for our solution we want all the points that generate values that are both less than and equal to ($\leq$) 0.

Let's choose −3 from the first interval, 0 from the second interval, and 3 from the third interval.

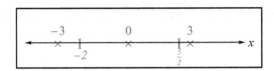

Step 4:

We proceed to test them.

Test $x = -3$: $\dfrac{2(-3)-5}{(-3)+2} = \dfrac{-11}{-1} = 11$, which is a positive number. We now know that every x-value in the interval $(-\infty, -2)$ will make $\dfrac{2x-5}{x+2} > 0$.

Test $x = 0$: $\dfrac{2(0)-5}{0+2} = \dfrac{-5}{2}$, which is a negative number. We now know that every x-value in the interval $\left(-2, \dfrac{5}{2}\right]$ will make $\dfrac{2x-5}{x+2} < 0$.

Test $x = 3$: $\dfrac{2(3)-5}{3+2} = \dfrac{1}{5}$, which is a positive number. We now know that every x-value in the interval $\left[\dfrac{5}{2}, \infty\right) > 0$.

Since we wanted $\dfrac{2x-5}{x+2} \leq 0$, our solution is the interval $\left(-2, \dfrac{5}{2}\right]$.

INTRA-SECTION EXERCISES

Solve the inequalities.

8. $-5 \leq 2x^2 + 11x$

9. $0 \leq \dfrac{x-3}{5+x}$

10. $0 \geq 4x + 16$

Solutions

8. We add 5 to both sides of the inequality: $0 \leq 2x^2 + 11x + 5$

We solve the related equation:

$$2x^2 + 11x + 5 = 0$$

$$(2x + 1)(x + 5) = 0$$

$$2x + 1 = 0; \ x + 5 = 0$$

$$x = -\frac{1}{2}, \ x = -5$$

We note that this equation is a continuous function. It is defined everywhere.

We divide the real numbers into three intervals: $\left(-\infty, -5 \right], \left[-5, -\frac{1}{2} \right], \left[-\frac{1}{2}, \infty \right) \right)$

We use square brackets around -5 and $-\frac{1}{2}$ because these are points that make our expression for y equal to zero, and for our solution we want values that make $2x^2 + 11x + 5$ less than 0 and also equal to 0 ($\leq$).

We choose a point from each interval. Let's choose $-6, -2,$ and 0.

We test $x = -6 : (2(-6) + 1)(-6 + 5) = (-11)(-1) = 11 > 0.$

Therefore, all x-values in the interval $(-\infty, -5)$ will generate positive values.

We test $x = -2 : (2(-2) + 1)(-2 + 5) = (-3)(3) = -9 < 0.$

Therefore, all x-values in the interval $\left(-5, -\frac{1}{2} \right)$ will generate negative values.

We test $x = 0 : (2(0) + 1)(0 + 5) = (1)(5) = 5 > 0.$

Therefore, all x-values in the interval $\left(-\frac{1}{2}, \infty\right)$ will generate positive values.

Since we want $0 \leq 2x^2 + 11x + 5$, or negative values and 0, our solution is the

interval $\left[-5, -\frac{1}{2}\right]$.

9. We need to solve the related equation $\frac{x-3}{5+x} = 0$, which occurs where $x - 3 = 0$,
or $x = 3$.

This equation is undefined where $5 + x = 0$, or at $x = -5$.

We divide the real numbers into the intervals: $(-\infty, -5), (-5, 3], [3, \infty)$.

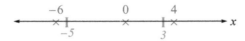

We choose a number from each interval. Let's choose −6, 0 and 4.

We test $x = -6 : \dfrac{-6-3}{5+(-6)} = \dfrac{-9}{-1} = 9 > 0.$

So every x-value in the interval $(-\infty, -5)$ will generate a positive value.

We test $0 : \dfrac{0-3}{5+0} = \dfrac{-3}{5} < 0.$

So every x-value in the interval $(-5, 3)$ will generate a negative value.

We test $4 : \dfrac{4-3}{5+4} = \dfrac{1}{9} > 0.$

So every x-value in the interval $(3, \infty)$ will generate a positive value.

Since we want $0 \leq \dfrac{x-3}{5+x}$, or negative and zero values, our solution is the interval
$(-5, 3]$. We use a round bracket around the endpoint −5 because it generates
an undefined y-value, something we don't want to include.

10. We need to solve the related equation:

$$4x+16=0$$

$$4x=-16$$

$$x=-4$$

We divide the real numbers into two intervals: $(-\infty,-4]$, $[-4, \infty)$.

We choose a number from each interval. Let's choose -5 and 0.

We test $x=-5: 4(-5)+16=-4<0$.

So every x-value in the interval $(-\infty,-4)$ will generate negative values.

We test $x=0: 4(0)+16=15>0$.

So every x-value in the interval $(-4, \infty)$ will generate positive values.

Since we want $0 \geq 4x+16$, or non-positive values, our solution is the interval $(-\infty,-4]$.

Now that we can solve inequalities, we'll return to our jewelry-making business in the next section when we determine where functions are increasing and decreasing algebraically.

IVR1 ANALYZING SLOPES ON GRAPHS AND SOLVING INEQUALITIES EXERCISES

1.

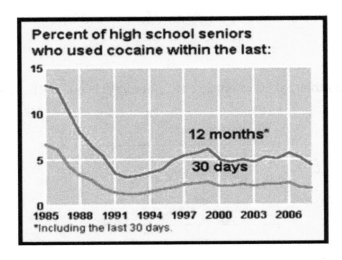

Source: University of Michigan, *Monitoring the Future National Results on Adolescent Drug Use: Overview of Key Findings 2008.*

    a. According to the graph above, the percent of high school seniors who used cocaine within the last 30 days was generally decreasing over the years _____.

    b. According to the graph above, the percent of high school seniors who used cocaine within the last 12 months was generally increasing over the years _____.

    c. According to the graph above, the percent of high school seniors who used cocaine within the last 30 days remained relatively constant for the years _____.

2.

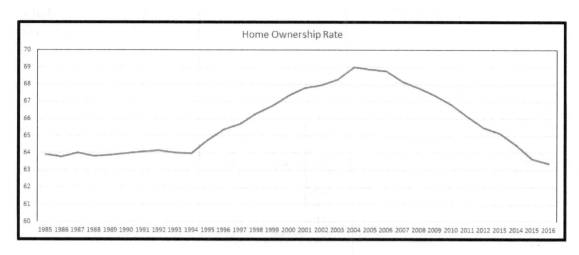

Source: US Bureau of the Census

a. The rate of home ownership in the United States generally decreased over the years _____.

b. The rate of home ownership in the United States generally increased over the years _____.

c. The rate of home ownership in the United States remained generally constant, increasing or decreasing only slightly over the years _____.

3. Where is the graph at right increasing, and where is it decreasing?

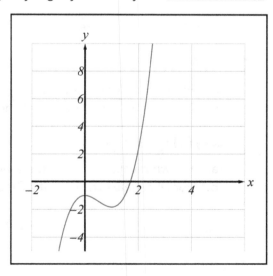

4.

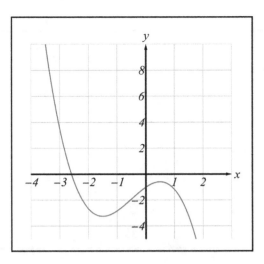

Where is the graph at left increasing, and where is it decreasing?

5. Sketch the graph of $f(x)=-(x+2)^2+3$. Where is it increasing, and where is it decreasing?

6. Sketch the graph of $f(x)=-(x-3)^3-5$. Where is it increasing, and where is it decreasing?

For numbers 7)–14), solve the inequalities, and write the solutions in interval notation.

7. $-4\leq 2x^2+11x+1$

8. $-4\geq x^2+5x$

9. $0\geq \dfrac{x-5}{3+x}$

10. $0\leq \dfrac{x-5}{3+x}$

11. $0\leq 3x-9$

12. $0>5x+15$

13. $0\leq x^2+7x$

14. $0<2x^2-6x$

15. Let $f(x)=x^2-x-12$.

    a. For what values of x will the function $y=f(x)$ generate positive y-values?

    b. For what values of x will the function $y=f(x)$ generate negative y-values?

16. Let $f(x)=x^2+x-12$.

    a. For what values of x will the function $y=f(x)$ generate positive y-values?

    b. For what values of x will the function $y=f(x)$ generate negative y-values?

IVR1 ANALYZING SLOPES ON GRAPHS AND SOLVING INEQUALITIES SOLUTIONS TO EXERCISES

1. a. 1985–1992   b. 1992–1999   c. 2000–2006
2. a. 2004–2016   b. 1994–2004   c. 1985–1994
3. Inc: $(-\infty, 0]$, $[1, \infty)$; Dec: $[0, 1]$ 4. Inc: $[-1.5, 0.5]$; Dec: $(-\infty, -1.5]$, $[0.5, \infty)$

5. 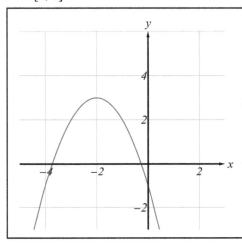   Inc: $(-\infty, -2]$; Dec: $[-2, \infty)$

6. 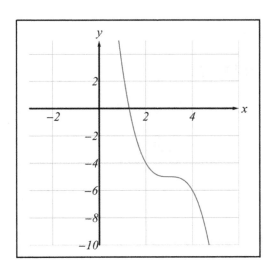   Inc: nowhere; Dec: $(-\infty, \infty)$

7. $-4 = 2x^2 + 11x + 1$
    $2x^2 + 11x + 5 = 0$
    $(2x+1)(x+5) = 0$

    $x = -\dfrac{1}{2}$, $x = -5$ produces intervals of:

    $(-\infty, -5], \left[-5, -\dfrac{1}{2}\right], \left[-\dfrac{1}{2}, \infty\right)$

    Choose $-6, -1$, and 0.
    Test $x = -6$: $(2(-6)+1)(-6+5) = (-11)(-1) = 11 > 0$,
    positive values
    Test $x = -1$: $(2(-1)+1)(-1+5) = (-1)(4) = -4 < 0$,
    negative values
    Test $x = 0$: $(2(0)+1)(0+5) = (1)(5) = 5 > 0$,
    positive values

8. $[-4, -1]$

Solution

$\left[-5, -\dfrac{1}{2}\right]$

9. $\dfrac{x-5}{3+x} = 0$; $x - 5 = 0$; $x = 5$

    y is undefined at $3 + x = 0$; $x = -3$

    produces intervals of: $(-\infty, -3), (-3, 5], [5, \infty)$;

    Choose $-4, 0$, and 6

    Test $x = -4$: $\dfrac{-4-5}{3+(-4)} = \dfrac{-9}{-1} = 9 > 0$, positive values

    Test $x = 0$: $\dfrac{0-5}{3+0} = \dfrac{-5}{3} < 0$, negative values

    Test $x = 6$: $\dfrac{6-5}{3+6} = \dfrac{1}{9} > 0$, positive values

10. $(-\infty, -3); [5, \infty)$

Solution

$(-3, 5]$

11. $3x-9=0$; $3x=9$; $x=3$
    intervals of $-\infty, 3]$, $[3, \infty)$ Choose 0 and 5
    Test $x=0$; $3(0)-9=-9<0$, negative values
    Test $x=5$; $3(5)-9=6>0$, positive values

12. $(-\infty, -3)$

Solution

    $[3, \infty)$

13. $x(x+7)=0$; $x=0$, $x=-7$
    intervals of: $(-\infty,-7]$,$[-7, 0]$,$[0, \infty)$
    Choose $-8, -1$, and 1
    Test $x=-8$: $-8(-8+7)=(-8)(-1)=8>0$,
    positive values
    Test $x=-1$: $-1(-1+7)=(-1)(6)=-6<0$,
    negative values
    Test $x=1$: $1(1+7)=8>0$, positive values

14. $(-\infty,0)$, $(3, \infty)$

Solution

    $(-\infty,-7]$, $[0, \infty)$

15. $x^2-x-12=0$
    $(x-4)(x+3)=0$; $x=4$, $x=-3$
    intervals of $(-\infty, -3)$, $(-3, 4)$, $(4, \infty)$
    Choose $-4, 0$, and 5
    Test $x=-4$: $(-4-4)(-4+3)=(-8)(-1)=8>0$,
    positive values
    Test $x=0$: $(0-4)(0+3)=-12<0$, negative values
    Test $x=5$: $(5-4)(5+3)=(1)(8)=8>0$,
    positive values

    a. $(-\infty,-3)$, $(4, \infty)$
    b. $(-3, 4)$

16.   a. $(-\infty, -4)$;$(3,\infty)$
      b. $(-4, 3)$

IVC2

Increasing and Decreasing Functions

We now return to our jeweler. Suppose his expenses for supplies can be represented by the function $f(x) = \dfrac{x^3}{3} - \dfrac{13}{2}x^2 + 40x.$

He wants to find for which size lots x this function $f(x)$ is increasing and decreasing.

Recall the functions are increasing where their slopes, or derivatives, are positive; i.e., where $f'(x) > 0$. Functions are decreasing where their slopes, or derivatives, are negative; i.e., where $f'(x) < 0$.

Our first step then is to find the derivative of $(x) = \dfrac{x^3}{3} - \dfrac{13}{2}x^2 + 40x.$ We find

$$f'(x) = \frac{3x^2}{3} - \frac{13}{2}(2)x + 40 = x^2 - 13x + 40.$$

Our next step is to find the set of x-values for which $f'(x) = x^2 - 13x + 40 > 0$, and for which $f'(x) = x^2 - 13x + 40 < 0$. Fortunately, we know how to solve inequalities.

Step 1:

We solve the related equation: $f'(x)=x^2-13x+40=0$.

$$(x-8)(x-5)=0$$

$$x=8, \ x=5$$

Step 2:

We note that $f'(x)=x^2-13x+40$ is defined everywhere. There are no x-values that will cause $f'(x)$ to be undefined.

The points where $f'(x)=0$, or where $f'(x)$ is undefined, are called **critical points**. The x-values of the critical points are called **critical values**.

The points where $f'(x)=0$ tell us where the slope equals 0; i.e., where the tangents of the curve have zero slope and are therefore horizontal lines.

On one side of each of these points, the slope increases, and on the other, it decreases. These critical points divide the curve into intervals having positive slopes and intervals having negative slopes. Observe the graph of $f'(x)$ at right. Note that it has horizontal tangents at $x=8$ and at $x=5$. To the left of $x=5$, the slope is positive everywhere and the function is increasing. This is also true for all x-values to the right of $x=8$. Between $x=8$ and $x=5$, the slope is negative everywhere and the function is decreasing. The dividing points for "increasing" and "decreasing," i.e., for positive and negative slopes, occur at the critical points.

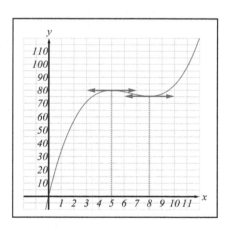

Suppose we didn't have the graph. We continue with our step method for solving inequalities.

Step 3:

We divide the real numbers into three intervals: $(-\infty, 5), (5, 8),$ and $(8, \infty)$.

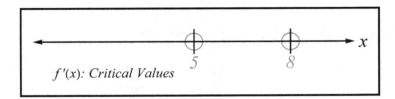

We have open circles at $x=5$ and $x=8$ because we are interested in the x-values that make $f'(x)>0$ and $f'(x)<0$. At the values $x=5$ and 8, $f'(x)=0$, which is neither positive nor negative.

Step 4:

We choose a test point from each interval. Let's choose 0, 6, and 10. These choices are arbitrary. We could have picked 2, 9, and 11. The choice doesn't matter as long as there is one choice from each line segment (if you're looking at the number line) or from each set (if you're looking at the subsets of real numbers). Note that *we will be testing these points in $f'(x)$, not in $f(x)$*, because it is the *derivative* that gives us slope and tells us where the function is increasing and decreasing.

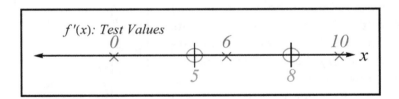

Step 5:

Test $x=0$: $f'(0)=(0-8)(0-5)=40>0$, positive slope → increasing expenses

Test $x=6$: $f'(6)=(6-8)(6-5)=-2<0$, negative slope → decreasing expenses

Test $x=10$: $f'(10)=(10-8)(10-5)=10>0$, positive slope → increasing expenses

We conclude that our jeweler should order supplies in lots of size somewhere between 5 and 8, because his expenses are falling within this interval.

Example 1:

Filbert is considering the purchase of a pizza chain. He is told that sales for the last several years can be represented by the function $s(t) = t^2 + t - 6$, where $t = 0$ represents the year 2012. He learns that the pizza chain underwent a significant change to their menu in the year 2011. Filbert would like to know when sales were increasing and decreasing. He needs to find when $s'(t) > 0$ and when $s'(t) > 0$.

The derivative is $s'(t) = 2t + 1$.

Step 1: Solve $s'(t) = 2t + 1 = 0$

$$2t = -1$$

$$t = -\frac{1}{2}$$

Step 2: There are no t's for which $s'(t)$ is undefined.

Step 3: The real numbers are divided into the intervals $\left(-\infty, -\frac{1}{2}\right), \left(-\frac{1}{2}, \infty\right)$.

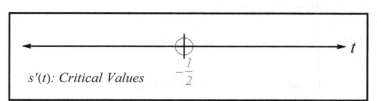

Step 4: We choose a point from each interval. Let's choose -2 and 0.

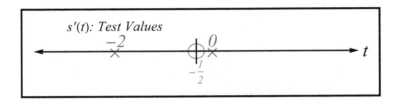

Step 5: Test $x=-2$: $m=s'(-2)=2(-2)+1=-3<0$, negative slope

Test $x=0$: $m=s'(0)=2(0)+1=1>0$, positive slope

Filbert now knows that sales were decreasing for the pizza chain in the years before $t=-\dfrac{1}{2}$, which would be before the last half of the year 2011. He also knows that sales were increasing for the pizza chain in the years after $t=-\dfrac{1}{2}$, or from the last half of 2011 onward.

If a quadratic function cannot be factored, we use the quadratic formula:

$$x=\frac{-b\pm\sqrt{b^2-4ac}}{2a}$$

to find the x-values that make the expression equal to zero. Actually, the quadratic formula works for any quadratic function whether it factors or not.

Example 2:

A minor recording studio tracks the number of on-line orders it receives for each recording per advertising dollar spent $D(A)$. This function can be approximated by the equation:

$$D(A)=-0.32A^3+4310A^2-14{,}300{,}900A.$$

The CEO would like to know when his advertising dollars are no longer effective at increasing sales. He needs to know where $D(A)$ is increasing and where $D(A)$ is decreasing or staying constant. To find out, we will need to investigate the slope. We need to find the derivative, $D'(A)$.

$$D'(A) = -0.32(3)A^2 + 4310(2)A - 14,300,900$$

$$D'(A) = -0.96A^2 + 8620A - 14,300,900$$

Step 1: We set $D'(A) = -0.96A^2 + 8620A - 14,300,900 = 0$.

Since it is doubtful that this equation factors, we will use the quadratic formula. We note that $a = 0.96$, $b = 8620$, and $c = -14,300,000$.

$$A = \frac{-8620 \pm \sqrt{(8620)^2 - 4(-0.96)(-14,300,900)}}{2(-0.96)} \approx 2196, 6783$$

Step 2: $D(A)$ is a continuous function. There are no values of A that will make $D(A)$ undefined.

Step 3: We divide the real numbers into the intervals:

$$(-\infty, 2196), \qquad (2196, 6783), \qquad (6783, \infty)$$

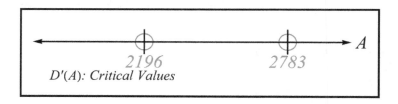

Step 4: We choose a number from each interval. Let's choose 0, 4,000, and 8,000.

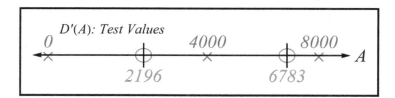

Test $A=0$: $D'(0)=-0.96(0)^2+8620(0)-14,300,900<0$, negative slope

Test $A=4,000$: $D'(4,000)=-0.96(4,000)^2+8620(4,000)-14,300,900$
$=4,819,100>0$, positive slope

Test $A=8,000$: $D'(8,000)=-0.96(8,000)^2+8620(8,000)-14,300,900$

$=-6,780,900<0$, negative slope

The CEO now knows that orders per advertising dollar increase as long as he spends between \$2,196 to \$6,783 per recording.

Example 3:

Find where the function $f(x)$ is increasing and decreasing if $f'(x)=\dfrac{2x-5}{x+2}$.

Step 1: We need to find where $f(x)$ equals zero. We recall that a fraction is zero where the numerator equals zero. We set: $2x-5=0$

$$2x=5$$

$$x=\frac{5}{2}$$

Step 2: We need to specify any x-values for which the expression is undefined. We recall that a fraction is undefined where the denominator equals zero.

We set: $x+2=0$

$x=-2$

Step 3: We divide the real numbers into the intervals:

$$(-\infty,-2),\left(-2,\frac{5}{2}\right),\left(\frac{5}{2},\infty\right)$$

We can also plot these two critical points on a number line.

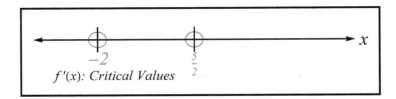

Step 4: We choose a point from each interval. Let's choose -3, 0, and 10.

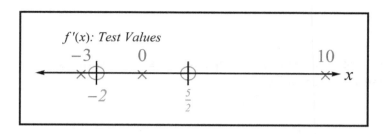

Test $x=-3$: $m=f'(-3)=\dfrac{2(-3)-5}{-3+2}=\dfrac{-11}{-1}=11>0$, positive slope, so $f(x)$ is increasing over the interval $(-\infty, -2)$.

Test $x=0$: $m=f'(0)=\dfrac{2(0)-5}{0+1}=-5<0$, negative slope, so $f(x)$ is decreasing over the interval $\left(-2, \dfrac{5}{2}\right)$.

Test $x=10$: $m=f'(10)=\dfrac{2(10)-5}{10+2}=\dfrac{15}{12}>0$, positive slope, so $f(x)$ is also increasing over the interval $\left(\dfrac{5}{2}, \infty\right)$.

In summary, $f(x)$ is increasing over the intervals $(-\infty, -2)$ and $\left(\dfrac{5}{2}, \infty\right)$ and $f(x)$ is decreasing over the interval $\left(-2, \dfrac{5}{2}\right)$.

INTRA-SECTION EXERCISES:

1. At a certain university, the number of students admitted from Middle Eastern countries can be expressed by the function $f(t)=2t^3-21t^2+72t+900$, where t represents years, and $t=0$ is the year 1998.

    Suppose we are interested in projecting future enrollment from different areas of the world. We want to know for which years the enrollment was increasing and for which years it was decreasing.

2. Where is the function $g(x)$ increasing and decreasing if $g'(x)=\dfrac{5x-10}{x+4}$?

Solutions

1. We want to know where the slope was positive and where it was negative. We will need the derivative.

$$f'(t)=6t^2-42t+72$$

Step 1: We solve the related equation:

$$6t^2-42t+72=0$$

We can factor out a 6:

$$6(t^2-7t+12)=0$$

$$6(t-3)(t-4)=0$$

We factor the quadratic:

$$t=3, t=4$$

Step 2: We note that $f'(t)$ is continuous. There are no t-values for which it is undefined.

Step 3: We divide the real numbers into the intervals $(-\infty,3), (3,4), (4,\infty)$.

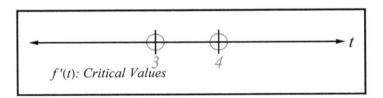

$f'(t)$: Critical Values

Step 4: We choose a point from each interval. Let's choose $0, 3.5$, and 10.

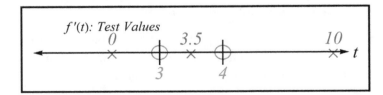

$f'(t)$: Test Values

Test $t=0$: $m=f'(0)=6(0-3)(0-4)=72>0$, positive slope, increasing function.

Test $t=3.5$: $m=f'(3.5)=6(3.5-3)(3.5-4)=-1.5<0$, negative slope, decreasing function.

Test $t=10$: $m=f'(10)=6(10-3)(10-4)=252>0$, positive slope, increasing function.

We now know that the number of students from the Middle East was rising before $t=3$, or the year 2001. The number fell between $t=3$ to $t=4$, or between the years 2001 and 2002, and the number rose again after $t=4$, or the year 2002.

2. We need to know where $g'(x)>0$ and where $g'(x)<0$.

   Step 1: We solve the related equation $g'(x)=\dfrac{5x-10}{x+4}=0$;

   Since a fraction equals zero where its numerator equals zero, we set: $5x-10=0$.

   $$5x=10$$
   $$x=2$$

   Step 2: Since a fraction is undefined where its denominator equals zero, we set: $x+4=0$.

   $$x=-4$$

   Step 3: We divide the real numbers into the intervals $(-\infty,-4)$, $(-4,2)$, $(2,\infty)$.

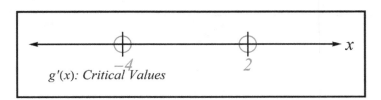
$g'(x)$: *Critical Values*

   Step 4: We choose a number to test from each interval. Let's choose $-6, 0$, and 5.

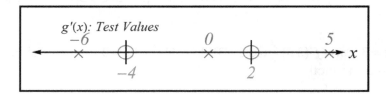

Test $x = -6$: $g'(-6) = \dfrac{5(-6)-10}{-6+4} = \dfrac{-40}{-2} = 20 > 0$, positive slope; $g(x)$ is increasing.

Test $x = 0$: $g'(0) = \dfrac{5(0)-10}{0+4} = \dfrac{-10}{4} = -\dfrac{5}{2} < 0$, negative slope; $g(x)$ is decreasing.

Test $x = 5$: $g'(5) = \dfrac{5(5)-10}{5+4} = \dfrac{15}{9} > 0$, positive slope; $g(x)$ is increasing.

The function $g(x)$ is increasing on the intervals $(-\infty, -4)$ and $(2, \infty)$.

The function $g(x)$ is decreasing on the interval $(-4, 2)$.

GRAPHING PIECEWISE DEFINED FUNCTIONS

Sometimes graphs are made up of several functions. Different intervals on the x-axis correspond to different functions of y. These are called **piecewise functions**.

The graph below represents the US minimum wage over the years 1991 to 2006.

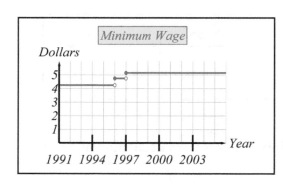

The function representing this graph can be written:

$$\text{Minimum wage} = y = \begin{cases} 4.25 & \text{for } 1991 \leq t < 1996 \\ 4.75 & \text{for } 1996 \leq t < 1997 \\ 5.15 & \text{for } 1997 \leq t \leq 2006 \end{cases}$$

Example 4:

A Very Moving Example

The function below represents the freight charges for a household moving company where x equals the number of miles from the point of origin to the new city.

$$f(x) = \begin{cases} \$350 & \text{for } 0 \leq x < 100 \text{ miles} \\ \$350 + \$5x & \text{for } 100 \leq x \leq 500 \text{ miles} \\ \$500 + \$5x & \text{for } x > 500 \text{ miles} \end{cases}$$

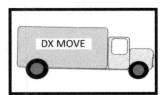

Three different functions are used by the moving company to determine the charges, depending on the miles moved.

To construct a piecewise graph, we have three functions:

(1) $f(x) = y = \$350$; (2) $f(x) = y = \$350 + \$5x$; and (3) $f(x) = \$500 + \$5x$.

They are all to be graphed on the same set of axes. The specifications regarding x tell us the intervals over which each segment will be graphed. Another way of looking at it is: the specifications regarding the x-axis tell us the endpoints for each segment.

The graph of (1), $f(x) = y = \$350$, is a straight line. It starts at $x = 0$ and ends at $x = 100$ because it is given that $350 is the cost for $0 \leq x < 100$ *miles,* giving us the two endpoints $(0, 350)$ and $(100, 350)$. The graph is below:

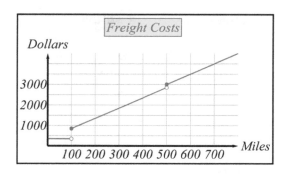

Since x cannot actually equal 100 miles on this function (because $x < 100$, not $x \leq 100$), we use an open dot at the point (100, 350). We have a closed dot at the endpoint (0,350) because we are given $0 \leq x$, so x can actually equal 0.

Also, since this graph is a horizontal line, we note that it is neither increasing nor decreasing.

The graph of (2), $f(x) = y = \$350 + \$5x$, is a linear function. We need two points to graph it, starting with an endpoint at $x = 100$ and ending with an endpoint at $x = 500$.

When $x = 100$ we solve for y to get $\$350 + \$5(100) = \$850$, giving us the point (100, 850).

When $x = 500$ we solve for y to get $\$350 + \$5(500) = \$2850$, giving us the point (500, 2850).

This time, we have a closed circle at each end because x can actually take on the values of 100 and 500, since our function specifies $30 \leq x \leq 500$.

For the third segment (3), we plot $f(x) = y = \$500 + \$5x$.

This is also a linear equation, so we need two points. We must start with the given endpoint of $x = 500$, but we will use an open circle for this endpoint because x can never actually take on the value of 500. (We were given $x < 500$, not $x \leq 500$).

We plot $y = f(500) = \$500 + \$5(500) = \$3,000$. We need a second point, but we must choose an $x > 500$. We'll choose $x = 600$.

Then $y = f(600) = \$500 + \$5(600) = \$3,500$. These points are entered in the box at right. We plot (500,3,000) using an open circle (because $x < 500$ not $x \leq 500$). Check out the finished graph again.

x	y
500	$3,000
600	$3,500

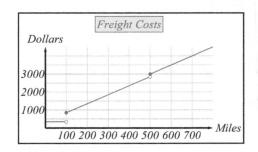

We note that the graph is increasing over the intervals (100,500) and (500,∞).

Just a technical note: We use square brackets for closed intervals and rounded parentheses for open intervals. Endpoints of infinity ($-\infty$ or ∞) always have rounded parentheses.

Example 5:

Suppose we need to graph the piecewise function:

$$f(x) = \begin{cases} x^2 + 2 \ f \ or \ x \geq 0 \\ -x + 2 \ f \ or \ x < 0 \end{cases}$$

The first half of the graph is $f(x) = y = x^2 + 2$.

We recognize this as the parabola at right.

Since we are restricted to $x \geq 0$, we use only the segment of the curve corresponding to x-values on the interval $[0, \infty)$. At the endpoint $x = 0$, we use a closed circle for the corresponding point on the graph of $y = f(0) = 0^2 + 2 = 2$.

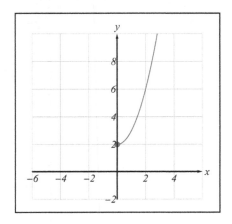

The left half of the graph is specified by the equation $f(x)=y=-x+2$. This is another linear equation so again, we need to find only two points. We must use the endpoint $x=0$ for one of the points. Because x cannot ever take on the actual value of 0 (because $x<0$, not $x\leq0$), we use an open circle on the graph at this point.

We find $y=f(0)=-0+2=2$.

For the second point, we must choose a value of x less than 0, say, -2.

We find $y=f(-2)=-(-2)+2=4$.

We summarize these points on the table at right.

x	y
0	2
-2	4

When we plot these last two points, we recognize that this graph extends over the interval $(-\infty, 0)$. Plotting these two points, we have the graph:

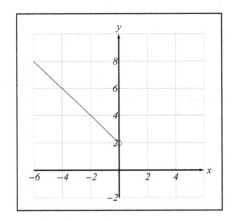

Put the two graph segments together to obtain the entire graph.

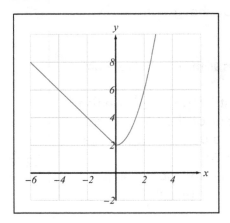

We note that this graph is increasing over the interval $(0, \infty)$ and decreasing over the interval $(-\infty, 0)$.

INTRA-SECTION EXERCISES:

3. Graph the function $f(x) = \begin{cases} 2x - 1 & f\!or \ x > 2 \\ 1 & f\!or \ -2 \leq x \leq 2 \\ -(x+2)^2 + 1 & f\!or \ x < -2 \end{cases}$

State where $f(x)$ is increasing and where $f(x)$ is decreasing.

Solutions

3. The function $f(x) = y = 2x - 1$ is a linear equation. We plot two points, $x = 2$, and a second point for which $x > 2$, such as 3. This gives us the points $(2,3)$ and $(3,5)$. There is an open circle on the point $(2,3)$ since $x > 2$, not $x \geq 2$.

The function $f(x) = y = 1$ is the horizontal line running from the point $(-2,1)$ to $(2,1)$. There are closed circles at each of these points since we are given $-2 \leq x$ and $x \leq 2$.

The function $f(x) = y = -(x+2)^2 + 1$ is a parabola with vertex shifted up one unit and two units to the left; i.e., at $(-2,1)$. It opens downward. We want only the left half of this parabola where $x < -2$. There would be an open circle at the point $(-2,1)$, but it has already been closed by the function $f(x) = 1$ for $-2 \leq x \leq 2$.

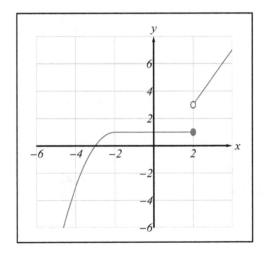

The graph is increasing over the intervals $(-\infty, -2)$. It is constant over the interval $(-2, 2)$, and it is increasing again over the interval $(2, \infty)$.

IVC2 INCREASING AND DECREASING FUNCTIONS EXERCISES

For numbers 1 through 10, using inequality tests for the derivative, find where the functions below are increasing and where they are decreasing.

1. $f(x) = -2x^2 + 4x + 3$

2. $f(x) = -4x^2 - 12x + 1$

3. $g(x) = x^2 + 8x + 10$

4. $g(x) = -3x^2 - 3x + 5$

5. $f(t) = t^4 - 2t^3$

6. $f(t) = 2t^4 + 4t^3$

7. $f(x) = x^{\frac{2}{3}}$

8. $f(x) = 3x^{\frac{1}{3}}$

9. $h(t) = -5t - 7$

10. $h(t) = 6t + 4$

11. Monthly revenue R (in thousands of dollars) for a shopping mall is projected by the equation $R(t) = 9.6t - 1.6t^2$ where t represents years, with $t = 0$ at the year 2020. For $t = 0$ to $t = 10$, find the intervals over which annual revenue is increasing and decreasing.

12. Annual concert attendance A (in millions) for a rising teenage pop singing group is projected by a publicity agent as $A(t) = 20.8t - 2.6t^2$ where t = years since the initial concert tour. For the years $t = 1$ to 10, in which years is attendance expected to increase, and in which years is it expected to decrease?

For numbers 13–18, graph the functions. State where they are increasing and where they are decreasing.

13. $f(x) = \begin{cases} (x-2)^3 + 1 & f\ or\ x > 2 \\ x - 1 & f\ or\ x \leq 2 \end{cases}$

14. $f(x) = \begin{cases} (x+2)^3 + 1 & f\ or\ x > -2 \\ x + 1 & f\ or\ x \leq -2 \end{cases}$

15. $f(x) = \begin{cases} 2x - 3 & f\ or\ x > 0 \\ 0 & f\ or\ -3 \leq x \leq 0 \\ -2x - 3 & f\ or\ x < -3 \end{cases}$

16. $f(x) = \begin{cases} -2x + 1 & f\ or\ x > 0 \\ 1 & f\ or\ -3 \leq x \leq 0 \\ 2x + 4 & f\ or\ x < -3 \end{cases}$

17. $f(x) = \begin{cases} -x^3 + 2 & f\ or\ x \geq 0 \\ x + 2 & f\ or\ x < 0 \end{cases}$

18. $f(x) = \begin{cases} x^3 + 2 & f\ or\ x \geq 0 \\ -x + 2 & f\ or\ x < 0 \end{cases}$

IVC2 INCREASING AND DECREASING FUNCTIONS SOLUTIONS TO EXERCISES

1. $f'(x) = -4x + 4 = 0$

   $-4x = -4$

   $x = 1$

   Divide real numbers into $(-\infty, 1)$ and $(1, \infty)$

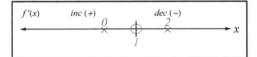

   Choose 0 and 2

   Test $x = 0$: $f'(0) = -4(0) + 4 = 4 > 0$, positive slope

   Test $x = 2$: $f'(2) = -4(2) + 4 = -4 < 0$, negative slope

   increasing: $(-\infty, 1)$ decreasing: $(1, \infty)$

2. increasing: $(-\infty, -1.5)$
   decreasing: $(-1.5, \infty)$

3. $g'(x) = 2x + 8 = 0$

   $2x = -8$

   $x = -4$

   Divide real numbers into $(-\infty, -4)$ and $(-4, \infty)$

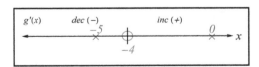

4. increasing: $\left(-\infty, -\dfrac{1}{2}\right)$

   decreasing: $\left(-\dfrac{1}{2}, \infty\right)$

Choose −5 and 0

Test $x = -5$: $g'(-5) = 2(-5) + 8 = -2 < 0$, negative slope

Test $x = 0$: $g'(0) = 2(0) + 8 = 8 > 0$, positive slope

increasing: $(-4, \infty)$ decreasing: $(-\infty, -4)$

5. $f'(t) = 4t^3 - 6t^2 = 0$

$2t^2(2t - 3) = 0$

$t = 0, t = \dfrac{3}{2}$

Divide real numbers into

$(-\infty, 0), \left[0, \dfrac{3}{2}\right], \left[\dfrac{3}{2}, \infty\right)$

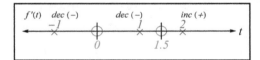

Choose −1, 1, and 2.

Test $x = -1$: $f'(-1) = 2(-1)^2(2(-1) - 3)$
$= 2(-5) < 0$, negative slope

Test $x = 1$: $f'(1) = 2(1)^2(2(1) - 3) = 2(-1) < 0$, negative slope

Test $x = 2$: $f'(2) = 2(2)^2(2(2) - 3) = 8(1) > 0$, positive slope

increasing: $\left[\dfrac{3}{2}, \infty\right)$ decreasing:

$(-\infty, 0), \left[0, \dfrac{3}{2}\right)$

6. increasing: $(-1.5, 0)(0, \infty)$
    decreasing: $(-\infty, -1.5)$

7. $f'(x) = \dfrac{2}{3}x^{-\frac{1}{3}} = \dfrac{2}{3\sqrt[3]{x}} = 0$

$f'(x)$ equals 0 nowhere, since the numerator will never equal 0, but it is undefined at $x = 0$, which is where the denominator equals 0.

Divide real numbers into: $(-\infty, 0), (0, \infty)$.

Choose 1 and -1.

Test $x = -1$: $f'(-1) = \dfrac{2}{3\sqrt[3]{-1}} = \dfrac{2}{-3} < 0$,

negative slope

Test $x = 1$: $f'(1) = \dfrac{2}{3\sqrt[3]{1}} = \dfrac{2}{3} > 0$,

positive slope

increasing: $(0, \infty)$; decreasing: $(-\infty, 0)$

8. increasing: $(-\infty, 0), (0, \infty)$
    decreasing: nowhere

9. $h'(t) = -5 \neq 0$

Because $h'(t)$ is negative everywhere, the function $h(t)$ is decreasing everywhere.

increasing: nowhere; decreasing: $(-\infty, \infty)$

10. increasing: $(-\infty, \infty)$
    decreasing: nowhere

11. $R'(t)=9.6-3.2t=0.$

$-3.2t=-9.6.$

$t=3.$

Divide real numbers into: $(0,3),(3,10)$.

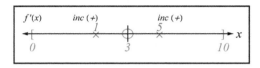

Choose 1 and 5.

Test $x=1: R'(1)=9.6-3.2(1)=6.4>0$, positive slope

Test $x=5: R'(5)=9.6-3.2(5)=-6.4<0$, negative slope

increasing: $(0,3)=$ years 2020 to 2023

decreasing: $(3,10)$ = years 2023 to 2030

12. increasing: $(1,4)$

decreasing: $(4,10)$

13.

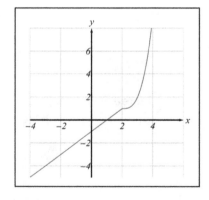

increasing: $(-\infty,\infty)$
decreasing: nowhere

14.

increasing: $(-\infty,-2),(-2,\infty)$
decreasing: nowhere

15.

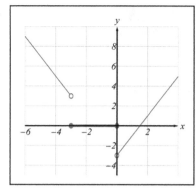

increasing: (0,∞)
decreasing: (−∞, −3)

16.

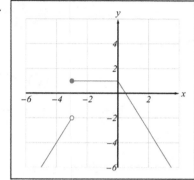

increasing: (−∞,−3)
decreasing: (0,∞)

17.

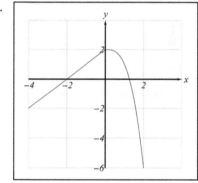

increasing: (−∞,0)
decreasing: (0,∞)

18.

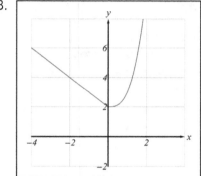

increasing: (0,∞)
decreasing: (−∞,0)

IVC3

Maxima, Minima, and the First Derivative Test

Ernest Larrabee raises roses to sell to local florists. The number of acres he plants has varied. If he doesn't plant enough acres, he foregoes some of the profit he could have made. If he plants too many acres, he incurs the costs of planting but has unsold roses, which lowers his profit for the season. Mr. Larrabee uses data he has collected from past years to plot his profits against acres planted.

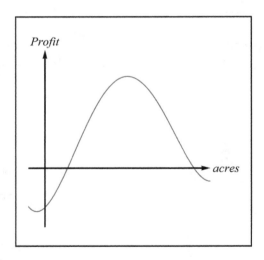

Mr. Larrabee would like to know which number of planted acres will yield the maximum revenue.

The graph below represents the average cost per student at a local junior college for enrollments between 100 and 1,000 students. Since each student pays tuition, as the number of students increases, the cost per student decreases, but at some point, adding additional students requires more classrooms and more professors, and possibly even another building.

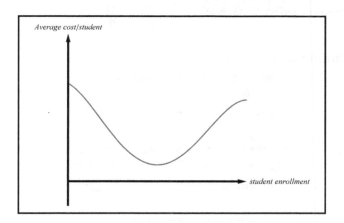

The administrators would like to determine the student enrollment that minimizes cost.

Suppose we find that student enrollment from Asian countries can be expressed by the function $f(t) = 2t^3 - 33t^2 + 60t + 900$ where t represents years, with $t = 0$ beginning in 1990.

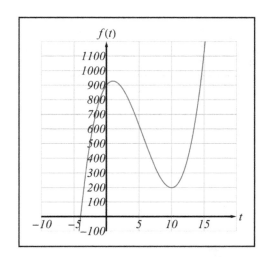

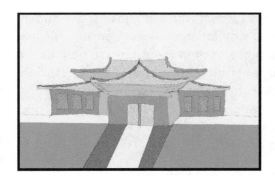

If we examine the graph of this function (above), we can see that there is a maximum at $t = 1$. The corresponding point on the graph is $(1,929)$. This is not the highest point on the graph, but it is higher than the points around it. It is a *relative maximum*; some texts call this a *local maximum*. The highest point on the graph is called the *absolute maximum*. Some texts call this the *global maximum*.

We can also see from the graph that there is a minimum at the point $(10,200)$. This is not the lowest point on the graph, but it is lower than the points around it. It is a *relative minimum*, also called a *local minimum*. The lowest point on the graph is the *absolute minimum*, also called a *global minimum*.

Sometimes a relative minimum is also an absolute minimum. Sometimes a relative maximum is also the absolute maximum. This is the case for the graph below. The relative maximum at x_0 is also the highest point on the graph.

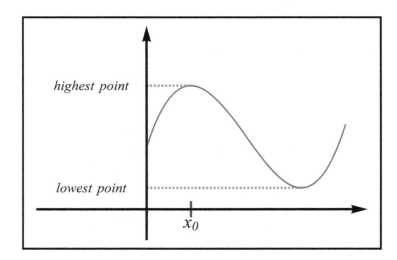

There can be more than one relative minimum or more than one relative maximum. Check out the graph below.

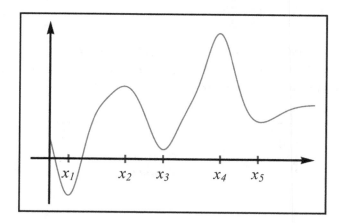

It has relative minima at x_1, x_3, and x_5. It has relative maxima at x_2 and x_4. The relative maxima at x_4 is also the absolute maximum and the relative minimum at x_1 is also an absolute minimum.

There can even be more than one absolute maximum or absolute minimum. There are three absolute maxima on the graph below. Two of them are also relative maxima. They occur at x_1, x_3, and x_5 because they are all equally high and are the highest points on the graph. At x_3 and x_5, these relative maxima are also absolute maxima.

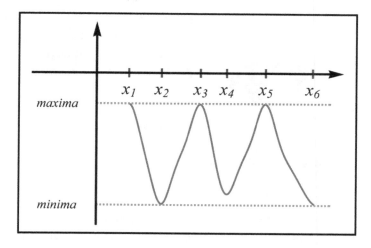

There are two absolute minima on the graph above. They occur at x_2 and x_6 because they are equally low and they are the lowest points on the graph. The absolute minimum at x_2 is also a relative minimum. Another relative minimum occurs at x_4, but it is not an absolute minimum.

To locate relative maxima and minima, collectively called relative extrema, we examine the slope. At a relative maximum the tangent to the curve is a horizontal line, which means the slope is zero at a maximum.

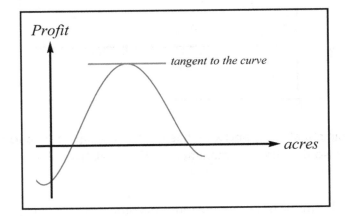

This is a good indicator! We also notice that on the left side of the relative maximum, the function is increasing, and on the right side of the relative maximum, the function is decreasing. We can now pinpoint where a relative maximum occurs, even if we don't have a graph, because we know two things about them:

1. At a relative maximum, the derivative equals 0 (when the derivative exists).
2. The derivative is positive on the left side of a relative maximum and negative on the right side.

If we are given a function without the graph, we could find the relative maxima by:

Step 1:

Setting the derivative equal to zero and solving for x. (Here we are assuming the derivative exists.) Suppose it happens at $x = x_1$.

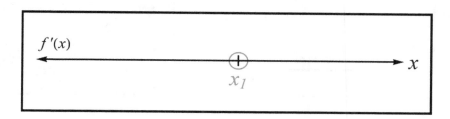

Step 2:

We check each side of x_1 to see if the slope is positive on the left of x_1 and negative on the right of x_1. If so, there is a relative maximum at x_1.

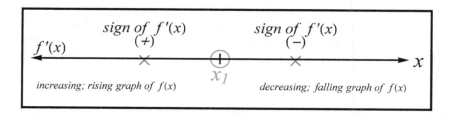

Step 3:

Since x_1 is only half of a point (x, y), we can find the y-value that corresponds to x_1 by going back to the original equation $y = f(x)$. To find y when x is x_1, we find $y = f(x_1)$. The relative maximum would be at $(x_1, f(x_1))$.

Recall: We use $f(x)$ when we want to find a y-value, or a height on a graph. We use $f'(x)$ when we want to find a slope.

Now examine the average cost/student graph. Notice that the tangent at the minimum is also a horizontal line. At minima, the derivative is also equal to 0.

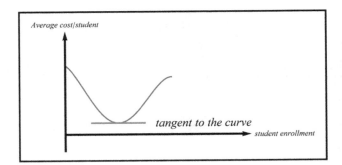

One difference is that the function is decreasing on the left side of the relative minimum, i.e., the slope is negative, and the function is increasing on the right side of the relative minimum, i.e., the slope is positive.

Now we know two things about a relative minimum:

1. The derivative equals 0 at a relative minimum (when the derivative exists).
2. The derivative is negative on the left and positive to the right of a relative minimum.

If we were given a function without its graph, we could still find any relative minima by:

Step 1:

Setting the derivative equal to zero and solving for x. (Here we are assuming the derivative exists.) Suppose that happens at $x = x_2$.

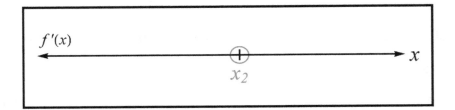

Step 2:

Checking each side of x_2 to see if the slope is negative on the left and positive on the right. If so, there is a relative minimum at x_2.

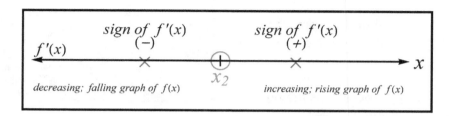

Step 3:

Since x_2 is only half of a point (x, y), we can find the y-value that corresponds to x_2 by going back to the original equation $y = f(x)$. To find y when x is x_2, we find $y = f(x_2)$. The relative minimum would be at $(x_2, f(x_2))$.

This method is called the **First Derivative Test** for finding *relative* extrema. (*Extrema* is a collective term for maxima and minima.)

Remember, at every *relative* maximum and *relative* minimum, the tangent is a horizontal line, so the derivative equals zero for every relative extrema (when the derivative exists). This is not necessarily true for *absolute* maxima and minima.

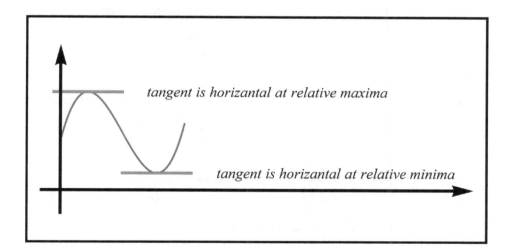

Example 1:

Suppose the market for newly constructed houses in a certain city can be represented by the function:

$f(t) = t^4 + 250$, where t represents the years 2005 to 2015 and $t = 0$ corresponds to 2010.

The function $f(t)$ represents the number of newly constructed houses.

Step 1: We take the derivative of $f(t)$ and set it equal to zero.

$f'(t) = 4t^3$. Dividing both sides by 4 and taking the cube root, we find $t = 0$. We plot this on a number line.

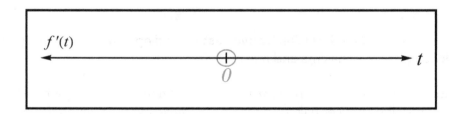

Step 2: We test a point from each side of 0 in the derivative because we want to know if the slope is positive or negative on each side. We choose -1 and 1.

Test $x = -1$: $f'(-1) = 4(-1)^3 < 0$, negative slope $\rightarrow$ falling number of homes. (Note that we don't really care what the slope is. We just want to know if it's positive or negative.)

Step 3: Test $x = 1$: $f'(1) = 4(1)^3 > 0$, positive slope $\rightarrow$ rising number of homes. (Once again, we don't really care what the slope is. We just want to know if it's positive or negative.)

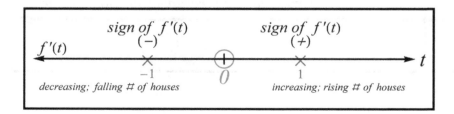

Since the graph is falling, or decreasing, on the left and rising, or increasing, on the right, we know there is a relative minimum at $t = 0$.

Step 4: To find the y-value when $t = 0$, we go back to the original function:

$$y = f(t) = t^4 + 250$$
$$y = f(0) = 0^4 + 250 = 250 \text{ new houses}$$

Therefore, when $t = 0$, $f(t) = 250$, so the relative minimum is at the point $(0, 250)$; i.e., in the year 2010, there were 250 new houses constructed, a relative minimum of new houses.

INTRA-SECTION EXERCISES:

Use the First Derivative Test to find the relative maxima and/or minima for the following functions.

1. $f(x) = \dfrac{x^2}{2} - 3x$
2. $g(t) = \dfrac{t^3}{3} + \dfrac{t^2}{2} - 6t$

Solutions

1. $f'(x) = x - 3 = 0$
   $x = 3$

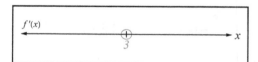

Choose 0 and 4.

Test $x = 0$: $f(0) = 0 - 3 < 0$, negative slope

Test $x = 4$: $f(4) = 4 - 3 > 0$, positive slope

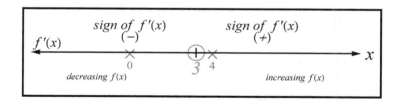

This pattern tells us there is a relative minimum where $x = 3$.

We also need to find $y = f(3) = \dfrac{3^2}{2} - 3(3) = -\dfrac{9}{2} = -4.5$.

Therefore, the relative minimum is at the point $(3, -4.5)$.

2. $g'(t) = t^2 + t - 6 = 0$ Choose -4, 0, and 3.
   $(t+3)(t-2) = 0$
   $t = -3, t = 2$

Test $t = -4$: $g'(-4) = (-4 + 3)(-4 - 2) = 6 > 0$, positive slope
Test $t = 0$: $g'(0) = (0 + 3)(0 - 2) = -6 < 0$, negative slope
Test $t = 3$: $g'(3) = (3 + 3)(3 - 2) = 6 > 0$, positive slope

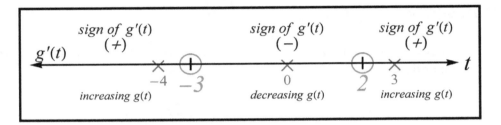

Relative maximum at $(-3, g(-3))$; relative minimum at $(2, g(2))$

$y = g(-3) = \dfrac{(-3)^3}{3} + \dfrac{(-3)^2}{2} - 6(-3) = -9 + 4.5 + 18 = 13.5$

$y = g(2) = \dfrac{(2)^3}{3} + \dfrac{(2)^2}{2} - 6(2) = 2.67 + 2 - 12 = -7.33$

Relative maximum at $(-3, 13.5)$; relative minimum at $(2, -7.33)$

ABSOLUTE MAXIMA AND MINIMA

Let's go back to our equation for Asian student enrollment:

$f(t) = 2t^3 - 33t^2 + 60t + 900$ where t represents years with $t = 0$ beginning in 1990.

Suppose we're interested in the maximum enrollment between the years 1990 and 2010; that is, between $t = 0$ and $t = 20$.

Recall that an absolute maximum is the highest point on a graph. According to a theorem offered here without proof, if there is an absolute maximum, it will occur either at a relative maximum or at an endpoint. Think about the figure below.

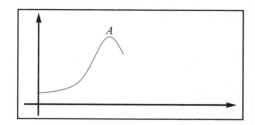

If the highest point, i.e., the absolute maximum, is not at point A, then the graph goes up even higher, to endpoint B.

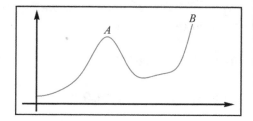

If the highest point is not at point B, an endpoint, then the graph goes down again and up even higher, making a relative maximum at B.

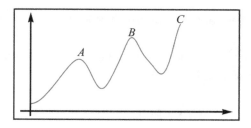

Similarly, an absolute minimum occurs either at a relative minimum or at an endpoint.

Since the *absolute* maximum is either at an endpoint or at a relative maximum, we begin by noting the given endpoints and then by finding where a relative maximum might occur. We already know that relative maxima have derivatives equal to zero (when the derivative exists), so we take the derivative of our function, set it equal to zero, and solve for x.

$f(t) = 2t^3 - 33t^2 + 60t + 900, \; [0, 20]$

$f'(t) = 6t^2 - 66t + 60 = 0$ We factor out 6.

$f'(t) = 6(t^2 - 11t + 10) = 0$ We factor the trinomial.

$f'(t) = 6(t - 10(t - 0) = 0$ Setting each factor equal to 0 we find:

$t = 10, \; t = 1$

We now know that the endpoints are at $t = 0$ and $t = 20$, and possible relative extrema occur at $t = 1$ and $t = 10$. Since we are looking for the highest point on the graph, we use $f(t)$ to give us the y-value (height) at each of these points.

Remember: We are looking for a height, or y-value, so we use $f(t)$. We are not looking for a slope, so we do not test in the derivative.

$y = f(0) = 2(0)^3 - 33(0)^2 + 60(0) + 900 = \mathbf{900}$

$y = f(20) = 2(20)^3 - 33(20)^2 + 60(20) + 900 = \mathbf{148,900}$

$y = f(1) = 2(1)^3 - 33(1)^2 + 60(1) + 900 = \mathbf{929}$

$y = f(10) = 2(10)^3 - 33(10)^2 + 60(10) + 900 = \mathbf{200}$

We look for the highest y-value in our set of: 900, 148,900, 929, and 200.

The highest point occurs when $y = f(20) = 148,900$. This occurred when $t = 20$, so the absolute maximum is $(20, 148,900)$.

To find the *absolute minimum*, we don't have to do any additional work.

We know that absolute minima occurs either at an endpoint or at a relative minimum, and we know that relative minima also occur where the derivative equals zero.

In the example above, we already know that the endpoints are at $t = 0$ and $t = 20$, and we know the derivative equals zero at $t = 1$ and $t = 10$. Next, we want to know which of these four points gives us the lowest height, or y-value. Fortunately, we've already found the y-value for each of these four points above.

We merely look for the lowest y-value in our set of 900, 148,900, 929, and 200.

The lowest height was 200, when $t = 10$. Therefore, the absolute minimum is $(10,200)$.

Note that after we set the derivative equal to zero, we didn't have to do the First Derivative Test to determine whether there was a relative maximum or a relative minimum at these points. We only check the heights.

If we examine the graph below, we can see that we found the correct absolute maximum and absolute minimum.

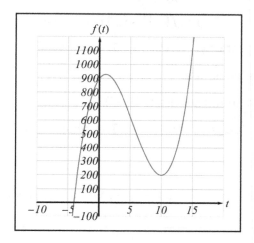

To summarize: To find the *absolute extrema*:

1. Note the given endpoints. We'll call them *a* and *b*.
2. Find the derivative and set it equal to zero. Suppose this occurs at x_1 and x_2.
3. Find the heights: $y = f(a)$ = height at the left endpoint.
                            $y = f(b)$ = height at the right endpoint
                            $y = f(x_1)$ = height at a relative extremum
                            $y = f(x_2)$ = height at a relative extremum

The absolute maximum is at the highest *y*-value. The absolute minimum is at the lowest *y*-value.

Example 2:

Suppose we're interested in $f(x) = x^2 + 2x - 4$ over the interval $[-2, 1]$ and we want to find the absolute extrema.

1. We note that the endpoints occur at $x = -2$ and $x = 1$.

2. We find the x-values where the derivative equals zero.

$$f'(x)=2x+2=0$$

$$2(x+1)=0$$

$$x=-1$$

3. We find the y-values, or heights, for each of these x-values (–2, 1, and –1).

$$y=f(-2)=(-2)^2+2(-2)-4=\mathbf{-4}$$

$$y=f(1)=(1)^2+2(1)-4=\mathbf{-1}$$

$$y=f(-1)=(-1)^2+2(-1)-4=\mathbf{-5}$$

We examine our set of y-values: –4, –1, and –5.

The highest y-value is –1 at $x=1$.

The absolute maximum occurs at (1, –1).

The lowest y-value is –5 at $x=-1$. The absolute minimum occurs at $(-1,-5)$.

To check our work, we can examine the graph of $y=f(x)=x^2+2x-4$.

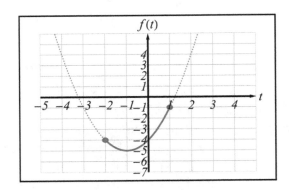

The graph is a parabola with vertex at $(-1,-5)$. If we consider the graph over the interval $[-2,1]$, we can see that the highest point on this interval, the absolute maximum, occurs at $(1,-1)$, and the lowest point, the absolute minimum, occurs at $(-1,-5)$.

> Remember: If you want a slope, use $f'(x)$. If you want a y-value, or height, use $f(x)$.

INTRA-SECTION EXERCISES:

Find the absolute extrema (x, y) over the given intervals $[a,b]$.

3. $f(x) = \dfrac{x^2}{2} - 3x, \quad [0, 4]$

4. $f(x) = -\dfrac{x^3}{3} - \dfrac{x^2}{2} + 12x, \quad [-2, 5]$

Solutions

3. $f'(x) = x - 3 = 0$

   $x = 3$

We check the y values at $x = 0, 3,$ and 4.

$$y = f(0) = \frac{(0)^2}{2} - 3(0) = 0$$

$$y = f(4) = \frac{(4)^2}{2} - 3(4) = -4$$

$$y = f(3) = \frac{(3)^2}{2} - 3(3) = -4.5$$

We examine our set of y-values: $0, -4,$ and -4.5. The highest is 0 at $x = 0$, and the lowest is -4.5 at $x = 3$. The absolute maximum is 0, and the absolute minimum is -45.

4. $f'(x) = -x^2 - x + 12 = 0$

   $-(x^2 + x - 12) = 0$

   $-(x + 4)(x - 3) = 0$

   $x = -4 \quad x = 3$

We check the y-values at $x = -2, 5,$ and 3.

$$y = f(-2) = -\frac{(-2)^3}{3} - \frac{(-2)^2}{2} + 12(-2) = -23.33$$

$$y = f(5) = -\frac{(5)^3}{3} - \frac{(5)^2}{2} + 12(5) = 5.83$$

$$y = f(3) = -\frac{(3)^3}{3} - \frac{(3)^2}{2} + 12(3) = 22.5$$

Since $x = -4$ is outside our interval $[-2, 5]$, it need not be tested.

We examine our set of y-values: $-23.33, 5.83,$ and, 22.5. The highest (22.5) is at $x = 3$, and the lowest (-23.33) is at $x = -2$. Therefore, the absolute maximum is 22.5, and the absolute minimum is -23.33.

Note: Any x-values where the derivative equals zero that are outside our interval [*a, b*] need not be tested.

IVC3 MAXIMA, MINIMA, AND THE FIRST DERIVATIVE TEST EXERCISES

For numbers 1–10, use the First Derivative Test to find any points of relative extrema (x, y) for the functions.

1. $f(x) = \dfrac{x^2}{2} - 5x$

2. $f(x) = \dfrac{x^2}{2} + 6x$

3. $f(x) = \dfrac{x^2}{2} - \dfrac{5x}{2}$

4. $f(x) = \dfrac{x^2}{2} + \dfrac{3x}{2}$

5. $g(x) = \dfrac{x^3}{3} - 4x$

6. $g(x) = \dfrac{x^3}{3} - 9x$

7. $f(t) = \dfrac{t^3}{3} + \dfrac{t^2}{2} - 6t$

8. $f(t) = \dfrac{t^3}{3} - \dfrac{t^2}{2} - 6t$

9. $f(x) = \dfrac{x^3}{3} - 3x^2 + 8x$

10. $f(x) = \dfrac{x^3}{3} - 2x^2 - 12x$

For numbers 11 through 22, find the points of absolute extrema (x, y) over the given intervals $[a, b]$.

11. $f(x) = \dfrac{x^2}{2} - 3x, [0, 4]$

12. $f(x) = \dfrac{x^2}{2} - 6x, [0, 7]$

13. $f(x) = \dfrac{x^2}{2} - 3x, [1, 5]$

14. $f(x) = \dfrac{x^2}{2} - 6x, [-1, 6]$

15. $g(x) = \dfrac{x^3}{3} - 4x, [-5, 2]$

16. $g(x) = \dfrac{x^3}{3} - 9x, [-4, 3]$

17. $g(x) = \dfrac{x^3}{3} - 4x, [0, 4]$

18. $g(x) = \dfrac{x^3}{3} - 9x, [0, 5]$

19. $f(t) = \dfrac{t^3}{3} + \dfrac{t^2}{2} - 6t, [-3, 0]$

20. $f(t) = \dfrac{t^3}{3} - \dfrac{t^2}{2} - 6t, [-3, 2]$

21. $h(x) = 5x + 10, [0, 10]$

22. $h(x) = -4x + 8, [-1, 4]$

23. Alice Sandringham, a caterer, incurs expenses per plate represented by the function $\bar{C}(p) = .01p^2 - 24 + \dfrac{1730}{p}$, where p equals the number of plates served.

For what number will her expenses per plate be at a minimum, if she requires a minimum number of 20 and a maximum of 150 plates?

24. George Watkinson can order assorted fireworks in a lot from 10 to 50 cases. If he orders too few, he will forego possible sales. If he orders too many, he will have unsold boxes since the sales season is limited. How many cases x should he order to maximize profit if his profit function is $P(x) = -\dfrac{p^3}{3} + 22.5p^2 - 450p + 5025$?

IVC3 MAXIMA, MINIMA, AND THE FIRST DERIVATIVE TEST SOLUTIONS TO EXERCISES

1. $f'(x) = x - 5 = 0$

   $x = 5$

   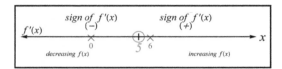

   Choose 0 and 6.

   Test $x = 0$: $f'(0) = 0 - 5 = -5 < 0$, negative slope

   Test $x = 6$: $f'(6) = 6 - 5 = 1 > 0$, positive slope

   relative minimum at $(5, f(5))$

   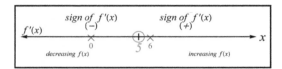

   $y = f(5) = \dfrac{(5)^2}{2} - 5 = -\dfrac{25}{2}$ or -12.5

   relative minimum at $(5, -12.5)$

2. relative minimum at $(-6, -18)$

3. $f'(x) = x - \dfrac{5}{2} = 0$

   $x = \dfrac{5}{2}$

   Choose 0 and 4.

   Test $x = 0$: $f'(0) = 0 - \dfrac{5}{2} < 0$, negative slope

   Test $x = 4$: $f'(4) = 4 - \dfrac{5}{2} > 0$, positive slope

   $y = f(2.5) = \dfrac{(2.5)^2}{2} - \dfrac{5(2.5)}{2} = -3.125$

   relative minimum at $(2.5, -3.125)$

4. relative minimum at $(-1.5, -1.125)$

5. $g'(x) = x^2 - 4 = 0$

$(x+2)(x-2)=0$

$x=2, -2$

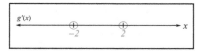

Choose $-3, 0,$ and $3.$
Test $x = -3$: $g'(-3) = (-3)^2 - 4$
$= 5 > 0$ positive slope
Test $x = 0$: $g'(0) = (0)^2 - 4 = -4 < 0 \to$ negative slope
Test $x = 3$: $g(3) = (3)^2 - 4 = 5 > 0,$ positive slope

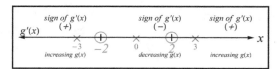

relative maximum at $(-2, g(-2)) = (-2, 5.33)$
relative minimum at $(2, g(2)) = (2, -5.33)$

6. relative max at $(-3, 18)$

relative min $(3, -18)$

7. $f'(t) = t^2 + t - 6 = 0$

$(t+3)(t-2)=0$

$x=-3, t=-2$

Choose $-4, 0,$ and $3.$
Test $t = -4$: $f'(-4) = (-4)^2 + (-4) - 6 = 6 > 0,$
positive slope
Test $t = 0$: $f'(0) = (0)^2 + 0 - 6 = -6 < 0,$
negative slope
Test $t = 3$: $f'(3) = (3)^2 + 3 - 6 = 6 > 0,$ positive slope

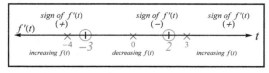

relative maximum at $(-3, f(-3)) = (-3, 13.5)$
relative minimum at $(2, f(2)) = (2, 7.33)$

8. relative max at
$(-2, 7.33)$
relative min $(3, -13.5)$

9. $f'(x) = x^2 - 6x + 8 = 0$

$(t-4)(t-2)=0$

$x=4, \quad t=2$

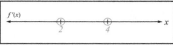

Choose $0, 3,$ and $5.$
Test $t = 0$: $f'(0) = 0^2 - 6(0) + 8 > 0,$ positive slope
Test $t = 3$: $f'(3) = 3^2 - 6(3) + 8 < 0,$ negative slope

10. relative max at
$(-2, 13.33)$
relative min at $(6, -72)$

Test $t = 5$: $f'(5) = 5^2 - 6(5) + 8 > 0$, positive slope

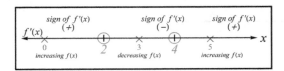

relative maximum at $(2, f(2)) = (2, 6.67)$
relative minimum at $(4, f(4)) = (4, 5.33)$

11. $f'(x) = x - 3 = 0$
    $x = 3$

    $height = f(3) = \dfrac{3^2}{2} - 3(3) = -4.5$ lowest

    $height = f(0) = \dfrac{0^2}{2} - 3(0) = 0$ highest

    $height = f(4) = \dfrac{4^2}{2} - 3(4) = -4$

    absolute maximum at $(0,0)$
    absolute minimum at $(3, -4.5)$

12. absolute max at $(0, 0)$
    absolute min at $(6, -18)$

13. $f'(x) = x - 3 = 0$
    $x = 3$

    $height = f(3) = \dfrac{3^2}{2} - 3(3) = -4.5$ lowest

    $height = f(1) = \dfrac{1^2}{2} - 3(1) = -2.5$ highest

    $height = f(5) = \dfrac{5^2}{2} - 3(5) = -2.5$ highest

    absolute maximum at $(1, -2.5)$ and $(5, -2.5)$
    absolute minimum at $(3, -4.5)$

14. absolute max at $(-1, 6.5)$
    absolute min at $(6, -18)$

15. $f'(x) = x^2 - 4 = 0$
    $(x + 2)(x - 2) = 0$
    $x = 2, -2$

    $height = f(2) = \dfrac{2^3}{3} - 4(2) = -5.33$

16. absolute max at $(-3, 18)$
    absolute min at $(3, -18)$

$height = f(-2) = \dfrac{(-2)^3}{3} - 4(-2) = 5.33$ highest

$height = f(-5) = \dfrac{(-5)^3}{3} - 4(-5) = -21.67$ lowest

absolute maximum at $(-2, 5.33)$

absolute minimum at $(-5, -21.67)$

17. $f'(x) = x^2 - 4 = 0$
    $(x+2)(x-2) = 0$
    $x = 2, -2$

    $height = f(2) = \dfrac{2^3}{3} - 4(2) = -5.33$ lowest

    $height = f(0) = \dfrac{(0)^3}{3} - 4(0) = 0$

    $height = f(4) = \dfrac{(4)^3}{3} - 4(4) = 5.33$ highest

    absolute maximum at $(4, \ 5.33)$

    absolute minimum at $(2, -5.33)$

    *Note: $x = -2$ need not be tested because it lies outside the given interval $[0,4]$

18. absolute max at $(0,0)$
     absolute min at $(3, -18)$

19. $f'(t) = t^2 + t - 6 = 0$
    $(t+3)(t-2) = 0$
    $x = -3, t = 2$

    $height = f(-3) = \dfrac{(-3)^3}{3} + \dfrac{(-3)^2}{2} - 6(-3) = 13.5$

    $height = f(0) = \dfrac{(0)^3}{3} + \dfrac{(0)^2}{2} - 6(0) = 0$

    absolute maximum at $(-3, 13.5)$

    absolute minimum at $(0,0)$

20. absolute max at $(-2, 7.33)$
     absolute min at $(2, -11.33)$

21. $h'(x) = 5 \neq 0$; *no relative extreme*
    $height = h(0) = 5(0) + 10 = 10$
    $height = h(10) = 5(10) + 10 = 60$
    absolute maximum at $(10, 60)$
    absolute minimum at $(0, 10)$

22. absolute max at $(-1, 12)$
     absolute min at $(4, -8)$

23. We need to find an absolute minimum over the interval [20, 150].

$$\overline{C}'(p)=0.02p-\frac{1730}{p^2}=0$$

$0.02p=\dfrac{1730}{p^2}$ We multiply both sides by p^2 and divide both sides by 0.02.

$p^3=86{,}500$ We take the cube root of both sides.
$p\approx44$

We compare: $C(44)=.01(44)^2-24+\dfrac{1730}{44}\approx\$34.68/plate$

$C(20)=.01(20)^2-24+\dfrac{1730}{20}\approx\$66.5/plate$

$C(150)=.01(150)^2-24+\dfrac{1730}{150}\approx\$212.53/plate$

Alice will minimize her expenses per plate at 44 plates.

24. We need to find an absolute maximum over the interval [10, 50].
$P'(x)=-p^2+45p-450=0$
$-(p^2-45p+450)=0$
$-(p-15)(p-30)=0$
$p=15; p=30$

We need to compare: $P(15)=-\dfrac{(15)^3}{3}+22.5(15)^2-450(15)+5025=\$2212.50$

$P(30)=-\dfrac{(30)^3}{3}+22.5(30)^2-450(30)+5025=\$2775.00$

$P(10)=-\dfrac{(10)^3}{3}+22.5(10)^2-450(10)+5025=\$2441.67$

$P(50)=-\dfrac{(50)^3}{3}+22.5(50)^2-450(50)+5025=\$-\$2891.67$

Profit is maximized when George orders 30 cases.

IVC4

Concavity and the Second Derivative Test

Consider the graphs below for three catering businesses, where *x* represents years and *f(x)* represents profits.

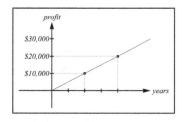

Carl's Catering

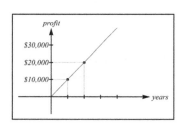

Carol's Catering

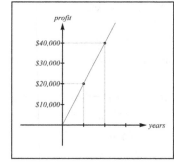

Cliff's Catering

All three functions represent increasing functions. They are increasing because *f(x)*, which is the *y*-value, or height, rises as they go from left to right.

In all three businesses, profits are growing at a constant rate. That is, they are increasing by the same amount each year. When the slope, or rate of change, is a constant, the graph is a straight line. We note that for Cliff's Catering, profits are increasing at a higher rate than either of the other businesses. Profits for Carl's Catering increase by $5,000 each year. Profits for Carol's Catering increase by $10,000 each year, but profits for Cliff's Catering increase by $20,000 each year.

The slope indicates the steepness of the curve—that is, the *rate of change* in profits. For the examples above, the slope indicates the amount by which the profits grow each year.

Now consider the graphs below. They represent the profits over time for three coffee bars.

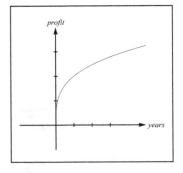 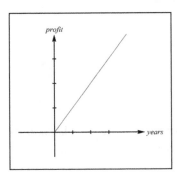 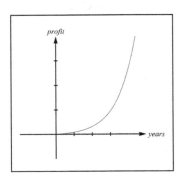

Claire's Coffees   *Cody's Coffees*   *Carmody's Coffees*

All the curves are increasing functions because they are rising as they travel from left to right. We notice that Cody's Coffees has a constant slope. The rate of change in profits is constant. Both Claire's Coffees and Carmody Coffees have increasing profits, but the slopes are changing.

If we remember that the slope at each point is represented by the tangent to the curve at that point, we can analyze the change in profit growth; i.e., we can analyze the way in which the growth rate changes.

Consider Claire's Coffees.

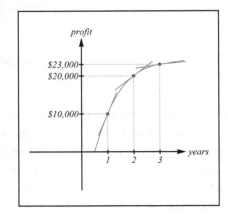

Traveling from left to right, the tangents are getting flatter. The slope is still positive, but the change in the slope is decreasing. Between years 1 and 2, profits increased from $10,000 to $20,000, a growth of $10,000. Between years 2 and 3, profits increased from $20,000 to $23,000, a growth of only $3,000. The rate of change is decreasing.

The term for the way in which the **slope** changes over time is *concavity*. For *Claire's Coffees*, the concavity is negative because the slope is decreasing.

To find concavity, we will need to take the second derivative, represented as $f''(x)$ or $\dfrac{d^2y}{dx^2}$, or sometimes by y''. The second derivative is found by taking the derivative of the derivative, so requires no new rules of computation. We may now call "the derivative" the first derivative. Since the first derivative gives the slope, the second derivative is the derivative of the slope; i.e., it measures the change in the slope.

The concavity of a curve is represented by its second derivative. A curve is **concave down** when the change in its slope is decreasing from left to right. For curves that are *concave down*, the second derivative is negative; i.e.,

for curves that are **concave down**, $f''(x) < 0$.

Examine the graph for Claire's Coffees once again. Notice that for graphs that are concave down, the curve lies below its tangents.

Now consider the slopes/tangents for *Carmody Coffees*.

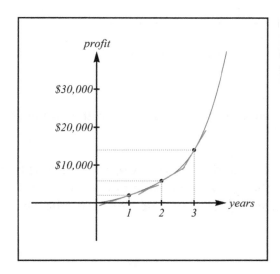

As we travel from left to right, the tangents are getting steeper; the slope is increasing. The change in profit is different every year. It is getting better and better.

A curve is said to be **concave up** when the change in slope increases from left to right. A curve is **concave up** when its second derivative is positive.

For curves that are **concave up**, $f''(x) > 0$.

Consider the graph for Carmody Coffees once again. Notice that for curves that are concave up, the curve lies above its tangents.

Now consider three businesses that are less successful.

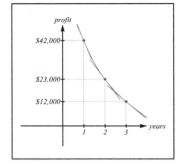

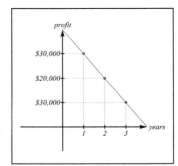

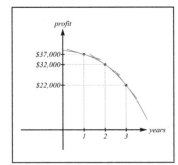

Cavity's Candies   *Corner Candies*   *Caddy's Candies*

Clearly, these are decreasing functions because the curves fall as we go from left to right.

Now consider Cavity's Candies. The slope, represented by the tangent to the curve at each point, changes as we travel from left to right. The slopes are getting flatter as we move from left to right. The slope, i.e., the rate of change in profits, is decreasing.

While profits are decreasing each year, the amount they decrease is getting less and less. Between *year 1* and *year 2*, profits fell from \$42,000 to \$23,000, a fall of \$19,000. Between *year 2* and *year 3*, profits fell from \$23,000 to \$12,000, a fall of \$11,000. Even though the slope is negative, because the curve falls as we go from left to right, this graph is **concave up** because the change in slope is decreasing. Hence, the second derivative will be positive.

To repeat, when a curve is concave up: $f''(x) > 0$.

Notice that, as before, the tangents lie below the curve when the curve is **concave up**.

Both curves below are concave up.

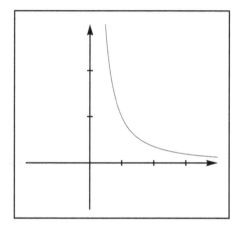 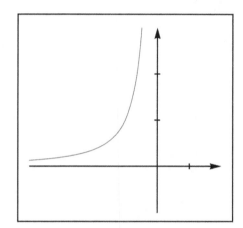

Now consider the change in slope for Caddy's Candies.

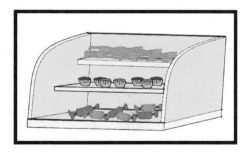 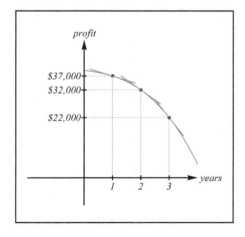

The slopes are negative and getting steeper. Between *year 1* and *year 2*, profit dropped from $37,000 to $32,000, a change of −$5,000. Between *year 2* and *year 3*, profit dropped from $32,000 to $22,000, a change of −$10,000. The change in profit is decreasing (getting more and more negative). Hence, the curve is **concave down**.

Again, when a curve is concave down: $f''(x) < 0$.

Notice that the curve continues to lie below its tangents when the curve is concave down.

Both curves below are concave down.

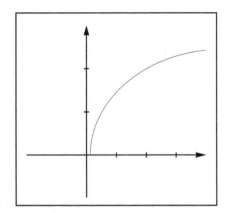 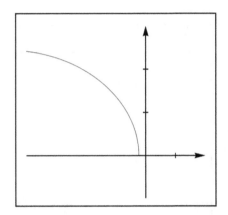

To summarize:

Graphs that are concave up

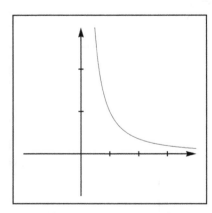 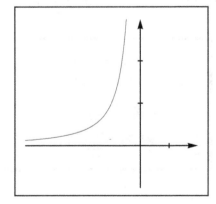

slope negative: $f'(x) < 0$ slope positive: $f'(x) > 0$
concave up: $f''(x) > 0$ concave up: $f''(x) > 0$

Graphs that are concave down

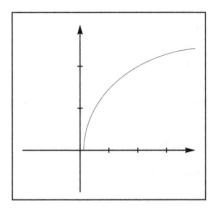

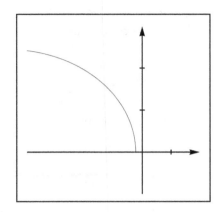

slope positive: $f'(x) > 0$
concave down: $f''(x) < 0$

slope negative: $f'(x) < 0$
concave down: $f''(x) < 0$

Note that for a concave up graph, the slope can be either positive or negative, and for a concave down graph, the slope can be either positive or negative.

INTRA-SECTION EXERCISES:

1. The graph below represents the US national debt.

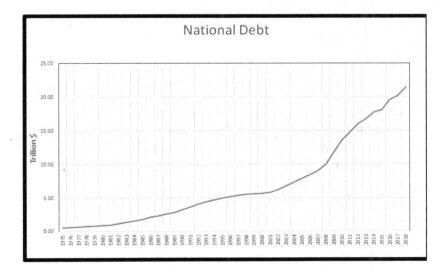

Examine the national debt line for the years 1975 through 2018.

   a. In general, is the slope positive or negative?
   b. Is the graph concave up or concave down?
   c. Is the second derivative positive or negative?
   d. Is $f''(x)>0$ or is: $f''(x)<0$?
   e. Is $f'(x)>0$ or is $f'(x)<0$?
   f. Is the debt increasing at a faster and faster rate, a slower and slower rate, or a constant rate?

2. Examine the curve for the years 2004 through 2006.

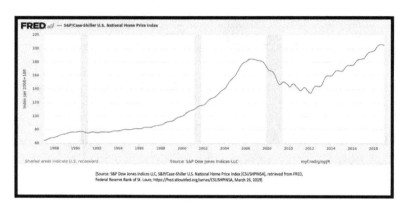

   a. In general, is the slope positive or negative?
   b. Is the graph concave up or concave down?
   c. Is the second derivative positive or negative?
   d. Is $f''(x)>0$ or is $f''(x)<0$?
   e. Is $f'(x)>0$ or is $f'(x)<0$?
   f. Is the index *increasing* at a faster and faster rate, a slower and slower rate, or a constant rate?

3. Examine the curve from exercise 2) for the years 2006 through 2009.

   a. In general, is the slope positive or negative?
   b. Is the graph concave up or concave down?
   c. Is the second derivative positive or negative?
   d. Is $f''(x)>0$ or is $f''(x)<0$?
   e. Is $f'(x)>0$ or is $f'(x)<0$?
   f. Is the index *decreasing* at a faster and faster rate, a slower and slower rate, or a constant rate?

4. Examine the cost of personal computers used for the Consumer Price Index represented by the graph above.

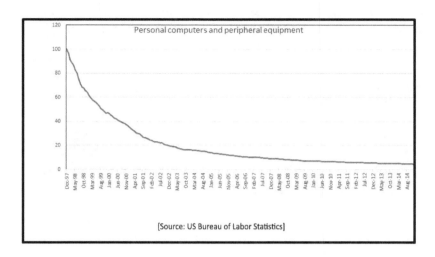

a. In general, is the slope positive or negative?
b. Is the graph concave up or concave down?
c. Is the second derivative positive or negative?
d. Is $f''(x)>0$ or is $f''(x)<0$?
e. Is $f'(x)>0$ or is $f'(x)<0$?
f. Is the price *decreasing* at a faster and faster rate, a slower and slower rate, or a constant rate?

Solutions

1. a. positive;   b. concave up;   c. positive;   d. $f''(x)>0$ e. $f'(x)>0$ f. faster and faster

2. a. positive;   b. concave down;   c. negative;   d. $f''(x)<0$ e. $f'(x)>0$ f. slower

3. a. negative;   b. concave down;   c. negative;   d. $f''(x)<0$ e. $f'(x)>0$ f. faster

4. a. negative;   b. concave up;   c. positive;   d. $f''(x)>0$ e. $f'(x)<0$ f. slower

THE SECOND DERIVATIVE TEST

The graph below represents the median price of houses over time in the fictional town of Matheapolis. In year x_1 there is a relative maximum, so $f'(x_1) = 0$.

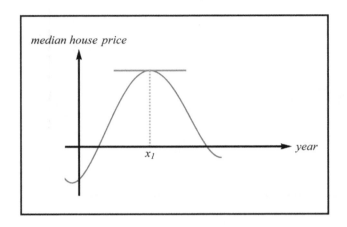

Relative maxima occur on graphs that are concave down. In year x_1 the second derivative will be negative, or $f''(x) < 0$.

The concavity gives us a new way to test for relative maxima. Instead of testing a point on either side of x_1 in the first derivative to find the slope, we test x_1 itself in $f''(x)$ to check whether or not it is negative. If $f''(x_1)$ is negative, f is concave down and has a relative maximum at x_1.

This method is called the **Second Derivative Test**.

The graph below represents the average monthly price of mobile phone service in Matheapolis.

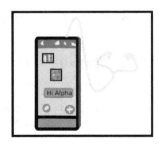

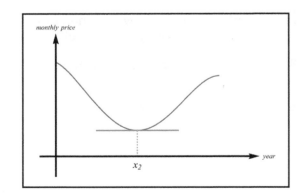

A relative minimum occurs in year x_2 so we know that $f'(x_2)=0$. Graphs with relative minima are concave up, so $f''(x)$ will be positive at x_2, or $f''(x)>0$.

This gives us a new way to test for relative minima. Instead of testing a point on either side of x_2 in the first derivative to find the slope, we test x_2 itself in $f''(x)$ to check whether or not it is positive. If $f''(x_2)$ is positive, f is concave up and has a relative minimum at x_2.

This new method is also the **Second Derivative Test**.

Suppose we don't have a graph, but we know $f(x)=3x^3+2x^2-5x+89$ and we want to locate the relative extrema.

Step 1:

> We set $f'(x)=0$ to find the possible values where an extrema occurs; i.e., the critical values.
>
> $$f'(x)=9x^2+4x-5=0$$
>
> We factor or use the Quadratic Formula: $(9x-5)(x+1)=0$
>
> $$9x-5=0 \text{ or } x+1=0$$
>
> $$x=\frac{5}{9}, x=-1$$

Step 2:

> To use the Second Derivative Test, we need to find $f''(x)$.
>
> $$f''(x)=18x+4$$
>
> Next, we test $\frac{5}{9}$ to see if it is a relative max or min by finding $f''\left(\frac{5}{9}\right)$. We use f $f''(x)$ (instead of $f(x)$ or $f'(x)$) because we are interested in the *concavity* at 5/9, not the slope (which equals $f'\left(\frac{5}{9}\right)$), or the corresponding y-value (which equals $f\left(\frac{5}{9}\right)$).

Also, we are only interested in whether $f''\left(\dfrac{5}{9}\right)$ is positive or negative. We don't really care about the actual value of $f''\left(\dfrac{5}{9}\right)$.

To continue: $f''\left(\dfrac{5}{9}\right)=18\left(\dfrac{5}{9}\right)+4$, which would equal a positive number. Therefore, the function is concave up at $x=\dfrac{5}{9}$ and a relative minimum occurs at $x=\dfrac{5}{9}$.

Step 3:

The corresponding y-value would be

$$y=f\left(\dfrac{5}{9}\right)=3\left(\dfrac{5}{9}\right)^{3}+2\left(\dfrac{5}{9}\right)^{2}-5\left(\dfrac{5}{9}\right)+89\approx87.4.$$

Therefore, the relative minimum occurs at the point $\left(\dfrac{5}{9},87.4\right)$.

Now we need to repeat steps (2) and (3) for the other relative extrema, $x=-1$.

Step 2:

We find that $f''(-1)=18(-1)+4$ is a negative number. Therefore, at $x=-1$ the curve is concave down and there must be a relative maximum at $x=-1$.

Step 3:

The corresponding y-value would be
$$y=f(-1)=3(-1)^{3}+2(-1)^{2}-5(-1)+89=93.$$

Therefore, the relative maximum occurs at the point $(-1,93)$.

The Second Derivative Test is easier to use than the first derivative test, but sometimes $f''(x_i)=0$ at a critical value x_i. Since zero is neither positive nor negative, we would have to revert to the first derivative test to determine if there is a relative maximum or a relative minimum at x_i.

INFLECTION POINTS

Consider the graph at right.

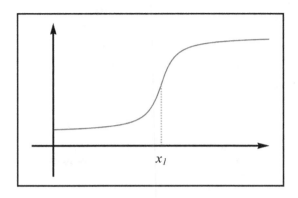

To the left of x_1, the graph is concave up and $f''(x)>0$. To the right of x_1, the graph is concave down and $f''(x)<0$. Where the curve shifts from concave up to concave down, $f''(x)=0$.

The point $(x_1, f(x_1))$ is called an **inflection point**. Inflection points also occur where curves shift from concave down $(f''(x)<0)$ to concave up $(f''(x)>0)$ as in the graphs below.

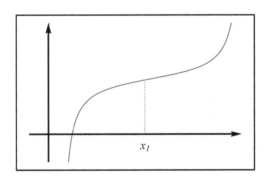 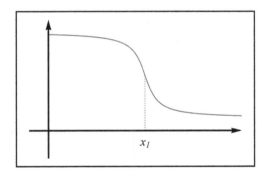

To find an inflection point, we locate any x-values where $f''(x)=0$. However, not all such points are inflection points, so we must test a point on each side in $f''(x)$ to make sure that $f''(x)$ is concave up on one side i.e. $f''(x)>0$, and concave down on the other, i.e., $f''(x)<0$.

Example 1:

Suppose the growth rate for newly discovered bacteria can be modeled by the equation $f(x)=-4x^5+32x^2+17900$, where x is the time in days and $f(x)$ is the bacterial population per square centimeter. To find the inflection point, we need the second derivative.

$$f'(x)=-20x^4+64x$$

$$f''(x)=-80x^3+64$$

We set the second derivative equal to zero. $f''(x)=-80x^3+64=0$

$$-80x^3=-64$$

$$x^3=\frac{-64}{-80}=0.8$$

We take the cube root of both sides. $x\approx0.928$.

It appears there is an inflection point at 0.928 days, but we must check.

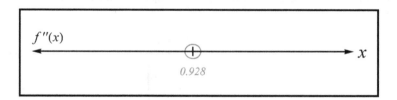

We need to test a number on the left side of 0.928 in $f''(x)$. It must be tested in the second derivative, rather than in $f(x)$ or in $f'(x)$ because we want to see if there is a change in concavity, not a corresponding y-value and not a slope.

For the left side of $f''(x)$, let's test 0

$f''(0)=-80(0)^3+64=$ a positive number.

Again, we are only interested in whether the second derivative is positive or negative. We are not really interested in the value of the second derivative at $x=0$.

Since $f''(x)>0$, the curve is concave up at less than 0.928 days.

On the right, we will test $x = 1$, although any number greater than 0.928 will do.

$f''(1) = -80(1)^3 + 64 =$ a negative number.

Therefore, the curve is concave down for more than 0.928 days.

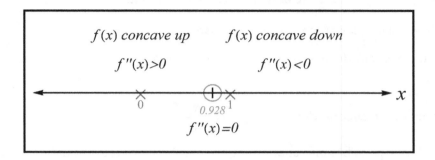

The graph looks something like the figure below. The bacteria population grows faster and faster until 0.928 days and then it increases, but at a slower and slower rate.

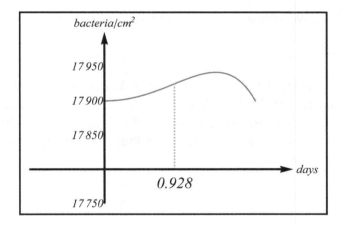

Example 2:

Consider the second derivative: $f''(x) = \dfrac{x+5}{4-x}$

To test the concavity, we need to find where the second derivative equals zero.

Back to the second derivative: $f''(x)=\dfrac{x+5}{4-x}$.

To find a possible inflection point, we set the numerator equal to zero.

$$x+5=0$$

$$x=-5$$

Since $x=-5$ will not turn the denominator into zero also (which would

give us $\frac{0}{0}$), we will plot $x=-5$ on a number line and test a point on each

side in $f''(x)$.

We note, however, that functions often change concavity on either side of a vertical asymptote. That would be where the denominator is undefined. Therefore, for fractions, we need to find all the places where the second derivative equals zero *and* places where the denominator equals zero.

$$4-x=0$$

$$4=x$$

We need to plot both $x=-5$ and $x=4$ on our number line and test a point from each segment.

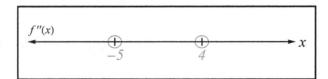

We test $x = -6$: $f''(-6) = \dfrac{-6+5}{4--6} =$ a negative number.

Therefore, the function is concave down when $x < -5$.

We test $x = 0$: $f''(0) = \dfrac{0+5}{4-0} =$ a positive number.

Therefore, the function is concave up when $-5 < x < 4$.

We test $x = 5$: $f''(5) = \dfrac{5+5}{4-5} =$ a negative number.

Therefore, the function is concave down when $x > 4$.

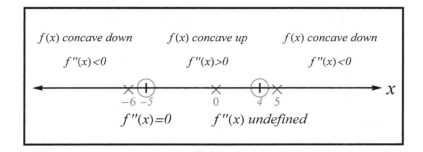

The concavity changes at $x = -5$, which gives us the inflection point $(-5, f(-5))$. [Since we were not given $f(x)$, we cannot find $f(-5)$.]

There is also a change in concavity at $x = 4$. However, since $f''(4) = \dfrac{4+5}{4-4}$ is undefined, there is not an inflection *point* at $x = 4$, although it is a place where the concavity might change, which could be very helpful to know.

INTRA-SECTION EXERCISES:

Find the inflection points and discuss the concavity for the functions below.

5. $f(x) = -3x^4 + 6x^2 - 6$ 6. $f(x) = x^3 + 3x^2$ 7. $f''(x) = \dfrac{x^2 - 25}{x+3}$

Solutions

5. Inflection points may occur where $f''(x)=0$. We need to find the second derivative.

$$f'(x)=-12x^3+12x$$

$$f''(x)=-36x^2+12=0$$

$$-36x^2=-12$$

$$x^2=\frac{1}{3}$$

$$x=\pm\sqrt{\frac{1}{3}}\approx 0.58-0.58$$

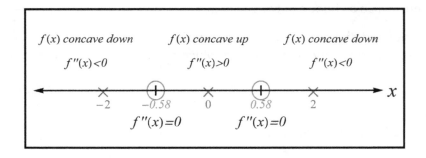

We test a point from each segment such as $-2, 0$, and 2, in $f''(x)$ to find the concavity.

Test -2: $f''(-2)=-36(-2)^2+12$ is a negative number. Hence, $f(x)$ is concave down for all numbers less than -0.58.

Test 0: $f''(0)=-36(0)^2+12$ is a positive number. Hence, $f(x)$ is concave up for all numbers between -0.58 and 0.58.

Test 2: $f''(2)=-36(2)^2+12$ is a negative number. Hence, $f(x)$ is concave down for all numbers greater than 0.58.

Inflection points occur at $(-0.58, f(-0.58))$ and at $(0.58, f(0.58))$
$y=f(-0.58)=-3(-0.58)^4+6(-0.58)^2-6=-4.32$
$y=f(0.58)=-3(0.58)^4+6(0.58)^2-6=-4.32$
Inflection points occur at $(-0.58,-4.32)$ and at $(0.58,-4.32)$

6. Inflection points may occur where $f''(x)=0$. We need to find the second derivative.

$$f'(x)=3x^2+6x$$

$$f''(x)=6x+6=0$$

$$6x=-6$$

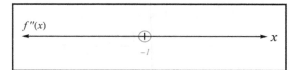

$$x=-1$$

We test a point from each segment such as -2 and 0, in $f''(x)$ to find the concavity.

Test -2: $f''(-2)=6(-2)+6=$ a negative number. Hence, $f(x)$ is concave down for all numbers x less than -1.

Test 0: $f''(0)=6(0)+6=$ a positive number. Hence, $f(x)$ is concave up for all numbers x greater than -1.

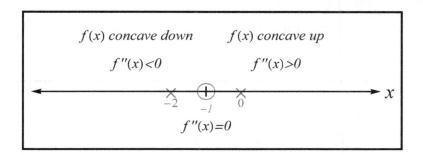

There is an inflection point at $(-1, f(-1))$.
$y=f(-1)=(-1)^3+3(-1)^2=-1+3=2$; the inflection point is at $(-1,2)$.

7. Note we are given the second derivative, not $f(x)$. We need to find where $f''(x)$ equals zero, and also where $f''(x)$ is undefined.

$$f''(x)=\frac{x^2-25}{x+3}=0 \text{ where } x^2-25=0.$$

$$(x+5)(x-5)=0$$

$$6x=-6x=5,-5$$

$f''(x) = \dfrac{x^2 - 25}{x+3}$ is undefined

where $x + 3 = 0$

$x = -3$

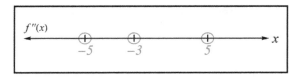

We need to test points from each segment, such as -6, -4, 0, and 6.

Test -6: $f''(-6) = \dfrac{(-6)^2 - 25}{-6+3} = \dfrac{11}{-3} =$ a negative number. Hence, $f(x)$ is concave down for all numbers x less than -5.

Test -4: $f''(-4) = \dfrac{(-4)^2 - 25}{-4+3} = \dfrac{-9}{-1} =$ a positive number. Hence, $f(x)$ is concave up for all numbers x between $x = -5$ and $x = -3$.

Test 0: $f''(0) = \dfrac{(0)^2 - 25}{0+3} = \dfrac{-25}{3} =$ a negative number. Hence, $f(x)$ is concave down for all numbers x between $x = -3$ and $x = 5$.

Test 0: $f''(6) = \dfrac{(6)^2 - 25}{6+3} = \dfrac{9}{9} =$ a positive number. Hence, $f(x)$ is concave up for all numbers x greater than 5.

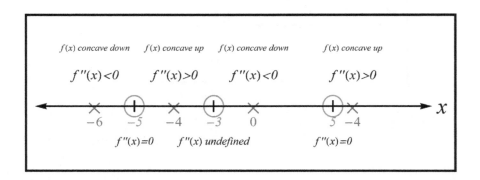

Inflection points occur at $(-5, f(-5))$ and $(5, f(5))$. They do not occur where $f''(x)$ is undefined. Since we have not been given $f(x)$, we will not be able to find the y-values at this time.

POINT OF DIMINISHING RETURNS

In business, this type of inflection point, where concavity changes from concave up to concave down, is called the *point of diminishing returns*.

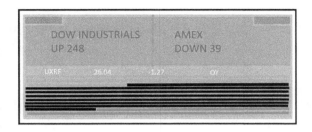

In many situations, $y = f(x)$ represents a system where inputs are represented by x and outputs are represented by y. The input can be capital investment dollars, such as the cost of buying stock shares, and output can be the return on the investment, the increase or decrease in the share values.

The derivative $f'(x)$ represents the change in the share values, the return on investment, relative to the amount of the investment. If the derivative $f'(x)$ is constant, as in a straight line, every one dollar change gives exactly the same change in stock values.

If the derivative $f'(x)$ is increasing, that is, $f(x)$ is concave up, every one dollar change gives a greater change in stock values, a greater return. If the derivative $f'(x)$ is decreasing; that is, $f(x)$ is concave down, every one dollar change gives a lesser change in stock values, a diminishing return. We would want to input more investment dollars only up to the point where $y = f(x)$ switches from concave up to concave down: the **point of diminishing returns**. A point of diminishing returns occurs where $f''(x) = 0$.

Example 3:

Suppose $r(x) = 3x^2 - \frac{1}{6}x^3$ gives the return in thousands of dollars on x millions of dollars invested. For what amount of investment x does the point of diminishing returns occur?

We will solve $r''(x) = 0$.

$$r'(x) = 6x - \frac{1}{2}x^2$$

$$r''(x) = 6 - x = 0$$

$$x = 6$$

Diminishing returns occur at $x = 6$. Any investment dollars beyond 6 million dollars should be used for another purpose.

INTRA-SECTION EXERCISES:

8. Find the point of diminishing returns for $f(x)=-2x^3+4x^2+11$.

Solutions

8. We need to find where $f''(x)=0$. $f'(x)=-6x^2+8x$

$$f''(x)=-12x+8=0$$

$$-12x=-8$$

$$x=\frac{-8}{-12}=\frac{2}{3}$$

The point of diminishing returns lies at $\left(\frac{2}{3}, f\left(\frac{2}{3}\right)\right)$.

$$y=f\left(\frac{2}{3}\right)=-2\left(\frac{2}{3}\right)^3+4\left(\frac{2}{3}\right)^2+11\approx 12.19$$

The point of diminishing returns lies at $\left(\frac{2}{3}, 12.19\right)$.

IVC4 CONCAVITY AND THE SECOND DERIVATIVE TEST EXERCISES

For numbers 1 through 10, use the Second Derivative Test to find the relative maxima and relative minima.

1. $f(x) = -\dfrac{x^3}{3} + 3x^2$

2. $f(x) = 3x^3 - \dfrac{x^2}{2}$

3. $g(x) = -2x^2 + 12x$

4. $g(x) = 3x^2 - 12x$

5. $f(x) = \dfrac{x^3}{3} - \dfrac{3x^2}{2} - 10x$

6. $f(x) = \dfrac{x^3}{3} + 2x^2 - 12x$

7. $g(t) = 3t - 4$

8. $g(t) = -4t + 5$

9. $f(x) = x^2 - 4x + 7$

10. $f(x) = x^2 - 8x - 3$

For numbers 11–20, find any inflection points, and note the concavity on a number line for each function.

11. $f(x) = -\dfrac{x^3}{3} + 3x^2$

12. $f(x) = 3x^3 - 9\dfrac{x^2}{2}$

13. $g(x) = -2x^2 + 12x$

14. $g(x) = 3x^2 - 12x$

15. $f(x) = \dfrac{x^3}{3} - \dfrac{3x^2}{2} - 10x$

16. $f(x) = \dfrac{x^3}{3} + 2x^2 - 12x$

17. $f(t) = t^4 - t^2$

18. $f(t) = t^3 + 5t$

19. $f(x) = x^{\frac{2}{3}} + 3$

20. $f(x) = x^{\frac{1}{2}} - 4$

For numbers 21–24, sketch a graph of a function having the following characteristics.

21. a. $f(-3) = 0$
    b. $f'(1) = 0; f'(5) = 0$
    c. $f''(1) < 0; f''(5) > 0$

22. a. $f(-1) = f(2) = 0$
    b. $f'(-1) = 0; f'(1) = 0$
    c. $f''(-1) > 0; f''(3) > 0$

23. a. $f'(2) = 0; f'(5) = 0$
    b. $f'(0) > 0; f'(4) < 0; f'(6) > 0$
    c. $f(0) = 6$

24. a. $f'(-3) = 0; f'(4) = 0$
    b. $f'(-4) < 0; f'(0) > 0; f'(6) < 0$
    c. $f(6) = 0$

25. $f'(x)=0$ at $x=-2, 4$, and 8
$f''(-2)=14, f''(4)=-12; f''(8)=10$
  a. For what values of x is there a relative minimum?
  b. For what values of x is there a relative maximum?

26. $f'(x)=0$ at $x=-3, 6$, and 9
$f''(-3)=-4, f''(6)=5; f(9)=-10$
  a. For what values of x is there a relative minimum?
  b. For what values of x is there a relative maximum?

27. $f'(x)=0$ at $x=-2, 4$, and 8
$f'(-3)<0; f'(0)<0;$
$f'(5)>0; f'(10)<0$
  a. For what values of x is there a relative minimum?
  b. For what values of x is there a relative maximum?

28. $f'(x)=0$ at $x=-3, 6$, and 9
$f'(-4)>0; f'(0)<0;$
$f'(7)<0; f'(10)>0$
  a. For what values of x is there a relative minimum?
  b. For what values of x is there a relative maximum?

29. $f'(x)=0$ at $x=-2, 4$, and 8
$f(-4)=5; f(-2)=10; f(4)=15$
$f(8)=20; f(10)=25$
  a. For what values of x in the interval $[-4,8]$ is there an absolute minimum?
  b. For what values of x in the interval $[-4,8]$ is there an absolute maximum?

30. $f'(x)=0$ at $x=-3, 6$, and 9
$f(-5)=4; f(-3)=8; f(6)=12$
$f(9)=16; f(11)=20$
  a. For what values of x in the interval $[-5,9]$ is there an absolute minimum?
  b. For what values of x in the interval $[-5,9]$ is there an absolute maximum?

For numbers 31 through 32, for what value of x is the point of diminishing returns reached?

31. $f(x)=-4x^3+5x^2-8x+13$

32. $f(x)=-5x^3+2x^2+6x-18$

33. When a new cell phone model is released, the number sold can be modeled by the function $N=-w^3+11w^2$ for $0\leq w\leq 10$, where N is the number sold, in thousands, and w is the number of weeks from launch.
  a. What is the maximum number of phones projected to be sold?
  b. When will the rate at which they are sold reach a maximum?

34. When a new car model is released, the number ordered can be modeled by the function $N=-w^3+15w^2$ for $0\leq w\leq 14$, where N is the number sold, in hundreds, and w is the number of weeks from release.
  a. What is the maximum number of cars projected to be ordered?
  b. When will the rate at which they are ordered reach a maximum?

35. Each year sales of watermelons in a certain market can be modeled by the function $S(t) = -0.5t^3 + 10.5t^2 - 10t, =$ where t is the number of weeks since June 1st, when watermelons first reach this market. If Carmody Phelps wishes to invest in watermelons in this market, at which week will sales reach the point of diminishing returns?

36. Each year, sales of fava beans in a certain market can be modeled by the function $S(t) = -0.17t^3 + 5.5t^2 + 18.5t,$ where t is the number of weeks since January 1st, when fava beans first reach this market. If Fenwick Costner wishes to invest in fava beans in this market, at which week will sales reach the point of diminishing returns?

IVC4 CONCAVITY AND THE SECOND DERIVATIVE TEST SOLUTIONS TO EXERCISES

1. $f'(x) = -x^2 + 6x = 0$
   $-x(x-6) = 0$
   $x = 0; \ x = 6$ at $\left(\dfrac{1}{9}, -0.002\right)$
   $f''(x) = -2x + 6$
   Test 0: $f''(0) = -2(0) + 6$ is a positive number. $f(x)$ is concave up at $x = 0$; therefore there is a relative minimum at $(0, f(0))$.

   $y = f(0) = -\dfrac{0^3}{3} + 3(0)^2 = 0$; **the relative minimum is at (0, 0).**

   Test 6: $f''(6) = -2(6) + 6$ is a negative number. $f(x)$ is concave down at $x = 6$; therefore there is a relative maximum at $(6, f(6))$.

   $y = f(6) = -\dfrac{6^3}{3} + 3(6)^2 = 36$; **the relative maximum is at (6, 36).**

2. relative maximum
   at $(0, 0)$
   relative minimum
   at $\left(\dfrac{1}{9}, -0.002\right)$

3. $g'(x) = -4x + 12 = 0$
   $-4x = -12$
   $x = 3$
   $g''(x) = -4$ $g(x)$ is concave down everywhere; therefore, there is a relative maximum at $(3, g(3))$ and no relative minimum.
   $y = g(3) = -2(3)^2 + 12(3) = 18$; **the relative maximum is at (3, 18).**

4. relative minimum
   at $(2, -12)$
   no relative maximum

5. $f'(x) = x^2 - 3x - 10 = 0$
   $(x-5)(x+2) = 0$
   $x = 5; -2$
   $f''(x) = 2x - 3$
   Test 5: $f''(5) = 2(5) - 3$ is a positive number. $f(x)$ is concave up at $x = 5$; therefore, there is a relative minimum at $(5, f(5))$.

6. relative minimum
   at $(2, -13.33)$
   relative maximum
   at $(-6, 72)$

$$y = f(5) = \frac{5^3}{3} - \frac{3(5)^2}{2} - 10(5) = -45.83.$$

The relative minimum is at (5, −45.83).

Test −2: $f''(-2) = 2(-2) - 3$ is a negative number. $f(x)$ is concave down at $x = -2$; therefore, there is a relative maximum at $(-2, f(-2))$.

$$y = f(-2) = \frac{(-2)^3}{3} - \frac{3(-2)^2}{2} - 10(-2) = 11.33.$$

The relative maximum is at $(-2, 11.33)$.

7. $g'(t) = 3 \neq 0$
   The slope is constant and has no relative extrema.

8. no relative extrema

9. $f'(x) = 2x - 4 = 0$
   $x = 2$
   $f''(x) = 2$ The graph is concave up everywhere.
   There is a relative minimum at $(2, f(2))$.
   $y = f(2) = 2^2 - 4(2) + 7 = 3$;
   The relative minimum is at (2, 3).
   There is no relative maximum.

10. relative minimum
    at $(4, -19)$
    no relative maximum

11. $f'(x) = -x^2 + 6x$
    $f''(x) = -2x + 6 = 0$
    $x = 3$
    Test 0: $f'(0) = -2(0) + 6 > 0$, concave up.
    Test 4: $f'(4) = -2(4) + 6 < 0$, concave down.

12.

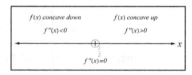

Inflection Point: $\left(\dfrac{1}{2}, -\dfrac{3}{4} \right)$

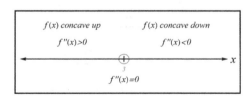

Inflection point at $(3, f(3))$

$$y = f(3) = -\frac{3^3}{3} + 3(3)^2 = 18;$$

inflection point at (3, 18).

13. $g'(x) = -4x + 12$
$g''(x) = -4 \neq 0$
There are no inflection points
The graph is concave down everywhere.

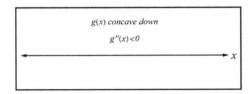

14.

No inflection points

15. $f'(x) = x^2 - 3x - 10$
$f''(x) = 2x - 3 = 0$

$x = \dfrac{3}{2} = 1.5$

Test 0: $f''(0) = 2(0) - 3 < 0 =$ concave down

Test 2: $f''(2) = 2(2) - 3 > 0 =$ concave up

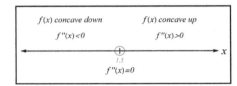

Inflection point at $(1.5, f(1.5))$

$y = f(1.5) = \dfrac{(1.5)^3}{3} - \dfrac{3(1.5)^2}{2} - 10(1.5) = -17.25$

Inflection point at (1.5, −17.25).

16.

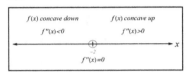

Inflection point:
$(-2, 29.33)$

17. $f'(t) = 4t^3 - 2t$
$f''(t) = 12t^2 - 2 = 0$
$12t^2 = 2$

$t^2 = \dfrac{2}{12} = \dfrac{1}{6}$

$t = \pm\sqrt{\dfrac{1}{6}} = 0.408, -0.408$

18.

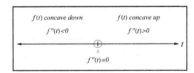

Inflection point: $(0, 0)$

Test $-1: f''(-1)=12(-1)^2-2>0$, concave up

Test $0: f''(0)=12(0)^2-2<0$, concave down

Test $1: f''(1)=12(1)^2-2>0$,
concave up

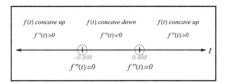

Inflection points at $(-0.408, f(-0.408))$
and $(0.408, f(0.408))$

$y = f(-0.408)=(-0.408)^4-(-0.408)^2=-0.139$

$y = f(0.408)=(0.408)^4-(0.408)^2=-0.139$

**Inflection points at $(-0.408, -0.139)$
and $(0.408, -0.139)$.**

19. $f'(x)=\dfrac{2}{3}x^{-\frac{1}{3}}$

$f''(x)=-\dfrac{2}{9}x^{-\frac{4}{3}}=-\dfrac{2}{9\sqrt[3]{x^4}}=0$

Since the numerator cannot equal zero,
there is no inflection point. However,
the fraction is undefined at $x=0$.

Test $-1: f''(-1)=-\dfrac{2}{9\sqrt[3]{(-1)^4}}<0$,

concave down

Test $1: f''(1)=-\dfrac{2}{9\sqrt[3]{(1)^4}}<0$,

concave down

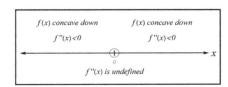

20.

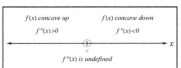

No inflection points

21.

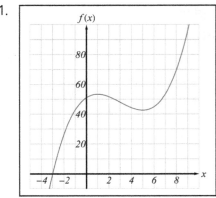

22.

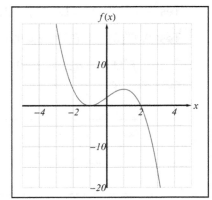

23.

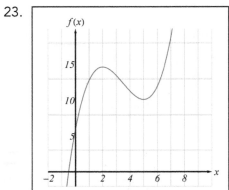

24.

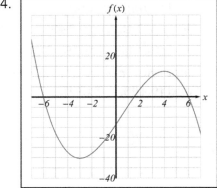

25. $f''(-2)>0$, concave up at $x=-2$
$f''(4)<0$, concave down at $x=4$
$f''(8)>0$, concave up at $x=8$
  a. relative minima at $x=-2$
    and $x=8$
  b. relative maximum at $x=4$

26. a. relative minimum at
    $x=6$
  b. relative maxima at
    $x=-3$ and at $x=9$

27.

  a. relative minimum at $x=4$
  b. relative maximum at $x=8$

28. a. relative minimum at
    $x=9$
  b. relative maximum
    at $x=-3$

29. a. absolute minimum at $x=-4$
     because $f(-4)$ has the lowest
     y-value of the numbers
     $5, 10, 15, 20,$ and 25.
   b. absolute maximum at $x=8$
     because $f(8)$ has the highest
     y-value of the numbers $5, 10, 15,$
     and 20. The y-value at $x=10$ is
     not considered since $x=10$ does
     not belong to the interval $[-4, 8]$.

30. a. absolute minimum:
     $x=-5$
   b. absolute maximum:
     $x=9$

31. $f'(x)=-12x^2+10x-8$
    $f''(x)=-24x+10=0$
    $-24x=-10$
    $x=\dfrac{-10}{-24}\approx.417$

32. $x=0.133$

33. The absolute maximum will occur either
    at a relative extremum (where $N'(w)=0$)
    or else at an endpoint.

    $N'(w)=-3w^2+22w=0$

    $w(-3w+22)=0$

    $w=0; w=\dfrac{22}{3}\approx7.33$

    Test: $7.33: N(7.33)=-(7.33)^3+11(7.33)^2\approx197$

    Test: $0: N(0)=-0^3+11(0)^2=0$

    Test: $20: N(10)=-(10)^3+11(10)^2=100$

    a. maximum number of phones
       sold will be about 197
    b. The rate is $N'(w)$. Its maximum
       will be where its derivative
       $(N''(w))$ equals zero.

    $N''(w)=-6w+22=0; \ w\approx3.67$

34. a. absolute maximum:
     $N=500$ *cars* at
     $w=10$
   b. rate is a maximum
     at $w=5$ *weeks*

We use the Second Derivative Test to determine if there is a relative maximum or relative minimum at $w \approx 3.67$. The second derivative of $N'(w)$ is $N''(w)$.

$N''(w) = -6$ implies $N'(w)$ is concave down at $w \approx 3.67$, so the rate is a maximum at $w \approx 3.67$ weeks.

35. $S'(t) = -1.5t^2 + 21t - 10$
$S''(t) = -3t + 21 = 0$
$t = 7$ *weeks*

36. $t \approx 11$ *weeks*

IVC5

Curve Sketching

While graphing calculators are very helpful at getting a look at the shape of a function, sometimes a quick sketch based on the characteristics of a curve is a more complete way to learn about the nature of a function.

Suppose Dr. F. Stein uses a catalyst to initiate a reaction that bonds limbs to a body until the body takes over the reaction and produces its own bonding compound. If he uses too much of his catalyst, the body is late in taking over the reaction. If he uses too little, the initial reaction might not get underway. Dr. Stein finds that the amount of bonding compound can be expressed by the function $B(x) = 5x^3 - 5x + 41$, where x represents the amount of catalyst. $B(0) = 41$ mg is the amount he is currently using.

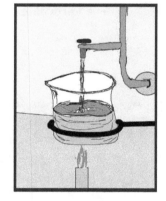

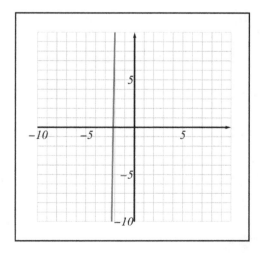

Using a standard graphing calculator with a 10 x 10 window, the graph of this function would look like that at left. It's not very helpful. Let's discuss how to do a quick sketch, not only because it can be helpful, but because it's a procedure that amalgamates all the information we've been accumulating so far.

507

Before beginning, make a list of the following curve characteristics down the side of your paper.

V.A. - This stands for **vertical asymptote**. They can occur where the denominator becomes equal to zero. More precisely, $x=c$ is a vertical asymptote if either $\lim_{x \to c^-} f(x)$ or $\lim_{x \to c^+} f(x)$ is infinite. For example, in the function $f(x)=\dfrac{4x}{x-5}$, a vertical asymptote could be $x=5$. In this case, $\lim_{x \to 5^-} f(x)=-\infty$, so $x=5$ is a vertical asymptote.

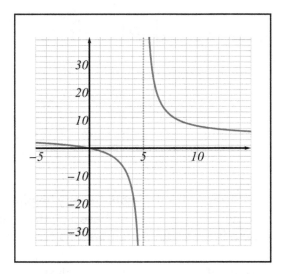

H.A. - This stands for **horizontal asymptote**. If the curve approaches a horizontal line as x goes toward ∞ or toward $-\infty$, then the horizontal line is an asymptote. In the graph at right, the horizontal asymptote is the line $y=3$. We can find horizontal asymptotes by examining the limits: $\lim_{x \to \infty} f(x)$ and $\lim_{x \to -\infty} f(x)$.

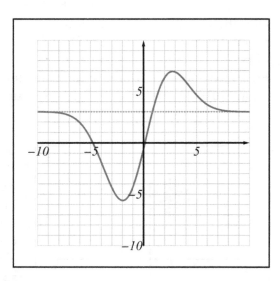

Rel Ext - Since we know **relative extrema** occur where the derivative equals zero, we set $f'(x)=0$, and note these x-values. We'll call them $x_i s$.

Rel Max - We can use the second derivative test to determine which of the x_i-values found above are **relative maxima**. These would be where $f''(x_i)<0$.

Further, we need to find the associated y-value for this point, or $f(x_i)$. This will tell us that the relative maximum is at the point $(x_i, f(x_i))$.

Rel Min - We can use the second derivative test to determine when of the x_i-values found above are **relative minima.** These would occur where $f''(x_i)>0$.

Further, we need to find the associated y-value for this point, or $f(x_i)$. This will tell us that the relative minimum is at the point $(x_i, f(x_i))$.

I.P.- **Inflection points** occur where the second derivative equals zero, so we set $f''(x)=0$. We'll call these x-values $x_j s$. Since not all places where $f''(x)=0$ are inflection points, we need to plot these $x_j s$ on the concavity line below, and test each side in $f''(x)$ to be sure the concavity changes on each side of any x_j. It should be concave up on one side of the x_j ($f''(x)>0$) and concave down on the other ($f''(x)<0$).

Further, we need to find the associated y-value for this point, or $f(x_j)$. This will tell us that an inflection point is at the point $(x_j, f(x_j))$.

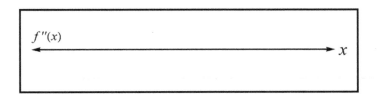

This is the concavity line.

On the concavity line, we plot any x_i-value; i.e., any place where $f''(x)=0$, and also, any x-value where the second derivative is undefined. This is also a place where the concavity may change. For $f''(x)=\dfrac{x+1}{x-4}$, we would plot $x=-1$ on the concavity line because $f''(x)=0$ at $x=-1$, and we would plot $x=4$ on the concavity line because $f''(x)$ is undefined at $x=4$. We would then test a point from each segment in the second derivative to determine where the curve is concave up and concave down.

This is the concavity line including the information for concave up, CU, and concave down, CD.

y-int - The **y-intercept** occurs where the curve crosses the y-axis. At this point, $x=0$, so we want to know "What is y when x is zero?" In other words, we find $f(0)$, which gives us the point $(0, f(0))$ for our graph.

WE RETURN TO DR. F. STEIN

We want to sketch the graph of the function $B(x)=5x^3-5x+41$. We make the list.

V.A.

H.A.

Rel Ext

   Rel Max

   Rel Min

I.P.

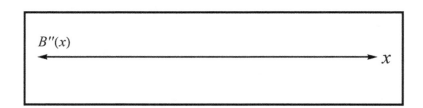

y-int.

V.A.   There is no denominator in our function, so there is no vertical asymptote.

H.A.   We examine $\lim\limits_{x \to \infty} 5x^3 - 5x + 41$. Because x approaches ∞, we can use the shortcut method. We need only consider $\lim\limits_{x \to \infty} 5x^3 = 5(\infty)^3 = \infty$. Thus, there is no limit as x gets very large, but it gives us valuable information. It tell us that as $x \to \infty$, the curve gets higher and higher, and the y-values also approach infinity.

For $\lim\limits_{x \to -\infty} 5x^3 - 5x + 41$, we can also use the shortcut method. $\lim\limits_{x \to -\infty} 5x^3 = 5(-\infty)^3 = -\infty$. Again, this means we have no actual limit as $x \to -\infty$, but it tells us that as the curve goes far to the left, the y-values go down forever; i.e., they approach $-\infty$.

Of course, this is exactly what we would expect for any third-degree equation with a positive leading coefficient.

So far we have:

V.A.   none

H.A. $x \to \infty$, $B(x) \to \infty$; $x \to -\infty$, $B(x) \to -\infty$

Rel Ext

Rel Max

Rel Min

I.P.

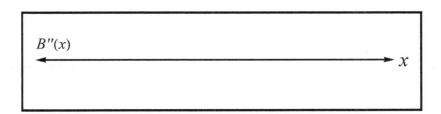

y-int

Now for the relative extrema—$B'(x) = 15x^2 - 5 = 0$

$$15x^2 = 5$$

$$x^2 = \frac{5}{15} \approx 0.333 \qquad \text{We take the square root of both sides.}$$

$$x \approx \pm\sqrt{0.333} = \pm 0.58$$

We can add this information to our list.

V.A.   none

H.A. $x \to \infty$, $B(x) \to \infty$; $x \to -\infty$, $B(x) \to -\infty$

Rel Ext $x = 0.58$; $x = -0.58$

    Rel Max

    Rel Min

I.P.

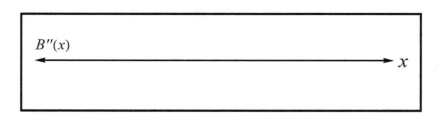

y-int

We suspect we have a relative maximum and a relative minimum. To test this assumption and to determine which is which, we can use the second derivative test.

$$B''(x) = 30x$$

We test 0.58: $B''(0.58)=30(0.58)$ is a positive number. Since $B''(0.58)>0$ the curve is concave up at $x=0.58$, and there is a relative minimum at the point $(0.58, B(0.58))$.

Since we will also need the corresponding y-value, we find $B(0.58) = 5(0.58)^3 - 5(0.58) + 41 \approx 43$.

We test -0.58: $B''(-0.58)=30(-0.58)$ is a negative number. Since $B''(-0.58)<0$ the curve is concave down at $x=-0.58$, and there is a relative maximum at the point $(-0.58, B(-0.58))$.

The y-value corresponding to $x=-0.58$ is $B(-0.58)=5(-0.58)^3 - 5(-0.58) + 41 \approx 39$.

We now have additional information for our list.

V.A.   none

H.A. $x \to \infty$, $B(x) \to \infty$; $x \to -\infty$, $B(x) \to -\infty$

Rel Ext $x=0.58$; $x=-0.58$

   Rel Max $(-0.58, 43)$

   Rel Min $(0.58, 39)$

I.P.

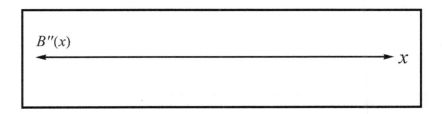

y-int

The next item on our list is the inflection point, which occurs where $B''(x)=0$. We set

$$B''(x)=30x=0$$
$$x=0$$

For the corresponding y-value, we find $B(0)=5(0)^3-5(0)+41=41$.

Before we know for sure that this is an inflection point, we use the concavity line test. Since $B''(x)$ equals zero at $x=0$, we plot 0 on the concavity line and test a point from each side. We also note that there is no point where $B''(x)$ is undefined.

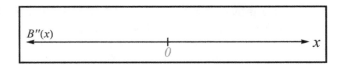

Let's test 1 and -1.

$B''(1)=30(1)>0$ so the curve is concave up from $x=0$ to ∞.

$B''(-1)=30(-1)<0$ so the curve is concave down from $-\infty$ to 0.

This confirms there is an inflection point at (0, 41). We add this information to the list.

V.A.   none

H.A. $x\to\infty$, $B(x)\to\infty$; $x\to-\infty$, $B(x)\to-\infty$

Rel Ext $x=0.58$; $x=-0.58$

    Rel Max $(-0.58, 43)$

    Rel Min $(0.58, 39)$

I.P. (0, 41)

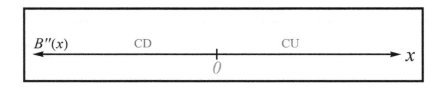

y-int

We have one last curve characteristic to find—the *y*-intercept.

We need $B(0) = 5(0)^3 - 5(0) + 41 \approx 41$, giving us a *y*-intercept of (0, 41), which also happens to be the inflection point in this case. Our list is now complete.

V.A.   none

H.A. $x \to \infty, B(x) \to \infty; x \to -\infty, B(x) \to -\infty$

Rel Ext $x = 0.58; x = -0.58$

Rel Max $(-0.58, 43)$

Rel Min $(0.58, 39)$

I.P. (0, 41)

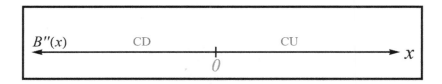

y-int (0, 41)

Plotting the points we've found and recognizing where the curve is concave up and down, we can sketch the curve.

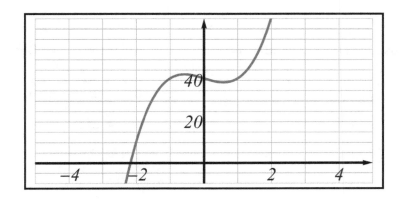

We can also recommend that Dr. F. Stein decrease the amount of catalyst he is using by 0.58 mg, since there is a relative maximum at -0.58. This would maximize the production of bonding compound.

ANOTHER EXAMPLE

Let's sketch the curve $f(x) = \dfrac{5}{x^5} + 6$. We start with the list.

V.A.

H.A.

Rel Ext

    Rel Max

    Rel Min

I.P.

y-int.

V.A. - Because $f(x)$ is undefined at $x = 0$, a vertical asymptote could be $x = 0$. Since $\lim\limits_{x \to 0^-} f(x) = -\infty$, so $x = 0$ is a vertical asymptote.

H.A. - We can use the shortcut method. We note that the term with the highest degree is $+6$. (It has a degree of 0, while the degree of the term $\dfrac{5}{x^5}$ is -5.) We take $\lim\limits_{x \to \infty} 6 = 6$. For $x \to -\infty$, the limit would also be 6. Our horizontal asymptote is therefore the line $y = 6$.

Rel Ext -   Since we'll be taking the derivative of $f(x)$, it will help to write it as:

$$f(x)=5x^{-5}+6$$

$$f'(x)=-25x^{-6}=\frac{-25}{x^6}=0$$

Recall that a fraction equals zero where its numerator equals zero, but the numerator above, -25, will never equal zero. Therefore, there are no relative extrema: no relative maxima and no relative minima.

I.P. $f''(x)=150x^{-7}=\frac{150}{x^7}$ Again, the fraction will never equal zero because the numerator will never equal zero, regardless of what value we might substitute for x. Therefore, there is also no inflection point. However, $f''(x)$ will be undefined when $x=0$ because the denominator will then equal zero. We need to plot $x=0$ on the concavity line.

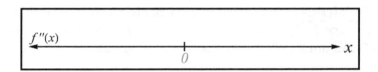

Let's test 1 and -1.

$f''(1)=\frac{150}{(1)^7}$ is a positive number. The curve is concave up from zero to infinity.

$f''(-1)=\frac{150}{(-1)^7}$ is a negative number. The curve is concave down from negative infinity to zero.

y-int $f(0)=\frac{5}{(0)^5}+6$, which is undefined. We also have no y-intercept.

We put this information on our list.

V.A. $x=0$

H.A. $y=6$

Rel Ext   none

   Rel Max   none

   Rel Min   none

I.P. none

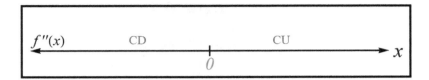

y-int none

Though it may seem like very little information, it is still enough to sketch the curve. The curve on the right side of 0 is concave up, but has no relative minimum. It must resemble "⌣" or "⌣". A configuration like the first would need to cross the asymptotes. A configuration like that on the right, however, would cross an asymptote if we try to fit it into the fourth quadrant, but it will fit nicely in the first quadrant.

Similarly, the curve on the left side of 0 is concave down, but has no relative maximum, so it must resemble "⌒" or "⌒". The first configuration will cross an asymptote whether we place it in Quadrant II or IV, but the second configuration will fit nicely in Quadrant II.

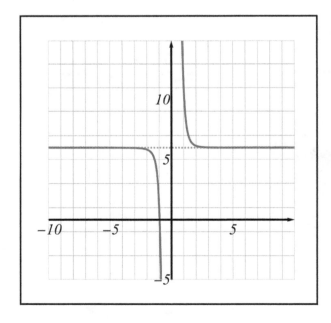

INTRA-SECTION EXERCISES:

1. Make a list of pertinent characteristics, and then sketch the graph of the function:

    $$f(x) = 2x^3 - 3x^2 - 36x + 14$$

2. Make a list of pertinent characteristics, and then sketch the graph of the function:

    $$f(x) = \frac{5}{x^2} - 4$$

Solutions

1. $f(x) = 2x^3 - 3x^2 - 36x + 14$

    V.A.   none

    H.A. $x \to \infty, f(x) \to \infty; x \to -\infty, f(x) \to -\infty$ because $\lim\limits_{x \to \infty} 2x^3 = 2(\infty)^3 = \infty$ and

    $$\lim\limits_{x \to -\infty} 2x^3 = 2(-\infty)^3 = -\infty$$

    Rel Ext $x = -2, 3$ because $f'(x) = 6x^2 - 6x - 36 = 0 = 6(x^2 - x - 6)$

    $$0 = 6(x-3)(x+2)0$$

    $$x = 3; x = -2$$

    Rel Max $(-2, 58)$ $f''(x) = 12x - 6$ Test -2: $f''(-2) = 12(-2) - 6$, CD, max

    $$y = f(-2) = 2(-2)^3 - 3(-2)^2 - 36(-2) + 14 = 58$$

    Rel Min $(3, -67)$ Test 3: $f''(-2) = 12(3) - 6$, CU, min

    $$y = f(3) = 2(3)^3 - 3(3)^2 - 36(3) + 14 = -67$$

    I.P. $(0.5, -4.5)$ $f''(x) = 12x - 6 = 0$

    $$12x = 6$$

    $$x = 0.5$$

    and there are no values of x where $f(x)$ is undefined.

Test -1: $f''(-1)=12(-1)-6=$ CD

Test 1: $f''(1)=12(1)-6=$ CU

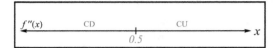

We conclude there is an inflection point at $x=0.5$.

$$y = f(0.5) = 2(0.5)^3 - 3(0.5)^2 - 36(0.5) + 14$$
$$= -4.5$$

y-int $(0, 14)$ $\qquad y = f(0) = 2(0)^3 - 3(0)^2 - 36(0) + 14 = 14$

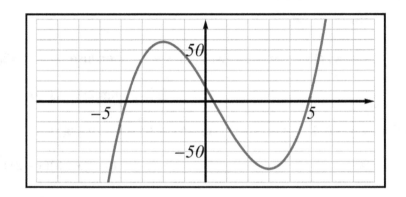

2. $f(x) = \dfrac{5}{x^2} - 4$; or $f(x) = 5x^{-2} - 4$

V.A. $\qquad x = 0$

H.A. $\qquad y = -4 \qquad$ because $\lim\limits_{x \to \infty} \dfrac{5}{x^2} - 4 = -4$ and $\lim\limits_{x \to -\infty} \dfrac{5}{x^2} - 4 = -4$

Rel Ext $\quad$ none $\qquad f'(x) = -10x^{-3} = \dfrac{-10}{x^3} \neq 0$

$\qquad\qquad$ Rel Max $\quad$ none

$\qquad\qquad$ Rel Min $\quad$ none

I.P. $\qquad$ none $\qquad f''(x) = 30x^{-4} = \dfrac{30}{x^4}$ is never zero, but is undefined at 0.

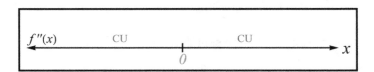

Test -1: $f''(-1) = \dfrac{30}{(-1)^4}$

is positive, CU

Test 1: $f''(1) = \dfrac{30}{(1)^4}$ is

positive, CU

y-int   none $y = f(0) = \dfrac{5}{0^2} - 4$ is undefined

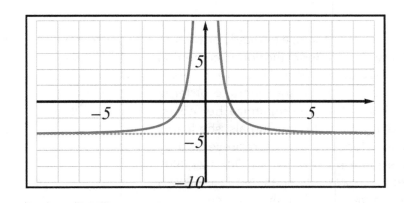

IVC5 CURVE SKETCHING EXERCISES

Make a list of the pertinent characteristics, and then sketch the curve of each function.

1. $y = \dfrac{2}{x^3}$

2. $y = \dfrac{3}{x^2}$

3. $g(x) = \dfrac{x^3}{3} - 9x + 11$

4. $g(x) = \dfrac{x^3}{3} + \dfrac{3x^2}{2} - 4x - 10$

5. $y = 2\sqrt{x} - 1$

6. $y = 3\sqrt{x} + 5$

7. $f(x) = \sqrt[3]{x} + 1$

8. $f(x) = \sqrt[3]{x} - 4$

9. Suppose Dr. Entricot, a pediatric orthodontist, wants to order orthodontic cement in bulk. Because of the discounts for various size quantities, she wants to order in a bulk size that will minimize her costs. Checking the industry journals, she learns the cost function can be represented by the equation $C(x) = 5x^3 - 1500x + 21{,}000$, where x represents units. Noting this is a third-degree equation, she suspects there is a relative minimum that will lower her costs. Make a list of the pertinent characteristics, and then sketch the curve. What quantity should be ordered to minimize costs?

10. Dr. Linderholt discovers a formula that seems to increase the IQ of subjects, but only to a certain point, represented by the function $I(x) = -\dfrac{4}{x^3} + 78$, where $I(x)$ represents increase in IQ and x represents the dosage in milligrams. Make a list of the pertinent characteristics, and then sketch the curve. Assume x must be a positive number.

IVC5 CURVE SKETCHING SOLUTIONS TO EXERCISES

1. $y = \dfrac{2}{x^3} = 2x^{-3}$

V.A. $x = 0$

H.A. $y = 0$ $\qquad$ $\displaystyle\lim_{x \to \infty} \dfrac{2}{x^3} = \dfrac{2}{\infty^3} = 0$ and $\displaystyle\lim_{x \to -\infty} \dfrac{2}{x^3} = \dfrac{2}{(-\infty)^3} = 0$

Rel Ext   none $\qquad$ $dy/dx = -6x^{-4} = \dfrac{-6}{x^4} \neq 0$

$\qquad$ Rel Max $\quad$ none

$\qquad$ Rel Min $\quad$ none

I.P. $\quad$ none $\qquad$ $d^2 y/dx^2 = 24x^{-5} = \dfrac{24}{x^5} \neq 0$ $\quad$ $y''(x)$ is undefined at $x = 0$.

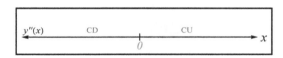

$\qquad$ Test -1: $\dfrac{24}{(-1)^3}$ is negative, CD

$\qquad$ Test 1: $\dfrac{24}{(1)^3}$ is positive, CU

y-int $\quad$ none $\qquad$ $y = \dfrac{24}{0^3}$ is undefined

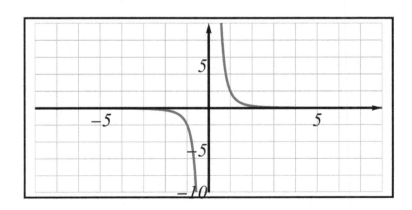

2. $y = \dfrac{3}{x^2}$

V.A. $x = 0$

H.A. $y = 0$

Rel Ext   none

         Rel Max   none

         Rel Min   none

I.P.   none

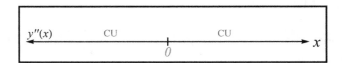

y-int   none

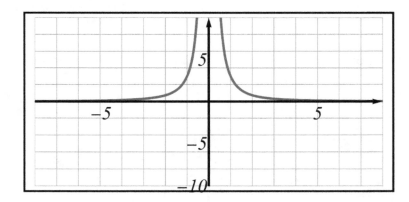

3. $g(x) = \dfrac{x^3}{3} - 9x + 11$

V.A.   none

H.A. $x \to \infty, g(x) \to \infty;\ x \to -\infty, g(x) \to -\infty$

Rel Ext $x = -3, 3$
$$g'(x) = x^2 - 9 = 0$$
$$(x+3)(x-3) = 0$$
$$x = -3;\ x = 3$$

Rel Max $(-3, 29)$ $g''(x) = 2x$

Test -3: $g''(-3) = 2(-3)$, CD, max

$$y = g(-3) = \frac{(-3)^3}{3} - 9(-3) + 11 = 29$$

Rel Min $(3, -7)$ Test 3: $g''(3) = 2(3)$, CU, min

$$y = g(3) = \frac{(3)^3}{3} - 9(3) + 11 = -7$$

I.P. $(0, 11)$ $g''(x) = 2x = 0$
$$x = 0$$

Test -1: $2(-1)$ is negative, CD

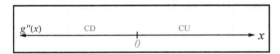

Test 1: $2(1)$ is positive, CU

$$y = g(0) = \frac{(0)^3}{3} - 9(0) + 11 = 11$$

y-int $(0, 11)$

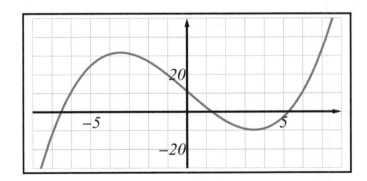

4. $g(x) = \dfrac{x^3}{3} + \dfrac{3x^2}{2} - 4x - 10$

V.A.   none

H.A. $x \to \infty, g(x) \to \infty; x \to -\infty, g(x) \to -\infty$

Rel Ext $x = -4, 1$

Rel Max $(-4, 8.67)$

Rel Min $(1, -12.17)$

I.P. $(-1.5, -1.75)$

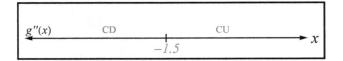

y-int $(0, -10)$

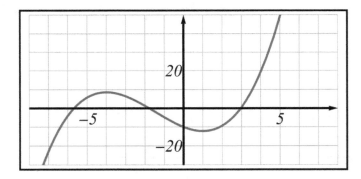

5. $y = 2\sqrt{x} - 1 = 2x^{\frac{1}{2}} - 1$ *Note the function is not defined for $x < 0$.

V.A.   none

H.A. $x \to \infty, y \to \infty$

Rel Ext   none $y'(x) = x^{-\frac{1}{2}} = \dfrac{1}{\sqrt{x}} \neq 0$

        Rel Max   none

        Rel Min   none

I.P.   none $y''(x) = -\dfrac{1}{2}x^{-\frac{3}{2}} = \dfrac{-1}{2\sqrt{x^3}} \neq 0$

$y''(x)$ is undefined where $x = 0$

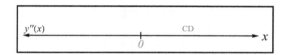

Test 1: $\dfrac{-1}{2\sqrt{(1)^3}}$ is negative, CD

y-int $(0, -1)$ $y = 2\sqrt{0} - 1 = -1$

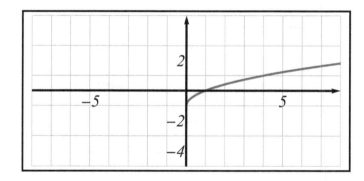

6. $y = 3\sqrt{x} + 5$ *Note the function is undefined for $x < 0$.

V.A.   none

H.A. $x \to \infty, y \to \infty$

Rel Ext   none

      Rel Max   none

      Rel Min   none

I.P.   none

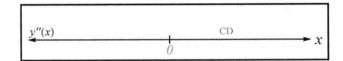

y-int $(0, 5)$

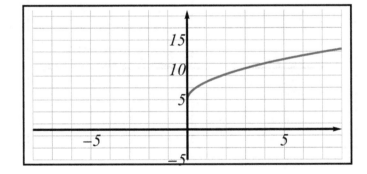

7. $f(x) = \sqrt[3]{x} + 1 = x^{\frac{1}{3}} + 1$

V.A.   none

H.A. $x \to \infty, f(x) \to \infty; x \to -\infty, f(x) \to -\infty$ $\lim_{x \to \infty} \sqrt[3]{x} + 1 = \infty; \lim_{x \to -\infty} \sqrt[3]{x} + 1 = -\infty$

Rel Ext   none $f'(x) = \frac{1}{3} x^{-\frac{2}{3}} = \frac{1}{3\sqrt[3]{x^2}} \neq 0$

    Rel Max   none

    Rel Min   none

I.P.   none $f''(x) = -\frac{2}{9} x^{-\frac{5}{3}} = \frac{-2}{9\sqrt[3]{x^5}} \neq 0$

$f''(x)$ is undefined at $x = 0$

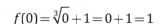

Test 1: $f''(1) = \frac{-2}{9\sqrt[3]{1^5}}$ is negative, CD

Test -1: $f''(-1) = \frac{-2}{9\sqrt[3]{(-1)^5}}$ is positive, CU

y-int $(0, 1)$ $f(0) = \sqrt[3]{0} + 1 = 0 + 1 = 1$

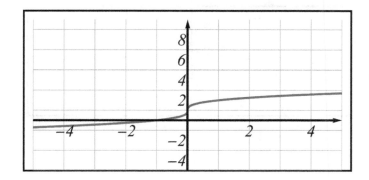

8. $f(x)=\sqrt[3]{x}-4$

V.A.   none

H.A. $x\to\infty, f(x)\to\infty; x\to-\infty, f(x)\to-\infty$

Rel Ext   none

      Rel Max   none

      Rel Min   none

I.P. $(0,-4)$

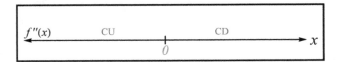

y-int $(0,-4)$

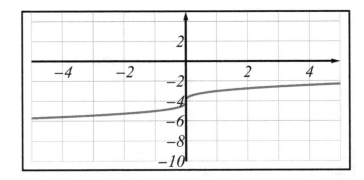

9. $C(x) = 5x^3 - 1500x + 21{,}000$

V.A. none

H.A. $x \to \infty,\ C(x) \to \infty;\ x \to -\infty,\ C(x) \to -\infty$

Rel Ext $x = -10, 10$

$$C'(x) = 15x^2 - 1500 = 0$$
$$15(x^2 - 100) = 0$$
$$15(x + 10)(x - 10) = 0$$
$$x = -10,\ x = 10$$
$$C''(x) = 30x$$

Rel Max $(-10, 31{,}000)$ Test -1: $C''(-10) = 30(-10)$ is negative, CD, relative max

Rel Min $(10, 11{,}000)$ Test 1: $C''(10) = 30(10)$ is positive, CU, relative min

I.P. $(0, 21{,}000)$

$$C''(x) = 30x = 0$$
$$x = 0$$
$$y = C(0) = 5(0)^3 - 1500(0) + 21{,}000$$
$$= 21{,}000$$

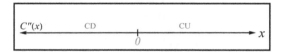

The y-intercept is the same point as the inflection point in this case.

y-int $(0, 21{,}000)$

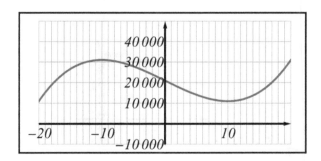

Dr. Entricot should order 10 units to minimize her costs. Dr. Entricot's problem is constrained by $x \geq 0$.

10. $I(x) = -\dfrac{4}{x^3} + 78 = -4x^{-3} + 78$

V.A.　　$x = 0$

H.A.　　$y = 78$

Rel Ext　none

　　　　Rel Max　　none

　　　　Rel Min　　none

I.P.　　none

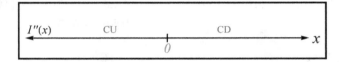

y-int　　none

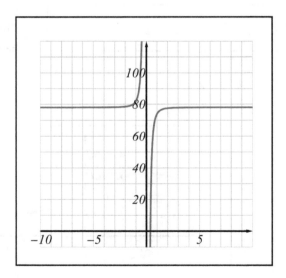

It appears Dr. Linderholt's formula will increase brain function, but only up to an increase of 78 points. The higher the dosage, the closer the increase will be to 78 points.

UNIT V

VC1

Business Applications

COST FUNCTIONS, AVERAGE COST FUNCTIONS, MARGINAL COST FUNCTIONS, REVENUE FUNCTIONS, AND PROFIT FUNCTIONS

Businesses that manufacture a product often have a *cost function* such as:

$C(x) = \$3500 + \$12x$, where x is the number of units manufactured.

The first term, $3500, would constitute the fixed costs, and $12 would constitute the variable costs; that is, $12 per unit in this case. While this example is a linear equation, the total cost function need not be. Suppose this is the cost function for *Smile Wide* Picture Framers.

The *Average Cost Function* lets us determine the cost per unit. It is denoted by $\bar{C}(x)$. The Average Cost Function, $\bar{C}(x)$, can be derived by dividing the total cost function, $C(x)$, by the number of units x. Using the total cost function above, we have:

$$\bar{C}(x) = \frac{C(x)}{x} = \frac{3500 + 12x}{x} = \frac{3500}{x} + \frac{12x}{x} = 3500x^{-1} + 12$$

$$\bar{C}(x) = \$3500x^{-1} + \$12$$

Suppose that Smile Wide is under contract to supply 800 frames to a retail customer, and suppose that their maximum capacity is 3000 frames. That is, $800 \leq x \leq 3,000$. How many units should be manufactured to minimize the average cost?

We know that relative extrema occur where the derivative equals zero, so we'll need to find $\bar{C}'(x)$.

$$\bar{C}'(x) = -\$3500x^{-2} = -\frac{\$3500}{x^2}.$$

This expression cannot equal zero; therefore, there are no relative extrema, hence no relative minima. In order to find the absolute minimum, we continue by testing each endpoint in $\bar{C}(x)$ to find the average cost.

$$\bar{C}(800) = \frac{\$3500 + \$12(800)}{800 \ units} = \$16.375/unit$$

$$\bar{C}(3000) = \frac{\$3500 + \$12(3000)}{3000 \ units} = \$13.17/unit$$

Smile Wide will have the minimum average cost of $\$13.17/unit$ when they make 3,000 frames.

The cost functions for businesses are often nonlinear functions. It is often the case that economies of scale cause larger batches to result in smaller costs per unit. Eventually, however, the need to add additional capacity will result in higher unit costs.

A typical cost function can be found at right. The y-axis represents the total cost to make x units. It is often useful to know the cost to make an additional unit,

$$\text{or} \ \frac{change \ in \ C(x)}{1 \ unit}.$$

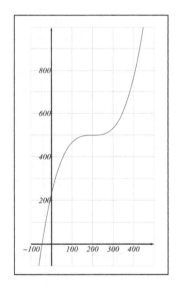

You probably recall that the slope of a curve is the limit of $\frac{change \ in \ whatever \ is \ on \ the \ y\text{-}axis}{change \ in \ units \ on \ the \ x\text{-}axis}$.

In this case, that would be approximately $\frac{change \ in \ total \ cost}{change \ of \ 1 \ unit \ on \ the \ x\text{-}axis}$, or in other

words, $\frac{change \ in \ C(x)}{1 \ unit}$, which is exactly what we were looking for. It is the *slope* of a Total Cost graph that gives us the projected cost to make an additional unit.

This cost to make the next unit is called the *marginal cost*. The steeper the slope, the higher the cost to make the next unit. Notice that on the graph above, between 0 and about 150 units, the cost to make the next unit is decreasing because the slope is getting flatter. Between about 150 and 250 units, the slope is almost flat. There is almost no cost to make another unit in this range. After 250 units, however, the slope begins to get steeper again. The cost to make an additional unit—i.e., the *marginal cost*—increases quickly.

On graphs, the slope is determined by the derivative of the function, so we obtain the marginal cost by finding $C'(x)$.

Suppose the Big Shot Binder Company has a cost function of

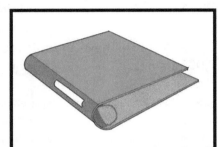

$$C(x) = .01x^3 - 2x + 30$$

for its 3-inch square-ring binders, where x equals the number of binders made.

If we wish to know the total cost of making 30 binders, we would find:

$$C(30) = .01(30)^3 - 2(30) + 30 = \$240.$$

To find the cost of making any individual binder, the marginal cost, we would need to find the derivative of the cost function.

$$C'(x) = .03x^2 - 2$$

To find the cost of making the next unit after the 30th, we find:

$$C'(30) = .03(30)^2 - 2 = \$25.$$

Cost Function: $C(x)$

Average Cost Function: $\bar{C}(x) = \dfrac{C(x)}{x}$

Marginal Cost Function: $C'(x)$

Businesses often have a *price function*, which is also called a *demand function*, such as:

$$\rho(x)=-0.03x+50.$$

Given a sales price of *p*, we can determine the corresponding demand *x*. (We know it would make more sense to have the equation solved for *x*, but this is the traditional and customary form.)

If we have a price/demand function, we can generate a *revenue function R(x)* because the revenue will be equal to the sales price of each unit times the number of units sold.

$$R(x)=\rho x$$

For Smile Wide, the revenue function would be:

$$R(x)=\rho x=(-0.03x+50)x=-\$0.03x^2+\$50x.$$

With a Revenue Function and a Cost Function, we can generate a *Profit Function* for the Smile Wide Company. After all, we know that profit will equal Revenue—Costs.

$$Pr(x)=R(x)-C(x)$$

$$Pr(x)=-\$0.03x^2+\$50x-(\$3500+\$12x)$$

$$Pr(x)=-\$0.03x^2+\$50x-\$3500-\$12x$$

Combining like terms:

$$Pr(x)=-0.03x^2+38x-\$3500$$

Now we can ask the burning question: How many frames should be made (and sold) to maximize profit?

Again, we are looking for an absolute maximum in the range $800 \leq x \leq 3,000$.

We start by looking for any relative extrema. We know these will occur where $Pr'(x)=0$.

$$Pr'(x)=-0.06x+38=0$$

$$-0.06x=-38$$

$$x \approx 633 \ frames$$

Now we determine which value of x produces the maximum profit, 633 (relative extrema), 800 (left endpoint), or 3,000 (right endpoint). At this point, we should note that 633 frames falls below the minimum possible, since Smile Wide is under contract to produce 800 frames. Therefore, we don't need to test $x=633$. However, we have decided to test this value for Smile Wide anyway.

$$Pr(633)=-0.03(633)^2+38(633)-\$3500=\$8,533$$

$$Pr(800)=-0.03(800)^2+38(800)-\$3500=\$7,700$$

$$Pr(3000)=-0.03(3000)^2+38(3000)-\$3500=-\$159,500$$

Smile Wide definitely does not want to produce 3,000 frames since they will lose money. For the maximum profit of \$8,533, they should make only 633 frames. However, since they are under contract, they must make the less profitable number of 800. We recommend that Smile Wide try to reduce their commitment when the contract comes up for renewal or else undertake cost-cutting measures that will change their profit function.

ANOTHER EXAMPLE

Suppose the Limber Summer Playground Manufacturers make playground sets to order. They must make at least 3 sets to be set up as models, and they can make a maximum of 200 sets in a summer.

Their cost function is $C(x)=\$148x+\$2500$, where x is the number of sets made.

Their price/demand function is $\rho(x) = -0.4x + 278$.

How many sets should be made and sold to maximize profit?

First, we build the revenue function. Since revenue equals the price per unit times the number sold,

$$R(x) = \rho x = (-0.4x + 278)x = -0.4x^2 + 278x.$$

Second, we build the profit function, recalling that profit equals revenue minus costs.

$$\text{Pr}(x) = R(x) = C(x)$$

$$\text{Pr}(x) = -0.4x^2 + 278x - (148x + 2500)$$

$$\text{Pr}(x) = -0.4x^2 + 278x - 148x - 2500$$

$$\text{Pr}(x) = -0.4x^2 + 130x - 2500$$

We find the relative extrema by setting the derivative of $\text{Pr}(x)$ equal to zero.

$$\text{Pr}'(x) = -0.8x + 130 = 0$$

$$-0.8x = -130$$

$$x \approx 163 \ playground \ sets$$

Finally, we check the profit at $x = 163$, and since $3 \le x \le 200$, we also compute the profit for $x = 3$, and $x = 200$. We'll round to the nearest dollar.

$$\text{Pr}(163) = -0.4(163)^2 + 130(163) - 2500 = \$8{,}062$$

$$\text{Pr}(3) = -0.4(3)^2 + 130(3) - 2500 = -\$2{,}114$$

$$\text{Pr}(200) = -0.4(200)^2 + 130(200) - 2500 = \$7{,}500$$

It would be best to take orders for 163 playground sets this summer.

USING THE SECOND DERIVATIVE TEST

Sometimes we aren't given endpoints to use in finding the absolute maximum or minimum for our profit function. When we set the derivative equal to zero and solve, we could be finding a relative maximum, relative minimum, or both. To determine which we have found, we can use the Second Derivative Test. For example, suppose our profit function is $Pr(x) = -0.03x^3 + 84.6x - 19$, where x represents the number of watermelon-flavored water bottles to be sold at a hockey game. We wish to know what number will generate the maximum profit. We find:

$$Pr'(x) = -0.09x^2 + 84.6 = 0$$

$$-.09x^2 = -86.6$$

$$x^2 = 940 \qquad \text{Next, we take the square root of both sides.}$$

$$x \approx 31 \; bottles$$

To determine if 31 bottles will give us a relative maximum or minimum, we use the second derivative test. We find the second derivative:

$$Pr''(x) = -0.18x \text{ and test } x = 31.$$

$Pr''(31) = (-0.18)(31)$, which yields a negative number, indicating the profit curve is concave down at $x = 31$, indicating that a relative maximum lies at $x = 31 \; bottles$.

INTRA-SECTION EXERCISES:

1. Suppose the Verdant Plains Manufacturing Corporation, maker of windmills, has a cost function of $C(x) = 800 + 90x + 0.02x_i^2$ where x equals the number of windmills made. Find the Average Cost Function. What is the average cost if 100 windmills are produced?

2. What is the cost to make the 101st unit; i.e., the one after the 100th unit? The 201st unit?

3. The Upside Construction Company converts warehouses into condos. Their cost function is $C(u) = 2400u + 5200$, where u is the number of condos per warehouse. Their demand function is $\rho(u) = -0.4u^2 + 6000$. For the warehouse under consideration, zoning requirements limit the maximum number of condos at 75. How many condos should be constructed to maximize profit?

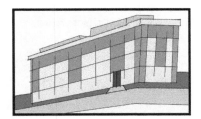

Solutions

1. $\bar{C}(x) = \dfrac{C(x)}{x} = \dfrac{800 + 90x + 0.02x^2}{x} = \dfrac{800}{x} + \dfrac{90x}{x} + \dfrac{0.02x^2}{x} = \dfrac{800}{x} + 90 + 0.02x$

   $\bar{C}(x) = \dfrac{800}{100} + 90 + 0.02(100) = 8 + 90 + 2 = \$100$ *per windmill*

2. $C'(x) = 90 + .04x$; $C'(100) = 90 + .04(100) = \$94$; $C'(200) = 90 + .04(200) = \$98$

3. $Pr(u) = R(u) - C(u)$
   $Pr(u) = (-0.4u^2 + 6000)u - (2400u + 5200)$
   $Pr(u) = -0.4u^3 + 6000u - 2400u - 5200$ We collect like terms.
   $Pr(u) = -0.4u^3 + 3600u - 5200$ = our profit function

   $Pr'(u) = -1.2u^2 + 3600 = 0$
   $\qquad 1.2u^2 = -3600$
   $\qquad u^2 = 3000$
   $\qquad u \approx 55 \ condos \qquad$ Since $0 \le u \le 75$, we test $u = 55, 0$, and 75.
   $Pr(55) = -0.4(55)^3 + 3600(55) - 5200 = \$126,250$
   $Pr(0) = -0.4(0)^3 + 3600(0) - 5200 = -\$5200$
   $Pr(75) = -0.4(75)^3 + 3600(75) - 5200 = \$96,050$
   Upside should construct 55 condos, for a profit of $126,500.

COEFFICIENT OF ELASTICITY

In general, the price of an item is related to the demand. This relationship is quantified by the *Coefficient of Elasticity*, defined as:

$$\eta = \frac{percent \ change \ in \ demand}{percent \ change \ in \ price}$$

This results in the formula:

Coefficient of Elasticity:

$$\eta = \frac{\dfrac{\rho}{x}}{\dfrac{d\rho}{dx}}$$

Proof:

For two fixed data values, this would be $\dfrac{\frac{\Delta x}{x}}{\frac{\Delta \rho}{\rho}}$, where x is the number demanded and ρ is the price/demand function.

The expression $\dfrac{\frac{\Delta x}{x}}{\frac{\Delta \rho}{\rho}}$ can be written as $\dfrac{\Delta x}{x} \div \dfrac{\Delta \rho}{\rho}$. When dividing fractions, we multiply by the divisor.

$$\frac{\Delta x}{x} \div \frac{\rho}{\Delta \rho} = \frac{(\Delta x)(\rho)}{(x)(\Delta \rho)} = \frac{(\rho)(\Delta x)}{(x)(\Delta \rho)} = \frac{\rho}{x} \cdot \frac{\Delta x}{\Delta \rho}$$

The next step is tricky—we "un-divide." $\dfrac{\rho}{x} \cdot \dfrac{\Delta x}{\Delta \rho} = \dfrac{\rho}{x} \div \dfrac{\Delta \rho}{\Delta x}$ which we can write as $\dfrac{\frac{\rho}{x}}{\frac{\Delta \rho}{\Delta x}}$

For the general continuous setting $\eta = \lim_{\Delta x \to 0} \dfrac{\frac{\rho}{x}}{\frac{\Delta \rho}{\Delta x}} = \dfrac{\frac{\rho}{x}}{\frac{d\rho}{dx}}$.

Q.E.D.

Curious student: "So what does Q.E.D. mean?"
Know-it-all: "It's Latin for *quod erat demonstrandum*."
Curious student: "Which means what?"
Know-it-all: "What was to be shown."
No-longer-curious student: "I see. It means, 'end of the proof.'"

SOME CHARACTERISTICS OF η, THE COEFFICIENT OF ELASTICITY

When η, the *Coefficient of Elasticity*, is negative, the demand and price move in opposite directions. When the price goes up, demand goes down. Conversely, when price goes down, demand goes up. Most products have negative elasticity. Stores run sales to increase demand by lowering the price. Some of the many products with negative Coefficients of Elasticity are bananas, ice cream, most clothes, admission prices to movies, and fast food.

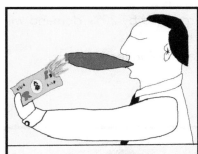

No one wants the cheapest yacht.

A few products, mostly luxury goods, have positive *Coefficients of Elasticity*. When the price goes up, demand goes up, and when the price goes down, the demand goes down. Examples include designer gowns, exotic high-end jewelry, penthouses, and (unfortunately for you) college tuition.

Another way we classify *Coefficients of Elasticity* is by their size.

If $|\eta| > 1$, then a product is said to be *elastic*. This means that if price is changed by, say, 10%, the demand will change by more than 10%. Elastic products include premium ice cream and vacation travel packages. In other words, the absolute value of η indicates how much demand will change when the price changes.

On the other hand, if $|\eta| < 1$, the product is said to be *inelastic*. If its price is changed by 10%, the demand will change by less than 10%. Products that are inelastic include items such as milk, bar soap, and salt. People tend to buy as much as they need and either have little use for extra (e.g., bar soap) or else the product will not keep, so there's no point in stocking up. While a sale might induce a customer to buy more soap, the percent increase in sales will not match the percent reduction in price.

If $|\eta| = 1$, then the product has *unit elasticity*. If price is changed by 10%, demand will also change by 10%.

Example 1:

Suppose an amusement park determines that the Coefficient of Elasticity $\eta = -2.31$ for its admission fee.

a. If a promotional discount coupon is offered for 20% off, will demand increase or decrease?

b. Will demand change by more than 20%, less than 20%, or exactly 20%?

c. Is this amusement park admission fee elastic, inelastic, or does it have unit elasticity?

a. Since η is a negative number, price and demand move in opposite directions. If the price is reduced, the demand will increase.

b. Since $|\eta| = |-2.31| = 2.31 > 1$, if the price is reduced by 20%, demand will increase by more than 20%.

c. Again, because $|\eta| = |-2.31| = 2.31 > 1$, the admission fee is elastic.

Example 2:

Suppose a customized limousine manufacturer determines that the Coefficient of Elasticity for its limos is 2.31. Due to some order cancellations, the manufacturer has an overstock of limos and decides to reduce the price of the limos in his inventory by 15%.

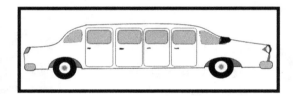

a. Will demand for these limos increase or decrease?

b. Will the change in demand be more than 15%, less than 15%, or exactly 15%?

c. In this case, are the customized limousines elastic, inelastic, or do they have unit elasticity?

a. Since η is a positive number, price and demand move in the same direction. If the price is reduced, the demand will also be reduced.

b. $|\eta| = |-2.31| = 2.31 > 1$, if the price is reduced by 15%, demand will decrease by more than 15%.

c. This product also has elasticity because $|\eta| = |-2.31| = 2.31 > 1$.

Example 3:

Suppose the Coefficient of Elasticity for packaged table salt $\eta = -0.205$. The grocer puts this item on sale for the week at 30% off.

   a. Will demand for the table salt increase or decrease?
   b. Will the change in demand be more than 30%, less than 30%, or exactly 30%?
   c. Is the table salt elastic, inelastic, or does it have unit elasticity?

a. The Coefficient of Elasticity is negative, so price and demand move in opposite directions. If the price is reduced, demand will increase.
b. Because the absolute value of the Coefficient of Elasticity is less than 1, ($|\eta| = |-0.205| = 0.205 < 1$) if the price is reduced, demand will increase, but not as much as 30%. It will increase, but by less than 30%.
c. Because $|\eta| = |-0.205| = 0.205 < 1$ the product is inelastic.

Example 4:

Suppose a type of packaged sea salt sold only in health food stores has a Coefficient of Elasticity $\eta = 0.88$. When the price of fuel rises, the cost of importing the salt rises, so the proprietor raises the price by 25%.

   a. Will demand for the sea salt increase or decrease?
   b. Will the change in demand be more than 25%, less than 25%, or exactly 25%?
   c. Is demand for the salt elastic, inelastic, or does it have unit elasticity?

a. Because the Coefficient of Elasticity is positive, demand and price move in the same direction. If the price is increased, demand will also increase.
b. Because $|\eta| = |.88| = .88 < 1$, although demand will rise, it will rise less than 25%.
c. The sea salt is an inelastic product because the absolute value of its coefficient is less than 1; i.e., $|\eta| = |.88| = .88 < 1$.

Example 5:

Sammy is a street vendor who sells hot dogs. He determines that his Coefficient of Elasticity $\eta = -1$. When construction makes travel difficult on his street, he decides to lower his price by 25%.

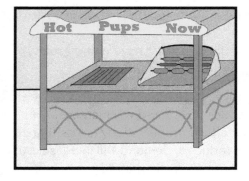

a. Will demand for his hot dogs increase or decrease?

b. Will the change in demand be more than 25%, less than 25%, or exactly 25%?

c. Are the hot dogs elastic, inelastic, or do they have unit elasticity?

a. Because the Coefficient of Elasticity is negative, price and demand move in opposite directions. If the price is reduced, demand will increase.

b. Because $|\eta| = |-1| = 1$ if price is reduced by 25%, demand will increase by 25%.

c. This type of elasticity where $|\eta| = 1$, is called *unit elasticity*.

INTRA-SECTION EXERCISES:

4. For Rio Bravo Custom-Made Saddles, the Coefficient of Elasticity is 0.75. If the price is increased by 12%, will demand increase or decrease? Will demand change by more than 12%, less than 12%, or exactly 12%? Is demand for Rio Bravo's saddles elastic, inelastic, or does it have unit elasticity?

5. For Nellie's Orange and Chocolate Chip Cookies, the Coefficient of Elasticity is −1.85. If the price is decreased by 20%, will demand increase or decrease? Will demand change by more than 20%, less than 20%, or exactly 20%? Is demand for Nellie's cookies elastic, inelastic, or does it have unit elasticity?

6. The Coefficient of Elasticity for Elias Arts' oil paints is −0.33. If the price is increased by 15%, will demand increase or decrease? Will demand change by more than 15%, less than 15%, or exactly 15%? Is demand for Elias Arts' oil paints elastic, inelastic, or does it have unit elasticity?

7. Holiday Fair Cruises has a Coefficient of Elasticity of −1.00. If the price is increased by 25%, will demand increase or decrease? Will demand change by more than 25%, less than 25%, or exactly 25%? Is demand for these cruises elastic, inelastic, or does it have unit elasticity?

Solutions

4. Because the Coefficient of Elasticity is positive, price and demand move in the same direction. If the price is increased, demand will increase. Because $|\eta|=|.75|=.75<1$, demand will change by less than 12%. It will increase, but not as much as 12%. The demand is inelastic.

5. Because the Coefficient of Elasticity is negative, price and demand move in opposite directions. Because the price is decreased, demand will increase. Because $|\eta|=|-1.85|=1.85>1$, demand will increase by more than 20%. The demand for Nellie's cookies is elastic.

6. Because the Coefficient of Elasticity is negative, price and demand move in opposite directions. Because the price is increased, the demand will decrease, but since $|\eta|=|-.33|=.33<1$, demand will not decrease as much as 15%. Demand for the oil paints is inelastic.

7. The Coefficient of Elasticity is negative, so price and demand move in opposite directions. Because the price is increased, the demand will decrease. Since $|\eta|=|-1|=1$, the decrease will be exactly 25%. Holiday Fair Cruises has unit elasticity.

Now to the calculations we need to determine Coefficients of Elasticity.

COEFFICIENT OF ELASTICITY—SOME CALCULATIONS

Recall that the Coefficient of Elasticity is computed from the equation $\eta=\dfrac{\frac{p}{x}}{\frac{dp}{dx}}$. Some examples follow.

Example 6:

The price function for Kay's Kiwi Lime Cakes is $\rho=-0.04x^2+486$ What is her Coefficient of Elasticity when she makes $x=100$ cakes? If she raises her price by 10%, will demand go up or down? Will it change by more than 10%, less than 10%, or exactly 10%? Recall that:

$$\eta=\dfrac{\frac{p}{x}}{\frac{dp}{dx}}$$

We substitute $\rho = -0.04x^2 + 486$; $x = 100$, and $\dfrac{dp}{dx} = -0.08x$ into the equation for η.

Then $\eta = \dfrac{\dfrac{-0.04(100)^2 + 486}{100}}{-0.08(100)} = \dfrac{0.86}{-8} = -0.1075$

If Kay raises her price by 10%, demand will go down, but not as much as 10% because η is negative and its absolute value is less than 1.

Example 7:

The Golden Memories Studio makes combination scrapbook and photo albums for forthcoming brides. They are also very popular wedding gifts. If the demand function is:

$$\rho = 0.15x^2 + 70x - 331,$$

determine the Coefficient of Elasticity for 50 orders.

Taking the derivative, we find that $\dfrac{d\rho}{dx} = 0.3x + 70$. Substituting ρ, x, and $\dfrac{d\rho}{dx}$ into the equation for Coefficient of Elasticity, we have:

$$\eta = \dfrac{\dfrac{p}{x}}{\dfrac{dp}{dx}} = \dfrac{\dfrac{(0.15)50^2 + 70(50) - 331}{50}}{0.3(50) + 70} = \dfrac{70.9}{85} \approx 0.834$$

Since η is positive, demand and price move in the same direction. Since $|\eta| < 1$, the product is inelastic. If Golden Memories raises their price of the albums by 10%, demand will increase, but not as much as 10%.

INTRA-SECTION EXERCISES:

8. The demand function for Andy's Edible Fruit Cakes is $\rho = -0.35x^2 + 924$. What is his Coefficient of Elasticity when he makes $x = 50$ cakes? If he lowers his price by 30%, will demand go up or down? Will it change by more than 30%, less than 30%, or exactly 30%? Is demand elastic, inelastic, or does it have unit elasticity?

9. The demand function for Adelaide's Custom-made Competition Ballgowns is $\rho = -0.34x^2 + 28$. What is her Coefficient of Elasticity when she makes $x = 10$ gowns? If she increases her price by 50%, will demand go up or down? Will it change by more than 50%, less than 50%, or exactly 50%? Is demand elastic, inelastic, or does it have unit elasticity?

Solutions

8. We substitute $\rho = -0.35x^2 + 924$; $x = 50$, and $\dfrac{dp}{dx} = -0.7x$ into the equation for η.

$$\text{Then } \eta = \frac{\dfrac{-0.35(50)^2 + 924}{50}}{-0.07(50)} = \frac{0.98}{-3.5} = -0.28$$

If the price is lowered by 30%, demand will increase, but less than 30%. Since $|\eta| = |-0.28| < 1$, demand is inelastic.

9. We substitute $\rho = -0.34x^2 - 26$; $x = 10$, and $\dfrac{dp}{dx} = -0.68x$ into the equation for η.

$$\text{Then } \eta = \frac{\dfrac{-0.34(10)^2 - 26}{10}}{-0.68(10)} = \frac{-6}{-6.8} = 0.88$$

If the price is increased by 50%, demand will increase by less than 50%. Since $|\eta| = |0.88| < 1$, demand is inelastic.

VC1 BUSINESS APPLICATIONS EXERCISES

1. R represents revenue generated from x motocross racing appearances for a manufacturer of racing motorbikes. If $R(x) = 36x^2 - 0.02x^3$, how many appearances will maximize revenue?

2. R represents revenue generated from x concert-goers for at the Fall Harvest Days Event Center. If $R(x) = 48x^2 - 0.08x^3$, how many concert-goers will maximize revenue?

3. Find the number of units x that produce the minimum average cost per unit $\overline{C}(x)$, if $C(x)$ represents the total cost for the Winterjoy Company to make x decorative sleighs. $C(x) = 0.02x^2 + 55x + 1250$. Maximum capacity for the company is 300.

4. Find the number of units x that produce the minimum average cost per unit $\overline{C}(x)$, if $C(x)$ represents the total cost for the Winterjoy Company to make x snow globes. $C(x) = 0.01x^2 + 27.5x + 625$. Maximum capacity for the company is 400.

5. The Half-Gauge Railway offers trips between two Western ghost towns. If the price/demand function and the cost functions are given below, how many tours will maximize profit, and what price does this number reflect? $C(x) = 17.5x + 200$; $p(x) = 155 - x$. Maximum tours available for the season is 70.

6. The Gastronomic Delight Company offers food tours in a major Midwestern city. If the price/demand function and the cost functions are given below, how many tours will maximize profit, and what price does this number reflect? $C(x) = 35x + 400$; $p(x) = 95 - x$. Maximum tours available for the season is 75.

7. The Land and River Company sells Missouri River rafting tours. If the price/demand function and the cost functions are given below, how many tours will maximize profit, and what price does this number reflect? $C(x) = 2400x + 6200$; $p(x) = 7200 - 0.4x^2$. Maximum tours possible is 70.

8. The Overland Adventure Company sells high-country jeep tours. If the price/demand function and the cost functions are given below, how many tours will maximize profit, and what price does this number reflect? $C(x) = 3600x + 9600$; $p(x) = 10{,}800 - 0.6x^2$. Maximum tours possible is 100.

9. Find the amount a of advertising dollars that maximize profit Pr for the Most News Radio Corporation. (Pr and a are in thousands of dollars.) $Pr(a) = -a^3 - 15a^2 + 3600a - 440$.

10. Find the amount a of advertising dollars that maximize profit Pr for the North Pacific Islands TV Network. (Pr and a are in thousands of dollars.) $Pr(a) = -3a^3 + 45a^2 + 10{,}800a - 2480$.

11. A commodity has a demand function modeled by $p = 200 - x$, and a total cost function modeled by $C(x) = 80x + 75$.

   a.   What price yields the maximum profit?
   b.   When the profit is maximized, what is the average cost per unit?

12. A commodity has a demand function modeled by $p = 50 - 0.25x$, and a total cost function modeled by $C(x) = 20x + 15$.

   a.   What price yields the maximum profit?
   b.   When the profit is maximized, what is the average cost per unit?

13. The price/demand function for a product is $\rho = 400 - 2x$.

   a.   For $x = 100$ determine the Coefficient of Elasticity of the product.
   b.   Is it elastic, inelastic, or does it have unit elasticity?

14. The price/demand function for a product is $\rho = 320 - 2x$.

   a.   For $x = 100$ determine the Coefficient of Elasticity for the prouduct.
   b.   Is it elastic, inelastic, or does it have unit elasticity?

15. The demand function for a product is: $\rho = \dfrac{100}{x^2} + 2$.

   a.   for $x = 10$, determine the Coefficient of Elasticity for the product.
   b.   Is it elastic, inelastic, or does it have unit elasticity?

16. The demand function for a product is $\rho = \dfrac{200}{x^2} + 2.7$.

   a.   for $x = 10$, determine the Coefficient of Elasticity for the product.
   b.   Is it elastic, inelastic, or does it have unit elasticity?

17. Demand for admission at a swimming pool is modeled by $x = 600 - 4p$, when the price p of admission is \$5. Can revenue be increased by lowering the price and thus attracting more customers? Use the Coefficient of Elasticity to determine your answer. Assume current demand is 50 swimmers.

18. Demand for admission at an ice skating rink is modeled by $x = 500 - 5p$, when the price p of admission is \$15. Can revenue be increased by lowering the price and thus attracting more customers? Use the Coefficient of Elasticity to determine your answer. Assume current demand is 75 skaters.

19. The cost function for a certain tablet is $C(x) = 13.50x + 47{,}750$, where $C(x)$ is measured in dollars and x is the number of tablets produced.

   a.   Find the Average Cost Function $\bar{C}$.
   b.   Find $\bar{C}$ when $x = 100$, when $x = 1{,}000$.
   c.   Determine the limit of the Average Cost Function as x approaches infinity.

20. The cost function for a certain speaker is $C(x)=24.50x+23{,}130$, where $C(x)$ is measured in dollars and x is the number of speakers produced.

   a. Find the Average Cost Function $\bar{C}$.
   b. Find $\bar{C}$ when $x=100$, when $x=1{,}000$.
   c. Determine the limit of the Average Cost Function as x approaches infinity.

21. The cost and revenue functions for certain silk scarves are $C=34.5x+1500$ and $R=74.2x$.

   a. Find the Average Profit Function: $\overline{Pr}=\dfrac{Pr}{x}$.
   b. Find the average profits when $x=100,\ 1000,\ and\ 10{,}000$.
   c. What is the limit of the Average Profit Function as x approaches infinity?

22. The cost and revenue functions for hand-painted neckties are $C=15.2x+1500$ and $R=51.5x$.

   a. Find the Average Profit Function: $\overline{Pr}=\dfrac{Pr}{x}$.
   b. Find the average profits when $x=100,\ 1000,\ and\ 10{,}000$.
   c. What is the limit of the Average Profit Function as x approaches infinity?

23. Suppose the Coefficient of Elasticity for Fi-Rich Energy Bars is -2.44. If the bars go on sale at 25% off,

   a. will demand increase or decrease?
   b. will demand change by 25%, more than 25%, or less than 25%?

24. Suppose the Coefficient of Elasticity for Renne-Cave 100-year-old vintage wine is 2.18. If the price for the wine is increased by 18%,

   a. will demand increase or decrease?
   b. will demand change by 18%, more than 18%, or less than 18%?

25. Suppose the Coefficient of Elasticity for Wren-Lu's designer gowns is 2.84. If the price for a Wren-Lu gown is increased by 24%,

   a. will demand increase or decrease?
   b. will demand change by 24%, more than 24%, or less than 24%?

26. Suppose the Coefficient of Elasticity for Walking Dog toys is -1.62. If the price is decreased by 14%,

   a. will demand increase or decrease?
   b. will demand change by 14%, more than 14%, or less than 14%?

27. Suppose the Coefficient of Elasticity for Dr. Ava's Vitamin Supplements is −0.76. If the price is decreased by 10%,

    a.   will demand increase or decrease?
    b.   will demand change by 10%, more than 10%, or less than 10%?

28. Suppose the Coefficient of Elasticity for Dr. Evan's hairpieces is 0.69. If the price is decreased by 50%,

    a.   will demand increase or decrease?
    b.   will demand change by 50%, more than 50%, or less than 50%?

29. Suppose the Coefficient of Elasticity for organically grown cotton sheets is 0.28. If the price is increased by 30%,

    a.   will demand increase or decrease?
    b.   will demand change by 30%, more than 30%, or less than 30%?

30. Suppose the Coefficient of Elasticity for Betsy's Dog Grooming is −0.28. If the price is increased by 5%,

    a.   will demand increase or decrease?
    b.   will demand change by 5%, more than 5%, or less than 5%?

VC1 BUSINESS APPLICATIONS SOLUTIONS TO EXERCISES

1. $R'(x)=72x-0.06x^2=0$ Second Derivative Test: $R''(x)=72-0.12x$
   $x(72-0.06x)=0$ Test 0: $R''(0)=72-(0.12)(0)$ is positive, Concave up
   $x=0; 72-0.06x=0$ There is a relative minimum at $x=0$
   $72=0.06x$ Test 1200: $R''(1200)=72-0.12(1200)=-72$ is neg-
   $1200=x$ ative, Concave down
   There is a relative maximum at $x=1200$

   12000 appearances will maximize revenue.

2. 400 concert-goers will maximize revenue.

3. $\bar{C}(x)=\dfrac{C(x)}{x}=\dfrac{0.02x^2+55x+1250}{x}=0.02x+55+\dfrac{1250}{x}=0.02x+55+1250x^{-1}$

   $\bar{C}'(x)=0.02-1250x^{-2}=0.02-\dfrac{1250}{x^2}=0$

$$0.02=\frac{1250}{x^2}$$

$$x^2=\frac{1250}{0.02}=62{,}500$$

$$x=250$$

   feasibility range: $0 \le x \le 300$

   $\bar{C}(250)=0.02(250)+55+\dfrac{1250}{250}=\$65/unit$

   $\bar{C}(0)=0.02(0)+55+\dfrac{1250}{0}=\pm\infty/unit$

   $\bar{C}(300)=0.02(300)+55+\dfrac{1250}{300}=\$65.17/unit$

   The Winterjoy Company should make 250 sleighs to minimize average cost per unit.

4. To minimize average cost per unit, the Winterjoy Company should make 250 snow globes.

5. $Pr(x)=x\rho(x)-C(x)=x(155-x)-(17.5x+200)=-x^2+137.5x-200$
   $Pr'(x)=-2x+137.5=0$

$$-2x=-137.5$$

$$x=68.75\approx 69\ tours$$

   $0\le x\le 70\ Pr(0)=-(0)^2+137.5(0)-200=-\$200$

   $Pr(69)=-(69)^2+137.5(69)-200=\$4526.50$

   $Pr(70)=-(70)^2+137.5(70)-200=\$4525$

   To maximize profit, Half-Gauge should offer 69 tours at $p(69)=155-69=\$86/tour$.

6. To maximize profit, Gastonomic Delight should offer 30 tours at $65 per tour.

7. $Pr(x) = x\rho(x) - C(x) = x(7200 - 0.4x^2) - (2400x + 6200)$

$$= 7200x - 0.4x^3 - 2400x - 6200$$

$$= -.4x^3 + 4800x - 6200$$

$Pr'(x) = -1.2x^2 + 4800 = 0$

$1.2x^2 = -4800$

$x \approx 63$ *tours*; number of tours: $0 \leq x \leq 70$

$Pr(63) = -0.4(63)^3 + 4800(63) - 6200 = \$196,181$

$Pr(70) = -0.4(70)^3 + 4800(70) - 6200 = \$192,600$

$Pr(0) = -.4(0)^3 + 4800(0) - 6200 = -\$6200$

To maximize profit, the land and River Company should sell 63 tours at a price of: $\rho(63) = 7200 - 0.4(63)^2 = \$5612.40$ *each.*

8. Overland Adventure should sell 63 tours at $8,418.60 each to maximize profit.

9. $Pr'(a) = -3a^2 - 30a + 3600 = -3(a^2 + 10a + 1200) = 0$

$$-3(a + 40)(a - 30) = 0$$

$$a = -40, 30 \text{ (We discard } -40)$$

Second Derivative Test: $Pr''(a) = -6a - 30$

Test 30: $Pr''(30) = -6(30) - 30$ *is negative, CD,* a relative maximum

The Most News Radio Corporation should spend $30,000 on advertising to maximize profit.

10. North Pacific should spend $40,000 on advertising to maximize revenue.

11. $Pr(x) = x\rho(x) - C(x) = x(200 - x) - (80x + 75) = -x^2 + 120x - 75.$

$Pr'(x) = -2x + 120 = 0$

$-2x = -120$

$x = 60$

Second Derivative Test: $Pr''(x) = -2, CD$ *everywhere,* relative maximum

a. $\rho(60) = 200 - 60 = \$140$

b. $\bar{C}(x) = \dfrac{80x + 75}{x} = 80 + \dfrac{75}{x}; \qquad \bar{C}(60) = 80 + \dfrac{75}{60} = \$81.25/unit$

12. a. $\$35/unit$ b. $\$20.25/unit$

13. a. $x = 100; \dfrac{d\rho}{dx} = -2; \qquad \eta = \dfrac{\dfrac{\rho}{x}}{\dfrac{d\rho}{dx}} = \dfrac{\dfrac{400 - 2(100)}{100}}{-2} = -1$

b. Because $|-1| = 1$, it has unit elasticity.

14 a. $\eta=-0.6$ b. It is inelastic.

15. a. $x=10;\ \dfrac{d\rho}{dx}=-200x^{-3}=\dfrac{-200}{x^3};\ \eta=\dfrac{\dfrac{\rho}{x}}{\dfrac{d\rho}{dx}}=\dfrac{\dfrac{\dfrac{100}{(10)^2}+2}{10}}{\dfrac{-200}{(10)^3}}=\dfrac{\dfrac{1+2}{10}}{-0.2}=\dfrac{0.3}{-0.2}=-1.5$

b. It is elastic.

16. a. $\eta=-1.175$ b. It is elastic.

17. $x-600=-4\rho$

$\dfrac{x-600}{-4}=\rho=\dfrac{x}{-4}-\dfrac{600}{-4}=-0.25x+150;\ x=50;\ \dfrac{d\rho}{dx}=-0.25;$

$\eta=\dfrac{\dfrac{\rho}{x}}{\dfrac{d\rho}{dx}}=\dfrac{\dfrac{-0.25(50)+150}{50}}{-0.25}=\dfrac{2.75}{-.25}=-11$

This is extremely elastic. Demand would definitely increase if the admission price were dropped.

18. $\eta=-5.7$ Demand will increase if the price is lowered.

19. a. $\bar{C}(x)=\dfrac{C(x)}{x}=\dfrac{13.50x+47{,}750}{x}$

b. $\bar{C}(100)=\dfrac{13.50(100)+47{,}750}{100}=\$491/unit$

c. $\bar{C}(1000)=\dfrac{13.50(1000)+47{,}750}{1000}=\$61.25/unit$

d. $\lim\limits_{x\to\infty}\dfrac{13.50x}{x}=\$13.50/unit$

20. a. $\bar{C}(x)=\dfrac{C(x)}{x}=\dfrac{24.50x+23{,}130}{x}$

b. $\bar{C}(100)=\$255.80/unit,\ \bar{C}(1000)=\$47.63/unit$

c. $\$24.50/unit$

21. $Pr(x) = R(x) - C(x) = 74.2x - (34.5x + 1500) = 39.7x - 1500$

    a. $\overline{Pr}(x) = \dfrac{Pr(x)}{x} = \dfrac{39.7x - 1500}{x}$

    b. $\overline{Pr}(100) = \dfrac{39.7(100) - 1500}{100} = \$24.70/scarf$;

        $\overline{Pr}(1000) = \dfrac{39.7(1000) - 1500}{1000} = \$38.20/scarf$

        $\overline{Pr}(10,000) = \dfrac{39.7(10,000) - 1500}{10,000} = \$39.55/scarf$

    c. $\lim\limits_{x \to \infty} \dfrac{39.7x}{x} = \$39.70/unit$

22. a. $\overline{Pr}(x) = \dfrac{36.3x - 1500}{x}$

    b. $\overline{Pr}(100) = \$21.30/tie$; $\overline{Pr}(1000) = \$34.80/tie$; $\overline{Pr}(10,000) = \$36.15/tie$

    c. $\$36.30/tie$

23. a. Demand will increase because η is negative.

    b. Because $|-2.44| > 1$, demand will increase by more than 25%.

24. a. increase

    b. Demand will increase by more than 18%.

25. a. Demand will increase because η is positive.

    b. Because $|2.84| > 1$, demand will increase by more than 24%

26. a. increase

    b. Demand will increase by more than 14%.

27. a. Demand will increase because η is negative.

    b. Because $|-0.76| < 1$, demand will increase, but by less than 10%.

28. a. decrease

    b. Demand will decrease by less than 50%.

29. a. Demand will increase because η is positive.

    b. Because $|0.28| < 1$, demand will increase, but by less than 30%.

30. a. decrease

    b. Demand will decrease by less than 5%.

VC2

Derivatives of Exponential and Log Functions

The function $f(x)=e^x$ is not a polynomial. To find its derivative, we cannot use the Power Rule.

The derivative of $f(x)=e^x$ is $f'(x)=e^x$. This is the only function that is its own derivative.

Hence, $f(x)=5e^x$ has the derivative $f'(x)=5e^x$.

The Hanger Hangar is a company that manufactures closet storage systems and containers. Since they have broken into the college dorm room market, their company has grown exponentially, approximated by the following function.

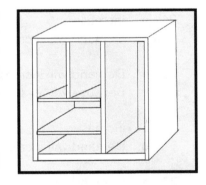

$$R(x)=\$900e^x-\$3,000x^2+\$7,600x$$

where x represents the years after startup, and $R(x)$ represents annual revenue.

The owners, Don and Dawn Davis, would like to know the average growth rate for their company. This calls for a derivative, since derivatives provide rates. However, since the first term cannot be written in the form ax^n, the Power Rule cannot be used. Note that the variable 'x' in the term $\$900e^x$ is in the exponent.

The function giving the growth rate for the Hanger Hangar Company is:

$$R'(x)=900e^x-6000x+7600$$

The company has been in business six years, so for $x=6$, the growth rate in revenue after six years is:

$$R'(6)=900e^6-6000(6)+7600\approx334{,}686$$

What about the concavity of this revenue function? Is it concave up ⌣ or concave down ⌢ ?

And what about a possible point where the concavity changes? We need to examine the second derivative for the answers.

$$R''(x)=900e^x-6000$$

To see if there is an inflection point, which indicates a change in concavity, we set

$$R''(x)=900e^x-6000=0$$

We add 6000 to both sides, $\qquad 900e^x=6000$

then divide both sides by 900 $\qquad e^x=\dfrac{20}{3}$

Since we are looking for a variable in the exponent, we will need to take the log or the ln (natural log) of both sides.

$$\ln e^x=\ln\dfrac{20}{3}$$

Since ln x and e^x are inverses, $\qquad x=\ln\dfrac{20}{3},$

$\qquad\qquad x\approx1.9$ years, which we get from a calculator.

We suspect that there has been a change in concavity; that is, an inflection point, after 1.9 years in business. We plot this on a number line and check the concavity on the right and left of 1.9.

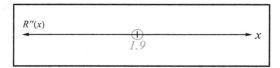

To find the concavity on the left, we use $x = 0$.

Concavity at $x = 0$: $R''(0) = \$900e^0 - \$6,000 = \$900(1) - \$6,000$, a negative number. So the growth was concave down until $x = 1.9$ years. Since $R(x)$ goes from a height of 900 at $x = 0$ to a higher value, 9627.3 at $x = 1.9$, and the concavity is negative, the first 1.9 years gives a growth something like: ⌠.

To find the concavity after 1.9 years, we use a number to the right of 1.9, like $x = 3$.

Concavity at $x = 3$: $R''(3) = 900e^3 - 6,000 \approx 12077$, a positive number.

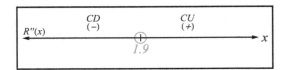

There is an inflection at $x = 1.9$ where concavity changes from down to up.

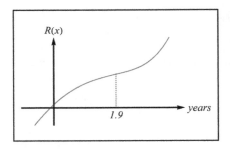

Business looks *really* good for the Hanger Hangar.

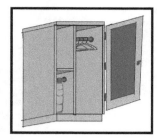

Now suppose the revenue stream is approximated by the function:

$$R(x) = \$1{,}200e^{0.3x} - \$38{,}000x^2$$

The first term is not e^x. It is e to the function 0.3x. We need a new rule.

The derivative of $f(x) = e^{g(x)}$ is $f'(x) = e^{g(x)}g'(x)$.

For the term $\$1{,}200e^{0.3x}$, $g(x) = 0.3x$ and $g'(x) = 0.3$. Therefore, the term $\$1{,}200e^{0.3x}$ has the derivative: $\$1{,}200e^{0.3x}(0.3)$.

We will return to the Hanger Hangar in a moment, but first, more examples.

Example 1:

    Suppose $f(x) = 4.6e^{x^2+3x}$. Then $g(x) = x^2 + 3x$ and $g'(x) = 2x + 3$.

    The derivative of $f(x) = f'(x) = 4.6(e^{x^2+3x})(2x + 3)$.

Example 2:

    Suppose $f(x) = 34e^{-x}$. Then $g(x) = -x$ and $g'(x) = -1$.

    The derivative of $f(x) = 34(e^{-x})(-1) = -34e^{-x}$.

Example 3:

    Let's use the other notation this time. Suppose $y = -4.2e^{3x-6}$.

    Then $g(x) = 3x - 6$ and $g'(x) = 3$.

    The derivative of $y = \dfrac{dy}{dx} = -4.2(e^{3x-6})(3) = -12.6(e^{3x-6})$.

Now back to the Hanger Hangar.

Since $R(x)=\$1{,}200e^{0.3x}-\$38{,}000x^2$, we have slope

$$R'(x)=1200(e^{0.3x})(0.3)-76000x$$

$$=360e^{0.3x}-76000x.$$

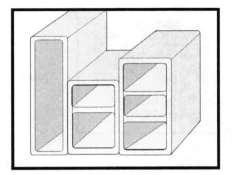

For $x=6$, $R'(6)=360e^{0.3(6)}-76000(6)\approx-453822$.

The slope $R'(6)$ is negative, hence $R(x)$ has a downward slope. This is a serious rate of loss. Can we expect a turnaround? We need to check the concavity. We take the derivative of $R'(x)$ to get:

$$R''(x)=360e^{0.3x}(0.3)-76000=108e^{0.3x}-76000$$

We set $R''(x)$ equal to zero to find a possible inflection point.

$R''(x)=108e^{0.3x}-76000=0$ We add 76000 to both sides.

$108e^{0.3x}=76000$ We divide both sides by 108.

$e^{0.3x}\approx703.70$ We take the natural log of both sides.

$\ln e^{0.3x}\approx\ln703.7$ We use $\ln e^u=u$ and $\ln703.7\approx6.56$.

$0.3x\approx6.56$ We divide both sides by 0.3.

$x\approx21.8$ We plot this on a number line.

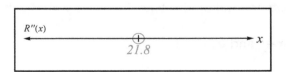

We test a number on the left, say, 1:

$R''(1) = 108e^{0.3(1)} - 76000 \approx 146 - 76000$, a negative number. So the graph is concave down for $x < 21.8$.

On the right, we test $x = 30$.

$R''(30) = 108e^{0.3(30)} - 76000 = 875133 - 76000$, a positive number. So the graph is concave up for $x > 21.8$.

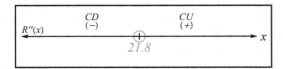

This means the Hanger Hangar will continue to lose money, but at a decreasing rate until it has been in business for 21.8 years. After that the concavity changes. We check the slope at $x = 21.8$ years.

For $x = 21.8$, $R'(21.8) = 360e^{0.3(21.8)} - 76000(21.8) \approx 249223 - 1656800$, a negative number.

At $x = 21.8$ years, the growth rate will be negative, but the revenue stream will change to concave up, promising less negative returns to come if the Hanger Hangar can hang on past 21.8 years. But it will still take almost 36 years to achieve a positive revenue stream.

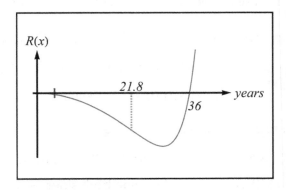

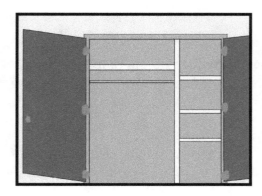

Twenty-one years is a long time, and the business climate might be radically different. Suppose the Hanger Hangar adopts a new strategy that generates the revenue function:

$$R(x) = \$1200(5^x) - \$2400x^2 - \$76,000.$$

To find the rate of revenue increase, we will need to take the derivative, since derivatives supply rates. We note that the function is not a polynomial and the first term is not in the form ae^x or $ae^{f(x)}$. The equation does not contain e^x. It contains 5^x. **To take the derivative of a term in the form $f(x)=a(b^x)$, we need $f'(x)=a(b^x)\ln b$.** For the function R(x) above, this gives us:

$$R'(x) = 1200(5^x)\ln 5 - 4800x$$

Since ln 5 is a number, let's combine $1200(\ln 5)$ to get approximately $1200(1.61)=1932$.

Substituting this into $R'(x)$, we get $R'(x) = 1932(5^x) - 4800x$.

If the new strategy has been in place for three years, we would like to find the rate of change in revenue at three years, so taking $x = 3$,

$$R'(3) = 1932(5^3) - 4800(3) = 241500 - 14400 = 227100.$$

This is a very good increase in revenue, but will it continue? What about the concavity?

We need the second derivative. Taking the derivative of $R'(x)$, we have:

$$R''(x) = 1932(5^x)(\ln 5) - 4800 \approx 1932(5^x)(1.61) - 4800.$$

$$R''(x) = 3110.52(5^x) - 4800$$

We set $R''(x)$ equal to zero to find possible inflection points.

$3110.52(5^x) - 4800 = 0$ We add \$4800 to both sides.

$3110.52(5x) = 4800$ We divide both sides by \$3110.52.

$5^x = 1.54$ We take the natural log of both sides.

*We could take the common log or the natural log, as long as we use the same type for both sides of the equation.

$$\ln(5^x) = \ln 1.54 \qquad \text{The exponent can now be a factor.}$$

$$x(\ln 5) = \ln 1.54 \qquad \text{We divide both sides by } \ln 5.$$

$$x = \frac{\ln 1.54}{\ln 5} \approx \frac{0.432}{1.61} \approx 0.268$$

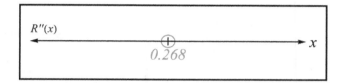

To the left we test $x = 0$:

$R''(0) = 3110.52(5^0) - 4800 = 3110.52 - 4800$, a negative number.
Before $x = 0.268$ years, the function is concave down.

To the right, we test $x = 1$:

$R''(1) = 3110.52(5^1) - 4800$, a positive number. After $x = 0.268$ years, the graph is concave up.

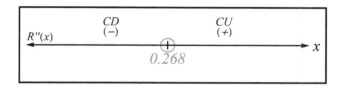

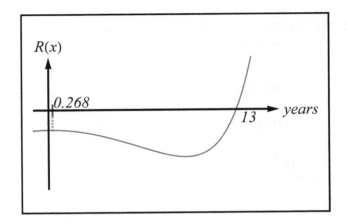

The new strategy is working out well.

TO SUMMARIZE:

If $y = ae^x$, $\dfrac{dy}{dx} = ae^x$ If $f(x) = ae^x$, $f'(x) = ae^x$

If $y = ae^{f(x)}$, $\dfrac{dy}{dx} = ae^{f(x)}f'(x)$ If $f(x) = ae^{g(x)}$, $f'(x) = ae^{f(x)}g'(x)$

If $y = ab^{f(x)}$, $\dfrac{dy}{dx} = ab^{f(x)}f'(x)\ln b$ If $f(x) = ab^{g(x)}$, $f'(x) = ab^{g(x)}g'(x)\ln b$

Example 1:

If $y = 7e^x$, find $\dfrac{dy}{dx}$.   Solution: $\dfrac{dy}{dx} = 7e^x$

Example 2:

If $y = 7e^{3x+8}$, find $\dfrac{dy}{dx}$.   Solution: $\dfrac{dy}{dx} = 7e^{3x+8}(3) = 21e^{3x+8}$

Example 3:

If $y = 2.5e^{x^2+3x}$, find $\dfrac{dy}{dx}$.   Solution: $\dfrac{dy}{dx} = 2.5e^{x^2+3x}(2x+3)$

Example 4:

If $f(x) = 7x^3 - 4x^2 + 9e^{-x}$, find $f'(x)$.

Solution: $f'(x) = 21x^2 - 8x + 9e^{-x}(-1) = 21x^2 - 8x - 9e^{-x}$

Example 5:

If $y = 7^x$, find $\dfrac{dy}{dx}$.   Solution: $\dfrac{dy}{dx} = 7^x \ln 7$

Example 6:

If $f(x) = 8(7^x)$, find $f'(x)$.   Solution: $f'(x) = 8(7^x)\ln 7$

Example 7:

If $f(x) = 8(7^{x^2+4x})$, find $f'(x)$.   Solution: $f'(x) = 8(7^{x^2+4x})(2x+4)\ln 7$

INTRA-SECTION EXERCISES:

Find the derivatives.

1. $y = 3e^x$

2. $y = 3e^{5x-4}$

3. $f(x) = 3(12^{5x-4})$

4. $f(x) = 8^x$

5. $f(x) = 8(14^x)$

6. $y = 1.6(9^{-4x+6})$

Solutions

1. $\dfrac{dy}{dx}=3e^x$

2. $\dfrac{dy}{dx}=3e^{5x-4}(5)=15e^{5x-4}$

3. $f'(x)=3(12^{5x-4})(5)\ln 12$
$\qquad =15(12^{5x-4})\ln 12$

4. $f'(x)=(8^x)\ln 8$

5. $f'(x)=8(14^x)\ln 14$

6. $\dfrac{dy}{dx}=1.6(9^{-4x+6})(-4)\ln 9$
$\qquad =-6.4(9^{-4x+6})\ln 9$

WHY IS *e* THE NATURAL NUMBER?

Let's look at the definition of the derivative for an exponential function $f(x)=b^x$:

$f'(x)=\lim\limits_{h\to 0}\dfrac{f(x+h)-f(x)}{h}=\lim\limits_{h\to 0}\dfrac{b^{x+h}-b^x}{h}=\lim\limits_{h\to 0}\dfrac{b^x b^h-b^x}{h}=\lim\limits_{h\to 0}\dfrac{b^x(b^h-1)}{h}$. We obtain

$f'(x)=b^x\lim\limits_{h\to 0}\dfrac{b^h-1}{h}$ since the factor b^x does not change as h approached 0. Further,

$\lim\limits_{h\to 0}\dfrac{b^h-1}{h}$ does not vary with x; that is, $\lim\limits_{h\to 0}\dfrac{b^h-1}{h}$ is a constant. We now have

$f'(x)=(constant)f(x)$, $\dfrac{f'(x)}{f(x)}=constant$. One of the pervasive models in the real world
is that of the amount, $f(x)$, being proportional to the rate of change in the amount, $f'(x)$. We could say the exponential functions are the most "natural." The natural

number e is defined so that $\lim\limits_{h\to 0}\dfrac{e^h-1}{h}=1$.

DERIVATIVE OF LOG FUNCTIONS

Etymology Enterprises is an online company that studies the origins of words and offers to supply several appropriate company names for startup businesses. In the past, they have supplied the name Orient Express for a tea shop and the name Straitlaced Enterprises for an orthopedic shoe manufacturer. After the first year, their revenue stream can be modeled by the equation.

$R(x)=\$290x^2+\$8,200\ln x-\$5,000$, where $x=$ number of years after startup.

To find the rate of growth in revenue for this company, we need the derivative. In examining the function, we see that it is not a polynomial. We will need to know how to find the derivative of ln x.

For the function $f(x) = \ln x,\ \ f'(x) = \dfrac{1}{x}$.

The function $f(x) = 7\ln x$ has the derivative $f'(x) = 7\left(\dfrac{1}{x}\right) = \dfrac{7}{x}$.

So how is Etymology Enterprises doing? Its growth rate would be:

$$R'(x) = 580x + 8200\left(\frac{1}{x}\right) \text{ or } R'(x) = -580x + 8200x^{-1}$$

The company has been in business four years, so we use $x = 4$ to find the growth rate at four years since startup.

$$R'(4) = 580(4) + 8200\left(\frac{1}{4}\right) = 2320 + 2050 = 4370.$$

After four years, the revenue stream is increasing at $4370 each year.

What about the concavity? Is there an inflection point? Again, we need the second derivative.

$$R''(x) = 580 - 8200x^{-2} = 580 - \frac{8200}{x^2}$$

If we set $R''(x)$ equal to zero, we have $580 - \dfrac{8200}{x^2} = 0,\ 580 = \dfrac{8200}{x^2}$

Multiply both sides by x^2 and divide both sides by 580; $x^2 = \dfrac{8200}{580}$, $x \approx 3.76$ years.

We'll test $x = 4$, $R''(x) = 580 - \dfrac{8200}{4^2} = 67.5$

Since $R''(x)$ is positive, the graph is concave up.

A curve that is concave up with positive slope resembles ⌡

Revenue will increase at a faster and faster rate.

The entrepreneurs should do very well.

PROOF FOR THE DERIVATIVE OF LOG FUNCTIONS

Here's a cute little proof.

If $y = \ln x$, prove that $\dfrac{dy}{dx} = \dfrac{1}{x}$.

Proof: Let $\ln x = y$. This is another way to write:

$e^y = x$.   We take the derivative of both sides with respect to x.

$e^y \dfrac{dy}{dx} = 1$ We divide both sides by e^y.

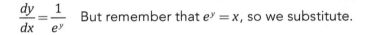

$\dfrac{dy}{dx} = \dfrac{1}{e^y}$ But remember that $e^y = x$, so we substitute.

$\dfrac{dy}{dx} = \dfrac{1}{x}$

Q.E.D.

Suppose that in addition to names, Etymology Enterprises designs and sells product logos. Suppose their annual revenue function (after year 1) becomes:

$$R(x) = -\$290x^2 + \$820\ln(6.8x^2) - \$5{,}000$$

Now the rate at which their revenue is increasing can be found from the derivative, if we learn how to find the derivative of the second term: $\$820\ln(6.8x^2)$.

For $y = a \ln f(x)$, the derivative is: $\dfrac{dy}{dx} = a\dfrac{1}{f(x)}f'(x).$

So the derivative of the second term is $820\dfrac{1}{6.8x^2}(13.6x) = 11152x\dfrac{1}{6.8x^2} = \dfrac{1640}{x}$ and the new rate of revenue is:

$$R'(x) = -580x + \dfrac{1640}{x}.$$

If this new strategy has been in effect for two years, we use $x=2$ to find:

$$R'(2)=-580(2)+\frac{1640}{x^2}=-1160+820=-340$$

The new product line is hemorrhaging considerably, but we'd better check the concavity to find out if the rate will continue to decline and whether or not there is an inflection point in the future for a possible rebound.

To take the derivative of $R'(x)$, we rewrite it as $R'(x)=-580x+1640x^{-1}$.

$$R''(x)=-580-1640x^{-2}=-580-\frac{1640}{x^2}$$

For $x=2$, we can see that $R''(2)$ is a negative number, so the revenue function is concave down. Revenue is decreasing at a faster and faster rate, like ⌐.

We might try looking for an inflection point. If we set $R''(x)=0$,

$$R''(x)=-580-\frac{1640}{x^2}$$

$$-580=\frac{1640}{x^2} \quad \text{Multiplying by } x^2 \text{ and dividing by } -580,$$

$$x^2=\frac{1640}{-580}\approx-2.83, \text{ but we can't take the square root of a negative number.}$$

Hence, we can't find an inflection point in the real number system. There won't be a turnaround for the plummeting revenue.

Suppose the revenue stream could be expressed by the function:

$$R(x)=-\$80x^2+\$820\log_8 x-\$5,000$$

To find the derivative of the second term, we need the derivative of a log value other than the natural log. Calculators and computers have functions only for computing *log* and *ln*. To compute a value such as $\log_3 5.2$, we need $\frac{\log 5.2}{\log 3}$ or $\frac{\ln 5.2}{\ln 3}$. In general, the base of a logarithm can be converted to another base using the equation $\log_c x = \dfrac{\log_b x}{\log_b c}$.

Therefore, for $f(x) = c \log_a x$, $f'(x) = c\dfrac{\ln x}{\ln a} = c\dfrac{1}{x} \cdot \dfrac{1}{\ln a}$.

The derivative of the second term in $R(x)$ would be:

$$820\frac{1}{x} \cdot \frac{1}{\ln 8} \approx 820\frac{1}{x}(0.481) \approx 394\frac{1}{x},$$

$$\text{and } R'(x) = -160x + 394\frac{1}{x}.$$

$$\text{For } x = 2: \; R'(2) = -\$160(2) + (394)\frac{1}{2} = -\$123$$

Revenue is still decreasing each year.

Here's another cute proof.

If $y = \log_a x$, prove $\dfrac{dy}{dx} = \dfrac{1}{x} \cdot \dfrac{1}{\ln a}$.

Only a mathematician would think a proof is "cute".

Let $y = \log_a x$. Then $a^y = x$. We take the natural log of both sides.

$\ln a^y = \ln x$ The exponent becomes a coefficient.

$y \ln a = \ln x$ We divide both sides by $\ln a$.

$$y = \frac{1}{\ln a}(\ln x)$$

Recall that the natural log of a number and its reciprocal are both just numbers.

We take the derivative of both sides to get:

$$\frac{dy}{dx} = \frac{1}{\ln a} \cdot \frac{1}{x} = \frac{1}{x} \cdot \frac{1}{\ln a}$$

$$\text{Q.E.D.}$$

If $f(x)=a\ln x$, $f'(x)=a\dfrac{1}{x}$ $\qquad$ If $y=a\ln x$, $\dfrac{dy}{dx}=a\dfrac{1}{x}$

If $f(x)=a\ln g(x)$, $f'(x)=a\dfrac{1}{g(x)}g'(x)$ $\qquad$ If $y=a\ln g(x)$, $\dfrac{dy}{dx}=a\dfrac{1}{g(x)}g'(x)$

If $f(x)=a\log_b x$, $f'(x)=a\dfrac{1}{x}\cdot\dfrac{1}{\ln b}$ $\qquad$ If $y=a\log_b x$, $\dfrac{dy}{dx}=a\dfrac{1}{x}\cdot\dfrac{1}{\ln b}$

If $f(x)=a\log_b g(x)$, $f'(x)=a\dfrac{1}{g(x)}\cdot g'(x)\cdot\dfrac{1}{\ln b}$ $\qquad$ If $y=a\log_b g(x)$, $\dfrac{dy}{dx}=a\dfrac{1}{g(x)}\cdot g'(x)\cdot\dfrac{1}{\ln b}$

Example 8:

If $f(x)=5\ln x$, find $f'(x)$.   Solution: $f'(x)=5\dfrac{1}{x}=\dfrac{5}{x}$

Example 9:

If $f(x)=5\ln(3x^2+7)$, find $f'(x)$.   Solution: $f'(x)=5\cdot\dfrac{1}{3x^2+7}6x=\dfrac{30x}{3x^2+7}$

Example 10:

If $y=5\log_9(3x^2+7)$, find $\dfrac{dy}{dx}$.   Solution: $\dfrac{dy}{dx}=5\dfrac{1}{3x^2+7}6x\dfrac{1}{\ln 9}=\dfrac{30x}{(3x^2+7)\ln 9}$

INTRA-SECTION EXERCISES

Find the derivatives.

7. $g(x)=7\ln x$ $\qquad$ 8. $g(x)=\ln(3x)$ $\qquad$ 9. $g(x)=5\ln(7x)$ $\qquad$ 10. $y=\log_3(5x)$

11. $f(x)=7\ln(4x)-3x^4+3e^{2x}$ $\qquad$ 12. $y=7\log_3(5x^2)$

Solutions

7. $g'(x) = \dfrac{7}{x}$

8. $g'(x) = \dfrac{1}{3x} \cdot 3 = \dfrac{1}{x}$

9. $g'(x) = 5\dfrac{1}{7x} \cdot 7 = \dfrac{5}{x}$

10. $\dfrac{dy}{dx} = \dfrac{1}{5x} \cdot 5 \cdot \dfrac{1}{\ln 3} = \dfrac{1}{x \ln 3}$

11. $f'(x) = 7\dfrac{1}{4x} \cdot 4 - 12x^3 + 3e^{2x}(2) = \dfrac{7}{x} - 12x^3 + 6e^{2x}$

12. $\dfrac{dy}{dx} = 7 \cdot \dfrac{1}{5x^2} \cdot 10x \cdot \dfrac{1}{\ln 3} = \dfrac{14}{x \ln 3}$

VC2 DERIVATIVES OF EXPONENTIAL AND LOG FUNCTIONS EXERCISES

Find the derivatives.

1. $f(x) = 4e^x$

2. $f(x) = -6e^x$

3. $y = -5e^{2x}$

4. $y = 6e^{7x}$

5. $g(x) = 5e^{3x-4}$

6. $g(x) = 2e^{3x+7}$

7. $y = -4e^{x^2-1}$

8. $y = 5e^{x^2+3}$

9. $h(x) = -7e^{3x^2+2x}$

10. $h(x) = 8e^{4x^2-x}$

11. $y = 5^x$

12. $y = 9^x$

13. $f(x) = 3(5^x)$

14. $f(x) = 5(6^x)$

15. $y = e(4^x)$

16. $y = 2e(5^x)$

17. $g(x) = 6^{5x}$

18. $g(x) = 5^{-4x}$

19. $y = 6^{5x^3+3}$

20. $y = 4^{3x^3-5}$

21. $h(x) = 7(8^{x^2-1})$

22. $h(x) = 6(5^{x^2+4})$

23. $y = x^3 + 5e^{4x-1}$

24. $y = 4x^3 + 5e^{3x-5.6}$

25. $f(x) = 8\ln x$

26. $f(x) = 12\ln x$

27. $y = 11\ln(6x)$

28. $y = 4\ln(9x)$

29. $h(x) = 4\log_7(13x)$

30. $h(x) = 4.2\log_8(5x)$

31. $y = \log_4(x^2+2)$

32. $y = \log_7(x^2-8)$

33. $f(x) = \log 3x$

34. $f(x) = \log 4x$

35. $y = 5.1\ln(4x^2-9)$

36. $y = 0.5\ln(2x^2-3)$

37. $g(x) = \log_3(5x^3 - 2x)$

38. $g(x) = \log_6(2x^3 - 5x)$

39. $y = \log_2 3x - 4x^2$

40. $y = \log_5 4x - 7x^2$

41. $h(x) = 4x^2 - 4\ln 4x + 5e^{-x}$

42. $h(x) = 4x^3 - 5\ln 2x + 6e^{-x}$

43. $y = \dfrac{1}{x} + 3\ln x + \dfrac{2}{x^2}$

44. $y = \dfrac{1}{x} - 4\ln x + \dfrac{3}{x^2}$

45. $f(x) = 6x + \dfrac{1}{3}\ln(x^2 + 6) - 12$

46. $f(x) = 9x + \dfrac{1}{4}\ln(x^2 - 12) + 8$

47. $y = 4e^{-3x^2} - 17.5 + 4\ln 2x$

48. $y = 2e^{6x^2} - 2.7 + 5\ln 2x$

49. What is the equation of the tangent line to the equation $f(x) = 3\ln(4x^2)$ at the point $(1, 4.2)$?

50. What is the equation of the tangent line to the equation $f(x) = 5\ln(4x^2)$ at the point $(1, 6.9)$?

51. What is the equation of the tangent line to the function $y = \log_4 x$ at the point $(2, 0.5)$?

52. What is the equation of the tangent line to the function $y = \log_7 x$ at the point $(2, 0.36)$?

53. Revenue for the Hallworth Historic Center can be modeled by the equation $R(x) = -800e^{-0.5x} + 2000$, where x is the number of years after startup. At what rate is revenue increasing after one year? After three years?

54. Revenue for the Central City Civic Center can be modeled by the equation $R(x) = -6000e^{-0.4x} + 3000$, where x is the number of years after startup. At what rate is revenue increasing after one year? After three years?

VC2 DERIVATIVES OF EXPONENTIAL AND LOG FUNCTIONS SOLUTIONS TO EXERCISES

1. $f'(x) = 4e^x$

2. $f'(x) = -6e^x$

3. $\dfrac{dy}{dx} = -5e^{2x}(2) = -10e^{2x}$

4. $\dfrac{dy}{dx} = 42e^{7x}$

5. $g'^{(x)} = 5(e^{3x-4})(3) = 15e^{3x-4}$

6. $g'(x) = 6e^{3x+7}$

7. $\dfrac{dy}{dx} = -4(e^{x^2-1})(2x) = -8xe^{x^2-1}$

8. $\dfrac{dy}{dx} = 10xe^{x^2+3}$

9. $h'^{(x)} = -7(e^{3x^2+2x})(6x+2)$

10. $h'(x) = 8(e^{4x^2-x})(8x-1)$

11. $\dfrac{dy}{dx} = 5^x \ln 5$

12. $\dfrac{dy}{dx} = 9^x \ln 9$

13. $f'(x) = 3(5^x)\ln 5$

14. $f'(x) = 5(6^x)\ln 6$

15. $\dfrac{dy}{dx} = e(4^x)\ln 4$ [Recall e is just a number.]

16. $\dfrac{dy}{dx} = 2e(5^x)\ln 5$

17. $g'^{(x)} = 6^{5x}(5)\ln 6 = (5\ln 6)(6^{5x})$

18. $g'(x) = (-4\ln 5)(5^{-4x})$

19. $\dfrac{dy}{dx} = (6^{5x^3+3})(15x^2)\ln 6$

20. $\dfrac{dy}{dx} = (4^{3x^3-5})(9x^2)(\ln 4)$

21. $\begin{aligned} h'^{(x)} &= 7(8^{x^2-1})(2x)\ln 8 \\ &= (\ln 8)(14x)(8^{x^2-1}) \end{aligned}$

22. $h'(x) = (\ln 5)(12x)(5^{x^2+4})$

23. $\dfrac{dy}{dx} = 3x^2 + 5(e^{4x-1})(4) = 3x^2 + 20e^{4x-1}$

24. $\dfrac{dy}{dx} = 12x^2 + 15e^{3x-5.6}$

25. $f'(x) = 8\dfrac{1}{x} = \dfrac{8}{x}$

26. $f'(x) = \dfrac{12}{x}$

27. $\dfrac{dy}{dx} = 11 \cdot \dfrac{1}{6x} \cdot 6 = \dfrac{11}{x}$

28. $\dfrac{dy}{dx} = \dfrac{4}{x}$

29. $h'(x) = 4 \cdot \dfrac{1}{13x} \cdot 13 \cdot \dfrac{1}{\ln 7} = \dfrac{4}{x\ln 7}$

30. $h'(x) = \dfrac{4.2}{x\ln 8}$

31. $\dfrac{dy}{dx} = \dfrac{1}{x^2+2} \cdot (2x) \cdot \dfrac{1}{\ln 4} = \dfrac{2x}{(x^2+2)\ln 4}$

32. $\dfrac{dy}{dx} = \dfrac{2x}{(x^2-8)\ln 7}$

33. $f'(x) = \dfrac{1}{3x} \cdot 3 \cdot \dfrac{1}{\ln 10} = \dfrac{1}{x \ln 10}$

34. $f'(x) = \dfrac{1}{x \ln 10}$

35. $\dfrac{dy}{dx} = 5.1 \cdot \dfrac{1}{4x^2 - 9} \cdot 8x = \dfrac{40.8x}{4x^2 - 9}$

36. $\dfrac{dy}{dx} = \dfrac{2x}{2x^2 - 3}$

37. $g'(x) = \dfrac{1}{5x^3 - 2x} \cdot (15x^2 - 2) \cdot \dfrac{1}{\ln 3} = \dfrac{15x^2 - 2}{(5x^3 - 2x)\ln 3}$

38. $g'(x) = \dfrac{6x^2 - 5}{(2x^3 - 5)\ln 6}$

39. $\dfrac{dy}{dx} = \dfrac{1}{3x}(3)\dfrac{1}{\ln 2} - 8x = \dfrac{1}{x \ln 2} - 8x$

40. $\dfrac{dy}{dx} = \dfrac{1}{x \ln 5} - 14x$

41. $h'(x) = 8x - 4\left(\dfrac{1}{4x}\right)(4) + 5e^{-x}(-1) = 8x - \dfrac{4}{x} - 5e^{-x}$

42. $h'(x) = 12x^2 - \dfrac{5}{x} - 6e^{-x}$

43. $y = x^{-1} + 3\ln x + 2x^{-2}; \ \dfrac{dy}{dx} = -x^{-2} + \dfrac{3}{x} - 4x^{-3}$

44. $\dfrac{dy}{dx} = -x^{-2} - \dfrac{4}{x} - 6x^{-3}$

45. $f'(x) = 6 + \dfrac{1}{3} \cdot \dfrac{1}{x^2 + 6} \cdot (2x) = 6 + \dfrac{2x}{3(x^2 + 6)}$

46. $f'(x) = 9 + \dfrac{x}{2(x^2 - 12)}$

47. $\dfrac{dy}{dx} = 4\,(e^{-3x^2})(-6x) + 4\dfrac{1}{2x}(2) = -24x(e^{-3x^2}) + \dfrac{4}{x}$

48. $\dfrac{dy}{dx} = 24xe^{6x^2} + \dfrac{5}{x}$

49. To find the equation of a line, we will need the slope, which we find from the derivative. $f'(x) = 3\dfrac{1}{4x^2}(8x) = \dfrac{6}{x}$ The slope at $x = 1$ is $m = f'(1) = \dfrac{6}{1} = 6$.

Next, we use the equation for finding lines:

$$y - y_1 = m(x - x_1)$$

We have $m = 6$ and $(x_1, y_1) = (1, 4.2)$:

$$y - 4.2 = 6(x - 1)$$
$$y - 4.2 = 6x - 6$$
$$y = 6x - 1.8$$

50. $y = 10x - 3.1$

51. To find the equation of a line, we will need the slope, which we find from the derivative. $\dfrac{dy}{dx} = \dfrac{1}{x \ln 4}$ The slope at $x = 2$ is $m = \dfrac{1}{2 \ln 4} \approx 0.36$.

Next, we use the equation for finding lines: $y - y_1 = m(x - x_1)$.

We have $m = 0.36$ and $(x_1, y_1) = (2, 0.5)$:

$$y - 0.5 = 0.36(x - 2)$$
$$y - 0.5 = 0.36x - 0.72$$
$$y = 0.36x - 0.22$$

52. $y = 0.26x - 0.16$

53. Rates call for derivatives. $R'(x) = -800(e^{-0.5x})(-0.5) = 400(e^{-0.5x})$

For $x = 1$: $R'(1) = 400(e^{-0.5(1)}) \approx \$242.61$. Revenue is increasing at $\$242.61/year$.

For $x = 3$: $R'(3) = 400(e^{-0.5(3)}) \approx \$89.25/year$. Revenue is increasing at $\$89.25/yr$.

54. For $= 1$, $R'(1) = \$1608.77/year$. For $x = 3$, $R'(3) = \$722.87/year$.

VC3

Product and Quotient Rules for Derivatives

Consider the function: $y = (3x^2 + 5x)(\ln x)$

This function is the product of two factors. The first factor is $(3x^2 + 5x)$ and the second factor is ln x. Suppose we need to find the derivative of y.

It would be nice if the derivative of y were the derivative of the first factor times the derivative of the second factor, **but it's not**. Instead, we must use the **Product Rule**.

PRODUCT RULE

The derivative of the product is the derivative of the first factor times the second factor, plus the first factor times the derivative of the second factor.
In mathematical notation:

For $y = u(x)v(x)$, $\dfrac{dy}{dx} = u'(x)v(x) + u(x)v'(x)$.

For the function above, $y = (3x^2 + 5x)(\ln x)$, $u(x) = (3x^2 + 5x)$ and $v(x) = \ln x$.

We'll need $u'(x) = 6x + 5$ and $v'(x) = \dfrac{1}{x}$.

Then $\dfrac{dy}{dx} = u'(x)v(x) + u(x)v'(x) = (6x + 5)\ln x + (3x^2 + 5x)\dfrac{1}{x}$

$$= (6x + 5)\ln x + (3x + 5).$$

Example 1:

$f(x) = 3e^x(4x^2 - 6)$ The first factor is: $3e^x$. Its derivative is: $3e^x$.

The second factor is: $(4x^2 - 6)$. Its derivative is: $8x$.

Using the Product Rule in words, we need:

(Derivative of 1st factor)(2nd factor) + (1st factor)(Derivative of 2nd factor)

$f'(x) = 3e^x(4x^2 - 6) + 3e^x(8x) = 3e^x(4x^2 + 8x - 6)$.

Let's do this again using mathematical notation instead; we have $f(x) = u(x)v(x)$.

$u(x) = 3e^x;\ u'(x) = 3e^x;\ v(x) = (4x^2 - 6);\ v'(x) = 8x$

We know $f'(x) = u'(x)v(x) + u(x)v'(x) = 3e^x(4x^2 - 6) + 3e^x(8x)$

Factoring, $f'(x) = 3e^x(4x^2 + 8x - 6)$

If our two factors are both polynomials such as $f(x) = (4x^2 + 3x - 5)(3 + 7 - 4x^2 - x^3)$, we could multiply them out, collect like terms, and then take the derivative as usual. This might get a little tedious, but it's possible to do it without the Product Rule. However, for a product like that in Example 1 above, we would have no choice but to use the Product Rule. Even if we distribute the $3e^x$, we would still have products.

$$f(x) = 3e^x(4x^2 - 6) = 12e^x x^2 - 18e^x$$

The term $12e^x x^2$ is still a product of $(12e^x)$ and (x^2) and we would need to use the Product Rule to find the derivative.

(Technically, there are three factors, 12, e^x, and x^2, but we don't need to use the Product Rule for a constant times a factor with a variable, such as $5x^3$, or $5e^x$. For products that have two or more factors which contain variables, such as $5xe^x$, or $2\pi rh$, we would need the Product Rule. For $5xe^x$ we would use the factors $5x$ and e^x. For the product $2\pi rh$, we would use the factors $2\pi r$ and h.)

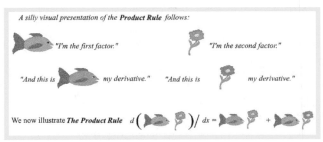

A silly visual presentation of the **Product Rule** follows:

"I'm the first factor."

"I'm the second factor."

"And this is   my derivative."   "And this is   my derivative."

We now illustrate **The Product Rule** $d\left(\ \ \ \ \right)/\ dx =$

Example 2:

Find the derivative of $y=(e^{-5x})(\ln 7x)$

The first factor is e^{-5x}. Its derivative is $e^{-5x}(-5)=-5e^{-5x}$.

The second factor is $\ln 7x$. Its derivative is $\dfrac{1}{7x}\cdot 7=\dfrac{1}{x}$.

Using the Product Rule in words, we need:

(Derivative of 1st factor)(2nd factor) + (1st factor)(Derivative of 2nd factor)

$$\frac{dy}{dx}=(-5e^{-5x})(\ln 7x)+(e^{-5x})\frac{1}{x}.$$

Example 3:

Find the derivative of $y=(e^{-5x})(\ln 7x)$

Again, here's another way to think of the Product Rule.

We think of the product as $y=u(x)v(x)$ where $u(x)=e^{-5x}$ and $v(x)=\ln 7x$.

We know $\dfrac{dy}{dx}=u'(x)v(x)+u(x)v'(x)$. We will need to find $u'(x)$ and $v'(x)$.

$u'(x)=e^{-5x}(-5)=-5e^{-5x}$ and $v'(x)=\dfrac{1}{7x}\cdot 7=\dfrac{1}{x}$.

Now we substitute into the Product Rule: $\dfrac{dy}{dx}=(-5e^{-5x})(\ln 7x)+(e^{-5x})\dfrac{1}{x}$.

Example 4:

Find the derivative for $f(x)=(2x+1)(x^2-3x)$.

Here $f(x)$ is expressed as the of two factors and we may use the Product Rule. Alternatively, we could simply multiply the two factors together and collect like terms to get the polynomial:

$f(x)=2x^3-5x^2-3x$ ⠀⠀⠀and then we could use the Power Rule.

$f'(x)=6x^2-10x-3,$ ⟵

or, using the Product Rule:

$f'(x)=2(x^2-3x)+(2x+1)(2x-3)$ Distributing the 2 and FOILing,

$f'(x)=2x^2-6x+4x^2-6x+2x-3.$ Combining like terms, we have:

$f'(x)=6x^2-10x-3$ which matches the result above. ⟵

Example 5:

Find the derivative of $y = 2\sqrt{x}(4x^5 - 3x^3 - 9)$.

We rewrite $y = 2x^{\frac{1}{2}}(4x^5 - 3x^3 - 9)$.

Then $u(x) = 2x^{\frac{1}{2}}$; $u'(x) = 2\left(\dfrac{1}{2}\right)x^{-\frac{1}{2}} = x^{-\frac{1}{2}}$,

and $v(x) = 4x^5 - 3x^3 - 9$; $v'(x) = 20x^4 - 9x^2$.

$$\frac{dy}{dx} = x^{-\frac{1}{2}}(4x^5 - 3x^3 - 9) + 2x^{\frac{1}{2}}(20x^4 - 9x^2) = \frac{4x^5 - 3x^3 - 9}{\sqrt{x}} + 2\sqrt{x}(20x^4 - 9x^2)$$

If we multiply the second term by $\dfrac{\sqrt{x}}{\sqrt{x}}$ so that both terms will have a common denominator, we have:

$$\frac{4x^5 - 3x^3 - 9}{\sqrt{x}} + 2\sqrt{x}(20x^4 - 9x^2)\frac{\sqrt{x}}{\sqrt{x}} = \frac{4x^5 - 3x^3 - 9 + 2x(20x^4 - 9x^2)}{\sqrt{x}}$$

We distribute the $2x$ and collect like terms to get:

$$\frac{44x^5 - 21x^3 - 9}{\sqrt{x}}, \text{ or } x^{-\frac{1}{2}}(44x^5 - 21x^3 - 9).$$

Example 6:

The weekly labor cost function for Harley's Tractors, Inc. can be modeled by the function $C(x) = (-2.5x^2 + 46x)(-0.08\ln x)$, where x represents number of employees. At what rate are Harley's labor costs increasing with respect to the number of employees? At what rate will the weekly cost increase if Harley employs 100 persons and wants to hire one more?

We need $C'(x)$, which will give us change in cost per change in number of employees, or additional cost per employee. To find $C'(x)$, we need the Product Rule.

$$C'(x) = (-5x + 46)(-0.08\ln x) + (-2.5x^2 + 46x)\left(-.08\frac{1}{x}\right)$$

For $x = 100$,

$$C'(100) = (-5(100) + 46)(-0.08\ln(100)) + (-2.5(100)^2 + 46(100))\left(-.08\frac{1}{100}\right)$$

$\approx \$184$

INTRA-SECTION EXERCISES:

Find the derivatives:

1. $f(x) = (3 - 2x)(3x^2 - 4x)$ 2. $g(x) = e^{2x}(x^2 - 3)$

3. $f(x) = (5 - 2x)(\ln 3x)$

Solutions

1. $f'(x) = -2(3x^2 - 4x) + (3 - 2x)(6x - 4) = -6x^2 + 8x + 18x - 12 - 12x^2 + 8x$
    $= -18x^2 + 34x - 12$

2. $g'(x) = 2e^{2x}(x^2 - 3) + e^{2x}(2x) = 2x^2e^{2x} - 6e^{2x} + 2xe^{2x}$ or $= 2e^{2x}(x^2 + x - 3)$

3. $f'(x) = -2\ln(3x) + (5 - 2x)\dfrac{1}{x}$

THE QUOTIENT RULE

Now consider the function: $y = \dfrac{u(x)}{g(x)}$

It would be nice if the derivative of a quotient were the derivative of the numerator over the derivative of the denominator, **but it isn't**. Instead, to take the derivative of a quotient, we must use the **Quotient Rule**.

QUOTIENT RULE

In words, the derivative of a quotient is the derivative of the numerator times the denominator, minus the derivative of the denominator times the numerator, all over the denominator squared.

In mathematical notation: For $f(x) = \dfrac{u(x)}{v(x)}$, $f'(x) = \dfrac{u'(x)v(x) - u(x)v'(x)}{[v(x)]^2}$

Note that no derivative appears in the denominator.

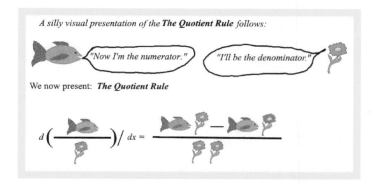

A silly visual presentation of the **The Quotient Rule** follows:

"Now I'm the numerator." "I'll be the denominator."

We now present: **The Quotient Rule**

Example 7:

Find the derivative for $= \dfrac{4x^2 + 2x - 3}{5 + 2x}$.

Let $u(x) = 4x^2 + 2x - 3$, then $u'(x) = 8x + 2$,

and let $v(x) = 5 + 2x$, then $v'(x) = 2$.

Substituting into the Quotient Rule: $\dfrac{dy}{dx} = \dfrac{u'(x)v(x) - u(x)v'(x)}{[v(x)]^2}$,

we have: $\dfrac{dy}{dx} = \dfrac{(8x + 2)(5 + 2x) - (4x^2 + 2x - 3)(2)}{(5 + 2x)^2}$

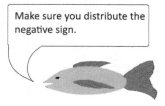

Make sure you distribute the negative sign.

We seldom FOIL the denominator, but we usually multiply out the numerator and collect like terms.

$$\frac{dy}{dx} = \frac{40x + 16x^2 + 10 + 4x - 8x^2 - 4x + 6}{(5 + 2x)^2} = \frac{8x^2 + 40x + 16}{(5 + 2x)^2}$$

Example 8:

Find the derivative for $y = \dfrac{5e^{3x+2}}{5x^2 - 6}$

Let $u(x) = 5e^{3x+2}$, then $u'(x) = (5e^{3x+2})(3) = 15e^{3x+2}$

and let $v(x) = 5x^2 - 6$, then $v'(x) = 10x$.

Substituting into the Quotient Rule: $\dfrac{dy}{dx}=\dfrac{u'(x)v(x)-u(x)v'(x)}{[v(x)]^2}$,

we have $\dfrac{dy}{dx}=\dfrac{(15e^{3x+2})(5x^2-6)-(5e^{3x+2})(10x)}{(5x^2-6)^2}=\dfrac{75x^2e^{3x+2}-90e^{3x+2}-50xe^{3x+2}}{(5x^2-6)^2}$

Example 9:

Find the derivative for $f(x)=\dfrac{\ln(x^2)}{5x^2-6}$.

We let $u(x)=\ln(x^2)$, then $u'(x)=\dfrac{1}{x^2}(2x)=\dfrac{2}{x}$.

We let $v(x)=5x^2-6$, then $v'(x)=10x$.

Substituting into the Quotient Rule: $\dfrac{dy}{dx}=\dfrac{u'(x)v(x)-u(x)v'(x)}{[v(x)]^2}$,

$\dfrac{dy}{dx}=\dfrac{\left(\dfrac{2}{x}\right)(5x^2-6)-\ln(x^2)(10x)}{(5x^2-6)^2}$. We have a complex fraction here, so to

simplify, we multiply the numerator and denominator by all subordinate denominators, in this case just x.

$\dfrac{dy}{dx}=\dfrac{\left[\left(\dfrac{2}{x}\right)(5x^2-6)-\ln(x^2)(10x)\right]}{(5x^2-6)^2}\cdot\dfrac{x}{x}=\dfrac{2(5x^2-6)-\ln(x^2)(10x^2)}{x(5x^2-6)^2}$

It would be "illegal" to cancel the (5x–6), since it is not a factor of both denominator terms.

$\dfrac{dy}{dx}=\dfrac{\left[\left(\dfrac{2}{x}\right)(5x^2-6)-\ln(x^2)(10x)\right]}{(5x^2-6)^2}\cdot\dfrac{x}{x}=\dfrac{2(5x^2-6)-\ln(x^2)(10x^2)}{x(5x^2-6)^2}$

Example 10:

Find the derivative for $f(x)=\dfrac{3}{4x-3}$.

We let $u(x)=3$, then $u'(x)=0$.

We let $v(x)=4x-3$, then $v'(x)=4$.

Substituting into the Quotient Rule: $f'(x) = \dfrac{u'(x)v(x) - u(x)v'(x)}{[v(x)]^2}$,

$$f'(x) = \frac{0(x-3) - 3(4)}{(4x-3)^2} = \frac{-12}{(4x-3)^2}$$

Example 11:

It is found that an experimental drug that promises to sharpen math skills is easily absorbed into the bloodstream. For doses greater than 1 *gram*, the amount absorbed in milligrams can be modeled by the function

$f(x) = \dfrac{.04e^x}{2x}$, where x represents the amount

of the dosage in grams, and $f(x)$ represents the amount absorbed in milligrams.

At what rate is the drug absorbed when the dosage is 5 grams?

To determine a rate, we will need the derivative of $f(x)$.

$$f'(x) = \frac{(.04e^x)(2x) - 2(.04e^x)}{4x^2} = \frac{.08xe^x - .08e^x}{4x^2}$$

For $x = 5$ *grams*, $f'(5) = \dfrac{.08(5)e^5 - .08e^5}{4(5)^2} \approx \dfrac{0.475 \, milligrams \; absorbed}{gram \; dosage}$

INTRA-SECTION EXERCISES:

Find the derivatives:

4. $y = \dfrac{4x}{2x-1}$

5. $f(x) = \dfrac{3e^x}{4x^2 - 7}$

6. $y = \dfrac{5\ln(2x)}{4x^2 - 7}$

Solutions

4. $\dfrac{dy}{dx} = \dfrac{4(2x-1) - 2(4x)}{(2x-1)^2} = \dfrac{8x - 4 - 8x}{(2x-1)^2} = \dfrac{-4}{(2x-1)^2}$

5. $f'(x) = \dfrac{3e^x(4x^2 - 7) - 3e^x(8x)}{(4x^2 - 7)^2} = \dfrac{12x^2e^x - 21e^x - 24xe^x}{(4x^2 - 7)^2}$

If desired, we can factor to: $f'(x) = \dfrac{3e^x(4x^2 - 7 - 8x)}{(4x^2 - 7)^2}$.

6. $\dfrac{dy}{dx} = \dfrac{\frac{5}{x}(4x^2-7)-(8x)(5\ln(2x))}{(4x^2-7)^2}$ Because this is a complex fraction,

we multiply by $\dfrac{x}{x}$.

$$\frac{dy}{dx} = \frac{\left[\frac{5}{x}(4x^2-7)-5(\ln 2x)(8x)\right]}{(4x^2-7)^2} \cdot \frac{x}{x} = \frac{5(4x^2-7)-40x^2\ln(2x)}{x(4x^2-7)^2}$$

$$= \frac{20x^2-35-40x^2\ln(2x)}{x(4x^2-7)^2}$$

PROOF OF THE PRODUCT RULE

In order to prove the Product Rule, it will be necessary to remember the definition of the derivative and the property often called the Zero Property of Addition. That is, adding zero to an algebraic expression does not change the value of the original expression. Neither does adding values with a net of zero.

Now on to the proof.

We let $f(x)=u(x)v(x)$. We will prove that $f'(x)=u'(x)v(x)+u(x)v'(x)$.

We must use the definition for derivative: $f'(x) = \lim\limits_{\Delta x \to 0} \dfrac{f(x+\Delta x)-f(x)}{\Delta x}$.

We note that $f(x+\Delta x)=u(x+\Delta x)v(x+\Delta x)$. We substitute into $f'(x)$.

$$\lim\limits_{\Delta x \to 0} \frac{u(x+\Delta x)v(x+\Delta x)-u(x)v(x)}{\Delta x}$$

Since it is legal to subtract and add the same quantity, for a net of zero, we subtract and add the quantity $u(x+\Delta x)v(x)$ right here: →

$$f'(x) = \lim\limits_{\Delta x \to 0} \frac{u(x+\Delta x)v(x+\Delta x)-u(x+\Delta x)v(x)+u(x+\Delta x)v(x)-u(x)v(x)}{\Delta x}$$

We factor $u(x+\Delta x)$ from the first two terms, and we factor $v(x)$ from the second two terms in the numerator to get:

$$f'(x)=\lim_{\Delta x \to 0} \frac{u(x+\Delta x)[v(x+\Delta x)-v(x)]+v(x)[u(x+\Delta x)-u(x)]}{\Delta x}$$

We decompose the fraction (we "un-add") and use the limit properties for the sum of terms.

$$f'(x)=\lim_{\Delta x \to 0} \frac{u(x+\Delta x)[v(x+\Delta x)+v(x)]}{\Delta x} + \lim_{\Delta x \to 0} \frac{v(x)[u(x+\Delta x)-u(x)]}{\Delta x}$$

We can decompose the function further.

$$f'(x)=\left[\lim_{\Delta x \to 0} u(x+\Delta x)\right]\left[\lim_{\Delta x \to 0} \frac{v(x+\Delta x)+v(x)}{\Delta x}\right] + \left[\lim_{\Delta x \to 0} v(x)\right]\left[\lim_{\Delta x \to 0} \frac{u(x+\Delta x)-u(x)}{\Delta x}\right]$$

We examine each term.

We note that $\lim\limits_{\Delta x \to 0} \dfrac{v(x+\Delta x)+v(x)}{\Delta x}$ is the definition of $v'(x)$, and

further, $\lim\limits_{\Delta x \to 0} \dfrac{u(x+\Delta x)-u(x)}{\Delta x}$ is the definition of $u'(x)$.

We can make these substitutions.

$$f'(x)=\lim_{\Delta x \to 0} u(x+\Delta x)v'(x) + \lim_{\Delta x \to 0} v(x)u'(x).$$

Now to evaluate the limits we replace Δx with 0.

$$f'(x)=u(x+0)v'(x)+v(x)u'(x)=u(x)v'(x)+v(x)u'(x)$$

We have only two steps left. Using the Commutative Law for Addition, we can rearrange the two terms.

$$f'(x)=v(x)u'(x)+u(x)v'(x)$$

Then using the Commutative Law for Multiplication, we have: $f'(x)=u'(x)v(x)+u(x)v'(x)$.

Q.E.D.

PROOF OF THE QUOTIENT RULE

We let $f(x)=\dfrac{u(x)}{v(x)}$. Then we will prove that $f'(x)=\dfrac{u'(x)v(x)-u(x)v'(x)}{[v(x)]^2}$.

Again, we must use the definition for the derivative: $f'(x)=\lim\limits_{\Delta x\to 0}\dfrac{f(x+\Delta x)-f(x)}{\Delta x}$.

Because $f(x)=\dfrac{u(x)}{v(x)}$, then $f(x+\Delta x)=\dfrac{u(x+\Delta x)}{v(x+\Delta x)}$. We substitute $f(x)$ and $f(x+\Delta x)$ into our definition.

$$f'(x)=\lim\limits_{\Delta x\to 0}\dfrac{\dfrac{u(x+\Delta x)}{v(x+\Delta x)}-\dfrac{u(x)}{v(x)}}{\Delta x}$$

This is definitely a complex fraction. We multiply the numerator and denominator by $v(x+\Delta x)v(x)$.

$$f'(x)=\lim\limits_{\Delta x\to 0}\dfrac{\left[\dfrac{u(x+\Delta x)}{v(x+\Delta x)}-\dfrac{u(x)}{v(x)}\right]}{\Delta x}\cdot\dfrac{[v(x+\Delta x)v(x)]}{[v(x+\Delta x)v(x)]}=$$

We distribute and then reduce. All the subordinate denominators should disappear.

$$f'(x)=\lim\limits_{\Delta x\to 0}\dfrac{\dfrac{u(x+\Delta x)v(x+\Delta x)v(x)}{v(x+\Delta x)}-\dfrac{u(x)v(x+\Delta x)v(x)}{v(x)}}{\Delta x[v(x+\Delta x)v(x)]}=$$

$$\lim\limits_{\Delta x\to 0}\dfrac{u(x+\Delta x)v(x)-u(x)v(x+\Delta x)}{\Delta x[v(x+\Delta x)v(x)]}$$

In the numerator, we are going to subtract and add $u(x)v(x)$.

$$f\Delta(x)=\lim\limits_{\Delta x\to 0}\dfrac{u(x+\Delta x)v(x)-u(x)v(x)+u(x)v(x)-u(x)v(x+\Delta x)}{\Delta x[v(x+\Delta x)v(x)]}$$

In the first two terms, we can factor out $v(x)$ and in the second two terms, we can factor out $u(x)$.

$$f'(x)=\lim\limits_{\Delta x\to 0}\dfrac{v(x)[u(x+\Delta x)-u(x)]+u(x)[v(x)-v(x+\Delta x)]}{\Delta x[v(x+\Delta x)v(x)]}$$

Let's switch the last two terms around (using the old Commutative Law for Addition) and factoring out a negative sign.

$$f'(x)=\lim\limits_{\Delta x\to 0}\dfrac{v(x)[u(x+\Delta x)-u(x)]-u(x)[v(x+\Delta)-v(x)]}{\Delta x[v(x+\Delta x)v(x)]}$$

We decompose the fraction (i.e., "un-adding") and use a limit law.

$$f'(x)=\lim_{\Delta x \to 0}\frac{v(x)[u(x+\Delta x)-u(x)]}{\Delta x[v(x+\Delta x)v(x)]}-\lim_{\Delta x \to 0}\frac{u(x)[v(x+\Delta)-v(x)]}{\Delta x[v(x+\Delta x)v(x)]}$$

We can decompose even further: $f'(x)$

$$=\left[\lim_{\Delta x \to 0}\frac{v(x)}{v(x+\Delta x)v(x)}\right]\left[\lim_{\Delta x \to 0}\frac{u(x+\Delta x)-u(x)}{\Delta x}\right]-\left[\lim_{\Delta x \to 0}\frac{u(x)}{v(x+\Delta x)v(x)}\right]\left[\lim_{\Delta x \to 0}\frac{v(x+\Delta x)-v(x)}{\Delta x}\right]$$

In the first term, we note that $\lim_{\Delta x \to 0}\dfrac{u(x+\Delta x)-u(x)}{\Delta x}$ is our definition of $u'(x)$,

and in the second term, we note that $\lim_{\Delta x \to 0}\dfrac{v(x+\Delta x)-v(x)}{\Delta x}$ is our definition of $v'(x)$.

Substituting, we have: $f'(x)=\lim_{\Delta x \to 0}\dfrac{v(x)}{[v(x+\Delta x)v(x)]}\cdot u'(x)-\lim_{\Delta x \to 0}\dfrac{u(x)}{\left[v(x+\Delta x)v(x)\right]}\cdot v'(x).$

But as $\Delta x \to 0$, $v(x+\Delta x)\to v(x)$ and $u(x+\Delta x)\to u(x)$, so the expression above becomes:

$$f'(x)=\frac{v(x)u'(x)}{v(x)v(x)}-\frac{u(x)v'(x)}{v(x)v(x)}.$$

Now we can use the old Commutative Law for Multiplication to rewrite the first numerator from $v(x)u'(x)$ to $u'(x)v(x)$ and the second numerator from $u(x)v'(x)$ to $v'(x)u(x)$. We also rewrite the denominators as $[v(x)]^2$.

$$f'(x)=\frac{u'(x)v(x)}{[v(x)]^2}-\frac{v'(x)u(x)}{[v(x)]^2}$$

Finally, since the fractions have a common denominator, we can combine the numerators.

$$f'(x)=\frac{u'(x)v(x)-u(x)v'(x)}{[v(x)]^2}$$

Q.E.D.

VC3 PRODUCT AND QUOTIENT RULES FOR DERIVATIVES EXERCISES

For numbers 1–16, find the derivatives.

1. $f(x)=\sqrt{x}(x^2-3)$

2. $f(x)=\sqrt{x}(x^2+4)$

3. $g(x)=4(x^2-3)$

4. $g(x)=7(x^2-5)$

5. $y=5e^x(x^2+3)$

6. $y=3e^x(x^2-7)$

7. $y=\dfrac{3x}{4x+2}$

8. $y=\dfrac{4x}{3x-2}$

9. $f(x)=\dfrac{7}{4x+2}$

10. $f(x)=\dfrac{4}{5x+2}$

11. $g(x)=\dfrac{4e^x}{5x-3}$

12. $g(x)=\dfrac{6e^x}{3x-5}$

13. $h(x)=\dfrac{4x}{6-\ln x}$

14. $h(x)=\dfrac{4x}{(\ln x)+6}$

15. $y=\dfrac{3x}{2x^2-6}$

16. $y=\dfrac{-4x}{3x^2-6}$

For numbers 17 through 20, find the value of the derivative at the given point.

17. $f(x)=\dfrac{2x-1}{5-x}$ (4, 7)

18. $f(x)=\dfrac{1-2x}{x+4}$ (−3, 7)

19. $g(t)=\dfrac{t^2-4}{t+1}$ (1, 2)

20. $g(t)=\dfrac{t^2-3}{t-2}$ (3, 2)

21. Find the equation of the tangent to the function $y=3e^x(2x-1)$ at the point (0,−3).

22. Find the equation of the tangent to the function $y=-2e^x(5x+1)$ at the point (0,−2).

23. Find the point(s) at which the graph of $f(x)$ has a horizontal tangent. $y=\dfrac{x^2}{x+1}$

24. Find the point(s) at which the graph of $f(x)$ has a horizontal tangent. $y = \dfrac{2x^2}{3+x}$

25. It is determined that the information disseminated through a certain televised ad will reach an audience of $P(t) = -3t^2 + 280.3t + 2400$, where t represents days since the ad is first aired, and P represents the number of people receiving the ad. At what rate will the audience (people receiving the ad) be growing after the ad has aired for 10 days? For 50 days?

26. It is determined that the information disseminated through a certain radio ad will reach an audience of $P(t) = -5.4t^2 + 460.8t + 3200$, where t represents days since the ad is first aired, and P represents the number of people receiving the ad. At what rate will the audience (people receiving the ad) be growing after the ad has aired for 10 days? For 50 days?

VC3 PRODUCT AND QUOTIENT RULES FOR DERIVATIVES
SOLUTIONS TO EXERCISES

1. $f(x) = x^{\frac{1}{2}}(x^2 - 3);\ f'(x) = \frac{1}{2}x^{-\frac{1}{2}}(x^2 - 3) + x^{\frac{1}{2}}(2x) = \frac{x^2 - 3}{2\sqrt{x}} + 2x\sqrt{x}$

2. $f'(x) = \frac{x^2 + 4}{2\sqrt{x}} + 2x\sqrt{x}$

3. $g'(x) = 0(x^2 - 3) + 4(2x) = 8x$ 4. $g'(x) = 14x$

5. $\frac{dy}{dx} = 5e^x(x^2 + 3) + 5e^x(2x) = 5x^2e^x + 15e^x + 10xe^x$ or $\frac{dy}{dx} = 5e^x(x^2 + 2x + 3)$

6. $\frac{dy}{dx} = 3x^2e^x - 21e^x + 6xe^x$ or $\frac{dy}{dx} = 3e^x(x^2 + 2x - 7)$

7. $\frac{dy}{dx} = \frac{3(4x + 2) - 4(3x)}{(4x + 2)^2} = \frac{12x + 6 - 12x}{(4x + 2)^2} = \frac{6}{(4x + 2)^2}$ 8. $\frac{dy}{dx} = \frac{-8}{(3x - 2)^2}$

9. $f'(x) = \frac{0(4x + 2) - 4(7)}{(4x + 2)^2} = \frac{-28}{(4x + 2)^2}$ 10. $f'(x) = \frac{-20}{(5x + 2)^2}$

11. $g'(x) = \frac{4e^x(5x - 3) - 5(4e^x)}{(5x - 3)^2} = \frac{20xe^x - 12e^x - 20e^x}{(5x - 3)^2} = \frac{20xe^x - 32e^x}{(5x - 3)^2}$ or

$g'(x) = \frac{4e^x(5x - 8)}{(5x - 3)^2}$

12. $g'(x) = \frac{18xe^x - 48e^x}{(3x - 5)^2}$ or $g'(x) = \frac{6e^x(3x - 8)}{(3x - 5)^2}$

13. $h'(x) = \frac{4(6 - \ln x) - \frac{1}{x}(4x)}{(6 - \ln x)^2} = \frac{24 - 4\ln x + 4}{(6 - \ln x)^2} = \frac{28 - 4\ln x}{(6 - \ln x)^2}$ or $h'(x) = \frac{4(7 - \ln x)}{(6 - \ln x)^2}$

14. $h'(x) = \frac{4\ln(x) + 20}{(\ln x + 6)^2}$ or $h'(x) = \frac{4(\ln(x) + 5)}{(\ln x + 6)^2}$

15. $\frac{dy}{dx} = \frac{3(2x^2 - 6) - 4x(3x)}{(2x^2 - 6)^2} = \frac{6x^2 - 18 - 12x^2}{(2x^2 - 6)^2} = \frac{-6x^2 - 18}{(2x^2 - 6)^2}$ or $\frac{dy}{dx} = \frac{-6(x^2 + 3)}{(2x^2 - 6)^2}$

16. $\frac{dy}{dx} = \frac{12x^2 + 24}{(3x^2 - 6)^2}$ or $\frac{dy}{dx} = \frac{12(x^2 + 2)}{(3x^2 - 6)^2}$

17. $f'(x) = \dfrac{2(5-x) - -1(2x-1)}{(5-x)^2} = \dfrac{10 - 2x + 2x - 1}{(5-x)^2} = \dfrac{9}{(5-x)^2}$;

   At $x = 4$, $f'(4) = \dfrac{9}{(5-4)^2} = 9$

18. $f'(-3) = -9$

19. $g'(t) = \dfrac{2t(t+1) - 1(t^2 - 4)}{(t+1)^2} = \dfrac{t^2 + 2t + 4}{(t+1)^2}$; At $t = 1$, $g'(1) = \dfrac{(1)^2 + 2(1) + 4}{(1+1)^2} = \dfrac{7}{4}$

20. $g'(3) = 0$

21. We will need the slope at $x = 0$. $\dfrac{dy}{dx} = 3e^x(2x-1) + 3e^x(2) = 6xe^x + 3e^x$

   For $x = 0$, $m = 6(0)e^0 + 3e^0 = 3$

   Then, to find the equation of the tangent we use: $y - y_1 = m(x - x_1)$,

   where $(x_1, y_1) = (0, -3)$ and $m = 3$. $y - -3 = 3(x - 0)$

   $$y = 3x - 3$$

22. $y = -12x - 2$

23. We need the points where the slope of the tangent equals zero, i.e., where

   $\dfrac{dy}{dx} = 0$.

   $\dfrac{dy}{dx} = \dfrac{2x(x+1) - x^2}{(x+1)^2} = \dfrac{x^2 + 2x}{(x+1)^2} = 0$ A fraction equals zero where its

   numerator equals zero, so we set: $x^2 + 2x = 0$

   $$x(x+2) = 0$$

   $x = 0, x = -2$ To find the points, we will also need the y-values.

   To find y at $x = 0$, we need $y = \dfrac{0^2}{0+1} = 0$ One of the points is (0, 0).

   To find y at $x = -2$, we need $y = \dfrac{(-2)^2}{(-2)+1} = -4$ The other point is $(-2, -4)$.

   One more thing—we want to make sure that the denominator of $y = \dfrac{x^2}{x+1}$ does not equal zero at either $x = 0$, or $x = -2$. It doesn't.

   Therefore, the function has horizontal tangents at the points (0, 0) and $(-2, -4)$.

24. (0,0) and $(-6, -24)$

25. To find a rate, we will need $P'(t) = -6t + 280.3$.

    At $t = 10$ *days*, $P'(10) = -6(10) + 280.3 \approx 220$. This represents an increase of 220 new audience members per day.
    At $t = 50$ *days*, $P'(50) = -6(50) + 280.3 \approx -20$. The audience is decreasing by 20 audience members per day.

26. At $t = 10$, there is an increase of approximately 353 new audience members per day. At $t = 50$, there is a decrease of approximately 79 audience members per day.

VC4

The Chain Rule

One of the algebraic operations on functions is composition: $f(g(x))$. It's read f of g of x.

For example, when $f(u)=\sqrt{u}$ and $g(x)=3x^2-5x$, we have the composition

$$y=f(g(x))=\sqrt{3x^2-5x}.$$

In a composition like this, one function, $3x^2-5x$, is inside another function, $\sqrt{}$.

The **Chain Rule** gives the derivative of a composition of functions in terms of the individual functions. The Chain Rule for the derivative of $y=f(g(x))$ is $\dfrac{dy}{dx}=f'(u)\cdot g'(x)$.

For $y=\sqrt{3x^2-5x}$, we have $f(u)=\sqrt{u}=u^{\frac{1}{2}}$, and $u=g(x)=3x^2-5x$.

Then $f'(u)=\dfrac{1}{2}u^{-\frac{1}{2}}$ and $g'(x)=6x-5$. We can substitute into: $\dfrac{dy}{dx}=f'(u)\cdot g'(x)$, where $u=g(x)$.

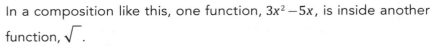

$$\frac{dy}{dx}=\left(\frac{1}{2}u^{-\frac{1}{2}}\right)(6x-5)=\frac{6x-5}{2\sqrt{u}}, \qquad \text{but } u=g(x)=3x^2-5x, \text{ so}$$

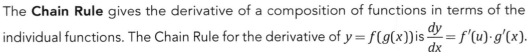

$$\frac{dy}{dx}=\frac{6x-5}{2\sqrt{u}}=\frac{6x-5}{2\sqrt{3x^2-5x}}.$$

Here's another way to look at it. Because of the position in the notation $f(g(x))$, $g(x)$ is referred to (loosely) as the "inside function," and $f(u)$ is referred to (loosely) as the "outside function." If $y=f(g(x))$, with these terms the Chain Rule is stated as the derivative of y equals the derivative of the "outside" function times the derivative of the "inside" function.

In the example above, $y = f(g(x)) = \sqrt{3x^2 - 5x}$.

The "outside function" would be: $\sqrt{inside\ function}$ or $(inside\ function)^{\frac{1}{2}}$.

Its derivative would be $\frac{1}{2}(inside\ function)^{-\frac{1}{2}}$ or $\frac{1}{2\sqrt{inside\ function}}$.

The "inside function" is $3x^2 - 5x$.

So the derivative of the "outside function" is: $\frac{1}{2\sqrt{3x^2 - 5x}}$.

The "inside function" would be: $g(x) = 3x^2 - 5x$. Its derivative is: $6x - 5$.

The derivative of the outside function times the derivative of the inside function is therefore:

$$\frac{dy}{dx} = \frac{1}{2\sqrt{3x^2 - 5x}}(6x - 5) = \frac{6x - 5}{2\sqrt{3x^2 - 5x}}, \text{ just as we had before.}$$

CHAIN RULE

For $y = f(g(x))$, $y'(x) = f'(u)g'(x)$ where $u = g(x)$.

In words, we could say if $y = f(g(x))$, then the derivative of y equals the derivative of the "outside" function times the derivative of the "inside" function.

Example 1:

Find the derivative of $y = (2x^3 - 3x + 7)^4$.

$f(u) = u^4$ and $g(x) = 2x^3 - 3x + 7$ Then $y = f(g(x))$.

$f'(u) = 4u^3$ and $g'(x) = 6x^2 - 3$ so that

$$\frac{dy}{dx} = f'(u)g'(x) = (4u^3)(6x^2 - 3) = (4(g(x)^3)(6x^2 - 3) =$$

$$(4(2x^3 - 3x + 7)^3)(6x^2 - 3)$$

Or using another method: Consider $y = (2x^3 - 3x + 7)^4$ as one function inside another.

The outside function is $(inside\ function)^4$ or some function to the 4th power. Its derivative would be $4(inside\ function)^3$. The inside function doesn't change, it remains $2x^3 - 3x + 7$.

So $4(\textit{inside function})^3 = 4(2x^3 - 3x + 7)^3$.

The inside function is $2x^3 - 3x + 7$. Its derivative is $6x^2 - 3$.

Remember the derivative of y equals the derivative of the outside function times the derivative of the inside function.

$$\frac{dy}{dx} = (4(2x^3 - 3x + 7)^3)(6x^2 - 3)$$

Example 2:

Find the derivative of $y = 4e^{2x^3 - 2x}$.

$f(u) = 4e^u$ and $g(x) = 2x^3 - 2x$ then $y = f(g(x))$.

Now $f'(u) = 4e^u$ and $g'(x) = 6x^2 - 2$ so that

$$\frac{dy}{dx} = f'(u)g'(x) = (4e^u)(6x^2 - 2) = (4e^{2x^3 - 2x})(6x^2 - 2).$$

The method used to find this derivative in Section VC2 was actually a use of the Chain Rule.

INTRA-SECTION EXERCISES:

Calculate the derivatives:

1. $y = (3x^2 + 4x)^5$
2. $y = \sqrt[3]{5x^2 + 6}$
3. $y = 6e^{-5x^2 + 7x}$

Solutions

1. $f(u) = u^5$; $g(x) = 3x^2 + 4x$ then $y = f(g(x))$.

   $f'(u) = 5u^4$; $g'(x) = 6x + 4$;

   $$\frac{dy}{dx} = f'(u)g'(x) = (5u^4)(6x + 4) = (5(3x^2 + 4x)^4)(6x + 4).$$

   (Alternative Method): We can use the Outside-Inside Method because we have one function inside another; that is, we have the composition of functions.

   The outside function is: $(\textit{inside function})^5$. Its derivative is: $5(\textit{inside function})^4$.

   The inside function is: $3x^2 + 4x$. Its derivative is: $6x + 4$. For $\dfrac{dy}{dx}$ we need the derivative of the outside function times the derivative of the inside function.

   $$\text{Therefore: } \frac{dy}{dx} = 5(3x^2 + 4x)^4(6x + 4).$$

2. $y = (5x^2 + 6)^{\frac{1}{3}}$; $f(u) = u^{\frac{1}{3}}$; $g(x) = 5x^2 + 6$; then $y = f(g(x))$.

$$f'(u) = \frac{1}{3}u^{-\frac{2}{3}}; \ g'(x) = 10x; \ \frac{dy}{dx} = f'(u)g'(x) = \left(\frac{1}{3}u^{-\frac{2}{3}}\right)(10x) = \left(\frac{1}{3}(5x^2 + 6)^{-\frac{2}{3}}\right)(10x)$$

(Alternative Method): We can use the Outside-Inside method because we have one function inside another; that is, we have the composition of functions.

First, we rewrite our function as: $y = (5x^2 + 6)^{\frac{1}{3}}$.

The outside function is: $(inside \ function)^{\frac{1}{3}}$. Its derivative is:

$\frac{1}{3}(inside \ function)^{-\frac{2}{3}}$.

The inside function is: $5x^2 + 6$. Its derivative is: $10x$.

For $\frac{dy}{dx}$ we need the derivative of the outside function times the derivative of the inside function.

$$\text{Therefore: } \frac{dy}{dx} = \frac{1}{3}(5x^2 + 6)^{-\frac{2}{3}}(10x)$$

3. $f(u) = 6e^u$; $g(x) = -5x^2 + 7x$; then $y = f(g(x))$

$f'(u) = 6e^u$; $g'(x) = -10x + 7$; then $y = f(g(x))$

$$\frac{dy}{dx} = f'(u)g'(x) = (6e^u)(-10x + 7) = (6e^{-5x^2 + 7x})(-10x + 7)$$

A silly visual presentation of **The Chain Rule** *follows:*

Let $g(x) =$ and its derivative be:

Let $f(u) =$ and its derivative be:

That gives us a *Chain Rule* for: $y = f(g(x)) =$ Couldn't find a ship in a *bottle*, eh?

Then $\frac{dy}{dx} =$

DERIVATIVES OF QUOTIENTS

The derivatives of some functions require the use of more than one derivative rule.

A new cartoon series is in production based on a very popular children's superhero movie. The number of viewers (in ten thousands) is projected as:

$$P(x) = \frac{(x^2 + 20)^{0.82}}{-e^{2x}} + 10,$$

where x represents the number of episodes aired. Suppose the producers want to find the rate at which viewership grows.

They will need the derivative of $P(x)$. Clearly, the Quotient Rule is needed. We also note that the numerator has one function inside another function, so the Chain Rule will also be needed.

We recall that the quotient rule for $f(x) = \dfrac{u(x)}{v(x)}$ is: $f'(x) = \dfrac{u'(x)v(x) - u(x)v'(x)}{[v(x)]^2}$.

We let $u(x) = (x^2 + 20)^{0.82}$, but this is the composition of two functions. We will need the Chain Rule, too.

> We let $f(\hat{u}) = \hat{u}^{0.82}$. [We've already used the letter u for the numerator, so we'll use the letter $\hat{u}$ for the inside function.]
>
> We let $g(x) = x^2 + 20$. Then we have $u(x) = y = f(g(x))$.
>
> $f'(\hat{u}) = 0.82\hat{u}^{-0.18}$ and $g'(x) = 2x$.
>
> Then $u'(x) = f'(\hat{u})g'(x) = (0.82\hat{u}^{-0.18})(2x) = 0.82(x^2 + 20)^{-0.18}(2x)$
>
> $\qquad = 1.64x(x^2 + 20)^{-0.18}$.

To continue with the Quotient Rule, we have our $u'(x) = 1.64x(x^2 + 20)^{-0.18}$.

We let $v(x) = -e^{2x}$. Then $v'(x) = -e^{2x}(2) = -2e^{2x}$.

$$f'(x) = \frac{u'(x)v(x) - u(x)v'(x)}{[v(x)]^2} = \frac{(1.64x(x^2 + 20)^{-0.18})(-e^{2x}) - (x^2 + 20)^{0.82}(-2e^{2x})}{[-e^{2x}]^2}$$

Since all three terms contain $-e^{2x}$, we can factor one $-e^{2x}$ from each term, giving us:

$$f'(x) = \frac{(-1.64x(x^2+20)^{-0.18}) + 2(x^2+20)^{0.82}}{-e^{2x}}.$$

Here's the same problem using the outside-inside method in conjunction with the Quotient Rule.

Recall: $P(x) = \dfrac{(x^2+20)^{0.82}}{-e^{2x}} + 10$

To begin the Quotient Rule, we need the derivative of the numerator, $u'(x)$, but we see that the numerator has one function inside another; i.e., the composition of functions.

The outside function is: $(inside\ function)^{0.82}$. $- - - - - - \blacktriangleright$

Its derivative is: $0.82 (inside\ function)^{-0.18}$. $- - - - - - \blacktriangleright$

The inside function is: (x^2+20). $- - - - - - - - \blacktriangleright$

Its derivative is: $2x$. $- - - - - - - - - - - \blacktriangleright$

For the derivative of the numerator, we need the derivative of the outside function times the derivative of the inside function.

Therefore, the derivative of the numerator is:

$$0.82(x^2+20)^{-0.18}(2x) = u'(x) = 1.64x(x^2+20)^{-0.18}.$$

Now to return to the Quotient Rule. We need:

$$\frac{dy}{dx} = \frac{u'(x)v(x) - u(x)v'(x)}{[v(x)]^2}.$$

The numerator $u(x) = (x^2+20)^{0.82}$.

Its derivative is $u'(x) = 1.64x(x^2+20)^{-0.18}$.

The denominator $v(x) = -e^{2x}$. Its derivative is $v'(x) = -e^{2x}(2) = -2e^{2x}$.

Therefore $\dfrac{dy}{dx} = \dfrac{[1.64x(x^2+20)^{-0.18}](-e^{2x})-[(x^2+20)^{0.82}(-2e^{2x})]}{[-e^{2x}]^2}$.

This brings us back to the same place as the preceding method, and we can once again factor $-e^{2x}$ from each term as before to yield:

$$f'(x) = \dfrac{(-1.64x(x^2+20)^{-0.18})+2(x^2+20)^{0.82}}{-e^{2x}}.$$

If we use the Chain Rule, we no longer need the Quotient Rule. Suppose we need the derivative of the function $y = \dfrac{3x^2-6x}{2x^2+5x-6}$. This expression for y can be written:

$$y = (3x^2-6x)(2x^2+5x-6)^{-1}.$$

The function y is now the product of two factors. We'll designate them $G(x) = 3x^2-6x$ and $H(x) = (2x^2+5x-6)^{-1}$. The Product Rule requires the derivative of $G(x)$ and the derivative of $H(x)$. [Recall: $\dfrac{dy}{dx} = G'(x)H(x)+G(x)H'(x)$.] The derivative of $G(x)$ is $6x-6$. The derivative of $H(x)$ requires the Chain Rule, where $H(x) = f(g(x))$, with $f(u) = u^{-1}$ and $g(x) = 2x^2+5x-6$.

Now $f'(u) = -u^{-2}$ and $g'(x) = 4x+5$,

so that $H'(x) = f'(u)g'(x) = (-u^{-2})(4x+5)$

$= (-(g(x))^{-2})(4x+5) = (-(2x^2+5x-6)^{-2})(4x+5)$

$= -(4x+5)(2x^2+5x-6)^{-2}$.

Returning to $y = (3x^2-6x)(2x^2+5-6)^{-1}$,

and the product rule $\dfrac{dy}{dx} = G'(x)H(x)+G(x)H'(x)$, we can substitute to get:

$\dfrac{dy}{dx} = (6x-6)(2x^2+5x-6)^{-1}+(3x^2-6x)(-(4x+5)(2x^2+5x-6)^{-2})$.

Next, we factor $(2x^2+5x-6)^{-2}$ from each term.

$\dfrac{dy}{dx} = (2x^2+5x-6)^{-2}[(6x-6)(2x^2+5x-6)^1-(3x^2-6x)(4x+5)]$

Then we FOIL.

$$\frac{dy}{dx} = (2x^2+5x-6)^{-2}[12x^3+30x^2-36x-12x^2-30x+36-12x^3-15x^2+24x^2+30x] \text{ and}$$

combine like terms: $\frac{dy}{dx} = (2x^2+5x-6)^{-2}[27x^2-36x+36]$.

Here's the same procedure by which we don't need the Quotient Rule using the Outside-Inside Method.

Recall: $y = \frac{3x^2-6x}{2x^2+5-6}$ but the expression can be written $y = (3x^2-6x)(2x^2+5x-6)^{-1}$.

We need to use the Product Rule. [Recall: $\frac{dy}{dx} = G'(x)H(x)+G(x)H'(x)$] The first factor, $G(x) = 3x^2-6x$, and $G'(x) = 6x-6$.

The second factor $H(x) = (2x^2+5x-6)^{-1}$. To find $H'(x)$, we need the Chain Rule.

The outside function is: (*inside function*)$^{-1}$

and its derivative is: $-($*inside function*$)^{-2}$.

The inside function is $(2x^2+5x-6)$ and its derivative is $4x+5$.

Therefore, the derivative of the second factor $H'(x) = -(2x^2+5x-6)^{-2}(4x+5)$.

Substituting into the Product Rule: $\frac{dy}{dx} = G'(x)H(x)+G(x)H'(x)$ yields:

$$\frac{dy}{dx} = (6x-6)(2x^2+5x-6)^{-1}+(3x^2-6x)[-(2x^2+5x-6)^{-2}(4x+5)] =$$

Factor out a common factor with the least exponent:

$$(2x^2+5x-6)^{-2}[(6x-6)(2x^2+5x-6)-(3x^2-6x)(4x+5)] =$$

Expand and collect like terms:

$$(2x^2+5x-6)^{-2}[(12x^3+30x^2-36x-12x^2-30x+36)-(12x^3+15x^2-24x^2-30x)]$$

$$= (2x^2+5x-6)^{-2}[27x^2-36x+36].$$

INTRA-SECTION EXERCISES:

Find the derivatives.

4. $y = \dfrac{(2x^2 + 5x)^5}{6x - 7}$ 5. $y = 6e^{5x^2 + 9}$ 6. $y = \dfrac{3x^2 - 4}{(5x + 6)^4}$

Solutions

4. We need the quotient rule plus the Chain Rule for the derivative of the numerator. Alternatively, we could write the problem as: $y = (2x^2 + 5x)^5(6x - 7)^{-1}$.

   Using the first method with the Quotient Rule, $y = \dfrac{u(x)}{v(x)}$ where $u(x) = (2x^2 + 5x)^5$

   and $v(x) = 6x - 7$. We know $\dfrac{dy}{dx} = \dfrac{u'(x)v(x) - u(x)v'(x)}{[v(x)]^2}$. We'll start with $u(x)$.

   We'll need the Chain Rule to find $u'(x)$. If $u(x) = f(\hat{u})g(x)$, then $f(\hat{u}) = \hat{u}^5$ and $g(x) = 2x^2 + 5x$.

   Then $f'(\hat{u}) = 5\hat{u}^4$ and $g'(x) = 4x + 5$.
   Then $u'(x) = f'(\hat{u})g'(x) = 5\hat{u}^4(4x + 5) = 5(2x^2 + 5x)^4(4x + 5)$.
   The denominator, $v(x) = 6x - 7$ has derivative: $v'(x) = 6$.

   $\dfrac{dy}{dx} = \dfrac{5(2x^2 + 5x)^4(4x + 5)(6x - 7) - (2x^2 + 5x)^5(6)}{(6x - 7)^2}$. We can factor $(2x^2 + 5x)^4$ from

   each term in the numerator. $\dfrac{dy}{dx} = \dfrac{(2x^2 + 5x)^4[5(4x + 5)(6x - 7) - (2x^2 + 5x)(6)]}{(6x - 7)^2}$

   Then by expanding and collecting like terms, we have:
   $\dfrac{dy}{dx} = \dfrac{(2x^2 + 5x)^4(108x^2 - 20x - 175)}{(6x - 7)^2}$.

5. If we use the Chain Rule here, $y = f(g(x))$, where $f(u) = 6e^u$ and $g(x) = 5x^2 + 9$.

   Then $f'(u) = 6e^u$ and $g'(x) = 10x$. $\dfrac{dy}{dx} = f'(u)g'(x) = 6e^u(10x) = (6e^{5x^2 + 9})10x$

   Therefore $\dfrac{dy}{dx} = 60xe^{5x^2 + 9}$.

6. We need the Quotient Rule plus the Chain Rule for the derivative of the denominator.

Alternatively, we could write the problem as: $y=(3x^2-4)(5x+6)^{-4}$ and use the Product Rule and the Chain Rule.

Using the second method, $y=G(x)H(x)$ where $G(x)=3x^2-4$. Then $G'(x)=6x$.

$H(x)=(5x+6)^{-4}$ and we'll use the Outside-Inside Method of the Chain Rule to find

$H'(x)$. The outside function is $(inside\ function)^{-4}$.

The derivative of the outside function is $-4(inside\ function)^{-5}$.

The inside function is $5x+6$. Its derivative is 5.

$H'(x)=(-4(inside\ function)^{-5})(5)=-20(5x+6)^{-5}$

For the product rule, $\dfrac{dy}{dx}=G'(x)H(x)+G(x)H'(x)$. Substituting gives us:

$\dfrac{dy}{dx}=6x(5x+6)^{-4}+(3x^2-4)[-20(5x+6)^{-5}]$.

We can factor $(5x+6)^{-5}$ from each term.

$\dfrac{dy}{dx}=(5x+6)^{-5}[(6x)(5x+6)^{1}+(3x^2-4)(-20)]$ and expand

$\dfrac{dy}{dx}=(5x+6)^{-5}[30x^2+36x-60x^2+80]=(5x+6)^{-5}(-30x^2+36x+80)$ or

$\dfrac{dy}{dx}=\dfrac{-30x^2+36x+80}{(5x+6)^5}$

THE CHAIN RULE WITH LOGARITHMS

Let $y=\ln(5x^2+6)$. In section VC2, we learned that $\dfrac{dy}{dx}=\dfrac{10x}{5x^2+6}$.

This was actually the Chain Rule at work because $y=\ln(5x^2+6)$ is a composition of the functions $f(u)=\ln u$, and $g(x)=(5x^2+6)$. To use the Chain Rule, we need $f'(u)=\dfrac{1}{u}$

and $g'(x)=10x$. Using $\dfrac{dy}{dx}=f'(u)g'(x)$, we find that $\dfrac{dy}{dx}=\dfrac{1}{u}(10x)=\dfrac{1}{5x^2+6}\cdot 10x=\dfrac{10x}{5x^2+6}$.

Using the Outside-Inside Method, the outside function is: ln(*inside function*).

Its derivative is $\dfrac{1}{(inside\ function)}$.

The inside function is: Its derivative is: $10x$.
$5x^2 + 6$.

Since $\dfrac{dy}{dx}$ equals the derivative of the outside function times the derivative of the inside function,

$$\frac{dy}{dx} = \frac{1}{(inside\ function)} \cdot 10x = \frac{10x}{5x^2 + 6}.$$

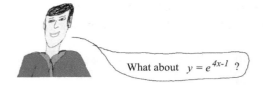

What about $y = e^{4x-1}$?

That's actually the use of the Chain Rule, too, although it doesn't really look like an "inside" and an "outside" function.

For $y = e^{4x-1}$, the outside function is $e^{(inside\ function)}$ and the inside function is $4x - 1$.

The derivative of $e^{(inside\ function)}$ is $e^{(inside\ function)}$.

The derivative of $4x - 1$ is 4.

Therefore $\dfrac{dy}{dx} = (e^{4x-1})(4)$ or $4(e^{4x-1})$.

One final example with logarithms.

Example 3:

Demand is growing for Aunt Ulalee's Frozen Frog Leg Dinners. Revenue can be modeled by the function $R(x) = 7\log_3(6.4x^2)$ where $R(x)$ represents revenue and x represents the number of years in business since 2000. Potential investors want to determine the growth rate for the company. At what rate is revenue expected to grow in the year 2020?

For the growth rate, we will need $R'(x)$.

If we think of $R(x)$ as the composition of functions, $R(x) = F(g(x))$ with $F(u) = 7\log_3 u$ and $g(x) = 6.4x^2$.

Then $R'(x) = F'(u)g'(x)$. $F'(u) = 7\frac{1}{u} \cdot \frac{1}{\ln 3} = \frac{7}{\ln 3} \cdot \frac{1}{u} = \frac{6.37}{u}$ and $g'(x) = 12.8x$.

$$R'(x) = \frac{6.37}{u}(12.8x) = \frac{81.54x}{u} = \frac{81.54x}{6.4x^2} = \frac{12.74}{x}.$$

At $x = 20$ years, $R'(20) = \frac{12.74}{20} = 0.637$ or 63.7%

Alternatively, we can think of $R(x)$ as the composition of functions with an outside function of $7\log_3(inside\ function)$ and an inside function of $6.4x^2$.

The derivative of the outside function would be:

$$7\frac{1}{\left(inside\ function\right)} \cdot \frac{1}{\ln 3} = (6.37)\frac{1}{inside\ function}.$$

The derivative of the inside function would be: $12.8x$.

Then $R'(x) =$ derivative of the outside function times the derivative of the inside function.

$$R'(x) = (6.37)\frac{1}{inside\ function}(12.8x) = \frac{81.54x}{6.4x^2} = \frac{12.74}{x}$$

At $x = 20$, $R'(20) = \frac{12.74}{20} = 0.637$ or 63.7%.

VC4 THE CHAIN RULE EXERCISES

Find the derivatives.

1. $f(x) = (5x^2 - 6)^3$

2. $f(x) = (7x^2 + 3)^4$

3. $y = \sqrt{3x^2 - 1}$

4. $y = \sqrt{5x^2 - 6}$

5. $f(x) = (4x^2 + 6x - 3)^{-6}$

6. $f(x) = (6x^2 - 5x + 3)^{-5}$

7. $g(x) = e^{5x^2 + 2}$

8. $g(x) = e^{7x^2 - 3}$

9. $y = (7x^2 + 2x)^4$

10. $y = (6x^2 - 3x)^4$

11. $f(x) = 3x(4x - 2)^5$

12. $f(x) = 8x(4x + 1)^7$

13. $y = \dfrac{7x}{(3x - 1)^2}$

14. $y = \dfrac{5x}{(3x + 2)^4}$

15. $h(x) = \dfrac{5x^2 + 1}{2x + 7}$

16. $h(x) = \dfrac{4x^2 - 5}{2x + 1}$

17. $f(x) = \dfrac{9}{5x^2 + 7x - 2}$

18. $f(x) = \dfrac{-6}{3x^2 + 5x + 2}$

19. $y = [\ln(5x^2 + 1)]^3$

20. $y = [\ln(5x^2 - 3)]^2$

21. A valley in California, which currently contains a two-lane highway, is under consideration for a multi-lane freeway. The average daily level of exhaust pollutants in the valley has been modeled by the equation $P(n) = 0.6\sqrt{0.4n^2 + 4n + 12}$, where n is the number of vehicles on the road per day in thousands. As a member of the planning board, find the rate the pollutants will increase as the number of vehicles increases; i.e., find $\dfrac{dP}{dn}$.

If the number of cars is 10,000 per day ($n = 10$), find the increase in pollutants.

22. Suppose the average number of pollutants in the air of a city on the edge of a national forest, caused by a forest fire in the adjacent forest, can be modeled by the equation:

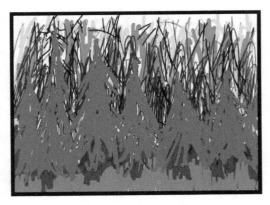

$P(a)=2.6\sqrt{0.3a^2+4a+15}$, where $P(a)$ is the number of pollutants per liter of air, and a is the number of acres burning. Find the rate the pollutants will increase as the number of burning acres increases; i.e., find $dP\!/\!da$

If the number of acres burning is 2000, find the increase in pollutants.

23. Find an equation of the tangent line to the graph of the function at the point $(5, 11)$.

$$g(x)=\frac{2x+1}{\sqrt{x-4}}$$

24. Find an equation of the tangent line to the graph of the function at the point $(1, 0.5)$.

$$g(x)=\frac{2x-1}{\sqrt{x+3}}$$

25. Find the relevant characteristics of the function $f(x)=\dfrac{2x}{x-5}$ and sketch.

26. Find the relevant characteristic of the function $f(x)=\dfrac{3x}{5-x}$ and sketch.

VC4 THE CHAIN RULE SOLUTIONS TO EXERCISES

1. $f'(x)=3(5x^2-6)^2(10x)=30x(5x^2-6)^2$

2. $56x(7x^2+3)^3$

3. $\dfrac{dy}{dx}=\dfrac{1}{2}(3x^2-1)^{-\frac{1}{2}}(6x)=\dfrac{3x}{\sqrt{3x^2-1}}$

4. $\dfrac{5x}{\sqrt{5x^2-6}}$

5. $f'(x)=-6(4x^2+6x-3)^{-7}(8x+6)$ or $\dfrac{-6(8x+6)}{(4x^2+6x-3)^7}$

6. $f'(x)=\dfrac{-5(12x-5)}{(6x^2-5x+3)^6}$

7. $g'(x)=(e^{5x^2+2})(10x)=10x(e^{5x^2+2})$

8. $g'(x)=14xe^{7x^2-3}$

9. $\dfrac{dy}{dx}=4(7x^2+2x)^3(14x+2)$

10. $\dfrac{dy}{dx}=4(6x^2-3x)^3(12x-3)$

11. $f'(x)=3(4x-2)^5+3x(5)(4x-2)^4(4)=(4x-2)^4[3(4x-2)^1+60x]$

    $=(4x-2)^4[12x-6+60x]=(4x-2)^4(72x-6)=6(12x-1)(2^4)(2x-1)^4$

    $=96(12x-1)(2x-1)^4$

12. $f'(x)=8(28x+1)(4x+1)^6$

13. $\dfrac{dy}{dx}=\dfrac{7(3x-1)^2-7x(2)(3x-1)^1(3)}{(3x-1)^4}$ We can factor our (3x-1) from each term.

    $\dfrac{dy}{dx}=\dfrac{7(3x-1)-42x}{(3x-1)^3}=\dfrac{21x-7-42x}{(3x-1)^3}=\dfrac{-21x-7}{(3x-1)^3}$ or $\dfrac{-7(3x+1)}{(3x-1)^3}$

14. $\dfrac{dy}{dx}=\dfrac{10-45x}{(3x+2)^5}$ or $\dfrac{5(2-9x)}{(3x+2)^5}$ or $\dfrac{dy}{dx}=5(2-9x)(3x+2)^{-5}$

15. $h'(x)=\dfrac{10x(2x+7)-2(5x^2+1)}{(2x+7)^2}=\dfrac{20x^2+70x-10x^2-2}{(2x+7)^2}$

    $=\dfrac{10x^2+70x-2}{(2x+7)^2}$ or $\dfrac{2(5x^2+35x-1)}{(2x+7)^2}$

16. $h'(x)=\dfrac{8x^2+8x+10}{(2x+1)^2}$ or $\dfrac{2(4x^2+4x+5)}{(2x+1)^2}$ or $\dfrac{dy}{dx}=2(4x^2+4x+5)(2x+1)^{-2}$

17. $f'(x)=\dfrac{0(5x^2+7x-2)-(10x+7)(9)}{(5x^2+7x-2)^2}$

    $=\dfrac{-9(10x+7)}{(5x^2+7x-2)^2}$ or $-9(10x+7)(5x^2+7x-2)^{-2}$

18. $f'(x) = \dfrac{6(6x+5)}{(3x^2+5x+2)^2}$ or $f'(x) = 6(6x+5)(3x^2+5x+2)^{-2}$

19. $\dfrac{dy}{dx} = 3[\ln(5x^2+1)]^2 \cdot \dfrac{1}{5x^2+1} \cdot (10x) = \dfrac{30x[\ln(5x^2+1)]^2}{5x^2+1}$

20. $\dfrac{dy}{dx} = \dfrac{20x[\ln(5x^2-3)]}{5x^2-3}$

21. $P(n) = 0.6(0.4n^2+4n+12)^{\frac{1}{2}}$ $\dfrac{dP}{dn} = 0.6\dfrac{1}{2}(0.4n^2+4n+12)^{-\frac{1}{2}}(0.8n+4)$

$\dfrac{dP}{dn} = \dfrac{0.3(0.8x+4)}{\sqrt{(0.4n^2+4n+12)}}$ At $n=10$, $\dfrac{dP}{dn} = \dfrac{0.3(0.8(10)+4)}{\sqrt{(0.4(10)^2+4(10)+12)}} = \dfrac{3.6}{\sqrt{92}} = 0.375$

increase of 375 pollutants / vehicle

22. $\dfrac{dP}{da} = \dfrac{1.3(0.6a+4)}{\sqrt{0.3a^2+4a+15}}$; increase of 1.42 pollutants/liter/burning acre

23. To find the equation of the tangent, we will use $y - y_1 = m(x - x_1)$ with $(x_1, y_1) = (5, 11)$. To find m, the slope, we will need $g'(x)$.

We first rewrite $g(x) = \dfrac{2x+1}{(x-4)^{\frac{1}{2}}}$ and use the Quotient Rule and Chain Rule, or

we rewrite $g(x) = (2x+1)(x-4)^{-\frac{1}{2}}$ and use the Product Rule and Chain Rule.

Using the second method, $g(x) = G(x)H(x)$ and $g'(x) = G'(x)H(x) + G(x)H'(x)$.

$G(x) = 2x+1$; $G'(x) = 2$; $H(x) = (x-4)^{-\frac{1}{2}}$; $H'(x) = -\dfrac{1}{2}(x-4)^{-\frac{3}{2}}(1)$

$g'(x) = 2(x-4)^{-\frac{1}{2}} + (2x+1)\left[-\dfrac{1}{2}(x-4)^{-\frac{3}{2}}\right] = (x-4)^{-\frac{3}{2}}\left[2(x-4)^1 - \dfrac{1}{2}(2x+1)\right]$

$= (x-4)^{-\frac{3}{2}}[2x-8-x-0.5] = (x-4)^{-\frac{3}{2}}(x-8.5)$

At $x=5$; $m = g'(5) = (5-4)^{-\frac{3}{2}}(5-8.5) = -3.5$

Then for $y - y_1 = m(x - x_1)$ we have $y - 11 = -3.5(x-5)$.

$$y - 11 = -3.5x + 17.5$$
$$y = -3.5x + 28.5$$

24. $y = 0.94x - 0.44$

25. V.A.: $x = 5$; H.A.: $y = 2$;

Rel Ext: none because $f'(x) = \dfrac{-10}{(x-5)^2} \neq 0$

I.P.: none because $f''(x) = \dfrac{20}{(x-5)^3} \neq 0$

However, $f''(x)$ is undefined at $x = 5$
CU: $x > 5$; CD: $x < 5$
y-intercept: $(0, 0)$

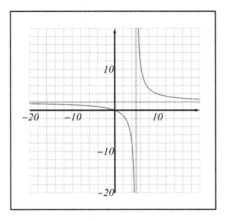

26. VA: $x = 5$; HA: $y = -3$; Rel Ext: none;

I.P.: none; CU: $x < 5$; CD: $x > 5$
y-intercept: $(0, 0)$

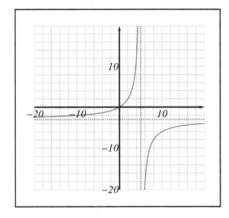

UNIT VI

VIC1

Implicit Differentiation

An equation such as $x^2 + 2xy - 4y^3 = 5 - 5y$ gives a relationship between two quantities x and y. Those quantities may be items like supply and demand or revenue and cost. The graph of the equation is a curve. To stay on the curve when x varies, y will be forced to vary; that is, for most parts of the curve, y is a function of x. But the explicit expression of x that gives y is not shown by the equation; in this case, the function of x is implied.

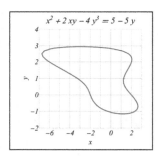

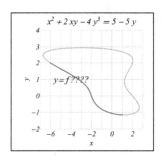

At most points on the curve, there is a direction or slope—that is, the derivative. Even though the function of x is implied, we can use the equation $x^2 + 2xy - 4y^3 = 5 - 5y$ to find the derivative $\dfrac{dy}{dx}$ without explicitly knowing y as a function x. The result can be called **implicit differentiation**.

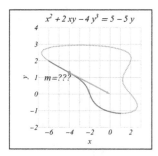

In this section, one method of finding a derivative implicitly is presented. In the next section, an alternative method is presented. Ether method can be used for section VIC3, so it is possible to skip over either section VIC1 or VIC2.

IMPLICIT DIFFERENTIATION AND THE CHAIN RULE

Implicit differentiation uses the Chain Rule. We can think of the Chain Rule as the derivative of the outside function times the derivative of the inside function.

Suppose we know that some quantity y is related to another quantity x. Perhaps y represents "burgers sold," and x represents "number of coupons distributed." So we know that y is related to x, but we're not sure how. Let the cloud represent y, an unknown function of x.

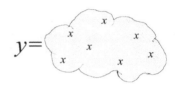
Now suppose we need y^5; that is:
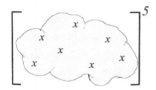

The outside function is $[cloud]^5$.   The inside function is
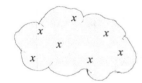

The derivative of the outside function is: $5[cloud]^4$ or

Remember, we need the derivative of the outside function times the derivative of the inside function. We now have the derivative of the outside function. Since we don't know exactly what is inside the cloud, the inside function, we just leave its derivative as:

$$\frac{d}{dx}\overbrace{[cloud]} = \frac{d}{dx}[cloud]$$

So the derivative of the outside function times the derivative of the inside function is:

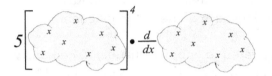

that is, $5[cloud]^4\dfrac{d}{dx}[cloud]=5y^4\dfrac{dy}{dx}$.

IMPLICIT DIFFERENTIATION—THE CHAIN RULE PROCESS

If our object is to find the change in some variable with respect to x, then any term containing a variable that is not x requires use of the Chain Rule. For example, consider the term $6y^3$. The derivative of the "outside" function is $18y^2$, and the derivative of the "inside function" y is $\dfrac{dy}{dx}$, assuming y is an unknown function of x.

Consider the equation $5x^3y^5-6x=7y-8$, and suppose we want to find $\dfrac{dy}{dx}$.

To find the derivative of the first term, we would need the Product Rule as well as the Chain Rule.

> The first term has factors $5x^3$, which we'll designate as $G(x)$. $G'(x)=15x^2$.
>
> The second factor is y^5, which we'll designate $H(x)$. $H'(x)=5y^4\dfrac{dy}{dx}$.
>
> Using the Product Rule, the derivative of the first term is then $G'(x)H(x)+G(x)H'(x)$.
>
> $G'(x)H(x)+G(x)H'(x)=15x^2y^5+5x^35y^4\dfrac{dy}{dx}=15x^2y^5+25x^3y^4\dfrac{dy}{dx}$

The derivative of both sides of our equation, $5x^3y^5-6x=7y-8$, is then:

$$15x^2y^5+25x^3y^4\frac{dy}{dx}-6=7(1)\frac{dy}{dx}-0.$$

To solve for $\dfrac{dy}{dx}$ we add or subtract to move all terms with $\dfrac{dy}{dx}$ to the left and all terms without $\dfrac{dy}{dx}$ to the right (or vice versa).

$$25x^3 y^4 \frac{dy}{dx} - 7\frac{dy}{dx} = -15x^2 y^5 + 6$$

We factor out $\dfrac{dy}{dx}$ from all terms on the left.

$$\frac{dy}{dx}(25x^3 y^4 - 7) = -15x^2 y^5 + 6$$

$$\frac{dy}{dx} = \frac{-15x^2 y^5 + 6}{25x^3 y^4 - 7}$$

If we know that $x = 1$ and $y = 1$, then $\dfrac{dy}{dx} = \dfrac{-15x^2 y^5 + 6}{25x^3 y^4 - 7} = \dfrac{-9}{18} = -\dfrac{1}{2}$.

Example 1:

Find $\dfrac{dy}{dx}$ if $3x^3 + 5y^2 - 3x + 7y = 4x^3 y^4 + 8$.

What is the slope at the point $(1, 1)$?

We want to know how the variable y changes with respect to x. We can see that if we could solve the equation for y, it would be a function of x

1st term: The derivative of the first term with respect to x would be $9x^2$.

2nd term: We use the Chain Rule to find the derivative of the second term. The inside function is y, the unknown function of x, and the outside function is $5(inside\ function)^2$. Its derivative is 10 $(inside\ function)^1$ or $10y$. The derivative of the inside function we leave merely as $\dfrac{dy}{dx}$. Then the derivative of the outside function times the derivative of the inside function is $10y\dfrac{dy}{dx}$.

3rd term: The derivative of $-3x$ is -3.

4rd term: Again, y is the inside function, and its derivative is $\dfrac{dy}{dx}$. The outside function is $7(inside\ function)^1$. Its derivative is 7. Then the derivative of the outside function times the derivative of the inside function would be $7\dfrac{dy}{dx}$

5th term: We need the Product Rule here. The first factor, $G(x)$ is $4x^3$ and the second factor, $H(x)$ is y^4. $G'(x) = 12x^2$. For $H'(x)$ we need the Chain Rule. The inside function is y, with derivative $\dfrac{dy}{dx}$. The outside function is $(inside\ function)^4$. Its derivative is $4(inside\ function)^3$, or $4y^3$. For $H'(x)$ we need the derivative of the outside function times the derivative of the inside function, which is $4y^3\dfrac{dy}{dx}$.

The Product Rule is $G'(x)H(x) + G(x)H'(x) = 12x^2y^4 + 4x^3 4y^3\dfrac{dy}{dx}$

$$= 12x^2y^4 + 16x^3y^3\frac{dy}{dx}$$

6th term: The derivative of 8 is 0.

We now have $9x^2 + 10y\dfrac{dy}{dx} - 3 + 7\dfrac{dy}{dx} = 12x^2y^4 + 16x^3y^3\dfrac{dy}{dx} + 0$.

To solve for $\dfrac{dy}{dx}$ we add or subtract to move all terms with $\dfrac{dy}{dx}$ to the left and all terms without $\dfrac{dy}{dx}$ to the right (or vice versa).

$$10y\frac{dy}{dx} + 7\frac{dy}{dx} - 16x^3y^3\frac{dy}{dx} = -9x^2 + 3 + 12x^2y^4$$

We factor out $\dfrac{dy}{dx}$.

$$\frac{dy}{dx}(10y + 7 - 16x^3y^3) = -9x^2 + 3 + 12x^2y^4$$

Now we just divide.

$$\frac{dy}{dx} = \frac{-9x^2 + 3 + 12x^2y^4}{10y + 7 - 16x^3y^3}$$

At $x = 1$ and $y = 1$, $\qquad \dfrac{dy}{dx} = \dfrac{-9(1)^2 + 3 + 12(1)^2(1)^4}{10(1) + 7 - 16(1)^3(1)^3} = \dfrac{6}{1} = 6$

Example 2:

Sometimes it is also implied that the variables change with time. In other words, the values change as time marches on.

Consider the equation $6a^3 + 5b^2 = -4a + 3b - 6$. Suppose we know that the variables a and b are both changing with time t, and we want to know in particular how a is changing with time. We use the Chain Rule to differentiate each term with respect to time t.

$$18a^2\frac{da}{dt} + 10b\frac{db}{dt} = -4(1)\frac{da}{dt} + 3\frac{db}{dt} - 0$$

We can solve for $\frac{da}{dt}$ by adding and/or subtracting terms until all the terms containing $\frac{da}{dt}$ are on one side of the equation and those terms that do not contain $\frac{da}{dt}$ are on the opposite side.

$$18a^2\frac{da}{dt} + 4\frac{da}{dt} = -10b\frac{db}{dt} + 3\frac{db}{dt}$$

We can then factor $\frac{da}{dt}$ from the terms on its side of the equation and then divide to solve for $\frac{da}{dt}$.

$$\frac{da}{dt}(18a^2 + 4) = (-10b + 3)\frac{db}{dt}$$

$$\frac{da}{dt} = \frac{(-10b + 3)\frac{db}{dt}}{18a^2 + 4}$$

If we are given a, b, and $\frac{db}{dt}$ at a particular time, we could then find $\frac{da}{dt}$.

VIC1 IMPLICIT DIFFERENTIATION EXERCISES

For numbers 1)–6), use the process of implicit differentiation to find $\dfrac{dy}{dx}$.

1. $3x + y^2 = 6$

2. $x^2 + 4y = 9$

3. $5xy^2 = 1$

4. $3x^2 y = 4$

5. $5x^2 y^3 + 2x - 3y = 7$

6. $-3x^3 y^2 - 4x + 3y = 8$

7. Find the slope of the curve $x^3 - xy + y^2 = 4$ at the point (0,2).

8. Find the slope of the curve $x^2 + xy + y^3 = 8$ at the point (0,2).

9. Find the slope of the curve $\sqrt{x} + \sqrt{y} = 9$ at the point (16, 25).

10. Find the slope of the curve $2\sqrt{x} + \sqrt{y} = 13$ at the point (16, 25).

11. Find the slope of the curve $x^{\frac{2}{3}} + y^{\frac{2}{3}} = 5$ at the point (8, 1).

12. Find the slope of the curve $x^{\frac{2}{3}} - 3y^{\frac{2}{3}} = -8$ at the point (8, 1).

13. Find the slope of the curve $x^2 y^2 - y = x$ at the point (0, 0).

14. Find the slope of the curve $x^2 y^3 + y = x$ at the point (0, 0).

15. The Cobb-Douglas Production Function, pictured at right, relates units of labor (x) to dollars invested (y) in a manufacturing process. When the number of units produced is 100,000, the function can be modeled by $74x^{0.75} y^{0.25} = 100{,}000$. Find the rate of change of y with respect to x when $x = 1500$ units and $y = \$1000$ (closely approximated by the model).

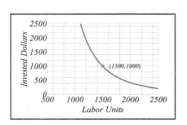

16. The Cobb-Douglas Production Function, pictured in #15) above, relates units of labor (x) to dollars invested (y) in a manufacturing process. When the number of units produced is 100,000, the function can be modeled by $74x^{0.75} y^{0.25} = 100{,}000$. Find the rate of change of y with respect to x when $x = 1200$ units and $y = \$1900$ (closely approximated by the model).

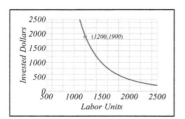

VIC1 IMPLICIT DIFFERENTIATION SOLUTIONS TO EXERCISES

For numbers 13) through 18), use the process of implicit differentiation to find $\dfrac{dy}{dx}$.

1. $3x + y^2 = 6$

$$3 + 2y\frac{dy}{dx} - 0 = 0$$

$$2y\frac{dy}{dx} = -3$$

$$\frac{dy}{dx} = \frac{-3}{2y}$$

2. $x^2 + 4y = 9$

$$\frac{dy}{dx} = -\frac{x}{2}$$

3. $5xy^2 = 1$

$$5y^2 + 5x(2y)\frac{dy}{dx} - 0 = 0$$

$$10xy\frac{dy}{dx} = -5y^2$$

$$\frac{dy}{dx} = \frac{-5y^2}{10xy} = -\frac{y}{2x}$$

4. $3x^2 y = 4$

$$\frac{dy}{dx} = -\frac{2y}{x}$$

5. $5x^2 y^3 + 2x - 3y = 7$

$$10xy^3 + 5x^2(3y^2)\frac{dy}{dx} + 2 - 3\frac{dy}{dx} = 0$$

$$15x^2 y^2\frac{dy}{dx} - 3\frac{dy}{dx} = -10xy^3 - 2$$

$$\frac{dy}{dx}(15x^2 y^2 - 3) = -10xy^3 - 2$$

$$\frac{dy}{dx} = \frac{-10xy^3 - 2}{15x^2 y^2 - 3}$$

6. $-3x^3 y^2 - 4x + 3y = 8$

$$\frac{dy}{dx} = \frac{9x^2 y^2 + 4}{-6x^3 y + 3}$$

7. Find the slope of the curve $x^3 - xy + y^2 = 4$ at the point (0,2).

$$3x^2 - (1)y - x(1)\frac{dy}{dx} + 2y\frac{dy}{dx} = 0$$

$$-x(1)\frac{dy}{dx} + 2y\frac{dy}{dx} = -3x^2 + y$$

$$\frac{dy}{dx}(-x + 2y) = -3x^2 + y$$

$$\frac{dy}{dx} = \frac{-3x^2 + y}{-x + 2y}$$

At $x = 0$ and $y = 2$, $\dfrac{dy}{dx} = \dfrac{-3(0)^2 + 2}{-(0) + 2(2)} = \dfrac{2}{4} = \dfrac{1}{2}$

8. Find the slope of the curve $x^2 + xy + y^3 = 8$ at the point $(0,2)$.

$$\frac{dy}{dx} = -\frac{2x + y}{x + 3y^2}, \quad m = -\frac{1}{6}$$

9. Find the slope of the curve $\sqrt{x} + \sqrt{y} = 9$ at the point $(16, 25)$.

$$x^{\frac{1}{2}} + y^{\frac{1}{2}} = 9$$

$$\frac{1}{2}x^{-\frac{1}{2}} + \frac{1}{2}y^{-\frac{1}{2}}\frac{dy}{dx} = 0$$

$$\frac{1}{2}y^{-\frac{1}{2}}\frac{dy}{dx} = -\frac{1}{2}x^{-\frac{1}{2}}$$

$$y^{-\frac{1}{2}}\frac{dy}{dx} = -x^{-\frac{1}{2}}$$

$$\frac{dy}{dx} = -\frac{x^{-\frac{1}{2}}}{y^{-\frac{1}{2}}} = -\frac{\sqrt{y}}{\sqrt{x}}$$

At $x = 16$ and $y = 25$, $-\dfrac{\sqrt{25}}{16} = -\dfrac{5}{4}$

10. Find the slope of the curve $2\sqrt{x} + \sqrt{y} = 13$ at the point $(16, 25)$.

$$\frac{dy}{dx} = -\frac{2x^{-1/2}}{y^{-1/2}}, \quad m = -\frac{5}{2}$$

11. Find the slope of the curve $x^{\frac{2}{3}} + y^{\frac{2}{3}} = 5$ at the point $(8, 1)$.

$$\frac{2}{3}x^{-\frac{1}{3}} + \frac{2}{3}y^{-\frac{1}{3}}\frac{dy}{dx} = 0$$

$$\frac{2}{3}y^{-\frac{1}{3}}\frac{dy}{dx} = -\frac{2}{3}x^{-\frac{1}{3}}$$

$$y^{-\frac{1}{3}}\frac{dy}{dx} = -x^{-\frac{1}{3}}$$

$$\frac{dy}{dx} = \frac{-x^{-\frac{1}{3}}}{y^{-\frac{1}{3}}} = -\frac{\sqrt[3]{y}}{\sqrt[3]{x}}$$

At $x = 8$ and $y = 1$, $-\dfrac{\sqrt[3]{1}}{\sqrt[3]{8}} = -\dfrac{1}{2}$

12. Find the slope of the curve $x^{\frac{2}{3}} - 3y^{\frac{2}{3}} = -8$ at the point $(8, 1)$.

$$\frac{dy}{dx} = \frac{y^{\frac{1}{3}}}{3x^{\frac{1}{3}}}, \quad m = \frac{1}{6}$$

13. Find the slope of the curve $x^2y^2 - y = x$ at the point $(0, 0)$.

$$2xy^2 + x^2(2y)\frac{dy}{dx} - (1)\frac{dy}{dx} = 1$$

$$2x^2y\frac{dy}{dx} - (1)\frac{dy}{dx} = -2xy^2 + 1$$

$$\frac{dy}{dx}(2x^2y - 1) = -2xy^2 + 1$$

$$\frac{dy}{dx} = \frac{-2xy^2 + 1}{2x^2y - 1}$$

At $x = 0$ and $y = 0$, $-\dfrac{2(0)(0)^2 - 1}{2(0)^2(0) - 1} = -1$

14. Find the slope of the curve $x^2y^3 + y = x$ at the point $(0, 0)$.

$$\frac{dy}{dx} = -\frac{2xy^3 + 1}{3x^2y^2 - 1}, \quad \text{At } (0, 0), \, m = 1$$

15. $F = 74x^{0.75}y^{0.25} - 100{,}000,$

$74x^{0.75}y^{0.25} = 100{,}000$

$$(0.75)74x^{-0.25}y^{0.25} + 74x^{0.75}(0.25)y^{-0.75}\frac{dy}{dx} = 0$$

$$74x^{0.75}(0.25)y^{-0.75}\frac{dy}{dx} = -[(0.75)74x^{-0.25}y^{0.25}]$$

$$\frac{dy}{dx} = -\frac{(0.75)74x^{-0.25}y^{0.25}}{74x^{0.75}(0.25)y^{-0.75}} = \frac{3y^{0.75}y^{0.25}}{x^{0.75}x^{0.25}} = \frac{3y}{x}$$

At $x = 1500$ and $y = \$1000$, $\dfrac{dy}{dx} = \dfrac{-3(1{,}000)}{1500} \approx -\$2\dfrac{dollars\ invested}{labor\ unit}$

There is a decrease of $2 invested per labor unit.

16. When $x = 1200$ units and $y = \$1900$,

$$\frac{dy}{dx} = -4.75 \; dollars\ invested\ per\ labor\ unit.$$

There is a decrease of $4.75 invested per labor unit.

VIC2

Partial Derivatives, Implicit Differentiation, Related Rates: an Alternative Approach

In this section, an alternative approach to implicit differentiation and related rates is given. This approach involves partial derivatives.

This section can be used in place of Section VIC1, or it can be used in conjunction with Section VIC1. Section VIC3 on related rates will follow from whichever section is used.

PARTIAL DERIVATIVES

For the function $f(x) = 2\pi^3 x^4 - 5\pi^2 x^2 - 7x + 9\pi$, since π and its powers are constant, the derivative is $f'(x) = 8\pi^3 x^3 - 10\pi^2 x - 7$.

For the function $g(y) = 2y^3\pi^4 - 5y^2\pi^2 - 7\pi + 9y$, since π and its powers are constant, the derivative is $g'(x) = 6y^2\pi^4 - 10y\pi^2 + 9$.

Now suppose $F = 2y^3 x^4 - 5y^2 x^2 - 7x + 9y$ and we ask: "What is the derivative?" The expression for F involves two symbols that we have used to represent variables—we need to know which one is the variable.

If x is the variable, we can proceed as we did with the function f above, treating the symbol y as a constant like π. In this case, the derivative is $8y^3 x^3 - 10y^2 x - 7$. We can denote this derivative F_x; $F_x = 8y^3 x^3 - 10y^2 x - 7$.

If y is the variable, we can proceed as we did with the function g above, treating the symbol x as a constant like π. In this case, the derivative is $6y^2 x^4 - 10yx^2 + 9$. We can denote this derivative F_y; $F_y = 6y^2 x^4 - 10yx^2 + 9$.

The expressions F_x and F_y are called *partial derivatives*. Both variables x and y may be variables, and the rate of change of F depends on both partial derivatives F_x and F_y.

Example 1:

Find the partial derivatives for $F = 2x^3 e^{2y-1} + xy - 7x$.

$$F_x = 6x^2 e^{2y-1} + y - 7$$

$$F_y = 4x^3 e^{2y-1} + x.$$

Example 2:

Find the partial derivatives for $G = \ln(x - 2y) + 2y - 7x$.

$$G_x = \frac{1}{x - 2y} - 7$$

$$G_y = \frac{-2}{x - 2y} + 2.$$

Example 3:

Find the partial derivatives for $F = 7r^3 s^2 - r^4 + 3s^5$.

$$F_r = 21r^2 s^2 - 4r^3$$

$$F_s = 14r^3 s + 15s^4.$$

INTRA-SECTION EXERCISES:

Find the partial derivatives for the following expressions.

1. $F = 3x^2 - 7y^3 + 4x + 12y$
2. $G = 2x^2 y^5 - 10xy^3 + 4\ln(x + y)$
3. $H = 0.34q^3 \sqrt{r} + e^{rq}$

Solutions

1. $F_x = 6x + 4$

   $F_y = -21y^2 + 12$

2. $G_x = 4xy^5 - 10y^3 + \dfrac{4}{x+y}$

   $G_y = 10x^2y^4 - 30xy^2 + \dfrac{4}{x+y}$

3. $H_q = 1.02q^2\sqrt{r} + re^{rq}$

   $H_r = 0.17q^3r^{-1/2} + qe^{rq}$

RELATED RATES AND PARTIAL DERIVATIVES

At the MAKATHING Corporation, it has been determined that sales, s, and production, q, are related by the equation $3s^2q^{3.2} + 2sq^{0.4} = s - q$. Neither is s explicitly set forth as a function of q, nor is q explicitly set forth as a function of s. But if s varies, it causes q to vary, and if q varies, it causes s to vary. In other words, it is *implied* that s is a function of q and q is a function of s. Furthermore, as time, t, changes, the values of s and q will change—it is *implied* that s and q are functions of t. The functions in this setting are *implicit* (implied) instead of being explicitly defined as an expression of a variable.

The word *rate* usually refers to the rate of change of a value, such as x, with respect to time, $\dfrac{dx}{dt}$ or $x'(t)$. Some familiar rates might be speed, the rate of change of distance with respect to time, or interest rate, the rate of change of an investment with respect to time.

For the MAKATHING Corporation, both s and q vary with time and so have rates $\dfrac{ds}{dt}$ and $\dfrac{dq}{dt}$. The relationship for s and q, $3s^2q^{3.2} + 2sq^{0.4} = s - q$, means that if either s or q varies over time, the other variable does. Hence, their rates are also related. We can obtain the relationship between the rates from the relationship between the variables.

Consider the relationship $3s^2q^{3.2} + 2sq^{0.4} = s - q$, and label the left side $F = 3s^2q^{3.2} + 2sq^{0.4}$ and the right side $G = s - q$. Since $F = G$, they should also have equal rates: $\dfrac{dF}{dt} = \dfrac{dG}{dt}$.

The equation $\dfrac{dF}{dt} = \dfrac{dG}{dt}$ is a related rate equation, but what is this equation in terms of s and q?

The expression F depends on s that depends on t; that is, a composition F of s of t. But the expression F also depends on q that depends on t; that is, a composition F of q of t. If s were the only variable, then the chain rule for derivatives of compositions would give $\dfrac{dF}{dt} \sim \dfrac{dF}{ds} \cdot \dfrac{ds}{dt}$. We did not place an equal sign between the expressions because q is also a variable, and in that light, we would see $\dfrac{dF}{dt} \sim \dfrac{dF}{dq} \cdot \dfrac{dq}{dt}$. We need to resolve the fact that there are two different views. First, the notations $\dfrac{dF}{ds}$ and $\dfrac{dF}{dq}$ are not correct; they should be the partial derivatives F_s and F_q. The total derivative is the sum of the two parts $\dfrac{dF}{dt} = F_s \cdot \dfrac{ds}{dt} + F_q \cdot \dfrac{dq}{dt}$.

The related rate equation $\dfrac{dF}{dt} = \dfrac{dG}{dt}$ now becomes

$$F_s \cdot \frac{ds}{dt} + F_q \cdot \frac{dq}{dt} = G_s \cdot \frac{ds}{dt} + G_q \cdot \frac{dq}{dt}$$

For $F = 3s^2q^{3.2} + 2sq^{0.4}$ and $G = s - q$;

$F_s = 6sq^{3.2} + 2q^{0.4}$, $G_s = 1$, $F_q = 9.6s^2q^{2.2} + 0.8sq^{-0.6}$, and $G_q = -1$.

This gives the related rate equation

$$(6sq^{3.2} + 2q^{0.4}) \cdot \frac{ds}{dt} + (9.6s^2q^{2.2} + 0.8sq^{-0.6}) \cdot \frac{dq}{dt} = 1 \cdot \frac{ds}{dt} + (-1) \cdot \frac{dq}{dt}.$$

Example 4:

Find the related rate equation for the relationship $3q^4r^2 - 4r = 2qr\ln(q - r^2)$.

Choose $F = 3q^4r^2 - 4r$ and $G = 2qr\ln(q - r^2)$.

Then $F_q = 12q^3r^2$, $F_r = 6q^4r - 4$,

$$G_q = 2r\ln(q - r^2) + 2qr\left(\frac{1}{q - r^2}\right) = 2r\ln(q - r^2) + \frac{2qr}{q - r^2},$$

and $G_r = 2q\ln(q - r^2) + 2qr\left(\frac{-2r}{q - r^2}\right) = 2q\ln(q - r^2) - \frac{4qr^2}{q - r^2}.$

The form of relationship for the rates is $F_q \cdot \dfrac{dq}{dt} + F_r \cdot \dfrac{dr}{dt} = G_q \cdot \dfrac{dq}{dt} + G_r \cdot \dfrac{dr}{dt}$.

The related rate equation is

$$12q^3r^2\frac{dq}{dt} + (6q^4r - 4)\frac{dr}{dt} = \left(2r\ln(q - r^2) + \frac{2qr}{q - r^2}\right)\frac{dq}{dt} + \left(2q\ln(q - r^2) - \frac{4qr^2}{q - r^2}\right)\frac{dr}{dt}.$$

Example 5:

Find the related rate equation for the relationship $= 4w^2 - 7\sqrt{2 - w}$.

Choose $F = v$ and $= 4w^2 - 7\sqrt{2 - w}$.

Notice that in this example, F and G depend on only one of the variables v or w. In this case, the partial derivatives become derivatives, $F_v = \dfrac{dF}{dv}$ and $G_w = \dfrac{dG}{dw}$ since $F_w = 0$ and $G_v = 0$.

Now the form of the relationship for the rates, $F_v \cdot \dfrac{dv}{dt} + 0 = 0 + G_w \cdot \dfrac{dw}{dt}$ or $\dfrac{dF}{dv} \cdot \dfrac{dv}{dt} = \dfrac{dG}{dw} \cdot \dfrac{dw}{dt}$.

The derivatives $\dfrac{dF}{dv} = 1$ and $\dfrac{dG}{dw} = 8w - 7\left(\dfrac{1}{2}\right)(2 - w)^{-\frac{1}{2}}(-1) = 8w + \dfrac{7}{2\sqrt{2 - w}}$

give the related rate equation $\dfrac{dv}{dt} = \left(8w + \dfrac{7}{2\sqrt{2 - w}}\right)\dfrac{dw}{dt}$.

Example 6:

Find the related rate equation for the relationship $2hr^3 - qw = w - \dfrac{r}{h}$.

Choose $F = 2hr^3 - qw$ and $G = w - \dfrac{r}{h}$. Now there are more than two variables, but there is a partial derivative for each variable:

$F_h = 2r^3$, $F_r = 6hr^2$, $F_q = -w$, $F_w = -q$, $G_h = \dfrac{r}{h^2}$, $G_r = -\dfrac{1}{h}$, $G_q = 0$, and $G_w = 1$.

The related rate equation includes terms for each partial derivative:

$$F_h\frac{dh}{dt} + F_r\frac{dr}{dt} + F_q\frac{dq}{dt} + F_w\frac{dw}{dt} = G_h\frac{dh}{dt} + G_r\frac{dr}{dt} + G_q\frac{dq}{dt} + G_w\frac{dw}{dt}.$$

Substituting the partial derivatives gives the related rate equation:

$$2r^3\frac{dh}{dt}+6hr^2\frac{dr}{dt}-w\frac{dq}{dt}-q\frac{dw}{dt}=\frac{r}{h^2}\frac{dh}{dt}-\frac{1}{h}\frac{dr}{dt}+\frac{dw}{dt}$$

INTRA-SECTION EXERCISES:

4. Find the related rate equation for the relationship $N-2k=3.2N^{0.23}k$
5. Find the related rate equation for the relationship $5p^3+2s^2=sp$.

Solutions

4. Choose $F=N-2k$ and $G=3.2N^{0.23}k$. Then $F_N=1$, $F_k=-2$, $G_N=0.736N^{-0.77}k$, and $G_k=3.2N^{0.23}$.

   The related rate equation is $\dfrac{dN}{dt}-2\dfrac{dk}{dt}=0.736N^{-0.77}k\dfrac{dN}{dt}+3.2N^{0.23}\dfrac{dk}{dt}$.

5. Choose $F=5p^3+2s^2$ and $G=sp$. Then $F_p=15p^2$, $F_s=4s$, $G_p=s$, and $G_s=p$.

   The related rate equation is $15p^2\dfrac{dp}{dt}+4s\dfrac{ds}{dt}=s\dfrac{dp}{dt}+p\dfrac{ds}{dt}$.

IMPLICIT DIFFERENTIATION—AN ALTERNATIVE METHOD USING PARTIAL DERIVATIVES

Look at the relationship $3xy^2-7x^3y^5=2x-4y$ and ponder the corresponding related rate equation. It can make things easier to change the form of the relationship by creating an equation where an expression is equal to zero. Here we could subtract $2x$ from both sides of the equation and add $4y$ to both sides of the equation, producing the equivalent equation $3xy^2-7x^3y^5-2x+4y=0$. Now label the left side $F=3xy^2-7x^3y^5-2x+4y$. The related rate equation is now $\dfrac{dF}{dt}=0$ or $F_x\cdot\dfrac{dx}{dt}+F_y\cdot\dfrac{dy}{dt}=0$.

What happens if $x=t$, i.e., the only variables, are really just x and y? In this case, $\dfrac{dx}{dt}=\dfrac{dx}{dx}=1$ and $\dfrac{dy}{dt}=\dfrac{dy}{dx}$. So the related rate equation becomes $F_x+F_y\cdot\dfrac{dy}{dx}=0$. We can solve for the derivative $\dfrac{dy}{dx}$. Subtract F_x from both sides, $F_y\cdot\dfrac{dy}{dt}=-F_x$. Finally, divide both sides by F_y to obtain the implicit form of the derivative $\dfrac{dy}{dt}=-\dfrac{F_x}{F_y}$.

Example 7:

Given $x^3 - 4y^2 = 7$, find $\dfrac{dy}{dx}$.

Manipulate the equation so that one side is zero: $x^3 - 4y^2 - 7 = 0$.

Choose $F = x^3 - 4y^2 - 7$, so that $F_x = 3x^2$ and $F_y = -8y$.

Thus, $\dfrac{dy}{dx} = -\dfrac{F_x}{F_y} = -\dfrac{3x^2}{-8y} = \dfrac{3x^2}{8y}$.

Example 8:

Suppose x represents the number of coffee shop outlets, and y represents the sales of lattes. Both x and y might depend on the population density.

Given the relationship $6 + x^3 y^2 = 3x - 4y$, find the derivative $\dfrac{dy}{dx}$.

Then find $\dfrac{dy}{dx}$ when $x = 2$ and $y = -0.5$.

Manipulate the equation so one side is zero: $6 + x^3 y^2 - 3x + 4y = 0$.

Choose $F = 6 + x^3 y^2 - 3x + 4y$ then $F_x = 3x^2 y^2 - 3$ and $F_y = 2x^3 y + 4$.

Thus, $\dfrac{dy}{dx} = -\dfrac{3x^2 y^2 - 3}{2x^3 y + 4}$.

When $x = 2$ and $y = -0.5$, $\dfrac{dy}{dx} = -\dfrac{3(2)^2(-0.5)^2 - 3}{2(2)^3(-0.5) + 4} = 0$.

Example 9:

Given the relationship $2e^{xy} = x - 2y$.

a. Find $\dfrac{dy}{dx}$.

b. Find $\dfrac{dy}{dx}$ when $x = 2$ and $y = 0$.

c. Find the equation of the tangent line to the curve at the point $(2, 0)$.

a. Manipulate the equation $2e^{xy} - x + 2y = 0$.

Choose $F = 2e^{xy} - x + 2y$ then $F_x = 2ye^{xy} - 1$ and $F_y = 2xe^{xy} + 2$.

$$\frac{dy}{dx} = -\frac{2ye^{xy} - 1}{2xe^{xy} + 2}.$$

b. When $x = 2$ and $y = 0$, $\dfrac{dy}{dx} = -\dfrac{2(0)e^{(2)(0)} - 1}{2(2)e^{(2)(0)} + 2} = \dfrac{1}{6}$

c. $y = \dfrac{1}{6}(x-2) + 0$, $y = \dfrac{1}{6}x - \dfrac{1}{3}$ or, in another form, $x - 6y = 2$.

Example 10:

Suppose x represents the number of burgers sold, and y represents the number of coupons redeemed. Both x and y might depend on the number of coupons distributed. Given the relationship $x^3 - xy = 2\ln y$

a. find $\dfrac{dy}{dx}$,

b. find $\dfrac{dy}{dx}$ at the point $(1,1)$,

c. find the equation of the tangent line to the curve at the point $(1,1)$.

a. Manipulate the equation $x^3 - xy - 2\ln y = 0$.

Choose $F = x^3 - xy - 2\ln y$ then $F_x = 3x^2 - y$ and $F_y = -x - \dfrac{2}{y}$.

$$\frac{dy}{dx} = -\frac{3x^2 - y}{-x - \dfrac{2}{y}}.$$

b. When $x = 1$ and $y = 1$, $\dfrac{dy}{dx} = -\dfrac{3(1)^2 - 1}{-1 - \dfrac{2}{1}} = \dfrac{2}{3}$

c. $y = \dfrac{2}{3}(x-1) + 1$, $y = \dfrac{2}{3}x + \dfrac{1}{3}$, or in another form, $2x - 3y = -1$.

Example 11:

Given the relationship $\sqrt{x+2}+\sqrt{3-y}=5$,

a. find $\dfrac{dy}{dx}$,

b. find $\dfrac{dy}{dx}$ at the point $(7,-1)$,

c. find the equation of the tangent line to the curve at the point $(7,-1)$.

a. Manipulate the equation $\sqrt{x+2}+\sqrt{3-y}-5=0$, $(x+2)^{\frac{1}{2}}+(3-y)^{\frac{1}{2}}-5=0$

Choose $F=(x+2)^{\frac{1}{2}}+(3-y)^{\frac{1}{2}}-5$ then $F_x=\dfrac{1}{2}(x+2)^{-\frac{1}{2}}(1)=\dfrac{1}{2}(x+2)^{-\frac{1}{2}}$ and

$F_y=\dfrac{1}{2}(3-y)^{-\frac{1}{2}}(-1)=-\dfrac{1}{2}(3-y)^{-\frac{1}{2}}$.

$\dfrac{dy}{dx}=-\dfrac{\dfrac{1}{2}(x+2)^{-\frac{1}{2}}}{-\dfrac{1}{2}(3-y)^{-\frac{1}{2}}}=\dfrac{(x+2)^{-\frac{1}{2}}}{(3-y)^{-\frac{1}{2}}}=\dfrac{(3-y)^{\frac{1}{2}}}{(x+2)^{\frac{1}{2}}}=\dfrac{\sqrt{3-y}}{\sqrt{x+2}}$.

b. When $x=7$ and $y=-1$, $\dfrac{dy}{dx}=\dfrac{\sqrt{3-(-1)}}{\sqrt{7+2}}=\dfrac{2}{3}$

c. $y=\dfrac{2}{3}(x-7)-1$, $y=\dfrac{2}{3}x-\dfrac{17}{3}$, or in another form, $2x-3y=17$.

INTRA-SECTION EXERCISES:

6. Given the relationship $2x^3-4x^2y^3=-16-3y+5x$, find $\dfrac{dy}{dx}$.

7. Given the relationship $4e^{3xy}=2x-y$, find $\dfrac{dy}{dx}$.

8. Given the relationship $2x^2-3xy=-1+5\ln y$,

a. find $\dfrac{dy}{dx}$,

b. find $\dfrac{dy}{dx}$ at the point $(1,1)$,

c. find the equation of the tangent line to the curve at the point $(1,1)$.

Solutions

6. $2x^3 - 4x^2y^3 + 16 + 3y - 5x = 0$,

   $F_x = 6x^2 - 8xy^3 - 5$ and $F_y = -12x^2y^2 + 3$,

   $\dfrac{dy}{dx} = -\dfrac{6x^2 - 8xy^3 - 5}{-12x^2y^2 + 3}$.

7. $4e^{3xy} - 2x + y = 0$,

   $F_x = 12ye^{3xy} - 2$ and $F_y = 12xe^{3xy} + 1$,

   $\dfrac{dy}{dx} = -\dfrac{12ye^{3xy} - 2}{12xe^{3xy} + 1}$.

8. a. $2x^2 - 3xy + 1 - 5\ln y = 0$,

   $F_x = 4x - 3y$ and $F_y = -3x - \dfrac{5}{y}$,

   $\dfrac{dy}{dx} = -\dfrac{4x - 3y}{-3x - \dfrac{5}{y}}$,

   b. When $x = 1$ and $y = 1$, $\dfrac{dy}{dx} = -\dfrac{4-3}{-3-\dfrac{5}{1}} = \dfrac{1}{8}$

   c. $y = \dfrac{1}{8}(x-1) + 1 = \dfrac{1}{8}x + \dfrac{7}{8}$ or $-8y = -7$.

VIC2 PARTIAL DERIVATIVES, IMPLICIT DIFFERENTIATION, RELATED RATES: AN ALTERNATIVE APPROACH EXERCISES

For numbers 1 through 6, find the partial derivatives of the expressions.

1. $F = 2x^3 y^4$

2. $G = 3x + 5y - 17$

3. $G = sw - 3e^{2sw}$

4. $H = \ln(3x^2 y^{-2} + y)$

5. $F = uv - 2u + 3v$

6. $G = 7p + 2q + p^2 q$

For numbers 7–12, find the related rate equation.

7. $2x^3 y^4 = 7x - 2y + 8$

8. $4p^5 q^2 = 7p + 2q + p^2 q$

9. $s^2 + \dfrac{2}{w} = sw - 3e^{2sw}$

10. $e^{2uv} = uv - 2u + 3v$

11. $3x^4 = 5y^2 - 17$

12. $W = 2r^2 - 7$

For numbers 13 through 18, use the process of implicit differentiation to find $\dfrac{dy}{dx}$.

13. $3x + y^2 = 6$

14. $x^2 + 4y = 9$

15. $5xy^2 = 1$

16. $3x^2 y = 4$

17. $5x^2 y^3 + 2x - 3y = 7$

18. $-3x^3 y^2 - 4x + 3y = 8$

19. Find the slope of the curve $x^3 - xy + y^2 = 4$ at the point $(0, 2)$.

20. Find the slope of the curve $x^2 + xy + y^3 = 8$ at the point $(0, 2)$.

21. Find the slope of the curve $\sqrt{x} + \sqrt{y} = 9$ at the point $(16, 25)$.

22. Find the slope of the curve $2\sqrt{x} + \sqrt{y} = 13$ at the point $(16, 25)$.

23. Find the slope of the curve $x^{\frac{2}{3}} + y^{\frac{2}{3}} = 5$ at the point $(8, 1)$.

24. Find the slope of the curve $x^{\frac{2}{3}} - 3y^{\frac{2}{3}} = -8$ at the point $(8, 1)$.

25. Find the slope of the curve $x^2 y^2 - y = x$ at the point $(0, 0)$.

26. Find the slope of the curve $x^2 y^3 + y = x$ at the point $(0, 0)$.

27. The Cobb-Douglas Production Function, pictured at right, relates units of labor (x) to dollars invested (y) in a manufacturing process. When the number of units produced is 100,000, the function can be modeled by: $74x^{0.75}y^{0.25} = 100,000$. Find the rate of change of y with respect to x when $x = 1500$ units and $y = \$1000$ (closely approximated by the model).

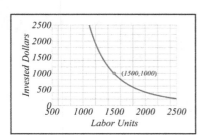

28. The Cobb-Douglas Production Function, pictured in #15 above, relates units of labor (x) to dollars invested (y) in a manufacturing process. When the number of units produced is 100,000, the function can be modeled by: $74x^{0.75}y^{0.25} = 100,000$. Find the rate of change of y with respect to x when $x = 1200$ units and $y = \$1900$ (closely approximated by the model).

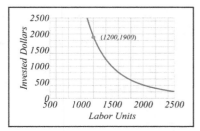

VIC2 PARTIAL DERIVATIVES, IMPLICIT DIFFERENTIATION, RELATED RATES: AN ALTERNATIVE APPROACH SOLUTIONS TO EXERCISES

For numbers 1 through 6, find the partial derivatives of the expressions.

1. $F = 2x^3 y^4$

   $F_x = 6x^2 y^4$, $F_y = 8x^3 y^3$

2. $G = 3x + 5y - 17$

   $G_x = 3$, $G_y = 5$

3. $G = sw - 3e^{2sw}$

   $G_s = w - 6we^{2sw}$, $G_y = s - 6se^{2sw}$

4. $H = \ln(3x^2 y^{-2} + y)$

   $H_x = \dfrac{6xy^{-2}}{3x^2 y^{-2} + y}$, $H_y = \dfrac{-6x^2 y^{-3} + 1}{3x^2 y^{-2} + y}$

5. $F = uv - 2u + 3v$

   $F_u = v - 2$, $F_v = u + 3$

6. $G = 7p + 2q + p^2 q$

   $G_p = 7 + 2pq$, $G_q = 2 + p^2$

For numbers 7–12, find the related rate equation.

7. $2x^3 y^4 = 7x - 2y + 8$

   $F = 2x^3 y^4$, $G = 7x - 2y + 8$

   $F_x = 6x^2 y^4$, $F_y = 8x^3 y^3$,

   $G_x = 7$, $G_y = -2$

   $6x^2 y^4 \dfrac{dx}{dt} + 8x^3 y^3 \dfrac{dy}{dt} = 7\dfrac{dx}{dt} - 2\dfrac{dy}{dt}$

8. $4p^5 q^2 = 7p + 2q + p^2 q$

   $20p^4 q^2 \dfrac{dp}{dt} + 8p^5 q \dfrac{dq}{dt}$

   $= (7 + 2pq)\dfrac{dp}{dt} + (2 + p^2)\dfrac{dy}{dt}$

9. $s^2 + \dfrac{2}{w} = sw - 3e^{2sw}$

   $F = s^2 + \dfrac{2}{w}$, $G = sw - 3e^{2sw}$

   $F_s = 2s$, $F_w = -\dfrac{2}{w^2}$

   $G_s = w - 6we^{2sw}$, $G_w = s - 6se^{2sw}$

   $2s\dfrac{ds}{dt} - \dfrac{2}{w^2}\dfrac{dw}{dt} = (w - 6we^{2sw})\dfrac{ds}{dt}$

   $\qquad + (s - 6se^{2sw})\dfrac{dw}{dt}$

10. $e^{2uv} = uv - 2u + 3v$

    $2ve^{2uv}\dfrac{du}{dt} + 2ue^{2uv}\dfrac{dv}{dt}$

    $= (v - 2)\dfrac{du}{dt} + (u + 3)\dfrac{dv}{dt}$

11. $3x^4 = 5y^2 - 17$

$F = 3x^4$, $G = 5y^2 - 17$

Here each of F and G depend on

only one variable: $F_x = \dfrac{dF}{dx} = 12x^3$,

$G_y = \dfrac{dG}{dy} = 10y$

$12x^3 \dfrac{dx}{dt} = 10y \dfrac{dy}{dt}$

12. $W = 2r^2 - 7$

$\dfrac{dW}{dt} = 4r \dfrac{dr}{dt}$

For numbers 13 through 18, use the process of implicit differentiation to find $\dfrac{dy}{dx}$.

13. $3x + y^2 = 6$, $F = 3x + y^2 - 6$

$F_x = 3$, $F_y = 2y$

$\dfrac{dy}{dx} = -\dfrac{3}{2y}$

14. $x^2 + 4y = 9$

$\dfrac{dy}{dx} = -\dfrac{x}{2}$

15. $5xy^2 = 1$, $F = 5xy^2 - 1$

$F_x = 5y^2$, $F_y = 10xy$

$\dfrac{dy}{dx} = -\dfrac{5y^2}{10xy} = -\dfrac{y}{2x}$

16. $3x^2 y = 4$

$\dfrac{dy}{dx} = -\dfrac{2y}{x}$

17. $5x^2 y^3 + 2x - 3y = 7$,

$F = 5x^2 y^3 + 2x - 3y - 7$,

$F_x = 10xy^3 + 2$, $F_y = 15x^2 y^2 - 3$

$\dfrac{dy}{dx} = -\dfrac{10xy^3 + 2}{15x^2 y^2 - 3}$

18. $-3x^3 y^2 - 4x + 3y = 8$

$\dfrac{dy}{dx} = \dfrac{9x^2 y^2 + 4}{-6x^3 y + 3}$

19. Find the slope of the curve $x^3 - xy + y^2 = 4$ at the point $(0, 2)$.

$F = x^3 - xy + y^2 - 4$, $F_x = 3x^2 - y$, $F_y = -x + 2y$,

$\dfrac{dy}{dx} = -\dfrac{3x^2 - y}{-x + 2y}$. At $(0,2)$, $m = \dfrac{dy}{dx} = -\dfrac{3(0)^2 - 2}{-0 + 2(2)} = \dfrac{1}{2}$.

20. Find the slope of the curve $x^2 + xy + y^3 = 8$ at the point $(0, 2)$.

$\dfrac{dy}{dx} = -\dfrac{2x + y}{x + 3y^2}$, $m = -\dfrac{1}{6}$

21. Find the slope of the curve $\sqrt{x}+\sqrt{y}=9$ at the point (16, 25).

$$F=\sqrt{x}+\sqrt{y}-9,\ F_x=\frac{1}{2}x^{-1/2},\ F_y=\frac{1}{2}y^{-1/2},$$

$$\frac{dy}{dx}=-\frac{\frac{1}{2}x^{-1/2}}{\frac{1}{2}y^{-1/2}}=-\frac{x^{-1/2}}{y^{-1/2}}.\ \text{At }(16,25),\ m=-\frac{16^{-\frac{1}{2}}}{25^{-\frac{1}{2}}}=-\frac{5}{4}$$

22. Find the slope of the curve $2\sqrt{x}+\sqrt{y}=13$ at the point (16, 25).

$$\frac{dy}{dx}=-\frac{2x^{-1/2}}{y^{-1/2}},\ m=-\frac{5}{2}$$

23. Find the slope of the curve $x^{\frac{2}{3}}+y^{\frac{2}{3}}=5$ at the point (8, 1).

$$F=x^{\frac{2}{3}}+y^{\frac{2}{3}}-5,\ F_x=\frac{2}{3}x^{-1/3},\ F_y=\frac{2}{3}y^{-1/3},$$

$$\frac{dy}{dx}=-\frac{\frac{2}{3}x^{-\frac{1}{3}}}{\frac{2}{3}y^{-\frac{1}{3}}}=-\frac{y^{\frac{1}{3}}}{x^{\frac{1}{3}}},\ \text{At }(8,1),\ m=-\frac{1^{\frac{1}{3}}}{8^{\frac{1}{3}}}=-\frac{1}{2}$$

24. Find the slope of the curve $x^{\frac{2}{3}}-3y^{\frac{2}{3}}=-8$ at the point (8, 1).

$$\frac{dy}{dx}=\frac{y^{\frac{1}{3}}}{3x^{\frac{1}{3}}},\ m=\frac{1}{6}$$

25. Find the slope of the curve $x^2y^2-y=x$ at the point (0, 0).

$$F=x^2y^2-y-x,\ F_x=2xy^2-1,\ F_y=2x^2y-1,$$

$$\frac{dy}{dx}=-\frac{2xy^2-1}{2x^2y-1},\ \text{At }(0,0),\ m=-1$$

26. Find the slope of the curve $x^2y^3+y=x$ at the point (0, 0).

$$\frac{dy}{dx}=-\frac{2xy^3+1}{3x^2y^2-1},\ \text{At }(0,0),\ m=1$$

27. $F=74x^{0.75}y^{0.25}-100,000,\ F_x=55.5x^{-0.25}y^{0.25},\ F_y=18.5x^{0.75}y^{-0.75},$

$$\frac{dy}{dx}=-\frac{55.5x^{-0.25}y^{0.25}}{18.5x^{0.75}y^{-0.75}}=-\frac{3y}{x},\ \text{When }x=1500\text{ units and }y=\$1000,$$

$$\frac{dy}{dx}=-\frac{3(1000)}{1500}=-2\ \textit{dollars invested per labor unit}$$

There is a decrease of $2 invested per labor unit.

28. When $x=1200$ units and $y=\$1900$, $\frac{dy}{dx}=-4.75$ *dollars invested per labor unit*..

There is a decrease of $4.75 invested per labor unit.

VIC3

Related Rates

RELATED RATES

A *rate* is a measure of the ratio of the change in the value of a quantity to the change in *time*. Some such rates are speed in kilometers per hour and interest rate in the change of an amount on deposit per year. In the language of calculus, a *rate* is the derivative of a function with respect to time $\frac{dy}{dt}$.

The equation $x^2 + 2xy - 4y^3 = 5 - 5y$ gives a relationship between two quantities x and y. If x also depends on time and is a function of t, and y also depends on time and is a function of t, we can use the equation $x^2 + 2xy - 4y^3 = 5 - 5y$ to find a relationship equation for the derivatives $\frac{dx}{dt}$ and $\frac{dy}{dt}$ without explicitly knowing $x(t)$ and $y(t)$. The resulting equation gives a relationship between $\frac{dx}{dt}$ and $\frac{dy}{dt}$, a related rate equation.

Related rate equations require implicit differentiation.

Typically, the varying quantities are not labeled generically x and y. Labels for quantities are more along the lines of s for supply, R for revenue, C for cost, and so forth.

RELATED RATE: SINGLE VARIABLE EXPRESSIONS

When the equation involved in a related rate problem can be separated into expressions of terms that only contain one variable, then the partial derivatives of section VIC2 are the same as the derivatives in section VIC1. We will proceed in these cases using the notation of section VIC1.

Example 1:

The sales s in hundreds of thousands of dollars at a company depends on the amount of advertising dollars x in thousands of dollars according to the model $s = 10 - 10e^{-0.05x^2}$. Dollars are invested in advertising at 2 thousand dollars per day. How fast are sales rising when five thousand dollars are invested in advertising?

We have an equation relating s and x. We are also given the fact that the change in thousands of advertising dollars invested per day is $\dfrac{dx}{dt} = 2$. The question asks how fast sales change. We will need to find the rate; that is, the change in sales per time, or $\dfrac{ds}{dt}$ when $x = 5$.

The solution uses the fact that we are differentiating with respect to t. Any term with a variable that is not t is considered the "outside function." For example, if r is a variable that changes with time, and we have the term $5r^3$, then $5r^3$ is the outside function, and the inside function is $\dfrac{dr}{dt}$. The derivative of $5r^3$ would be $\dfrac{dF}{dr}\dfrac{dr}{dt} = 15r^2 \dfrac{dr}{dt}$.

From the perspective of section VIC2 with partial derivatives, the "outside" function is $F = 5r^3$ and $F_r = \dfrac{dF}{dr}$. Since there is only one variable, r, the total derivative $F_r \dfrac{dr}{dt} = 15r^2 \dfrac{dr}{dt}$. We will now proceed without partial derivative notation and use derivative notation.

Solution to Example 1

We are given $s = 10 - 10e^{-0.05x^2}$, $\dfrac{dx}{dt} = 2$, and $x = 5$. We are asked to find $\dfrac{ds}{dt}$.

$(1)\dfrac{ds}{dt} = 0 - 10e^{-0.05x^2}(-0.10)x\dfrac{dx}{dt}$.   We substitute $\dfrac{dx}{dt} = 2$, and $x = 5$.

$\dfrac{ds}{dt} = -10e^{-0.05(5)^2}(-0.10)(5)(2) \approx 2.865$ hundreds of thousands of dollars per day.

Example 2:

A manufacturing plant output y relates to raw material input x by the equation $y^3 = 0.35x^2 - 0.2x$.

Raw material available is declining at 3 units per hour.

How fast is output declining when output is 40 units?

The question is: How fast is output declining? This is asking for the rate:

change in output per time, or $\dfrac{dy}{dt}$.

We are given a change in raw material input with time, or $\dfrac{dx}{dt} = -3 \; units/hour$ and $y = 40 \; units$.

Solution for Example 2

We are given a change in raw material input with time, or $\dfrac{dx}{dt} = -3 \; unit/hour$ and $y = 40 \; units$.

We need to find the change in y with time, or $\dfrac{dy}{dt}$.

$y^3 = 0.35x^2 - 0.2x$

$3y^2\dfrac{dy}{dt} = 0.70x\dfrac{dx}{dt} - 0.2\dfrac{dx}{dt}$

$$\frac{dy}{dt} = \frac{0.70x\frac{dx}{dt} - 0.2\frac{dx}{dt}}{3y^2}$$ We substitute $\frac{dx}{dt} = -3$ *unit/hour* and $y = 40$ *units*.

$$\frac{dy}{dt} = \frac{0.70x(-3\,units/hr) - 0.2(-3\,units/hr)}{3(40\,units)^2}$$

We are still missing a value for x. However, by substituting $y = 40$ *units* into the original equation, we can solve for the current x.

$(40)^3 = 0.35x^2 - 0.2x$

$64,000 = 0.35x^2 - 0.2x$

This is a quadratic equation. We will need to use the quadratic formula.

$0 = 0.35x^2 - 0.2x - 64,000$

$$x = \frac{-b \pm \sqrt{b^2 - 4ac}}{2a} = \frac{--0.2 \pm \sqrt{(-0.2)^2 - 4(0.35)(-64,000)}}{2(0.35)} \approx -427.3,\ 427.9$$

Since $x > 0$, $x \approx 427.9$. Returning to our output over time equation:

$$\frac{dy}{dt} = \frac{.070(427.9)(-3\,units/hr) - 0.2(-3\,units/hr)}{3(40\,units)^2} \approx -0.187\ units/hour$$

Output is decreasing at 0.187 units/hour.

INTRA-SECTION EXERCISES:

1. The Champignon Mushroom Company has invested in a promotional hot air balloon with the company name and logo. The balloon is spherical, and when it is being inflated, the radius increases at 0.6 meters/minute. How fast is the volume increasing when the radius is 2 meters? (Hint: for a sphere, $V = \frac{4}{3}\pi r^3$.)

Champion
Champignons

2. A conical pile of sandy talus is accumulating at the bottom of an overhanging cliff on which a housing subdivision is built. The city engineer would like to know how fast the volume of talus is growing. The height seems to remain at a constant ratio of 1.6 times the radius. The radius is currently 4 feet and growing at 0.3 feet per year.

How fast is the volume growing? (Hint: for a cone, $V = \frac{1}{3}\pi r^2 h$.)

3. After a serious flood has receded, the landing of an exterior metal fire escape at the Corrighan Company began slowly sliding down the wall as the foot began sliding away from the wall in the thick mud. If the foot of the fire escape was moving away at a rate of 0.22 *feet/day*, how fast was the landing moving down the wall when it was 11 feet above the ground? The fire escape remained a constant 20 *feet* long.

Solutions

1. We are given: $\frac{dr}{dt} = 0.6m/min$ and $r = 2$ *meters*. We need $\frac{dV}{dt}$.

   The equation, which relates the "given" quantities and the "needed" quantities, is $V = \frac{4}{3}\pi r^3$.

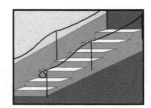

Champion
Champignons

   We take the derivative of both sides with respect to *t*, so any variable that is not *t* is an "outside" function and *t* is the "inside" function. These variables are *V* and *r*.

   $1\frac{dV}{dt} = (3)\frac{4}{3}\pi r^2 \frac{dr}{dt}$ We are looking for $\frac{dV}{dt}$, so we need not solve for it further.

   $\frac{dV}{dt} = 4\pi r^2 \frac{dr}{dt}$ We substitute $\frac{dr}{dt} = 0.6$ m/min and $r = 2$ *meters*.

   $\frac{dV}{dt} = 4\pi(2\ m)^2\left(0.6\frac{m}{min}\right) \approx 30.16 m^3/min.$

2. We are given $h = 1.6r$, $r = 4$ *ft*, and $\frac{dr}{dt} = 0.3\ ft/yr$. We need $\frac{dV}{dt}$.

   An equation that relates the "given" quantities with the "needed" quantities is $V = \frac{1}{3}\pi r^2 h$.

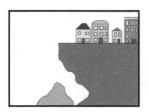

   We first substitute the relationship $h = 1.6r$.

   $$V = \frac{1}{3}\pi r^2(1.6r) = (1.6)\frac{1}{3}\pi r^3$$

We take the derivative of both sides with respect to t, so any variable that is not t is an "outside" function and t is the "inside" function. These variables in our equation are V and r.

$$1\frac{dV}{dt}=(1.6)\frac{1}{3}\pi(3)r^2\frac{dr}{dt}=(1.6)\pi r^2\frac{dr}{dt} \quad \text{We are looking for } \frac{dV}{dt}.$$

$$\frac{dV}{dt}=(1.6)\pi r^2\frac{dr}{dt} \quad \text{We substitute } r=4 \text{ ft and } \frac{dr}{dt}=0.3 \text{ ft/yr.}$$

$$\frac{dV}{dt}=(1.6)\pi((4 \text{ ft})^2)\left(0.3\frac{ft}{yr}\right)\approx 24.1 \text{ ft}^3/yr$$

The talus cone is accumulating 24.1 cubic feet per year, which might soon have serious consequences for the homeowners on top of the cliff.

3. We are given $l=20$ ft, a constant; $\frac{dx}{dt}=0.22$ ft/da; and $y=11$ ft.

    We need $\frac{dy}{dt}$. We can use the Pythagorean theorem: $x^2+y^2=l^2$ which will relate the "given" and "needed" quantities.

    Because l is a constant 20 feet, we can substitute this value directly into our equation.

    $x^2+y^2=20^2$ Next, we take the derivative of both sides with respect to t, so any variable that is not t is an "outside" function and t is the "inside" function. These variables in our equation are x and y.

    $$2x\frac{dx}{dt}+2y\frac{dy}{dt}=0 \quad \text{We need to solve for } \frac{dy}{dt}.$$

    $$2y\frac{dy}{dt}=-2x\frac{dx}{dt}$$

    $$\frac{dy}{dt}=-\frac{x}{y}\frac{dx}{dt}$$

We can substitute $y=11$ ft and $\frac{dx}{dt}=0.22$ ft/da, but as yet we do not know the value of x. However, at this instant, we do know the values of x and l, so we can use the Pythagorean theorem again to find x when $y=11$ feet.

$x^2 + 11^2 = 20^2$; this gives us $x \approx 16.7$ ft. when $y = 11$ ft.

$$\frac{dy}{dt} = -\frac{x}{y}\frac{dx}{dt} = -\frac{16.7\,ft}{11\,ft}\left(0.22\frac{ft}{da}\right) \approx -0.334\ ft/day$$

The fire escape landing is sliding down at a rate of 0.334 feet per day at this rate. It should be stabilized immediately.

RELATED RATE: MULTI-VARIABLE EXPRESSIONS

Suppose the BugOut Company bottles a spray to eliminate bed bugs. They market it in airport kiosks near the check-in counters. Their ads advise customers to spray their luggage and pack a bottle of the spray before the customers check in their luggage.

BugOut has determined that sales depend on the number of outgoing flights. Sales also depend on the number of bed bug reports in online reporting sites. Assume sales S (in thousands of dollars) can be modeled by the equation $S = 0.2F^2 + 0.014FB + 75$, where F is the number of outgoing flights per year at the local airport, and B is the number of bed bug reports logged in the past year. If the number of outgoing flights is currently 55 per day and increasing at an average of one per year, and the number of bed bug reports in the last year is 170 but decreasing at a rate of 26 per year, and sales last year were $53,000, find the rate at which sales will increase or decrease.

The expression $0.2F^2 + 0.014FB + 75$ involves two independent variables F and B. We can generate the related rate equation using either the methods of section VIC1 or section VIC2, but they are now different processes. We will find the rate of sales using the methods of section VIC1 to find the rate of sales, and then we will go back and find the rate of sales using the methods of section VIC2.

Section VIC1 Methods:

We need to find $\frac{dS}{dt}$. We note all the information that is "given":

$F = (55)(365) = 20075$ for one year, $\frac{dF}{dt} = 1$, $B = 170$, $\frac{dB}{dt} = -26$, $S = \$53,000$.

We generate the related rate equation from the relationship

$$S = 0.2F^2 + 0.014FB + 75$$

We use the chain rule to find the derivative of $0.2F^2$ and the product rule to find the derivative of FB.

$$\frac{dS}{dt} = 0.2(2)F^1\frac{dF}{dt} + 0.014\left(\frac{dF}{dt} + \frac{dB}{dt}\right) + 0$$

$$\frac{dS}{dt} = 0.4F\frac{dF}{dt} + 0.014\left(B\frac{dF}{dt} + F\frac{dB}{dt}\right)$$

Substitute the given values into the related rate equation.

$$\frac{dS}{dt} = 0.4(20075)(1) + 0.014((170)(1) + (20075)(-26)) = 725.08 \text{ bottles per year.}$$

Section VIC2 Methods:

We need to find $\frac{dS}{dt}$. We note all the information that is "given":

$F = (55)(365) = 20075$ for one year, $\frac{dF}{dt} = 1$, $B = 170$, $\frac{dB}{dt} = -26$, $S = \$53,000$.

We generate the related rate equation from the relationship

$$S = 0.2F^2 + 0.014FB + 75$$

Choose $G = 0.2F^2 + 0.014FB + 75$ then $G_F = 0.2(2)F + 0.014B$ and $G_B = 0.014F$.

The related rate equation is $\frac{dS}{dt} = (0.4F + 0.014B)\frac{dF}{dt} + 0.014F\frac{dB}{dt}$.

Substitute the given values into the related rate equation.

$$\frac{dS}{dt} = (0.4(20075) + 0.014(170))(1) + 0.014(20075)(-26) = 725.08.$$

At this point, we will proceed using the methods of section VIC2 with more complicated expressions in multiple variables on both the left and right sides on an equation.

Example 3:

The number of shoes, s, that ACM Corporation supplies weekly to Shoes 'R' US' and the price of a pair of shoes, p, are related by the equation $50(p+30)^2 s^{0.2} + 28120 = 9\ s^3 + s\ \ln(sp-2)$. If the price is rising at the rate of \$0.60 per week, how is the supply changing when the current price is \$100 and the current number of shoes supplied per week is 60?

Choose $F = 50(p+30)^2 s^{0.2} + 28120$ and $G = s^3 + s\ln(sp-2)$, then

$$F_p = 50(2)(p+30)s^{0.2} = 100(p+30)s^{0.2}\ ,$$

$$F_s = 50(p+30)^2(0.2)s^{-0.8} = 10(p+30)^2 s^{-0.8}$$

$$G_p = s\frac{s}{sp-2} = \frac{s^2}{sp-2} \quad G_s = 3s^2 + \ln(sp-2) + s\frac{p}{sp-2} = 3s^2 + \ln(sp-2) + \frac{sp}{sp-2}.$$

The related rate equation:

$$F_p\frac{dp}{dt} + F_s\frac{ds}{dt} = G_p\frac{dp}{dt} + G_s\frac{ds}{dt}$$

$$100(p+30)s^{0.2}\frac{dp}{dt} + 10(p+30)^2 s^{-0.8}\frac{ds}{dt} = \frac{s^2}{sp-2}\frac{dp}{dt} + \left(3s^2 + \ln(sp-2) + \frac{sp}{sp-2}\right)\frac{ds}{dt}$$

Substitute the given information:

$$100(100+30)(60)^{0.2}(0.60) + 10(100+30)^2(60)^{-0.8}\frac{ds}{dt}$$

$$= \frac{60^2}{60(100)-2}(0.60) + \left(3(60)^2 + \ln(60(100)-2) + \frac{6(100)}{60(100)-2}\right)\frac{ds}{dt}$$

$$17689.8786 + 6388.0117\frac{ds}{dt} = 0.36012004 + 10808.7992\frac{ds}{dt}$$

$$6388.0117\frac{ds}{dt} - 10808.7992\frac{ds}{dt} = 0.36012004 - 17689.8786$$

$$\left(6388.0117 - 10808.7992\right)\frac{ds}{dt} = 0.36012004 - 17689.8786$$

$$-4420.7875\frac{ds}{dt} = -17689.5185,$$

$$\frac{ds}{dt} = -\frac{17689.5185}{-4420.7875} \approx 4.0014 \text{ shoes per week increase.}$$

VIC3 RELATED RATES EXERCISES

1. A popular restaurant chain has determined that its customer base spreads out in the year after its initial opening and can be modeled by an expanding circle, in which the area of the circle is analogous to the number of customers, and the radius is the farthest distance from the restaurant. At what rate is the area (number of customers) increasing if the farthest distance of customers from the restaurant (radius) is currently at 2 miles and expanding at 0.5 miles/month? If each square mile represents 25 customers, how fast is the customer base increasing?

2. A popular restaurant chain has determined that its customer base spreads out in the year after its initial opening and can be modeled by an expanding circle, in which the area of the circle is the number of customers, and the radius is the farthest distance from the restaurant. At what rate is the area (number of customers) increasing if the farthest distance of customers from the restaurant (radius) is currently at 1.5 miles and expanding at 0.25 miles/month? If each square mile represents 20 customers, how fast is the customer base increasing?

3. A construction company is building a cylindrical tower. The tower is rising at 3 meters per week, and the radius is a constant 20 meters. How fast is the volume of the tower increasing? (Hint: The volume of a cylinder is $\pi r^2 h$.)

4. A construction company is building a cylindrical tower. The tower is rising at 2.6 meters per week, and the radius is a constant 18 meters. How fast is the volume of the tower increasing?

5. A cubical primitive structure, possibly an aboriginal temple, is disintegrating due to the incursion of vegetation. If each dimension is shrinking at a rate of 0.3 meters per year, at what rate is the volume diminishing if each edge is currently 12 meters?

6. A cubical primitive structure, possibly a native multifamily complex, is disintegrating due to its inundation by a recently dammed river. If each dimension is shrinking at a rate of 0.2 meters per year, at what rate is the volume diminishing if each edge is currently 15 meters?

7. A retail furniture store estimates that its weekly sales S and weekly advertising costs a are related by the equation $S = 1500 + 30a - 0.01a^2$. The current weekly advertising costs are $1200, and these costs are increasing at a rate of $120 per week. Find the current rate of change of weekly sales.

8. A retail furniture store estimates that weekly sales S and weekly advertising costs a are related by the equation $S = 1500 + 50a - 0.02a^2$. The current weekly advertising costs are $1100, and these costs are increasing at a rate of $130 per week. Find the current rate of change of weekly sales.

9. A company that manufactures trading card packs calculates that its costs and revenue can be modeled by the equations $C = 50,000 + 1.1x$ and $R = 500x - 0.008x^2$, where x is the number of cards. If production in one particular week is 20,000 cards and is increasing at a rate of 1200 cards per week, find the following:

   a. the rate at which the cost is changing.
   b. the rate at which the revenue is changing.
   c. the rate at which the profit is changing.

10. A company that manufactures packs of gum calculates that its costs and revenue can be modeled by the equations $C = 40,000 + 1.3x$ and $R = 550x - 0.0087x^2$, where x is the number of gum sticks. If production in one particular week is 25,000 gum sticks and is increasing at a rate of 1400 gum sticks per week, find the following:

   a. the rate at which the cost is changing.
   b. the rate at which the revenue is changing.
   c. the rate at which the profit is changing.

11. The number of shoes, s, that ACM Corporation supplies weekly to Shoes 'R' US and the price of shoes, p, are related by the equation $3p^2 + 19500 = 4s^3$. If the price is rising at the rate of $0.50 per week, how is the supply changing when the current price is $69?

12. The number of blades (b) that ACM Corporation supplies weekly to Ice Skates 'R' Us and the price of blades (p) are related by the equation $2.8p^2 + 24,000 = 4b^3$. If the price is rising at the rate of $.50 per week, how is the supply of blades changing when the current price is $26?

13. The number of hats, h, that Habadashes sells monthly and price of hats, p, are related by the equation $2h^2 + 2500 = 4p^2$. If the price is rising at the rate of $1.25 per month, how is the number of hats sold changing when the current price is $80?

14. The monthly sales of pullets, s, by D & O Produce and the price of pullets, p, are related by the equation $2s^2 + 3.2 = 38p^2$. If the price is rising at the rate of $0.25 per month, how are the sales changing when the current price is $1.80?

15. At a manufacturing company, the number of workers n, and the amount of resources available, x, are related by the equation $\sqrt{3n} + 600 = 5x - 0.005xn$. Find $\dfrac{dn}{dt}$ when the work force is at 50 and the amount of resources is changing at a rate of 20 units per day.

16. At a retail firm, the number of online orders, n, and the number of online hits, h, are related by the equation $\sqrt{3n} + 600 = 5h - 0.0005hn$. Find $\dfrac{dn}{dt}$ when the number of online orders is 500 and the number of online hits is increasing at a rate of 200 hits per day.

17. Easy Park is an alternative to the airport parking garage. Patrons who use their services park in Easy Park's lot and take a shuttle to the airport. Easy Park has determined that the number of patrons N depends on the average number of daily flights F, the number of competitor lots C, and the cost differential between the airport garage's hourly rate and Easy Park's hourly rate, according to the function:

$$N = 0.21F - 50C + 30D.$$

If the current number of daily flights is 80 but is increasing at a rate of 2/*year*, the current number of competitors is 3 but is likely to increase by 1 per year, and the current differential is $1.30 but is likely to decrease by $0.20 per year, determine the expected change in the number of patrons for Easy Park.

18. Easy Park is an alternative to the airport parking garage. Patrons who use their services park in Easy Park's lot and take a shuttle to the airport. Easy Park has determined that the number of patrons N depends on the number of average number of daily flights F, the number of competitor lots C, and the cost differential between the airport garage's hourly rate and Easy Park's hourly rate, according to the function:

$$N = 56F - 50C + 30D.$$

If the current number of daily flights is 85 but is increasing at a rate of 2/*year*, the current number of competitors is 2 but is likely to increase by 2 per year and the current differential is $.80 but is likely to decrease by $0.10 per year, determine the expected change in the number of patrons for Easy Park.

19. The Fennel-Harrith Company measures water quality in number of pollutants P in ppm (parts per million). Compounds A, B, and C are possible contaminants, and the company's filtration system can clean F ppm hourly. Some of the contaminants can bond and reduce the filtration efficiency and also increase the amount of pollutants in the system by making flow-through more difficult. The system has been modeled by the following equation:

$$30A + 20B + 80C - 50F = P + AB^2 - 10ABF - 5ACF$$

The current level of A is 14 ppm. Adding a new production line will cause an increase of contaminants A and B. A is expected to increase by 0.005 ppm/hour; B is currently 23 ppm and expected to increase by 0.02 ppm/hour; C is currently 52 ppm and expected to decrease by 0.04 ppm/hour. If the filtration system currently processes 100 ppm, but its deficiency decreases over time at 0.003 ppm/hour, determine the expected change in pollutants P in ppm/hour.

20. The Fennel-Harrith Company measures water quality in number of pollutants P in ppm (parts per million). Compounds A, B, and C are possible contaminants, and their filtration system can clean F ppm hourly. Some of the contaminants

can bond and reduce the filtration efficiency and also increase the amount of pollutants in the system by making flow-through more difficult. The system has been modeled by the following equation:

$$20A + 30B + 40C - 100F = P + AC^2 - 10ACF - 5ABF$$

The current level of A is 14 ppm. Adding a new production line will cause an increase of contaminants A and B. A is expected to increase by 0.005 ppm/hour; B is currently 23 ppm and expected to increase by 0.02 ppm/hour; C is currently 52 ppm and expected to decrease by 0.04 ppm/hour. If the filtration system currently processes 100 ppm, but its deficiency decreases over time at 0.003 ppm/hour, determine the expected change in pollutants P in ppm/hour.

21. For planning purposes, the Welsh-Jordan Private Academy would like to know how its student population is expected to change. The projected number of students depends on the population in its district, P, the percent of the population in the district with income above the median income level I, and the number of alumni, A. These relationships can be modeled by the function:

$$N = 0.012P + 0.04IP + 0.002A^2 + 300.$$

If the population is currently 8,000 but is decreasing at 100 per year, the percent above the median income is currently 0.7, but is decreasing at 0.15 per year, and the number of alumni is 3,500 and increasing at a net of 7 per year, find the projected annual change in projected number of students N.

22. For planning purposes, the Welsh-Jordan Private Academy would like to know how its student population is expected to change. The projected number of students depends on the population in its district, P, the percent of the population in the district with income above the median income level, I, and the number of alumni, A. These relationships can be modeled by the function:

$$N = 0.012P + 0.04IP + 0.0002A^2 + 300.$$

If the population is currently 3,200 but is decreasing at 28 per year, the percent above the median income is currently 0.7, but is decreasing at .08 per year, and the number of alumni is 5,500 and increasing at a net of 5 per year, find the projected annual change in projected number of students N.

23. The Sorrel Corporation manufactures veterinary pharmaceuticals. Their profit depends on the cost of ingredients, I, and the cost of labor, w. The price of beef b has been found to be a good predictor of how likely livestock producers are to purchase veterinary supplies. Profit has been determined to be modeled by the equation:

$$P + \$8900 = 1.4b^2I - 0.2b - 0.3Iw^2 - 0.6w$$

where P represents profit in thousands of dollars. The current price of beef is $3.20 per pound, ingredients are $38.50 per pound produced, and labor is approximately $12.50 per pound produced. Compute the expected change in profit per year if the price of beef is expected to fall $0.05 per pound yearly, the cost of ingredients is expected to rise $1.20 per pound yearly, and the cost of labor is expected to rise $0.80 per pound yearly.

24. The Sorrel Corporation manufactures veterinary pharmaceuticals. Their profit depends on the cost of ingredients, I, and the cost of labor, w. The price of beef b has been found to be a good predictor of how likely livestock producers are to purchase veterinary supplies. Profit has been determined to be modeled by the equation:

$$P + \$6900 = 1.6b^2 - 0.2bI - 0.3Iw^2 - 0.6w$$

where P represents profit in thousands of dollars. The current price of beef is $3.40 per pound, ingredients are $22.50 per pound produced, and labor is approximately $12.80 per pound produced. Compute the expected change in profit per year if the price of beef is expected to fall $0.06 per pound yearly, the cost of ingredients is expected to fall $.20 per pound yearly, and the cost of labor is expected to rise $0.25 per pound yearly.

25. The Great Shakes Shop estimates that quantity demanded, q, is dependent on the number of coupons redeemed, r, the number of online hits at their website, h, and the number of coupons distributed by their competitors, c, modeled by the following equation:

$$0.41r + \frac{600h}{c} - 0.07c - q = 1500$$

If r is currently 4,000, and expected to remain steady, h is 3300 but expected to increase by 500 per year, c is 2,000 and expected to increase by 1,000 per year, and q is currently 45,000, determine the expected change in demand per year.

26. The Gourmet Meatball Bistro estimates that quantity demanded, q, is dependent on the number of coupons redeemed, r, the number of online hits at their website, h, and the number of coupons distributed by their competitors, c, modeled by the following equation.

$$0.41r - \frac{800h}{c} - 0.07c - 0.25q = 1500.$$

If r is currently 2,000, and expected to remain steady, h is 5300 but expected to increase by 500 per year, c is 400 and expected to increase by 200 per year, and q is currently 95,000, determine the expected change in demand per year.

VIC3 RELATED RATES: SOLUTIONS TO EXERCISES

1. We are given $r = 2$ *miles* and $\dfrac{dr}{dt} = 0.5$ *miles/month*. We need $\dfrac{dA}{dt}$.

   For a circle $A = \pi r^2$. We differentiate both sides implicitly with respect to t.

   (1)$\dfrac{dA}{dt} = 2\pi r \dfrac{dr}{dt}$ We substitute $r = 2$ *miles* and $\dfrac{dr}{dt} = 0.5$ *miles/month*.

   $$\dfrac{dA}{dt} = 2\pi(2 \ miles)\left(0.5\dfrac{miles}{month}\right) \approx 6.28\dfrac{miles^2}{month} = 6.28 \ square \ miles \ per \ month$$

   If there are 25 customers/square mile, the base is increasing at

   $$\dfrac{25 \ customers}{sq \ mile} \ x \ \dfrac{6.28 \ sq \ miles}{month} = 157 \ customers/month$$

2. $\dfrac{dA}{dt} \approx 2.36 \ square \dfrac{miles}{month}$.

   This represents an increase in approximately 47 customers/month.

3. We are given $\dfrac{dh}{dt} = 3 \ m/wk$ and a constant $r = 20 \ meter$. We need $\dfrac{dV}{dt}$.

   $V = \pi r^2 h$ We can substitute the constant $r = 20 \ m$ immediately.

   $V = \pi(20 \ m)^2 h$ We take the derivative of both sides implicitly with respect to t.

   (1)$\dfrac{dV}{dt} = \pi(20 \ m)^2(1)\dfrac{dh}{dt}$ We substitute $\dfrac{dh}{dt} = 3 \ m/wk$.

   $$\dfrac{dV}{dt} = \pi(20 \ m)^2(1)\left(\dfrac{3m}{wk}\right) \approx 3769.9 \ meters^3/week$$

4. $\dfrac{dV}{dt} \approx 2646.5 \ meter^3/week$

5. We are given $\dfrac{de}{dt} = -0.3m/yr$ and $e = 12 \ meters$. We need $\dfrac{dV}{dt}$.

   For a cube, $V = e^3$ where e equals the length of each edge.

   $V = e^3$ We take the derivative of each side of the equation implicitly with respect to t.

   (1)$\dfrac{dV}{dt} = 3e^2 \dfrac{de}{dt}$ We substitute $\dfrac{de}{dt} = -0.3m/yr$ and $e = 12 \ meters$.

   $$\dfrac{dV}{dt} = 3(12m)^2\left(-\dfrac{0.3m}{yr}\right) \approx -129.6\dfrac{(meters)^3}{year}$$

   The ruin is losing 129.6 cubic meters per year.

6. $\dfrac{dV}{dt} = -135 \ (meters)^3 / year$

The ruin is losing 135 cubic meters per year.

7. $(1)\dfrac{dS}{dt} = 0 + 30\dfrac{da}{dt} - 0.02a\dfrac{da}{dt}$; at $a = \$1200$ and $\dfrac{da}{dt} = \$120/week$,

$\dfrac{dS}{dt} = 30(\$120) - 0.02(\$1200)(\$120) = \$720$ per week

8. $\dfrac{dS}{dt} = \$780/week$; sales are increasing at $780/week

9. a. We need $\dfrac{dC}{dt}$ and we are given $x = 20,000 \ cards$; $\dfrac{dx}{dt} = 1200 \ cards/week$.

$C = 50,000 + 1.1x$

$(1)\dfrac{dC}{dt} = 0 + 1.1\dfrac{dx}{dt}$

$\dfrac{dC}{dt} = 1.1(1200) = \$1320/week$ Costs are increasing at $1320/week$.

b. $R = 500x - 0.008x^2$

$(1)\dfrac{dR}{dt} = 500\dfrac{dx}{dt} - 0.016x\dfrac{dx}{dt}$

$\dfrac{dR}{dt} = 500(1200) - 0.016(20,000)(1200) = \$216,000/week$

Revenue is increasing at $216,000/week$.

c. Profit = Revenue – Cost; $P(x) = 500x - 0.008x^2 - (50,000 + 1.1x)$

$P(x) = -0.008x^2 + 498.9x - 50,000$

$(1)\dfrac{dP}{dt} = -0.016x\dfrac{dx}{dt} + 498.9\dfrac{dx}{dt}$

$(1)\dfrac{dP}{dt} = -0.016(20,000)(1200) + 498.9(1200) = \$214,680/week$

Profits are increasing at $214,680/week$.

10. a. $\dfrac{dC}{dt} = \$1820/week$ Costs are increasing at $1820/week$.

b. $\dfrac{dR}{dt} = \$161,000/week$ Revenue is increasing at $161,000/week$.

c. $\dfrac{dP}{dt} = \$159,180/week$ Profit is increasing at $159,180/week$.

11. We are given $\frac{dp}{dt}=\$0.50/week$ and $p=\$69$. We need $\frac{ds}{dt}$.

$$3p^2+19500=4s^3$$

$$6p\frac{dp}{dt}=12s^2\frac{ds}{dt}$$

$$\frac{6p\frac{dp}{dt}}{12s^2}=\frac{ds}{dt}=\frac{p}{2s^2}\frac{dp}{dt}=\frac{(\$69)}{2s^2}(\$0.50/week)$$

To find s, we use the original equation, $3p^2+19500=4s^3$ and solve for s when $p=\$69$.

$$3(\$69)^2+19500=4s^3;\ s=\sqrt[3]{\frac{3(\$69)^2+19500}{4}}\approx\$20.36$$

Back to $\frac{ds}{dt}=\frac{(\$69)}{2(20.36)^2}\left(\frac{\$0.50}{week}\right)\approx.042\,shoes/week$.

The supply of shoes is increasing by approximately 0.042shoes per week.

12. $\frac{db}{dt}\approx0.175\ supply\ of\ blades/week$

The supply of blades is increasing by approximately 0.175/week.

13. We are given $\frac{dp}{dt}=\$1.25/mo$ and $p=\$80$. We need $\frac{dh}{dt}$.

$$2h^2+2500=4p^2$$

$$4h\frac{dh}{dt}+0=8p\frac{dp}{dt}$$

$$\frac{dh}{dt}=\frac{8p}{4h}\frac{dp}{dt}=\frac{2p}{h}\frac{dp}{dt}=\frac{2(80)}{h}(1.25)$$

To find h we use the original equation $2h^2+2500=4p^2$.

$$2h^2=4p^2-2500;\ h=\sqrt{\frac{4p^2-2500}{2}};\ h=\sqrt{\frac{4(80)^2-2500}{2}}\approx107.47$$

Back to $\frac{dh}{dt}=\frac{2(\$80)}{107.47}\left(\frac{\$1.25}{mo}\right)\approx1.86\ hats/month$

The number of hats sold is increasing by approximately 1.86 hats per month.

14. $\dfrac{ds}{dt} \approx 1.10 \; pullets/month$

Then number of pullets sold is increasing by approximately 1.10 per month.

15. <u>Solution using section VIC2</u>: We are given $n = 50$ and $\dfrac{dx}{dt} = 20 \dfrac{units}{day}$. We need $\dfrac{dn}{dt}$.

Choose $F = \sqrt{3n} + 600 = (3n)^{\frac{1}{2}} + 600$ and $G = 5x - 0.005xn$, then

$$F_n = \frac{1}{2}(3n)^{-\frac{1}{2}}(3) + 0 = \frac{3}{2}(3n)^{-\frac{1}{2}}, \; F_x = 0, \; G_n = -0.005x, \; G_x = 5 - 0.005n.$$

The related rate equation is $\dfrac{3}{2}(3n)^{-\frac{1}{2}}\dfrac{dn}{dt} + 0\dfrac{dx}{dt} = -0.005x\dfrac{dn}{dt} + (5 - 0.005n)\dfrac{dx}{dt}$

Substitute $n = 50$ and $\dfrac{dx}{dt} = 20\dfrac{units}{day}$,

$$\frac{3}{2}(3(50))^{-\frac{1}{2}}\frac{dn}{dt} + 0\frac{dx}{dt} = -0.005x\frac{dn}{dt} + (5 - 0.005(50))(20)$$

$$\frac{3}{2}(150)^{-\frac{1}{2}}\frac{dn}{dt} = -0.005x\frac{dn}{dt} + 95$$

To find x we use the original equation when $n = 50$.

$$\sqrt{3n} + 600 = 5x - 0.005xn,$$

$$\sqrt{3(50)} + 600 = 5x - 0.005x(50)$$

$$\sqrt{150} + 600 = x(5 - 0.25) = 4.75x$$

$$x = \frac{\sqrt{150} + 600}{4.75} \approx \frac{612.24}{4.75} \approx 128.89$$

We return to the related rate equation,

$$\frac{3}{2}(150)^{-\frac{1}{2}}\frac{dn}{dt} = -0.005(128.89)\frac{dn}{dt} + 95$$

$$\frac{3}{2}(150)^{-\frac{1}{2}}\frac{dn}{dt} + 0.005(128.89)\frac{dn}{dt} = 95$$

$$\left(\frac{3}{2}(150)^{-\frac{1}{2}} + 0.005(128.89)\right)\frac{dn}{dt} = 95$$

$$0.7669\frac{dn}{dt} \approx 95$$

$$\frac{dn}{dt} \approx \frac{95}{0.7669} \approx 123.87 \text{ workers per day.}$$

Solution using section VIC1: We are given $n=50$ and $\frac{dx}{dt}=20 \text{ } units/day$. We need $\frac{dn}{dt}$.

$$\sqrt{3n}+600=5x-0.005xn$$

$(3n)^{\frac{1}{2}}+600=5x-0.005xn$ We use the Chain Rule to find the derivative of $(3n)^{\frac{1}{2}}$ and the Product Rule to find the derivative of $-0.005xn$.

$$\frac{1}{2}(3n)^{-\frac{1}{2}}(3)\frac{dn}{dt}+0=5\frac{dx}{dt}-(0.005)\frac{dx}{dt}n-(0.005x)(1)\frac{dn}{dt}$$

$$\frac{1}{2}(3n)^{-\frac{1}{2}}(3)\frac{dn}{dt}+(0.005x)(1)\frac{dn}{dt}=5\frac{dx}{dt}-(0.005)\frac{dx}{dt}n$$

$$\frac{dn}{dt}\left[\frac{1}{2}(3n)^{-\frac{1}{2}}(3)+0.005x\right]=5\frac{dx}{dt}-(0.005)\frac{dx}{dt}n$$

$$\frac{dn}{dt}=\frac{5\frac{dx}{dt}-(0.005)\frac{dx}{dt}n}{\frac{1}{2}(3n)^{-\frac{1}{2}}(3)+0.005x}=\frac{5(20)-(0.005(20)(50)}{\frac{3}{2}(3(50))^{-\frac{1}{2}}+0.005x}$$

To find x we use the original equation when $n=50$.

$$\sqrt{3n}+600=5x-0.005xn$$

$$\sqrt{3n}+600=x(5-0.005n)$$

$$\frac{\sqrt{3n}+600}{5-0.005n}=x=\frac{\sqrt{3(50)}+600}{5-0.005(50)}\approx\frac{612.24}{4.75}\approx128.89$$

We return to: $\dfrac{dn}{dt}=\dfrac{5(20)-(0.005(20)(50)}{\frac{3}{2}(3(50))^{-\frac{1}{2}}+0.005(128.89)}\approx123.87 \text{ } workers \text{ } per \text{ } day$

16. $\dfrac{dn}{dt}\approx8971 \text{ } orders/day$

The number of online hits is increasing by approximately 8971 orders per day.

17. We are given: $F=80$; $\dfrac{dF}{dt}=2$; $C=3$; $\dfrac{dC}{dt}=1$; $D=1.30$; $\dfrac{dD}{dt}=-0.20$, and

$N=0.21F-50C+30D$. We need $\dfrac{dN}{dt}$.

Choose $G=0.21F-50C+30D$ then $G_F=0.21$, $G_C=-50$, and $G_D=30$.

The related rate equation is $\dfrac{dN}{dt}=0.21\dfrac{dF}{dt}-50\dfrac{dC}{dt}+30\dfrac{dD}{dt}$

Substitute the given values

$\dfrac{dN}{dt}=0.21(2)-50(1)+30(-\$0.20)=-55.58$

The number of patrons is expected to decrease by approximately 56 per year. This figure is driven largely by the term representing growth in number of competitors. Easy Park may need to develop a definite competitive advantage.

18. The number of patrons is expected to increase by approximately 9 customers per year. This indicates that demand will essentially remain the same.

19. We are given: $A=14$; $\dfrac{dA}{dt}=0.005$; $B=23$; $\dfrac{dB}{dt}=0.02$; $C=52$; $\dfrac{dC}{dt}=-0.04$;

$F=100$; $\dfrac{dF}{dt}=-0.003$ and $30A+20B+80C-50F=P+AB^2-10ABF-5ACF$.

We need $\dfrac{dP}{dt}$.

Choose $Q=30A+20B+80C-50F$ and $G=P+AB^2-10ABF-5ACF$ then

$Q_A=30$, $Q_B=20$, $Q_C=80$, $Q_F=-50$, $Q_P=0$, $G_A=B^2-10BF-5CF$,

$G_B=2AB-10AF$, $G_C=-5AF$, $G_F=-10AB-5AC$, and $G_P=1$.

The related rate equation is:

$30\dfrac{dA}{dt}+20\dfrac{dB}{dt}+80\dfrac{dC}{dt}-50\dfrac{dF}{dt}+0\dfrac{dP}{dt}$

$=(B^2-10BF-5CF)\dfrac{dA}{dt}+(2AB-10AF)\dfrac{dB}{dt}-5AF\dfrac{dC}{dt}+(-10AB-5AC)\dfrac{dF}{dt}+1\dfrac{dP}{dt}$

Substitute the given values:

$30(0.005)+20(0.02)+80(-0.04)-50(-0.003)$

$=(23^2-10(23)(100)-5(52)(100))(0.005)+(2(14)(23)-10(14)(100))(0.02)$

$-5(14)(100)(-0.04)+(-10(14)(23)-5(14)(52))(-0.003)+\dfrac{dP}{dt}$

$$-2.5 = -242.355 - 267.12 + 280 + 20.58 + \frac{dP}{dt}$$

$$\frac{dP}{dt} = 206.395$$

An increase in pollutants of 206.395 ppm/hour is expected. Fennel-Harrith may want to invest in a better filtration system.

20. $\frac{dP}{dt} = 860.05$. An increase in pollutants of 860.05 ppm/hour is expected.

21. We are given $P = 8,000$; $\frac{dP}{dt} = -100$; $I = 0.7$; $\frac{dI}{dt} = -0.15$; $A = 3,500$; $\frac{dA}{dt} = 7$

and $N = 0.012P + 0.04IP + 0.002A^2 + 300$. We need $\frac{dN}{dt}$.

Choose $F = 0.012P + 0.04IP + 0.002A^2 + 300$ then $F_P = 0.012 + 0.04I$, $F_I = 0.04P$, and $F_A = 0.004A$.

The related rate equation is $\frac{dN}{dt} = (0.012 + 0.04I)\frac{dP}{dt} + 0.04P\frac{dI}{dt} + 0.004A\frac{dA}{dt}$.

Substitute the given values:

$$\frac{dN}{dt} = (0.012 + 0.04(0.7))(-100) + 0.04(8000)(-0.15) + 0.004(3500)(7) = 46$$

An increase of 46 students per year is expected. The academy might want to do some long-range planning for an addition and more staff.

22. $\frac{dN}{dt} = -0.36$. It appears the enrollment will remain steady for the foreseeable

future, despite an expected loss in population and higher-income residents in the future.

23. We are given: $b = \$3.20$; $I = \$38.50$; $w = \$12.50$; $\frac{db}{dt} = -\$0.05$; $\frac{dI}{dt} = \$1.20$;

$\frac{dw}{dt} = \$0.80$ and $P + \$8900 = 1.4b^2I - 0.2b - 0.3Iw^2 - 0.6w$. We need $\frac{dP}{dt}$.

Choose $F = P + \$8900$ and $G = 1.4b^2I - 0.2b - 0.3Iw^2 - 0.6w$ then $F_P = 1$, $F_I = 0$, $F_b = 0$, $F_w = 0$, $G_P = 0$, $G_I = 1.4b^2 - 0.3w^2$, $G_b = 2.8bI - 0.2$, and $G_w = -0.6Iw - 0.6$.

The related rate equation is $1\frac{dP}{dt} + 0\frac{dI}{dt} + 0\frac{db}{dt} + 0\frac{dw}{dt} = 0\frac{dP}{dt} + (1.4b^2 - 0.3w^2)$.

$\frac{dI}{dt} + (2.8bI - 0.2)\frac{db}{dt} + (-0.6Iw - 0.6)\frac{dw}{dt}$.

Substitute the given values:

$$\frac{dP}{dt} = (1.4(3.20)^2 - 0.3(12.50)^2)(1.20) + (2.8(3.20)(38.50) - 0.2)(-0.05)$$

$$+ (-0.6(38.50)(12.50) - 0.6)(0.80) = -287.7648$$

A decrease in profit of $287,764.80 is expected per year, driven largely by the cost of ingredients. Sorrel should implement cost-cutting policies or consider raising their prices.

24. $\frac{dP}{dt} = -33.7664$. A decrease in profit of $33,766 is expected annually, driven largely by the cost of ingredients. Sorrel should implement cost-cutting policies or consider raising their prices.

25. We are given: $r = 4000$; $\frac{dr}{dt} = 0$; $h = 3300$; $\frac{dh}{dt} = 500\big/_{yr}$; $c = 2000$;

$\frac{dc}{dt} = 1000\big/_{yr}$; $q = 45{,}000$ and $0.41r + \frac{600h}{c} - 0.07c - q = 1500$. We need $\frac{dq}{dt}$.

choose $F = 0.41r + \frac{600h}{c} - 0.07c - q = 0.41r + 600hc^{-1} - 0.07c - q$ then

$F_r = 0.41$, $F_h = \frac{600}{c}$, $F_c = -600hc^{-2} - 0.07$, and $F_q = -1$.

The related rate equation is $0.41\frac{dr}{dt} + \frac{600}{c}\frac{dh}{dt} + (-600hc^{-2} - 0.07)\frac{dc}{dt} - \frac{dq}{dt} = 0$.

Substitute the given values:

$$0.41(0) + \frac{600}{2000}(500) + (-600(3300)(2000)^{-2} - 0.07)(1000) - \frac{dq}{dt} = 0$$

$$\frac{dq}{dt} = -415$$

Demand is expected to decrease by approximately 415 shakes per year.

26. Demand is expected to grow by 17,144 meatballs per year.

VIC4

Indefinite Integrals

Consider the functions below and their derivatives.

Do you agree that the derivative of $f(x)=3x^2+6x-1$ is $f'(x)=6x+6$?

Do you agree that the derivative of $f(x)=3x^2+6x+5$ is also $f'(x)=6x+6$?

Would you further agree that the derivative of $f(x)=3x^2+6x$ is again $f'(x)=6x+6$?

In fact, the derivative for the function $f(x)=3x^2+6x+C$, where C is any constant, will always be $f'(x)=6x+6$.

INDEFINITE INTEGRALS

We say that the function $F(x)=3x^2+6x+C$ is the antiderivative of $f(x)=6x+6$. If we're going backward from a derivative function to its antiderivative, we'll need to recognize that the antiderivative could contain a constant we can't determine from the derivative alone, so we add a generic "$+C$." It's called the *constant of integration*. Antiderivatives are also called *Indefinite Integrals*. In what follows, we will see why this name makes sense. We use the integral notation $\int f(x)\,dx$ for the antiderivative (indefinite integral) of the function $f(x)$.

Example 1:

If $f'(x) = x^5$, then $f(x) = \frac{1}{6}x^6 + C$.

To check, we can take the derivative of $f(x) = \frac{1}{6}x^6 + C$.

Does it equal $f'(x) = x^5$?

$$\int_a^b f(x)\, dx$$

Definite Integral

Example 2:

If $f'(x) = x^{-4}$, then $f(x) = \frac{x^{-3}}{-3} + C$.

To check, we can take the derivative of $f(x) = \frac{x^{-3}}{-3} + C$.

Does it equal $f'(x) = x^{-4}$?

$$\int f(x)\, dx$$

Indefinite Integral

Indefinite integration is the inverse operation of differentiation. In mathematical terms,

$$\int f'(x)\, dx = f(x) + C.$$

If $f'(x)$ is in the form $f'(x) = bx^n$, then $\int bx^n\, dx = b\frac{x^{n+1}}{n+1} + C.$

Recall the Power Rule for Integration from Chapter I. We were finding areas between known x-values a and b. When the integrals are without these values of a and b, then they are indefinite integrals.

The **Fundamental Theorem of Calculus** formalizes the relationship of the indefinite integral and the definite integral. It tells us that if we can find an antiderivative for a function f, then we can use the antiderivative to evaluate $\int_a^b f(x)\, dx = F(b) - F(a)$ where $F'(x) = f(x)$ for all x in [a,b].

THE FUNDAMENTAL THEOREM OF CALCULUS

Suppose we have a continuous function $y = f(x)$, as in the graph at right. We define $A(x)$ to be a function equal to the area under the curve from a to x.

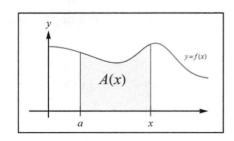

Now suppose we let x increase by an amount Δx. Then $A(x)$ is increased by ΔA.

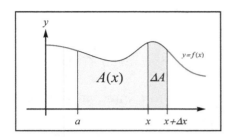

Let us designate $f(m)$ as the minimum height for the area added and $f(M)$ as the maximum height for the area added.

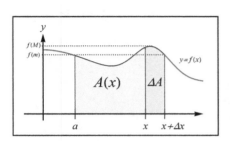

Then the minimum area added would be: $f(m) \cdot \Delta x$

[height times width for minimum area],

and the maximum area added would be: $f(M) \cdot \Delta x$

[height times width for maximum area].

This gives us: $f(m) \cdot \Delta x \leq \Delta A \leq f(M) \cdot \Delta x$. We can divide all three "sides" by Δx.

$$f(m) \leq \frac{\Delta A}{\Delta x} \leq f(M)$$

We can take the limit as $\Delta x \to 0$ for every term.

$$\lim_{\Delta x \to 0} f(m) \leq \lim_{\Delta x \to 0} \frac{\Delta A}{\Delta x} \leq \lim_{\Delta x \to 0} f(M)$$

We note that $\lim_{\Delta x \to 0} \frac{\Delta A}{\Delta x} = A'(x)$, and $\lim_{\Delta x \to 0} f(m) = f(m)$ since it contains no Δx's.

Similarly, $\lim_{\Delta x \to 0} f(M) = f(M)$, giving us:

$$f(m) \leq A'(x) \leq f(M)$$

But as $\Delta x \to 0$, $f(x + \Delta x) \to f(x)$, and $f(m) \to f(M) = f(x)$. Then,

$$f(x) \leq A'(x) \leq f(x)$$

Since $A'(x)$ cannot be both greater and less than $f(x)$, $A'(x) = f(x)$.

We know that $\int f(x)dx = A(x)$ so $\int A'(x)dx = A(x)$.

Therefore, integrating the derivative of a function gives us the function itself.

Also, if $F'(x) = f(x)$ then $A(x) = F(x) + C$. The derivative of C would be zero.

Furthermore, $\int_a^x f(t)dt = A(x) = F(x) + C$, so $F(b) - F(a) = [A(b) - C] - [A(a) - C]$

$$= A(b) - A(a) = \int_a^b f(t)dt - \int_a^a f(t)dt = \int_a^b f(t)dt - 0 = \int_a^b f(t)dt.$$

THE FUNDAMENTAL THEOREM OF CALCULUS

If F is any function such that $F'(x) = f(x)$ for all x in $[a,b]$ then $\int_a^b f(x)dx = F(b) - F(a)$

Example 1:

$$\int x^3 dx$$

$$\int x^3 dx = \frac{x^4}{4} + C$$

Example 2:

$$\int (3x^2 - 5)dx$$

$$\int (3x^2 - 5)dx = 3\frac{x^3}{3} - 5x + C = x^3 - 5x + C$$

Example 3:

$$\int 3^x - \frac{5}{x} dx$$

$$\int 3^x - \frac{5}{x} dx = \frac{3^x}{\ln 3} - 5\ln|x| + C$$

Example 4:

$$\int_{-2}^{3} x^3 dx = \left[\frac{x^4}{4}\right]_{-2}^{3} = \frac{(3)^4}{4} - \frac{(-2)^4}{4} = \frac{81}{4} - \frac{16}{4} = \frac{65}{4}$$

INTRA-SECTION EXERCISES:

1. $\int (x^3 - 5x + 4) dx$ 2. $\int \frac{2}{x^3} + 4e^x dx$ 3. $\int 3^x - \frac{5}{x} dx$

Solutions

1. $\int (x^3 - 5x + 4) dx = \frac{x^4}{4} - 5\frac{x^2}{2} + 4x + C$

2. $\int 2x^{-3} + 4e^x dx = 2\frac{x^{-2}}{-2} + 4e^x + C = -\frac{1}{x^2} + 4e^x + C$

3. $\int_{1}^{2}\left(3^x - \frac{5}{x}\right) dx = \left[\frac{3^x}{\ln 3} - 5\ln|x|\right]_{1}^{2} = \left(\frac{3^2}{\ln 3} - 5\ln|2|\right) - \left(\frac{3^1}{\ln 3} - 5\ln|1|\right) =$

    $= 8.19 - 5(0.69) - \left[2.73 - 5(0)\right] \approx 2.01$

PROBLEMS WITH GIVEN CONDITIONS

For indefinite integrals, if we are given conditions, we can determine "C." Suppose it is known that $f'(x) = 2x + 3$. Suppose we also know that $f(1) = 8$. Our task is to find $f(x)$. We can find $f(x)$ by integrating $f'(x)$.

$$f(x) = \int f'(x) dx = \int (2x + 3) dx = \frac{2x^2}{2} + 3x + C$$

$$f(x) = x^2 + 3x + C$$

Because we also know that when $x=1$, $f(x)=8$, we can substitute these values to solve for C.

$$8=1^2+3(1)+C$$

$$4=C$$

We substitute our newly found C. We have determined that $f(x)=x^2+3x+4$.

Example 5:

Suppose we know that the rate at which a vineyard's yield of grapes is increasing has been modeled by the function $G'(t)=0.12t-0.06$ tons per acre per year, where t is the number of years after the first year of production. We also know that two years after the first year of production, the yield was 2.3 tons per acre. We would like to determine a function for total tons of grapes per acre.

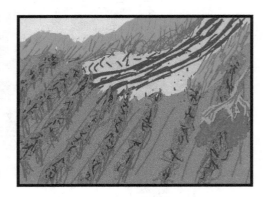

We are given $G'(t)=0.12t-0.06$ and the condition $G(2)=2.3$.

To find $G(t)$, we need $\int G'(t)dt$.

$$G(t)=\int G'(t)dt=\int(0.12t-0.06)dt=\frac{0.12t^2}{2}-0.06t+C$$

$$=G(t)=0.06t^2-0.06t+C$$

We also know that when $t=2$, $G(t)=2.3$. If we substitute these values, we can solve for C.

$$G(t)=0.06t^2-0.06t+C$$

$$2.3=0.06(2)^2-0.06(2)+C$$

$$2.3=0.24-0.12+C$$

$$2.18=C$$

Now that we know C, we can substitute it into our equation for $G(t)$ to get the projected grape yield for any year t after first production.

$$G(t)=0.06t^2-0.06t+2.18 \; tons \; per \; acre$$

Example 6:

If $f''(x)=x^2+2$, $f'(0)=8$, and $f(0)=5$, find $f(x)$.

$$f'(x)=\int f''(x)dx=\int (x^2+2)dx=\frac{x^3}{3}+2x+C$$

We know $f'(0)=8$. That is, $f'(x)=8$ when $x=0$. We substitute these values and solve for C.

$$8=\frac{0^3}{3}+2(0)+C; \text{ thus } 8=C.$$

We substitute this value of C into our equation for $f'(x)$.

$$f'(x)=\frac{x^3}{3}+2x+8$$

Now to find $f(x)$ we need to integrate $f'(x)$.

$$f(x)=\int f'(x)dx=\int \left(\frac{x^3}{3}+2x+8\right)dx=\int \frac{1}{3}x^3+2x+8dx$$

$$f(x)=\frac{1}{3}\cdot\frac{x^4}{4}+\frac{2x^2}{2}+8x+C=\frac{x^4}{12}+x^2+8x+C$$

We know $f(0)=5$. That is, $f(x)=5$ when $x=0$. We substitute these values and solve for C.

$$5=0^2+8(0)+C$$

We substitute this value of C into our equation for $f(x)$.

$$f(x)=\frac{x^4}{12}+x^2+8x+5$$

INTRA-SECTION EXERCISES:

4. If $f'(x)=6x^2+4x$ and $f(1)=10$, find $f(x)$.

5. If $f''(x)=5x-2$, $f'(0)=3$, and $f(1)=7$, find $f(x)$.

Solutions

4. $f(x)=\int f'(x)dx=\int (6x^2+4x)dx=6\dfrac{x^3}{3}+4\dfrac{x^2}{2}+C=2x^3+2x^2+C$

$10=2(1)^3+2(1)^2+C$

$6=C$ Therefore, $f(x)=2x^3+2x^2+6$.

5. $f'(x)=\int f''(x)dx=\int (5x-2)dx=5\dfrac{x^2}{2}-2x+C$

$3=5\dfrac{(0)^2}{2}-2(0)+C;$ $C=3$ Therefore, $f'(x)=5\dfrac{x^2}{2}-2x+3$

$f(x)=\int f'(x)dx=\int \left(5\dfrac{x^2}{2}-2x+3\right)dx=\dfrac{5}{2}\cdot\dfrac{x^3}{3}-2\dfrac{x^2}{2}+3x+C$

$=\dfrac{5}{6}x^3-x^2+3x+C;$

$7=\dfrac{5}{6}(1)^3-(1)^2+3(1)+C;\ 7=\dfrac{17}{6}+C;\ \dfrac{42}{6}-\dfrac{17}{6}=C;\ \dfrac{25}{6}=C$

Therefore, $f(x)=\dfrac{5}{6}x^3-x^2+3x+\dfrac{25}{6}$

VIC4 INDEFINITE INTEGRALS EXERCISES

For numbers 1) through 10), integrate.

1. $\int (4x^3 - 2x^2 + 5x - 4)dx$

2. $\int (5x^3 - 3x^2 + 6x - 5)dx$

3. $\int \left(\dfrac{6}{x^4} + \sqrt[3]{x} \right)dx$

4. $\int \left(\dfrac{5}{x^4} + \sqrt{x} \right)dx$

5. $\int (4e^x + 6)dx$

6. $\int (7e^x + 9)dx$

7. $\int \left(\dfrac{3}{x^4} - \dfrac{3}{x} \right)dx$

8. $\int \left(\dfrac{4}{x^5} - \dfrac{4}{x} \right)dx$

9. $\int (4^x - 4e^x)dx$

10. $\int (3^x - 3e^x)dx$

11. Find the area under the curve $f(x) = 3x^2 - 8x$ from $x = 1$ to $x = 2$.
12. Find the area under the curve $f(x) = 3x^2 + x$ from $x = 0$ to $x = 3$.
13. A university cafeteria keeps track of pounds of bread used per day, b, over the course of a semester. If $B'(t) = -0.4t^2 + 40.6t - 38.1$, and t represents the number of days, how many total pounds of bread will be used during the first 30 days?
14. An airport parking garage keeps track of the number of vehicles entering the lot per day over the course of a year. If $V'(t) = -0.2t^2 + 36t - 51$, where t represents days, how many total vehicle parkings, V, occur in the first 60 days of the year?

For numbers 15) through 22), calculate $f(x)$ using the given conditions.

15. $f'(x) = 3x^2 + 4x;\ f(1) = 10$

16. $f'(x) = 3x^2 + 6x;\ f(1) = 12$

17. $f'(x) = \dfrac{3}{x^4} + 3x^2 - 2;\ f(1) = 10$

18. $f'(x) = \dfrac{2}{x^3} + 4x + 3;\ f(1) = 8$

19. $f''(x) = 6x - 2;\ f'(0) = 3;\ f(0) = 8$

20. $f''(x) = 8x + 2;\ f'(0) = -4;\ f(0) = 1$

21. $f''(x) = 4x + 1;\ f'(1) = 4;\ f(1) = 5$

22. $f''(x) = 6x - 3;\ f'(0) = 4;\ f(1) = 5$

23. The marginal cost function for Roaren Industries is $\dfrac{dC}{dx} = \dfrac{1}{18\sqrt{x}} + 6$. If fixed costs are \$350, find the cost function.

24. The marginal cost function for Delta Base Industries is $\dfrac{dC}{dx} = \dfrac{1}{10\sqrt{x}} + 16$. If fixed costs are \$850, find the cost function.

25. The national debt, D, in millions, of a small country is increasing at a rate modeled by the equation $\frac{dD}{dy} = 1.04y^2 - 0.04y + 0.7$, where y indicates the year. If the year 2000 is represented by $y = 0$, and the national debt was $5 (million) in 2001, find an equation to represent the national debt for any year, y, assuming the rate of increase remains constant.

26. National debt, D, in millions, of a small country is increasing at a rate modeled by the equation $\frac{dD}{dt} = 1.61y^2 - 0.02y + 0.3$, where y indicates the year. If the year 2000 is represented by $y = 0$, and the national debt was $25 (million) in 2001, find an equation to represent the national debt for any year, y, assuming the rate of increase remains constant.

27. Administrative costs for the Lentroven Medical Provider Network are changing at a rate modeled by the function $C'(r) = 30.3r^2$, where r represents the number of government regulations requiring paperwork. If the administrative costs were $56,000 when the number of regulations was $r = 14$, find the total Administrative Cost Function.

28. Administrative costs for the Bodrick Medical Provider Network are changing at a rate modeled by the function $C'(r) = 123r^2$, where r represents the number of government regulations requiring paperwork. If the administrative costs were $27,000 when the number of regulations was $r = 9$, find the total Administrative Cost Function.

29. After the first airing of an ad on a highly rated television program, the customer base for a computer repair store increased according to the function $\frac{dn}{dt} = 8.3t^2$ where t represents months since first airing and n represents number of customers. If the initial customer base was 1450, find a function to represent the number of customers t months after first airing.

30. After the first airing of an ad on a highly rated television program, the customer base for a dance studio increased according to the function $\frac{dn}{dt} = 4.06t^2$ where t represents months since first airing and n represents number of customers. If the initial customer base at the time of airing was 850, find a function to represent the number of customers after t months.

31. Suppose bacterial contaminants are infecting trout at a rate of $1.04t^2$ trout hatcheries infected per month. If there were 22 hatcheries infected when the bacteria were first observed, formulate a function to determine the number of hatcheries, h, infected at t months after initial observation.

32. Suppose invasive gall worms are infecting banana groves at a rate of $1.15t^2$ groves infected per month. If there were 46 groves infected when the worms were first detected, formulate a function to determine the number of groves infected, g, at t months after initial detection.

VIC4 INDEFINITE INTEGRALS SOLUTIONS TO EXERCISES

1. $4\dfrac{x^4}{4} - 2\dfrac{x^3}{3} + 5\dfrac{x^2}{2} - 4x + C = x^4 - 2\dfrac{x^3}{3} + 5\dfrac{x^2}{2} - 4x + C$

2. $5\dfrac{x^4}{4} - x^3 + 3x^2 - 5x + C$

3. $\displaystyle\int \left(6x^{-4} + x^{\frac{1}{3}}\right) dx = 6\dfrac{x^{-3}}{-3} + \dfrac{x^{\frac{4}{3}}}{\frac{4}{3}} + C = -\dfrac{2}{x^3} + \dfrac{3}{4}x^{\frac{4}{3}} + C$

4. $-\dfrac{5}{3x^3} + \dfrac{2}{3}x^{\frac{3}{2}} + C$ 5. $4e^x + 6x + C$ 6. $7e^x + 9x + C$

7. $\displaystyle\int \left(3x^{-4} - 3\dfrac{1}{x}\right) dx = 3\dfrac{x^{-3}}{-3} - 3\ln|x| + C = -\dfrac{1}{x^3} - 3\ln|x| + C$

8. $\dfrac{-1}{x^4} - 4\ln|x| + C$ 9. $4^x(\ln 4) - 4e^x + C$ 10. $3^x(\ln 3) - 3e^x + C$

11. $\left[3\dfrac{x^3}{3} - 8\dfrac{x^2}{2}\right]_1^2 = [x^3 - 4x^2]_1^2 = 2^3 - 4(2)^2 - [1^3 - 4(1)^2] = 8 - 16 - 1 + 4 = -5$

12. 31.5

13. $B(t) = \displaystyle\int_0^{30} -0.4t^2 + 40.6t - 38.1\, dt = \left[-0.4\dfrac{t^3}{3} + 40.6\dfrac{t^2}{2} - 38.1t\right]_0^{30}$

$= -0.4\dfrac{(30)^3}{3} + 40.6\dfrac{(30)^2}{2} - 38.1(30) - \left[-0.4\dfrac{0^3}{3} + 40.6\dfrac{0^2}{2} - 38.1(0)\right]$

$= 13{,}527\ pounds$

14. 47,340 vehicles

15. $f(x) = \displaystyle\int (3x^2 + 4x)dx = 3\dfrac{x^3}{3} + 4\dfrac{x^2}{2} + C = x^3 + 2x^2 + C$

$10 = 1^3 + 2(1)^2 + C;\ \ 7 = C;$ therefore, $f(x) = x^3 + 2x^2 + 7.$

16. $f(x) = x^3 + 3x^2 + 8$

17. $f(x)=\int (3x^{-4}+3x^2-2)dx=3\dfrac{x^{-3}}{-3}+3\dfrac{x^3}{3}-2x+C=-\dfrac{1}{x^3}+x^3-2x+C$

$10=-\dfrac{1}{1^3}+1^3-2(1)+C;\ 12=C;$ therefore, $f(x)=-\dfrac{1}{x^3}+x^3-2x+12.$

18. $f(x)=-\dfrac{1}{x^2}+2x^2+3x+4$

19. $f'(x)=\int (6x-2)dx=6\dfrac{x^2}{2}-2x+C=3x^2-2x+C$

$3=3(0)^2-2(0)+C;\ 3=C;$ therefore, $f'(x)=3x^2-2x+3$

$f(x)=\int (3x^2-2x+3)dx=3\dfrac{x^3}{3}-2\dfrac{x^2}{2}+3x+C=x^3-x^2+3x+C$

$8=0^3-0^2+3(0)+C;\ 8=C;$ therefore, $f(x)=x^3-x^2+3x+8$

20. $f(x)=\dfrac{4x^3}{3}+x^2-4x+1$

21. $f'(x)=\int (4x+1)dx=4\dfrac{x^2}{2}+x+C=2x^2+x+C;$

$4=2(1)^2+1+C;\ 1=C$ Therefore $f'(x)=2x^2+x+1$

$f(x)=\int (2x^2+x+1)\,dx=2\dfrac{x^3}{3}+\dfrac{x^2}{2}+x+C$

$5=2\dfrac{(1)^3}{3}+\dfrac{(1)^2}{2}+1+C;\ \dfrac{17}{6}=C;$ therefore, $f(x)=2\dfrac{x^3}{3}+\dfrac{x^2}{2}+x+\dfrac{17}{6}$

22. $f(x)=x^3+3\dfrac{x^2}{2}+4x+1.5$

23. We are given the condition that for $x=0,\ C(x)=\$350.$

$C(x)=\int \left(\dfrac{1}{18}x^{-\frac{1}{2}}+6\right)dx=\dfrac{1}{18}\cdot\dfrac{x^{\frac{1}{2}}}{\left(\dfrac{1}{2}\right)}+6x+C'=\dfrac{1}{9}\sqrt{x}+6x+C'$

Since the variable C is used for cost, we designate the constant as C'.

$\$350=\dfrac{1}{9}\sqrt{0}+6(0)+C';\ \ \$350=C';$ therefore, $C(x)=\dfrac{1}{9}\sqrt{x}+6x+350$

24. $C(x) = \dfrac{\sqrt{x}}{5} + 16x + 850$

25. $D(y) = \int \dfrac{dD}{dy} dy = \int (1.04y^2 - 0.04y + 0.7)dy = 1.04\dfrac{y^3}{3} - 0.04\dfrac{y^2}{2} + 0.7y + C$

   We are given $D(y) = \$5$ *million* when $y = 1$.

   $\$5m = 1.04\dfrac{1^3}{3} - 0.04\dfrac{1^2}{2} + 0.7(1) + C; C = \$3.97\ m;$

   therefore, $D(y) = 1.04\dfrac{y^3}{3} - 0.02y^2 + 0.7y + 3.97\overline{3}$ *million*

26. $D(y) = 1.61\dfrac{y^3}{3} - 0.01y^2 + 0.3y + 24.17\overline{3}$ *million*

27. $C(r) = \int 30.3r^2 dr = 30.3\dfrac{r^3}{3} + C' = 10.1r^3 + C'$

   Since the variable C is used for cost, we designate the constant as C'.

   $\$56{,}000 = 10.1(14^3) + C'; C' = \$28{,}285.6;$ therefore, $C(r) = 10.1(r^3) + 28{,}285.6.$

28. $C(r) = 41r^3 - 2889$

29. $n(t) = \int 8.3t^2 dt = 8.3\dfrac{t^3}{3} + C;$ we are given that $n = 1450$ when $t = 0$.

   $1450 = 8.3\dfrac{0^3}{3} + C; 1450 = C;$ therefore, $n(t) = 8.3\dfrac{t^3}{3} + 1450.$

30. $n(t) = 4.06\dfrac{t^3}{3} + 850$

31. $h(t) = \int 1.04t^2 dt = 1.04\dfrac{t^3}{3} + C$ We are given $h = 22$ when $t = 0$.

   $22 = 1.04\dfrac{0^3}{3} + C; 22 = C;$ therefore, $h(t) = 1.04\dfrac{t^3}{3} + 22.$

32. $g(t) = 1.15\dfrac{t^3}{3} + 46$

VIC5

Integration by Substitution

Unlike for differentiation, there is no Product Rule or Quotient Rule for integration. However, there are special functions which can still be integrated. If the integrand contains both a function, which we'll designate as u, and its derivative, which we'll designate as u' or $\frac{du}{dx}$, then we may be able to integrate. (The integrand is the function to be integrated.) For example, we could integrate:

$$\int (2x+1)(2)dx$$

because it contains a function $u = 2x+1$, and the derivative of that function, $\frac{du}{dx} = 2$. Of course, this is a very trivial example because it would be easier to integrate if we just distributed the 2 to get $\int (4x+2)dx$ and integrated normally.

Example 1:

$$\int 3x^2 e^{x^3} dx$$

We designate x^3 as our function u, i.e. $u = x^3$.

Then $u'(x) = 3x^2$ or $du = 3x^2 dx$.

If we substitute u for x^3, and du for $3x^2 dx$, our integrand becomes:

$\int e^u du$.   When we integrate with respect to u we have:

$\int e^u du = e^u + C$. The last step is to replace u with x^3.

$$\int e^u du = e^{x^3} + C$$

These problems are like puzzles.

So why does this work? It's just a case of using the Chain Rule in reverse. Recall the Chain Rule gave us the derivative of $F(u(x))$. It was $\frac{d}{dx}F(u(x))=F'(u)\cdot u'(x)$. Also recall that if we integrate the derivative of a function, we get the function itself back. That is: $\int g'(x)dx=g(x)+C$. So the integral of $F'(u)\cdot u'(x)$ gives us its antiderivative, or

$$\int F'(u)\cdot u'(x)dx = F(u(x))+C.$$

It's not always easy to decide on the function u. If one function is inside another, the inside function is a good place to start. Our steps will be the following.

Step 1: Choose a function $u(x)$ (consider the "inside" function of a composition).

Step 2: Convert all functions of "x" into functions of u.

Step 3: Integrate the function of u.

Step 4: Substitute the original function of "x" back in for u.

Example 2:

$$\int 6x(3x^2-5)^7\,dx$$

Let $u=3x^2-5$　　So far, our original integral is: $\int 6x(u)^7\,dx$.

$u'(x)=6x;\;\;du=6xdx$. Replacing the $6x$ and dx, we now have: $\int (u)^7\,du$,

which we can integrate. $\int (u)^7\,du=\dfrac{u^8}{8}+C=\dfrac{(3x^2-5)^8}{8}+C$

Example 3:

$$\int 5x\sqrt{4x^2-3}\,dx$$

We rewrite. $\int 5x(4x^2-3)^{\frac{1}{2}}\,dx$　　Let $u=4x^2-3$

$\int 5x(u)^{\frac{1}{2}}\,dx$　　　　$u'(x)=8x;\;\;du=8xdx$

We need to replace $5xdx$ but we have $du=8xdx$,

so we multiply both sides by $\frac{5}{8}$.

$\frac{5}{8}du = \frac{5}{8} \cdot 8xdx;$ or $\frac{5}{8}du = 5xdx$

Substituting $\frac{5}{8}du$ for the $5x$ and the dx, our integral becomes:

$\int (u)^{\frac{1}{2}} \frac{5}{8} du$ or $\int \frac{5}{8}(u)^{\frac{1}{2}} du$ which we can integrate.

$\int \frac{5}{8}(u)^{\frac{1}{2}} du = \frac{5}{8} \frac{(u)^{\frac{3}{2}}}{\frac{3}{2}} + C = \frac{5}{12}(u)^{\frac{3}{2}} + C = \frac{5}{12}(4x^2 - 3)^{\frac{3}{2}} + C$

Example 4:

$\int \frac{4x - 8}{3x^2 - 12x + 23} dx$ We let $u = 3x^2 - 12x + 23$
    $u'(x) = 6x - 12;$ or $du = (6x - 12)dx$

$\int \frac{4x - 8}{u} dx$

We need to replace $(4x - 8)dx$ but we have $du = (6x - 12)dx$.
We factor each expression. $4(x - 2)dx$ and $du = 6(x - 2)dx$.

We multiply both sides by $\frac{4}{6}$ or $\frac{2}{3}$. $\frac{2}{3}du = \frac{2}{3} \cdot 6(x - 2)dx = 4(x - 2)dx$.

Substituting $\frac{2}{3}du$ for $(4x - 8)dx$ we have the integral: $\int \frac{2}{3} \cdot \frac{1}{u} du$

which we can integrate, if we remember that $\int \frac{1}{x} dx = \ln|x| + C$.

$\int \frac{2}{3} \cdot \frac{1}{u} du = \frac{2}{3}\ln|u| + C = \frac{2}{3}\ln|3x^2 - 12x + 23| + C$

Example 5:

$\int \frac{\ln x}{x} dx$ We let $u = \ln x$

    $u'(x) = \frac{1}{x};$ $du = \frac{1}{x}dx$

$\int \ln x \cdot \frac{1}{x} dx = \int u\, du = \frac{u^2}{2} + C = \frac{(\ln x)^2}{2} + C$

Example 6:

The rate at which a certain textile mill can produce yarn (in kilograms) is approximated by the function:

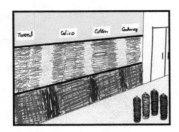

$$Y'(x) = (0.084x - 3.3)(0.042x^2 - 3.3x)^2$$

where x equals the number of spindle shifts. One spindle shift represents one spindle in operation and spinning for a duration of eight hours. Find a function for the total amount of yarn produced in terms of spindle shifts.

$$Y(x) = \int Y'(x)\,dx = \int (0.084x - 8.25)(0.042x^2 - 8.25x)^2\,dx$$

Let $u = 0.042x^2 - 8.25x$

$du = (0.084x - 8.25)dx$ We substitute into the integrand.

$$Y(x) = \int u^2 du = \frac{u^3}{3} + C = \frac{(0.042x^2 - 8.25x)^3}{3} + C$$

If we know that 9,420 kg of yarn was produced using 200 spindle shifts, we can determine C.

$$9{,}420 = \frac{[0.042(200)^2 - 8.25(200)]^3}{3} + C$$

$9{,}420 = 9000 + C; \quad 420 = C$

Therefore $Y(x) = \dfrac{(0.042x^2 - 8.25x)^3}{3} + 420$

Example 7:

$$\int_0^2 (7x^2 + 2x)^3 (7x + 1)dx$$

We let $u = 7x^2 + 2x$
$du = (14x + 2)dx$

$\dfrac{1}{2}du = (7x + 1)dx$

This is a definite integral. The upper and lower endpoints are currently values of x and must also be converted to values of u. Fortunately, in $u = 7x^2 + 2x$, we already have a template for doing just that.

$$\text{For } x=2, \; u=7(2)^2+2(2)=32$$

$$\text{For } x=0, \; u=7(0)^2+2(0)=0$$

Substituting, our integral becomes:

$$\int_0^{32} \frac{1}{2} u^3 du = \left[\frac{u^4}{8}\right]_0^{32} = \frac{(32)^4}{8} - \frac{(0)^4}{8} = 131{,}072$$

We did not need to covert u back into a function of x because we are substituting in number values for u.

INTRA-SECTION EXERCISES:

1. $\int (2x^2+3x)^5(4x+3)dx$

2. $\int \frac{2x}{(x^2+3)^2} dx$

3. $\int \frac{x^2+1}{\sqrt{x^3+3x}} dx$

4. $\int_0^1 5(5x-2)^4 dx$

Solutions

1. Let $u=2x^2+3x$

   $du=(4x+3)dx$

   $$\int (2x^2+3x)^5(4x+3)dx = \int u^5 du = \frac{u^6}{6}+C =$$

   $$\frac{(2x^2+3x)^6}{6}+C$$

2. Let $u=x^2+3$

   $du=2xdx$

   $$\int \frac{2x}{(x^2+3)^2} dx = \int \frac{1}{u^2} du = \int u^{-2} du = \frac{u^{-1}}{-1} = -\frac{1}{u} =$$

   $$-\frac{1}{x^2+3}+C$$

3. Let $u=x^3+3x$

   $du=(3x^2+3)dx$

   $\frac{1}{3}du=(x^2+1)dx$

   $$\int \frac{x^2+1}{\sqrt{x^3+3x}} dx = \int \frac{1}{\sqrt{u}} \cdot \frac{1}{3} du = \frac{1}{3} \int u^{-\frac{1}{2}} du$$

   $$= \frac{1}{3} \frac{u^{\frac{1}{2}}}{\frac{1}{2}} + C = \frac{2}{3}\sqrt{u}+C = \frac{2}{3}\sqrt{x^3+3x}+C$$

4. Let $u = 5x - 2$
    $du = 5dx$
    $x = 1 : u = 5(1) - 2 = 3$
    $x = 0 ; u = 5(0) - 2 = -2$

$$\int_0^1 5(5x - 2)^4 \, dx = \int_{-2}^3 u^4 \, du = \left[\frac{u^5}{5} \right]_{-2}^3 =$$

$$= \frac{(3)^5}{5} - \frac{(-2)^5}{5} = 48.6 - -6.4 = 55$$

VIC5 INTEGRATION BY SUBSTITUTION EXERCISES

For numbers 1 through 22, integrate.

1. $\int (5x^3+8x)^6(15x^2+8)dx$

2. $\int (6x^3-7x)^5(18x^2-7)dx$

3. $\int -2xe^{-2x^2-4}dx$

4. $\int 6x^2e^{2x^3+5}dx$

5. $\int 10^{6x^5-3}(30x^4)dx$

6. $\int 20^{4x^5+11}(20x^4)dx$

7. $\int \dfrac{4x+8}{(x^2+4x)^6}dx$

8. $\int \dfrac{4x-10}{(x^2-5x)^7}dx$

9. $\int 21x^2\sqrt{7x^3-2}dx$

10. $\int 18x^2\sqrt{6x^3+5}dx$

11. $\int x^2\sqrt{3x^3-4}dx$

12. $\int x^2\sqrt{4x^3-7}dx$

13. $\int \dfrac{2x}{x^2-6}dx$

14. $\int \dfrac{6x}{x^2+3}dx$

15. $\int \dfrac{y^2}{y^3+4}dy$

16. $\int \dfrac{y^3}{y^4-6}dy$

17. $\int \dfrac{u^2}{(u^3+4)^5}du$

18. $\int \dfrac{u^2}{(u^3+8)^7}du$

19. $\int_{0}^{1} \dfrac{2z}{(z^2-3)^2}dz$

20. $\int_{0}^{1} \dfrac{2z}{(z^2+4)^3}dz$

21. $\int_{\sqrt{2}}^{2} 2x\sqrt{x^2-2}dx$

22. $\int_{\sqrt{2}}^{2} 6x\sqrt{3x^2+3}dx$

23. Find the area under the curve $f(x)=9x(4x^2-6)^6$ from $x=0$ to $x=1$.

24. Find the area under the curve $f(x)=5x(4x^2+2)^6$ from $x=0$ to $x=1$.

25. Find the output of paper clips $x = f(m)$ that satisfies the initial conditions.

$\dfrac{dx}{dm} = 12m\sqrt{3m^2 + 6}$; output: $x = 1000$ when materials $m = 5$.

26. Find the output of paper clips $x = f(m)$ that satisfies the initial conditions.

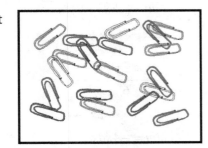

$\dfrac{dx}{dm} = 16m\sqrt{4m^2 + 41}$; output: $x = 12{,}500$ when materials $m = 10$.

VIC5 INTEGRATION BY SUBSTITUTION
SOLUTIONS TO EXERCISES

1. Let $u = 5x^3 + 8x$

   $du = (15x^2 + 8)dx$

   $$\int (5x^3 + 8x)^6 (15x^2 + 8)dx = \int u^6 du = \frac{u^7}{7} + C$$

   $$= \frac{(5x^3 + 8x)^7}{7} + C$$

2. $\dfrac{(6x^3 - 7x)^6}{6} + C$

3. Let $u = -2x^2 - 4$

   $du = -4xdx$

   $\dfrac{1}{2}u = -2xdx$

   $$\int -2xe^{-2x^2 - 4}dx = \int e^u \left(\frac{1}{2}\right)du = \frac{1}{2}e^u + C$$

   $$= \frac{1}{2}e^{-2x^2 - 4} + C$$

4. $e^{2x^3 + 5} + C$

5. Let $u = 6x^5 - 3$

   $du = 30x^4 dx$

   $$\int 10^{6x^5 - 3}(30x^4)dx = \int 10^u du = 10^u / (\ln 10) + C$$

   $$= 10^{6x^5 - 3} / (\ln 10) + C$$

6. $20^{4x^5 + 11} / (\ln 20) + C$

7. Let $u = x^2 + 4x$

   $du = (2x + 4)dx$

   $2du = (4x + 8)dx$

   $$\int \frac{4x + 8}{(x^2 + 4x)^6}dx = \int \frac{1}{u^6}(2)du = \int 2u^{-6}du = 2\frac{u^{-5}}{-5} + C$$

   $$= -\frac{2}{5u^5} + C = -\frac{2}{5(x^2 + 4x)^5} + C \text{ or } -\frac{2}{5}(x^2 + 4x)^{-5} + C$$

8. $-\dfrac{1}{3(x^2 - 5x)^6} + C$ or $-\dfrac{1}{3}(x^2 - 5x)^{-6} + C$

9. Let $u = 7x^3 - 2$

   $du = 21x^2 dx$

   $$\int 21x^2 \sqrt{7x^3 - 2}dx = \int \sqrt{u}du = \int u^{\frac{1}{2}}du = \frac{u^{\frac{3}{2}}}{\frac{3}{2}} + C$$

   $$= \frac{2}{3}(7x^3 - 2)^{\frac{3}{2}} + C$$

10. $\dfrac{2}{3}(6x^3 + 5)^{\frac{3}{2}} + C$

11. Let $u = 3x^3 - 4$

    $du = 9x^2 dx$

    $$\int x^2 \sqrt{3x^3 - 4}dx = \int \frac{1}{9}\sqrt{u}du = \int \frac{1}{9}u^{\frac{1}{2}}du = \frac{1}{9}\frac{u^{\frac{3}{2}}}{\frac{3}{2}}$$

    $$= \frac{1}{9} \cdot \frac{2}{3}(3x^3 - 4)^{\frac{3}{2}} + C = \frac{2}{27}(3x^3 - 4)^{\frac{3}{2}} + C$$

12. $\dfrac{1}{18}(4x^3-7)^{\frac{3}{2}}+C$

13. Let $u=x^2-6$
$du=2xdx$

$$\int \frac{2x}{x^2-6}dx = \int \frac{1}{u}du = \ln|u|+C$$
$$=\ln|x^2-6|+C$$

14. $3\ln|x^2+3|+C$

15. Let $u=y^3+4$
$du=3y^2dy$

$$\int \frac{y^2}{y^3+4}dy = \int \frac{1}{u}\left(\frac{1}{3}\right)du = \frac{1}{3}\ln|u|+C$$
$$=\frac{1}{3}\ln|y^3+4|+C$$

16. $\dfrac{1}{4}\ln|y^4-6|+C$

17. Let $v=u^3+4$
$dv=3u^2du$
$\dfrac{1}{3}dv=u^2du$

$$\int \frac{u^2}{(u^3+4)^5}du = \int \frac{1}{v^5}\frac{1}{3}dv = \int \frac{1}{3}v^{-5}du = \frac{1}{3}\frac{v^{-4}}{(-4)}+C$$
$$=-\frac{1}{12v^4}+C=-\frac{1}{12(u^3+4)^4}+C \text{ or } -\frac{1}{12}(u^3+4)^{-4}+C$$

18. $-\dfrac{1}{18(u^3+8)^6}+C$ or $-\dfrac{1}{18}(u^3+8)^{-6}+C$

19. Let $u=z^2-3$
$du=2zdz$
$x=1:\ u=1^2-3=-2$
$x=0:\ u=0^2-3=-3$

$$\int_0^1 \frac{2z}{(z^2-3)^2}dz = \int_{-3}^{-2} \frac{1}{u^2}du = \int_{-3}^{-2} u^{-2}du = \left[\frac{u^{-1}}{-1}\right]_{-3}^{-2}$$
$$=\left[-\frac{1}{u}\right]_{-3}^{-2}=-\frac{1}{-2}-\left(-\frac{1}{-3}\right)=\frac{3}{6}-\frac{2}{6}=\frac{1}{6}$$

20. $\dfrac{9}{800}$ or 0.01125

21. Let $u=x^2-2$
$du=2xdx$
$x=2:\ u=2^2-2=2$
$x=\sqrt{2};u=\sqrt{2}^2-2=0$

$$\int_{\sqrt{2}}^2 2x\sqrt{x^2-2}dx = \int_0^2 \sqrt{u}du = \int_0^2 u^{\frac{1}{2}}du = \left[\frac{u^{\frac{3}{2}}}{\frac{3}{2}}\right]_0^2 =$$
$$=\left[\frac{2}{3}u^{\frac{3}{2}}\right]_0^2 = \frac{2}{3}(2)^{\frac{3}{2}}-\frac{2}{3}(0)^{\frac{3}{2}} \approx 1.89-0=1.89$$

22. ≈ 20.7

23. Let $u = 4x^2 - 6$

$du = 8xdx$

$\dfrac{9}{8}du = \dfrac{9}{8}8xdx = 9xdx$

$x = 1$: $u = 4(1)^2 - 6$
$= -2$

$x = 0$: $u = 4(0)^2 - 6$
$= -6$

$\displaystyle\int_0^1 9x(4x^2 - 6)^6\,dx = \int_{-6}^{-2} u^6 \dfrac{9}{8}\,du = \left[\dfrac{9}{8}\cdot\dfrac{u^7}{7}\right]_{-6}^{-2} =$

$= \dfrac{9}{56}(-2)^7 - \dfrac{9}{56}(-6)^7 \approx 44969.14$

24. $\approx 24{,}982.86$

25. $x = \displaystyle\int \dfrac{dx}{dm}dm$

$= \displaystyle\int 12m\sqrt{3m^2 + 6}\,dm$

Let $u = 3m^2 + 6$
$du = 6mdm$
$2du = 12mdm$

$\displaystyle\int 12m\sqrt{3m^2 + 6}\,dm = \int 2\sqrt{u}\ du = \int 2u^{\frac{1}{2}}\ du$

$= 2\dfrac{u^{\frac{3}{2}}}{\frac{3}{2}} + C = \dfrac{4}{3}u^{\frac{3}{2}} + C =$

$= \dfrac{4}{3}(3m^2 + 6)^{\frac{3}{2}} + C$

At $x = 1000$ and $m = 5$, $1000 = \dfrac{4}{3}(3(5)^2 + 6)^{\frac{3}{2}} + C$; $1000 - 972 = C$; $C = 28$

Therefore: $x = \dfrac{4}{3}(3m^2 + 6)^{\frac{3}{2}} + 28$.

26. $x = \dfrac{4}{3}(4m^2 + 41)^{\frac{3}{2}} + 152$

VIC6

Higher-Order Derivatives

Consider the function $g(x) = 5x^5 - x^4 + 2x^3 + 3x^2 - 4x + 75$.

It has a derivative function: $g'(x) = 25x^4 - 4x^3 + 6x^2 + 6x - 4$. This is the **first derivative** of $g(x)$.

The function $g'(x)$ also has a derivative: $(g')'(x) = g''(x) = 100x^3 - 12x^2 + 12x + 6$. The derivative of the derivative is called the **second derivative**. The function $g''(x)$ is the second derivative of $g(x)$.

The function $g''(x)$ also has a derivative: $(g'')'(x) = g'''(x) = 300x^2 - 24x + 12$. The derivative of the second derivative is called the **third derivative**. The function $g'''(x)$ is the third derivative of $g(x)$. [It is also the first derivative of $g''(x)$ and the second derivative of $g'(x)$.]

An Order

The process can be continued to generate the fourth, fifth, sixth, … derivatives.

The original function $\quad g(x) = 5x^5 - x^4 + 2x^3 + 3x^2 - 4x + 75$

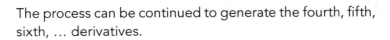

A Higher Order

first derivative $\quad g'(x) = 25x^4 - 4x^3 + 6x^2 + 6x - 4$

second derivative $\quad g''(x) = 100x^3 - 12x^2 + 12x + 6$

third derivative $\quad g'''(x) = 300x^2 - 24x + 12$

fourth derivative $\quad g^{(4)}(x) = 600x - 24$

fifth derivative $g^{(5)}(x)=600$

sixth derivative $g^{(6)}(x)=0$

seventh derivative $g^{(7)}(x)=0$

Notice that the notation changes a bit. The seventh derivative of $g(x)$ is $g^{(7)}(x)$. It is not $g''''''''(x)$.

Notice also that the degree of each successive derivative is one less than the preceding derivative; i.e., $g(x)$ was a fifth degree polynomial, $g'(x)$ is a fourth degree polynomial, $g''(x)$ is a third degree polynomial, $g'''(x)$ is a second degree polynomial, $g^{(4)}(x)$ has degree 1, and $g^{(5)}(x)$ has degree zero, as do all succeeding derivatives.

For any polynomial $f(x)$ of degree n, we will always reach a derivative of 0 when we get to the derivative $f^{(n+1)}(x)$. For example, the polynomial $f(x)=3x^3-4x$ has degree 3, so its fourth derivative will equal zero.

$$f'(x)=9x^2-4; \ f''(x)=18x; \ f'''(x)=18, f^{(4)}=0$$

We can use the alternate notation for these derivatives as well.

An Order of Monks

$$y=5x^5-x^4+2x^3+3x^2-4x+75$$

First Derivative $\dfrac{dy}{dx}=25x^4-4x^3+6x^2+6x-4$

Second Derivative $\dfrac{d^2y}{dx^2}=100x^3-12x^2+12x+6$

Third Derivative $\dfrac{d^3y}{dx^3}=300x^2-24x+12$

A Higher Order

Fourth Derivative $\dfrac{d^4y}{dx^4}=600x-24$

Fifth Derivative $\dfrac{d^5y}{dx^5}=600$

Sixth Derivative $\dfrac{d^6 y}{dx^6} = 0$

Seventh Derivative $\dfrac{d^7 y}{dx^7} = 0$

Both systems of notation are widely used. Leibniz's notation $\dfrac{dy}{dx}$ is very helpful for multivariable calculus. When a function contains several variables—e.g., x, y, and z,—this notation makes it easy to see which variable is being differentiated while the others are held constant. The $f'(x)$ notation was popularized by LaGrange. It easily indicates which variables are being evaluated, e.g., $f'(5)$. There is even a hybrid notation. The first derivative is denoted y'; the second derivative is y''; the third derivative is y'''; etc.

While derivatives of polynomials get simpler as one takes higher and higher derivatives, functions that involve products, quotients, or transcendental functions are often more complicated.

Example 1:

  $g(x) = 3x^2 - 5x + 7$ Find the third derivative.

  We find the first derivative: $g'(x) = 6x - 5$,

  and then the second derivative: $g''(x) = 6$.

  The third derivative is the derivative of the second derivative: $g'''(x) = 0$.

Example 2:

  $\varphi(t) = 7t^{\frac{11}{3}}$ Find the third derivative.

  $\varphi'(t) = 7\left(\dfrac{11}{3}\right)t^{\frac{8}{3}} = \dfrac{77}{3}t^{\frac{8}{3}}$ = the first derivative

  $\varphi''(t) = \dfrac{77}{3}\cdot\dfrac{8}{3}t^{\frac{5}{3}} = \dfrac{616}{9}t^{\frac{5}{3}}$ = the second derivative

  $\varphi'''(t) = \dfrac{616}{9}\cdot\dfrac{5}{3}t^{\frac{2}{3}} = \dfrac{3080}{27}t^{\frac{2}{3}}$ = the third derivative

Example 3:

$$f(x) = \frac{3x^2 - 6x + 1}{4x + 3}$$ Find the third derivative.

If we use the quotient rule, $u(x) = 3x^2 - 6x + 1$ and $v(x) = 4x + 3$.

Then $u'(x) = 6x - 6$ and $v'(x) = 4$. For $f'(x) = \dfrac{u'(x)v(x) - u(x)v'(x)}{[v(x)]^2}$:

$$f'(x) = \frac{(6x-6)(4x+3) - (3x^2 - 6x + 1)(4)}{(4x+3)^2}$$

$$= \frac{24x^2 + 18x - 24x - 18 - 12x^2 + 24x - 4}{(4x+3)^2} = \frac{12x^2 + 18x - 22}{(4x+3)^2}.$$

$$f''(x) = \frac{(24x+18)(4x+3)^2 - (12x^2 + 18x - 22)2(4x+3)(4)}{(4x+3)^4}$$

We factor $(4x+3)$ from each term.

$$f''(x) = \frac{(24x+18)(4x+3) - (12x^2 + 18x - 22)(2)(4)}{(4x+3)^3}$$

$$= \frac{96x^2 + 72x + 72x + 54 - 96x^2 - 144x + 176}{(4x+3)^3} = \frac{230}{(4x+3)^3}.$$

$$f'''(x) = \frac{0(4x+3)^3 - (230)(3)(4x+3)^2(4)}{(4x+3)^6} = \frac{-(230)(4x+3)^2(12)}{(4x+3)^6}$$

We factor $(4x+3)^2$.

$$f'''(x) = \frac{-2760}{(4x+3)^4}.$$

Alternatively, we could write $f(x) = (3x^2 - 6x + 1)(4x+3)^{-1}$ and use the product rule.

Then $G(x) = 3x^2 - 6x + 1$, and $G'(x) = 6x - 6$.

$H(x) = (4x+3)^{-1}$ and $H'(x) = -(4x+3)^{-2}(4) = -4(4x+3)^{-2}$

$f'(x) = (6x-6)(4x+3)^{-1} + (3x^2 - 6x + 1)(-4)(4x+3)^{-2}$

Factoring $(4x+3)^{-2}$ from each term yields:

$f'(x) = (4x+3)^{-2}[(6x-6)(4x+3)^1 - 4(3x^2 - 6x + 1)]$

$= (4x+3)^{-2}[24x^2 + 18x - 24x - 18 - 12x^2 + 24x - 4]$

$= (4x+3)^{-2}(12x^2 + 18x - 22)$ or $(12x^2 + 18x - 22)(4x+3)^{-2}$.

For $f''(x)$, $G(x)=12x^2+18x-22$ and $G'(x)=24x+18$

$H(x)=(4x+3)^{-2}$ and $H'(x)=-2(4x+3)^{-3}(4)=-8(4x+3)^{-3}$

$f''(x)=(24x+18)(4x+3)^{-2}+(12x^2+18x-22)(-8)(4x+3)^{-3}$

Factoring $(4x+3)^{-3}$ from each term yields:

$f''(x)=(4x+3)^{-3}[(24x+18)(4x+3)^1-8(12x^2+18x-22)]$

$\quad\quad =(4x+3)^{-3}(96x^2+72x+72x+54-96x^2-144x+176)$

$\quad\quad =(4x+3)^{-3}(230)$ or $230(4x+3)^{-3}$

$f'''(x)=-690(4x+3)^{-4}(4)=-2760(4x+3)^{-4}$

Example 4:

$F(x)=\log_3(2x-5)$ Find the third derivative.

$\dfrac{dF}{dx}=\dfrac{2}{(2x-5)\ln 3}$

$\dfrac{d^2F}{dx^2}=\dfrac{0(2x-5)\ln 3-2(\ln 3)(2)}{[(2x-5)\ln 3]^2}=\dfrac{-4\ln 3}{[(2x-5)\ln 3]^2}$ We factor $(\ln 3)$ from each term.

$\dfrac{d^2F}{dx^2}=\dfrac{-4}{(\ln 3)(2x-5)^2}$

$\dfrac{d^3F}{dx^3}=\dfrac{0(\ln 3)(2x-5)^2-(-4)(\ln 3)(2)(2x-5)(2)}{(\ln 3)^2(2x-5)^4}=\dfrac{16(\ln 3)(2x-5)}{(\ln 3)^2(2x-5)^4}=\dfrac{16}{(\ln 3)(2x-5)^3}$

Alternatively, we could rewrite $\dfrac{dF}{dx}$ as $\dfrac{2}{\ln 3}(2x-5)^{-1}$. Then

$\dfrac{d^2F}{dx^2}=-\dfrac{2}{\ln 3}(2x-5)^{-2}(2)=-\dfrac{4}{\ln 3}(2x-5)^{-2}$

$\dfrac{d^3F}{dx^3}=\dfrac{8}{\ln 3}(2x-5)^{-3}(2)=\dfrac{16}{\ln 3}(2x-5)^{-3}$

VIC6 HIGHER-ORDER DERIVATIVES EXERCISES

Find the first, second, and third derivatives for each function below.

1. $y = 3x^4 - 2x^3 + 7x^2 + 9x - 12$

2. $y = 12x^4 - 9x^3 + 7x^2 - 2x + 3$

3. $f(x) = 6x^4 + 4x^2 - 10$

4. $f(x) = 7x^5 - 4x^3 - 11x$

5. $y = 4x^2 + 7x - 18$

6. $y = 3x^2 - 11x - 4$

7. $g(x) = 2\ln x$

8. $g(x) = 5\ln x$

9. $y = 2\ln(3x)$

10. $y = -\ln(2x)$

11. $f(x) = 3^{2x-3}$

12. $f(x) = 5^{3x-2}$

13. $y = \sqrt{5x^2 - 2}$

14. $y = \sqrt{4x^2 - 6}$

15. $f(x) = 4x^2 e^{2x}$

16. $f(x) = 5x^2 e^{3x}$

17. $y = \log(3 - x^2)$

18. $y = \log(7 - 3x^2)$

VIC6 HIGHER-ORDER DERIVATIVES SOLUTIONS TO EXERCISES

1. $\dfrac{dy}{dx} = 12x^3 - 6x^2 + 14x + 9;\quad \dfrac{d^2y}{dx^2} = 36x^2 - 12x + 14;\quad \dfrac{d^3y}{dx^3} = 72x - 12$

2. $\dfrac{dy}{dx} = 48x^3 - 27x^2 + 14x - 2;\quad \dfrac{d^2y}{dx^2} = 144x^2 - 54x + 14;\quad \dfrac{d^3y}{dx^3} = 288x - 54$

3. $f'(x) = 24x^3 + 8x;\quad f''(x) = 72x^2 + 8;\quad f'''(x) = 144x$

4. $f'(x) = 35x^4 - 12x^2 - 11;\quad f''(x) = 140x^3 - 24x;\quad f'''(x) = 420x^2 - 24$

5. $\dfrac{dy}{dx} = 8x + 7;\quad \dfrac{d^2y}{dx^2} = 8;\quad \dfrac{d^3y}{dx^3} = 0$

6. $\dfrac{dy}{dx} = 6x - 11;\quad \dfrac{d^2y}{dx^2} = 6;\quad \dfrac{d^3y}{dx^3} = 0$

7. $g'(x) = 2\dfrac{1}{x} = 2x^{-1};\quad g''(x) = -2x^{-2};\quad g'''(x) = 4x^{-3}$ or $g'''(x) = \dfrac{4}{x^3}$

8. $g'(x) = \dfrac{5}{x} = 5x^{-1};\quad g''(x) = -5x^{-2};\quad g'''(x) = 10x^{-3}$ or $g'''(x) = \dfrac{10}{x^3}$

9. $\dfrac{dy}{dx} = 2\dfrac{1}{3x}(3) = \dfrac{2}{x} = 2x^{-1};\quad \dfrac{d^2y}{dx^2} = -2x^{-2};\quad \dfrac{d^3y}{dx^3} = 4x^{-3}$ or $\dfrac{d^3y}{dx^3} = \dfrac{4}{x^3}$

10. $\dfrac{dy}{dx} = -\dfrac{1}{x} = -x^{-1};\quad \dfrac{d^2y}{dx^2} = x^{-2};\quad \dfrac{d^3y}{dx^3} = -2x^{-3}$ or $\dfrac{d^3y}{dx^3} = \dfrac{-2}{x^3}$

11. $f'(x) = 3^{2x-3}(2)\ln 3 = 2(\ln 3)3^{2x-3};\quad f''(x) = 2(\ln 3)3^{2x-3}(2)(\ln 3) = 4(\ln 3)^2 3^{2x-3}$

    $f'''(x) = 4(\ln 3)^2 3^{2x-3}(2)(\ln 3) = 8(\ln 3)^3 3^{2x-3}$

12. $f'(x) = 3(\ln 5)5^{3x-2};\quad f''(x) = 9(\ln 5)^2 5^{3x-2};\quad f'''(x) = 27(\ln 5)^3 5^{3x-2}$

13. $y = (5x^2 - 2)^{\frac{1}{2}};\quad \dfrac{dy}{dx} = \dfrac{1}{2}(5x^2 - 2)^{-\frac{1}{2}}(10x) = 5x(5x^2 - 2)^{-\frac{1}{2}}$

    For $\dfrac{d^2y}{dx^2}$ we must use the product rule. $G(x) = 5x$, and $G'(x) = 5$.

    $H(x) = (5x^2 - 2)^{-\frac{1}{2}}$, and $H'(x) = -\dfrac{1}{2}(5x^2 - 2)^{-\frac{3}{2}}(10x) = 5x(5x^2 - 2)^{-\frac{3}{2}}$

    $\dfrac{d^2y}{dx^2} = 5(5x^2 - 2)^{-\frac{1}{2}} + 5x\left(-\dfrac{1}{2}(5x^2 - 2)^{-\frac{3}{2}}\right)(10x) = 5(5x^2 - 2)^{-\frac{1}{2}} - 25x^2(5x^2 - 2)^{-\frac{3}{2}}$

We can factor $5(5x^2-2)^{-\frac{3}{2}}$ from each term.

$$\frac{d^2y}{dx^2}=5(5x^2-2)^{-\frac{3}{2}}[(5x^2-2)^1-5x^2]=5(5x^2-2)^{-\frac{3}{2}}[5x^2-2-5x^2]$$

We then collect like terms.

$$\frac{d^2y}{dx^2}=5(5x^2-2)^{-\frac{3}{2}}(-2)=-10(5x^2-2)^{-\frac{3}{2}}$$

$$\frac{d^3y}{dx^3}=-10\left(-\frac{3}{2}\right)(5x^2-2)^{-\frac{5}{2}}(10x)=150x(5x^2-2)^{-\frac{5}{2}}$$

14. $\dfrac{dy}{dx}=4x(4x^2-6)^{-\frac{1}{2}}$; $\dfrac{d^2y}{dx^2}=-24(4x^2-6)^{-\frac{3}{2}}$; $\dfrac{d^3y}{dx^3}=288x(4x^2-6)^{-\frac{5}{2}}$

15. We must use the product rule. $G(x)=4x^2$, and $G'(x)=8x$.

$H(x)=e^{2x}$, $H'(x)=e^{2x}(2)=2e^{2x}$.

$f'(x)=8xe^{2x}+4x^2(2e^{2x})=8xe^{2x}+8x^2(e^{2x})$

For $f''(x)$ we must use the Product Rule for each term, then we collect like terms.

$f''(x)=8e^{2x}+8xe^{2x}(2)+16xe^{2x}+8x^2e^{2x}(2)$

$\quad=8e^{2x}+16xe^{2x}+16xe^{2x}+16x^2e^{2x}=8e^{2x}+32xe^{2x}+16x^2e^{2x}$

For $f'''(x)$ we will use the product rule for the second and third terms.

$f'''(x)=8e^{2x}(2)+32e^{2x}+32xe^{2x}(2)+32xe^{2x}+16x^2e^{2x}(2)$

$\quad=16e^{2x}+32e^{2x}+64xe^{2x}+32xe^{2x}+32x^2e^{2x}$

$\quad=48e^{2x}+96xe^{2x}+32x^2e^{2x}$ or $f'''(x)=16e^{2x}(3+6x+2x^2)$

16. $f'(x)=10xe^{3x}+15x^2e^{3x}$; $f''(x)=10e^{3x}+60xe^{3x}+45x^2e^{3x}$;

$f'''(x)=90e^{3x}+270xe^{3x}+135x^2e^{3x}$ or $f'''(x)=45e^{3x}(2+6x+3x^2)$

17. $\dfrac{dy}{dx}=\dfrac{1}{(3-x^2)}(-2x)\dfrac{1}{\ln 10}=\dfrac{-2x}{\ln 10}\cdot(3-x^2)^{-1}$

For $\dfrac{d^2y}{dx^2}$, the product rule is necessary. $G(x)=\dfrac{-2x}{\ln 10}$. Recalling that $\dfrac{-2}{\ln 10}$ is merely a constant,

$G'(x)=\dfrac{-2}{\ln 10}$. $H(x)=(3-x^2)^{-1}$, and $H'(x)=-(3-x^2)^{-2}(-2x)=2x(3-x^2)^{-2}$.

$\dfrac{d^2y}{dx^2}=\dfrac{-2}{\ln 10}(3-x^2)^{-1}+\dfrac{-2x}{\ln 10}(2x)(3-x^2)^{-2}=\dfrac{-2}{\ln 10}(3-x^2)^{-1}+\dfrac{-4x^2}{\ln 10}(3-x^2)^{-2}$

We factor $\dfrac{-2}{\ln 10}(3-x^2)^{-2}$ from each term and then collect like terms.

CPSIA information can be obtained
at www.ICGtesting.com
Printed in the USA
LVHW061105180822
726219LV00005B/11

$$\frac{d^2y}{dx^2}=\frac{-2}{\ln 10}(3-x^2)^{-2}[(3-x^2)^1+2x^2]=\frac{-2}{\ln 10}(3-x^2)^{-2}(3+x^2)$$

For $\dfrac{d^3y}{dx^3}$ we use the product rule again. $G(x)=\dfrac{-2}{\ln 10}(3-x^2)^{-2}$ and $H(x)=(3+x^2)$.

$$G'(x)=\frac{4}{\ln 10}(3-x^2)^{-3}(-2x)=\frac{-8x}{\ln 10}(3-x^2)^{-3}; \; H'(x)=2x$$

$$\frac{d^3y}{dx^3}=\frac{-8x}{\ln 10}(3-x^2)^{-3}(3+x^2)+\frac{-2}{\ln 10}(3-x^2)^{-2}(2x)$$

$$=\frac{-8x}{\ln 10}(3-x^2)^{-3}(3+x^2)-\frac{4x}{\ln 10}(3-x^2)^{-2} \text{ If we factor out } -\frac{4x}{\ln 10}(3-x^2)^{-3},$$

$$\frac{d^3y}{dx^3}=-\frac{4x}{\ln 10}(3-x^2)^{-3}[2(3+x^2)+(3-x^2)^1]$$

$$=-\frac{4x}{\ln 10}(3-x^2)^{-3}[6+2x^2+3-x^2]=-\frac{4x}{\ln 10}(3-x^2)^{-3}(9+x^2)$$

18. $\dfrac{dy}{dx}=\dfrac{-6x}{\ln 10}(7-3x^2)^{-1}$; $\dfrac{d^2y}{dx^2}=\dfrac{-6}{\ln 10}(7+3x^2)(7-3x^2)^{-2}$; $\dfrac{d^3y}{dx^3}=\dfrac{-36x(21+3x^2)}{(\ln 10)(7-3x^2)^3}$